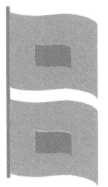

Proceedings of the 2010
CGO

The Eighth International Symposium on Code Generation
and Optimization

April 24–28, 2010, Toronto, Ontario, Canada

**Association for
Computing Machinery**

Advancing Computing as a Science & Profession

IEEE
COMPUTER
SOCIETY

Co-sponsored by ACM SIGMICRO, ACM SIGPLAN,
and the IEEE Computer Society TC-uARCH.

Association for Computing Machinery

Advancing Computing as a Science & Profession

The Association for Computing Machinery
2 Penn Plaza, Suite 701
New York, New York 10121-0701

Notice to Past Authors of ACM-Published Articles
ACM intends to create a complete electronic archive of all articles and/or other material previously published by ACM. If you have written a work that has been previously published by ACM in any journal or conference proceedings prior to 1978, or any SIG Newsletter at any time, and you do NOT want this work to appear in the ACM Digital Library, please inform permissions@acm.org, stating the title of the work, the author(s), and where and when published.

ISBN: 978-1-60558-635-9

Additional copies may be ordered prepaid from:

ACM Order Department
PO Box 30777
New York, NY 10087-0777, USA

Phone: 1-800-342-6626 (USA and Canada)
+1-212-626-0500 (Global)
Fax: +1-212-944-1318
E-mail: acmhelp@acm.org
Hours of Operation: 8:30 am – 4:30 pm ET

ACM Order Number 528103

Printed in the USA

Message from the General Co-Chairs

On behalf of the organizing committee, we welcome you to the Eighth International Symposium on Code Generation and Optimization (CGO 2010) and to the vibrant city of Toronto.

We were fortunate to have an excellent organizing committee, and we are extremely thankful for their efforts and dedication. We warmly thank the program chairs Kim Hazelwood and David Kaeli for their hard work in recruiting a strong program committee and their passion and leadership throughout the program selection process. We owe our sincere gratitude to the authors who submitted to CGO, and the program committee and external reviewers for their thoughtful reviews and diligent creation of an excellent technical program.

We also owe a huge thanks to the members of the conference team for their efforts in making CGO possible. We thank John Cavazos and Yiannis Kalamatianos for soliciting proposals and selecting several quality workshops and tutorials respectively. We thank Tipp Moseley for managing the student poster session by soliciting and selecting proposals, and also for managing the student travel grants. Tor Aamodt was in charge of publications; we thank him for assembling and formatting the proceedings, and ensuring that deadlines were met. We thank Koushik Chakraborty for setting up and managing the registration system, and we thank Jason Zebchuk for managing the CGO website. Natalie Enright Jerger served as the publicity chair, and we thank her for ensuring that CGO was well advertised. Once again, we are really grateful to have had such a dedicated organizing committee.

We would like to express our gratitude to the steering committee for their guidance, and for the opportunity to serve as general co-chairs. We also thank our corporate sponsors for their generous financial support, making it possible to provide student travel grants and to keep the cost of student registration low. We thank ACM and IEEE for their continued support of CGO.

Finally, we extend our welcome and thanks to all of the attendees of CGO, and we hope that you enjoy the conference and your time in Toronto.

Andreas Moshovos
CGO 2010 General Co-Chair
University of Toronto

Greg Steffan
CGO 2010 General Co-Chair
University of Toronto

Message from the Program Co-Chairs

On behalf of the entire Program Committee, it is our pleasure to present the final program of papers selected for CGO 2010. This year we received a total of 70 submissions. Program Committee members were provided the opportunity to "bid" on the papers to review. Each paper was assigned to 4 PC members, with an additional review assigned to an expert solicited by the Program Chairs. Each paper received on average 4.94 reviews. The entire review process was double-blind. Papers receiving reviews with large deviations were discussed by PC members through email prior to the Program Committee Meeting.

The CGO 2010 Program Committee Meeting was held in Boston, MA on Saturday November 7th. 27 of the 31 PC members attended in-person, with one person attending electronically. We particularly want to acknowledge those PC members that traveled long distances and internationally to be present at the meeting.

This year CGO received a high number of quality papers. 29 papers were selected for the final program. CGO continues to draw a high percentage of international submissions; 44.3% of the submissions had at least one author from outside of the US. CGO also maintained its tradition of drawing contributions from industry, with 14.3% of the submissions having at least one author from industry.

We are also happy to present two stimulating keynote talks from industry leaders. Ben Zorn from Microsoft Research will talk to us about a new definition of performance for future applications. CJ Newburn from Intel will present his perspectives on heterogeneous computing systems, and specifically the role that Intel technology will play. We thank our keynotes for agreeing to spend their time sharing their thoughts with the CGO community.

A lot of hard work went into putting together this technical program, and many people deserve thanks for their help. Again, we want to acknowledge the time and effort of the PC and we also want to thank the many external expert reviewers. We would like to thank all authors who submitted papers to CGO 2010 for their hard work and commitment to the CGO community. Finally, we would like to especially thank Dana Schaa who handled many of the details of the submission website and the smooth running of the Program Committee Meeting.

We hope you will enjoy the CGO 2010 program.

Kim Hazelwood
CGO 2010 Program Co-Chair
University of Virginia

David Kaeli
CGO 2010 Program Co-Chair
Northeastern University

Table of Contents

Keynote I

Session 1: Dynamic Optimization and Analysis

Session 2: Feedback-Directed and JIT Compilation

Session 3: Memory Optimizations and Synchronization

Keynote II

Session 4: Speculative and Automatic Parallelization

Session 5: Register Allocation

Session 6: Static Optimizations

Session 7: Mathematical/Statistical Approaches

Session 8: Runtime Techniques

CGO 2010 Organizing Committee

General Co-Chairs:	Andreas Moshovos, University of Toronto
	Greg Steffan, University of Toronto
Program Co-Chairs:	Kim Hazelwood, University of Virginia
	David Kaeli, Northeastern University
Registration Chair:	Koushik Chakraborty, Utah State University
Student Posters/Grants:	Tipp Moseley, Google
Workshops Chair:	John Cavazos, University of Delaware
Tutorials Chair:	Yiannis Kalamatianos, AMD
Publicity Chair:	Natalie Enright Jerger, University of Toronto
Web Chair:	Jason Zebchuk, University of Toronto
Publications Chair:	Tor Aamodt, University of British Columbia
Steering Committee:	David August, Princeton University
	Tom Conte, Georgia Tech
	Evelyn Duesterwald, IBM
	Wen-mei Hwu, University of Illinois – Urbana Champaign
	Chris J. Newburn, Intel
	Michael D. Smith, Harvard
	Ben Zorn, Microsoft

Program Committee

Matthew Arnold, IBM Research

Derek Bruening, VMware

John Cavazos, University of Delaware

Brad Chen, Google

Fred Chong, University of California – Santa Barbara

Nate Clark, Georgia Tech

Robert Cohn, Intel

Jack Davidson, University of Virginia

Saumya Debray, University of Arizona

Angela Demke Brown, University of Toronto

Amer Diwan. University of Colorado - Boulder

Lieven Eeckhout, Ghent University

Antonio Gonzalez, Intel & Universitat Polytechnia Catalunya

Rajiv Gupta, University of California - Riverside

Sam Guyer, Tufts University

Wei Hsu, National Chao-Tung University

Wen-Mei Hwu, University of Illinois – Urbana Champaign

Martha Kim, Columbia University

Jim Larus, Microsoft Research

Tipp Moseley, University of Colorado - Boulder

Satish Narayanasamy, University of Michigan

Michael O'Boyle, University of Edinburgh

Keshav Pingali, University of Texas - Austin

Alasdair Rawsthorne, University of Manchester

Norm Rubin, AMD

Vivek Sarkar, Rice University

Olin Shivers, Northeastern University

David Whalley, Florida State University

Mohamed Zahran, City University of New York

Additional Reviewers

Tarek Abdelrahman
Jaume Abella
Alex Aleta
Erik Altman
Rajkishore Barik
Steve Blackburn
Preston Briggs
David Brooks
Zoran Budimlic
Mihai Budiu
Calin Cascaval
Francisco J Cazorla
Joao Dias
Chen Ding
Paul Drongowski
Evelyn Duesterwald
Alexandre Eichenberger
Alexandra Fedorova
Michael Franz
Joshua Fryman
Grigori Fursin
Enric Gibert
Dominic Grewe
Yi Guo
Ben Hardekopf
Michael Hind
Jason Hiser
Josh Hodosh
Kun-Yuan Hsieh
Xiaohuang Huang

Robert Hundt
Nikolas Ioannou
Byunghyun Jang
Marta Jimenez
Lizy John
Changhee Jung
Andreas Krall
Dimitrij Krepis
Chandra Krintz
Miriam Leeser
Marc Lupon
Carlos Madriles
Scott Mahlke
Jenny Mankin
Milo Martin
Sally McKee
Mario Mendez
Maged Michael
Seung-Jai Min
Perhaad Mistry
Tali Moreshet
Eliot Moss
Onur Mutlu
Deepthi Nandakumar
V. Krishna Nandivada
Nicholas Nethercote
Donald Nguyen
Naddy Obeid
Guilherme Ottoni
Jens Palsberg

Santosh Pande
Alexandros Papakonstantinou
Fernando Pereira
Ramesh Peri
Louis-Noel Pouchet
Raghavan Raman
Chris Rodrigues
Sara Sadeghi
Jesus Sanchez
Ron Sass
Timothy Sherwood
Mary Lou Soffa
Yan Solihin
Daniel Sorin
Kyriakos Stavrou
Mark Stephenson
Edward Suh
I-Jui Sung
Steven Swanson
Peter Sweeney
Rich Uhlig
Neil Vachharajani
Dimitrios Vardoulakis
Clark Verbrugge
Emmett Witchel
Haicheng Wu
Xiao-Long Wu
Pen-Chung Yew
Jie Yu
Jisheng Zhao

CGO 2010 Sponsors & Supporters

Sponsors:

IEEE CS TC-uARCH

Supporters:

Google

intel

IBM Research

Microsoft Research

Keynote I

Performance is Dead, Long Live Performance!

Benjamin Zorn

Microsoft Research
zorn@microsoft.com

In a world of social networking, security attacks, and hot mobile phones, the importance of application performance appears to have diminished. My own research agenda has shifted from looking at the performance of memory allocation to building runtime systems that are more resilient to data corruption and security attacks. In my talk, I will outline a number of areas where code-generation and runtime techniques can be successfully applied to areas for purposes other than performance, such as fault tolerance, reliability, and security. Along the way, I will consider such questions as "Does it really matter if this corruption was caused by a software or hardware error?" and "Is it okay to let a malicious person allocate arbitrary data on my heap?".

Despite these other opportunities, the importance of performance in modern applications remains undiminished, and current hardware trends place an increasing burden on software to provide needed performance boosts. In concluding, I will suggest several important trends that I believe will help define the next 10 years of code generation and optimization research.

Ben Zorn is a Principal Researcher at Microsoft Research. After receiving a PhD in Computer Science from UC Berkeley in 1989, he served eight years on the Computer Science faculty at the University of Colorado in Boulder, receiving tenure and being promoted to Associate Professor in 1996. He left the University of Colorado in 1998 to join Microsoft Research, where he currently works. Ben's research interests include programming language design and implementation and performance measurement and analysis. He has served as an Associate Editor of the ACM journals Transactions on Programming Languages and Systems and Transactions on Architecture and Code Optimization and he currently serves as a Member-at-Large of the SIGPLAN Executive Committee. For more information, visit his web page at http://research.microsoft.com/~zorn/.

Categories and Subject Descriptors D.3.4 [**Programming Languages**]: Processors – code generation

General Terms Performance, Security, Reliability, Languages.

Keywords *Code generation*

PinPlay: A Framework for Deterministic Replay and Reproducible Analysis of Parallel Programs

Harish Patil, Cristiano Pereira, Mack Stallcup, Gregory Lueck, James Cownie

Intel Corporation

{harish.patil, cristiano.l.pereira, t.mack.stallcup, gregory.m.lueck, james.h.cownie}@intel.com

Abstract

Analysis of parallel programs is hard mainly because their behavior changes from run to run. We present an execution capture and deterministic replay system that enables repeatable analysis of parallel programs. Our goal is to provide an easy-to-use framework for capturing, deterministically replaying, and analyzing execution of large programs with reasonable runtime and disk usage. Our system, called PinPlay, is based on the popular Pin dynamic instrumentation system hence is very easy to use. PinPlay extends the capability of Pin-based analysis by providing a tool for capturing one execution instance of a program (as log files called *pinballs*) and by allowing Pin-based tools to run off the captured execution. Most Pintools can be trivially modified to work off pinballs thus doing their usual analysis but with a guaranteed repeatability. Furthermore, the capture/replay works across operating systems (Windows to Linux) as the pinball format is independent of the operating system. We have used PinPlay to analyze and deterministically debug large parallel programs running trillions of instructions. This paper describes the design of PinPlay and its applications for analyses such as simulation point selection, tracing, and debugging.

Categories and Subject Descriptors   D.2.5 [*Software Engineering*]: Testing and Debugging—Debugging aids, Tracing

General Terms   design, experimentation

Keywords   deterministic replay, dynamic program analysis, repeatable simulation point selection, reproducible debugging

1. Introduction

With multi-core processors becoming the norm, there is a renewed interest in writing parallel programs. One of the many challenges in writing parallel programs is their non-repeatable behavior. Although a parallel program may produce the same result on multiple runs, its threads/processes may actually execute differently on each run. This non-repeatability may be introduced by the synchronization mechanisms, such as locks, used in parallel programs or it can be the result of unsynchronized access to shared data ("data race"). In either case, the non-repeatability makes analysis and debugging of parallel programs extremely challenging. So, there is an acute need for a framework for deterministic replay and analysis of par-

allel programs. Further, such a framework needs to be easy to use, have reasonable runtime and disk space overhead and should be widely available.

There are a number of papers proposing hardware support for deterministic replay, however those ideas are still at the research stage. There are software-based deterministic replay approaches based on virtualization ([27], [7]) although they require special environments or modification to the operating system which can be a hurdle for many users. Microsoft has developed a deterministic replay system called *iDNA* [2] which is based on dynamic instrumentation; however it is currently an internal tool hence is not widely available. The goal of our work is to provide easy-to-use tools for capturing, deterministically replaying, and analyzing the execution of large parallel programs with reasonable overhead. We have used the Pin dynamic instrumentation system [11] to implement a framework called PinPlay that is easy to use, and will be made widely available with the Pin distributions in the future.

PinPlay consists of two Pintools [1] a *logger* that records an execution of a program in a set of files collectively called a *pinball* and [2] a *replayer* that runs off a pinball repeating the corresponding captured execution. However, merely logging and replaying executions is not very useful; those functionalities need to be combined with some useful analysis. To this end, we can combine the logger and replayer with most existing Pintools with only small changes to the Pintool sources. Thus a PinPlay-enabled Pintool can function in one of four modes [1] as a regular Pintool running a native program, [2] as a logger where it creates a pinball, [3] as a replayer where it runs off a previously captured pinball, and [4] as a *relogger* (replayer and logger) where the Pintool runs off a pinball and generates another pinball (possibly for a selected region). For the last three modes, the Pintool could optionally carry out its regular analysis. We have found this ability to combine Pintools with PinPlay to be very useful for many analyses.

We are successfully using PinPlay for two major purposes [1] Repeatable PinPoints : finding representative simulation regions (*PinPoints*) and re-visiting them to generate checkpoints for simulation, and [2] Replay debugging : capturing a buggy execution of a parallel program and repeating it multiple times under a debugger.

Since PinPlay tools are based on Pin they are very easy to use; they do not require any special hardware or special operating system support. PinPlay tools work at binary level with previously built program images and do not require access to program sources. The PinPlay logger only records the minimal information necessary to reproduce the non-deterministic events and relies on the replayer to recreate the rest of the program state. A pinball needs to be "executed" by the replayer to regenerate program state, only reading non-deterministic events from PinPlay logs. This makes the pinball format relatively small (average pinball size of 39MB for SPEC2006 "reference" runs with 924 billion instructions on average). However, the analysis required for captur-

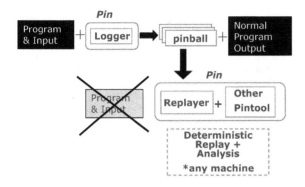

Figure 1: PinPlay: Integration with Pin

ing non-deterministic events is expensive. Typically each memory access in the program needs to be monitored which causes at least a double-digit factor slowdown in execution time. Although there are opportunities for optimizing PinPlay implementation the overheads cannot match those expected with hardware support for deterministic replay. This means that PinPlay functionality cannot be "always on". We believe that for the two major purposes for which we are currently using PinPlay the slowdowns are acceptable.

In this paper, we will present details of how PinPlay tools work and how we are using them for reproducible analyses of large programs. The main contributions of this paper are :

1. We describe user-level execution capture and deterministic replay tools based on the Pin dynamic instrumentation toolkit. We show how Pintools can be extended, as shown in Figure 1, to use replay capability thereby providing reproducible analyses. No other software-based deterministic replay technique (except iDNA) provides such an easy-to-use framework for replay-based analysis.

2. We show how we are using PinPlay with large serial and parallel programs (some commercial) for two major purposes: (i) finding representative simulation regions, and then re-visiting them for validation, tracing, and simulation, and (ii) reproducible debugging of bugs that only occasionally show up in some parallel programs. PinPlay also provides the option of doing per thread/process replay of parallel programs which can be useful in some contexts.

3. We introduce the pinball format used for capturing executions which has some interesting properties: (a) it is independent of the operating system, and (b) it is self-contained, i.e. the program binary, input files, special licenses are not needed during replay. This makes a pinball an ideal way to share workloads for Pin-based analyses among researchers : once captured a pinball can be analyzed multiple times, anywhere!

2. How PinPlay Works

Since we use the Pin dynamic instrumentation system which only analyzes user-level code, PinPlay can log and replay only the user-level code. The Pin team graciously added a few features to Pin to ease the implementation of PinPlay and we will describe those new Pin features in this section. We will also discuss various design choices available for a deterministic replay system and describe the design we implemented for PinPlay first on Linux and then on the Windows operating system. Our design choices were mainly driven by the purposes for which PinPlay was developed; namely reproducible simulation point selection/analysis and reproducible debugging.

There are two extreme ways in which a replay system can be implemented:

- *record-all-recompute-nothing*: If the register and memory state before each instruction executed is recorded, the execution can be reproduced by restoring the state before each instruction replayed. The space and time overhead of such handling of register and memory state will of course be very high.

- *record-little-recompute-everything*: if only the register and memory state at the beginning of the execution, and only truly non-deterministic events (such as input values) are recorded, the exact instruction sequence can be reproduced by loading the initial state and injecting the non-deterministic events at the right time.

There are many design points in between these two extremes. We chose an implementation closer to the second extreme.

For a single-threaded program, PinPlay reproduces the exact same sequence of instructions that was observed during logging. For multi-threaded/multi-process programs, there are two ways in which replay can be provided. We can either replay individual threads/processes in isolation (*parallel logging isolated replay*) or replay them together (*parallel logging parallel replay*). For the latter case, possible designs are either to preserve a total global order of instructions in all threads/processes, or only to preserve the order between specific inter-thread/inter-process events. For multi-threaded programs, we chose to provide parallel logging and parallel replay, with the order of shared-memory accesses repeated among various threads. Thus, instructions in each thread are repeated exactly during replay, however instructions from different threads do not follow a strict order with respect to one another – the only guarantee is that the accesses to shared-memory locations by multiple threads are repeated exactly as they were observed during logging. On the other hand, for multi-process programs, we chose to implement parallel logging and isolated replay where each process is replayed in isolation without any interaction with other replayed processes.

2.1   Controlling Non-determinism

Non-determinism in programs arises from either sources internal to the program, e.g. order of shared memory access by multiple threads, or from external sources such as system calls. In particular, we observed that the execution of a program is not completely reproducible because across different runs the following can happen:

1. *Initial stack location changes*: the stack location is assigned by the operating system kernel and we observed that for each run the kernel may assign a different location for the program stack.

2. *Text and data location changes*: shared-library load locations (due to address space randomization done by some operating systems) and location of dynamically allocated memory (heap location) may change. The fact that Pin and Pintool are pre-loaded in the same address space as the test program makes shared-library load location changes more likely under Pin.

3. *Program binary/shared-library code changes*: change over time or from machine to machine.

4. *Processor-specific instruction behavior changes*: Output of IA-32 instructions such as CPUID, RDTSC, RDPMC depends on the processor version.

5. *Signals*: Signals are not guaranteed to arrive at the same execution points across runs. Signals result in arbitrary memory, register, and control-flow changes.

6. *Un-initialized memory location reads*.

7. *Differing behavior of system calls*: Certain system calls depend on the environment in which they are running and hence are non-deterministic. Examples on Linux are *gettimeofday()* and *uname()*.

8. *Different access order of shared memory locations*: In shared memory parallel programs, different threads or processes may read/write shared memory locations in different order on different runs.

In order to guarantee repeatability across runs, the sources of non-determinism listed above are tracked and logged by PinPlay's logger and injected by PinPlay's replayer. Here's an overview of how this is done:

- For handling changing stack, text, and data locations, the PinPlay logger logs the addresses of the memory ranges that are used for the stack, dynamically allocated memory, and shared libraries using operating system independent techniques. The Linux PinPlay replayer uses a newly added Pin feature to pre-allocate the logged ranges making sure that the replay run uses the same stack, heap, and text area as the logged run. The Windows PinPlay replayer uses another new Pin feature to relocate stack, data, and text.

- Program binary/shared-library code is captured during logging and restored during replay.

- Processor-specific instructions change known registers whose values are logged and restored during replay.

- The point where a signal arrives during logging is recorded using the instruction count along with the register value changes. During replay, the logged effects of the signal are repeated at the right instruction count.

- To log the un-initialized memory values needed during replay, PinPlay applies a technique based on [13]. The technique only logs memory values which are read for the first time, without any prior write. The insight is that all the other memory values will be recalculated during replay because all the instructions executed during logging will be re-executed. Hence the values of the writes will be recalculated and written to memory deterministically. The technique is explained in section 2.1.1.

- System calls modify both register state and memory values. The technique to record memory values is described in section 2.1.1. In addition, system calls change the register state. During replay, PinPlay completely skips most of the system calls (except those for thread creation/termination and a few others) and simply restores the logged register changes.

- For handling the run-to-run variation in shared memory access order by different threads/processes, PinPlay logger records the order of shared memory read/writes and the replayer obeys them during replay. Recording the execution of PinPlay's shared-memory order logging scheme is a software-implementation of the scheme described in [26]. The logger simulates a cache-coherency protocol noting the last reader/writer for address ranges used in the program at a tunable granularity. It uses this information to compute read/write, write/write, and write/read dependences for shared-memory address ranges and records a subset of them (others are implied). The replayer obeys the recorded dependences, possibly stalling threads/processes if needed.

2.1.1 Memory Value Logging

PinPlay logs memory values based on the technique which is explained in detail in [14]. Here is a brief overview. The PinPlay logger maintains a copy *UserMem* of all memory changes made by the user-level code in the input program. After a *store* in the program *UserMem* is updated with the stored value. On a *load*, *UserMem* is consulted; if the loaded location is not found, it is an uninitialized read and the value is logged. If the loaded location is in *UserMem* but the value there differs from the value loaded, then the value is logged since the location must have been changed by some external entity (either a system call or another thread/process [in case of per-thread/process logging]). *UserMem* is always updated with the logged value to avoid duplicate logging in the future.

Maintaining *UserMem* doubles the memory requirement of the program being logged. That will rule out logging some 32-bit programs that use more than half their virtual address space. While 64-bit programs are unlikely to run out of virtual address space, increasing the memory footprint above the physical memory available on the logging machine can result in major slowdown during logging due to excessive page thrashing.

2.2 Sources of Slowdown

The Pin dynamic instrumentation system, while providing a very flexible interface for analysis can cause noticeable slowdown depending on the analysis done in the Pintool. There is a fixed run-time translation overhead common to all Pintools and a variable Pintool-specific overhead. In this sub-section, we will discuss the sources of run-time overhead specific to the PinPlay tools and ways to alleviate the resulting slowdowns.

For finding un-initialized reads and memory changed by system calls, we implement the scheme described above (2.1.1). The advantage of this scheme is that it records only the minimal set of memory values needed for replaying the execution so is good for limiting log sizes. However, the scheme involves maintaining a copy of all user-level memory accessed and instrumenting all loads/stores in the program for detecting un-initialized reads and system-call side-effects. This is a major source of slowdown for the logger. We can greatly reduce this slowdown as described below:

[A] The instrumentation for un-initialized reads can be avoided by recording initial values of all data and text pages as program images get loaded under Pin. That way only a callback on image loads is needed as opposed to instrumenting each load and store. Logging initial pages could increase the size of the logs. However, such logging of entire images is also desirable for replay-based debugging as the user may want to explore memory locations not otherwise touched by the replayed execution which would not be recorded by the scheme from [14].

[B] The instrumentation for system-call side-effect detection could be avoided if we precisely knew the memory locations changed by each system call. That way, only monitoring system calls under Pin and recording the locations changed by each system call will be needed. Such ad-hoc system-call analysis is only possible for operating systems such as Linux where system calls are well documented.

With [A] and [B] above, we can have a logger for serial codes that only monitors image loads, system calls, and processor-specific instructions such as RDTSC all of which are relatively infrequent events and hence the logger will have very low overhead. We are currently implementing such a *fast logger* for Linux.

For multi-threaded programs, the PinPlay logger currently acquires a lock before each memory operation and releases it afterwards. This is necessary to prevent possible modification of the memory location being analyzed by another thread between the time of analysis and the time of execution of the instruction. We identify this problem as *Analysis-Atomicity Problem*, which is illustrated in Figure 2. Thread 1 executes a memory operation reading a value from memory location *A*. This memory location is initialized to 0. Its analysis routine, represented by the function call *BeforeAnalysisRoutine*, executes before the instruction executes. The

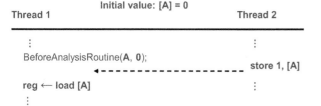

Initial value: [A] = 0

Thread 1	Thread 2
⋮	⋮
BeforeAnalysisRoutine(**A**, **0**);	
◄- store 1, [A]	
reg ← load [A]	⋮
⋮	

Figure 2: Analysis-Atomicity Problem

analysis routine knows the effective address and the value that will be read by the instruction, which is 0 in the example. However, before the load instruction executes, thread 2 modifies the value to 1. Consequently, the analysis routine sees the load reading the value 0 but the actual instruction reads the value 1, which is incorrect. The locks to prevent the problem above are maintained for fixed sized chunks (tunable) of memory addresses so as to minimize contention. However, acquiring and releasing a lock around each memory operation causes a large amount of slowdown. We can reduce this slowdown by using the new "memory redirection" feature in Pin. The idea is to translate each memory load instruction to first copy the value into a thread-private location and then do the actual load from the thread-private location. Any analysis that is done before the instruction can then look at the thread-private location, with the guarantee that the instruction will see the same value that the analysis function saw.

During replay, each memory read is instrumented to first check the recorded log to see if any value needs to be injected and, if required, to do a memory injection. Instrumenting every memory read is quite expensive. For single-threaded programs without signals, we can avoid the instrumentation of memory reads by only monitoring system calls and combining all the memory injections between a system call and the next into one big "lump-sum" memory injection. This works because (in the absence of signals and shared memory with other processes) system calls are the only external entities that can change memory in single-threaded programs. Thus there can only be one log entry for a given address between two system calls, and this is why we can safely restore all entries between two system calls. We have implemented such a "fast replayer" on Linux for single-threaded programs. We can extend the lump-sum injection scheme to multi-threaded programs by doing some extra book-keeping for instructions that access shared memory. This would allow one to determine which memory locations can be restored from the logs in one "lump-sum".

For recording the order of shared memory accesses in multi-threaded programs, the PinPlay logger simulates a cache coherency protocol in software. This allows us to capture all read-read, read-write, write-write, and write-read dependencies precisely. This helps in faithful replay of these dependencies later on but the analysis is quite expensive. To reduce the number of dependencies logged, the logger uses the well-known Netzer optimization [15] at the cost of additional slowdown. Precise recording of shared-memory dependencies is required only if the program threads are to be replayed in parallel. For multi-process programs, we currently only allow per-process replay in isolation and hence do not need to pay the cost of recording shared memory dependencies during logging.

2.3 Microsoft Windows® Port

We have ported the PinPlay logger and replayer to Microsoft Windows. We can currently log multi-threaded Windows programs and replay them on Windows or Linux. There are a number of issues which are specific to the Windows port of PinPlay; the issues, and our solutions are described here.

2.3.1 Handling Windows System Calls

As described earlier, PinPlay logs system-call side-effects without requiring any a-priori knowledge of how a system call modifies memory. This is especially beneficial on Windows, where the details of the kernel interface are neither public nor fixed. This logging is sufficient for most system calls, since the only requirement at replay time is that the replayed code sees the same effects on memory and the registers as occurred at record time (the actual effects of the system call on the kernel and the outside world are not required). Therefore, there is no need to execute most system calls at replay time. Currently we do execute even uninteresting system calls, because we want Pin to notice them, and call any system call related callbacks registered by the Pintool running on top of the replayer. We expect to remove the need to execute the system calls by adding a call to the Pin API to allow PinPlay directly to request that Pin execute the relevant callbacks. To ensure that the system call has no side effects, we force the system call number to be that of the *NtYieldExecution* system call, which has no arguments. This only affects thread scheduling which does not matter to us since we explicitly enforce inter-thread data dependencies.

However there are a few system calls which do have critical effects that must be recreated at replay time, (e.g. thread creation, thread exit and process exit). To support cross operating system replay, we have designed the system call information in the pinball format to include semantic tags for these critical system calls. Thus, rather than simply recording that a system call instruction was executed with a specific set of register values changed, we record that a thread creation system call was made, capturing the semantics of the system call, as well as the details of its invocation.

This additional information allows the replayer to translate the system call into one which has the same effect on the host operating system during replay. Thus a thread creation call on Windows is mapped at replay time on Linux into a suitable *clone()* system call. Since the replayer restores all of the machine registers after the system call has been made to the values they had after the corresponding system call at record time, the replayed code cannot detect that the system call was actually executed in a completely different way by a different operating system. However the critical semantic effects of the system call (creating a new thread) take place as required.

On Windows, the precise system call numbers used to implement the system calls in *ntdll* may change with each Windows service pack. Therefore converting from a system call number to the system call semantics is not as easy as on Linux, where the system call numbers are fixed and well known. Fortunately Pin has already solved this problem for a small set of critical system calls which are a superset of those which PinPlay needs to understand. We have therefore been able to expand the Pin API to allow PinPlay to extract this information from Pin, and determine the system call semantics from the system call number.

The same interface is used at replay time to translate back from the semantics to the system call number required to implement it on the replaying machine. In effect we treat all replay on Windows as if it were a cross OS replay, because we cannot rely on the stability of the system call numbers.

2.3.2 Placement of Code and Data in Memory at Replay Time

One of the critical issues in supporting replay is that the code in Pin and the PinPlay replayer Pintool occupy parts of the address space which were not used by the program being replayed. On Linux this can be achieved by ensuring that all of the regions of the address space which were used by the recorded process are reserved (using a newly added Pin switch) before Pin injects any code into the newly created replay process. Since Pin and PinPlay tools are all position independent, they can then be placed in the gaps which remain in the address space.

However, on Windows, Pin cannot take control of the process as early in its creation as it can on Linux. Therefore by the time Pin takes control of the process, the address space is already likely to contain code which occupies addresses that were used by the recorded process. To overcome this problem we have extended Pin's existing interface to memory operand rewriting to allow it to handle the memory operands of all instructions (with the exception of "enter" with a non-zero second immediate operand, which we have, luckily, never seen used). This is complex because the Intel® 64 and IA-32 architectures have a significant number of instructions which access memory without having an explicit memory operand that could be edited (for example, PUSH, POP, CALL, RETURN, ENTER, LEAVE, MOVS, STOS, SCAS,...). To rewrite the memory operands of these instructions at JIT time, Pin has to remove the source instruction and replace it with a suitable sequence of instructions which implement the semantics of the original instruction while allowing the memory operand to be explicitly specified.

Using memory operand rewriting, we are able to introduce a layer of software controlled address translation between the replayed code, and the replaying process. By using this, and Pin's existing interface to allow tools to intercept its instruction fetch mechanism, we can place the recorded process' code and data anywhere in the replaying process' address space. This avoids areas of the address space which are occupied by Pin, the replay Pin tool, and associated system libraries, while maintaining the appearance to the recorded code that everything is where it was at record time.

Of course, altering the placement of data would cause us a problem if we were executing system calls, since the kernel would be unaware of the additional layer of address translation. Our code is unable to make translations before the system call since we have no knowledge of which system call arguments require address translation. However this is not a problem because (as discussed above) the only system calls we execute at replay time are those with specific semantics whose arguments we construct explicitly.

2.3.3 Treatment of the Thread Environment Block at replay time

Windows Thread Environment Block (TEB) is a critical data structure which is accessed both by Windows runtime libraries and the Windows kernel. A pointer to the TEB is maintained in one of the segment registers [1] (FS on a 32 bit kernel, GS on a 64 bit one), so that fields in the TEB can be rapidly accessed using instructions like

```
mov     eax, DWORD PTR fs:[0]
```

If the replaying process' TEB were replaced by that of the recorded process, the replaying process would rapidly crash, since the kernel and runtime libraries must see the correct value for the active process. Therefore we must ensure at replay time that the recorded process' execution sees one set of TEB values, while the replaying process sees another. The memory address rewriting we have previously discussed provides half of the solution here, allowing us to place the replayed process' TEB anywhere in the replaying process memory. However, we still have the problem that the two pieces of code must see different addresses when accessing via the relevant segment register. The solution to this problem is for Pin to virtualize the critical segment register, so that all accesses from the Pinned code (in this case the recorded process' code)

---

[1] The details of segmented addressing and how segment registers work is more complex than this, however thinking of them as pointers is sufficient for this discussion.

to the segment register are not to the hardware register, but to a separate value maintained by Pin. Thus the hardware segment register continues to hold the correct value, ensuring the kernel and runtime are happy, while the replayed process accesses the TEB at the address which was recorded and therefore sees the same values as at record time.

2.3.4 Thread Creation at Replay Time

Unlike Linux, where thread creation can be achieved with a single *clone* system call, Windows thread creation is presented as a runtime library call *CreateThread*, which may make multiple system calls, allocate memory and so on. This presents a problem for PinPlay replay, since we need to create threads in the context of the replayed process, but cannot insert library calls there. This would cause them to be instrumented and their instructions and memory accesses would be seen by tools sitting on top of the replay, even though they didn't happen at record time. (Also, the recorded process cannot execute code from the replaying tool because of the address translation between the two). To overcome this problem when the PinPlay replayer starts up on Windows it reads the number of required threads from the logs, and creates all of them in a suspended state before it starts the replay. When a thread creation system call is then required, it can be mapped into a single *NtResumeThread* system call. This causes the pre-created thread to start executing in user space at which point it is picked up by Pin. The replayer can then force its register state to that required to replay the thread's execution.

2.4 Combining PinPlay with other Pintools

To perform repeatable analysis of parallel programs, we combine PinPlay functionality with other Pintools. The only requirement is that the tool not change the control flow of the program in any manner. The PinPlay framework provides a library and a well-defined application programmer's interface (API) to enable logging and replaying capability that other Pintools can utilize. Only minimal source changes are needed to the sources of the Pintool to make it PinPlay-enabled. Once PinPlay-enabled, a Pintool can operate in any of the following four modes [1] as a regular Pintool running a program binary, [2] as a logger creating PinPlay logs (pinball), [3] as a replayer running off a pinball, and [4] as a relogger running off a pinball and creating another pinball (for a selected region). For the last three modes, the Pintool can optionally do its regular analysis. The ability to run a Pintool in these modes can be useful in certain cases. If a Pintool encounters a problem at a user site, it can be switched to the logger mode and the resulting pinball can be shipped back to the developer site. The developers can then run the Pintool in replay mode and reproduce the problem. Since the pinball is self-contained, no additional information (program binaries, licenses, special operating environment, input files) are needed to reproduce the problem. If the pinball for the entire program run is too big to transfer, selective logging, using the relogger mode, can be done to capture just the region that shows the problem.

2.5 Selective Logging

The logging capability in the PinPlay logger is quite flexible. In addition to logging the entire execution of a program, one can be more selective about what part of the execution to log. Logging can be done for just an interval specified, say, by providing the number of instructions to skip and the number of instructions to log. Such selective logging creates a pinball for the region which can then be processed by other Pintools avoiding the need for fast-forwarding. When used for reproducible debugging, selective logging of the region showing a bug can be helpful in creating a pinball that is small enough to be transferred to the developer site.

Selective logging can also be done to exclude some part of the program code, say a function body. The basic idea is to treat a specified code range like a system call by turning off all the analysis in the code range. Just like system calls, the logger takes a difference in register states before and after the specified region and logs the register values changed. Any memory changed by the excluded code range will be discovered by the algorithm that detects system-call side effects. During replay, the code range will be completely skipped and its side-effects restored. We have used this ability of code range exclusion to discard spin-loops in large parallel programs to ease simulation.

3. Applications of PinPlay

We are using PinPlay for two different purposes: [1] Finding representative simulation regions and analyzing them with a guarantee of repeatability and [2] reproducible debugging of large parallel programs. In this section we briefly describe these two applications.

3.1 Repeatable PinPoints

Most programs are long-running (trillions of instructions) and given the complexity of the processors that are being designed, detailed simulation is quite slow. Traditionally, architects have used program knowledge or sampling (random or uniform) to specify regions for simulation which may or may not be representative of the whole-program behavior. Luckily, all large programs show unique repetitive behaviors or phases. An approach called *SimPoint* [23] identifies such program phases and selects simulation regions representing each phase.

We are using the PinPoints [18] methodology which combines Pin and SimPoint for finding representative regions of large programs and generating traces for them. The PinPoints methodology involves running two Pintools – one for generating program profiles and another for generating traces for simulation. The profile generated by the first Pintool is analyzed by SimPoint to find representative regions, or PinPoints, which are described in a PinPoints file. The tracing tool then reads the region description from the PinPoints file and generates traces for the representative regions. Additional Pintools may be run to evaluate the quality of the simulation regions selected. In the PinPoints methodology, the input program is run at least twice, once for profiling and once for trace generation. The assumption is that the two runs are identical so that the PinPoints regions found after the first run are reachable in the second run. However, we found that for many programs, even single-threaded programs, the two runs differ sufficiently between the profiling and the tracing run to make PinPoints un-reachable or be reached out of order. In an experiment with SPEC2006 programs, we found non-repeatability of PinPoints to be an issue in 27 of 55 reference runs. Although some workarounds do exist, the PinPlay framework completely solves this non-repeatability problem.

We have combined our versions of the PinPoints tools with PinPlay and we run them in replay mode. We first use the PinPlay logger to capture a pinball for a whole-program execution and then do all the PinPoints analysis using the whole-program pinball. After finding suitable PinPoints, we use the PinPlay relogger to selectively log just the PinPoints regions of interest. Just like *Suite-Specks* in [20], this saves fast-forwarding time for future analysis of the regions. We have also modified our simulators to accept pinball format directly so that the exact same region can be simulated with the simulators and analyzed under Pintools. For multi-process programs, we do per-process replay and can run PinPoints tools on the pinballs for individual processes in isolation. For multi-threaded programs, we do parallel replay, and can choose to collect traces either for each thread in isolation or to generate combined traces for all the threads. Using the pinballs as inputs to simulators enables

deterministic simulation of multi-threaded programs by controlling thread order during simulation as described in [19].

3.2 Replay Debugging

Another useful application of PinPlay is to facilitate the debugging of non-deterministic multi-threaded programs. Such programs are difficult to debug because failures can be intermittent and the events leading up to a failure can vary for each run. Our replay debugging feature removes the non-determinism of such programs, making them much easier to debug. The basic idea is to capture a failing execution with PinPlay and then debug the problem from the recorded log files.

The Pin team has recently extended Pin to allow it to connect to the Gnu debugger (GDB), or other debuggers, and to provide a "pure" view of the program running under Pin. This allows one to debug the program at the source level even while it is instrumented with a Pintool. Combining this feature with PinPlay allows "replay debugging" of a program execution. Nearly all debugger features work normally under this scenario. The debugger can print variables, examine the stack, set breakpoints, advance the execution with *continue* or *single-step* commands, etc. However, since the pinball being replayed is a recording of a previous run, the debugger cannot modify variables or change the program's control flow in any way. These limitations do not seem serious, though, since debuggers are more often used to observe the state of a program than to modify it.

3.2.1 Implementation of the Debugger Extensions

Pin connects to GDB via its remote debugging protocol. When using this protocol, GDB sends Pin a command for each low-level debugging operations: reading memory, reading a register, setting a breakpoint, single-stepping, etc. Since GDB implements all of its high-level operations on top of these low-level commands, Pin does not need to understand complex debugger tasks like stack backtrace or symbol resolution. Pin treats each of these low-level commands as a request to its virtual machine. For example, a request to read a register really returns Pin's emulated copy of the program's register. When the debugger asks to single-step the program, Pin fetches a single instruction from the program image loaded in memory, asks the PinPlay replayer to instrument the instruction, and then executes the resulting instrumented trace. The communication with the debugger is two-way. GDB sends commands to Pin, and Pin sends notifications back whenever the program stops or terminates. It is important to note that every program instruction that is executed under control of the debugger is still instrumented with the PinPlay replayer. Therefore, the debugger sees all the memory values the replayer restores from its log files. Also, the replayer still synchronizes the replayed threads to ensure they execute in the same order as the recorded execution. In fact, we prevent the debugger from advancing the threads out of order. If the debugger attempts to advance a thread beyond a recorded synchronization point, the replayer delays that thread until the other thread catches up. The overall setup for replay debugging is shown in Figure 3.

3.2.2 Typical Use

Imagine that you have an intermittently failing program. You start by running the program under the PinPlay logger until it fails. If the failure is rare, you can do this by running an automated script overnight. When it does fail, PinPlay has captured the exact sequence of events that lead up to the failure and you can reproduce the failure from the log files.

Now you can run the PinPlay replayer in debug mode, which causes it to stop immediately before the program's first instruction. You then start GDB and attach to Pin / PinPlay with the "target remote" command. We have not made any modifications to GDB

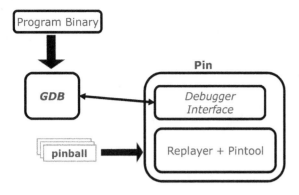

Figure 3: PinPlay-based debugging.

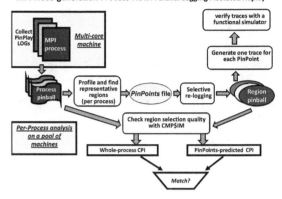

Figure 4: PinPlay-based simulation region selection and tracing of MPI programs

to enable replay debugging, so any modern version of GDB will work. You can then continue execution up to the point of the failure and look at the program state to understand the immediate cause. Often this will be some sort of unexpected value in memory. In this case, you can rerun the program and use a conditional debugger breakpoint to find the point at which this value was written, even if it is written by some other thread. Since PinPlay guarantees a reproducible replay, the program is guaranteed to write the same bad value to the same memory location when the program is rerun. In this way, it is easy to peel back the layers of the bug until you find the root cause.

A central feature of replay debugging is that each time you run the debugger, you see exactly the same program behavior. Each thread allocates exactly the same memory locations on each execution, and any data races between threads are resolved in exactly the same way each time. This means you can use repeated debugger sessions without worrying that the dynamically allocated memory addresses or thread interleavings might change from run to run.

3.2.3 Extended Debugger Commands

In a typical scenario, it is common to use conditional breakpoints to peel back the layers of your bug. For example, you may want to conditionally stop when some thread writes an unexpected value to a shared variable. You can use the debugger's conditional breakpoints for this, but that can be slow because GDB triggers the breakpoint unconditionally and then checks the condition from inside the debugger.

As a performance enhancement, we have written a PinPlay replayer tool that uses a new Pin API to receive interactive commands from the GDB prompt. We used this mechanism to add faster conditional breakpoint commands, where the condition is checked inside the Pintool. These breakpoints are more than 1000 times faster than traditional conditional breakpoints, but they currently require you to express the condition at the assembly level. We have added other extended debugger commands too. For example, we have a command that stops the debugger immediately before a jump to an invalid address. This allows you to stop at a breakpoint immediately before calling through an invalid function pointer or corrupt C++ v-table entry. We expect to develop a small collection of similar extended commands as we refine our replay debugging paradigm.

4. Results

In this section we summarize the overhead (runtime and disk space) for a number of programs we tested. Table 1 describes the single and multi-threaded Linux 64-bit programs we tested and the average logging/replaying overhead and size of pinballs. Table 2 lists the same data for four multi-process (using *Message Passing Inter-*

face (MPI)) Linux 64-bit programs we tested. There are a number of observations we can make from Tables 1 and 2:

1. The pinball sizes are for bzip2-compressed files (which the replayer can read directly). The individual pinball files are currently in text format (for the ease of debugging) which we are planning to convert to a binary format and expect noticeable reduction in size.

2. The pinball size is not a function of instruction count but of the memory behavior of the programs.

3. In general, logging is more expensive than replaying. This is because there is more analysis done during logging.

4. For single-threaded SPEC2006 programs, we tried the *fast* replayer doing *lump-sum* memory restores at system calls as described in section 2.2. The resulting slowdown (1.4X) is very small and is similar to the average slowdown (1.3X) of running the programs under Pin alone. Since the *fast* replayer only requires instrumenting system calls that are quite infrequent in SPEC, the runtime overhead is low.

5. MPI programs use the message passing paradigm for communication among parallel processes. When run on a multiprocessor machine (as opposed to a distributed processing system) the MPI run-time system implements message passing using inter-process shared memory. We implemented the *parallel logging isolated replay* model for MPI programs where each MPI process is run by a separate instance of Pin and the logger Pintool and creates its own pinball. Since shared-memory dependences are not recorded for isolated replay, the logging in MPI programs is not as expensive as the multi-threaded cases (SPECOMP2001 and McBench). Further, for MPI programs the logger can figure out which memory address ranges are shared. This, it only needs to handle the Analysis-Atomicity Problem for those address ranges. The pinballs are noticeably larger for MPI programs. That is because each process logs modification to shared memory by another process as if it were modified by some system call. Depending on the interleaving of accesses to shared memory by different processes, many of shared memory locations may get logged increasing pinball size. Also, a per process pinball ends up logging program text multiple times even though the program binary is the same for all the processes. We believe the sizes of MPI pinballs will be

Program Suite	Average Instruction Count	Average pinball size	Logger slowdown (X native)	Replayer slowdown (X native)
SPEC2006: Single-threaded CPU benchmarks: 55 *reference* runs	924 billion	39 MB	80 X	26 X (1.4 X with *fast replayer*)
SPECOMP2001: 4-threaded *openmp* benchmarks: 8 *train* runs	307 billion	91 MB	117 X	25 X
McBench: 4-threaded "recognition mining synthesis" benchmarks: 5 runs	156 billion	396 MB	146 X	36 X

Table 1: Average slowdowns and disk usage: single/multi-threaded program suites.

MPI Program (8 processes)	Average Instruction Count	Average pinball size	Logger slowdown (X native)	Replayer slowdown (X native)
MILC: A large-scale numerical simulator for quantum chromodynamics	109 billion	2.09 GB	93 X	18 X
POP: An ocean circulation model simulator	952 billion	1.09 GB	147 X	10 X
WRF: A generation mesoscale numerical weather prediction system	755 billion	5.1 GB	36 X	14 X
EnergyApp: A commercial energy exploration program	693 billion	1.95 GB	68 X	12 X

Table 2: Slowdowns and disk usage: MPI programs (*parallel logging isolated replay*).

reduced drastically when we implement *parallel logging parallel replay* for multi-process programs.

We analyzed the commercial MPI application (EnergyApp) with PinPlay-based PinPoints on 4-24 process runs as shown in Figure 4. The steps we ran were: PinPlay logger, per-process profiling, simulation-point selection, relogging to create pinballs for just the simulation regions, running a Pin-based fast simulator, CMP$IM [8], on whole-program and simulation region pinballs to evaluate performance projection error, trace generation from the region pinballs, and verification of the traces with a functional simulator. The turnaround time for running all these steps was at most a couple of days which was acceptable to our end users (computer architects). The PinPoints selected could be accurately reached multiple times thanks to the repeatability provided by PinPlay. After some tuning, the PinPoints selection was deemed accurate based on the small (less than 5%) difference between whole-program performance, and performance projected by PinPoints.

After simulating the EnergApp traces generated by PinPlay-based PinPoints, the architects noticed that some of the traces showed a large number of instructions in a spin-loop indicating the process traced was busy-waiting for some other process. This behavior was more pronounced for runs with higher number of processes. This busy-waiting was natural behavior for the program (albeit perturbed by the slowdown under Pin). Unfortunately, traces mostly showing busy-waiting were useless for projection. So the architects changed their analytical projection model to account for busy-waiting separately and requested traces without busy waiting from PinPlay-based PinPoints. We could exclude the code-range that did busy waiting as described earlier in section 2.5. Figure 5 shows the per process instruction count as measured by a replay-based tool for EnergyApp processes logged with and without spin-loops. When spin-loops are removed by the PinPlay logger, there is a noticeable reduction in instruction count per process especially with larger numbers of processes. This is expected because only the code doing actual work remains in the pinball, and since the total work is constant, the per process share of the work reduces.

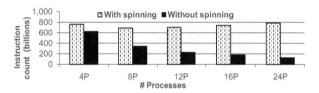

Figure 5: EnergyApp: Effect of spin-loop removal on average per process instruction count.

5. Related Work

In this section, we will describe other software-only deterministic replay techniques and how they relate to our work.

Boothe [3] used copy-on-write check-pointing based on the UNIX `fork` system call, which is used to capture memory locations touched by the program. Boothe also proposed to capture the side-effects of system calls by instrumenting each system call in the system and capturing the register and memory side-effects. Although this handles the non-determinism of system calls during replay, this is operating system dependent (e.g. would not work on Windows) and hard to maintain (because OS interfaces change over time). Michiel *et al.* [6] implemented a solution which avoids instrumenting every system call. Their solution is based on modifying the Linux kernel and instrumenting a single point of execution, where memory values changed by a system call are copied from kernel space to user-space. Srinivasan *et al.* introduced *Flashback* [24], which is similar to Boothe's solution. Flashback allows check-pointing the state of a multi-threaded programs, but does not support replaying it deterministically on a multi-processor. More recently, Montesinos *et al.* [12] proposed a solution that also instruments the Linux kernel. Montesinos also presents an interface and implementation which allows the OS to record and replay multiple processes in the same system by separating them into replay *spheres*. None of these software solutions supports deterministic replay of multi-threaded or multi-process programs on a multi-processor system. Some solutions to allow replay of a multi-threaded program on a single-processor system have been introduced in the past. Choi *et al* [4] and Russinovich *et al* [22] proposed recording the thread schedule and reproducing it during replay.

In the context of multi-core processors, LeBlanc *et al.* [10] proposed *Instant Replay*, which was used to debug multi-process programs that exchange data through shared objects (e.g. message passing buffers, shared segments). Instant Replay records the order of every access to the shared objects. This only works well if the sharing is coarse grain because of the amount of information logged can be significant. Additionally, Instant Replay assumes no data races. Pan *et al.* developed Recap [17], which records input values for every instruction that reads from shared-memory in a multi-process system. Recap relies on compiler analysis and code modification to identify shared memory accesses and record their values. This allows replaying each process independent of the others. Ronsee *et al.* proposed RecPlay [21], which uses JIT compilation to instrument synchronization operations and record the order in which they occur using *Lamport clocks*. None of these approaches allows replaying data races.

More recently, Bhansali *et al.* developed iDNA [2]. iDNA logs memory instruction input values in a manner similar to our approach. It maintains a copy of user-level memory, which is used to identify system-call side-effects. This is very beneficial because it is OS independent and handles other side-effects such as DMA transfers and direct mapped I/O. iDNA's focus is on performance and hence the copy of user-level memory is implemented as a direct-mapped cache, which is more efficient than PinPlay, but results in larger log files. Each thread of execution maintains its own copy, thus allowing threads to be replayed independently from one another, but this also enlarges the log files. iDNA monitors synchronization operations and records the total order in which they execute. Although programs with data races can be recorded, additional analysis is required to repeat the data races exactly during replay.

Triage [25] is a system that allows for periodic checkpoint and deterministic replay for bug analysis in production runs. Once a bug is detected, analysis to identify the type, trigger and the where the bug happens is performed. Triage allows exploring different control paths during replay to help identify the root cause of a bug. By augmenting PinPlay's logs, similar techniques could be applied. One of the limitation of Triage is that it only works on uni-processors and it is OS dependent, which allows for lower overheads. On the other hand, while PinPlay has higher overheads, it is OS independent and works on multi-processors as well.

Kendo [16] proposes an algorithm to increment a logical clock in a deterministic manner during the execution of a program. Kendo does it by assigning deterministic identifiers for each thread and by designing an algorithm to increase the logical clock of each thread in a deterministic way. The logical clocks are incremented when acquiring locks, thus guaranteeing locks are acquired in the same order. For applications with data races, Kendo provides an API for ensuring deterministic reads. While Kendo provides low-overhead deterministic execution, it requires OS and application modification to ensure determinism. PinPlay, on the other hand, is mostly OS independent and works without modifying the application.

All the approaches above record the execution of user-level instructions and some capture operating system side-effects to replay them correctly. Another approach is to record the whole execution of the operating system as well as the user-level instructions. Revirt [7, 9] and VMWare's [27] systems are approaches that record the operating system by monitoring the execution at the virtual machine monitor (VMM). All external inputs (e.g. internet packets, disk I/O, etc) are observed by the VMM, which records them. Both approaches also record multi-threaded shared-memory interleaving by monitoring accesses to OS-level pages and triggering interrupts. These solutions require the entire system to run above a VMM.

In [5] Chow *et al.* describe the idea of separating execution from analysis and allowing multiple accurate off-line analyses of a prior application execution. They use VMWare Workstation for recording which only supports uni-processor machines. The replay-time analysis can be done using binary translators implemented either on VMWare or a simulator (QEMU [1]). The VMWare binary translator is implemented in the most privileged protection layer (ring 0) where dynamic memory allocation is heavily constrained hence doing a general-purpose analysis is not feasible there. Doing analysis with QEMU requires an extra re-logging step. PinPlay-based analysis, while only user level, requires no extra steps.

6. Summary and Future Work

As parallel programming becomes more popular, there is an increasing need to analyze parallel programs in a repeatable manner. We have presented PinPlay which is a framework for deterministic capture and reproducible analysis of parallel programs. PinPlay is based on the popular Pin dynamic instrumentation system and hence is very easy to use.

As part of the PinPlay work, we have identified sources of non-determinism in serial and parallel programs and have devised ways to control the non-determinism. PinPlay captures an execution of a program in a set of files collectively called a pinball. A pinball is self-contained, operating system independent, and can be generated selectively for only part of the execution. PinPlay integrates seamlessly with other Pintools. We have extended many Pintools to run off pinballs and used the tools for two purposes on large parallel programs: [1] reproducible simulation point selection, tracing, and simulation, and [2] repeatable debugging.

We have identified many opportunities for reducing the overhead in PinPlay logger and replayer and plan to work on them in the future. We also want to support *parallel logging parallel replay* for multi-process (MPI and other) programs. Eventually we want to make PinPlay publicly available along with Pin distributions.

Acknowledgments

This work has benefited tremendously from the support, contribution, and suggestions of many individuals over the years. We sincerely thank all of them. In particular, we would like to acknowledge Geoff Lowney, Moshe Bach, Robert Cohn, Brad Calder, Satish Narayanasamy, Chitra Natarajan, Mike Greenfield, Aamer Jaleel, Sam Strom, and Alex Skaletsky. We also thank the anonymous reviewers for their comments and suggestions.

References

[1] F. Bellard. Qemu, a fast and portable dynamic translator. In *USENIX Annual Technical Conference, FREENIX Track*, pages 41–46. USENIX, 2005.

[2] S. Bhansali, W.-K. Chen, S. de Jong, A. Edwards, R. Murray, M. Drinić, D. Mihočka, and J. Chau. Framework for instruction-level tracing and analysis of program executions. In *Proceedings of the 2nd international conference on Virtual execution environments (VEE)*, pages 154–163, 2006.

[3] B. Boothe. Efficient algorithms for bidirectional debugging. In *Proceedings of the ACM SIGPLAN 2000 conference on Programming language design and implementation(PLDI)*, pages 299–310, 2000.

[4] J.-D. Choi, B. Alpern, T. Ngo, and J. Vlissides. A perturbation-free replay platform for cross-optimized multithreaded applications. *Parallel and Distributed Processing Symposium, International*, 1:10023a, 2001.

[5] J. Chow, T. Garfinkel, and P. M. Chen. Decoupling dynamic program analysis from execution in virtual environments. In R. Isaacs and Y. Zhou, editors, *USENIX Annual Technical Conference*, pages 1–14. USENIX Association, 2008. ISBN 978-1-931971-59-1.

[6] F. Cornelis, M. Ronsse, and K. D. Bosschere. Tornado: A novel input replay tool. In *In Proceedings of the 2003 International Conference on Parallel and Distributed Processing Techniques and Applications (PDPTA)*, pages 1598–1604, 2003.

[7] G. W. Dunlap, S. T. King, S. Cinar, M. A. Basrai, and P. M. Chen. Revirt: Enabling intrusion analysis through virtual-machine logging and replay. In *In Proceedings of the 2002 Symposium on Operating Systems Design and Implementation (OSDI)*, volume 36, pages 211–224, 2002.

[8] A. Jaleel, R. S. Cohn, C.-K. Luk, and B. Jacob. Cmp$im: A pin-based on-the-fly single/multi-core cache simulator. In *Proceedings of the 4th Annual Workshop on Modeling, Benchmarking and Simulation, MoBS*, 2008.

[9] S. T. King, G. W. Dunlap, and P. M. Chen. Debugging operating systems with time-traveling virtual machines. In *In USENIX Annual Technical Conference*, pages 1–15, 2005.

[10] T. J. LeBlanc and J. M. Mellor-Crummey. Debugging parallel programs with instant replay. *IEEE Trans. Comput.*, 36(4):471–482, 1987.

[11] C.-K. Luk, R. S. Cohn, R. Muth, H. Patil, A. Klauser, P. G. Lowney, S. Wallace, V. J. Reddi, and K. M. Hazelwood. Pin: building customized program analysis tools with dynamic instrumentation. In V. Sarkar and M. W. Hall, editors, *PLDI*, pages 190–200, 2005.

[12] P. Montesinos, M. Hicks, S. T. King, and J. Torrellas. Capo: a software-hardware interface for practical deterministic multiprocessor replay. In *Proceeding of the 14th international conference on Architectural support for programming languages and operating systems (ASPLOS)*, pages 73–84, 2009.

[13] S. Narayanasamy, G. Pokam, and B. Calder. Bugnet: Continuously recording program execution for deterministic replay debugging. In *Proceedings of the 32nd annual international symposium on Computer Architecture(ISCA)*, pages 284–295, 2005.

[14] S. Narayanasamy, C. Pereira, H. Patil, R. Cohn, and B. Calder. Automatic logging of operating system effects to guide application-level architecture simulation. In *Proceedings of the joint international conference on Measurement and modeling of computer systems(SIGMETRICS)*, pages 216–227, 2006.

[15] R. H. B. Netzer. Optimal tracing and replay for debugging shared-memory parallel programs. In *Proceedings of the ACM/ONR Workshop on Parallel and Distributed Debugging*, pages 1–11, 1993.

[16] M. Olszewski, J. Ansel, and S. P. Amarasinghe. Kendo: efficient deterministic multithreading in software. In M. L. Soffa and M. J. Irwin, editors, *ASPLOS*, pages 97–108. ACM, 2009. ISBN 978-1-60558-406-5.

[17] D. Z. Pan and M. A. Linton. Supporting reverse execution for parallel programs. *SIGPLAN Not.*, 24(1):124–129, 1989.

[18] H. Patil, R. Cohn, M. Charney, R. Kapoor, A. Sun, and A. Karunanidhi. Pinpointing representative portions of large Intel Itanium programs with dynamic instrumentation. In *MICRO-37*, 2004.

[19] C. Pereira, H. Patil, and B. Calder. Reproducible simulation of multi-threaded workloads for architecture design exploration. In *IISWC*, pages 173–182, 2008.

[20] J. Ringenberg and T. N. Mudge. Suitespecks and suitespots: A methodology for the automatic conversion of benchmarking programs into intrinsically checkpointed assembly code. In *ISPASS*, pages 227–237. IEEE, 2009.

[21] M. Ronsse and K. De Bosschere. Recplay: a fully integrated practical record/replay system. *ACM Trans. Comput. Syst.*, 17(2):133–152, 1999.

[22] M. Russinovich and B. Cogswell. Replay for concurrent non-deterministic shared-memory applications. In *PLDI '96: Proceedings of the ACM SIGPLAN 1996 conference on Programming language design and implementation*, pages 258–266, 1996.

[23] T. Sherwood, E. Perelman, G. Hamerly, and B. Calder. Automatically characterizing large scale program behavior. In *ASPLOS-X*, 2002.

[24] S. M. Srinivasan, S. Kandula, S. K, C. R. Andrews, and Y. Zhou. Flashback: A lightweight extension for rollback and deterministic replay for software debugging. In *In USENIX Annual Technical Conference, General Track*, pages 29–44, 2004.

[25] J. Tucek, S. Lu, C. Huang, S. Xanthos, and Y. Zhou. Triage: diagnosing production run failures at the user's site. In T. C. Bressoud and M. F. Kaashoek, editors, *SOSP*, pages 131–144. ACM, 2007. ISBN 978-1-59593-591-5.

[26] M. Xu, R. Bodik, and M. D. Hill. A "flight data recorder" for enabling full-system multiprocessor deterministic replay. In *Proceedings of the 30th annual international symposium on Computer architecture(ISCA)*, pages 122–135, 2003.

[27] M. Xu, V. Malyugin, J. Sheldon, G. Venkitachalam, B. Weissman, and V. Inc. Retrace: Collecting execution trace with virtual machine deterministic replay. In *In Proceedings of the 3rd Annual Workshop on Modeling, Benchmarking and Simulation, MoBS*, 2007.

TAO: Two-level Atomicity for Dynamic Binary Optimizations

Edson Borin   Youfeng Wu   Cheng Wang   Wei Liu   Mauricio Breternitz Jr.   Shiliang Hu
Esfir Natanzon   Shai Rotem   Roni Rosner

Intel Corporation

{edson.borin, youfeng.wu, cheng.c.wang, wei.w.liu, mauricio.breternitz.jr, shiliang.hu, esfir.natanzon, shai.rotem,
roni.rosner}@intel.com

Abstract

Dynamic binary translation is a key component of Hardware/Software (HW/SW) co-design, which is an enabling technology for processor microarchitecture innovation. There are two well-known dynamic binary optimization techniques based on atomic execution support. Frame-based optimizations leverage processor pipeline support to enable atomic execution of hot traces. Region level optimizations employ transactional-memory-like atomicity support to aggressively optimize large regions of code. In this paper we propose a two-level atomic optimization scheme which not only overcomes the limitations of the two approaches, but also boosts the benefits of the two approaches effectively. Our experiment shows that the combined approach can achieve a total of 21.5% performance improvement over an aggressive out-of-order baseline machine and improve the performance over the frame-based approach by an additional 5.3%.

Categories and Subject Descriptors   B.1.4 [*Microprogram Design Aids*]: Languages and compilers

General Terms   Design, Experimentation, Measurement, Performance

Keywords   Hardware/software co-design, dynamic binary optimization, atomic execution, large region optimization

1. Introduction

Hardware/software co-design is a promising technology for processor microarchitecture innovations [7, 9, 15, 16, 25, 27]. In this technology, the traditional source ISA, e.g. x86, is dynamically translated into an internal implementation ISA, and may be optimized by SW before the implementation ISA is executed on the microarchitecture. Intel's P6 microarchitecture family converts x86 instructions into internal micro-operations (called μops), and may apply a number of μop level optimizations in the HW pipeline when they are executed [6]. This can be viewed as an early dynamic optimization system, although the optimizations are simple and done by HW.

Frame-level optimizations (FAO), explored by rePLay [25, 29] and PARROT [1, 27], rely on atomic execution support to enable aggressive μop optimizations. For example, rePLay collects frequently executed μop traces, or frames, and converts branches in them into "asserts" to verify the branch conditions [26]. When a frame executes, its results, e.g. store values, are buffered in pipeline buffers (re-order buffer, store/load buffers, etc). If an assert fails to verify the branch condition, the architectural state is rolled back to the beginning of the frame, the buffered results are discarded, and the execution is steered to the corresponding non-optimized μops. If no failure is detected, the frame can commit its results after the last μop is executed. The frame level atomicity support enables fast and aggressive optimizations within the frame without concern about control flow among the μops as well as the memory order among the memory operations being optimized. Another key feature explored by rePLay and PARROT is that they use well known branch prediction techniques to predict future paths and their associated frames, which enables path-based optimizations. Slechta [29] et al. and Almog [1] et al. showed that μop optimizations with frame level atomicity support can improve performance by ~17% on machine models that implement the x86 ISA.

Buffering the results of frame execution into the processor's pipeline buffers enables fast checkpointing, commit and rollback. However, the pipeline buffers are limited in size, which restrict the size of the frames, reducing the scope for optimizations. Furthermore, a frame of μops is a straight-line of code that can only commit at the end of the frame. This requires that only highly predictable branches be included inside the frame and must be converted into assertions. Fahs et al. [10] shows that partial matching, i.e. allowing a frame to optionally exit early, may significantly improve the potential performance.

Region level atomic execution, such as implemented by Transmeta Efficeon [16], supports a fully programmable internal ISA. The internal ISA allows branches within a region, which enables partial match. A region is also normally larger than a frame. Consequently, it increases the optimization scope for advanced optimizations. To support atomic execution, region level atomic execution usually utilizes a speculative data cache to buffer the execution results until the whole region is committed. A checkpoint is created at the beginning of the region execution. When unexpected execution events happen, such as exceptions or uncacheable memory accesses, the data in the speculative cache is discarded, the execution rolls back to the beginning of the region and continues with less aggressive optimizations, e.g. interpretation. Due to its larger scope, region level atomic execution is likely to have higher checkpointing, rollback, and commit overheads.

Clearly, frame-level and region-level atomic execution have their respective advantages and disadvantages. Frame-level atomic execution benefits greatly from path based optimizations, asserts, and fast checkpointing/commit. Region level atomic execution enables large region optimizations, supports internal branches and enables memory optimizations across large code regions.

In this paper, we propose an integrated Two-level Atomic Optimization approach, or TAO for short. We support frame-level atomicity with processor pipeline buffers, and region level atomicity with speculative cache HW support to optimize large regions constructed from frames. TAO not only achieves the advantages of both approaches, but also enhances each so the combined benefits are higher. For example, the combined approach enables even larger region level optimizations because the frame level atomicity support allows partial commit of the region execution, which minimizes the overhead caused by the region roll back.

The contributions of the paper can be summarized as follows.

- We developed a framework to extend frame level optimizations to large region optimizations, which takes advantage of both levels of support for atomic execution.

- We implemented a list of global optimizations to optimize large regions of code dynamically, and also extended several frame level optimizations to the region level.

- We demonstrated the potential benefit of TAO over frames by measuring the performance improvements of two-level atomic optimizations using an industrial strength cycle accurate simulator. Our experiments show that TAO can achieve a total of 21.5% performance gain over an aggressive out-of-order baseline machine and improve upon the FAO approach by an additional 5.3%.

The paper is organized as follows. Section 2 provides an overview of the frame based optimizations framework and Section 3 shows how we extended the frame based framework to optimize and execute large regions. Section 4 discusses the two-level atomicity support and its benefits for global region optimizations. Section 5 depicts the TAO framework, including the optimizations used to optimize large regions and the hardware support to execute the regions. Section 6 discusses the experimental results. Section 7 describes the related work and Section 8 concludes the paper.

2. Frame-level Atomic Optimizations

Frame-level Atomic Optimizations (FAO) were previously introduced in [1, 25, 27, 29]. It extends the trace cache [28] idea to store decoded and optimized μop traces in a processor local frame cache to reduce instruction decoding overhead as well as benefit from μop optimizations. We implemented a FAO framework on top of an x86 out-of-order simulator with the following HW support.

Frame formation logic: This logic collects profile information for retired μops, and uses branch predictability information to form hot frames. This logic also tracks the branch direction history to train the frame prediction logic.

Frame optimizer: Once the frames are collected, they are optimized. The optimizer converts predictable branches into asserts and optimizes the frame code as a single basic block, which can be done easily and efficiently. Since the μops are beneath the x86 ISA, many microarchitecture level resources, such as internal extra registers, and special operations, such as fused and SIMDized μops, can be used. The optimized μops are stored in a frame cache.

Frame cache: Since frames have variable sizes, the frame cache organizes frames into chunks of fixed number of μops each. When the size of a frame is not a multiple of the chunk size, the last chunk may be not fully utilized, causing frame cache and fetching fragmentation. This could be more severe for smaller frames.

Since the atomic scope for frames is constrained inside the HW pipeline, the checkpointing and commit can be done as efficiently as those for branch misprediction handling. Specifically, the checkpointing only needs to remember a few points in the pipeline, e.g.

renaming buffer, re-order buffer location, etc. The commit allows buffered stores to be retired to cache and memory.

Frame predictor: Given an x86 instruction pointer (IP) and the current global branch history, the frame predictor tries to predict a frame for execution. If the prediction fails, regular branch prediction is used to predict x86 code for execution. Note that it is possible to have multiple frames starting at the same x86 IP, distinguished only by the internal branch directions. This allows specialized frames with the same starting IP to be formed for path-specific optimizations. For a correctly predicted frame, the direction information for the branches (converted to assert) within the frame is used to update the global history register for future branch and frame prediction. The predicted frame is fetched from the frame cache and fed into the processor pipeline for execution.

2.1 Limitations of frame-level optimizations

Although FAO has distinctive advantages, such as fast checkpointing/commit, straight-line code optimizations and path-specialized optimizations, it also has several limitations.

First, it does not allow internal branches inside frames. This forces frames to be terminated at un-predictable branches, leading to smaller frames. Small frames can limit optimization benefits and reduce the effective frame fetch bandwidth. Not being able to partially execute a frame can constrain the frame execution coverage as the partial execution has to abort and execute un-optimized code.

Second, there are other issues caused by relatively small size of frames. For example, when the iTLB (instruction translation lookaside buffer) flushes (e.g. due to process context switches), the page mapping for the x86 instructions may be changed and the translation may be invalidated. This may require flushing the frame cache. One optimization is to add "page mapping check" (PMC) code in the beginning of a frame to examine whether or not the page mapping has changed for the frame code and only if the mapping has changed the optimized code would be discarded. The checking can quickly verify if the iTLB changed since the last time the frame was executed. If so, a more complete check, including the mapping of all the pages that contain the frame code, must be performed. As our experiments in Section 6.4 indicate, this checking cost is usually negligible for large regions but it can be significant for small frames. Notice that PMC does not handle self-modifying code (SMC). To handle SMC we may use techniques such as described by Dehnert et al. [7].

3. Extending FAO to Region Level

The two-level atomic optimization (TAO) framework extends the FAO framework to enable global optimizations on regions composed of multiple atomic frames. A TAO region (or region for short) is defined as a set of frames connected by control-flow edges.

In this section, we describe the extensions to the FAO framework to enable the optimizations and execution of TAO regions. We believe this approach can overcome most of the FAO limitations.

Public and private frames: We use the terms public frame and private frame to distinguish the region entry frames from the internal frames. A public frame is defined as a frame that can be reached from outside of the region (through un-optimized code or any other frame), while a private frame is a frame that can only be reached though one of its predecessor frames in the region control flow graph. A region may contain multiple public (entry) and private (internal) frames. Figure 1 (a) shows a region composed of one public (F_1) and two private frames (F_2 and F_3). In this region, the private frame F_2 can only be reached through its predecessor frame F_1. We represent public frames as boxes with a black circle and

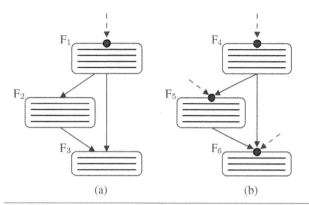

(a)   (b)

Figure 1. TAO regions. Boxes with black circles (F_1, F_4, F_5, and F_6) represent public frames and boxes without the circles (F_2 and F_3) represent private frames.

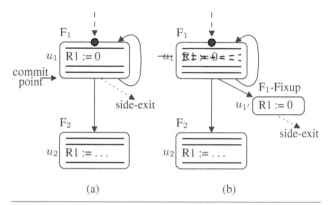

(a)   (b)

Figure 2. (a) Region with partially dead code. (b) Region after partial dead code elimination.

a dashed income edge. The dashed edge indicates that the control flow can reach the frame from outside of the region.

Private frames are basically used to trim side entries in the control flow graph, creating more optimization opportunities. The region at Figure 1 (a) illustrates the benefits of private frames. Suppose that frame F_1 computes a value that is recomputed at F_3. Since F_1 dominates F_3, we can apply common sub-expression elimination (CSE) to remove the redundant computation in F_3. The key property that enables the CSE and other forward optimizations (like partial redundancy elimination - PRE) is that F_1 dominates F_3. It is easy to see that, if all frames are public, as shown in Figure 1(b), a frame cannot dominate other frame in the region. Notice that all the frames can be directly reached from outside of the region (dashed edges), therefore they cannot be dominated by the other frames in the region.

Fixup code: We introduce the concept of fixup code to allow the execution of compensation code on side-exits of regions. As we show below, the fixup code mechanism relaxes the frame commit semantics, enabling more aggressive optimizations to be performed.

In the FAO framework, the architectural state (registers, memory, etc.) is required to be precise at frame boundaries, as the code executed after a frame may rely on precise architectural state for correct execution. As an example, assume the region in Figure 2 (a). If frame F_2 raises an exception, the framework rolls the architectural state back to the last checkpoint (beginning of F_2) and transfers the execution to un-optimized code, which properly handles the exception. Since the framework supports precise exceptions, the architectural state has to be precise when the execution is transferred to un-optimized code, therefore, the commit points must hold precise architectural states.

Requiring precise architectural state on commit points prevents many optimizations from being applied to the region. As an example, the value produced by μop u_1, in the region at Figure 2 (a), is killed by itself (through the back-edge) and by μop u_2 (in frame F_2). Unfortunately, u_1 cannot be eliminated, as the value of R1 would not be precise at the commit point.

To model the potential control transfer to un-optimized code, we annotate commit points with implicit side-exits to un-optimized code (as seen in Figure 2 (a)). Also, to ensure precise architectural state on the side-exits, we modify the global optimizations to assume that all the architectural values (memory and architectural registers) are alive on the side-exits.

The fixup code is a piece of compensation code associated with a commit point and it is executed whenever the execution rolls

back and the precise architectural state is required. Figure 2 (b) shows how the fixup code can be used to optimize the dead code in Figure 2 (a). Notice that μop u_1 was removed from F_1 and the μop $u_{1'}$ was inserted into the fixup code (F_1-Fixup). After the removal of u_1, the commit point at the end of F_1 does not hold the precise architectural state anymore (R1 value is not precise). However, in case F_2 fails and the execution rolls back to F_2 checkpoint, F_1-Fixup is identified and executed, computing the precise value for R1 and recovering the precise architectural state. For simplicity, since F_1 commit happens immediately before F_2 checkpoint, we may say that the execution was rolled back to F_1 commit point, instead of F_2 checkpoint.

We can see from the previous example that the fixup code allows the F_1 commit point to hold an imprecise architectural state. This is possible because before any external inspection to the value of register R1 (exception handler, context switch, etc.) the framework executes the fixup code and corrects the value of R1.

Although fixup code enables more optimizations across frames, it is limited by the fact that it cannot contain μops that may generate exceptions (Divide by zero, loads, stores, etc.). Notice that if an exception happens in the fixup code, the valid architectural state cannot be recovered, which could cause an incorrect execution.

Besides the limitation on the fixup code, the global optimizations are also limited by the fact that optimizing memory operations across frames may violate the memory ordering. This happens because whenever a frame commits, the memory state becomes visible to other processors. In order to remove these limitations, we propose the usage of a second level of atomicity support at region level.

Region atomicity support: To provide atomic execution at region level, a checkpoint is created whenever the execution enters the region, the data is buffered during execution and committed when the execution leaves the region. The region atomicity support provides two main benefits:

- The memory operations inside the region are only made visible to other processors when the execution leaves the region. This semantic enables the aggressive optimizations to freely optimize (reorder, remove or insert) memory operations across frames inside the region without compromising the memory ordering. In case there is a memory ordering conflict, the execution rolls back to the checkpoint at the beginning of the region. This semantics also allows instructions with lock prefix to be included into the atomic regions.

- The region checkpoint provides a secondary valid architectural state that can be used to recover the execution in case the fixup code cannot perform the architectural state recovery. This property enables the optimizations to insert code that may generate exceptions inside the fixup code. Notice that if the fixup code for a frame fails, the TAO framework can still recover the architectural state saved by the checkpoint at the region entry.

Successor list: In order to represent the control-flow edges of the region we annotate each frame in the region with a list of successor frames. In this sense, each frame in a region has a list of identifiers representing its valid successor frames in the region. The framework uses the successor list to check if the next predicted frame is a valid successor frame. If not, the framework takes a side-exit and executes the proper fixup code to fix the architectural state.

Region formation: The TAO framework builds and optimizes atomic frames for hot code. In order to form regions, TAO profiles the retired frames and triggers the region optimizer.

TAO collects hot frames and stores them into a hot frame buffer. Whenever the buffer is full, or one of the frames becomes very hot, the region formation module is triggered. The region formation module uses the edge frequency information between frames to analyze the hot frames in the buffer and forms one or more connected regions. Non-cacheable memory operations, I/O operations and system calls should not be included in the region, otherwise, the region will abort when they are executed.

Region optimizer: Once a region is formed, the region optimizer is invoked to optimize the region. Section 5.3 describes the optimizations implemented into our TAO Framework.

Gear shifting: The TAO framework implements a system that executes the code using three gears. Unlike Transmeta Efficeon [16], our first gear is the native execution of x86 code (a.k.a. un-optimized code), rather than interpretation. The second gear is the execution of optimized frames. The third gear is the execution of hot regions. The frame profiler shifts the gear from 1 to 2 by building and optimizing hot frames. The region profiler shifts the gear from 2 to 3 by building and optimizing hot regions. Besides the profilers shifting the gears up, the TAO framework also employs a gear down profiler to detect bad frames/regions that frequently roll back. The gear down profiler triggers the removal of frames/regions from the frame cache and prevents the bad frames/regions from being formed again. Although the shift down rarely happens, it is important for certain benchmarks.

4. Benefit of Two-level Atomicity

The two-level atomicity consists of a mechanism to provide atomicity at region and frame levels. In this section we describe the importance of providing the two-level atomicity support for efficient region and frame execution and how the two atomicity mechanisms can make each other more effective.

Region level atomicity: As discussed at Section 3, the main benefit of region level atomicity is that it enables the optimizations to freely optimize memory operations across frames.

Frame level atomicity: TAO framework provides atomicity support at frame level similar to FAO. The frame μops are executed speculatively and the frame commits only if all the μops were executed successfully.

The TAO framework relies on the frame atomicity and the fixup code support to record local checkpoints that enable the recovery of precise architectural states without rolling the execution back to the beginning of the region. This is important to minimize the amount of work discarded during a roll back. As an example, Figure 3 (a) shows a region with a loop that was optimized by sinking the store μop from loop F_2 to frame F_3. There is a region checkpoint in the

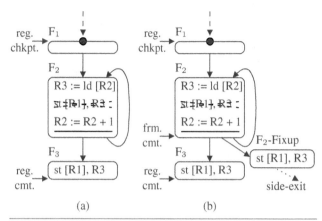

Figure 3. (a) optimized loop region. (b) optimized loop region after introducing the speculative checkpoint.

beginning of the region execution and a region commit in the end of the region. After entering the region, the loop starts to run and all the memory operations are stored in the speculative cache. Suppose that, after 1000 loop iterations, the speculative cache runs out of resources and the execution cannot proceed. A safe way to proceed is to roll the execution back to the last checkpoint (region entry) and continue the execution with un-optimized code. However, in this case, the amount of work wasted due to the roll back to the region entry would be very large (1000 loop iterations).

In order to reduce the amount of work discarded on a roll back, we use the frame atomicity support to record a speculative checkpoint that enables us to recover a more recent precise architectural state, instead of rolling back to the beginning of the region. The speculative checkpoint is recorded by the frame checkpoint mechanism and is called speculative because it contains speculative states. Figure 3 (b) shows how the speculative checkpoint is used to recover the precise architectural state. In this figure, F_2-Fixup is the fixup code associated with the commit point at frame F_2. Whenever a roll back is required, the framework rolls the execution back to the last frame checkpoint and execute the fixup code associated with the previously executed frame to recover the full precise architectural state. Different from the example in Figure 3 (a), if the speculative cache runs out of resource after 1000 loop iterations, the execution rolls back to the last frame checkpoint (entry of F_2 at iteration 999), executes the fixup code associated with the previously executed frame (F_2-Fixup) and commits the region. Although the execution leaves the region, it managed to commit the work produced by 999 loop iterations. This ability to save useful work even when overflowing the speculative cache is important, as it gives the TAO optimizer the freedom to construct large regions without concern about speculative cache capacity.

If the recovery is not possible (e.g. the fixup code fails), the framework rolls the execution back to the checkpoint in the beginning of the region. In this sense, the fixup code is allowed to contain μops that may generate exceptions, like memory μops.

Similar to FAO, the results produced by the frame execution are buffered by the pipeline buffers until the frame commits. However, when the frame commits, the retired memory data is transferred to the speculative cache. Figure 4 shows the storage and migration of computed data. The data generated by frames execution is buffered on the pipeline until the frame commits. After the frame commits, the data produced by store operations is migrated to the speculative cache. After the region commits, the speculative data is promoted to non-speculative and becomes visible to other processors.

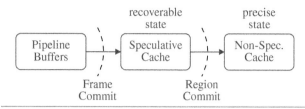

Figure 4. Storage and migration of computed data.

With region level atomicity support, frame level optimizations can also be more effective. For example, the fixup code at frame level could not contain any potential excepting operations, as the fixup code is meant to recover precise architectural state. Consequently, frame level optimizations cannot optimize memory operations across frame boundary even with fixup code support. If the frames are inside a region, however, the fixup code is allowed to have operations that may potentially generate exceptions. So if no exception happens in the fixup code for a frame, the execution can fix the precise machine state and exit the region. If an exception happens, the execution can roll back to the region entry and then exit the region.

The two-level atomicity support could be implemented using a multi-version speculative cache [11], dedicating one version for the frame level atomicity and another to the region level atomicity. Although this approach may remove the size limitation of the frames, it would be certainly more expensive in terms of hardware, and the checkpoint/commit overhead for the frame could be significantly increased, diminishing the benefits of the frame execution.

5. TAO Implementation

As we described in Section 4, the TAO framework relies on the frame atomicity support to record speculative checkpoints that enable the recovery of precise architectural states without rolling the execution back to the beginning of the region. However, these speculative checkpoints add side-exits to the control flow graph, which may reduce the optimization opportunities in the region. Section 5.1 discusses the limitations imposed by these side-exits and shows that sinking and some speculative hoisting optimizations can still be applied after the introduction of speculative checkpoints with fixup code.

5.1 Speculative checkpoint limitation on optimizations

In order to ensure that the fixup code can recover the full architectural state, the optimizations must ensure that the transformations applied to the region do not prevent the architectural state from being recovered. As an example, Figure 5 shows a hoisting transformation that prevents the architectural state from being recovered by the fixup code. In this example, the store operation u_1 was hoisted out of the loop. In this case, u_1 changes the contents of the cache when F_1 commits, however, the fixup code cannot undo this speculative cache write, which prevents the precise architectural state from being recovered by the F_1 fixup code.

In Section 4 we showed that if the architectural state cannot be recovered for the side-exit, the execution can still roll back to the beginning of the region. This is also valid for the example of Figure 5. In case the transformation prevents the fixup code from recovering the architectural state, we could simply force the fixup code to fail, which would roll the execution back to the beginning of the region in case the fixup code is executed. However, this behavior may cause performance degradation (as discussed in Section 4), thus, we avoid transformations that prevent the fixup code from recovering the precise state.

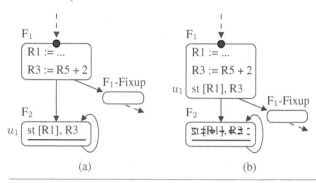

Figure 5. Hoisting transformation that prevents the fixup code from recovering the precise architectural state.

Sinking optimizations: Optimizations that sink code in the control flow graph, like the partial dead code elimination in Figure 2, are known as sinking optimizations. These optimizations do not cause unrecoverable modifications to the architectural state before the frame commits. In fact, they eliminate or postpone these modifications to after the commit point. Therefore, they do not prevent the fixup code from recovering the architectural state.

Hoisting optimizations: Optimizations that perform code hoisting, like the loop invariant code motion in Figure 5, are known as hoisting optimizations. As seen before, these optimizations could speculatively modify the architectural state, preventing it from being recovered by the fixup code. In order to avoid this scenario, we adopt the following rules in our hoisting optimizations:

- *Rename the destination register when hoisting μops that write to architectural registers:* whenever hoisted across a commit point, the destination register is renamed to a non architectural temp register and a new μop is introduced to copy the value from the temp register to the architectural register.

- *Do not hoist μops that have unrecoverable side-effects:* these μops include store μops and μops in which the destination architectural register cannot be renamed. The optimizations do not hoist these μops.

Figure 6 (b) shows an example where a load that modifies an architectural register (R1) is hoisted from a loop. The load μop (u_1) is hoisted out of the loop and a copy μop (u_2) is introduced to copy the value from the temp register (T4) to the architectural register (R4). Although the load is speculatively executed, the architectural state is not modified by the hoisted operation.

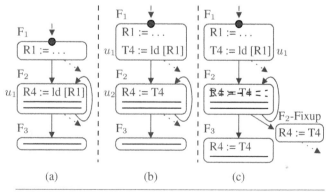

Figure 6. (a) Original code. (b) Hoisted load. (c) Partially dead code eliminated.

The copy operation introduced by the hoisting transformation is dead across the loop back edge and we remove it by applying partial dead code elimination to the region. Figure 6 (c) shows the region code after applying partial dead code elimination.

Although we do not hoist store operations, often, these μops can be sunk in order to achieve the same benefits of hoisting. Notice that the store μop at Figure 5 could be sunk out of the loop, instead of hoisted. In fact, our framework implements the partial dead store elimination (PDSE), an optimization that performs this sinking transformation.

5.2 Hardware support for TAO regions

In this section we describe the extra hardware proposed to support building and executing regions on top of a frame-level optimizations framework.

Prediction of private frames: During the region formation, if a frame is not chosen to be one of the entry frames, it is privatized into the region, and the original frame is left in the frame cache as a stand-alone frame. For a given stand-alone (public) frame, there may be multiple private copies in multiple regions, each with a unique identifier (ID). Since the frame predictor only predicts public frames in the FAO framework, we need an additional mechanism to determine whether the predicted frame should be one of the privatized versions of the frame. This is accomplished by keeping a list of valid successor frames. If the predicted frame matches one of the valid successors of the last predicted frame, then the private frame corresponding to the valid successor should be the predicted. The IDs of the valid successor frames are stored in each frame, in the "successor list", as described in Section 3. After a private frame is predicted, it is fetched and executed in the same way as public frames. This approach enables us to keep the same frame prediction accuracy achieved by FAO.

The frame predictor could also be modified to directly predict private frames. In this case, the frame predictor would have to be trained with private frame IDs. The direct private frame prediction eliminates the match operation on the successor frames list, but may require a bigger prediction table in order to store the extra frame IDs and could affect the frame prediction accuracy. Other IP remapping techniques could also be used to predict private frames [14, 21], however, we leave the evaluation of these approaches for future work.

Execution of fixup code: Fixup code will only be executed when one of the following unexpected region exit events happens: 1) a frame misprediction, 2) a frame cache fetch miss, 3) a roll back caused by a frame control assert failure, an exception or interrupt, or by lack of speculative cache resources. When this happens, the fixup code associated with the previous frame will be injected into the fetch flow in the processor. If an exception occurs inside the fixup code, the execution rolls back to the region entry and exits the region.

Region formation profilers: The FAO framework uses branch predictability information to form hot traces before converting the highly predictable branches into asserts. For region level optimizations, branch frequency/probability information is necessary for constructing tight regions where the execution stays inside for extended time before exiting. We currently maintain the edge frequency information for all frames retired since the last time a region was constructed. When enough hot frames are collected, new regions are formed for optimizations and the edge frequency information is cleared. Although the edge frequency information is convenient for region formation, it may be inefficient in HW implementation. We leave the evaluation of more efficient region profiling techniques, like in [20], for future work.

Memory disambiguation: Many memory optimizations, such as load hoisting, redundant and dead loads/stores eliminations, etc, require precise memory alias information. We use "alias assertions" to dynamically detect if any memory dependency is violated in an optimization range. For example, if we move a load from frame B to frame A, assertions are inserted to monitor all of the potentially aliased stores to ensure that no stores from A to B may store to the same location as the load. If any assert fails during execution, the execution needs to roll back. If a memory optimization range is within a frame, only the frame needs to be rolled back. Otherwise the whole region needs to be aborted and rolled back.

Atomic region execution: In our framework, TAO relies on a speculative cache and a register checkpoint mechanism to provide atomic region execution support. Notice that regions may execute loops with thousands of μops and it would be impractical to buffer the execution using the processor's pipeline buffers. Speculative caches usually require more hardware than traditional, non-speculative caches, however, we expect that more and more processors will readily provide speculative caches for hardware transactional memory support (HTM) [11] on multi-cores. In this sense, the TAO framework can take advantage of HTM support.

5.3 TAO optimizations

TAO includes most of the frame level optimizations as described in [1]. In addition, it supports a number of region level optimizations. Here we outline the region level transformations and optimizations implemented for our TAO. All the optimizations are implemented by a processor internal software, like the Transmeta Code Morphing Software [7].

Before a region is optimized, the region is transformed to enable optimizations. Specifically, a fake entry frame is created and connected to every public frame in the region, and empty fixup frames are created and connected to each frame in the region. The fixup frames and the fake entry are removed if they stay empty after applying the optimizations to the region. These created entry frame and fixup frames allow code to be hoisted to the region entry or sunk to the fixup frame after the exit frames. The following is a brief description of the region level optimizations.

Once the control flow graph for a region is constructed, function inlining is applied. This optimization expands non-recursive functions into their call sites, to 1) reduce function call/return overhead, 2) provide context sensitive data analysis information surrounding the called functions.

For every post-test loop inside a region, a pre-header frame is created. This frame initially is empty, and later optimizations, such as partial redundancy elimination, may move code from inside the loop to the pre-header frame. The pre-header is removed if it remains empty after all the optimizations are applied. Pre-test loops can be converted into post-test loops by applying the loop inversion transformation [23], however, we did not find a significant number of pre-test loops in our experiments and we did not implement this transformation.

Partial Redundancy Elimination (PRE) aggressively removes redundant operations by hoisting code upward to remove redundant computations along some of the paths reaching the split node. This operation subsumes traditional invariant and load hoisting, redundant load/store elimination, and forward propagations.

Partial Dead Code Elimination (PDE) pushes operations, including loads and stores, downwards to remove dead computations in some of the successor paths. When pushing an operation across a commit point of a frame, the operation is also pushed into the fixup frame, generating fixup code.

In addition to the above optimizations, global transformations could extend some of the frame level optimizations to region level. For example, frame level μop fusion [1] combines two or more

μops within the same frame to a single new μop that can be scheduled and/or executed as a single μop to reduce scheduling slots and execution delay. Global optimization framework can be leveraged to hoist or sink fuseable μops into the same frame and apply frame level fusion to accomplish the final fusions. Similarly, code motion can extend frame level SIMDization to region level.

6. Experimental Results

In this section we describe the infrastructure used and the results achieved with TAO. We first introduce our experimental framework and show the performance improvements, measured in terms of instructions per cycle (IPC), for FAO and TAO. Then, we compare the average dynamic sizes and the execution coverage for regions and frames. Finally, we discuss the impact of page mapping check on frames and regions.

We implemented the TAO framework on top of an x86 simulator. The simulator is a very detailed execution driven cycle accurate timing simulator for an out-of-order microarchitecture. The simulator was first modified to include the FAO framework, similar to PARROT [1, 27], and later extended to support the TAO framework. The atomicity for FAO and the first level atomicity for TAO is provided by the re-order buffer. The second level atomicity for TAO is modeled using a speculative cache with unbounded resources. We used the product quality simulation methodology, which includes around 350 single-threaded simulation traces distributed among 140 applications. The 140 applications belong to 8 different benchmark classes: SPEC 2006 floating point (FSPEC06) and integer (ISPEC06) applications, games, multimedia, office, productivity, server and workstation.

In our experiments, we use the following configurations:

- *base:* models an aggressive state-of-the-art 4-wide out-of-order microarchitecture.

- *FAO:* extends the base configuration by adding support for atomic frame execution, as described in Section 2. The frame optimizations are simple and mostly performed by hardware and the optimization overheads are modeled in the simulation.

- *TAO:* extends the FAO configuration by profiling and building large regions composed of frames, as described in Section 5. The TAO configuration uses the same size of frame cache, frame predictor and associated structures as the FAO configuration. We also charge an extra checkpoint operation when entering a region. The overhead associated with software optimizations for TAO is not measured in our experiments.

6.1 IPC improvement

Figure 7 shows the IPC improvement of FAO and TAO over the base microarchitecture. On average (geometric mean), FAO improves the base IPC by 16.3% and TAO increases another 5.3%, a total of 21.5% IPC improvement.

6.2 Dynamic sizes

Figure 8 shows the average dynamic size for TAO regions using the arithmetic mean. On average, each region executes about 8,900 x86 instructions before exiting the region.

Figure 9 shows that the average dynamic size for FAO frames is 27 instructions. The average size for regions is much bigger than for frames, which not only provides a larger optimization scope for TAO, but also helps to hide the extra overhead associated with "page mapping check" (see the effects of this property at Section 6.4).

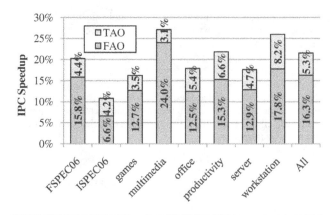

Figure 7. IPC speedup achieved by FAO and TAO.

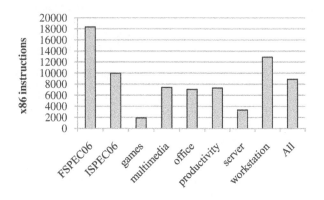

Figure 8. Dynamic region sizes for TAO.

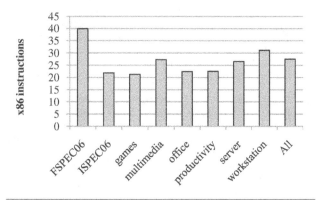

Figure 9. Dynamic frame sizes for FAO.

6.3 Execution coverage

Figure 10 shows the execution coverage for FAO and TAO. TAO has both region and frame coverage because the frames that could not be connected to other frames during the region formation step are left as stand-alone frames in the frame cache. On the average (arithmetic mean), TAO can cover ~84% of dynamic instructions. Note that the coverage for FAO and TAO are very similar. This happens because our current implementation only allows hot frames in regions. We are investigating techniques to also include small basic blocks that are not qualified as frames, despite hot, into regions to further improve region coverage and performance.

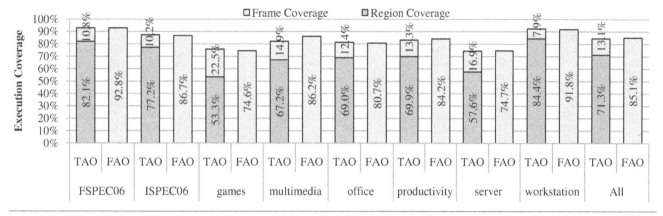

Figure 10. Frame and Region execution coverage for FAO and TAO.

6.4 Page mapping check (PMC)

The frame predictor mechanism predicts frames based on a virtual instruction pointer (IP). In this sense, whenever a frame is executed, the framework needs to ensure that the virtual IP still maps to the same physical address that it mapped during the region/frame formation. We call this task "Page Mapping Check". We experimented with two approaches for PMC:

- *Explicit PMC:* Every time a region or a stand-alone frame is executed, we check if the set of IPs represented by the region/frame still maps to the same physical addresses. In this case, there is an extra overhead for checking the physical IP for every region or stand-alone frame executed. The results reported before assume this approach.

- *Frame Cache Flush:* Every time the iTLB changes, we flush the frame cache. The disadvantage of this approach is the loss of coverage due to the reduced utilization of optimized frames.

Figure 11 shows the results for FAO when performing explicit PMC (FAO-PMC) and when flushing the frame cache on iTLB changes (FAO-Flush). Notice that the overall performance is very similar, but the IPC speedup varies for different classes of workloads. Specifically, for games and server benchmarks, the flush approach is worse due to reduced frame coverage caused by excessive frame cache flushes. The large code footprint in these benchmarks causes an increased amount of iTLB updates, which leads to frame cache flushes on the FAO-Flush. The FAO-Flush approach is better for Spec 2006, office and workstation benchmarks, which have very few iTLB flushes, due to the extra overhead associated with the explicit PMC in the FAO-PMC approach.

Figure 12 shows the results for TAO when performing the explicit PMC (TAO-PMC) and when flushing the frame cache on iTLB updates (TAO-Flush). Notice that the TAO-PMC is often better than TAO-Flush, and the performance difference is bigger than in the FAO experiment. The explicit PMC overhead for regions is amortized due to the large dynamic region size. On average, the checking is only performed at every 8,900 x86 dynamic instructions. As opposed to the FAO experiment, the checking overhead in TAO does not cause significant impact to the IPC speedup on the Spec 2006, office and workstation benchmarks.

7. Related Work

This work is related to several research areas, such as dynamic binary translation, dynamic optimization, atomic execution, and nested atomic execution.

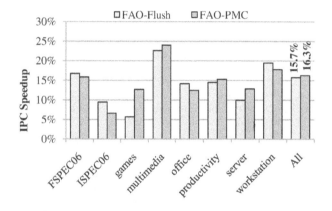

Figure 11. IPC Speedup for FAO-PMC and FAO-Flush.

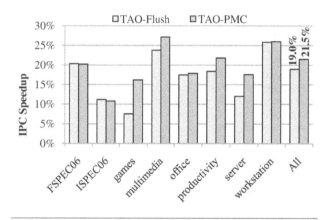

Figure 12. IPC Speedup for TAO-PMC and TAO-Flush.

The frame-level atomic optimizations were previously introduced by Patel and Lumetta [25] and latter explored by others [1, 27, 29]. Similar to PARROT [27], our experimental results show that frame-level atomic optimizations can achieve an average of 16% IPC improvement. The TAO approach enables large region optimizations and boosts IPC improvement to 21.5%.

HW/SW co-designed systems [7, 15, 16] leverage DBT SW and special HW support to enable efficient emulation of source ISA code at system level and can potentially improve performance, reduce energy and processor silicon. For example, Transmeta Efficeon [16] used a DBT SW layer to implement x86 processors. The DBT SW translates x86 code into an internal VLIW code for execution with promising power/performance benefits.

IBM Research's DAISY and BOA projects [9] utilize a VLIW architecture to emulate PowerPC processors. A similar project [12] proposed binary translation assistance for an IBM System/390 mainframe design.

In addition to HW based dynamic optimization, such as rePLay [25, 29] and PARROT [1, 27], SW based dynamic optimizations can be done at user level as well as at system level. There are many research papers and systems on dynamic binary translation (DBT), e.g. IA32-EL [2], StarDBT [31], HDTrans [30], DynamoRIO [3], and Pin [18]. User level DBT might not easily benefit from internal HW support and thus usually suffers from translation and emulation overhead. For example, IA32-EL [2] runs IA32 applications on Intel IPF platforms, achieving 40% to 60% of native performance.

Speculative optimizations enabled by atomic execution demonstrate benefits at both source level and binary level. Chen et al. [4] proposed atomicity support in a static compiler to optimize and parallelize C/C++ program aggressively. Neelakantam et al. used HW atomicity to optimize Java programs in a JVM [24] and reported 10-15% average speedup, however, the optimizations were done at bytecode level and cannot be applied to legacy C/C++ and binary code. TAO is implemented at microarchitecture level and can optimize legacy binary code transparently. Although rePLay [25, 29], and PARROT [1, 27] also used atomic HW support at binary (μop) level, TAO enables the optimization of large regions of code (including loops).

Atomicity and recovery are also the foundation of thread-level speculations (TLS) [5, 8, 17, 19]. TLS speculatively runs potentially conflicting regions of code in parallel, and when dependency violation is detected at runtime, some of the threads may roll back to the beginning of the region using the HW atomicity support.

Transactional memory (TM) [13] supports atomicity, isolation and consistency. These features allow TM to achieve opportunistic parallelism in places where locks used to be required. When conflicting data accesses happen within a TM region, the atomicity support allows the transaction to abort and recover from the conflict. Because of its atomicity, a transactional memory system can be leveraged to support atomic optimizations [24].

Transactional memory may also allow nested atomicity [22]. Specifically, closed nested transactions may allow partial abort of inner transactions and roll back to the beginning of the inner transactions (nested atomicity). However, nested atomicity may result in deadlock when an inner transaction aborts and re-executes the same code. Some implementations may flatten nested transactions into the top-level transaction, resulting in a complete abort on conflict (single level atomicity). Although TAO employs two-level atomicity, it avoids any dead lock by fixing the architectural state and going to un-optimized code when an inner atomic frame aborts.

8. Conclusions and Future Work

Dynamic binary optimizations benefit greatly from atomicity support to achieve performance gain. Both frame-level and region level atomic optimizations have their advantages and limitations respectively. Frame-based optimizations can leverage processor's pipeline buffers to support atomic execution of hot traces of straight-line code. It is efficient, but the optimization scope is small and performs poorly when branches are unpredictable. Region level optimizations can aggressively optimize large regions of code, but may suffer from higher rollback overheads. We have not seen any previous attempt to combine the two approaches. In this paper, we present TAO, a two-level atomic optimization framework, which

not only overcomes the limitations of the two approaches, but also boosts the benefits of the two approaches effectively. Our experiment shows that the combined approach can significantly improve the frame-based approach by 5.3%, and has the potential to enhance the region level atomic optimization.

This work can be expanded in several directions. First, our current regions consist of frames only. Since frames have to be larger than a minimal size, some hot small blocks are not transformed into frames and excluded from our regions. In the future, we may also include these hot basic blocks into our regions, which would potentially increase region coverage, make regions larger and improve TAO's performance gain. Second, more elaborated optimizations, like code vectorization and parallelization, could also be employed to improve the execution of the atomic regions. These optimizations can take advantage of the region atomicity support, which avoids memory ordering issues. Third, in our current implementation of TAO, a speculative checkpoint is recorded at the entry of every frame. We could assigning speculative checkpoints to only a few selected frames to reduce the constraints imposed on the region optimizations. These checkpoints should be carefully assigned so that the amount of speculative data produced between checkpoints is small enough to fit the pipeline buffers. Finally, HW and SW trade-offs for frames storage (HW frame cache versus memory code cache) and region optimizations (HW versus SW optimizers) should be investigated more closely.

Acknowledgments

We would like to thank the anonymous reviewers for their valuable comments and discussions. We also appreciate the support provided by Jesse Fang at the Programming System Laboratory and colleagues at the Mobility Group at Intel.

References

[1] Almog, Y., Rosner, R., Schwartz, N., and Schmorak, A. Specialized Dynamic Optimizations for High-Performance Energy-Efficient Microarchitecture. In Proceedings of the international symposium on code generation and optimization (CGO'04), Palo Alto, CA, 2004.

[2] Baraz, L., Devor, T., Etzion, O., Goldenberg, S., Skalesky, A., Wang, and Y., Zemach, Y. IA-32 Execution Layer: A Two Phase Dynamic Translator Designed to Support IA-32 Applications on Itanium-based Systems. In Proceedings of the 36th international symposium on microarchitecture (MICRO'03). San Diego, CA, 2003.

[3] Bruening, D. L. Efficient, Transparent, and Comprehensive Runtime Code Manipulation. Ph.D thesis, Massachusetts Institute of Technology, 2004.

[4] Chen, L-L. and Wu, Y. Aggressive Compiler Optimization and Parallelization with Thread-Level Speculation. In Proceedings of international conference on parallel processing (ICPP'03). Kaohsiung, Taiwan, 2003.

[5] Chen, M. K. and Olukotun, K. The Jrpm System for Dynamically Parallelizing Java Programs. In Proceedings of the 30th annual international symposium on computer architecture (ISCA'03). San Diego, CA, 2003.

[6] Colwell, B., and Steck, R. A 0.6 um BiCMOS processor with dynamic execution. In Digest of Technical Papers of 1995 IEEE international solid-state circuits conference (ISSCC'95). San Francisco, CA, 1995.

[7] Dehnert, J. C, Grant, B., Banning, J. P., Johnson, R., Kistler, T, Klaiber, A., and Mattson, J. The Transmeta Code Morphing Software: Using Speculation, Recovery, and Adaptive Retranslation to Address Real-Life Challenges. In Proceedings of the international symposium on code generation and optimization (CGO'03). San Francisco, CA, 2003.

[8] Du, Z.-H., Lim, C.-C., Li, X.-F., Yang, C., Zhao, Q., and Ngai, T.-F. A cost-driven compilation framework for speculative parallelization of sequential programs. In Proceedings of the ACM SIGPLAN 2004

conference on programming language design and implementation (PLDI'04). Washington, DC, 2004.

[9] Ebcioglu, K., Altman, E., Gschwind, M., and Sathaye, S. Dynamic Binary Translation and Optimization. IEEE Transactions on Computers.50, 6 (Jun. 2001), 529-548.

[10] Fahs, B., Mahesri, A., Spadini, F., Patel, S., and Lumetta, S. The Performance Potential of Trace-based Dynamic Optimization. Tech. report, University of Illinois at Urbana-Champaign, 2005.

[11] Gopal, S., Vijaykumar, T. N., Smith, J.E., and Sohi, G.S. Speculative Versioning Cache. In Proceedings of the 4th international symposium on high performance computer architecture (HPCA'98). Las Vegas, NV, 1998.

[12] Gschwind, M., Ebcioglu, K., Altman, E., and Sathaye, S. Binary Translation and Architecture COnvergence issues for IBM System 390. In Proceedings of International Converence on Supercomputing, Santa Fe, NM, 2000.

[13] Herlihy, M., and Moss, J. E. B. Transactional memory: Architectural support for lock-free data structures. In Proceedings of the 20th annual international symposium on computer architecture (ISCA '93). New York, NY, 1993.

[14] Kim, H-S. and Smith, J. Hardware Support for Control Transfers in Code Caches. In proceedings of the 36th annual IEEE/ACM International Symposium on Microarchitecture (MICRO'03). Washington, DC, 2003.

[15] Klaiber, A. The Technology Behind the Crusoe Processors. White Paper, http://www.charmed.com/PDF/CrusoeTechnologyWhitePaper_1-19-00.pdf, Jan. 2000.

[16] Krewell, K. Transmeta Gets More Efficeon. Microprocessor report. v.17, October, 2003

[17] Liu, W., Tuck, J., Ceze, L., Ahn, W., Strauss, K., Renau, J., and Torrellas, J. POSH: a TLS compiler that exploits program structure. In Proceedings of the 11th ACM SIGPLAN symposium on Principles and practice of parallel programming (PPOPP'06). New York, NY, 2006.

[18] Luk, C., Cohn, R., Muth, R., Patil, H., Klauser, A., Lowney G., Wallace, S., Reddi, V., and Hazelwood K. Pin: Building Customized Program Analysis Tools with Dynamic Instrumentation. In Proceedings of the 2005 ACM SIGPLAN conference on programming language design and implementation (PLDI'05). New York, NY, 2005.

[19] Luo, Y., Packirisamy, V., Hsu, W.-C., Zhai, A., Mungre, N., and Tarkas, A. Dynamic performance tuning for speculative threads. In Proceedings of the 36th annual international symposium on computer architecture (ISCA'09). Austin, TX, 2009.

[20] Merten, M. C., Trick, A. R., George, C. N., Gyllenhaal, J. C., and Hwu, W-m. W. A Hardware-Driven Profiling Scheme for Identifying Program Hot Spots to Support Runtime Optimization. In Proceedings of the 26th annual international symposium on computer architecture (ISCA'99). Atlanta, GA, 1999.

[21] Merten, M. C., Trick, A. R., Nystrom, E. M., Barnes, R. D., and Hwu, W-m. W. A hardware mechanism for dynamic extraction and relayout of program hot spots. In Proceedings of the 27th annual international symposium on computer architecture (ISCA'00). Vancouver, Canada, 2000.

[22] Moravan, M., Bobba, J., Moore, K., Yen, L., Hill, M., Liblit, B., Swift, M., and Wood, D. Supporting nested transactional memory in logTM. In Proceedings of the 12th international conference on architectural support for programming languages and operating systems (ASPLOS'06). San Jose, CA, 2006.

[23] Muchnick, S. S. Advanced compiler design and implementation, Morgan Kaufmann Publishers Inc., San Francisco, CA, 1998

[24] Neelakantam, N., Rajwar, R., Srinivas, S., Srinivasan, U., and Zilles, C. B. Hardware atomicity for reliable software speculation. In Proceedings of the 34th annual international symposium on computer architecture (ISCA'07). San Diego, CA, 2007.

[25] Patel, S. J. and Lumetta, S. S. rePLay: A Hardware Framework for Dynamic Optimization. IEEE Transactions on Computers.50, 6 (Jun. 2001), 590-608.

[26] Patel, S., Tung, T., Bose, S., and Crum, M. Increasing the size of atomic instruction blocks using control flow assertions. In Proceedings of the 33rd annual ACM/IEEE international symposium on microarchitecture (MICRO'00), Monterey, CA, 2000.

[27] Rosner, R., Almog, Y., Moffie, M., Schwartz, N., and Mendelson, A. Power Awareness through Selective Dynamically Optimized Frames. In Proceedings of the 31st annual international symposium on computer architecture (ISCA'04). Mnchen, Germany, 2004.

[28] Rotenberg, E., Bennett, S., and Smith, J. Trace cache: A low latency approach to high bandwidth instruction fetching. In Proceedings of the 29th international symposium on microarchitecture (MICRO'29). Paris, France, 1996.

[29] Slechta, B., Crowe, D., Fahs, B., Fertig, M., Muthler, G., Quek, J., Spadini, F., Patel, S. J., and Lumetta, S. S. Dynamic Optimization of Micro-Operations. In Proceedings of the 9th international symposium on high-performance computer Architecture (HPCA'03), Washington, DC, 2003.

[30] Sridhar, S., Shapiro, J. S., Northup, E., and Bungale, P. HDTrans: An Open Source, Low-Level Dynamic Instrumentation System. In Proceedings of the 2nd international conference on virtual execution environments (VEE'06), Ottawa, Canada, 2006.

[31] Wang, C., Hu, S., Kim, H-S., Nair, S. R., Breternitz Jr., M., Ying, Z., and Wu, Y. StarDBT: An Efficient Multi-platform Dynamic Binary Translation System. In Proceedings of Asia-pacific computer systems architecture conference, 2007.

Umbra: Efficient and Scalable Memory Shadowing

Qin Zhao

CSAIL
Massachusetts Institute of Technology
Cambridge, MA, USA
qin_zhao@csail.mit.edu

Derek Bruening

VMware, Inc.
bruening@vmware.com

Saman Amarasinghe

CSAIL
Massachusetts Institute of Technology
Cambridge, MA, USA
saman@csail.mit.edu

Abstract

Shadow value tools use metadata to track properties of application data at the granularity of individual machine instructions. These tools provide effective means of monitoring and analyzing the runtime behavior of applications. However, the high runtime overhead stemming from fine-grained monitoring often limits the use of such tools. Furthermore, 64-bit architectures pose a new challenge to the building of efficient memory shadowing tools. Current tools are not able to efficiently monitor the full 64-bit address space due to limitations in their shadow metadata translation.

This paper presents an efficient and scalable memory shadowing framework called *Umbra*. Employing a novel translation scheme, Umbra supports efficient mapping from application data to shadow metadata for both 32-bit and 64-bit applications. Umbra's translation scheme does not rely on any platform features and is not restricted to any specific shadow memory size. We also present several mapping optimizations and general dynamic instrumentation techniques that substantially reduce runtime overhead, and demonstrate their effectiveness on a real-world shadow value tool. We show that shadow memory translation overhead can be reduced to just 133% on average.

Categories and Subject Descriptors D.3.4 [*Programming Languages*]: Processors – Optimization, Run-time environments

General Terms Performance

Keywords Shadow Memory, Dynamic Optimization

1. Introduction

Shadow value tools store information about every application data location accessed by an application. This information, or *shadow metadata*, is tracked at the granularity of individual instructions as the application executes. Shadow value tools have been created for a wide variety of purposes, including finding memory usage errors [21, 24], tracking tainted data [5, 18, 20], detecting race conditions [9, 12, 22, 23], and many others [3, 14, 15, 29].

Although hardware-supported shadow value frameworks have been proposed both for specific tools [7, 8, 26, 27, 30] and general tool classes [4, 6, 31], shadow value tools in use today are implemented entirely in software. This allows them to run on com-

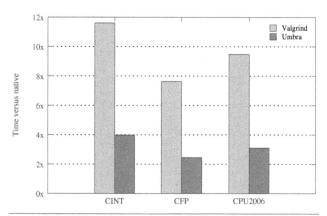

Figure 1. The performance of Umbra compared to Valgrind on 64-bit Linux on the SPEC CPU2006 benchmarks, focusing on shadow metadata mapping. Umbra is configured to use 2 shadow bits per application byte, to match the setup of the Valgrind MemCheck tool [24]. As shown in Section 4, Umbra achieves even better performance when using one shadow byte per application byte.

modity hardware, thereby broadening their reach. Software-based shadow value tools are typically implemented using a dynamic binary instrumentation system like DynamoRIO [2], Pin [13], or Valgrind [17]. By inserting additional instructions to be executed along with the application's code, a shadow value tool can update shadow metadata during program execution.

The inserted instrumentation code performs two tasks: *mapping*, which maps from an application data location to the corresponding shadow metadata location, and *updating*, which performs customized metadata updates and checks. These two tasks are also the major source of runtime overhead in software shadow value tools. In the current state-of-the-art tools, full memory shadowing results in one or two orders of magnitude slowdown. This prohibitive overhead results in infrequent deployment of shadow value tools, even though they can potentially lead to important insights about an application's behavior that in turn can be used for performance tuning or debugging. In this paper, we describe how our framework reduces the metadata mapping overhead. Figure 1 compares the mapping overhead of Umbra to the most widely-used memory shadowing framework, Valgrind. Umbra is *three times faster*.

1.1 Shadow Metadata Mapping Schemes

Shadow metadata mapping is the process of translating an application data location to its corresponding shadow metadata location. Shadow value tools typically use either a one-level or two-level mapping scheme. In a one-level scheme, the entire application address space is shadowed with a single, contiguous shadow address space. Mapping becomes a simple offset with a scaling factor, depending on the relative sizes of the spaces. However, reserving such a large piece of address space endangers the robustness of some applications. Furthermore, operating systems often impose requirements on where certain structures are located, which constrains the deployment of a one-level scheme.

A two-level mapping scheme splits up the shadow memory into regions with the first level of translation used to determine which region is to be used for a particular memory address. All existing two-level schemes map the address space uniformly. This works well for 32-bit address spaces but cannot scale up to full 64-bit address spaces. A key insight of Umbra is to allocate and perform mappings based on the application's memory allocations.

1.2 Contributions

The following are the key contributions of this paper:

- We propose a flexible shadow memory mapping scheme that does not rely on idiosyncrasies of the operating system or underlying architecture and is not limited to specific shadow metadata sizes or semantics. To the best of our knowledge, it is the first software shadow memory mapping scheme that scales to both 32-bit and full 64-bit address spaces efficiently.

- We present several novel optimizations to improve the speed of shadow metadata mapping.

- We present a general 3-stage code layout strategy for efficient dynamic instrumentation.

- We show that shadow memory translation can be implemented with low average overhead of 133%.

- We study the trade-off between metadata space usage and metadata mapping efficiency.

- We demonstrate the usefulness of Umbra by implementing a shared data reference detection tool that is suitable for analyzing multi-threaded application data access behavior.

1.3 Outline

The rest of the paper is organized as follows: Section 2 describes the basic framework of Umbra. Section 3 then presents optimizations to improve the basic system. Section 4 evaluates the performance of Umbra. Section 5 discusses related work and Section 6 concludes the paper.

2. Base System

We designed Umbra with the following goals in mind:

Flexibility. Umbra should be a general-purpose memory shadowing framework and not be tied to any particular use case. It should support a wide range of shadow metadata sizes a tool might need, from a single shadow bit per application byte to several shadow bytes per application byte. Many prior systems were built with only one application in mind and only work well with certain predetermined metadata sizes.

Platform independence. Umbra should be platform independent and not rely on features of a particular platform in order to achieve efficiency. This makes the system easy to port.

Efficiency. Umbra's runtime overhead should be as low as possible.

2.1 Base System Overview

There are two basic components to Umbra. The *shadow metadata manager* is in charge of shadow memory management, including

allocating and de-allocating shadow metadata, as well as maintaining the mapping information between application data and shadow metadata. The *instrumenter* instruments the program during its execution. The inserted instructions perform metadata mapping and updating for each instruction in the application.

2.2 Shadow Metadata Manager

An application's data is stored either in registers or in memory. These are dealt with differently.

2.2.1 Metadata Management for Registers

Most modern processors have a fixed and limited number of registers that can be used by a program. Furthermore, the registers used by every instruction can be determined by inspection. Thus we are able to statically allocate shadow metadata for every register and bind it accordingly. If an instruction uses any registers, we can insert metadata updating code to update or check the corresponding metadata directly without any metadata mapping code.

2.2.2 Metadata Management for Memory

Unlike registers, a single instruction can access dynamically varying memory locations. Thus, the shadow metadata for application memory must be managed dynamically. The Shadow Metadata Manager dynamically allocates and frees shadow metadata and must perform metadata mapping to locate the appropriate shadow metadata before that metadata can be updated. In Umbra, metadata mapping is achieved via a *shadow memory mapping table*.

We observe that the application memory is organized into a number of memory modules, including stacks, heaps, data and code segments of executables and shared libraries, etc. This observation inspires us to use a simple yet novel shadow memory mapping scheme that uses the application memory module as a mapping unit: for each such module the Shadow Metadata Manger allocates a shadow memory module and associates it with the application memory module. For example, Table 1 shows that the simple program `HelloWorld` running on Linux has five application memory modules. We simply associate each module with one shadow memory module.

Module	Application Memory	Shadow Memory
HelloWorld	08048000-0804b000	28048000-2804b000
[heap]	097a3000-097c4000	297a3000-297c4000
libc.so	b7e20000-b7f7f000	57e20000-57f7f000
ld.so	b7f8b000-b7fab000	57f8b000-57fab000
[stack]	bfb95000-bfbaa000	5fb95000-5fbaa000

Table 1. Application memory modules for a simple application.

By focusing on allocated memory regions rather than on the entire address space, this approach scales to large 64-bit address spaces without requiring multiple translation steps or extremely large tables: the table scales with the application's memory use, independently of the maximum size of the address space.

The module level mapping can be further improved by moving to a more coarse-grained mapping: address space unit mapping. The idea is to virtually split the whole process address space into two address spaces: the application address space and the shadow address space, as was implemented by TaintTrace [5]. However, unlike TaintTrace, which splits the space into two equally-size pieces, we carve up the address space in a much more flexible and efficient manner.

We treat the whole process address space as a collection of address space units. Each address space unit has three possible states:

- An *application address space unit* is used for hosting application modules. The size of each application address space unit is fixed, e.g., 256MB for 32-bit architectures and 4GB for 64-bit architectures, and its start address must be unit-aligned. This restriction is to enable a fast check to determine whether a memory address is in an application unit.

- A *shadow address space unit* is reserved for storing shadow memory metadata. The size of the shadow units depends on the size of the shadow metadata. For example, when using one shadow bit per application byte, the shadow units are one-eighth the size of the application units.

- An *unused unit* is memory that is not yet used.

At the start of application execution, we first obtain information about all of the application memory modules. We assign those address space units that contain application modules as application address space units. Then we reserve new shadow address space units for each application unit. If an application memory module spans multiple units, we reserve multiple contiguous shadow units for its metadata. Table 2 shows the address space units and the modules inside each for the HelloWorld example of Table 1.

	Application Memory	Shadow Memory
Unit	00000000-10000000	20000000-30000000
Module	08048000-0804b000	28048000-2804b000
	097a3000-097c4000	297a3000-297c4000
Unit	b0000000-c0000000	50000000-60000000
Module	b7e20000-b7f7f000	57e20000-57f7f000
	b7f8b000-b7fab000	57f8b000-57fab000
	bfb95000-bfbaa000	5fb95000-5fbaa000

Table 2. Address space units and the modules inside each for the HelloWorld example of Table 1.

When the application requests a new piece of memory from the operating system via a system call, the Shadow Metadata Manager intercepts the the system call and ensures that the application receives that new memory from either an application address space unit or an unused unit that then becomes an application unit. The Manager then adjusts the shadow units to maintain the corresponding shadow memory. If the application resizes an existing piece of memory, the Manager performs the same actions on the shadow memory. This may require relocating the shadow memory if there is a conflict between application memory and shadow memory. To detect and handle cases where the application obtains new memory without using system calls, e.g., during stack expansion, we use a signal handler to catch and resolve the access violation signal raised by accessing the unallocated corresponding shadow memory.

This simple mapping scheme allow us to use a small shadow memory mapping table to maintain the translation information between application and shadow memory modules. Table 3 shows the mapping table of the HelloWorld example. Each application address space unit has one entry in the mapping table, which stores two values:

- $base_{app}$ is the start address of the application address space unit, which is used for table entry lookup.

- *offset* is an offset value for address translation.

When translating from an application address $addr_{app}$ to its corresponding shadow address $addr_{shd}$, we first identify in which application unit $addr_{app}$ is contained by using a mask to calculate $addr_{app}$ aligned to the unit size. We compare that value with the $base_{app}$ of each table entry, and then calculate $addr_{shd}$ using

$base_{app}$	$Offset$
0x00000000	0x20000000
0xb0000000	-0x60000000

Table 3. Shadow memory mapping table for HelloWorld example.

$addr_{app}$ and *offset* from the matched entry based on the equation below:

$$addr_{shd} = addr_{app} \times scale + offset \qquad (1)$$

Scale is the scale factor from application memory to shadow memory, and it is 1 in the HelloWorld example for one shadow byte per application byte mapping. If we restrict the shadow metadata unit size to be a power of 2, this equation can be optimized using a shift as shown below, which is a faster operation than multiply on most architectures:

$$addr_{shd} = addr_{app} \ll scale_{shift} + offset \qquad (2)$$

2.3 Instrumenter

The *instrumenter* inserts the *metadata tracking* (i.e., metadata mapping and updating) code into the application code stream. Metadata updating code varies depending on the shadow value tool. Here we focus on the metadata mapping code. In particular, we focus on code for application memory accesses, since metadata for registers is statically bound. For each application memory reference, the instrumented code performs a sequence of operations as shown in Figure 2:

Metadata Tracking(Instr)
1: Save application context
2: Calculate $addr_{app}$ from Instr and saved context
3: Search mapping table for the correct entry
4: Calculate $addr_{shd}$
5: Update metadata at $addr_{shd}$
6: Restore application context

Figure 2. Pseudocode for metadata tracking instrumentation.

Steps 1 and 6 preserve the application's context. Step 2 calculates the memory address $addr_{app}$ from the instruction and the application's context (e.g., the register value used as a base register in the instruction's address operand). Step 3 walks the mapping table to find the containing application address space unit and its translation information. Step 4 then calculates the corresponding shadow memory address $addr_{shd}$ using $addr_{app}$ and the translation information found in Step 3. Step 5 performs metadata update operations, which are specified by the Umbra client.

2.4 Client Interface

Umbra's memory shadowing framework is combined with a *client* to produce a complete shadow value tool. Umbra provides a simple interface that allows the tool developer to concentrate on inserting code for the client's metadata updates (Step 5 in Figure 2) without worrying about the details of mapping between application data and shadow metadata.

The interface includes a data structure umbra_client_t and a list of event callback hooks. The umbra_client_t structure, shown in Figure 3, allows a client to specify the parameters of the desired shadow memory mapping, such as the number of registers to be used, the unit size of application data and of shadow metadata, and the events of interest. In theory, Umbra could allow the application data unit size (app_size) and shadow metadata size (shd_size) to be any value. In our current version we restrict the value to a power of two in order to simplify the implementation and

```
struct umbra_client_t {
  /* shadow memory specification */
  int num_regs;   /* number of registers to use */
  int app_size;   /* application data unit size */
  int shd_size;   /* shadow metadata unit size */
  /* event callback hooks */
  ...
}
```

Figure 3. A client specifies desired parameters of Umbra's memory shadowing framework using the `umbra_client_t` data structure.

provide better performance. Most tools desire a power-of-two size regardless.

An Umbra client must export an initialization function named `umbra_client_init`, which is called by Umbra at application start time. The function fills in the fields of `umbra_client_t` and registers event hooks to point at client-provided callback functions. Umbra then sets up the shadow memory and instruments the application code according to the client specifications. Umbra also calls the provided callback functions when the indicated events occur. Examples of commonly used event hooks are listed in Table 4.

Event Hooks	Description
`client_exit`	Process exit
`client_thread_init`	Thread initialization
`client_thread_exit`	Thread exit
`shadow_memory_create`	Shadow memory creation
`shadow_memory_delete`	Shadow memory deletion
`instrument_update`	Insert metadata update code

Table 4. Umbra client event callback hooks.

The `instrument_update` event is the most important callback function to be implemented by a client. Umbra passes needed information to the client via callback function arguments, including the memory reference instruction to be instrumented and an array of registers whose first register will contain the address of the corresponding shadow metadata during execution of the instruction. The client-implemented callback function inserts metadata update code, which will be executed immediately prior to the application's memory reference instruction each time that instruction is invoked. The `shadow_memory_create` and `shadow_memory_delete` events allow a client to perform metadata initialization and collect or report results, respectively, while the thread and process events allow the client to update any bookkeeping it maintains.

3. Optimization

The framework described in Section 2 works correctly, but it incurs large time and space overheads. We can significantly reduce these overheads using a number of techniques. Performance is improved in two different ways:

- We present several mapping improvements that speed up or even avoid walking the mapping table during translation.

- We optimize the inserted instrumentation itself to reduce overhead.

3.1 Translation Optimizations

We use a number of caching strategies to eliminate translation overhead.

3.1.1 Thread-Private Mapping Table (O1)

To support multi-threaded applications, any query or update of the shadow memory mapping table must be guarded by a lock. This incurs locking overhead and may suffer from lock contention. We use a thread-private mapping table to reduce such overhead. The thread-private table caches the information from the global table. Any application memory update by a thread is immediately pushed to the global mapping table. The thread-private table only pulls updates from the global table when necessary. The rest of the data structures described in this section are thread-private, thereby avoiding the complexity and overhead of synchronization.

3.1.2 Metadata Lookup Hashtable (O2)

Traversing the mapping table for every memory reference can cause large overheads. A *metadata lookup hashtable* is introduced to improve lookup speed. This table serves a similar role as the translation lookaside buffer (TLB) does for virtual page table lookup. The lookup hashtable has a fixed number of slots that store pointers to thread-private mapping table entries. It uses a unit-aligned application address as search key, and returns the mapping table entry pointer if the requested address is present in the hashtable. If the address is absent, a mapping table traversal is performed, and the hashtable is updated with the newly found pointer.

3.1.3 Last Unit (Memoization) Check (O3)

Each thread also stores the memory mapping found in the previous translation lookup. Before performing any lookup, we first check if it is the memory unit we found last time. This optimization takes advantage of the reference locality of the overall application execution.

3.1.4 Reference Cache (O4)

Our final translation optimization tries to avoid the mapping table lookup by taking advantage of each individual instruction's reference locality: an instruction typically accesses memory at the same location or at a nearby location on each subsequent execution.

A *reference cache* is a software data structure containing the same information as the mapping table entry:

```
struct reference_cache_t {
  void *base;
  void *offset;
}
```

`base` is a unit-aligned application memory address while `offset` holds the corresponding mapping information to its shadow memory.

We associate each memory reference instruction with a reference cache that stores the memory reference and translation information from the instruction's previous execution. When translating a memory address, we first check the reference cache to see if it accesses the same unit as its previous execution. If it matches, we use the stored `offset` directly. Otherwise, the translation proceeds to the lookup, and the reference cache is updated with the new mapping information. Because the total number of static application instructions that are executed in any one run is small, the total memory usage for the reference cache is small as well, only a few kilobytes for most applications.

As stack memory references in one thread all access the same memory unit, they all share one reference cache. If the application swaps stacks, only one reference cache miss will occur followed by a series of hits once the new stack's information is in the cache.

3.2 Instrumentation Optimizations

In addition to improving the performance of the metadata mapping scheme, we also apply several general optimizations to our inserted instrumentation.

3.2.1 Context Switch Reduction (O5)

Previous work [5, 20, 29] proposed optimization to reduce context switch overhead by analyzing register usage and utilizing dead registers whenever possible. We further extend this optimization. In the case that we have to save and restore a register for stealing, we expand the register steal range as far as possible. Typically, more than one application memory reference falls in the range, allowing us to share the save and restore cost across multiple shadow memory translations. Careful attention must be paid to fault handling, where the register's value may need to be restored even when there is no explicit use in the regular execution path.

3.2.2 Reference Group (O6)

We observe that it is often the case that, in the same basic block, several instructions reference memory close to each other: e.g., function local variables, or different fields of the same object. If we statically know that two memory references access the same application address space unit or two contiguous units, we cluster these two instructions into one *reference group*. All the memory references in a reference group share the same reference cache. In addition, only the first reference need perform a mapping lookup. All subsequent references can use the translation information from that first lookup.

A *trace* is a code fragment with a single entry but multiple exits. DynamoRIO builds traces from several frequently executed basic blocks. Reference group optimization can be extended over multiple basic blocks of a trace due to the single entry property.

This optimization assumes that shadow memory is allocated contiguously if its application memory is allocated together, which is guaranteed to be true in Umbra's mapping scheme.

3.2.3 3-Stage Code Layout

The metadata mapping pseudocode from Figure 2 is updated in Figure 4 with the addition of the optimizations presented in Section 3.1.

If we inlined all 27 steps for every memory reference instruction, the code size expansion would be prohibitive, causing poor performance in both the software code cache and hardware instruction cache. Instead, we split the instrumentation into three parts, resulting in a *3-stage code layout*:

- The first stage (*inline stub*) is inlined for fast execution at a small space cost and minimal context switch; this stage includes the address check in steps 3–4.

- The second stage (*lean procedure*) is invoked if the inlined check of the first stage misses. It uses shared code with a fast function call protocol to execute the code and return with small context switch overhead. This stage is used for steps 5–19. The fast function call protocol includes only a partial context switch and uses a memory store and jump instructions to perform a call and return without requiring a stack. The callee cannot use the stack but has several saved registers available for scratch space.

- The third stage (*callout*) performs a full context switch and invokes shared code that is implemented in C rather than hand-coded in machine instructions. This stage is invoked only if the second stage lookup fails; it covers step 20–24.

In this way, we are able to strike a balance between performance and space requirements, reducing the size of instrumented code

Metadata Tracking(Instr)
1:   Save application context
2:   Calculate $addr_{app}$ from Instr and saved context
Inline stub:
3:   (O4) Check Instr's Reference Cache
4:   Jump to 25 if hits
Lean procedure:
5:   (O3) Check Last Unit
6:   Jump to 9 if no match
7:   Update Instr's Reference Cache
8:   Jump to 25
9:   (O2) Search Metadata Lookup Hashtable
10: Jump to 14 if not found
11: Update Instr's Reference Cache
12: Update Last Unit
13: Jump to 25
14: (O1) Search Thread Private Mapping Table
15: Jump to 20 if not found
16: Update Hashtable
17: Update Last Unit
18: Update Instr's Reference Cache
19: Jump to 25
Callout:
20: Search Global Mapping Table
21: Update Thread-Private Mapping Table
22: Update Hashtable
23: Update Last Unit
24: Update Instr's Reference Cache
$addr_{shd}$ calculation:
25: Calculate $addr_{shd}$
26: Update metadata at $addr_{shd}$
27: Restore application context

Figure 4. Pseudocode for optimized shadow metadata tracking instrumentation.

without compromising the optimizations. In most cases, only the first stage is executed, allowing us to avoid large overheads due to context switches. This 3-stage code layout strategy can also be applied to general dynamic instrumentation tasks for better performance without sacrificing functionality, where an inline stub performs simple common-case actions and a lean procedure and callout are used for less common and more complex situations.

3.3 Mapping Table Update

Although the performance of mapping table lookups is improved, the multiple levels of cache increase the complexity of updating the shadow memory mapping table when the application memory layout changes.

Adding a new application address space unit is normally cheap, requiring only a new entry in the global mapping table. The new information will be propagated into every level of cache lazily as the application accesses the newly allocated memory.

In contrast, removing an entry is much more expensive, requiring that we suspend all threads while we update every level of cache in every thread. We try to delay such updates on the mapping table for better performance. For example, if the application de-allocates (unmaps) a piece of memory, we delete the corresponding shadow memory, but do not change the mapping table even if there is no application memory in the application address space unit. If the application later allocates memory from that same application address space unit, the same shadow address space unit and mapping table entry are used.

In some cases an expensive update is unavoidable. For example, if an application requests memory from a fixed address that was reserved for shadow memory; or an application expands its memory across a unit boundary and causes a conflict with shadow memory. For such cases, we suspend all the threads, move the shadow memory, relabel the address space units, and update every level of cache in all threads. These are extremely rare events with our large mapping units and as such they have negligible impact on overall performance. In contrast, if we used a finer-grained module-level mapping, we would have to update all of the cached mapping information on every module change, including each call to `mremap`.

3.4 Discussion

This mapping scheme and optimization works well even for large applications with complex memory usage. It avoids updating the mapping table when an application repeatedly allocates and deallocates memory in the same address space unit, and it is flexible enough to handle rare conflicts by relocating the shadow memory and updating the mapping table. In a 64-bit architecture, the available address space is much larger than current applications use and even larger than current hardware's physical capacity, so our scheme can easily handle large applications without any problem. In contrast, it is possible that a 32-bit address space might be exhausted by the application and Umbra together. However, this possibility is present for any shadow value framework, including the widely used MemCheck [24]. Umbra's shadow memory layout can be configured to match Memcheck's second-level shadow memory layout, and Umbra's small mapping table occupies less space than MemCheck's first-level table. Thus, Umbra should be able to operate on any application that runs successfully under MemCheck.

In addition to simplifying the handling of memory map updates, address space unit mapping has other performance advantages over module level mapping. Because one application address space unit often contains several memory modules, it not only makes table traversal faster due to fewer entries, but also increases the hit ratio of the hashtable, last unit cache, and the reference cache.

We can further reduce the memory used by our mapping scheme. For example, it is possible to allocate shadow memory in a lazy way by not allocating it until its corresponding application memory is accessed and an access violation signal is raised for accessing the metadata.

4. Evaluation

In this section, we evaluate the performance of Umbra on a number of benchmarks.

4.1 Experimental Setup

We have implemented Umbra on top of DynamoRIO version 1.4.0 [1] for Linux. We used the SPLASH-2 [28] and SPEC CPU2006 suite [25] [1] with the reference input sets to evaluate Umbra. All the benchmarks are compiled as 64-bit using gcc 4.1 -O2. We ran our experiments on dual-die quad-core Intel Xeon processors with 3.16GHz clock rates, 12MB L2 cache on each die, and 8GB total RAM. The operating system is 64-bit Debian GNU/Linux 5.0. We configured Umbra to use 4GB as the address space unit size.

4.2 Performance Evaluation

In the first experiment, we assess the translation overhead. For every memory reference performed by the application we calculate the corresponding shadow memory address without any further operation being done on the shadow memory. The resulting performance normalized to native execution is shown in Table 5. The second column (DR) shows that the DynamoRIO core has an average

slowdown of 14%. The third (1B-1B) and fourth (1B-2b) columns list the performance of Umbra mapping every byte of application memory into 1-byte and 2-bit shadow memory, respectively. The slowdown varies from about 10% to 6x, and the benchmarks that run slower in DynamoRIO usually suffer more runtime overhead under Umbra, implying that the sources of overhead are similar in both Umbra and DynamoRIO.

| Benchmark | DR | Umbra | | Valgrind | |
		1B-1B	1B-2b	base	map
400.perlbench	1.76	4.57	6.12	10.00	19.20
401.bzip2	1.07	2.75	3.75	6.43	10.06
403.gcc	1.20	2.24	2.80	4.23	7.40
429.mcf	1.08	1.75	1.92	2.40	2.78
445.gobmk	1.59	5.01	6.82	10.93	15.96
456.hmmer	1.01	2.85	3.79	5.31	8.82
458.sjeng	1.50	4.91	6.63	10.81	14.85
462.libquantum	0.98	1.07	1.11	2.55	3.02
464.h264ref	1.29	4.00	5.57	8.47	37.04
471.omnetpp	1.20	2.44	3.41	3.68	6.84
473.astar	1.05	2.15	2.62	3.89	5.55
483.xalancbmk	1.28	2.57	3.25	4.60	7.76
CINT Average	**1.25**	**3.03**	**3.98**	**6.11**	**11.61**
410.bwaves	1.04	1.52	1.89	3.64	5.67
416.gamess	0.96	2.33	3.21	4.63	8.37
433.milc	1.00	1.23	1.38	2.04	3.05
434.zeusmp	0.99	1.36	1.66	—	—
435.gromacs	1.03	1.84	2.77	8.20	12.31
436.cactusADM	1.00	2.04	4.49	3.79	8.62
437.leslie3d	1.00	1.51	1.99	3.20	5.91
444.namd	1.00	1.11	1.37	3.59	5.53
447.dealII	1.18	2.98	3.77	—	—
450.soplex	1.02	1.46	1.64	2.85	3.88
453.povray	1.38	3.51	4.74	7.44	13.05
454.calculix	1.00	1.33	1.80	3.26	5.51
459.GemsFDTD	1.01	1.39	1.70	2.36	4.55
465.tonto	1.19	2.34	3.21	5.41	12.75
470.lbm	1.00	1.05	1.12	1.90	2.60
482.sphinx3	1.04	1.98	2.45	12.38	15.01
CFP Avg	**1.05**	**1.81**	**2.45**	**4.62**	**7.63**
SPEC Avg	**1.14**	**2.33**	**3.11**	**5.31**	**9.47**

Table 5. Performance summary on the SPEC CPU2006 benchmarks for DynamoRIO (DR), Umbra configured for byte-to-byte shadowing (1B-1B), Umbra configured for byte-to-2-bit shadowing (1B-2b), Valgrind base, and Valgrind performing shadow metadata mapping (map). Valgrind's shadow mapping is byte-to-2-bit. 434.zeusmp and 447.dealII fail to run under Valgrind.

We also measure the running time of the Valgrind base and of Valgrind's MemCheck tool [24] modified to only perform address mapping (byte-to-2-bit). The resulting data are presented in the fifth (base) and sixth (map) columns of Table 5. The Valgrind base performs extra operations targeted at shadow value tools that the DynamoRIO core does not and which Umbra must perform itself, making the core-to-core comparison less meaningful than the Umbra-to-Valgrind-with-mapping comparison. Valgrind's mapping overheads are much higher than Umbra's, ranging from 2x to over 30x, with an average 8.47x slowdown [2].

---

[1] wrf is excluded because it cannot be compiled by gcc 4.1

[2] 434.zeusmp and 447.dealII are not included as they fail to run under Valgrind

4.3 Optimization Impact

We next conduct a set of experiments to quantify the impact of our optimizations described in Section 3. These experiments perform translation for a 1-byte to 1-byte mapping. Figure 5 shows the performance normalized to native execution of base DynamoRIO and of each optimization added to the set of prior optimizations.

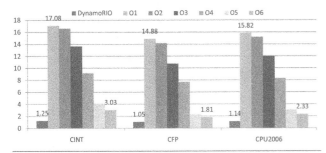

Figure 5. Impact of optimizations from Section 3, applied cumulatively: O1 (Thread Private Mapping Table), O2 (Hashtable), O3 (Last Unit Check), O4 (Reference Cache), O5 (Context Switch Reduction), and O6 (Reference Cache Group).

The figure shows that O2 (Hashtable) has only a marginal improvement over O1 (Thread-Private Mapping Table). In these benchmarks the mapping table is small (< 10 entries), making the table walk inexpensive. O2 would show more improvement over O1 with a larger mapping table. O3 (Last Unit Check) and O4 (Reference Cache) take advantage of application reference locality on the overall application as well as individual instructions, which improves performance significantly: they halve the overall running time on average. O5 (Context Switch Reduction) has the biggest impact and further halves the runtime overhead. The context switch overhead is expensive, as register saving and restoring requires memory load and store operations. Adding several extra memory operations, especially stores, for every application memory reference can easily saturate the memory bus and cause long delays. O6 (Reference Cache Group) removes another 20% of running time by further taking advantage of reference locality over basic blocks and avoiding redundant runtime checks via static analysis. When all optimizations are applied, the overall average runtime overhead is reduced to 133% over native execution.

To better understand the quality of these optimizations, we collect a number of statistics about the benchmark characteristics and the optimization effects. Table 6 presents the ratio of these statistics relative to the total number of application instructions executed.

The flags stolen and registers stolen ratios show the effect of the Context Switch Reduction optimization (O5). The flags stolen ratio is reduced from 41.79% (save and restore on every memory reference) to 2.55% and the register save and restore is reduced from 41.79% to 8.20%. This significantly reduces the pressure on the memory bus and thus reduces runtime overhead, and explains why context switch reduction has the biggest improvement. The reference cache check ratio shows that the Reference Cache Group optimization (O6) effectively removes 19% (41.79% - 22.76%) of redundant reference cache checks.

We also collect the hit ratio of our cache lookups, which are presented in Table 7.

We expected the Last Unit Check to experience some thrashing when an application accesses alternating memory units, e.g., interleaving stack and heap accesses. In contrast, each instruction usually accesses the same type of memory and thus the same memory unit. Table 7 confirmed our expectations. The Reference Cache

Metric	CINT	CFP	All
memory references	40.34%	42.88%	41.79%
flags stolen	3.17%	2.07%	2.55%
registers stolen	11.44%	5.77%	8.20%
ref cache checks	25.70%	20.56%	22.76%

Table 6. Optimization statistics normalized to the total number of application instructions executed.

Metric	CINT	CFP	All
ref cache hit ratio	99.91%	99.94%	99.93%
last check hit ratio	66.26%	69.98%	68.93%

Table 7. Hit ratio of the Reference Cache (O4) and the Last Unit Check (O3).

hit ratio is extremely high (> 99.9%), while the Last Unit Check hit ratio is much lower.

4.4 Impact of Shadow Metadata Size

The shadow metadata size chosen can significantly impact the mapping overhead. To evaluate that impact we measure the following shadow sizes:

1B-to-1B maps 1 byte of application memory to 1 byte of shadow memory. This is the fastest mapping because only a simple offset is required.

1B-to-4B maps 1 byte of application memory to 4 bytes of shadow memory. This requires one left shift and one addition, as shown in Section 2.

4B-to-1B maps 4 bytes of application memory to 1 byte of shadow memory. It is similar to the 1B-to-4B mapping but uses a right shift.

1B-to-2b maps 1 byte of application memory to 2 bits of shadow memory. It first performs a 4B-to-1B mapping and then uses an extra register to hold the bit position. This incurs additional overhead for register stealing and bit position calculation.

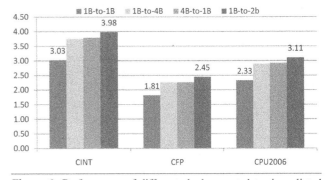

Figure 6. Performance of different shadow metadata sizes, listed as *application size*-to-*shadow size* where *B* is *byte* and *b* is *bit*.

Figure 6 shows the normalized performance. As expected, the 1B-to-1B mapping has the best performance, and 1B-to-2b has the worst, a 30% slowdown compared to 1B-to-1B.

4.5 Code Cache Expansion

In the experiments above, the instrumented code is organized into three stages (Section 3.2.3). The Reference Cache check (O4) is inlined and only one register is stolen for use. The Thread-Private Table walk (O1), Hashtable search (O2), and Last Unit Check (O3) are implemented as a shared lean procedure, where two registers are used. The global mapping table lookup is implemented as a C function, where a full context switch is required. Umbra's code cache size on average is about 4 times that of the base DynamoRIO. In contrast, inlining all instrumented code instead of using a 3-stage layout would result in a more than 100 times code expansion.

4.6 Example Tool

We used Umbra to build a sample shadow value tool called *SDRD*, or Shared Data Reference Detector. This tool identifies which memory is referenced by which threads. We designed the shadow metadata as a bitmap, representing each thread with a different bit. On every application memory access, Umbra translates the application memory address into a shadow memory address and passes it to SDRD. By setting the appropriate bit for the current thread in the shadow metadata, SDRD is able to tell which threads have accessed this data. We use a 4-byte application memory to 4-byte shadow metadata mapping scheme (4B-to-4B), so we are able to keep track of up to 32 threads per 32-bit word accessed. If the application access size is smaller than 4 bytes we align it to 4 bytes, resulting in a single-word granularity.

The implementation of SDRD using Umbra is straightforward. We fill the `umbra_client_t` data structure with appropriate values as shown below:

```
num_regs = 1;  /* 1 scratch register required */
app_size = 32; /* 4-byte application data    */
shd_size = 32; /* 4-byte metadata            */
```

SDRD's `instrument_update` function inserts 3 metadata update instructions for every application memory reference, as shown in Figure 7. `reg` is the register provided by Umbra that will point to the metadata address during execution. `thread_bit` is a thread private variable that holds a bitmap with only one bit set to represent the thread itself. This bitmap can be a constant when using DynamoRIO's thread-private code caches. The first metadata update instruction is a `test` instruction [3] that checks via the metadata pointed at by `reg` whether the current thread has accessed the application data being accessed. If it has not, the metadata is updated using an atomic `or` operation. If the thread has already accessed this application data, the metata write is avoided. As shown below, the cost of the check is significantly less than the cost of performing a metadata write every time.

```
test [reg], thread_bit
jnz  skip_update
or   [reg], thread_bit => [reg]
skip_update:
 ...
```

Figure 7. Instrument metadata update code for SDRD.

In addition to `instrument_update`, SDRD also implements a callback function for the event `shadow_memory_delete` in order to report which data has been accessed by which thread when the memory is de-allocated.

We evaluate the performance of SDRD using the SPLASH-2 benchmarks with 8 threads on our 8-core system. As shown in Figure 8, Umbra works well on multi-threaded applications. Umbra by itself causes a 3x slowdown, which is consistent with the slowdown measured from the single-threaded SPEC benchmarks.

---

[3] The `test` instruction computes the bit-wise logical AND of two operands and sets the conditional flags according to the result. The result is then discarded.

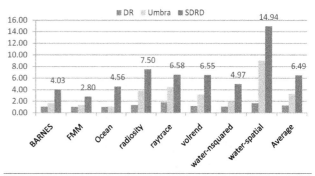

Figure 8. Performance of base DynamoRIO (DR), shadow metadata mapping (Umbra), and our Shared Data Reference Detector shadow value tool (SDRD) performing metadata updates.

The metadata updating by SDRD incurs another 3x slowdown. The water-spatial benchmark shows a larger slowdown because its running time is too short (< 0.3 second) for Umbra's initialization overhead to be amortized. We found that using the test-and-set approach shown is much faster than directly updating the metadata without testing, which incurs an average $30\times$ slowdown. This is primarily because the metadata update can easily cause expensive cache coherence maintenance and memory bus saturation.

5. Related Work

Existing shadow value tools employ shadow metadata mapping schemes consisting typically of either one or two levels of translation. When using one level of translation, the full user address space is mapped into a single shadow address space. This simplifies translation, requiring only an offset and potentially a scale if the shadow metadata size does not match its corresponding application size. However, using a single shadow region sacrifices robustness, as it requires stealing a large chunk of space from the application.

TaintTrace [5], Hobbes [3], and Eraser [23] all use one-level translation with one shadow byte per application byte. They assume a 3GB 32-bit user address space and take 1.5GB for shadow memory. Their shadow metadata mapping involves a simple offset and incurs little overhead. However, claiming a full half of the address space gives up flexibility and presents problems supporting applications that make assumptions about their address space layout. Such a design is problematic on operating systems that force various structures to live in certain parts of the address space or use different address space splits for kernel versus user space.

LIFT [20] uses one-level translation, but shadows each application byte with only one shadow bit. Consequently its mapping uses both a scale and an offset, and its shadow region only requires one-eighth of the user address space.

Several shadow value tools, like Umbra, use two-level translation schemes for flexibility. Using two levels gives up some performance but provides support for a wider range of applications and platforms. Unlike Umbra, other tools map the entire address space uniformly, rather than mapping regions based on application memory allocation.

MemCheck [24] employs a two-level translation scheme [16]. Memcheck's scheme was designed for a 32-bit address space. It splits the space into 64K regions of 64KB each. A first-level table points at the shadow memory for the 64KB region containing the address in question. Memcheck originally kept all of its shadow memory in a single contiguous region but was forced to split it up in order to support a wider range of applications and platforms, due to the limitations discussed earlier with claiming too large of a contiguous fraction of the application address space.

Memcheck uses several optimizations to reduce overhead, but most of them are specific to Memcheck's particular metadata semantics. It saves memory and time by pointing shadow memory regions that are filled with a single metadata value to a shared shadow memory structure. For aligned memory accesses it processes all bytes in a word simultaneously. And it maintains bit-level shadowing granularity without requiring shadow bits for every application bit by compressing the shadow metadata to only use such granularity when byte-level granularity is not sufficient.

Memcheck extends its scheme to 64-bit address spaces with a larger first-level table that supports the bottom 32GB of the address space. It uses a slower translation path for addresses above 32GB, and attempts to keep as much memory as possible in the lower 32GB. The Memcheck authors report problems with their approach on other platforms and suggest it may need improvement [16]: "It is unclear how this shadow memory scheme can best be scaled to 64-bit address spaces, so this remains an open research question for the future."

The TaintCheck [18], Helgrind [12], and Redux [15] tools are all built on the same Valgrind [17] dynamic binary instrumentation platform as Memcheck. They all use the same two-level translation scheme as Memcheck.

pinSel [14] uses a two-level translation scheme similar to Memcheck's, but with 4KB shadow units rather than 64KB units. VisualThreads [9] uses 16MB units in its two-level approach.

DRD [22] uses a nine-level table to hold its shadow memory, which shadows memory accessed during each unit of time.

Commercial shadow value tools include Purify [21], Intel Parallel Inspector [11], Insure++ [19], and Third Degree [10]. Unfortunately, their shadow translation details are not published.

EDDI [29] shadows each memory page with a shadow page that stores for each application byte whether a data watchpoint has been set. A table is used to locate the shadow page for each memory page, with multiple levels used for 64-bit.

MemTracker [27] and HARD [30] propose using additional hardware to provide low-overhead shadow value tools: memory access monitoring (but not propagation) for MemTracker, and data race detection for HARD. The introduced hardware is targeted to a specific tool in each case.

Metadata management and propagation directly in hardware [7, 8, 26] imposes limitations on the metadata format but can reduce overheads significantly for tools that can use the supported formats. Other hardware proposals support a wider range of shadow value tools by targeting the costs of dynamic binary instrumentation [6, 31] or providing metadata support independently of the metadata structure [4].

Umbra is implemented entirely in software using the DynamoRIO [2] dynamic binary instrumentation system. It could be implemented using other binary instrumentation systems such as Pin [13] or Valgrind [17].

6. Conclusion

In this paper we presented Umbra, the first shadow memory mapping scheme that supports both 32-bit and full 64-bit address spaces efficiently. This flexible and scalable approach does not rely on any specific operating system or architectural features or specific shadow metadata sizes or semantics. We have described several novel optimizations that improve the speed of Umbra's shadow metadata mapping and detailed the contributions of each optimization.

This paper focused on efficient shadow metadata mapping. Future work includes providing a flexible interface for shadow metadata updating to allow building a wide range of tools with our framework. We are also continuing to improve the mapping performance of Umbra.

We have implemented and evaluated Umbra and shown that it is three times faster than the most widely-used shadow value framework today, Valgrind. We hope that by reducing the prohibitive overhead of shadow value tools we can increase the frequency with which these powerful tools can be deployed.

References

[1] DynamoRIO dynamic instrumentation tool platform, February 2009. http://dynamorio.org/.

[2] Derek Bruening. *Efficient, Transparent, and Comprehensive Runtime Code Manipulation*. PhD thesis, M.I.T., September 2004.

[3] Michael Burrows, Stephen N. Freund, and Janet L. Wiener. Run-time type checking for binary programs. In *Proc. of the 12th International Conference on Compiler Construction (CC '03)*, pages 90–105, 2003.

[4] Shimin Chen, Michael Kozuch, Theodoros Strigkos, Babak Falsafi, Phillip B. Gibbons, Todd C. Mowry, Vijaya Ramachandran, Olatunji Ruwase, Michael Ryan, and Evangelos Vlachos. Flexible hardware acceleration for instruction-grain program monitoring. In *Proc. of the 35th International Symposium on Computer Architecture (ISCA '08)*, pages 377–388, 2008.

[5] Winnie Cheng, Qin Zhao, Bei Yu, and Scott Hiroshige. Tainttrace: Efficient flow tracing with dynamic binary rewriting. In *Proc. of the Proceedings of the 11th IEEE Symposium on Computers and Communications (ISCC '06)*, pages 749–754, 2006.

[6] Marc L. Corliss, E. Christopher Lewis, and Amir Roth. Dise: a programmable macro engine for customizing applications. In *Proc. of the 30th International Symposium on Computer Architecture (ISCA '03)*, pages 362–373, 2003.

[7] Jedidiah R. Crandall and Frederic T. Chong. Minos: Control data attack prevention orthogonal to memory model. In *Proc. of the 37th International Symposium on Microarchitecture (MICRO 37)*, pages 221–232, 2004.

[8] Michael Dalton, Hari Kannan, and Christos Kozyrakis. Raksha: a flexible information flow architecture for software security. In *Proc. of the 34th International Symposium on Computer architecture (ISCA '07)*, pages 482–493, 2007.

[9] Jerry J. Harrow. Runtime checking of multithreaded applications with visual threads. In *Proc. of the 7th International SPIN Workshop on SPIN Model Checking and Software Verification*, pages 331–342, 2000.

[10] Hewlett-Packard. Third Degree. http://h30097.www3.hp.com/developerstoolkit/tools.html.

[11] Intel. Intel Parallel Inspector. http://software.intel.com/en-us/intel-parallel-inspector/.

[12] OpenWorks LLP. Helgrind: A data race detector, 2007. http://valgrind.org/docs/manual/hg-manual.html/.

[13] Chi-Keung Luk, Robert Cohn, Robert Muth, Harish Patil, Artur Klauser, Geoff Lowney, Steven Wallace, Vijay Janapa Reddi, and Kim Hazelwood. Pin: Building customized program analysis tools with dynamic instrumentation. In *Proc. of the ACM SIGPLAN Conference on Programming Language Design and Implementation (PLDI '05)*, pages 190–200, June 2005.

[14] Satish Narayanasamy, Cristiano Pereira, Harish Patil, Robert Cohn, and Brad Calder. Automatic logging of operating system effects to guide application-level architecture simulation. In *Proc. of the Joint International Conference on Measurement and Modeling of Computer Systems (SIGMETRICS '06/Performance '06)*, pages 216–227, 2006.

[15] Nicholas Nethercote and Alan Mycroft. Redux: A dynamic dataflow tracer. In *Electronic Notes in Theoretical Computer Science*, volume 89, 2003.

[16] Nicholas Nethercote and Julian Seward. How to shadow every byte of memory used by a program. In *Proc. of the 3rd International Conference on Virtual Execution Environments (VEE '07)*, pages 65–74, June 2007.

[17] Nicholas Nethercote and Julian Seward. Valgrind: A framework for heavyweight dynamic binary instrumentation. In *Proc. of the ACM SIGPLAN Conference on Programming Language Design and Implementation (PLDI '07)*, pages 89–100, June 2007.

[18] James Newsome. Dynamic taint analysis for automatic detection, analysis, and signature generation of exploits on commodity software. In *Proc. of the Network and Distributed System Security Symposium (NDSS 2005)*, 2005.

[19] Parasoft. Insure++. http://www.parasoft.com/jsp/products/insure.jsp?itemId=63.

[20] Feng Qin, Cheng Wang, Zhenmin Li, Ho-seop Kim, Yuanyuan Zhou, and Youfeng Wu. Lift: A low-overhead practical information flow tracking system for detecting security attacks. In *Proc. of the 39th International Symposium on Microarchitecture (MICRO 39)*, pages 135–148, 2006.

[21] Rational Software. Purify: Fast detection of memory leaks and access errors, 2000. http://www.rationalsoftware.com/products/whitepapers/319.jsp.

[22] Michiel Ronsse, Bastiaan Stougie, Jonas Maebe, Frank Cornelis, and Koen De Bosschere. An efficient data race detector backend for diota. In *Parallel Computing: Software Technology, Algorithms, Architectures & Applications*, volume 13, pages 39–46. Elsevier, 2 2004.

[23] Stefan Savage, Michael Burrows, Greg Nelson, Patrick Sobalvarro, and Thomas Anderson. Eraser: a dynamic data race detector for multithreaded programs. *ACM Trans. Comput. Syst.*, 15(4):391–411, 1997.

[24] Julian Seward and Nicholas Nethercote. Using Valgrind to detect undefined value errors with bit-precision. In *Proc. of the USENIX Annual Technical Conference*, pages 2–2, 2005.

[25] Standard Performance Evaluation Corporation. SPEC CPU2006 benchmark suite, 2006. http://www.spec.org/osg/cpu2006/.

[26] G. Edward Suh, Jae W. Lee, David Zhang, and Srinivas Devadas. Secure program execution via dynamic information flow tracking. In *Proc. of the 11th International Conference on Architectural Support for Programming Languages and Operating Systems (ASPLOS '04)*, pages 85–96, 2004.

[27] Guru Venkataramani, Brandyn Roemer, Yan Solihin, and Milos Prvulovic. Memtracker: Efficient and programmable support for memory access monitoring and debugging. In *Proc. of the 2007 IEEE 13th International Symposium on High Performance Computer Architecture (HPCA '07)*, pages 273–284, 2007.

[28] Steven Cameron Woo, Moriyoshi Ohara, Evan Torrie, Jaswinder Pal Singh, and Anoop Gupta. The SPLASH-2 programs: characterization and methodological considerations. In *Proc. of the 22nd International Symposium on Computer Architecture (ISCA '95)*, pages 24–36, 1995.

[29] Qin Zhao, Rodric M. Rabbah, Saman P. Amarasinghe, Larry Rudolph, and Weng-Fai Wong. How to do a million watchpoints: Efficient debugging using dynamic instrumentation. In *Proc. of the 17th International Conference on Compiler Construction (CC '08)*, pages 147–162, 2008.

[30] Pin Zhou, Radu Teodorescu, and Yuanyuan Zhou. Hard: Hardware-assisted lockset-based race detection. In *Proc. of the 2007 IEEE 13th International Symposium on High Performance Computer Architecture (HPCA '07)*, pages 121–132, 2007.

[31] Yuanyuan Zhou, Pin Zhou, Feng Qin, Wei Liu, and Josep Torrellas. Efficient and flexible architectural support for dynamic monitoring. *ACM Transactions on Architecture and Code Optimization (TACO)*, 2(1):3–33, 2005.

Large Program Trace Analysis and Compression with ZDDs

Graham Price and Manish Vachharajani

University of Colorado at Boulder
Department of Electrical and Computer Engineering
{graham.price, manishv} @colorado.edu

Abstract

Prior work has shown that reduced, ordered, binary decision diagrams (BDDs) can be a powerful tool for program trace analysis and visualization. Unfortunately, it can take hours or days to encode large traces as BDDs. Further, techniques used to improve BDD performance are inapplicable to large dynamic program traces. This paper explores the use of ZDDs for compressing dynamic trace data. Prior work has show that ZDDs can represent sparse data sets with less memory compared to BDDs. This paper demonstrates that (1) ZDDs do indeed provide greater compression for sets of dynamic traces (25% smaller than BDDs on average), (2) with proper tuning, ZDDs encode sets of dynamic trace data over $9\times$ faster than BDDs, and (3) ZDDs can be used for all prior applications of BDDs for trace analysis and visualization.

Categories and Subject Descriptors   D.2.2 [*Software Engineering*]: Design Tools and Techniques

General Terms   Performance

Keywords   parallel programming, trace compression

1. Introduction

Prior work showed that reduced, ordered, binary decision diagram (ROBDDs) [2], originally developed for hardware verification, can be a powerful tool for static and dynamic program analysis because BDDs can provide compression for large sets of data whose size would otherwise make analysis intractable. For example, BDDs in hardware verification and validation allow equivalence checking of circuits with many states in constant time [1]. In program analysis, BDDs have been used to store program contexts for each object in a program analysis lattice object [16]. When BDDs are used for the analysis of large program traces [11, 13, 18], the size of dynamic program traces can be reduced by up to 60x when encoded as a BDD [11]. Further, this compressed representation can be analyzed without decompression, with algorithmic complexity that is a function of the compressed size [11].

Unfortunately, encoding large traces as BDDs can be time consuming, requiring hours to days to complete [12]. This in turn makes tools that use BDD-based representations less effective than they otherwise could be. Prior applications of BDDs depend on three methods to mitigate BDD creation time: (1) search for a vari-

able order that allows for fast BDD creation, (2) tune the tables and caching systems used in many BDD packages, and (3) encode an abstraction of the original data set, instead of the raw data.

The order in which variables occur in a BDD data structure affect both the size of the BDD [5, 9] as well as BDD creation time for BDD compressed traces [12]. Unfortunately, it is difficult to find a fast BDD variable order because a fast order, if it exists, does not guarantee good compression. Further, some algorithms are dependent on a specific variable order and these fail if the variable order is changed [13].

Tuning a BDD package can also reduce BDD creation time [3, 14]. BDD creation packages often use hash tables to maintain unique representations for each boolean function, as well as a separate cache to contain recently computed values. This is the unique table and the computed cache, respectively. These structures can be tuned in a variety of ways to increase the efficiency of BDD creation. However, caches only help if the working set does not greatly exceed the available RAM and induce thrashing [3]. BDD packages attempt to avoid memory thrashing and memory exhaustion by garbage collecting dead nodes[1]. Unfortunately, the garbage collection process itself can dominate BDD creation time.

Another method used to reduce BDD creation time is to abstract the data set, throwing away information, and encoding this abstraction [8]. Unfortunately, this method may remove information that a user of the compressed trace later discovers they want or need. For example, the ParaMeter tool [13] needs all of the dependence information from a trace in order to create an accurate visualization of potential parallelism. Abstracting this data may obscure the very parallelism opportunities the visualization is trying to uncover. Similarly, when applying Zhang et al.'s [18] debugging tools to a BDD-compressed trace, abstracting dependence information may obscure the source of the observed bug.

This paper explores zero-suppressed BDDs (ZDDs) as an alternative to BDDs in order to reduce creation time for large traces. Prior work has shown that ZDDs can reduce the final BDD size for sparse data and context data used during static program analysis [4, 7], though this work has not applied ZDDs to compressing dynamic trace data. This paper shows that, without any data abstraction:

1. ZDD-based SPEC INT 2000 benchmark traces are 25% smaller than BDD-based traces.

2. ZDD-based trace compression algorithms have a smaller working set size making tuning possible for large traces, resulting in a $9\times$ reduction in compression time.

3. The authors' high-performance algorithm for visualizing parallelism in traces [13] can be adapted to ZDDs.

---

[1] Note, deciding when to garbage collect is also non-trivial as aggressive garbage collection can be problematic – although collected nodes are dead, they may be resurrected from the cache.

CGO'10   April 24-28, 2010, Toronto, Canada
Copyright © 2010 ACM 978-1-60558-635-9/10/04...$10.00

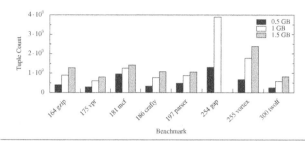

Figure 1. Number of Tuples for Fixed Memory Bound

4. Application of existing program analysis techniques to ZDD-based traces is a straight-forward adaptation of applying the techniques to BDD-based traces.

The rest of this paper is organized as follows. Section 2 briefly motivates compression for traces. Section 3 reviews BDD-based trace compression and explains why BDD compression is so time consuming. Section 4 demonstrates how ZDD construction differs from BDD-based construction resulting in a 25% reduction in BDD size and a 9x reduction in trace compression time. Section 5 shows how to adapt prior BDD-based trace visualization algorithms to ZDDs without loss of performance. Section 6 concludes.

2. Background

Analysis of dynamically generated traces is difficult because the generated data, even for short collection times, can grow to terabytes in size depending on the information collected and the duration of traced execution. In fact, even intermediate analysis data can become become prohibitively large. In response researchers have turned to BDDs to reduce the size of these data sets. Zhang et al. use BDDs for just the intermediate data showing an improvement in analysis memory usage and performance [18]. Subsequently, Price et al. showed that BDDs can represent entire program traces [11].

BDDs provide good compression levels for traces, and allow analysis without decompressing the trace. BDDs can also be used for many program and trace analyses [11, 17].

2.1 BDD Space Efficiency

The authors' previously show BDD encoded trace sizes of 12x to 60x less than a naïve representation [11]. In Figure 1 ([11]) shows the number of (DIN,DIN) data-dependence graph tuples that fit into a fixed amount of memory (512 MB, 1 GB, and 1.5 GB). DINs are discussed in detail in Section 3. Note, 1 GB can store 500 million to 4 billion data-dependence edges for up to 1.04 billion instructions.

Subsequently, the paper [13] used BDD-compressed traces to visualize and extract potential parallelism from programs. However, this paper does not discuss the time required to create a BDD representation of trace information. Figure 2 shows that, using a Intel Xeon E5420 2.5Ghz Linux machine with 8 GB of RAM, trace-BDD creation time is prohibitively large, exceeding 76 hours for 176.gcc DINxDIN trace. The traces used in this figure are from gcc-compiled SPEC 2000 integer benchmarks run with the reference inputs.

3. BDD Compression Time

To understand why BDD-based compression is time-consuming, this section begins by first describing BDD-based trace representation [11]. This section then analyzes the BDD-trace creation algorithm and shows that inefficient trace BDD compression is primarily caused by:

- Frequent garbage collection of dead BDD nodes

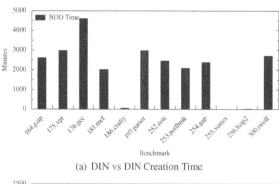

(a) DIN vs DIN Creation Time

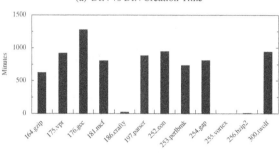

(b) DIN vs SIN Creation Time

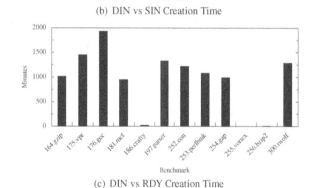

(c) DIN vs RDY Creation Time

Figure 2. BDD Creation Time

- The deallocation of potentially reusable dead BDD nodes and corresponding BDD system cache entries

3.1 Traces as Boolean Functions

BDDs represent boolean functions, and thus, to represent traces as BDDs, let us review how to represent trace data as a boolean function [11].

Observe that boolean functions can encode arbitrary binary data. For example, as explained by authors explain in [11], if the represented universe, Ω, consists of 4 elements $\Omega = \{a, b, c, d\}$, then a 2-bit encoding can be used to represent each element, $\{a \mapsto 00, b \mapsto 01, c \mapsto 10, d \mapsto 11\}$. With this encoding, they create a boolean indicator function (i.e., characteristic function) that evaluates to true for any subset of the Ω. For example, the indicator function for the set $\{a, b\}$ is $I_{\{a,b\}} = x'$ where x is the variable for the most-significant bit (MSb) of the set encoding and x' is read as not x.

The authors' extend this simple notion to encode different data sets necessary for representing and analyzing the trace. All trace data is encoded by a set of tuples $(DIN, data)$ where the DIN is the dynamic instruction number (i.e., the position in the trace, the first instruction has DIN 0, the second DIN 1, and so on). Therefore, a simple instruction trace is encoded as (DIN, PC), where

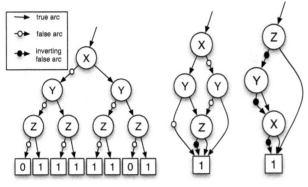

(a) Binary Decision Tree (b) Naïve Order (c) Better Order

Figure 3. A Three-variable Binary Decision Tree and BDDs

the PC is the program counter value. Similarly, more complex data relationships can be encoded by simply joining the binary representations of arbitrary tuples into a single equation.

In this paper we discusses three types of data tuples. The first is (DIN, SIN), where the SIN is the static instruction number or PC (Note that the paper will use PC and SIN interchangeably). The second tuple type is (DIN, DIN), which is used to represent edges of the trace's dynamic data dependence graph. If a decision diagram (DD) encodes an edge set E, if $(10, 24)$ is in the edge set then the 24th instruction in the trace depends on the 10th instruction in the trace. If we wish to know the PC of either of these instructions, we can refer to the (DIN, SIN) tuple set. Finally, the paper will evaluate (DIN, RDY) tuple sets, which encode the ideal schedule for the trace, i.e., for each DIN, RDY is the earliest time a scheduler could execute that DIN given an ideal machine [13].

3.2 Boolean Functions as BDDs

BDDs can be viewed as compressed versions of binary decision trees. Figure 3(a) shows a binary tree for the three variable function $f(x, y, z) = x'y + xy' + z$. For example, traversing the left edges of the graph we evaluate $f(0, 0, 0)$ as 0. BDDs are a graph data structure in which each node corresponds to a boolean function (just as each node in a binary decision tree does) [2]. Converting a decision tree to an ROBDD (BDD henceforth) is done by following two reduction rules

1. When two BDD nodes p and q are identical, edges leading to q are changed to lead to p and q is removed

2. If both edges from a node p go to child node q, then p is eliminated and all nodes that go to p are redirected to q.

The last reduction rule is commonly referred to as the *S-deletion* rule [4]. Figure 3(b) shows the BDD for f under the variable ordering (x, y, z) with additional compression provided by inverting edges. To compute $f(0, 0, 0)$ with the BDD, we traverse the 0, or false, arc of the X node, the false arc of the rightmost Y node and the inverting false arc of the Z node. Because we reached the constant 1 node through an odd number of inverting arcs, we find $f(0, 0, 0) = 0$ as before. BDD creation is covered in more detail in the literature [2, 11, 15].

3.3 BDD Unique Tables

Prior work shows how to encode trace data as BDDs. However, the encoding processes can take an unreasonable amount of time. Inefficient encoding is primarily caused by the interaction of garbage

collection and BDD system caches, specifically the unique table and the operation cache.

The *S-deletion* rule used to reduce a binary tree into a BDD is realized through the *unique table*. The unique table enforces strong canonicity because each new node has a unique location in the table. If a node is a duplicate of an existing table node (i.e., it represents the same boolean function), the node is reused from the unique table [2]. The unique table also increases the efficiency of BDD creation. If a BDD node already exists a BDD package, such as CUDD [15] (a state of the art, high-performance, BDD package), saves time by reusing the existing node and avoiding recomputation for the remainder of the nodes below the cached one.

The unique table can be used to tune the overall creation time of the BDD by altering its size. The size of the unique table must at least be large enough to contain all of the live BDD nodes. With CUDD, however, nodes contained in the subtable can also be dead. Upon garbage collection, these dead nodes are added to *death row*, which is an additional cache used to hold recently invalidated nodes. The nodes on death row can also be resurrected and reused.

In addition to a simple node cache, BDD packages, including CUDD, also have an operation cache which caches the results of BDD operations. For example, if one requests a computation of $B \wedge C$ and the result is A, then CUDD will cache that $A = B \wedge C$. If $B \wedge C$ is requested again, it will immediately return BDD A from this cache, and perform the potentially exponential recursion required to recompute A. This cache gives BDDs their polynomial time complexity [2].

Unfortunately, garbage collection frees the nodes on death row in order to free memory, which, in turn evicts corresponding results from the operation cache. As we will see, the eviction of useful results caused by accumulation of real garbage ultimately hinders BDD creation efficiency.

3.4 Garbage Collection and Compression Time

Garbage collection allows BDD packages to control memory consumption and free the dead nodes on death row. The CUDD package uses a saturating reference counter to keep track of the amount of node use, and to determine if a node is safe to delete. A reference counting system also aids other BDD functions related to automatic variable ordering.

CUDD uses plain pointers to `DdNodes` as a handle to an entire BDDs. If A, B, and C have different pointer values they will represent different BDDs. In the pseudo code presented above, the B and C BDDs have their reference counts increased to prevent them from being garbage collected. B and C are then combined using a boolean $\wedge$ operator to create the new BDD A. A then also has its reference count increased to prevent garbage collection, but the code now decreases the reference count of B and C. If B and C now have reference counts equal to zero they are considered *dead*, and could be removed by garbage collection.

To explain how BDD trace creation produces garbage, we first must consider the BDD creation algorithm. The algorithm is simple. For each tuple, a BDD is created to represent the single element tuple (see the work [11] for details), call it E, and this BDD is or'ed into the set of all tuples, call it Ω. Thus, the pseudo-code for the algorithm using CUDD calls is:

```
DdNode * buildSet()
{
    DdNode *Omega = getEmptySetBdd()
    while(!done) {
        DdNode *OmegaOld = Omega;
        DdNode *E = getNextTupleBdd();
        Cudd_Ref(E);
        Omega = Cudd_or(OmegaOld, E);
        Cudd_Ref(Omega);
        Cudd_RecursiveDeref(E);
```

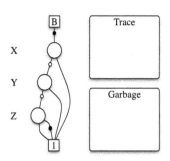

Figure 4. A BDD for $\bar{X} \wedge \bar{Y} \wedge \bar{Z}$

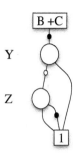

Figure 6. A BDD for $(\bar{X} \wedge \bar{Y} \wedge \bar{Z}) \vee (X \wedge \bar{Y} \wedge \bar{Z})$

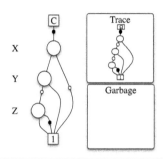

Figure 5. A BDD for $(X \wedge \bar{Y} \wedge \bar{Z})$

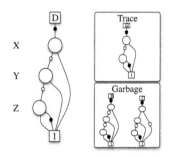

Figure 7. A BDD for D

```
      Cudd_RecursiveDeref(OmegaOld);
   }
   return Omega;
}
```

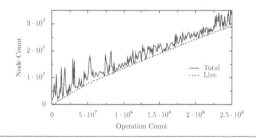

Figure 8. BDD Total and Live Nodes

Notice that at the end of each loop iteration the only live nodes are those that are part of the BDD for the current Ω; every other node is dead.

Now, let us examine how this algorithm interacts with the BDD package and its data structures. Let us set $E = \bar{X} \wedge \bar{Y} \wedge \bar{Z}$ which is exactly the shape of a tuple BDD assuming that we only had 8 possible tuples and thus 3 boolean variables (in practice there are typically 64-128 variables per tuple). In Figure 4 we can see the BDD representation of the boolean function for $E = \bar{X} \wedge \bar{Y} \wedge \bar{Z}$.

As shown in the figure, at the start of the algorithm, the trace BDD is empty, and there is no garbage. After the BDD is created for E, E is added to the trace BDD by computing $\Omega = E \vee 0$, as shown in the pseudo-code earlier.

Now we need to add our second tuple to the set, call it E'. The BDD for E' is shown in Figure 5 along with the BDD for Ω and the garbage created so far.

Figure 6 shows the trace BDD Ω after adding E'. In this new BDD, the X term is now a *don't - care* value because the result of the function no longer depends on the value of X. The *S-deletion* rule removes *don't care* values from the BDD structure. Figure 6 shows the BDD for the function $(\bar{X} \wedge \bar{Y} \wedge \bar{Z}) \vee (X \wedge \bar{Y} \wedge \bar{Z})$ with the X node removed.

In Figure 7 we show yet another tuple $E'' = \bar{X} \wedge \bar{Y} \wedge \bar{Z}$, which will be added to Ω along with the current trace BDD and the dead BDD nodes. At this point, notice that the entire BDD for both E and E' is dead and will be garbage collected.

Now, notice that E'' is exactly the same as E. However, the BDD for E is garbage and is on death row. If no garbage collection operation has taken place between the creation of E and the creation of E'', the BDD package can quickly resurrect E''. If death row has been cleared by garbage collection, then the BDD for function $\bar{X} \wedge \bar{Y} \wedge \bar{Z}$ must be recreated. Furthermore, though not shown

in this simple example, a similar effect may occur even without repeated tuples. If Ω from prior iterations of the trace creation loop contained sub-BDDs that would be useful for future $\Omega's$, they too may be garbage collected and thus have to be recreated.

The garbage collection process is triggered when system memory is running low, or when the amount of garbage reaches a threshold set by the BDD package. This threshold is generally tuned to balance garbage collection time and frequency. If the working set of trace-BDD creation is less than the threshold for garbage collection, then the results of many BDD operations will be cached in death row and in the operation cache. However, if the working set size of BDD creation is larger than this threshold the BDD will free the nodes on death row. Furthermore, if the working set size of the BDD continues to grow throughout the trace-BDD creation process, then garbage collection will occur more often as well exacerbating the problem and increasing runtime.

To get an idea of the working set size, we can look at the amount of garbage produced during trace-BDD construction. Figure 8 shows the number of live BDD nodes and the total number of BDD nodes present at each sample point in a trace compression run with automatic garbage collection enabled (a run without garbage collection quickly exhausts all system memory) vs. the number of instructions processed in for the (DIN, DIN) BDD for 164.gzip. Graphs for trace creation in other SPEC INT benchmarks look simi-

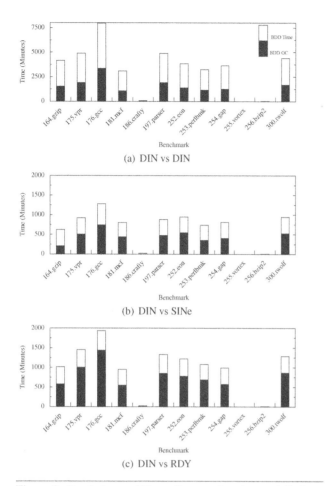

(a) DIN vs DIN

(b) DIN vs SINe

(c) DIN vs RDY

Figure 9. Break-down of Trace Compression time and Garbage Collection time for select SPEC INT benchmarks.

lar to 164.gzip. From the graph we can see that while the number of live nodes is small, the working set size grows quickly (the spikes in the graph) until automatic garbage collection reclaims the nodes. Because the BDD package must manage this garbage, the package (1) spends most of its time in garbage collection (see Figure 9 for a breakdown of garbage collection time vs. total trace creation time), and (2) during garbage collection free's the fraction of nodes that could accelerate BDD creation.

4. ZDD Compressed Traces

ZDDs are a variant of BDDs where the *S-deletion* compression rule is replaced by the use of the *pD-deletion* compression rule. In this section we see that ZDDs provide better compression than BDDs for trace data, and over $9\times$ faster creation times.

4.1 BDDs vs. ZDDs

Zero-suppressed BDDs, or ZDDs, replace the *S-deletion* rule with a the *pD-deletion* rule. This rule states the following:

- If the *1* edge from a node p leads to a zero terminal node and whose *0* edge a child node q, then p is eliminated and all nodes that lead to p are redirected to q.

Furthermore, ZDDs do not typically implement the inverting arcs optimization, i.e., ZDDs have no inverting arcs, only plain *then* and *else* arcs. To see how this rule change results in a different decision diagram, consider, once again, the function $f(x, y, z)$ whose

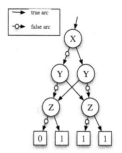

Figure 10. A ZDD for $f(x, y, z)$

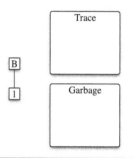

Figure 11. A ZDD for $\bar{X} \wedge \bar{Y} \wedge \bar{Z}$

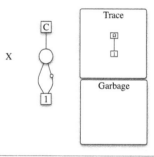

Figure 12. A ZDD for $X \wedge \bar{Y} \wedge \bar{Z}$

binary decision tree was shown in Figure 3a. Figure 10 shows the ZDD for this function. Note, for this function, ZDDs are bad, as most of the values for (x, y, z) cause the function to evaluate to 1. However, for sparse functions (i.e., those with few 1's in the range), such as trace data, ZDDs are far better.

4.2 Traces as ZDDs

To see the advantage of ZDDs for trace creation, let us revisit the equation $E = \bar{X} \wedge \bar{Y} \wedge \bar{Z}$ from Section 3. The ZDD, with trace-ZDD and garbage, is shown in Figure 11.

ZDD construction does not apply the *S-deletion* rule, therefore the resulting graph does contain Boolean *don't-care* values. However, if a node's *then* arc terminates at the Boolean false value, that node is removed. In the equation $B = \bar{X} \wedge \bar{Y} \wedge \bar{Z}$ all *then* arcs terminate at 0, therefore the X, Y and Z nodes are removed, leaving a very small ZDD. We can now construct the trace ZDD for the equation $E' = X \wedge \bar{Y} \wedge \bar{Z}$, as shown in Figure 12.

The ZDD for $E' = X \wedge \bar{Y} \wedge \bar{Z}$ now contains a node for X. Notice X is a boolean *don't-care*, but the BDD *don't-care* reduction rule has been replaced by the ZDD's *zero-suppression* rule. Therefore X is not removed and the *then* and *else* arcs point to the same node.

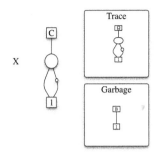

Figure 13. A ZDD for $B \wedge C$

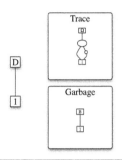

Figure 14. A ZDD for $B \wedge C \wedge D$

Figure 13 shows the state of the trace ZDD after the addition of E'. Notice how little garbage is produced after this addition. Now, like the example from Section 3, we can add the function $E'' = \bar{X} \wedge \bar{Y} \wedge \bar{Z}$, where E'' is equal to E. Like trace-BDD creation, the efficiency of this final step will depend if garbage collection has occurred between the creation of E, E', and the trace BDD. However, the ZDD creation of this trace ZDD produced less garbage than the BDD, therefore it is less likely to invoke garbage collection.

In both functions $(\bar{X} \wedge \bar{Y} \wedge \bar{Z})$ and $(X \wedge \bar{Y} \wedge \bar{Z})$ most *then* arcs terminate at the false, or constant zero node. Note that the trace representation method described in Section 3 uses nodes that with zero terminating arcs to represent the binary 0 in a trace. Therefore, as long as the binary representation of such trace data contains many zeros, and is therefore sparse, ZDDs can achieve good compression levels. In fact, ZDDs have been found achieve better compression levels than BDDs for sets of combinations, as long as the data remains sparse [4].

Figure 15, as well as Table 1, shows that for same set of traces studied in the work in [13] ZDDs achieve approximately 25% better compression. Figure 15 shows the number of nodes required to represent the BDDs required for various trace analyses and visualizations. The data is for 250 million instruction traces from the SPEC INT 2000 benchmark suite.

4.3 ZDD Variable Order, Visualization, and Analysis

It is important to note that ZDD and BDD size can vary significantly depending on the choice variable order. Furthermore, the choice of the best variable order for a ZDD may not be the same as the best order for the equivalent BDD. This can be problematic, for, as discussed in Section 5, certain visualization algorithms depend on the variable order in the ZDD. Fortunately, Lhoták et al. found that in many cases the best BDD variable order is also the best ZDD variable order [7]. Lhoták et al. also show that it is trivial to convert any BDD-based program analysis into a ZDD-based analysis. Applying Lhoták et al.'s insight and the authors' prior work [11], all the standard analyses can also be applied to ZDD compressed traces. The

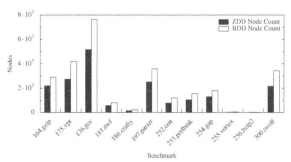

(a) DIN vs DIN Node Count

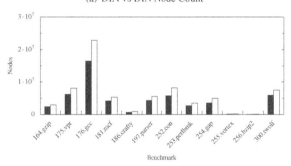

(b) DIN vs SIN Node Count

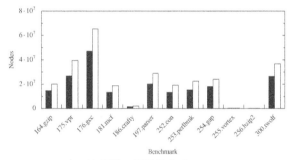

(c) DIN vs RDY Node Count

Figure 15. DD Node Count

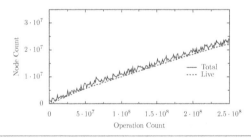

Figure 16. ZDD Total and Live Nodes

one non-trivial algorithm is the trace visualization algorithm developed by the authors [13]. However, Section 5 shows how to adapt this algorithm used for ZDDs.

4.4 ZDD Compression Time

BDD compression time may increase as node count decreases [12]. However, the ZDD unique table growth in Figure 16 (compared to Figure 8) shows that far less garbage is produced during trace-ZDD creation. Because there is far less garbage produced, the ZDD-based trace compressor spends far less time collecting garbage. Fig-

(a) DIN vs RDY

Benchmark	ZDD	BDD
164.gzip	14776031	20191795
175.vpr	26758473	39488720
176.gcc	47191021	65452369
181.mcf	13371337	18857151
186.crafty*	1426447	1989019
197.parser	20298664	28928181
252.eon	13438978	19243812
253.perlbmk	15447265	22507110
254.gap	18167754	24067457
255.vortex*	193184	260701
256.bzip2*	101730	138353
300.twolf	26470707	36674682

(b) DIN vs SIN

Benchmark	ZDD	BDD
164.gzip	2395329	2954172
175.vpr	6220387	8094630
176.gcc	16477762	22851246
181.mcf	4166872	5302426
186.crafty*	664726	944032
197.parser	4346929	5561810
252.eon	5758390	8175031
253.perlbmk	2728992	3490785
254.gap	3563179	4998176
255.vortex*	140930	212049
256.bzip2*	61088	89025
300.twolf	5912991	7515602

(c) DIN vs DIN

Benchmark	ZDD	BDD
164.gzip	22014614	28903561
175.vpr	27382836	41901557
176.gcc	51666471	76472039
181.mcf	5669206	8109996
186.crafty*	1438765	2081447
197.parser	25075154	35929906
252.eon	7925540	12075596
253.perlbmk	10525806	15667727
254.gap	13014623	17960509
255.vortex*	226433	312175
256.bzip2*	113627	157461
300.twolf	21568405	34202383

*Full benchmark trace, benchmark ran to completion.

Table 1. BDD vs ZDD Node Count

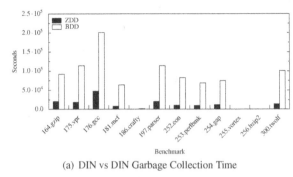

(a) DIN vs DIN Garbage Collection Time

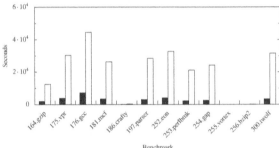

(b) DIN vs SIN Garbage Collection Time

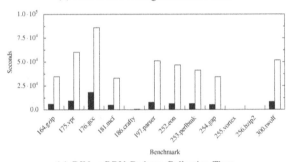

(c) DIN vs RDY Garbage Collection Time

Figure 17. DD Garbage Collection Time

ure 17 compares the amount of time required for garbage collection for ZDD and BDD encoded traces for the set of trace data used by the authors in prior work [13]. These figures are also presented in Table 2. Notice that the ZDD-based code spends far less time collecting garbage.

Now that we know that ZDDs have a small working set size and that the amount of garbage produced stays almost flat during trace-ZDD creation, it is possible to further accelerate ZDD trace creation by adjusting the size of the unique table so that it will contain the working set of the trace-ZDD.

In Figure 18, and Table 3, we can see the time, in seconds, required to encode 250 million trace instructions into a ZDD compared to the time required by BDDs. In this figure the size of the unique table was manually increased to be initially 100x the normal size for both BDD and ZDD based creation. The data collected for Figure 17 and 18 was for the same computer system described in Section 2. Notice that because BDDs generate so much garbage, their working size is much larger than available RAM, mean-

ing that they gain little benefit from the 100x increase in table size. ZDDs on the other hand are much faster because the larger unique table can fit almost the entire working set of useful BDD nodes, and garbage does not cause these nodes to be reaped from death row and the operation cache.

5. ZDD Dependence Visualization

Section 4 described how to trivially extend BDD-based trace analysis to ZDDs by leveraging prior work. In prior work, the authors propose a visualization scheme that allows interactive identification, analysis, and extraction of parallelism based on BDD-compressed traces [13]. However, this visualization algorithm is specific to BDDs, but given the promise of this approach, we show that it is possible to apply the same with techniques on ZDDs with only slight modifications.

5.1 DINxRDY Visualization

The authors' visualization system is based on the DINxRDY plot, originally introduced by Postiff et al. [10]. An example DINxRDY plot is shown in Figure 19.

DINxRDY plots can show potential regions of parallelism as follows (as first described by Iyer et al. [6]). Lines in a DINxRDY plot that run from the lower-left to upper right form dependence chains

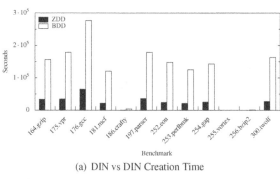

(a) DIN vs DIN Creation Time

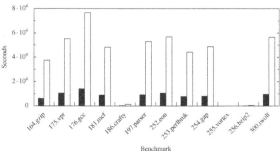

(b) DIN vs SIN Creation Time

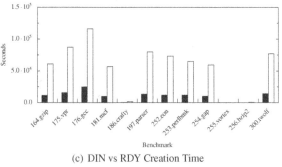

(c) DIN vs RDY Creation Time

Figure 18. DD Creation Time

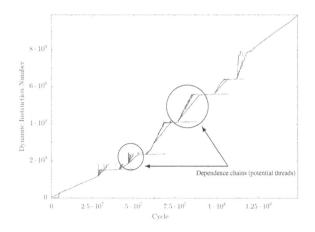

Figure 19. Dynamic instruction number vs. ready-time plot of SPEC CINT 2000 benchmark 254.gap. Circled areas represent potential threads

(a) DIN vs RDY

Benchmark	ZDD	BDD
164.gzip	6149	34744
175.vpr	9395	60352
176.gcc	18260	86119
181.mcf	4970	33083
186.crafty*	69	505
197.parser	7881	51172
252.eon	6478	46865
253.perlbmk	6417	41291
254.gap	5232	34420
255.vortex*	1	10
256.bzip2*	14	97
300.twolf	8511	51914

(b) DIN vs SIN

Benchmark	ZDD	BDD
164.gzip	20522	92132
175.vpr	18718	114093
176.gcc	47518	201188
181.mcf	7704	63987
186.crafty*	143	1196
197.parser	20720	114329
252.eon	10218	82897
253.perlbmk	9549	68938
254.gap	11944	75353
255.vortex*	3	19
256.bzip2*	38	216
300.twolf	13663	100911

(c) DIN vs DIN

Benchmark	ZDD	BDD
164.gzip	1964	12410
175.vpr	3879	30428
176.gcc	7184	44513
181.mcf	3447	26368
186.crafty*	69	262
197.parser	3042	28573
252.eon	4001	32793
253.perlbmk	2298	21147
254.gap	2547	24172
255.vortex*	2	9
256.bzip2*	18	90
300.twolf	3315	31596

*Full benchmark trace, benchmark ran to completion.

Table 2. BDD vs ZDD Garbage Collection Time (Seconds)

of relatively nearby instructions [6]. Iyer et. al found that diagonal lines with overlapping x-extents could potentially represent regions of code that have the potential to be parallelized (circled in the Figure). The authors later confirmed that DINxRDY plots can be used to find and extract parallelism by locating a region in a DINxRDY plot with overlapping x-extents in the 175.vpr benchmark [13]. Using classic program analyses applied to traces, they extracted both data and pipeline parallelism from the benchmark.

5.2 Extended Visualization Algorithm

In prior work, the authors generate visualizations from trace-BDDs in milliseconds by treating the BDD structure like a quad-tree [13]. To understand this algorithm, consider Figures 20 and 21.

In graphics, a a quad-tree decomposes two-dimensional image data into hierarchical regions. Figure 21 shows a quad tree for the DINxRDY graph shown in Figure 20. The region outlined on Figure 20 represents its decomposition, where node Ni corresponds to the region i in the figure.

(a) DIN vs RDY

Benchmark	ZDD	BDD
164.gzip	11487	61046
175.vpr	15699	87107
176.gcc	24612	116137
181.mcf	9995	57038
186.crafty*	219	1495
197.parser	13392	79809
252.eon	11817	73301
253.perlbmk	11773	64993
254.gap	10145	59557
255.vortex*	5	25
256.bzip2*	50	469
300.twolf	14125	77106

(b) DIN vs SIN

Benchmark	ZDD	BDD
164.gzip	6100	37454
175.vpr	10532	55314
176.gcc	14015	76713
181.mcf	8974	48328
186.crafty*	268	1385
197.parser	9214	52987
252.eon	10503	56826
253.perlbmk	7779	44185
254.gap	8013	48764
255.vortex*	7	25
256.bzip2*	71	526
300.twolf	9558	56593

(c) DIN vs DIN

Benchmark	ZDD	BDD
164.gzip	33581	156663
175.vpr	34234	178788
176.gcc	64607	276295
181.mcf	21517	121063
186.crafty*	521	3711
197.parser	35717	178564
252.eon	24280	147433
253.perlbmk	21072	125391
254.gap	25234	143287
255.vortex*	10	61
256.bzip2*	132	1099
300.twolf	27167	162679

*Full benchmark trace, benchmark ran to completion.

Table 3. BDD vs ZDD Creation Time (Seconds)

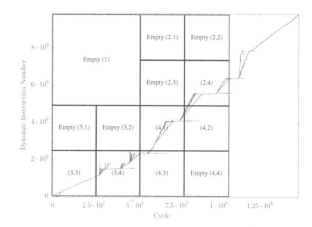

Figure 20. Sample partial quad-tree regions superimposed a DINxRDY plot of SPEC CINT 2000 benchmark 254.gap. (Not to scale)

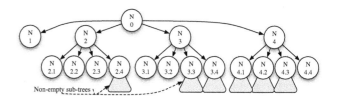

Figure 21. Sample partial quad-tree for regions in Figure 20

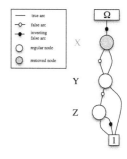

Figure 22. Graph BDD With Missing Node

The visualization algorithm used by ParaMeter is straightforward. Under the variable ordering used in this work, if a BDD is traversed like a tree, then the even levels correspond to bisecting each region horizontally, and the odd levels correspond to bisecting each region vertically. Thus traversing two levels of the BDD corresponds to traversing a single level of the corresponding quad tree. However, since BDDs use the *S-deletion* rule to eliminate nodes, this algorithm must account for eliminated nodes. Since ZDDs use a *pD-deletion* rule, the authors' algorithm for BDDs applies to ZDDs with only a change to how missing levels in the ZDD traversal are handled and what to do when the terminal state is reached.

Recall that the *S-deletion* rule removes nodes from a BDD when both the 1 and 0 outgoing branches lead to the same child node. The quad-tree graphing algorithm must detect removed BDD nodes before graphing the extracted data. For example, consider the indicator function $(\bar{X} \wedge \bar{Y} \wedge \bar{Z}) \vee (X \wedge \bar{Y} \wedge \bar{Z})$. This function represents the set of two numbers $\{000, 100\}$. In the BDD for this function, shown in Figure 6 the node for X was removed because it is a boolean *don't care*. Thus, the algorithm used by ParaMeter has to virtually traverse the graph shown in Figure 22 instead. To do this, ParaMeter detects that a variable was skipped during traversal and then orchestrates its traversal to virtually traverse outgoing arcs from the removed node, which is shown in grey. If a traversal through the BDD reveals many removed nodes, the number of new arcs grows exponentially in the number of *don't care* values, however, ParaMeter implements a number of optimizations to terminate traversals early, limiting the exponential explosion.

To adapt this algorithm to ZDDs we must understand how to deal with missing nodes. In practice, the final algorithm is simpler than that for BDDs because the *pD-reduction* rule does not have to be undone like the *S-deletion* rule.

In Figure 23 we can see the ZDD for the function $(\bar{X} \wedge \bar{Y} \wedge \bar{Z}) \vee (X \wedge \bar{Y} \wedge \bar{Z})$ with removed nodes also highlighted in grey. Notice that, as per the pD-deletion rule, all of the removed nodes have *then* branches leading to the 0 terminal case. Therefore, any

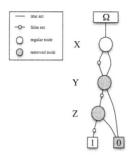

Figure 23. Graph ZDD With Missing Nodes

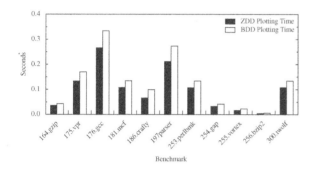

Figure 24. ZDD and BDD Visualization Time for SPEC CINT 2000 benchmarks

time the graphing algorithm detects a removed node, it knows that there is no need to traverse the half of the region where the variable of the missing node is true, and thus needs to do no work. For the half where the variable is false, the algorithm virtually traverses the else-edge of the missing node, just as the BDD-based algorithm traversed both the then and the else edges. Accordingly, Figure 24 shows ZDD rendering is slightly faster than BDDs. Data is from a 2.8 GHz Intel Core i7 with 12 GB of RAM running Linux.

6. Conclusion

Previous works have found BDDs useful in program analysis [8, 13, 17]. For many applications, ZDDs can achieve even greater compression levels while allowing for the same analysis types used with BDDs [7]. The results in this paper show that ZDD-based trace compression results in 25% smaller representation compared to BDD-based traces. Further, ZDDs have a smaller working set, thus the ZDD creation package can tuned to cache the working set of the trace-ZDD during creation. This reduces the number of garbage collection operations and removal of useful dead nodes. This reduces ZDD creation by up to $9\times$. This paper also extends the authors' algorithm for visualizing parallelism in BDD-compressed traces to ZDDs [13]. The resulting algorithm results in trace times as fast or faster than BDDs.

Acknowledgments

The authors thank the reviewers for their insightful comments, Fabio Somenzi for his advice, and Chinmay Ashok, Matthew Iyer, Josh Stone, and Neil Vachharajani for the Adamantium framework.

References

[1] BRAYTON, R. K., HACHTEL, G. D., SANGIOVANNI-VINCENTELLI, A. L., SOMENZI, F., AZIZ, A., CHENG, S.-T., EDWARDS, S. A., KHATRI, S. P., KUKIMOTO, Y., PARDO, A., QADEER, S., RANJAN, R. K., SARWARY, S., SHIPLE, T. R., SWAMY, G., AND VILLA, T. Vis: A system for verification and synthesis. In *CAV '96: Proceedings of the 8th International Conference on Computer Aided Verification* (London, UK, 1996), Springer-Verlag, pp. 428–432.

[2] BRYANT, R. E. Graph-based algorithms for Boolean function manipulation. *IEEE Transaction on Computers C-35*, 8 (August 1986), 677–691.

[3] BWOLEN YANG YIRNG-AN CHEN BRYANT, R.E. O'HALLARON, D. Space- and time-efficient bdd construction via working set control. In *ASP-DAC '98:Design Automation Conference 1998. Proceedings of the ASP-DAC '98. Asia and South Pacific* (Feb 1998), pp. 423–432.

[4] ICHI MINATO, S. Zero-suppressed bdds and their applications. *International Journal on Software Tools for Technology Transfer 3*, 2 (May 20), 156–70.

[5] III, J. H., AND BRGLEZ, F. Design of experiments in bdd variable ordering:lessons learned. In *Computer-Aided Design, 1998. ICCAD 98. Digest of Technical Papers. 1998 IEEE/ACM International Conference on* (1998), pp. 646–652.

[6] IYER, M., ASHOK, C., STONE, J., VACHHARAJANI, N., CONNORS, D. A., AND VACHHARAJANI, M. Finding parallelism for future EPIC machines. In *Proceedings of the 4th Workshop on Explicitly Parallel Instruction Computing Techniques (EPIC)* (March 2005).

[7] LHOTÁK, O., CURIAL, S., AND AMARAL, J. N. Using zbdds in points-to analysis. 338–352.

[8] LHOTÁK, O., AND HENDREN, L. Jedd: a bdd-based relational extension of java. In *PLDI '04: Proceedings of the ACM SIGPLAN 2004 conference on Programming language design and implementation* (New York, NY, USA, 2004), ACM, pp. 158–169.

[9] PANDA, S., AND SOMENZI, F. Who are the variables in your neighborhood. In *ICCAD '95: Proceedings of the 1995 IEEE/ACM international conference on Computer-aided design* (Washington, DC, USA, 1995), IEEE Computer Society, pp. 74–77.

[10] POSTIFF, M., TYSON, G., AND MUDGE, T. Performance limits of trace caches. Tech. Rep. CSE-TR-373-98, University of Maryland, Department of Electrical Engineering and Computer Science, CSE, September 1998.

[11] PRICE, G., AND VACHHARAJANI, M. A case for compressing traces with BDDs. *Computer Architecture Letters 5* (November 2006).

[12] PRICE, G. D. Enabling advanced program analysis with bdds. Master's thesis, Department of Electrical and Computer Engineering, University of Colorado at Boulder, Boulder, CO, 2008.

[13] PRICE, G. D., GIACOMONI, J., AND VACHHARAJANI, M. Visualizing potential parallelism in sequential programs. In *PACT '08: Proceedings of the 17th international conference on Parallel architectures and compilation techniques* (New York, NY, USA, 2008), ACM, pp. 82–90.

[14] SENTOVICH, E. A brief study of bdd package performance. In *FMCAD '96: Proceedings of the First International Conference on Formal Methods in Computer-Aided Design* (London, UK, 1996), Springer-Verlag, pp. 389–403.

[15] SOMENZI, F. CUDD: Colorado University Decision Diagram package, release 2.42. Tech. rep., University of Colorado at Boulder, http://vlsi.colorado.edu/~fabio/CUDD/, 2009.

[16] WHALEY, J. *Context-sensitive pointer analysis using binary decision diagrams.* PhD thesis, Stanford, CA, USA, 2007. Adviser-Lam, Monica.

[17] WHALEY, J., AND LAM, M. S. Cloning-based context-sensitive pointer alias analysis using binary decision diagrams. In *PLDI '04: Proceedings of the ACM SIGPLAN 2004 conference on Programming Language Design and Implementation (PLDI)* (2004), pp. 131–144.

[18] ZHANG, X., GUPTA, R., AND ZHANG, Y. Efficient forward computation of dynamic slices using reduced ordered binary decision diagrams. In *Procedings of the 26th International conference on Software Engineering (ICSE)* (2004).

Taming Hardware Event Samples for FDO Compilation

Dehao Chen[1]   Neil Vachharajani[2]   Robert Hundt[2]   Shih-wei Liao [2]   Vinodha Ramasamy

Paul Yuan[3]   Wenguang Chen[2]   Weimin Zheng[2]

[1]Tsinghua University, [2]Google, [3]Peking University

chendh05@mails.tsinghua.edu.cn, {nvachhar, rhundt, sliao}@google.com, vinodha23@gmail.com,
yingbo.com@gmail.com, {cwg,zwm-dcs}@tsinghua.edu.cn

Abstract

Feedback-directed optimization (FDO) is effective in improving application runtime performance, but has not been widely adopted due to the tedious dual-compilation model, the difficulties in generating representative training data sets, and the high runtime overhead of profile collection. The use of hardware-event sampling to generate estimated edge profiles overcomes these drawbacks. Yet, hardware event samples are typically not precise at the instruction or basic-block granularity. These inaccuracies lead to missed performance when compared to instrumentation-based FDO. In this paper, we use multiple hardware event profiles and supervised learning techniques to generate heuristics for improved precision of basic-block-level sample profiles, and to further improve the smoothing algorithms used to construct edge profiles. We demonstrate that sampling-based FDO can achieve an average of 78% of the performance gains obtained using instrumentation-based exact edge profiles for SPEC2000 benchmarks, matching or beating instrumentation-based FDO in many cases. The overhead of collection is only 0.74% on average, while compiler based instrumentation incurs 6.8%–53.5% overhead (and 10x overhead on an industrial web search application), and dynamic instrumentation incurs 28.6%–1639.2% overhead.

Categories and Subject Descriptors C.4 [*PERFORMANCE OF SYSTEMS*]: Reliability, availability, and serviceability; C.4 [*PERFORMANCE OF SYSTEMS*]: Modeling techniques; D.3.4 [*PROCESSOR*]: Optimization; D.3.4 [*PROCESSOR*]: Compilers

General Terms Algorithms, Design, Performance

Keywords Feedback-Directed Optimization, Sampling Profile, Performance Counters

1. Introduction

Many compiler optimizations, for example procedure inlining, instruction scheduling, and register allocation benefit from dynamic information such as basic block frequency and branch taken / not taken ratios. This information allows the compiler to optimize for the frequent case, rather than using probabilistically estimated frequencies or conservatively assuming that all code is equally likely to execute. Profiling is used to provide this feedback to the compiler.

The traditional approach to profile-guided optimization involves three steps. First, the application is compiled with special flags to generate an instrumented version of the program (*instrumentation build*). Next, the instrumented application is run with training data to collect the profile. Finally, the application is recompiled using the profile to make better optimization decisions (*feedback-directed optimization (FDO) build*).

Unfortunately, there are several shortcomings in this approach. First, it requires compiling the application twice. For applications with long build times, doubling the build time can significantly degrade programmer productivity.

Second, the instrumentation and optimization builds are tightly coupled, thereby preventing reuse of previous profile collection. For example GCC requires that both builds use the same inline decisions and similar optimization flags to ensure that the control-flow graph (CFG) that is profiled in the instrumentation build matches the CFG that is annotated with the profile data in the FDO build.

Third, collecting the profiles requires the appropriate execution environment and *representative* input. For example, profiling a transaction processing application may require an elaborate database setup and a representative set of queries to exercise the application. Creating such an environment and identifying a set of representative input can be very difficult.

Fourth, the instrumentation build of an application typically incurs significant overhead (reported as 9% to 105% [3, 4], but observed to be as much as 10x on an industrial web search application) due to the additional instrumentation code that is executed. While scaling down inputs may ameliorate the problem, for the profiles to be useful, they must accurately reflect the application's real usage. Crafting an input that is sufficiently scaled down to facilitate fast and easy profiling while retaining high fidelity to the real workload is difficult. The problem is exacerbated by constant application changes potentially making old profiling inputs inapplicable to new versions of the application. Furthermore, the high run-time overhead can alter the critical path of time critical routines, e.g., OS kernel codes, for which getting an instrumentation based profile is not easily possible in the first place.

These limitations often lead developers to avoid FDO compilation and forgo its associated performance benefits. To overcome these limitations, we propose skipping the instrumentation step altogether, and instead rely on sampling events generated by the performance monitoring units (PMU) of modern processors to obtain estimated edge profiles. The sample data does not contain any information on the intermediate representation (IR) used by the compiler. Instead, source position information in the debug section of unstripped binaries is used to correlate the samples to the corresponding basic blocks during the FDO build.

This approach has two key benefits. First, since source position information is used to correlate the profile to the program being compiled, this approach eliminates the tight coupling between the instrumentation and FDO builds. Profiles collected on older versions of a program can be used by developers, thus eliminating dual compilation in the normal workflow. Second, the overhead of profile collection is significantly lower since no instrumentation code is inserted, typically in the range of 2% or less.

The low overhead of profiling together with a loose coupling between the profiling build and the FDO build offer compelling use cases. For example, in an Internet company, profile collection can occur by infrequently attaching to standard binaries running on production systems. The data collected can be stored in a profile database for future FDO builds. This usage model further eliminates any potential discrepancy between profile input data and actual usage patterns observed in the deployed application.

Using hardware performance monitoring events to estimate execution profiles is, however, not a panacea. First, sampling provides instruction frequencies, rather than edge frequencies, and it has been shown that it is not possible to transform statement profiles into exact edge profiles in general [15]. Second, to avoid having performance monitoring slow the processor's execution, many tradeoffs are made in the design of modern PMUs leading to imprecise sample attribution. The instruction address associated with an event by the PMU is often not the true address at which the event occurred. To complicate matters further, the distance between the instruction that caused an event and the instruction to which event is attributed is typically variable. Our experiments show that even when using advanced PMU features (e.g., Precise Event-Based Sampling (PEBS) mode on Intel Core 2 processors), events aggregate on particular instructions and are missing on others. While these phenomena may not be problematic for performance debugging, they create significant challenges for using sample profiles in FDO.

In this paper, we present methods to mitigate these problems and use heuristics to derive relative basic block and edge frequency count estimates from the sample profiles. Below, we summarize the primary contributions of this work.

1. We develop a machine learning approach to identify the hardware event most closely correlated to the true execution frequency of program instructions.

2. We identify hardware effects which negatively influence sample distribution, namely synchronization, sample skid, and aggregation/shadow effects.

3. We introduce a hueristic approach, based on sampling multiple hardware events, that mitigates the systematic bias introduced by these hardware effects. Specifically, we show how sample profiles from ancillary hardware events can be used to predict which basic blocks are over/under-sampled, and how this prediction can be used to tune parameters in MCF, the algorithm used to smooth inconsistencies in the primary sample profile.

4. We build a framework to study the limits of the accuracy that can be achieved with the currently available sampling quality and intra-procedural analysis scope.

5. Finally, we present an evaluation of the efficacy of the proposed approach. We present results from an implementation of sample-based FDO in the GCC compiler. Overall, we show that PMU sampling-based FDO, combined with the proposed smoothing heuristics, can achieve 78% of the performance gains obtained using instrumentation-based FDO for SPEC2000 benchmarks. However, sampling-based FDO, on average, incurs only a 1% profiling overhead (2.47% in the worst case) as compared to the 22% profiling overhead (10x on an industrial web search application) incurred by compiler-based instrumentation.

The rest of the paper is organized as follows: Section 2 describes hardware event sampling and explains how it can be used to estimate a basic block profile and derive an estimated edge profile. Section 3 then describes anomalies observed in the raw PMU samples. Section 4 proposes several heuristics to improve the quality of the edge profiles inferred from the raw data. Section 5 then describes the experimental evaluation of PMU sampling-based FDO. Section 6 describes related work in the area. Finally, Section 7 discusses conclusions and future work in sampling-based FDO.

2. Inferring Profiles with the PMU

This section describes how sampling works with most modern performance monitoring units, and how PMU sampling can be used to devise an edge profile for an application.

2.1 Hardware Event Sampling

The performance monitoring unit on a modern micro processor is usually organized as a collection of counters that can be configured to increment when certain *hardware events* occur. For example, counters can be configured to increment on each clock cycle, each time an instruction retires, for every L2 cache miss, etc. The raw contents of these counters can be dumped at program exit to get summary information about how the program executed. Alternatively, the counters can be used for sampling. In this mode, the PMU is configured to generate an interrupt whenever a counter overflows. When the interrupt triggers, performance monitoring software can record the system state (e.g., the program counter (PC), register contents, etc.). This recorded data forms the sample profile for the application.

Sampling a counter that increments each time an instruction retires (e.g., `INST_RETIRED` on x86 processors) provides a natural way to estimate a basic block profile. Each time the counter overflows, the PC is recorded. Then, for each basic block, the sample counts for all the instructions in the basic block are summed and normalized by the number of instructions in the block. This guarantees that large basic blocks do not receive higher profile weights than smaller blocks. In the literature, this approach to sampling has been called *frequency-based* sampling [22]. An alternative to this approach is *time-based* sampling [22], where processor cycles, rather than instructions, are counted. Unfortunately, time-based sampling biases the sample towards basic blocks that take longer to run than others. Section 4.1 compares both approaches and confirms the hypothesis that the frequency-based approach most closely approximates the true basic block frequencies. The remainder of section 4 examines how other counters may be used to correct for anomalies observed in the frequency-based sample profiles.

2.2 Using the Profile in the Compiler

For the sampling-based profile to be usable by the compiler, the instruction-level profile must be converted into a profile annotated onto the compiler's intermediate representation (IR). To achieve this, the instruction-level samples are first attributed to the corresponding program source line using the source position information present in the debug information. The execution frequency for each source line is stored in the feedback data file.

During the FDO build, the compiler reads the profile data to annotate the CFG. Each basic block consists of a number of IR statements. The source line information associated with the individual IR statements is used to determine the list of source lines corresponding to a basic block. The basic block sample count is then determined by the frequency of source lines corresponding to it. Theoretically, the frequency of all source lines corresponding to a basic block should be the same. However, as will be discussed in Section 5.2, source correlation can be skewed. A voting algorithm (e.g., average or max) is designed to assign the most reliable frequency as the basic block sample count.

By using source line information to record profiles, the coupling between the binary used for profile collection and the FDO build is greatly relaxed. This allows effective reuse of the collected profiles. For example, when there are minor source code changes between profile collection and the FDO build, the list of source code changes (change-list descriptions) can be used to update the profile recorded to better match the source code being compiled with FDO.

2.3 Constructing Edge Profiles

Due to errors and noise in sampling, the basic block counts obtained via sampling may not be consistent. That is to say, for a given block, its sample count will not always equal the sum of the sample counts of its successor or predecessor blocks. To make the counts consistent and to obtain an edge profile from the basic block profile, we translate the problem into an instance of the minimum cost flow (MCF) problem. In our implementation, we use MCF twice. First, before creating the sample feedback file, an MCF prepass is performed on instruction level profile. During the prepass, a binary level CFG is built for each procedure, the instruction level profile is annotated on the CFG, and MCF is used to refine the profile (detailed in Section 4). This refined profile is used to create the profile feedback file. Second, after reading the profile feedback file, the compiler uses MCF to translate the basic block profile into an edge profile. The details of formulating the basic block to edge profile conversion problem as an MCF problem can be found in the literature [12, 16]. Here, we describe a few salient details.

An instance of the MCF problem consists of a graph $G = (V, E)$, where each edge has a capacity and a cost function. The objective is to assign a flow to each edge such that for each edge, (a) the flow is less than the edge's capacity, (b) for a given vertex, the sum of the flows on incoming edges equals the sum of the flows on outgoing edges, and (c) that over the whole graph, the sum of the costs is minimized.

For profile smoothing, the graph used in MCF is known as the residual graph and it is based on a function's CFG. However, each basic block is split into two nodes, the incoming edges to the block connect to the first node in the pair, and the outgoing edges originate at the second node in the pair. The two nodes are connected with a forward and reverse edge. Sending flow through the forward edge corresponds to increasing the basic block count, and sending flow through the reverse edge corresponds to decreasing the basic block count. Since a solution to MCF seeks to minimize cost, the solution can be biased in favor of raising a particular block's weight by assigning its forward edge a low cost. Similarly, one can bias in favor of lowering a block's weight by assigning its reverse edge a low cost. Additionally, the solution can be biased towards altering a specific block's weight by giving its forward and reverse edges a higher cost. We exploit this property of MCF in Section 4.

3. Problems Observed

Sampling is a statistical approach and therefore its results are not exact. However, we observe hardware induced problems that go well beyond plain statistical inaccuracies. For example, consider the loop shown in Figure 1. The loop is comprised of one basic block that iterates 104166667 times. If the loop is sampled using a sampling period of 202001, then one would expect each instruction in the loop's body to receive approximately $\frac{104166667}{202001} = 515.67$ samples. The two columns

Fixed Sample Period		Random Sample Period		PEBS		
Abs.	Norm.	Abs.	Norm.	Abs.	Norm.	Loop
267	0.52	577	1.13	1554	3.01	00: add $0x1,%rdx
142	0.28	95	0.19	0	0.00	04: or $0x2,%rdx
1212	2.35	237	0.46	0	0.00	08: add $0x3,%rdx
272	0.53	532	1.04	447	0.87	0c: or $0x4,%rdx
0	0.00	523	1.02	1438	2.79	10: add $0x5,%rdx
1252	2.43	475	0.93	66	0.13	14: or $0x6,%rdx
269	0.52	502	0.98	1	0.00	18: add $0x7,%rdx
149	0.29	454	0.89	46	0.09	1c: or $0x8,%rdx
1197	2.32	512	1.00	504	0.98	20: add $0x9,%rdx
9	0.02	498	0.98	1402	2.72	24: or $0xa,%rdx
327	0.63	487	0.95	3	0.01	28: add $0xb,%rdx
48	0.09	724	1.42	116	0.22	2c: or $0xc,%rdx
1504	2.92	633	1.24	1833	3.55	30: add $0xd,%rdx
266	0.52	565	1.11	19	0.04	34: or $0xe,%rdx
141	0.27	762	1.49	260	0.50	38: add $0xf,%rdx
1219	2.36	999	1.96	1675	3.25	3c: or $0x10,%rdx
268	0.52	532	1.04	35	0.07	40: add $0x1,%esi
0	0.00	0	0.00	0	0.00	43: cmp %rcx,%rdx
1255	2.43	591	1.16	398	0.77	46: jbe 0
515.63		510.42		515.63		Average
541.21		222.45		677.56		StdDev

Figure 1. The sample counts measured on an Intel Clover-town for a loop consisting of one basic block.

INST_RETIRED	CPU_CLK_UNHALTED	DTLB_MISS	Source
1957	5801	0	m = m + i;
1958	5965	0	m = m + i;
1942	5764	0	m = m + i;
3947	11634	0	x = rand() % size;
68551	340252	1047	m = m + test_v[x];
38	2042	0	m = m + i;
105	5835	0	m = m + i;
13	5846	0	m = m + i;
7	5813	0	m = m + i;
3	5901	0	m = m + i;
3040	5912	0	m = m + i;
2027	5875	0	m = m + i;
2057	5883	0	m = m + i;

Figure 2. Aggregation Effect due to long latency instructions measured on an Intel Clovertown.

of numbers labeled Fixed Sample Period in the figure show the actual samples collected on an Intel Clovertown machine. The first column shows the raw count for each instruction and the second shows the count normalized by the expected count (i.e., 1.0 is the correct count, < 1.0 means the instruction was undersampled, and > 1.0 means the instruction was oversampled). We can see from this data, that the sample counts vary by a factor of 2–3 from what they ought to be. In this section, we describe these artifacts, and posit causes for these anomalies. Section 4 will then introduce various approaches to achieve more precise profiles at both the basic block level and CFG level. We observed similar effects on a variety of architectures from Intel and AMD.

3.1 Synchronization

If one selects a period that is *synchronized* with a piece of the application, a few instructions will receive all of the samples. For example, if a loop contains k dynamic instructions per iteration, and the sampling period is selected as a multiple k, then only one instruction in the loop will be sampled.

Randomization can avoid synchronization. Instead of using a constant sampling period, the PMU is configured so the number of events between samples is the user provided sampling period plus a randomly chosen delta. After each sample, a new random delta is selected. Since the number of events between each sample is not constant, periodic properties in the program being measured do not skew the sample.

Additionally, our empirical results show that random sampling improves the uniformity of samples even in the absence of synchronization. In the example in Figure 1, there are 19 instructions in the loop and the sampling period used was 202001 which is not a multiple of 19. Consequently, the unexpected results should not be due to synchronization. However, when random sampling is used, one obtains the results shown in the two columns labeled Random Sample Period

in the figure. With randomization, the samples are more uniformly distributed. The average number of samples per instruction changed because the average sampling period was 204080 (rather than 202001) due to randomization. However, notice that random sampling reduced the standard deviation by a factor of almost 2.5.

Further experiments reveal that non-random sampling leads to a form of pseudo-synchronization. Although a particular sampling period is requested, due to skid (described in the next section) that is variable, yet systematic, the actual sampling period is ultimately partially synchronized with the loop. While this can be mitigated through careful non-random adjustment of the sampling period for the particular code in the example, random sampling proves more effective when dealing with code with complex control flow and with varying amounts instruction-level parallelism.

3.2 Sample Skid

Ideally the PC reported when a counter overflows would be the PC associated with the instruction that triggered the overflow. Unfortunately, the reported PC is often for an instruction that executes many cycles later. This phenomenon is referred to as *skid*. For example, previous work shows that on an Alpha 21064, the recorded PC corresponds to the instruction that is at the head of the instruction queue 6-cycles after the one that triggered the overflow [7]. On an Intel Clovertown machine, we observed a similar phenomenon. The reported PC corresponds to the instruction that is at the head of the instruction queue some number of cycles (often approximately 30-cycles) after the one that overflows the counter.

When using time-based sampling, this phenomenon is not important as it only skews the sampling period [2]. However, for frequency-based sampling, the effects of skid are important. Figure 2 shows how this effect interacts with a long latency instruction. Because long latency instructions sit at the head of the instruction queue for long periods of time, they are sampled disproportionately more than other instructions. Consequently, instructions that trigger long stalls such as cache or TLB misses will have abnormally higher sample counts compared to other instructions in the same basic block. We refer to this as the *aggregation effect*. These additional samples should have been attributed to instructions *after* the stalled instruction, however since they accumulate on the stalled instruction, instructions in the shadow of the stalled instruction frequently have unusually low sample counts. We refer to this as the *shadow effect*.

Previous work suggests accounting for this phenomenon by approximating the amount of time that an instruction spends at the head of the instruction queue [2]. Unfortunately, estimating this quantity on a modern out-of-order, superscalar processor with a deep cache hierarchy is difficult. In the next section, we show how measuring other performance counters can be used to help correct for this bias.

Modern Intel x86 processors provide *precise event based sampling* (PEBS) which guarantees that the address reported for a counter overflow corresponds to a dynamic instruction that caused the counter to increment. Provided sufficient delay between two back-to-back events, the address reported corresponds to the instruction immediately after the one that overflowed the counter [6]. Unfortunately, when measuring instruction retirement, as the two columns labeled PEBS in Figure 1 show, sampling with PEBS actually yields *lower* accuracy than sampling without PEBS. This occurs due to bursts of instruction retirement events near the counter overflow. These instructions will not be sampled, once again leading to asymmetric sampling. Since PEBS does not support randomized sampling periods, non-PEBS sampling with randomized sampling periods appears to be a more promising approach.

AMD processors, on the other hand, provide *instruction-based sampling* (IBS) which is similar to the ProfileMe approach [7]. Unfortunately, this facility only allows sampling instructions fetched (which include instructions on mispredicted paths) or μops retired (which are at a finer granularity than ISA instructions). Since the number of μops per instruction is unknown, using IBS also proves problematic [8].

3.3 Multi-Instruction Retirement

On most modern superscalar processors, more than one instruction can retire in a given cycle. For example, on Intel's Clovertown processor, up to four instructions can retire each cycle. Unfortunately, the interrupt signaling the overflow of a performance counter happens immediately before or after a group of committing instructions, and the performance monitoring software records only one PC associated with the group. Consequently, if a set of instructions always retire together, only one instruction in the group will have samples attributed to it, and these samples will be the aggregation of all the samples for the instructions it retired with. For example, in Figure 1, observe that the `cmp` instruction receives no samples. While the precise cause cannot be known, it is likely because it commits with the instruction immediately preceding it (they are not data dependent) or with the instruction immediately following it (due to fused compare and branch in the processor backend). Further, since the other instructions are data-dependent, the instruction with address `0x30` will execute approximately 30-cycles later, and the data shows that it

has accumulated additional samples. We find similar effects on other x86 architectures such as AMD.

Fortunately, as Figure 1 shows, this aggregation is frequently contained within a single basic block due to the serialization caused by branches. Consequently, while the sample counts for individual instructions may show significant variation due to this effect, the *basic block* profiles derived by averaging these samples across each block's instructions exhibit significantly less variability.

4. Improving Profile Precision

From the previous section, it may seem that profiles derived from PMU sampling will be fraught with inaccuracies. However, as Levin et al. show MCF is an effective algorithm to derive completely consistent basic block and edge profiles from potentially inaccurate basic block profiles [12]. However, as they also demonstrate, the quality of the derived profiles heavily depend on the specific cost functions used in MCF. In general, if the sample counts for a particular basic block are accurate, the corresponding edges in the residual graph used during MCF should be assigned a high cost. Conversely, if the sample count is inaccurate, depending on whether the sample count is too high or too low, the corresponding forward or reverse edge in the residual graph should have a lower cost. Based on the observation that basic blocks are often missed during profiling (and therefore have a profile that is too small), prior work uses a fixed cost for all edges, with forward edges having a significantly lower cost than reverse edges. This section details an alternate approach for assigning edge costs. By sampling multiple performance counters, one can compute a confidence in the accuracy of the profile for a basic block, and estimate if the sample count is too high or too low. As our results indicate, adjusting the cost functions used in MCF according to these predictions significantly improves the quality of the derived profiles.

4.1 Choosing the Profiles

As was discussed in Section 2, there are two primary approaches for obtaining a sample profile using hardware-event sampling, the frequency-based approach and the time-based approach. More generally, any of the myriad hardware events exposed by the PMU can be used to derive a sample profile. Consequently, it is unclear which event is best for estimating the execution count of basic blocks. We propose using machine learning during compiler tuning to find the most relevant events automatically. We use linear support vector regression (SVR) [11] to quantify how various hardware events correlate with the execution count of a basic block. SVR is similar to the common least-squares linear regression, but uses a different cost function for evaluating the deviation of predictions [18]. SVR is applied to a training set of hardware event values and the exact execution counts of basic blocks obtained through instrumentation (note, the instrumentation is only necessary when *training* the regression model). Given a training set with the true execution frequency of a basic block, and the normal-

Event	Mask	Counter Incremented	Weight
INST_RETIRED	None	when an instruction retires	0.43
INST_RETIRED	PEBS	when an instruction retires	0.272
INST_RETIRED	0	when no instruction retires in a cycle	-0.1247
INST_RETIRED	4	when 4 instructions retire in 1 cycle	-0.1887
CPU_CLK_ UNHALTED	None	each CPU cycle	0.2131
DTLB_MISS	None	when there is an DTLB miss	-0.1124
L1I_MISS	None	when there is an L1 I-Cache miss	0.0092

Table 1. Events and related weights from the SVM regression model.

ized values of various sampled performance counters, SVR attempts to find a vector of weights such that

$$F \approx \sum_i w_i c_i + b$$

where F is the true execution frequency of a block, w_i is the weight for the ith sampled event, c_i is the corresponding sample count, and b is a constant offset. The absolute value of a weight signifies how well the particular sampled event correlates with the true execution frequency; the sign of the weight indicates whether the correlation is positive or negative.

Table 1 shows the results of applying this approach with the SPEC CINT2000 benchmarks used as training data. Four different hardware events were sampled, and the INST_RETIRED event was configured with 4 different masks leading to a total of 7 different profiles.

As expected, sampling the INST_RETIRED event with randomization has the best correlation to the true execution frequency of a basic block. The DTLB miss event has a negative weight because it leads to many cycles of stall, and consequently leads to aggregation effects. Other events such as zero and multiple instruction retirements result in a negative factor because of the aggregation effect. The CPU_CLK_UNHALTED profile has a positive factor, but it is less significant than random sampling of the INST_RETIRED event since, as was discussed earlier, time-based sampling correlates with execution time not execution frequency. As the micro-benchmark from Section 3 showed, using precise event based sampling (PEBS) on the instruction retired event has a lower positive factor than the corresponding event without PEBS.

The automatically trained model shows which events could serve as the principal ones to sample to estimate basic block frequencies, and it also provides information about which events can be used to supplement the principal profile. Unfortunately, the SVM model cannot directly be used to convert a collection of profiles into a basic block frequency estimate because of the regression constant b. This constant implies that the estimated frequency of a block is non-zero even if no sample (across all the measured events) was attributed to it. Since there are many blocks in a program which truly do not get executed, using the model directly would yield poor results. The next section describes an alternate strategy for using additional hardware events to supplement the primary count.

4.2 Classifying Basic Blocks

Since the instruction retired event with random sampling showed highest correlation to the actual execution frequency of a basic block, we chose it as the base profile to estimate basic block counts. Here, we present heuristics to predict the confidence level of the instruction retired profile for a specific basic block. High confidence means that the basic block sample count is predicted to be close to the real execution count. Basic blocks with low confidence are further divided into two categories, blocks where the sample count is predicted to be larger(smaller) than the true execution count. The basic block classification information is used by the edge cost functions in the MCF algorithm to help make better smoothing decisions.

As was described earlier, there are two principal biasing effects in the INST_RETIRED based profile: the aggregation effect and the shadow effect. Recall that the aggregation effect leads to larger sample counts, and the shadow effect leads to smaller sample counts. However, both these effects usually coexist for a single basic block. Consequently, the goal of the heuristic is to determine which effect, if any, is dominant for a particular basic block.

Recall that aggregation occurs for long-latency instructions. For a fixed skid, D, a unit-latency instruction will be sampled if the instruction that retired D cycles earlier overflowed the performance counter. However, since an instruction with latency L remains at the head of the instruction window between times t and $t + L - 1$, it will be sampled if the counter overflowed anywhere between D and $D - L - 1$ cycles before the instruction issued. Consequently, an instruction's chance of getting sampled increases proportionally to its latency. To model this aggregation, the compiler must estimate the latency of each instruction. However, it is hard to measure latency since stall events are not attributed to the correct instruction due to skid. However, our observations show that most aggregation is caused by instructions that stall for significant amounts of time (e.g., stalling due to a DTLB miss). Events measuring these long stalls are generally unaffected by skid and therefore are attributed to the instruction that caused the overflow of the performance counter. Consequently, the heuristic to model aggregation is restricted to events that lead to significant stalls. The set of such events is selected once when a compiler is being tuned for a specific architecture.

For each such event e, the stall duration (obtained from processor manuals), stall_duration$_e$, multiplied by the sample count for the event, count$_{e,i}$, gives the total number of cycles that a particular instruction i stalled due to event e. Summing over all such stall events for all instructions in a basic block gives us an aggregation factor, A.

$$A = \sum_e \text{stall\_duration}_e \times \left(\sum_{i \in BB} \text{count}_{e,i} \right)$$

The shadow effect can be modeled by comparing the total number of cycles spent in a basic block (as measured by sampling CPU_CLK_UNHALTED) to the number of instruction retired events attributed to the block. The difference between these two sample counts is the shadow factor, S. Recall, that the delay in attribution does not affect time-based sampling, implying that the CPU_CLK_UNHALTED sample count should have proper attribution. Consequently, if S is large, two possibilities exist. First, the basic block could legitimately have experienced high CPI. Alternatively, its instruction retirement samples could have been shadowed. In the first case, A should also be large. Consequently if $S \gg A$ then it is likely that the block's samples have been shadowed. In our implementation, if $S - A$ is greater than twice the raw basic block count, the block is classified as under-sampled. Conversely, if $A > S$ and A is a significant fraction of the total number of cycles spent in the block, then it is likely that the block has aggregated too many instruction retirement samples[1]. In our implementation, if $A > S$ and A accounts for more than 50% of the cycles spent in the block, it is classified as over-sampled.

Based on this classification, an MCF prepass is performed on the binary level profile, with adjusted cost function for basic blocks that are predicted to be over-/under-sampled. For over-sampled blocks, its corresponding forward edge in the residual graph is set as the maximum cost in the CFG, while its reverse edge is set to 0 (and vice-versa for under-sampled basic blocks).

5. Experimental Results

We evaluated the framework described in the previous sections by comparing the quality of refined sample profiles to raw sample profiles and instrumentation profiles. Additionally, we evaluated the performance of sampling-based FDO by comparing the runtime performance of sample-FDO builds with instrumented-FDO builds. All binaries were produced using GCC version 4.3.2 targeting an x86_64. The sample profiles were collected using perfmon2 on an Intel Core2 Quad 2.4 GHz machine with a prime sampling period of 202001. Random sampling, with a randomization mask of 0xFFF, was used to improve the quality of the samples. With these parameters, a sample was taken after every 202001 + (rand() & 0xFFF) instructions retired. All runtime performance measurements were run on the Intel Core2 Quad 2.4GHz machine used to collect profiles.

5.1 Precision of the profile

We used the *degree of overlap* metric [12] to evaluate the quality of the profiles independent of the FDO optimizations with which they will be used. The degree of overlap metric compares the similarity of two edge profiles annotated onto a

common CFG. The definition is as follows:

$$\mathrm{PW}\,(e, W) = \frac{W(e)}{\sum_{e' \in E} W(e')}$$

$$\mathrm{overlap}\,(W_1, W_2) = \sum_{e \in E} \min\left(\mathrm{PW}\,(e, W_1), \mathrm{PW}\,(e, W_2)\right)$$

where W is a map from edges to weights, E is the set of edges in the CFG, and PW computes the normalized weight of an edge. If two profiles agree exactly, the overlap is equal to 1 (or 100%), the sum of the normalized edge weights over the CFG. Conversely, if the profile weights differ for some edge, since the minimum of the two is selected the overlap will decrease. Consequently, the overlap can vary between 0% and 100%.

Figure 3 shows the overlap between the sample profiles and the instrumented profiles for the SPEC CINT2000. The first four bars are measured at binary level, which are derived by comparing sampled profiles to edge profiles derived using Pin [13]. We evaluate binary level overlap to isolate the PMU sampling precision problem from source correlation problems (see Section 5.2), and show how refinements can improve the precision incrementally. The first bar shows the quality of the raw profiles (converted to an edge profile using static profile heuristics [21]). Comparing the first and second bar shows that, on average, the MCF algorithm (as presented in the literature [12]) improves the overlap by 17.8% when compared with static estimation. Comparing the second and third bars shows that by classifying basic blocks as over-/under-sampled using multiple PMU profiles, the precision can be further improved by 5.5%. The fourth bar shows the potential of our refinement approach by classifying blocks as over-/under-sampled using perfect profiles (obtained from Pin) rather than using additional hardware events. Comparing the third and fourth bars shows that our approach is only 2.3% worse (80.5% to 82.8%) than using perfect profiles for basic block classification. However, as shown by the 5th bar, when the profile is transformed to the source level and used to annotate the CFG in GCC, the precision decreases by 4.6% due to source correlation problems (see Section 5.2).

To estimate the potential for futher improvement, we computed the function-level overlap of the sampled profile and the true function profiles obtained using Pin. Function-level overlap is defined identically to the edge overlap except that W is a mapping from a procedure to its weight. Since the heuristics used to infer edge profiles from the sample profiles are intra-procedural, the function-level overlap is an upper bound to the edge overlap. The function-level overlap was measured to be 91.7%, making the smoothed edge profile obtained using our algorithms within 10% of optimal. The imprecision in the function-level profile can be explained by aggregation/shadow effects crossing procedure boundaries. The overlap when using a more aggressive compiler inline heuristic (which reduces the chances of aggregation/shadowing across procedure boundaries) increases the function-level overlap to 94.1%. These results suggest that inter-procedural smooothing algorithms may be a promising avenue of future research.

---

[1] The aggregation factor A may over-estimate the number of cycles spent in a basic block due to stalls if some of the stalls are overlapped. In such cases, our heuristic may assert that a block has aggregated too many samples when in fact it has not. Our experience has shown that this mischaracterization occurs rarely, if at all.

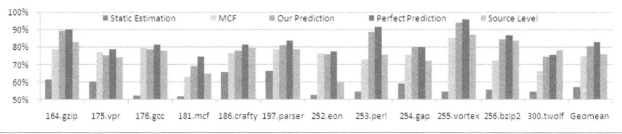

Figure 3. Edge overlap measures for SPEC CINT2000 benchmarks. Sampled FDO reaches an overlap of 80.5%.

Finally, to experimentally verify that using INST_RETIRED as the primary profile is best, we measured the overlap using other hardware events. Since our enhancements to MCF are tuned specifically for the INST_RETIRED hardware event, for fairness, the results presented here were obtained using the original MCF algorithm. As expected, using INST_RETIRED with randomization achieved the best average overlap (75.1%), while using PEBS is slightly worse (74.2%), and using CPU_CLK_UNHALTED achieved an average overlap of (72.6%) even with randomization.

5.2 Issues with Source Position Information

In addition to the challenges imposed by issues inherent to hardware-event sampling, there are other challenges due to inaccuracies in the source position information used to correlate samples to the compiler's IR. These challenges are outlined here.

Insufficient Source Position Information One line of source code can embody multiple basic blocks (e.g., consider any use of the ternary ? : operator). In our current implementation, samples originating from instructions corresponding to such lines of code will be attributed to all of the corresponding basic blocks in the compiler's IR instead of the specific block for the instruction. We currently use source formatting to mitigate this issue, and, in the future, will rely on basic-block discriminators[2] to distinguish the different code regions.

Missing/Incorrect Source Position Information Source formatting does not help in cases where there is incorrect source position information. For example, even if each clause in a ? : expression is on a separate line, GCC attributes all the code for the expression with the first line. In other cases, source position information is completely lost during optimization [16].

Over/Under Sampling Due to Optimization Optimizations such as loop unrolling etc., lead to some statements being duplicated in different basic blocks in the optimized binary used for profile collection. Because the multiple basic blocks in the binary correspond to one basic block in the compiler's IR, the profile normalization strategy will cause the profile for these basic blocks to be too low. Conversely, optimizations like if-conversion promote conditionally executed code to uncondi-

---

[2] Currently being implemented in GCC.

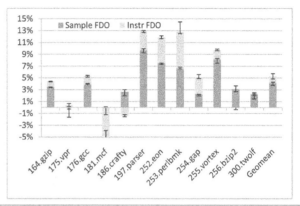

Figure 4. Speedup for SPEC CINT2000 benchmarks. Sampled FDO achieves 78% of instrumented FDO.

tionally executed code. This increases the likelihood that it will be sampled thus causing its profile count to be too high.

5.3 Effectiveness of the framework

The true measure of quality for the profiles is how well they enable feedback-directed optimizations. Figure 4 shows the speedup obtained by using FDO over a baseline binary compiled without FDO. The baseline and FDO binaries were all compiled using GCC with the -O2 flag.

On average, using profiles collected on an Intel Core2 processor, sample-based FDO with our refinements provides an absolute speedup of 4.106%. This is 78% of the speedup obtained by instrumentation-based FDO.

For some benchmarks (e.g. 186.crafty), sample-based FDO outperforms its instrumentation-based counterpart. Since many feedback-directed optimizations in GCC are driven by threshold based heuristics, this difference is not surprising as subtle differences in the profile can lead to substantially different optimization decisions.

Detailed investigation into several benchmarks revealed that most of the performance gap between sample-based FDO and instrumentation-based FDO can be attributed to source correlation problems. For 181.mcf, instrumentation based FDO suffers a significant performance loss compared to the baseline binary. Code layout decisions change a conditional back edge jump in the baseline binary to a conditional loop exit followed by an unconditional back edge jump in an important loop. The latter code sequence suffers from sig-

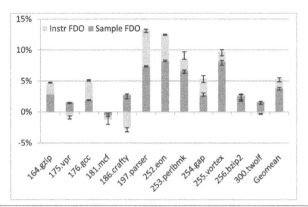

Figure 5. Cross-validation of the speedup for SPEC CINT2000 benchmarks. Sampled FDO achieves 72% of instrumented FDO.

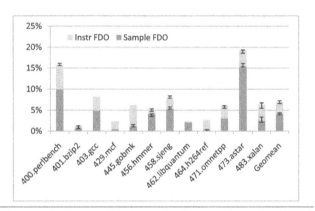

Figure 6. Cross-validation of the speedup for SPEC CINT2006 benchmarks. Sampled FDO achieves 60% of instrumented FDO.

nificantly higher branch misprediction leading to the performance degradation. For the 252.eon and 253.perlbmk, the gap between the instrumentation-based approach and sampling-based approach is due to frequent use of the ternary(?:) operator in one of the hottest functions in the benchmark. Unfortunately, samples for all instructions participating in the statement will be allocated to a single source line (even after source formatting) even though it corresponds to several basic blocks. These benchmarks' performance would no doubt improve with better source position information. Further study of an industrial application shows that loop unrolling is another important source for the performance gap between the two approaches. The instrumentation based profile can derive exact loop trip counts, while the trip counts derived using the sampling based profile is often off by a small amount. As a result, with instrumented FDO, a loop may be fully-unrolled for most frequent situations, while in sampled FDO it may have some "left-over" iterations that degrade the performance. Tuning the compiler's unroll heuristics for the sample based behavior could potentially ameliorate this problem.

One thing to note is that the above evaluations were not cross-validated. However, they are good indicators of the ef-

fectiveness of our approach because FDO (both instrumented and sample-based) performs best when the input data used for profile collection is also used for performance evaluation. However, to make the evaluation complete, we cross-validated the performance improvements on both SPEC CINT2000 and SPEC CINT2006 benchmarks. "Train" data sets are used to collect both sampled and instrumented profiles. These profiles are used in the FDO builds and performance is measured using the "Ref" data sets. As shown in Figures 5 and 6, sampling based FDO can achieve 72% and 60% speedup of instrumentation based FDO, respectively.

We also evaluated the overhead incurred by profile collection. Using a sampling rate of 202001, the overhead of sampling ranges from 0.44% to 2.47%, averaging 0.74%. On the SPEC benchmarks, compiler-based instrumentation incurs an overhead between 6.8% and 53.5%, and dynamic instrumentation tools, such as Pin, incur an overhead between 28.6% and 1639.2%. On an industrial web search application, the compiler-based instrumentation suffered a 10x overhead, compared to just over 2% overhead when profiled using hardware PMU sampling.

6. Related Work

In a recent paper, Levin, Newman, and Haber [12] use sampled profiles of the instruction retirement hardware event to construct edge profiles for feedback-directed optimization in IBM's FDPR-Pro, post-link time optimizer. The samples can be directly correlated to the corresponding basic blocks without using source position information, as this is done post-link time. As is done in this paper, the problem of constructing a full edge profile from basic block sample counts is formalized as a Minimum Cost Circulation problem. In this paper, we extend their work by applying sampling to higher level compilation (as opposed to post-link optimization) and show how sampling additional performance counters can improve the quality of sample profiles.

Others have proposed sampling approaches without relying on performance counters. For example, the Morph system [22] collects profiles via statistical sampling of the program counter on clock interrupts. Alternatively, Conte et al. proposed sampling the contents of the branch-prediction hardware using kernel-mode instructions to infer an edge profile [5]. In particular, the tags and target addresses stored in the branch target buffer (BTB) serve to identify an arc in an application, and the branch history stored by the branch predictor can be used to estimate each edge's weight. Both of these works require additional information to be encoded in the binary to correlate instruction-level samples back to the compiler's IR rather than using source position information present in unstripped binaries. Additionally, neither work investigates the intrinsic bias of the sampling approach nor attempts to correct the collected profiles heuristically. We do however believe that edge sampling is a promising approach and are evaluating extending our infrastructure using hardware support for branch recording (for example the LBR stack on Intel Core2 processors) to enable the approach with unmodified commodity operating systems.

Other profiling methods build on ideas from both program instrumentation and statistical sampling. For example, Traub, Schechter, and Smith propose periodically inserting instrumentation code to capture a small and fixed number of the branch's executions [19]. A post-processing step is used to derive traditional edge profiles from the sampled branch biases collected. Their experiments show that the derived profiles show competitive performance gains when compared with using complete edge profiles to drive a superblock scheduler. Rather than dynamically modifying the binary, others have proposed a similar framework that performs code duplication and uses compiler-inserted counter-based sampling to switch between instrumented and non-instrumented code in a controlled, fine-grained manner [10]. Finally, stack sampling has been used, without the use of any instrumentation, to implement a low-overhead call path profiler [9].

Similarly, there have been proposals that combine instrumentation and hardware performance counters. Ammons, Ball, and Larus proposed instrumenting programs to read hardware performance counters [1]. By selecting where to reset and sample the counters, the authors are able to extract flow and context sensitive profiles. These profiles are not limited to simple frequency profiles. The authors show, for example, how to collect flow sensitive cache miss profiles from an application.

Not surprisingly, performance counter sampling has also been used in the context of just-in-time (JIT) compilation. For example, Schneider, Payer, and Gross sample cache miss performance counters to optimize locality in a garbage collected environment [17]. Like our work, the addresses collected during sampling have to be mapped back to the source code (in their case, Java bytecode). However, since their optimizations were implemented in a JIT, they simply augmented the information stored during dynamic compilation to perform the mapping.

Specialized hardware has also been proposed to facilitate PMU-based profiling. ProfileMe was proposed hardware support to allow accurate instruction-level sampling [7] for Alpha processors. Merten et al. also propose specialized hardware support for identifying program hot spots [14]. Unfortunately, the hardware they propose is not available in today's commercial processors.

Orthogonal to collecting profiles, recent work has studied the stability and accuracy of hardware performance counters [20]. In that work, the authors measured the total number of instructions retired across a range of benchmarks on various x86 machines running identical binaries. Their results show that subtle changes to the heap layout, the number of context switches and page faults, and differences in the definition of one instruction can lead to substantial variability in even the total number of instructions retired as reported by the performance counters. Unfortunately, the authors do not study the artifacts in sampling the performance counters, and the results on the aggregate data do not explain the anomalous behavior observed in our experiments

7. Conclusion and Future Work

We designed and implemented a framework to use hardware event sampling and source position information to drive feedback-directed optimizations. By using multiple profiles and supervised learning to refine the profile precision, sampling-based FDO can achieve good overlap with the true execution frequencies and competitive speedups when compared with the instrumentation-based approach. Moreover, sampling-based FDO provides better portability and usability while incurring negligible overhead. Our experiments show that the proposed techniques are feasible for production use on out-of-order platforms, and the precision/performance can be further improved with more precise source position information.

The results presented here represent an initial implementation. Our ongoing work is exploring the possibility of using algorithms other than MCF to refine the precision of the profile in the CFG. We are also investigating heuristics to avoid precision loss due to code duplicating optimizations.

Further, while our current implementation focuses on generating edge profiles, we plan on exploring using other types of profiles, such as cache miss profiles to guide code- and data-layout optimizations, and branch misprediction profiles to guide if-conversion. Ultimately, we believe these additional profiles facilitated by hardware event sampling will significantly improve the profitability of feedback-directed optimization.

8. Acknowledgments

We want to thank all the reviewers for their insightful reviews and suggestions, which are integrated into the final version of this paper. We would like to thank all the people on the Google compiler team. Special thanks to Stephane Eranian for his help in analyzing the behaviour of PMU based sampling.

References

[1] Glenn Ammons, Thomas Ball, and James R. Larus. Exploiting Hardware Performance Counters with Flow and Context Sensitive Profiling. *Proc. of SIGPLAN Conference on Programming Language Design and Implementation*, Las Vegas, Nevada, June 1997.

[2] Jennifer M. Anderson, Lance M. Berc, Jeffrey Dean, Sanjay Ghemawat, Monika R. Henzinger, Shun-Tak A. Leung, Richard L. Sites, Mark T. Vandevoorde, Carl A. Waldspurger, and William E. Weihl. Continuous Profiling: Where Have All the Cycles Gone? *ACM Transactions on Computer Systems*, 15(4):357–390, 1997.

[3] Thomas Ball and James R. Larus. Optimally Profiling and Tracing Programs. *ACM Transactions on Programming Languages and Systems*, 1994.

[4] Thomas Ball and James R. Larus. Efficient Path Profiling. *Proc. of ACM/IEEE International Symposium on Microarchitecture*, IEEE Computer Society, 1996.

[5] Thomas M. Conte, Burzin A. Patel, Kishore N. Menezes, and J. Stan Cox. Hardware-Based Profiling: An Effective Technique for Profile-Driven Optimization. *International Journal of Parallel Processing*, 24(2):187–206, 1996.

[6] Intel Corporation. Volume 3B: System Programming Guide, Part 2. *Intel 64 and IA-32 Architectures Software Developer's Manual*, 2008.

[7] Jeffrey Dean, James E. Hicks, Carl A. Waldspurger, William E. Weihl, and George Chrysos. ProfileMe: Hardware Support for Instruction-Level Profiling on Out-of-Order Processors. *Proc. of ACM/IEEE International Symposium on Microarchitecture*, IEEE Computer Society, 1997.

[8] Paul J. Drongowski. Instruction-Based Sampling: A New Performance Analysis Technique for AMD Family 10h Processors. Advanced Micro Devices, Inc., November 2007.

[9] Nathan Froyd, John Mellor-Crummey, and Rob Fowler. Low-Overhead Call Path Profiling of Unmodified, Optimized Code. *Proc. of International Conference on Supercomputing*, Arvind and Larry Rudolph, eds., ACM, Cambridge, Massachusetts, June 2005.

[10] Nick Gloy, Zheng Wang, Catherine Zhang, J. Bradley Chen, and Michael D. Smith. Profile-Based Optimization with Statistical Profiles. Harvard University, Cambridge, Massachusetts, April 1997.

[11] Steve R. Gunn. Support Vector Machines for Classification and Regression. Ph.D. Thesis, University of Southampton, 1998.

[12] Roy Levin, Gad Haber, and Ilan Newman. Complementing Missing and Inaccurate Profiling using a Minimum Cost Circulation Algorithm. *Proc. of International Conference on High Performance Embedded Architectures and Compilers*, Göteborg, Sweden, January 2008.

[13] Chi-Keung Luk, Robert Cohn, Robert Muth, Harish Patil, Artur Klauser, Geoff Lowney, Steven Wallace, Vijay Janapa Reddi, and Kim Hazelwood. Pin: Building Customized Program Analysis Tools with Dynamic Instrumentation. *Proc. of SIGPLAN Conference on Programming Language Design and Implementation*, pages 190–200, Chicago, Illinois, June 2005.

[14] Matthew C. Merten, Andrew R. Trick, Christopher N. George, John C. Gyllenhaal, and Wen-mei W. Hwu.
A Hardware-Driven Profiling Scheme for Identifying Program Hot Spots to Support Runtime Optimization. *Proc. of International Symposium on Computer Architecture*, IEEE Computer Society, Atlanta, Georgia, 1999.

[15] R. L. Probert. Optimal Insertion of Software Probes in Well-Delimited Programs. *IEEE Transactions on Software Engineering.*, 8(1):34–42, 1982.

[16] Vinodha Ramasamy, Paul Yuan, Dehao Chen, and Robert Hundt. Feedback-Directed Optimization in GCC with Estimated Edge Profiles from Hardware Event Sampling. *Proc. of GCC Developers' Summit*, Ottawa, Canada, June 2008.

[17] Florian T. Schneider, Mathias Payer, and Thomas R. Gross. Online Optimizations Driven by Hardware Performance Monitoring. *Proc. of SIGPLAN Conference on Programming Language Design and Implementation*, 2007.

[18] Alex J. Smola and Bernhard Scholkopf. A Tutorial on Support Vector Regression. *Statistics and Computing*, 14(3):199–222, 2004.

[19] Omri Traub, Stuart Schechter, and Michael D. Smith. Ephemeral Instrumentation for Lightweight Program Profiling. Harvard University, Cambridge, Massachusetts, June 2000.

[20] Vincent M. Weaver and Sally A. McKee. Can Hardware Performance Counters Be Trusted? *Proc. of IEEE International Symposium on Workload Characterization*, IEEE Computer Society, Seattle, Washington, September 2008.

[21] Youfeng Wu and James R. Larus. Static Branch Frequency and Program Profile Analysis. *Proc. of ACM/IEEE International Symposium on Microarchitecture*, IEEE Computer Society, 1994.

[22] Xiaolan Zhang, Zheng Wang, Nicholas Gloy, J. Bradley Chen, and Michael D. Smith. System Support for Automatic Profiling and Optimization. *SIGOPS Operating Systems Review*, 31(5):15–26, 1997.

Lightweight Feedback-Directed Cross-Module Optimization

Xinliang David Li, Raksit Ashok, Robert Hundt

Google
1600 Amphitheatre Parkway
Mountain View, CA, 94043
{davidxl, raksit, rhundt}@google.com

Abstract

Cross-module inter-procedural compiler optimization (IPO) and Feedback-Directed Optimization (FDO) are two important compiler techniques delivering solid performance gains. The combination of IPO and FDO delivers peak performance, but also multiplies both techniques' usability problems. In this paper, we present LIPO, a novel static IPO framework, which integrates IPO and FDO. Compared to existing approaches, LIPO no longer requires writing of the compiler's intermediate representation, eliminates the link-time inter-procedural optimization phase entirely, and minimizes code re-generation overhead, thus improving scalability by an order of magnitude. Compared to an FDO baseline, and without further specific tuning, LIPO improves performance of SPEC2006 INT by 2.5%, and of SPEC2000 INT by 4.4%, with up to 23% for one benchmarks. We confirm our scalability results on a set of large industrial applications, demonstrating 2.9% performance improvements on average. Compile time overhead for full builds is less than 30%, incremental builds take a few seconds on average, and storage requirements increase by only 24%, all compared to the FDO baseline.

Categories and Subject Descriptors   D.3.4 [*Processors*]: Compilers;   D.3.4 [*Processors*]: Optimization

General Terms   Performance

Keywords   Inter-procedural, Feedback-directed, Cross-module, Optimization

1. Introduction

A static compiler's ability to optimize code is limited by the scope of code it can see. Typically, compilers translate one source file at a time, operating at function granularity. Most compilers, often at higher optimization levels, start to gradually enable intra-module inter-procedural optimizations. For languages supporting independent compilation of separate source files, such as C, C++, or Fortran, source boundaries become an optimization blocker.

For example, consider the artificial code in Figure 1 with two source files a.c and b.c. While compiling a.c, the compiler has no knowledge of the body of function bar() and will have to emit two standard calling sequences to bar(), passing two parameters

```
a.c:
   int foo(int i, int j) {
      return bar(i,j) + bar(j,i);
   }

b.c:
   int bar(int i, int j) {
      return i-j;
   }
```

Figure 1. Simple example to illustrate benefits of IPO

to each. If bar() had been inlined into foo(), across the module boundary, the body of foo() could have been reduced to a simple return 0 statement.

Over the years, a large array of inter-procedural (IP) optimizations has been developed. The typical techniques are inlining and cloning, indirect function call promotion, constant propagation, alias, mod/ref, and points-to analysis, register allocation, register pressure estimation, global variable optimizations, code and data layout techniques, profile propagation techniques, C++ class hierarchy analysis and de-virtualization, dead variable and function elimination, and many more.

To study the effectiveness of some of these transformations, we used the open64 [19] compiler, release 4.1 (SVN revision r1442), and compiled SPEC2000 INT in a set of experiments. All experiments were run on an Intel Pentium 4, 3.4 GHz, with 4GB of memory. In each experiment, we disabled one inter-procedural optimization pass and measured the expected performance degradations. Since there are interactions between the various passes' performance contributions, this study can only give an approximation.

Our baseline is compiled at -O2 with IPO and feedback directed optimization (FDO). We evaluated the eight inter-procedural passes inlining, indirect call promotion, alias analysis, copy propagation, as well as function reordering, class hierarchy analysis, dead code analysis, and dead function elimination. Early inlining (at the single module level) remained enabled for all experiments. Only the first four inter-procedural optimizations showed measurable performance impact on these benchmarks, summarized in Figure 2. Correspondingly, we omit the results for the other four optimizations.

We find that two of the more important IPO passes are inlining, as turning it off results in a 17% performance degradation overall, with 252.eon degrading by 70%, as well as indirect function call promotion (3% degradation overall when turned off). Correspondingly, we focused on these two in our initial implementation of LIPO. All performance numbers presented later result from improved performance enabled by these two passes.

Inlining improves performance by eliminating procedure call overhead, adding context sensitivity, and creating larger optimiza-

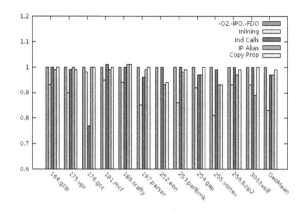

Figure 2. Effects of turning off individual IPO optimizations and analysis passes. Shown are relative regressions against normalized performance, 1.0 means no loss.

Experiment	SPEC score	Improvement
-O2	12.69	
-O2 -FDO	12.60	-1%
-O2 -IPO	13.46	6%
-O2 -FDO -IPO	14.27	12%

Table 1. $p(FDO + IPO) > p(FDO) + p(IPO)$

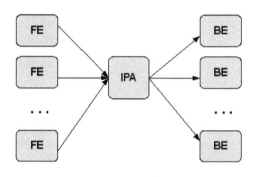

Figure 3. Traditional IPO model

tion and scheduling regions. Added context sensitivity can improve alias and points-to information and enables more constant propagation, redundancy elimination, dead code and unreachable code elimination. It can also serve as an enabler for other major phases, such as the loop optimizer.

Indirect call promotion is an enabler for inlining. It replaces an indirect, hot call having a limited set of target addresses, with a cascade of tests guarding direct calls to those targets, plus a fall through branch containing the original indirect branch. The introduction of these direct calls enables further inlining (see also [1]).

1.1 Feedback Directed Optimization (FDO)

In this section we briefly describe feedback directed optimization (FDO) and study its impact on IPO. FDO imposes a dual build model. In a first *instrumentation build* the compiler inserts code into the binary, typically to count edges or to collect value profiles. The instrumented binary is run on a representative set of training input in a *training phase*. At the end of this execution, all collected edge counts and value information are written and aggregated in a profile database. In a second *optimization build*, the compiler uses the generated profile to make better optimization decisions. Many compiler phases can benefit from more exact information then estimated heuristics, e.g., the inliner and indirect call promotion, where knowing the exact distribution of targets is essential, the loop optimizer, where distinguishing loops with low or high trip count can be beneficial, and many other optimizations, at both high and low level.

IP optimizations strongly benefit from FDO. To illustrate the effects, we used the same open64 compiler to benchmark SPEC2000 INT and compared the baseline to builds using IPO and FDO turned on, individually and combined. In these experiments, plain FDO actually decreased performance slightly, indicating that our open64 version was not tuned well towards this set of benchmarks. We believe this only strengthens our argument, as less of the typical SPEC specific optimizations were perturbing the results. Our claim that IPO needs FDO is supported by the winning 12% performance (p) increase in Table 1, which almost doubles the effects of plain IPO alone.

1.2 Existing IPO Frameworks

In Section 2 we discuss some of the existing inter-procedural compilation frameworks in more detail, in particular HLO [2, 3], the old high-level optimizer from HP, its successor SYZYGY [16],

the open source frameworks open64, gcc's *-combine* feature, gcc's LTO framework, and LLVM. We find that all existing infrastructures represent a variation of a standard IPO model, as presented in [16]. This model distinguishes three major phases, a front-end phase, an IPO phase, and a back-end phase.

In the parallelizable front-end phase, the compiler performs a reasonable amount of optimizations for code cleanup and canonicalization. It may also compute summary information for consumption by IPO. This phase writes the compiler intermediate representation (IR) to disk as fake ELF object files, which allows seamless integration into existing build systems.

The IPO phase is typically executed at link time. IPO reads in the fake object files, or parts of them, e.g., sections containing summary data. It may perform type unification and build an inter-procedural symbol table, perform analysis, either on summaries, IR, or combined IR, make transformation decisions or perform actual transformations, and readies output for consumption by the back-end phase.

The parallelizable back-end phase accepts the compiler IR from IPO, either directly out of memory or via intermediate fake object files, and performs a stronger set of scalar, loop, and other optimizations, as well as code generation and object file production. These final object files are then fed back to the linker to produce the final binary.

All these tasks are points of distinction between the various frameworks. What all these frameworks have in common is that they write the compiler IR to disk, putting pressure on disk and network bandwidth. Because the compiler IR usually contains more information than a simple object file, e.g., full type information, IR files are typically larger than regular object files by factors ranging on average from 4x to 10x, with potential for pathological cases.

At IPO start, the IR files have to be read/mapped in, which can consume a significant amount of time, e.g., in the range of minutes, and even hours for large applications. While the front-end and back-end phase can be parallelized, IPO typically cannot, or only to a limited extent, representing a bottleneck with runtimes ranging again from minutes to hours.

Since the effects and dependencies of source changes aren't modeled, even insignificant code changes lead to full invocations of IPO and the complete back-end phase, which can also take very long for large applications. Overall, this design allows effective cross-module inter-procedural optimizations at the cost of very long overall compile/link cycles. We provide detailed examples for compile and link times for existing infrastructures in Section 2

Debugging of the IPA infrastructure is cumbersome, because of the many intermediate steps and the many files involved, as well as the high runtime of IPO itself. Maintaining debug information can be complicated for some compilers, depending on how they maintain or generate debug information (e.g., via callbacks into the compiler front-end). Combining FDO and IPO multiplies the usability problems, as now two IPO builds have to be performed, at least for compilers that expect identical control flow graphs during the FDO instrumentation and profile annotation phase.

1.3 Contribution

In this paper, we make the following contributions:

- We present our novel IPO framework, which seamlessly integrates IPO with FDO.

- We evaluate the infrastructures properties of our approach using the SPEC benchmark suite. We show that our approach performs an order of magnitude better than existing approaches in terms of compile time and storage requirements. Furthermore, our approach is amenable to distributed build systems.

- We demonstrate the immediate performance benefits from improved inlining and indirect call promotion, the only two optimizations we focused on in this paper.

- We confirm our results on a set of very large industrial applications, and provide further analysis results.

The rest of this paper is organized as follows. We first ask the reader for patience as we detail key design decisions of several existing IPO frameworks. These descriptions allow drawing a sharp contrast to our work, which we describe in Section 3. Readers familiar with existing frameworks can safely skip Section 2 and proceed directly to Section 3. We provide a thorough experimental evaluation in Section 4, before we conclude.

In this paper we always include cross-module optimizations when referring to IPO, unless noted otherwise. We use the term inter-procedural analysis (IPA) in cases where we refer to inter-procedural analysis only. While we used open64 for illustration above, all subsequent results reference our implementation based on gcc 4.4. All performance effects come from improved inlining and indirect call promotion only.

2. Related Work

Early work in inter-procedural optimization was done by Hall [13]. This work focused mainly on core IPO algorithms, such as call graph construction and inlining. Early studies of inlining have been done in [6, 9, 10] , and more recently in [5]. It became clear early on that even minor code changes would make a full IPO and back-end phase necessary. [8] tried to solve this problem by maintaining proper or approximated dependencies. While this certainly is a path to reducing the compile time of IPO, to our knowledge no commercially successful system has been deployed using such techniques. There have also been approaches to do IPO at link time on regular object files or fully built executables. A good example of such an approach is [18]. To a certain extent, dynamic optimizers could be considered inter-procedural optimizers, as they see the whole program at execution time. However, this field is far removed from the topic of this paper and we won't discuss it further here.

The earliest reference to feedback directed optimization was made by no other than Knuth [14], Ball and Larus had a seminal paper on optimal profile code insertion [4]. FDO is available in most modern compilers, with the notable exception of LLVM. A detailed description and evaluation of techniques to eliminate C++ virtual calls can be found in [1], class hierarchy analysis has been studied in [11].

We believe the most relevant and directly comparable pieces of work are the fully developed and deployed commercial and open source frameworks. In the next few sections, we detail key design choices made by HLO, an older inter-procedural optimizer from HP, its successor SYZYGY, the open source frameworks open64, gcc's *-combine* feature, gcc's LTO framework, and LLVM. We won't discuss other commercial compilers, e.g., from Intel, or Microsoft, but are confident that many of them implement a variation of the described general IPO model.

The HP High-Level Optimizer (HLO) [2, 3] maps in all input files at link time, and offers a compiler controlled swapping mechanism in order to scale to large applications, hoping that domain knowledge would beat the standard virtual memory management system. Code generation is an integral part of HLO, not parallelized, and a bottleneck in terms of compile time. On average, to compile SPEC2000 INT, HLO imposed a 2.5x overhead in compile time on full rebuilds, with up to 6x for larger benchmarks. For incremental builds, the compile time overhead factor is orders of magnitudes higher, as full IPO and backend phase have to be executed. HLO did not scale to the larger SPEC2006 INT benchmarks.

SYZYGY [16] is the successor of HLO and significantly improves compile time and scalability. It has a two-part IPO model. The first half operates on summaries only and makes most optimization decisions. During this time, no more than two IR files are opened at any given time. The second half of IPO consists of the inliner, which operates on summaries first to compute inlining decisions, before using actual compiler IR to make the transformations. In order to scale to very large applications, even with a constricted memory space, it maintains a pool of no more than a few dozen open IR files and algorithms were developed to minimize the file open and closing times [5]. At the end of IPO, final transformation decisions are written back to temporary IR files, and the back-end phase is parallelized over these files.

On average, to compile SPEC2000 INT, SYZYGY imposes a 2.3x overhead for full rebuilds at (backend) parallelism level 1, but only a 1.2x overhead at parallelism level 4. Again, for incremental builds, the compile time overhead factor is orders of magnitudes higher. The IR file to object file ratio was about 5x. Compiling a large shared library of a commercial database application, consisting of several thousand C input files, took around 4 hours for full builds, and 2 hours for incremental builds. The file overhead led to exceeding of the file size limit on the system, and build system changes were necessary to break this large library apart.

Open64's IPO maps in all IR files at link time. Its IPA phase runs comparatively fast, seeking to operate on summary data only. It writes back intermediate object files, and the back-end phase is parallelized over these files, similar to SYZYGY. One interesting design decision has been made for the inter-procedural symbol and type tables. Open64 produces a single intermediate object file containing all statically promoted and global variables, as well as the IP symbol and type table. In the parallelized backend phase, this file is compiled first, before all other intermediate files are compiled in parallel. All of these compilations pass a temporary IR file plus the symbol table file to the compiler. For large applications, the symbol table file can become many hundred MB in size, and as a result this design can significantly slow down compile time.

We used open64 (SVN revision 1442) to compile the C++ "Search" application presented in table 6 on a 4-core AMD Opteron machine, running at 2.2GHz, with 32GB of memory. Reading in and mapping of all input files required 6.5GB and took 59 minutes. Building other inter-procedural data structures required another 6.4GB of memory. The symbol table intermediate file ended up at 384 MB and took 53 minutes to compile. The resulting assembly file had 23 mio lines. The rest of the backend and code generation took many hours to complete, compiling an average of 5 files per minute per core (running 5 processes in parallel).

The recently started gcc LTO effort writes *fat* object files to disk in the front-end phase, containing both compiler IR and regular object file sections. This allows LTO to use the same object files for regular builds or IPO builds. LTO has a very narrow IPO phase, which works on summaries only and makes mostly grouping decisions, before parallelizing the back-end over these groups. The back-end is an extended gcc compiler, which accepts multiple IR files as a combined input and performs existing inter-procedural transformations. This is somewhat similar to the *-combine* support described below. At time of this writing, no scalability results were available.

LLVM [15] also has a traditional link time optimizer. It keeps the full compiler IR in core, alongside analysis data structures, such as use-def chains. Because of this design, the LLVM IR has been specifically optimized for memory footprint. In practice, LLVM is capable of optimizing mid-size programs (500K - 1M LOC) on desktop workstations. For example, compiling 176.gcc requires roughly 40MB of memory to hold in core. LLVM also performs code generation sequentially in core and produces one large assembly file. While efforts are underway to parallelize LLVM, in particular code generation, its current architecture is not capable of distributing to more than one machine [7].

The gcc C front-end supports the `-combine` option, allowing to combine sources into one compilation process in an all-in-memory model. This model differs from the general IPA approach, as users must manually partition the source files into sets, a labor intensive process which is unrobust against program evolution and obtrusive to the build system. The implementation is unloved by the gcc community because of its lack of robustness, falsely reported errors, and restriction to C.

3. Lightweight IPO

In this section we detail the design of our novel lightweight inter-procedural optimizer LIPO. The key design decisions can be summarized the following way:

- We seamlessly integrate IPO and FDO.

- We move the IPA analysis phase into the binary and execute it at the end of the FDO training run.

- We add aggregated IPA analysis results to the FDO profiles.

- During the FDO optimization build, we use these results to read in additional source modules and form larger pseudo modules to extend scope and to enable more intra-module inter-procedural optimizations.

We now discuss this design in detail with focus on the two key IP optimizations inlining and indirect call promotion.

Since IPO needs FDO to maximize its performance potential, integrating these two techniques becomes a logical design choice. Existing FDO users can get IPO almost for free by adding an option.

LIPO no longer needs an explicit inter-procedural optimizer to be executed at link time. Instead, the IPA analysis phase now runs at the end of the FDO training run, with negligible performance overhead. At this point, the analysis phase can see the complete results of the binaries' execution, in particular, all profile counters,

debug and source information, as well as summary information, which may have been stored in the binary.

From this information, LIPO constructs a full dynamic call graph and performs a greedy clustering algorithm to determine beneficial groupings for inlining and indirect call promotion. The clustering information, and further analysis results, are stored alongside regular FDO counters in augmented FDO profiles. To use the initial example in Figure 1, since `foo()` contains hot calls to `bar()`, the files `a.c` and `b.c` would end up in the same cluster to enable cross module inlining later.

During the FDO optimization build, the compiler continues to compile one file at a time and reads in the augmented profiles. If a cluster has been formed in the step above, auxiliary source modules were specified in the profiles and are now read in and added to the compilation scope of the first, main module. This step sounds simpler than it actually is. This process can be conceptually thought of as combining multiple source files into one big one. Just as when doing this manually, problems with multiple definitions, identically named static variables, and type mismatches must be resolved by the compiler. To avoid redundant computation later, the compiler needs to keep track of what was specified in the main module.

Now the compiler has a greatly extended scope and intra-module inter-procedural optimizations can be performed. In our initial implementation we focused on the existing optimization passes inlining and indirect call promotion. Both passes had to be augmented to be able to handle functions from out of (original) scope.

After all transformations have been performed, unnecessary auxiliary functions are deleted to avoid redundant time spent in further optimization and code generation passes. Referencing the example in Figure 1 again, while compiling `a.c`, the compiler will read the auxiliary module `b.c`. After `bar()` has been inlined into `foo()`, the compiler can safely delete `bar()` from its current scope and not pass it on to later compilation phases. If it is referenced somewhere else, the body of `bar()` will still become available when module `b.c` is being compiled and linked in later.

The implementation of LIPO consists of three major blocks. Support for LIPO in the language frontend, where parsing of multiple modules must be supported, a runtime component, and compiler extensions to support optimizations. We will discuss details of these in the next sections.

3.1 Language Front-End Support

The main task for the language front-end is to support parsing of multiple source modules. This requires more than concatenating all source modules together, e.g., via include directives, and parsing the combined file. For languages like C++ the name lookup rules are very complicated and simply combining all sources and treating them as one extended translation unit won't work. For simpler languages such as C, gcc offers support with its `-combine` option, yet, even though this option has been implemented years ago, it is fragile, unrobust, and generally unused.

Our solution is to parse each module in isolation, i.e., we added support in the front-end to allow independent parsing of source modules. For gcc, this required clearing of the name bindings for global entities after parsing of each module. We shifted type unification and symbol resolution to the backend, which greatly simplified the required implementation overhead in the front-ends. Compilers with separated front- and back-end, e.g., open64, will pass compiler IR around and LIPO can be added easily as a simple extension.

3.2 LIPO Runtime

At the end of the program execution in the FDO training phase, before profiles are written, the IPA analysis takes place. For inlining we build the dynamic call graph. For indirect calls, we use the existing FDO value profiling to obtain the branch targets. For direct calls we don't rely on the existing edge profiles, but add new instrumentation for direct call profiling. The resulting counters are for consumption by LIPO only. This design sacrifices training phase execution speed in favor of smaller profile sizes, a decision we may revisit in the future.

Source module affinity analysis is now performed on this dynamic call graph. To obtain best module groupings, e.g., for inlining, it would be appropriate to model the inlining heuristics in the clustering algorithm. We, instead, use the simple greedy algorithm outlined in Figure 4. The computed module groups are written into the augmented profiles.

There is an interesting observation in regards to summaries. In traditional IPA, summary information is typically written to the IR object files in some encoding, and the link-time IPO has to read, decode and store this information in its internal data structures. Since LIPO runs at program runtime, summary information can be stored as program data and be used directly by LIPO, without the need for further decoding.

3.3 Optimization Extensions

There are several LIPO specific tasks in the compiler middle-end and back-end to enable cross module optimizations, to ensure correct code generation, and to reach a successful final program link.

3.3.1 In-core Linking

An in-core linking phase merges global functions, variables, and types across modules. Undefined symbols are resolved to their definition, if one exists in a module group. If function references can be resolved before the call graph is built, the implementation may chose to directly resolve calls in the intermediate representation.

As for the traditional link time IPO, type merging is also needed for LIPO. In this process, types from different modules are merged into a global type equivalence table, which is used by the compiler middle-end and back-end for tasks like type based aliasing queries, or useless type cast removal.

3.3.2 Handling Functions with Special Linkage

Functions defined in auxiliary modules have special linkage. Most of the functions are treated as inline functions, they are not not needed for code expansion and can be deleted after the final inline phase. COMDAT functions need to be expanded if they are still reachable after inlining. There may be multiple copies of a COMDAT function in a LIPO compilation. The compiler will pick one instance and discard the rest, similar to what the linker would have done in a regular link. Compiler-created functions, e.g., function clones after constant propagation, can never be 'external'. They can be deleted only if there is no remaining reference after inlining.

3.3.3 Static Promotion and Global Externalization

A *static* entity has internal linkage and a name that is either file- or function-scoped. Static variables and static functions need special handling in both main and auxiliary modules. Global variables need special handling in auxiliary modules as well. We distinguish these cases:

- For any module that is imported as an auxiliary module, static variables and functions defined in it need to be promoted to globals, both when the module is compiled as the main module and as an auxiliary module. The problem is that a unique, non-conflicting linker id for the static entities must be created that both caller and callee module can agree upon. Our solution is to postfix the original, mangled names with the keyword

"lipo/cmo" and the main module's linker id. It is possible for multiple static variables in different scopes to share the same name. We therefore add sequence numbers to the names, following the variables' declaration order.

- When a module is never imported, no promotion needs to happen when that module is compiled as the primary module.

- Static functions in auxiliary modules are externalized, same as variables, but their function bodies are kept for the purpose of inlining. The naming convention is similar to the one for static variables described above.

- Global variables in auxiliary modules should be treated as, and converted to, extern.

3.4 Build System Integration

In this section we discuss integrating LIPO into build systems. We distinguish the three cases of a local fresh build, a local, but incremental build, and a distributed build.

For fresh builds on a local system, LIPO works without problems and, e.g., Makefile-based systems do not have to change. All sources are available, LIPO will find all auxiliary modules, and the dependence checking at the main module level (as opposed to including the auxiliary modules) is sufficient.

For incremental builds, the situation is slightly different. If a main module is part of a group and auxiliary modules are brought in during compilation, a modification of an auxiliary module makes a recompilation of the main module necessary. In order to maintain these dependencies, we developed a small tool that reads module profile information and dumps the full list of auxiliary dependencies. A common paradigm in Makefile based systems is to generate source dependencies. This tool can be added to this process. Dependencies should be refreshed whenever the FDO profiles are being regenerated, as modified profiles can lead to modified grouping decisions.

Integrating LIPO into a distributed build system, e.g., distcc [12], poses a similar problem. For such systems, the main module and all auxiliary files, headers, and profiles, need to be distributed across build machines. We can use the same tool introduced before and only minor modifications to these build systems are necessary to allow distributed LIPO builds.

4. Experimental Evaluation

In this section we analyze various aspects of our infrastructure, such as module grouping properties, IPA analysis overhead, compile time and file size overheads, as well as runtime performance. Most experiments were run on SPEC 2006 INT, using a cutoff ratio of 95% in our greedy clustering algorithm. We also present performance numbers for SPEC2000 INT, as well as interesting analysis results for a set of large industrial applications. For all these sets of benchmarks, we only compiled the C/C++ benchmarks, and only formed non-mixed language module groups. All experiments were run on an 8-core Intel Core-2 Duo, running at 2.33 GHz, with 32 GB of memory.

4.1 Module Groups

We analyze how the cutoff threshold in the greedy algorithm influences the module grouping. We compile all of SPEC2006 INT with cutoff thresholds of 80%, 90%, and 95%. The results are summarized in Table 2. For each experiment, we compute the total number of auxiliary modules used (column *Aux*), the number of trivial module groups, which are groups with only 1 module (column *Trv*), the maximum size of a module group for a benchmark (column *Mx*), and the average size of module groups (column *Avg*). To put these

1. Compute the sum total of all dynamic call edge counts.
2. Create an array of sorted edges in descending order of their call counts.
3. Find the cutoff call count:
   (a) Iterate through the sorted edge array and add up the call counts.
   (b) If the current total count reaches 95% of the count computed at step 1, stop. The cutoff edge count is the count of the current edge. A edge is considered *hot* if its count is greater than the cutoff count.
4. Start module grouping: For each call graph node, find all nodes that are reachable from it in a reduced call graph, which contains only hot edges. Add the defining modules of the reachable nodes to the module group of the node being processed.

Figure 4. Greedy clustering algorithm for module group formation.

numbers into context, we also provide the total number of modules for each benchmark (column *Mods*).

The experiments show that the average size of module groups is small, averaging (geometric mean) 1.3 for a cutoff of 80%, 1.5 for 90%, and 1.6 for 95%. The notable exception is the benchmark 403.gcc, which has oversized module groups because of remarkably flat profiles. Clearly, the graph partitioning algorithm has to improve in order to handle such cases properly. Another interesting benchmark is 473.astar, which only forms trivial program groups. Discounting 403.gcc, the largest module group consists of 11 files (in 483.xalancbmk at 95%).

4.2   IPA Analysis Overhead

LIPO's runtime overhead on the training phase consists of two components, the overhead from additional instrumentation to count direct calls, and the overhead from running the IPA analysis at the end of execution. The instrumentation runtime overhead is shown in Table 3, it amounts to 32.5% on average, with one case increasing by 2.6x. This overhead is a result of our design decision to not rely on basic block counts for direct call profiling, but to add more instrumentation instead.

We determine the IPA analysis overhead by measuring the difference in execution time of the instrumented binary, with and without the IPA analysis. This overhead is generally minimal. We show the runtimes without IPA in the *No IPA* column and overheads (comparing *LIPO* against *NoIPA*) larger than 1% in the following *Ov.* column.

4.3   Compile Time Overhead

We measured the overhead for full and incremental builds for SPEC2006 INT. For full rebuilds, we compare in Table 4 a regular build at -O2, a regular full FDO optimization build, and a full LIPO build. Since with FDO and LIPO there is generally more aggressive inlining, we would expect the FDO times to be higher than the -O2 times. The average group size at 95% cutoff was 1.6, which would lead us to expect a 60% compile overhead over FDO. However, we see a lower overhead of only 28%, as we are removing unnecessary code before it enters further optimization and code generation passes. Assuming unlimited parallelism in a distributed build infrastructure, a lower bound for full build times on such systems is the longest time it takes to compile any given module group. Since module groups are generally small, distributed build times can be a fraction of undistributed build times.

To measure the overhead for incremental builds, we run N experiments for each benchmarks, where N is the number of C/C++ files in this benchmark. In each experiment, we touch one source module, find all other groups containing this source file, and additionally touch each of these groups' main module, modeling the

full dependencies in a build system. We then compute maximum and average rebuild overhead at parallelism levels 1 and 2 (indicated by letter 'j'). The results are also in Table 4.

The incremental build times are on average surprisingly low, less than 2 seconds on average, less than 20 seconds on average for the worst cases for sequential rebuilds, and less than 12 seconds on average for the worst cases at parallelism level 2. This number continues to decline at higher levels of build parallelism. The expected outlier is again 403.gcc, where too many large module groups were formed.

The columns *imax* and *iavg* further analyze the inclusion patterns and show to what extent modules are part of other module groups. We show maximum and average numbers, which help explain the incremental compile time overhead. For example, for 403.gcc, modifying a particular (unfortunate) file may cause 33 other files to be recompiled, roughly 22% of this benchmark's overall modules. We want to emphasize that even this pathological case is still significantly better than previous approaches, as outlined in Section 2, where all modules have to be rebuilt after IPO, even after insignificant code changes.

4.4   File Size Overhead

We analyze the changes in object file sizes and profile sizes for LIPO compared to a standard FDO build. In Table 5 we list these values for the SPEC2006 INT benchmarks. Column *objects* lists the sizes of the object files produced by the FDO-optimize build. The gcc compiler stores profile information in *gcda* files, and correspondingly, the column *profiles* lists the profile sizes. The following column shows the relation of these two in percent. The same data is shown for the LIPO object files, LIPO profiles, and the corresponding percentages.

Profiles add up to about 18% of the object file sizes for FDO. The file sizes for the LIPO objects increase by about 8% due to more aggressive inlining. The relative profile sizes for LIPO amount to 36% of the LIPO object files, as IPA information has been added to them. The LIPO profiles are about 2.1x larger than the FDO profiles. In total, LIPO imposes a total increase in file sizes of only 25% over the FDO baseline.

4.5   Performance

We analyze how the grouping cutoff threshold affects performance. In this paper we didn't add any novel optimizations, all gains come from more aggressive inlining and additional indirect call promotion.

For the cutoff values of 80%, 90%, and 95%, on the C/C++ SPEC2006 INT programs, we show the improvements of LIPO over the FDO baseline in Figure 5. For this particular comparison,

Clustering Cutoff:		80%				90%				95%			
Benchmark	Mods	Aux	Trv	Mx	Avg	Aux	Trv	Mx	Avg	Aux	Trv	Mx	Avg
400.perlbench	50	18	41	5	1.4	28	38	5	1.6	38	34	6	1.7
401.bzip2	7	3	4	2	1.4	4	4	3	1.6	4	4	3	1.4
403.gcc	143	216	82	13	2.5	365	65	18	3.6	524	54	26	4.4
429.mcf	11	1	10	2	1.1	3	9	3	1.3	3	9	3	1.3
445.gobmk	62	11	54	4	1.2	16	50	4	1.3	21	47	5	1.3
456.hmmer	56	1	55	2	1.0	1	55	2	1.0	1	55	2	1.0
458.sjeng	19	12	14	9	1.6	12	14	9	1.6	12	14	9	1.6
462.libquantum	16	1	15	2	1.1	1	15	2	1.1	1	15	2	1.1
464.h264ref	42	1	41	2	1.0	3	39	2	1.1	5	37	2	1.1
471.omnetpp	83	48	66	7	1.6	63	62	8	1.8	73	60	10	1.9
473.astar	11	0	11	1	1.0	0	11	1	1.0	0	11	1	1.0
483.xalancbmk	693	97	660	9	1.1	133	657	11	1.2	147	654	11	1.2
Geo Mean					1.3				1.5				1.6

Table 2. Module grouping information for SPEC2006 at 80%, 90%, and 95%

Benchmark	FDO	LIPO	Ov.	NoIPA	Ov.
400.perlbench	41.5	66.5	60.3%	64.3	3.4%
401.bzip2	70.3	75.1	6.8%	74.8	< 1%
403.gcc	2.0	2.6	29.2%	2.6	< 1%
429.mcf	41.5	40.4	-2.7%	40.5	< 1%
445.gobmk	173.9	208.0	19.6%	207.2	< 1%
456.hmmer	106.5	106.9	0.4%	107.5	< 1%
458.sjeng	236.3	290.3	22.9%	290.9	< 1%
462.libquantum	2.8	2.9	5.4%	2.9	< 1%
464.h264ref	148.5	241.1	62.3%	241.0	< 1%
471.omnetpp	110.8	209.6	91.3%	208.3	< 1%
473.astar	150.1	161.9	7.9%	160.7	< 1%
483.xalancbmk	175.8	456.8	159.8%	447.4	2.1%
GeoMean			32.5%		

Table 3. Training phase runtimes, in [*sec*], and overhead from additional instrumentation, and IPA.

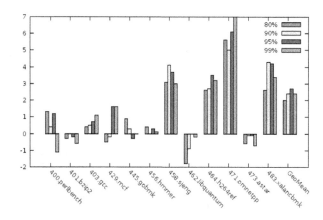

Figure 5. Performance improvements in [%] over FDO, for SPEC2006 INT, at cutoff thresholds of 80% (2.0%), 90% (2.4%), 95% (2.7%), and 99% (2.4%)

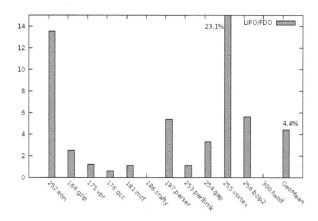

Figure 6. Performance improvements in [%] over FDO, for SPEC2000 INT

we also add the performance numbers generated with a cutoff of 99%. All experiments were compiled with -O2.

We see several degradations at a cutoff threshold of 99% over 95%. Clearly, the compiler can benefit from better tuning for larger compilation scopes. For now, we picked a default threshold of 95% in our implementation. As other IP optimization heuristics improve, this value will be subject of further tuning. The threshold of 95% also results in good performance results on SPEC2000 INT, shown in Figure 6, which yields an overall performance improvement of about 4.4%..

4.6 Large Applications

We verified – and confirmed – the presented results on a set of larger, industrial C++ applications running in Google's datacenters. In Table 6 we present the performance numbers for seven large and two smaller benchmarks. Average performance on these benchmarks improves by 2.9% (over the FDO baseline). In this table we also show the module grouping information, similar to Table 2.

The average module groups sizes are, again, surprisingly small at 1.24. To find out why we show the total number of dynamic call graph edges, their sum total edge counts, and the number and percentage of hot call edges, as filtered out by our greedy algorithm (Table 4). We find that on average only about 5% of all edges are *hot* (3.6% if we discard the smaller Video Converter benchmark).

	Full Builds, j1				Incremental Builds					
Benchmark	-O2	FDO	LIPO	Overhead	j1 max	j1 avg	j2 max	j2 avg	imax	iavg
400.perlbench	42.3	43.9	56.7	29.0%	29.3	3.1	16.3	2.1	12	1.7
401.bzip2	3.0	4.6	5.9	41.7%	2.5	1.1	1.9	1.0	3	1.4
403.gcc	108.0	129.0	255.0	97.7%	126.1	7.7	68.1	4.8	33	4.4
429.mcf	1.0	1.6	2.6	60.0%	1.6	0.4	1.1	0.3	2	1.3
445.gobmk	30.4	35.4	41.0	15.7%	16.6	1.4	8.7	1.1	9	1.3
456.hmmer	12.0	11.3	11.5	1.3%	1.1	0.3	1.1	0.3	2	1.0
458.sjeng	4.4	5.1	6.6	30.0%	3.1	1,0	2.2	0.8	4	1.6
462.libquantum	1.8	1.8	1.8	0.0%	0.6	0.1	0.5	0.2	2	1.1
464.h264ref	20.6	26.7	27.7	3.7%	7.2	1.1	5.4	1.0	3	1.1
471.omnetpp	39.5	38.8	63.6	64.0%	18.2	3.1	10.6	2.0	7	1.9
473.astar	2.0	2.6	2.6	-0.4%	0.5	0.3	0.5	0.3	1	1.0
483.xalancbmk	278.7	257.0	333.5	29.8%	63.3	2.5	35.3	2.0	16	1.2
Geo Mean				28.0%	18.8	1.9	11.5	1.3		1.6

Table 4. Full and incremental rebuild times for SPEC 2006 INT, in $[sec]$, at parallelism level 1, 2

	FDO			LIPO		
Benchmark	objects	profiles	%	objects	profiles	%
400.perlbench	2406827	491960	20.4%	2660211	876172	33.0%
401.bzip2	113082	18028	15.9%	141074	33852	24.0%
403.gcc	8145095	1450064	17.8%	10081375	3036424	30.1%
429.mcf	49456	4436	8.0%	63176	17048	27.0%
445.gobmk	5631666	353504	6.3%	5845274	632056	10.8%
456.hmmer	560264	101948	18.2%	561944	225048	40.1%
458.sjeng	341184	39020	11.4%	372416	83156	22.3%
462.libquantum	86424	13800	16.0%	86408	40272	46.6%
464.h264ref	1098496	136244	12.4%	1094216	261684	23.9%
471.omnetpp	2160915	423876	19.6%	2585539	1053220	40.7%
473.astar	98920	17436	17.6%	98272	51892	52.8%
483.xalancbmk	17856968	3975728	22.3%	18399040	8669508	47.1%
Total	38549297	7026044	18%	41988945	14980332	36%
Overhead	45575341			56969277		25%

Table 5. Object and profile file sizes in [byte], and overhead, for SPEC2006 INT, for FDO and LIPO

We attribute the small average group size to the fact that this C++ source base has been tuned for years, and, in absence of an inter-procedural optimizer, all performance critical code has been moved into C++ header files.

5. Discussion

In this paper we made a case for combining inter-procedural optimization with FDO and describe and contrast existing IPO frameworks with our new LIPO approach. Compared to existing approaches, we no longer require writing of the compiler IR to disk, no longer need a link time optimizer, and minimize code regeneration overhead. This design leads to improvements of an order of magnitude for compile time and resource requirement and makes IPO amenable to distributed build systems.

Training phase runtime overhead is 32% on average. We made an explicit design decision to trade in this runtime penalty against small profile file sizes, assuming that training runs are generally short. This is a decision we may want to revisit in the future, or offer under an option.

The file size overhead is at 25%. This is an order of magnitude smaller than the 4x to 10x overheads of existing infrastructures. The compile time overhead for full builds is less than 30%, compared

to factors of 2x and higher for existing infrastructures, and builds can be distributed, which is not easily possible in existing systems. Incremental builds are done in seconds on average, compared to minutes and hours in existing approaches, which always have to run a full IPO and a full code generation phase, even after small code changes. This fast behavior is enabled by small average module groups containing only 1.3 - 1.6 files, and deletion of redundant compiler IR.

LIPO's current main disadvantages are the following.

- We currently don't support full program analysis. While of course all program modules can be grouped into a single compilation, e.g., similar to LLVM's approach, such an approach won't scale to very large applications.

- LIPO does require FDO.

- Mixed language support is hard, in particular for compilers that maintain language-specific front-ends. In this paper, we only generated non-mixed language module groups.

The results presented in this paper are based on gcc 4.4. An updated implementation for gcc 4.5 is available on the public gcc branch *lw-ipo*. We believe that the concepts in LIPO are general and can be implemented in other compilers.

Benchmark	Perf	Mods	Aux	Triv	Mx	Avg	CG Edg	Sum Total	Hot	%
BigTable	-0.73%	1803	1519	1613	63	1.84	52576	2077481070	4223	8.0%
Ad Delivery	+4.56%	2441	329	2365	18	1.13	28014	8660809169	934	3.3%
Indexer	+0.54%	3631	514	3471	18	1.14	56937	1325046290	1594	2.8%
Search	+1.48%	2410	369	2323	20	1.15	28748	3067176774	1003	3.5%
OCR	+3.61%	1029	322	952	20	1.31	7226	290777838	476	6.6%
Search Quality	+3.19%	1232	36	1218	10	1.02	15540	3272632527	95	0.6%
Sawzall	+0.62%	2285	103	2254	15	1.04	30072	435312950	227	0.7%
Video Converter	+6.52%	86	39	78	13	1.45	1797	358857930	306	17.0%
Compression	+6.99%	224	15	218	7	1.06	2271	126211312	81	3.6%
Geo Mean	+2.94%					1.24				5.0%

Table 6. Industrial applications performance, module grouping information, and statistics on dynamic call graph edges, sum total of all edge weights, and number/percentage of hot edges.

6. Future Work

Besides fine tuning of the clustering algorithm and relevant heuristics, we will gradually add existing IP optimizations to LIPO, many of which have been mentioned in the introduction. We plan to work on some of LIPO's disadvantages, in particular, we are evaluating summary based approaches to allow classic IPO optimizations that need whole program analysis. We're also interested in using sample based profiling instead of instrumented FDO, as this would eliminate the FDO instrumentation and training phase [17]. The fact that the IPA analysis phase runs at execution time allows for the development of interesting new techniques, which we are evaluating. This should become a rich area of research.

7. Acknowledgements

We wanted to thank Urs Hoelzle for his early comments on this paper, as well as the anonymous reviewers for their invaluable feedback.

References

[1] Gerald Aigner and Urs Hölzle. Eliminating virtual function calls in C++ programs. In *ECCOP '96: Proceedings of the 10th European Conference on Object-Oriented Programming*, pages 142–166, London, UK, 1996. Springer-Verlag. ISBN 3-540-61439-7.

[2] Andrew Ayers, Richard Schooler, and Robert Gottlieb. Aggressive inlining. *SIGPLAN Not.*, 32(5):134–145, 1997. ISSN 0362-1340. doi: http://doi.acm.org/10.1145/258916.258928.

[3] Andrew Ayers, Stuart de Jong, John Peyton, and Richard Schooler. Scalable cross-module optimization. *SIGPLAN Not.*, 33(5):301–312, 1998. ISSN 0362-1340. doi: http://doi.acm.org/10.1145/277652.277745.

[4] Thomas Ball and James R. Larus. Optimally profiling and tracing programs. In *POPL '92: Proceedings of the 19th ACM SIGPLAN-SIGACT symposium on Principles of programming languages*, pages 59–70, New York, NY, USA, 1992. ACM. ISBN 0-89791-453-8. doi: http://doi.acm.org/10.1145/143165.143180.

[5] Dhruva R. Chakrabarti, Luis A. Lozano, Xinliang D. Li, Robert Hundt, and Shin-Ming Liu. Scalable high performance cross-module inlining. In *PACT '04: Proceedings of the 13th International Conference on Parallel Architectures and Compilation Techniques*, pages 165–176, Washington, DC, USA, 2004. IEEE Computer Society. ISBN 0-7695-2229-7. doi: http://dx.doi.org/10.1109/PACT.2004.25.

[6] P. P. Chang and W.-W. Hwu. Inline function expansion for compiling C programs. In *PLDI '89: Proceedings of the ACM SIGPLAN 1989 Conference on Programming language design and implementation*, pages 246–257, New York, NY, USA, 1989. ACM. ISBN 0-89791-306-X. doi: http://doi.acm.org/10.1145/73141.74840.

[7] Chris Lattner, Private Communication.

[8] Keith D. Cooper, Ken Kennedy, and Linda Torczon. Interprocedural optimization: Eliminating unnecessary recompilation. In *SIGPLAN '86: Proceedings of the 1986 SIGPLAN symposium on Compiler construction*, pages 58–67, New York, NY, USA, 1986. ACM. ISBN 0-89791-197-0. doi: http://doi.acm.org/10.1145/12276.13317.

[9] Keith D. Cooper, Mary W. Hall, and Linda Torczon. An experiment with inline substitution. *Softw. Pract. Exper.*, 21(6):581–601, 1991. ISSN 0038-0644. doi: http://dx.doi.org/10.1002/spe.4380210604.

[10] Jack W. Davidson and Anne M. Holler. A study of a C function inliner. *Softw. Pract. Exper.*, 18(8):775–790, 1988. ISSN 0038-0644. doi: http://dx.doi.org/10.1002/spe.4380180805.

[11] Jeffrey Dean, David Grove, and Craig Chambers. Optimization of object-oriented programs using static class hierarchy analysis. In *ECOOP '95: Proceedings of the 9th European Conference on Object-Oriented Programming*, pages 77–101, London, UK, 1995. Springer-Verlag. ISBN 3-540-60160-0.

[12] distcc, A fast free distributed C/C++ compiler. http://distcc.samba.org. URL http://distcc.samba.org.

[13] M.W. Hall. Managing interprocedural optimization. In *PhD Dissertation*, 1991.

[14] Donald E. Knuth. An empirical study of FORTRAN programs. *Software: Practice and Experience*, 1(2):105–133, 1971. doi: 10.1002/spe.4380010203. URL http://dx.doi.org/10.1002/spe.4380010203.

[15] Chris Lattner and Vikram Adve. LLVM: A compilation framework for lifelong program analysis and transformation. In *Proceedings of the 2004 International Symposium on Code Generation and Optimization (CGO04)*, March 2004.

[16] Sungdo Moon, Xinliang D. Li, Robert Hundt, Dhruva R. Chakrabarti, Luis A. Lozano, Uma Srinivasan, and Shin-Ming Liu. SYZYGY - a framework for scalable cross-module IPO. In *CGO '04: Proceedings of the international symposium on Code generation and optimization*, page 65, Washington, DC, USA, 2004. IEEE Computer Society. ISBN 0-7695-2102-9.

[17] Vinodha Ramasamy, Paul Yuan, Dehao Chen, and Robert Hundt. Feedback-directed optimizations in gcc with estimated edge profiles from hardware event sampling. In *Proceedings of GCC Summit 2008*, 2008.

[18] Amitabh Srivastava and David W. Wall. A practical system for inter-module code optimization at link-time. In *Journal of Programming Language*, pages 1–18, 1992.

[19] The Open64 Compiler Suite. www.open64.net. URL http://www.open64.net.

Automated Just-In-Time Compiler Tuning

Kenneth Hoste   Andy Georges   Lieven Eeckhout

Ghent University, Belgium

{kehoste, ageorges, leeckhou}@elis.ugent.be

Abstract

Managed runtime systems, such as a Java virtual machine (JVM), are complex pieces of software with many interacting components. The Just-In-Time (JIT) compiler is at the core of the virtual machine, however, tuning the compiler for optimum performance is a challenging task. There are (i) many compiler optimizations and options, (ii) there may be multiple optimization levels (e.g., -O0, -O1, -O2), each with a specific optimization plan consisting of a collection of optimizations, (iii) the Adaptive Optimization System (AOS) that decides which method to optimize to which optimization level requires fine-tuning, and (iv) the effectiveness of the optimizations depends on the application as well as on the hardware platform. Current practice is to manually tune the JIT compiler which is both tedious and very time-consuming, and in addition may lead to suboptimal performance.

This paper proposes automated tuning of the JIT compiler through multi-objective evolutionary search. The proposed framework (i) identifies optimization plans that are Pareto-optimal in terms of compilation time and code quality, (ii) assigns these plans to optimization levels, and (iii) fine-tunes the AOS accordingly. The key benefit of our framework is that it automates the entire exploration process, which enables tuning the JIT compiler for a given hardware platform and/or application at very low cost.

By automatically tuning Jikes RVM using our framework for average performance across the DaCapo and SPECjvm98 benchmark suites, we achieve similar performance to the hand-tuned default Jikes RVM. When optimizing the JIT compiler for individual benchmarks, we achieve statistically significant speedups for most benchmarks, up to 40% for start-up and up to 19% for steady-state performance. We also show that tuning the JIT compiler for a new hardware platform can yield significantly better performance compared to using a JIT compiler that was tuned for another platform.

Categories and Subject Descriptors D.3.4 [*Programming Languages*]: Processors—Run-time environments

General Terms Design, Experimentation, Measurement, Performance

Keywords Java Virtual Machine (JVM), Just-In-Time (JIT) compiler, compiler tuning, evolutionary search, machine learning

1. Introduction

One of the key advantages of managed programming languages, such as Java, is that programs are compiled to an intermediate machine-independent level, called bytecode, enabling cross-platform portability. However, this requires a process virtual machine—a Java virtual machine or JVM for short—to translate bytecode to executable code. Modern JVMs tend to follow a mixed-mode execution scheme in which application methods are first interpreted, or compiled with a baseline non-optimizing compiler. If a method is sufficiently *hot*, i.e., is executed frequently, it will likely be a candidate for (re)compilation by the optimizing JIT compiler. In this paper, we refer to a set of optimizations used together during the (re)compilation of a method as an *optimization plan*. Modern JVMs [3, 19, 21] employ multiple *optimization levels* (e.g., -O0, -O1 and -O2), in which each level comprises a successively more aggressive optimization plan. In other words, more aggressive optimizations are performed on more frequently executed code: higher optimization levels result in longer compilation times, yet they supposedly yield better code, thereby further speeding up the execution of the hot methods.

Tuning the VM's JIT compiler is a challenging task for a number of reasons. For one, to ensure good performance, the VM developer has to carefully tune each of the optimization levels, choosing the right optimizations at each level and tweaking their settings and controls. This is far from trivial because of the large number of available optimizations and their complex interactions. Second, the Adaptive Optimization System (AOS), i.e., the engine that decides which methods to optimize to which optimization level, needs to be fine-tuned. This is non-trivial as well because the optimum AOS configuration is highly dependent on the compilation plans at each optimization level and it is crucial to take full advantage of the available optimization levels. Third, this tuning process needs to be done for every possible optimization target of interest. In particular, the optimal VM configuration may be specific to a particular hardware platform because different hardware platforms come with different memory hierarchies, microarchitecture, etc. which requires the JIT compiler to be tuned differently. Different applications may need the JIT compiler to be tuned differently as well. For example, servers often run a single application or a limited number of applications, such as middle-ware or business applications, over and over again. As such, it makes sense to tune the VM for a particular application or set of applications.

Current practice is to manually tune the JIT compiler. Arnold et al. [4] and Ishizaki et al. [16] describe such a manual process for the Jikes RVM and the IBM JDK production VM, respectively. This process is both tedious, time-consuming and costly, and may lead to sub-optimal performance. Moreover, tuning needs to be done for every new processor on the market as well as for different applications and application domains.

This paper proposes automated JIT compiler tuning. This is done in two steps. The first step identifies optimization plans that are Pareto-optimal in terms of compilation time and code quality—a Pareto-optimal plan is defined such that there exists no optimization plan that performs better on both compilation time *and* code quality. We use a multi-objective evolutionary search algorithm to efficiently search the large optimization space: starting from a set of randomly generated optimization plans, we let the algorithm evolve until it converges on a set of Pareto-optimal plans. We subsequently retain a limited number of optimization plans that cover the Pareto frontier well. The second major step is to search for the optimum JIT compiler. This involves assigning Pareto-optimal compilation plans to optimization levels (-O0, -O1 and -O2), and fine-tuning the AOS. Again, we use evolutionary search for doing so. The end result is a VM that is optimized for the optimization target(s) of interest, i.e., for a given hardware platform and/or application domain.

Our experimental results using the Jikes RVM, the DaCapo and SPECjvm98 benchmarks, and four different hardware platforms demonstrate the value of the proposed framework. The key experimental results from this paper are as follows:

- We show that the framework succeeds in automatically tuning a modern JIT compiler. We report similar average performance compared to the manually tuned Jikes RVM.

- Tuning for a particular benchmark and a particular hardware platform yields statistically significant speedups of up to 19% for steady-state and 40% for start-up performance.

- Tuning a VM for a new hardware platform yields significantly better performance compared to a VM that was tuned for another platform.

Overall, this paper makes the following key contributions:

- We are the first to propose a framework for automatically tuning a JIT compiler with multiple optimization levels for optimum performance. The key benefit is that the exploration is fully automated and enables tuning the JIT compiler for a given hardware platform and/or (set of) application(s) at very low cost.

- We provide empirical evidence that substantial performance gains can be obtained by tuning the JIT compiler for a particular hardware platform and/or application.

- We make the case that tuning a dynamic (JIT) compiler is much more complicated than tuning a static compiler because of the tight interaction between the optimization plans and levels and the AOS. This insight motivated us to propose a two-step process in which we first identify Pareto-optimal optimization plans, and subsequently assign plans to levels and fine-tune the AOS.

Although this paper uses the Jikes RVM for driving the experiments, we strongly believe that the overall framework and conclusion is applicable to other Java virtual machines. Moreover, similar JIT compiler tuning can be applied on other process virtual machines, such as the Common Language Runtime (CLR) of the Microsoft's .NET initiative.

The remainder of this paper is organized as follows. Section 2 gives a detailed description of the organization of a modern JVM, namely Jikes RVM. In Section 3, we present our JIT optimization space exploration algorithm. In Section 4, we describe our experimental setup, and we present the results in Section 5. Finally, we discuss related work in Section 6 and conclude in Section 7.

2. Java Virtual Machine

Before presenting the proposed JIT compiler optimization framework, we first briefly describe the organization of a modern Java virtual machine, namely Jikes RVM [3]. This will enable us to better understand the complexity of JIT compiler tuning.

Optimization plans and levels. Jikes RVM is a compilation-only VM. Methods are initially compiled using a fast but non-optimizing baseline compiler that generates relatively inefficient machine code. To improve performance, Jikes RVM employs an JIT optimization strategy for optimizing hot methods using three optimization levels (-O0, -O1, and -O2). We refer to the baseline compilation level as base.

Each optimization level -On is defined by an optimization plan P_{On} that enumerates the optimizations at that level along with several values that further steer their use. In the default Jikes RVM configuration, optimization plans for higher levels include the optimizations for the lower levels. Each optimization level also has a corresponding *aggressiveness* assigned to it that influences the use of various optimizations, e.g., more copy propagation passes are done at higher opti-

	base	-O0	-O1	-O2
compilation rate (bs/ms)	909.46	39.53	18.48	17.28
speedup vs. base	1.0	4.03	5.88	5.93

Table 1: Default compiler DNA values for Jikes RVM.

mization levels. In Jikes RVM (version 3.0.1), there are 33 boolean options available, each of which turns an optimization on or off, and 10 value options that control the optimizations[1]. Thus, per optimization plan, we have 2^{33} possible combinations of boolean flags and a space spanned by eight positive integer values and two positive floating-point values. This results in a huge search space.

Compiler DNA. A compilation plan is characterized using two metrics: the compilation rate (i.e., bytecodes compiled per millisecond (bc/ms)), and the improvement in code quality (i.e., speedup in execution time over base). Combined, these two metrics are referred to as the *compiler DNA* associated with the optimization plan.

The compiler DNA for each optimization plan/level in Jikes RVM is measured as follows. The compilation rate is obtained by compiling *all* methods at the specified optimization level upon first execution. The speedup is the ratio between the execution time obtained by executing the optimized code and the execution time for a VM using the base compiler only. The DNA in Jikes RVM for x86, see Table 1, was computed on an LS41 type 7972 blade, equipped with an AMD Opteron 8218 with 4MB L2 cache and 4GB RAM, using the SPECjvm98 benchmarks[2].

Sample-based JIT optimization. Jikes RVM uses OS-timer triggered sampling to identify hot methods. When the timer fires, the method on top of the stack is sampled the moment a yield point[3] is reached [4, 5]. When sufficient samples have been gathered for a method, the VM uses the AOS to decide whether or not to optimize the method to a particular optimization level.

Adaptive Optimization System. The AOS decides whether or not to optimize a method, and if so, to which optimization level the method should be optimized. There are five value options in total that control the AOS. There are three positive integer values, and two positive floating-point values in total, again, a large space to explore. The AOS parameters control when the engine finds a method to be hot enough to be considered for optimization to a higher level. The AOS uses the compiler DNA to make a trade-off in compilation cost

(i.e., how long does it take to optimize the method at a given optimization level?) and code quality (i.e., how much faster will the code run once optimized?).

3. JIT Compiler Tuning

We now present our framework for automatically optimizing a JIT compiler. This includes identifying the compilation plans, optimization levels and AOS settings. Before describing the overall framework in great detail, we first motivate the need for a two-step process.

3.1 Why a two-step process?

As mentioned earlier in the introduction, optimizing a dynamic compiler is substantially more complicated than optimizing a static compiler because of the tight interaction between optimization plans and levels, and the AOS settings. For example, including a compiler optimization at one level changes the compilation rate versus code quality trade-off, which in its turn changes which methods are optimized to which optimization level. This leads to complex interactions which severely complicate the search process. Our initial approach to this problem was to use an evolutionary algorithm to optimize the compilation plans, plan-to-level assignments, the number of optimization levels, and the AOS settings in a single go. In fact, we used the previously proposed COLE approach [15] which was developed for a static compiler, and naively applied it to a dynamic compiler. However, we encountered three significant problems. First, the automatically derived JIT compiler did not perform better (and for many benchmarks significantly worse) than the manually tuned Jikes RVM. Second, the search process took extremely long to converge. Third, expressing the optimization problem in a format that could be handled by COLE's evolutionary search algorithm was non-trivial, e.g., it is unclear how to sensibly define crossover across two JIT compiler settings with a different number of optimization levels. This motivated us to come up with a two-step process in which we first focus on code quality versus compilation rate while excluding dynamic compilation and GC activity, and subsequently assign plans to levels and optimize the AOS settings while considering dynamic compilation and GC activity. The two-step process enables a higher performance JIT compiler to be derived in a shorter amount of time.

3.2 Pareto-optimal optimization plans

The goal of the first step is to identify optimization plans that are Pareto-optimal in terms of compilation time and code quality. Figure 1 shows an illustrative example of a Pareto frontier in the dual-objective search space, namely compilation rate (i.e., number of bytecodes compiled per unit of time) versus speedup (i.e., performance improvement compared to non-optimized code). A compilation plan is Pareto-optimal if there is no other plan that performs better both in terms of compilation rate and speedup. When constructing the Pareto frontier, we consider a setup in which we first

---

[1] These are the options we have used in the exploration. There are other options we did not use because they are either unstable, not meant to be changed from outside the VM or can activate options that result in breaking the Java language specification.

[2] The Jikes RVM compiler DNA for the PowerPC platform specifies different values.

[3] A yield point in Jikes RVM is a point during the execution where the scheduler can safely switch threads. It is placed at the beginning and the end of methods and at loop back-edges.

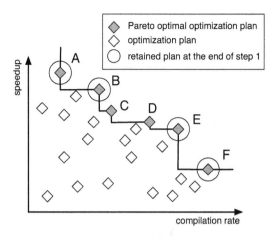

Figure 1: An example of a Pareto frontier in our dual-objective exploration space. The circled plans are those retained at the end of the first step to bootstrap the second step.

compile all the code according to the optimization plan and subsequently execute the optimized code—we do not consider JIT compilation (for now) and consider a large heap size (8 times the minimum heap size) to minimize GC activity. This is to understand the basic trade-off in code quality versus optimization overhead.

For identifying the Pareto frontier, we use the SPEA2 multi-objective evolutionary search algorithm [27], which was also used in the COLE framework [15]. In our implementation, the algorithm starts with a *generation* of 25 compilation plans: one plan with all compilations turned on, one plan with all optimizations turned off, and 23 randomly generated compilation plans. Each of these plans are evaluated in terms of compilation rate and speedup. The best compilation plans seen so far are retained in an *archive*, which contains the Pareto-optimal plans. The next generation is formed by probabilistically mutating plans and combining them using crossover. In our setup, we use mutation to construct $1/10$ of the plans in the next generation with a mutation rate of 25%, and crossover for $9/10$ of the plans with a crossover rate of 25%. After evaluating this new generation, we retain the Pareto-optimal entities in the new archive. This iterative process is repeated until convergence, i.e., until there is no further improvement in the Pareto frontier. The final Pareto frontier contains all the Pareto-optimal optimization plans ever seen during the exploration.

3.3 Limiting the number of Pareto-optimal optimization plans

The end result of the multi-objective evolutionary search as described above is a fairly large set of Pareto-optimal optimization plans; in our experiments, we obtained up to 80 Pareto-optimal plans. From this set, we select a subset such that the Pareto frontier is covered well. We found this Pareto frontier reduction procedure to be an important step in the

overall JIT exploration in order to limit the total exploration time.

The rationale behind the Pareto frontier reduction procedure is to prefer optimization plans that result in high code quality at roughly the same compilation rate, and compile bytecode faster while attaining roughly the same speedup. We therefore use an iterative selection algorithm. In the first iteration, we pick the two adjacent plans on the Pareto frontier that lie closest to each other along the X axis. We drop the plan that scores worst along the Y axis. We then select the two plans that lie closest to each other along the Y axis, and drop the one that scores worst along the X axis. This iterative process stops when the number of retained plans drops below a given number. We limit the number of retained Pareto-optimal compilation plans to 8.

In our running example, see Figure 1, this means we first select the pair (B,C) because they lie closest on the X axis and drop C. The next pair is (D, E) because they lie closest on the Y-axis and we only retain E. After two iterations, the list of retained optimization plans equals {A, B, E, F}.

3.4 JIT compiler tuning

The second step in the proposed JIT compiler tuning framework is to (i) assign the Pareto-optimal optimization plans to optimization levels (-O0, -O1 and -O2), and (ii) optimize the JIT AOS accordingly. In contrast to the first step, we now consider adaptive JIT compilation, i.e., the JIT compiler optimizes the most frequently executed methods at run time, and we consider heap sizes that introduce GC activity in order to achieve representative performance numbers. In other words, compilation and optimization time as well as GC time become part of the overall execution time.

Assigning compilation plans to optimization levels is fairly straightforward: given the limited number of retained Pareto-optimal optimization plans we can easily consider all possible assignments of plans to levels. In our setup, this means we need to assign 8 optimization plans to 1 through 3 optimization levels. There are 92 possible assignments. We use an evolutionary search algorithm to identify the best AOS settings.

4. Experimental Setup

In this section, we describe our experimental setup in terms of the benchmarks, the hardware platforms, the Jikes RVM version, and the data analysis method used.

4.1 Benchmarks

Table 2 shows the benchmarks used in this study. We use the SPECjvm98 benchmarks [23] (top seven rows), as well as nine DaCapo benchmarks [7] (bottom nine rows). SPECjvm98 is a client-side Java benchmark suite consisting of seven benchmarks. We run all SPECjvm98 benchmarks with the largest input set (-s100). The DaCapo benchmark suite is an open-source benchmark suite; we use release version 2006-10-MR2. We use the nine benchmarks that exe-

benchmark	description	min heap size (MB)
compress	file compression	24
jess	puzzle solving	16
db	database	32
javac	Java compiler	32
mpegaudio	MPEG decompression	16
mtrt	raytracing	24
jack	parsing	24
antlr	parsing	32
bloat	Java bytecode optimization	56
fop	PDF generation from XSL-FO	56
hsqldb	database	176
jython	Python interpreter	72
luindex	document indexing	32
lusearch	document search	32
pmd	Java class analysis	64
xalan	XML to HTML transformer	40

Table 2: SPECjvm98 (top seven) and DaCapo (bottom nine) benchmarks considered in this paper.

cute properly on the 3.0.1 version of Jikes RVM. We use the default (medium size) input set for the DaCapo benchmarks unless mentioned otherwise.

4.2 Hardware platforms

We use four different hardware platforms in this study:

- an AMD Opteron 242 clocked at 1.6GHz with 1MB L2 cache and 4GB RAM running Linux 2.6.9;

- an Intel Pentium 4 clocked at 3GHz with 1M L2 cache and 1.5GB RAM running Linux 2.6.19;

- an Intel Core 2 based Xeon L5420 clocked at 2.5GHz with 6MB L2 cache and 16GB RAM running Linux 2.6.18; and

- an Intel Core i7 920 based machine clocked at 2.6GHz with 256KB L2, 8MB L3 and 12GB RAM running Linux 2.6.27.

4.3 Jikes RVM

We use Jikes RVM version 3.0.1, released on November 18th, 2008. We patched Jikes RVM such that optimizations can be set on a per-optimization level basis at the command line. The virtual machine was built using the *production* profile, which uses the GenMS garbage collector and compiles the VM methods using the optimizing compiler with the default P_{02} optimization plan. During the first step of the exploration algorithm, we use a heap size that is 8 times the minimum size required to run the benchmark; this is to eliminate the effect of garbage collection, as mentioned earlier. We do vary the heap size (i.e., $2\times$, $4\times$, and $8\times$ the minimum heap size) during the second step and during evaluation, following current practice [7].

Plan	Compilation rate	Speedup (over base)
-O0	53.12	1.86
-O1	21.84	2.14
-O2	20.81	2.13
A	59.70	1.77
B	57.62	1.86
C	50.86	1.89
D	41.07	2.00
E	37.42	2.02
F	28.70	2.05
G	25.90	2.08
H	19.11	2.13

Table 3: Compilation rates and speedups over base on the Intel Core 2 for the compilation plans used by default in Jikes RVM (top rows), and the compilations plans obtained through our exploration (bottom rows).

4.4 Statistically rigorous performance evaluation

To deal with the non-determinism that is due to timer-based sampling and adaptive optimization in Jikes RVM, we use both multiple VM invocations and multiple benchmark iterations per VM invocation in our experiments, following the statistically rigorous performance evaluation methodology proposed by Georges et al. [13]. When reporting start-up performance we consider the average execution time for the first benchmark iteration across 20 VM invocations. When reporting steady-state performance we consider the arithmetic mean across the final 5 out of 15 benchmark iterations across 20 VM invocations. We also report 95% confidence intervals which are indicated through error bars in the graphs.

5. Results

We now evaluate the proposed JIT compiler tuning framework. We consider three cases: (i) tuning for average performance across all benchmarks, (ii) tuning for a particular benchmark, and (iii) tuning for a specific hardware platform. We consider experimental setups both with and without cross-validation. Finally, we discuss the exploration time.

5.1 Tuning for a benchmark suite

For now, we use all the benchmarks from the SPECjvm98 and DaCapo suites, and aim at finding a JIT compiler setting that performs well on average across all of the benchmarks. Our goal is to demonstrate that automated JIT compiler tuning performs at least as well as a manually tuned JIT compiler. This exploration was conducted on the Intel Core 2 platform.

Pareto-optimal optimization plans. Table 3 lists the three default compilation levels as well as the compilation plans we obtained from the first step in our exploration process in terms of compilation rate and speedup (code quality). The automatically derived Pareto-optimal compilation plans are comparable to the manually tuned compilation plans in default Jikes RVM, and are well spread in terms of compilation rate and code quality.

Optimum JIT compiler. The second step is to identify optimum plan-to-level assignments and AOS settings. We denote the JIT compiler that optimizes start-up performance as C_{ST}; the JIT compiler that optimizes steady-state performance is denoted as C_{SS}. These settings are shown in Table 4; interestingly, the optimum start-up JIT compiler C_{ST} has three levels with plans E, C and A, whereas the optimum steady-state JIT compiler C_{SS} has only two levels with plans E and A. We found the automatically tuned JIT compiler to achieve significantly better performance than the manually tuned Jikes RVM for a couple benchmarks, e.g., mtrt (30% for start-up and 7% for steady-state), hsqldb (10% for start-up) and bloat (3% for steady-state). For some benchmarks, we observe slightly worse performance, e.g., lusearch and xalan for steady-state; performance degradation is limited to 3% to 4% though. However, for the majority of the benchmarks, we do not observe statistically significantly better or worse performance. Overall, the end conclusion is that *automated JIT compiler tuning is feasible and achieves similar performance compared to a manually tuned JIT compiler.*

5.2 Cross-validation experiment

The evaluation described so far assumed that the JIT compiler was tuned and evaluated using the same set of benchmarks, namely DaCapo and SPECjvm98. Even more relevant is to study whether one could tune the JIT compiler with one set of benchmarks and then achieve good performance for other benchmarks. We now employ such a cross-validation setup: we tune the JIT compiler using the DaCapo benchmark suite and then evaluate the tuned JIT compiler using the SPECjvm98 benchmark suite, and vice versa. Figure 2 shows the results of this cross-validation experiment along with the results of a non cross-validation experiment (i.e., the JIT compiler is tuned and evaluated using the same set of benchmarks), which serves as a point of reference. For SPECjvm98 (top row), we observe that the automatically tuned JIT compiler achieves good performance even in a cross-validation experiment (compare Figure 2(a) to the non cross-validation experiment in Figure 2(b)). The automatically tuned JIT compiler achieves substantial speedups for mtrt and compress. We observe a slowdown for mpegaudio in the cross-validation setup. The performance picture is mixed for the DaCapo benchmark suite (bottom row): when tuned for SPECjvm98, the JIT compiler performs worse for some of the DaCapo benchmarks, see for example bloat, jython, lusearch and pmd. For the other benchmarks, we observe similar (or similarly good, see hsqldb) performance under cross-validation. The reason for the different performance picture for DaCapo compared to SPECjvm98 is due to the significant differences in workload characteristics be-

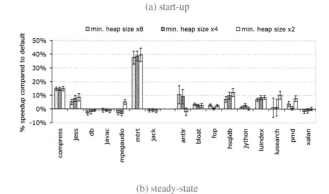

(a) start-up

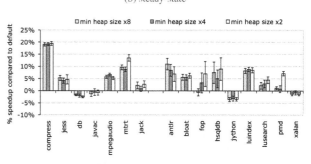

(b) steady-state

Figure 3: Speedup on the Intel Core 2 compared to default Jikes RVM for start-up and steady-state performance when tuning the JIT compiler for optimum performance on a per-benchmark basis.

tween DaCapo and SPECjvm98: Blackburn et al. [7] demonstrate that DaCapo shows more complex code, has richer object behaviors, and has more demanding memory system requirements. This result motivates the need for representative benchmarks when (automatically) tuning a JIT compiler—this is a general concern for feedback-loop based optimization and tuning.

5.3 Tuning for a single benchmark

An important benefit from automated JIT compiler tuning is that it enables the optimization for specific applications as well as for specific hardware platforms at very low cost, given that the tuning process is completely automated. In this section, we discuss the results we obtain when we tune the JIT compiler for a specific benchmark; we discuss the case in which we tune for a specific hardware platform later.

Figure 3 shows the speedup on the Core 2 platform when comparing the best Pareto-optimal configuration tuned per benchmark for (a) start-up and (b) steady-state performance against the default Jikes RVM. The automated exploration yields JIT compilers that outperform the default Jikes RVM for a good portion of the benchmarks, and up to 40% for start-up and up to 19% for steady-state.

5.4 Cross-input validation

In the previous section, we considered the same benchmark inputs when tuning the JIT compiler as during evaluation.

	default	C_{ST}	C_{SS}
number of levels	3	3	2
level 0	P_{00}	plan E	plan E
level 1	P_{01}	plan C	plan A
level 2	P_{02}	plan A	–
Number of clocks ticks after which call graph decays	100	52	26
Call graph decay rate	1.10	1.10	1.10
Call graph update frequency in timer ticks	20	3	4
Initial edge weight in call graph	3	3	3
Percentage of edges that mark hotness	0.01	0.0136	0.0098

Table 4: The JIT compiler configurations that are optimal in terms of startup (C_{ST}) and in terms of steady-state (C_{SS}).

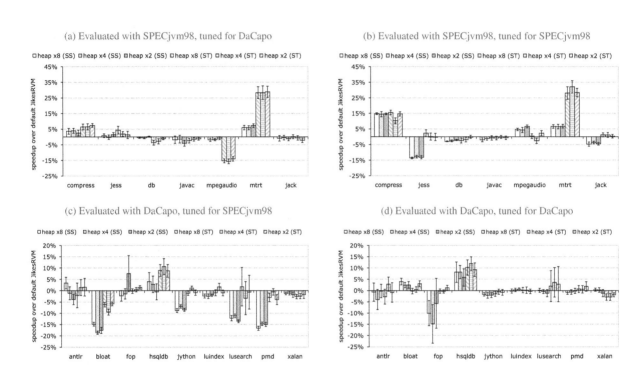

Figure 2: Per-benchmark performance speedups on the Intel Core 2 compared to default Jikes RVM when tuning Jikes RVM in a cross-validation setup (left column: (a) + (c)), and a non cross-validation setup (right column: (b) + (d)). These graphs show results for both startup (ST) and steady-state (SS) performance, across three heap sizes.

Figure 4 reports performance results when considering a different input during the tuning process and evaluation, i.e., we now consider a cross-input validation setup. We limit ourselves to the DaCapo benchmarks in this experiment: we use the medium inputs during JIT compiler tuning and use the large inputs during evaluation. Two DaCapo benchmarks are excluded, namely fop and luindex, because the medium input is equal to the large input. We do not consider SPECjvm98 here because of lack of inputs: the -s1 and -s10 inputs are too small and only stress virtual machine startup performance and do not stress code quality [12].

Comparing Figures 3 and 4, we observe roughly the same speedup for the medium inputs (Figure 3) as for the large input (Figure 4) for some benchmarks, e.g., hsqldb. For other benchmarks, we observe a slight performance drop, e.g., bloat. This motivates the need for representative inputs when tuning a JIT compiler for a particular application — an input that yields substantially different program behavior than the input used during the tuning process may result in suboptimal performance. As mentioned before, this is a general concern for feedback-loop based optimization and tuning.

5.5 Tuning for a specific hardware platform

We now explore the potential performance benefit by tuning the JIT compiler for a specific hardware platform. In this case study, we examine the effects of tuning for a particular platform using two benchmarks: (i) mtrt, and (ii)

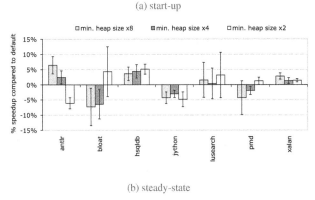

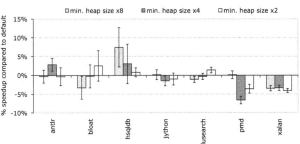

Figure 4: Per-benchmark start-up and steady-state speedup through a cross-input validation experiment.

luindex. During the benchmark suite wide exploration on the Intel Core 2 (see Figure 2), the optimum JIT compiler did very well for mtrt, yet it failed to improve performance for luindex. In the per-benchmark exploration, mtrt improves further, while luindex gains 9% in both start-up performance and in steady-state performance on the Core 2, see Figure 3. Thus, these two benchmarks make for two excellent cases for examining the effect of exploring benchmark-specific tuning across different hardware platforms.

Per-platform tuning. Our first experiment tunes the JIT compiler for a specific hardware platform and compares performance against the default JIT compiler (which was manually tuned for another hardware platform). The results of this hardware-specific exploration are shown in Figure 5 for (a) start-up and (b) steady-state performance. There is significant benefit in start-up performance for mtrt: performance speedups range from 19% to 40%. For luindex we observe performance benefits in the 4% to 12% range. For steady-state performance, we observe substantial performance benefits for both mtrt and luindex: performance improves by up to 13% for mtrt and up to 17% for luindex. These examples make the case that significant speedups can be obtained from tuning a JIT compiler for a specific hardware platform.

This result is further illustrated in Figure 6 which shows the per-platform Pareto-optimal optimization plans in terms of compilation rate versus performance speedup over base. There are two observations we can immediately draw from

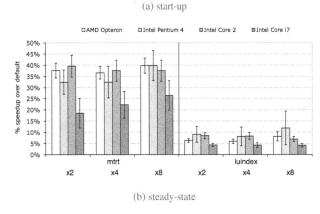

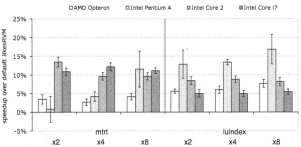

Figure 5: This graph shows speedup numbers across different heap sizes on all hardware platforms for mtrt and luindex for (a) start-up and (b) steady-state performance.

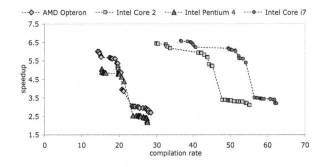

Figure 6: The Pareto frontiers for the optimization plans tuned for mtrt on each of the platforms in our experimental setup.

this graph. First, the frontier shifts to the upper right for more recent platforms. As a consequence, if one tunes the compiler DNA on an older platform, the cost for optimization is over-estimated and the potential benefit the optimization reaps is under-estimated. This results in optimizing either later—more samples are required to overcome the decision threshold—or optimizing to a lower level. Conversely, if the VM is tuned for a more recent platform, the VM might optimize too soon and/or too much, potentially offsetting the gain the adaptive framework might bring. Second, we see that on each platform the Pareto frontier is well spread across

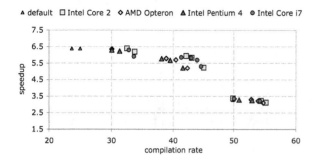

(a) Optimization plans

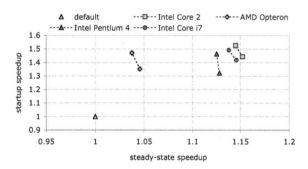

(b) Tuned JIT compilers

Figure 7: Graph (a) shows compilation rate versus performance speedup for the Pareto-optimal compilation plans determined on the AMD Opteron, Pentium 4 and Core i7 when run on the Core 2 platform. Graph (b) shows start-up versus steady-state performance for the AMD Opteron, Pentium 4 and Core i7 tuned JIT compilers when evaluated on the Core 2. These graphs consider `mtrt`.

the space, suggesting that a few optimizations might have a large effect.

Employing tuned JIT compilers across platforms. Using a JIT compiler that was tuned for a particular hardware platform on another hardware platform may yield suboptimal results. This is illustrated in Figure 7(a) where the Pareto-optimal plans tuned for `mtrt` for each platform have been evaluated on the Intel Core 2 platform. The optimization plans tuned for the Intel Pentium 4 and AMD Opteron platforms are suboptimal, i.e., they perform worse than the ones that were tuned for the Core 2. We observe a similar result when looking into tuned JIT compilers, see Figure 7(b) which compares the performance of a JIT compiler tuned for the Pentium 4, AMD Opteron and Core i7 when run on a Core 2 machine against a JIT compiler that was tuned on the Core 2. Clearly, the JIT compiler tuned for the Core 2 yields the best possible performance on the Core 2—the JIT compilers tuned for the other platforms perform worse. In particular, the JIT compiler that was tuned for the Core 2 yields approximately 5% better start-up performance and 10% better steady-state performance compared to the JIT compiler

that was tuned for the Pentium 4. We thus conclude that *platform-specific JIT compiler tuning can yield substantial performance benefits and transferring JIT settings across platforms may lead to suboptimal performance.*

5.6 Exploration time

Finally, we discuss how much time is needed to complete the JIT compiler tuning.

Performing the first step for all of the DaCapo and SPECjvm98 benchmarks on the Core2 platform took 33 generations to converge. During each generation, 25 new optimization plans are constructed, each of which requires roughly 40 minutes to measure the compiler DNA. This means that about 550 machine hours are needed to run the first step of the tuning process to convergence. Note however, that this tuning process is embarrassingly parallel, i.e., all plans can be measured in parallel and independently from each other. Having sufficient machine resources available, this first step takes 22 hours only.

The second exploration step, which tunes the plan-to-level assignment and AOS, converges significantly faster: only 8 generations are required. Evaluating a single JIT compiler setting takes about 400 minutes on average. This results in an additional exploration time of about 1320 hours. Again, because each generation can be evaluated in parallel, the exploration can be performed in about 53 hours.

Thus, the entire exploration for a set of 16 benchmarks on a particular hardware platform takes around 75 hours or roughly 3 days. Performing the exploration for a single application only, as we did for the experiments described in Section 5.3, is a matter of hours.

6. Related Work
6.1 Dynamic optimization

Most modern Java virtual machines implement multiple levels of optimization, see for example [4, 6, 19, 24]. Since compilation time is an integral part of the total execution time in a dynamic compiler, it is of utmost importance to make a good trade-off between compilation time and code quality when proposing optimization levels in a optimizing dynamic compiler. Arnold et al. [6] and Ishizaki et al. [16] describe how optimization levels are determined manually for the Jikes RVM and IBM DB production VM, respectively.

Cavazos and O'Boyle [9] take a different approach to optimizing JIT compilers. They apply a different optimization plan for each method. The optimizations in these plans are determined by using a logistic regression function that predicts which optimizations are most useful for the given method based on bytecode features. They report speedups of 4%, 2% and 29% on average compared to optimizing all methods at the -O0, -O1, and -O2 levels, respectively. When considering adaptive optimization, they report a 1% improvement over default Jikes RVM for SPECjvm98; for the DaCapo benchmarks, they report a 4% average performance improvement. Our JIT tuning approach does not apply different compilation plans to individual methods which simplifies JIT compiler tuning. In addition, Cavazos and O'Boyle do not make the case that JIT compilers that are tuned for particular hardware platforms and/or applications can yield substantial performance benefits. In their follow-on work [10], Cavazos and O'Boyle use a genetic algorithm to automatically tune the heuristics of the inliner in a dynamic Java compiler. Our work is not limited to the inliner; we instead tune the entire JIT optimization system.

6.2 Multi-objective iterative compilation

The basic idea of iterative compilation is to explore the compiler optimization space by iteratively compiling and measuring the effectiveness of optimization sequences. A large body of work has been done on iterative compilation over the past few years, and many researchers have reported impressive results showing significant performance, energy or code size improvements over standard optimization sequences, see for example [1, 2, 8, 11, 17, 25].

What all of this prior work on iterative compilation has in common is that it focuses on a single objective function to be optimized. For example, researchers typically focus on a single optimization criterion such as performance [1, 8, 9, 11, 25], or energy consumption [14], or code size [11]. And some researchers focus on optimizing a single objective function that combines multiple optimization criteria such as code quality and compilation time [9, 10], or code quality and code size [17].

Very recently, Hoste and Eeckhout [15] proposed the COLE framework which explores a multi-objective compiler optimization space, unlike prior work which focuses on single-objective optimization. The key innovation compared to COLE is that this paper studies multi-objective compiler optimization in a dynamic compiler; the COLE work focused on static compilers for programming languages such as C, C++, Fortran, etc. A dynamic compiler poses several new challenges compared to a static compiler which complicates the search process, which, as mentioned before, motivated us for the two-step process proposed in this paper.

7. Conclusion

This paper proposed a framework for automatically tuning dynamic compilers. The framework uses evolutionary searching and tunes the JIT compiler for a given hardware platform and a given application or application domain. This is done through a two-step process in order to manage the complexity in exploring the huge optimization space: we first identify Pareto-optimal compilation plans, and subsequently assign plans to optimization levels and fine-tune the AOS. Our experimental results using the Jikes RVM, four hardware platforms and the SPECjvm98 and DaCapo benchmarks, demonstrate that the proposed framework identifies JIT compiler configurations that achieve significantly bet-

ter performance compared to a manually tuned VM. When optimizing for individual applications, we achieve performance improvements up to 40% and 19% for start-up and steady-state performance, respectively. Also, optimizing for a specific hardware platform leads to significantly better performance. Our framework is completely automated and explores the complex JIT compiler space in approximately 3 days for the collection of DaCapo and SPECjvm benchmarks; tuning the JIT compiler for individual applications is done in a few hours.

Acknowledgements

We would like to thank Brad Chen and the anonymous reviewers for their thoughtful comments and valuable suggestions. Kenneth Hoste is supported by the Institute for the Promotion of Innovation by Science and Technology in Flanders (IWT). Andy Georges is supported through a post-doctoral fellowship by the Research Foundation–Flanders (FWO). Additional support is provided by the FWO projects G.0232.06, G.0255.08, and G.0179.10, and the UGent-BOF projects 01J14407 and 01Z04109. Computational resources and services used in this work were provided by Ghent University.

References

[1] F. Agakov, E. Bonilla, J. Cavazos, B.Franke, G. Fursin, M. O'Boyle, J. Thomson, M. Toussaint, and C. Williams. Using machine learning to focus iterative optimization. In *CGO*, pages 295–305, Mar. 2006.

[2] L. Almagor, K. D. Cooper, A. Grosul, T. J. Harvey, S. Reeves, D. Subramanian, L. Torczon, and T. Waterman. Compilation order matters: Exploring the structure of the space of compilation sequences using randomized search algorithms. In *LCTES*, pages 231–239, June 2004.

[3] B. Alpern, C. R. Attanasio, J. J. Barton, M. G. Burke, P. Cheng, J.-D. Choi, A. Cocchi, S. J. Fink, D. Grove, M. Hind, S. F. Hummel, D. Lieber, V. Litvinov, M. F. Mergen, T. Ngo, J. R. Russell, V. Sarkar, M. J. Serrano, J. C. Shepherd, S. E. Smith, V. C. Sreedhar, H. Srinivasan, and J. Whaley. The Jalapeño Virtual Machine. In *IBM System Journal*, 39(1), Feb. 2000.

[4] M. Arnold, S. Fink, D. Grove, M. Hind, and P. F. Sweeney. Adaptive optimization in the Jalapeño JVM. In *OOPSLA*, pages 47–65, Oct. 2000.

[5] M. Arnold, S. Fink, D. Grove, M. Hind, and P. F. Sweeney. A Survey of Adaptive Optimization in Virtual Machine. In *Proceedings of the IEEE*, 93(2), 2005

[6] M. Arnold, M. Hind, and B. G. Ryder. Online Feedback-Directed Optimization in Java. In *OOPSLA*, pages 111–129, 2002

[7] S. M. Blackburn, R. Garner, C. Hoffmann, A. M. Khang, K. S. McKinley, R. Bentzur, A. Diwan, D. Feinberg, D. Frampton, S. Z. Guyer, M. Hirzel, A. Hosking, M. Jump, H. Lee, J. E. B. Moss, A. Phansalkar, D. Stefanovic, T. VanDrunen, D. von Dincklage, and B. Wiedermann. The DaCapo benchmarks: Java benchmarking development and analysis. In *OOPSLA*, pages 169–190, Oct. 2006.

[8] F. Bodin, T. Kisuki, P. Knijnenburg, M. O'Boyle, and E. Rohou. Iterative compilation in a non-linear optimisation space. In *PACT*, Oct. 1998.

[9] J. Cavazos, and M. O'Boyle Method-Specific Dynamic Compilation using Logistic Regression. In *OOPSLA*, pages 229–240, Oct. 2006.

[10] J. Cavazos and M. O'Boyle. Automatic tuning of inlining heuristics. In *Proceedings of the ACM/IEEE SC2005 Conference on High Performance Networking and Computing*, Nov. 2005.

[11] K. D. Cooper, P. J. Schielke, and D. Subramanian. Optimizing for reduced code space using genetic algorithms. In *LCTES*, pages 1–9, May 1999.

[12] L. Eeckhout, A. Georges, and K. De Bosschere. How Java programs interact with virtual machines at the microarchitectural level. In *OOPSLA*, pages 169–186, Oct. 2003.

[13] A. Georges, D. Buytaert, and L. Eeckhout. Statistically rigorous Java performance evaluation. In *OOPSLA*, pages 57–76, Oct. 2007.

[14] S. V. Gheorghita, H. Corporaal, and T. Basten. Iterative compilation for energy reduction. *Journal of Embedded Computing*, 1(4):509–520, July 2005.

[15] K. Hoste and L. Eeckhout. COLE: Compiler Optimization Level Exploration In *CGO*, pages 165–174, Apr. 2008.

[16] K. Ishizaki, M. Takeuchi, K. Kawachiya, T. Suganuma, O. Gohda, T. Inagaki, A. Koseki, K. Ogata, M. Kawahito, T. Yasue, T. Ogasawara, T. Onodera, H. Komatsu, T. Nakatani Effectiveness of cross-platform optimizations for a java just-in-time compiler. In *OOPSLA*, pages 187–204, Oct. 2003.

[17] P. Kulkarni, S. Hines, J. Hiser, D. Whalley, J. Davidson, and D. Jones. Fast searches for effective optimization phase sequences. In *PLDI*, pages 171–182, June 2004.

[18] Y. Luo, and L.K. John. Efficiently Evaluating Speedup Using Sampled Processor Simulation. In *IEEE Computer Architecture Letters*, 3, 2004

[19] D. Maier, P. Ramarao, M. Stoodley, and V. Sundaresan. Experiences with Multithreading and Dynamic Class Loading in a Java Just-In-Time Compiler. In *CGO*, pages 87–97, Mar. 2006.

[20] J. Neter, M. H. Kutner, W. Wasserman, and C. J. Nachtsheim. *Applied Linear Statistical Models*. McGraw-Hill, 1996.

[21] M. Paleczny, C. Vick, and C. Click. The Java Hotspot server compiler. In *JVM*, pages 1–12, Apr. 2001.

[22] Standard Performance Evaluation Corporation. SPECjbb2000 Benchmark. http://www.spec.org/jbb2000.

[23] Standard Performance Evaluation Corporation. SPECjvm98 Benchmarks. http://www.spec.org/jvm98.

[24] T. Suganuma, T. Yasue, M. Kawahito, H. Komatsu, and T. Nakatani. Design and evaluation of dynamic optimizations for a Java Just-In-Time compiler. *ACM Transactions on Programming Languages and Systems (TOPLAS)*, 27(4):732–785, July 2005.

[25] S. Triantafyllis, M. Vachharajani, and D. I. August. Compiler optimization-space exploration. *Journal of Instruction-level Parallelism*, Jan. 2005. Accessible at http://www.jilp.org/vol7.

[26] E. Zitzler and L. Thiele. Multiobjective evolutionary algorithms: a comparative case study and the strength Pareto approach. In IEEE Transactions on Evolutionary Computation, 3(4), pages 257–271, Nov. 1999.

[27] E. Zitzler, M. Laumanns and L. Thiele. SPEA2: Improving the Strength Pareto Evolutionary Algorithm. Technical Report TIK-Report 103, May 2001.

Hybrid Java Compilation and Optimization for Digital TV Software Platform

Dong-Heon Jung, Soo-Mook Moon, Hyeong-Seok Oh
School of Electrical Engineering and Computer Science
Seoul National University, Seoul 151-742, Korea
{clamp, smoon, oracle}@altair.snu.ac.kr

Abstract

The Java software platform for the interactive digital TV (DTV) is composed of the system/middleware classes statically installed on the DTV set-top box and the *xlet* classes dynamically downloaded from the TV stations, where xlets are executed only when the TV viewer initiates the interaction. In order to achieve high performance on this dual-component, user-initiated system, existing just-in-time compilation is not enough, but idle-time compilation and optimization as well as ahead-of-time compilation are also needed, requiring a *hybrid compilation and optimization environment*. We constructed such a hybrid environment for a commercial DTV software platform and experimented with real, on-air xlet applications. Our experimental results show that the proposed hybrid environment can improve the DTV Java performance by as much as an average of 150%, compared to the JITC-only environment.

Categories & Subject Descriptors D.3.4[Processors]; Compilers; Code generation; Run-time environments; D.4.7[Organization and Design]; Real-time systems and embedded systems

General Terms Design, Languages, Performance

Keywords Digital TV Java, ahead-of-time compiler, idle-time compiler, just-in-time compiler, xlets

1. Introduction

The *digital TV* (DTV) presents a new paradigm of a TV by sending and receiving digital signals instead of analog signals [1]. Since digital signals consume less bandwidth due to digital video compression, the TV stations can broadcast a higher definition picture and a clearer sound with reduced noises and ghosts, providing a high-definition TV (HDTV). In addition to the picture and the sound, we can use the remaining bandwidth for sending and receiving *data*, such as the traffic/weather/news/stock information, the program-specific information synchronized to the video, and the interaction with the viewers using a return channel (T-commerce, T-

banking, T-government), providing the *data broadcasting TV* or the *interactive TV (i*TV*)* [2].

One key technology underneath the data broadcasting is ***Java***, such that many open standards for the iTV is based on Java [3]. Sun Microsystems announced Java API for data broadcasting in 1998 and published the Java TV specification in 1999 [4]. Then, Multimedia Home Platform (MHP) based on Java TV API was developed by DVB [5]. MHP-DVB become the basis for other iTV platforms such as Open Cable Application Platform (OCAP) by Cablelabs [6], or Advanced Common Application Platform (ACAP) by ATSC [7]. As of 2006, more than three million Java-enabled set-tops are shipped world-wide [8].

The Java-based data broadcasting is programmed using the *xlet application*, which is composed of the xlet classes and image/text files. The xlet application is broadcasted to the DTV set-top box and executed there interacting with system/middleware classes, on a user request to display the chosen information. Consequently, there exist two types of Java classes in the DTV platform: (1) the system and middleware classes installed on the DTV set-top box, and (2) the *xlet* classes broadcasted from the TV station. Also, the xlet application is executed only when the user initiates the interaction, even after the xlet application is completely downloaded. As usual, Java performance is also an issue in the DTV platform and causes a substantial delay in responding to the user's request, requiring acceleration.

The most common wisdom of Java acceleration employed commercially by most DTV manufacturers is simply resorting to *just-in-time compilation* (JITC) included in the Java virtual machine (JVM), which translates Java bytecode to machine code on an as-needed basis. However, we think that JITC is not enough for accelerating the DTV Java, but *idle-time compilation* and *optimization* as well as *ahead-of-time compilation* are also needed. That is, the system and middleware classes can be compiled and installed ahead-of-time with better code optimizations and no JITC overhead. The downloaded xlet classes can be compiled during the idle-time while the TV viewer watches the TV program before initiating the xlet execution. The images and the texts included in the xlet application can also be processed in advance during the idle-time, and this is beneficial because loading/decoding of the images or creating the fonts for the texts cause a serious runtime overhead.

In this paper, we propose such a *hybrid compilation and optimization environment* for the DTV Java platform. We actually constructed one for a commercial DTV set-top box and evaluated it with real, on-air xlet applications. A big improvement of the response time could be observed when the xlet applications are executed, with little change to other DTV behavior. We analyzed the performance improvement and evaluated it. As far as we know, there have been no research or commercial effort to address the DTV Java performance.

This work was supported in part by the Korea Research Foundation Grant funded by the Korean Government (MOEHRD, KRF-2007-313-D00628), by the IT R&D program of MKE/KEIT [2009-S-036-01, Development of New Virtual Machine Specification and Technology], and by LG electronics.

We provided an elaborate and efficient engineering solution based on the compilation technology for this real-life problem, which is our contribution.

The rest of this paper is as follows. Section 2 describes the background of the DTV Java platform and its possible acceleration solutions. Section 3 describes the proposed hybrid environment. Section 4 shows our evaluation results. Related work is in Section 5 and a summary is in Section 6.

2. DTV Java Platform and Its Acceleration

In this section, we describe some background for the DTV Java platform and the xlet applications. We also explore Java acceleration choices for the DTV platform.

2.1 DTV Software Architecture and the xlet Lifecycle

Our target DTV Java platform is the ACAP, a standard terrestrial DTV and IPTV platform in Korea. It is similar to other Java-based standard platforms (OCAP for cable TVs and DVB-MHP for satellite TVs). The ACAP middleware on the DTV set-top box is primarily based on GEM (globally executable MHP) [5], the common Java-based application environment across MHP-based platforms.

For data broadcasting in the ACAP, DTVs receive an xlet application, which consists of xlet class files, image files for screen menus or icons, and text files for titles and subtitles. These files are organized in a hierarchical structure. The xlet application is sent via the object/data carousel mechanism of MPEG-2 DSM-CC (digital storage media command and control) standard, such that a stream of xlet files is sent repetitively in a round-robin manner, as if they are put on a "carousel" and sent. Since the DTV can receive xlet files starting from the middle of the stream, we need to manage those received xlet files. The *object carousel file manager* in the set-top

box picks up the xlet files, identifies their names, properties, directory locations, and the version numbers, and rebuilds their original hierarchical structure. Each channel has a different xlet application, so if the channel is switched, a new xlet application is downloaded.

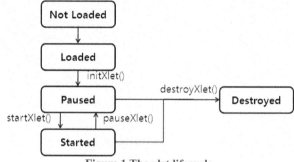

Figure 1 The xlet lifecycle

When the DTV is turned on, the JVM starts and a Java program called an application manager is initiated. Then, the xlet application for the current channel will start its lifecycle, as depicted in Figure 1. When the user explicitly requests data broadcasting (usually by pressing a button in the remote control) or when the DTV is set up to request it automatically when turned on, the xlet application starts being downloaded, entering in the "*Not Loaded*" state. When the application manager loads xlet's main class file and creates the xlet object, the xlet is in the "*Loaded*" state. Then, the application manager will call *initXlet()* method in the xlet application for its initialization. The xlet is in the "*Paused*" state when the initialization completes. Finally, the application manager calls the *startXlet()*, converting the xlet in the "*Started*" state.

(a) Display Red-Dot

(b) Display xlet Menu

(c) Select xlet Menu

(d) Display Selected Menu

Figure. 2. Flow of xlet execution

At this point, a message (usually a red-dot) appears on the upper left corner of the TV screen, indicating that the xlet application is ready for execution and waiting for the TV viewer's request (by pressing the red-button in the remote control). An example of the start screen with the red-dot is depicted in Figure 2 (a). When the viewer presses the red button, a menu appears on the screen as shown in Figure 2 (b) where the weather, stock, news, and traffic menus are displayed. If the user chooses one of them (e.g., stock) by moving the cursor as in Figure 2 (c), the corresponding information will appear as in Figure 2 (d).

If the viewer switches to a different channel, or if some xlet file of the current channel is updated (i.e., a modified xlet file is sent via the carousel which is detected by the carousel file manager), the xlet is stopped and its state is transferred to a "*Destroyed*" state, where all the resources for the xlet is released. A new xlet application for the changed channel will start its lifecycle.

2.2 DTV Java Acceleration

There are some performance issues with the DTV Java. For example, displaying Figure 2 (d) takes 17 seconds in our target DTV (released last year), which would make viewers bored. So, we need to accelerate the DTV Java.

One notable characteristic of the DTV Java is that two types of Java classes that have different origins are executed. One is the system and middleware classes statically installed at the DTV set-top box. The other is the xlet classes dynamically downloaded from the TV station to the DTV. In fact, this occurs in other embedded systems. For example, a software platform for mobile phones is composed of the MIDP middleware installed on the phone and *midlets* downloaded wirelessly [9]. Bluray disks also consist of the BD-J middleware on the BD player and *xlet*s on the BD titles [10]. So, this *dual-component* Java architecture is a trend of embedded Java platforms.

Another trend of this dual-component system is that both the system/middleware classes and the downloaded classes become more complex and substantial. The initial downloaded Java classes were mainly for displaying idle screen images or for delivering simple contents, but now more substantial Java classes such as games or interactive contents are being downloaded with a longer execution time. In order to reduce the network bandwidth for downloading, the Java middleware also gets more substantial to absorb the size and the complexity of downloaded classes. In mobile phones, for example, the first MIDP middleware provided libraries for user interfaces only, yet its successor middleware called JTWI provided an integrated library with music players and SMS [11]. Now a more substantial middleware called MSA is being introduced with more features [12]. This is also true for DTVs and BD players.

Consequently, accelerating DTV Java can be generalized to accelerating Java on these substantial, dual-component systems. Generally, Java's popularity as an embedded software platform is due to the advantage of platform independence, which is achieved by using the JVM that executes Java's compiled executable called the *bytecode*. The bytecode is a stack-based instruction set which can be executed by an interpreter on any platform without porting the original source code. Since this software-based execution is obviously much slower than hardware-based execution, compilation techniques for translating bytecode into machine code have been used, such as *just-in-time compilation* (JITC) [13,20] and *ahead-of-time compilers* (AOTC) [14,15,16,17]. In embedded systems, JITC means performing an online translation at the client device at runtime, while AOTC means performing an offline translation before runtime and the translated machine code is installed at the client device.

Obviously, we can simply employ JITC for DTVs such that both the xlet class methods and the system/middleware class methods are compiled just when they are found to be hot. As to AOTC, although we cannot employ AOTC for xlet classes since they are available at runtime only, we can compile the system/middleware class methods ahead-of-time. In fact, AOTC is more advantageous in embedded systems since it obviates the runtime translation overhead of JITC, which would waste the limited computing power and runtime memory, and may affect the real time behavior. Therefore, it will be desirable to use AOTC for the middleware/system classes while using JITC for the xlet classes, thus employing *hybrid compilation*.

We can extend hybrid compilation further. Another unique characteristic of the DTV Java is that even after the xlets are downloaded, the TV viewer does not necessarily execute the xlets right away. It means that there can be an idle time between the time when the xlets are downloaded and the time when the user really executes them. During the idle-time, the CPU of the set-top box is really idle, so we can do some useful work, like compiling the xlet methods in advance, i.e., *idle-time compilation* (ITC). Also, we can perform other optimizations as well, such as pre-processing of images and texts in the xlet applications, i.e., *idle-time optimization* (ITO). Consequently, we are proposing a hybrid compilation and optimization environment for the DTV Java platform, which is depicted in Figure 3.

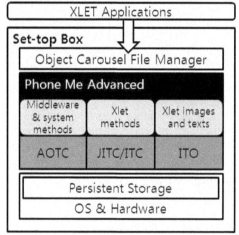

Figure 3. Hybrid compilation and optimization for DTV

3. Hybrid Java Compilation and Optimization

The previous section provided the background of DTV Java platform with the xlet lifecycle, and motivated a hybrid compilation and optimization environment. This section describes the details of the proposed environment, which are composed of three parts: (1) JITC for hot xlet methods, (2) AOTC for system/middleware methods, (3) ITC for xlet methods and ITO for images and texts.

3.1 JITC for Hot xlet Methods.

Our target DTV platform employs an open source version of Sun's Connected Device Configuration (CDC) JVM, called the phoneMe Advanced [18]. It includes an adaptive JITC based on Sun's HotSpot technology, where a Java method is first executed by the interpreter but when it is detected as a hot spot, it is compiled to machine code and saved at the **code cache** in the JVM, which is executed thereafter. In our DTV environment, a hot xlet method will be handled by the JITC, unless it is compiled earlier by the ITC, which will be described shortly.

3.2 AOTC for System/Middleware Methods.

The system and the middleware classes provide DTV-related APIs for easier programming of xlets and are installed at the DTV set-top box. As such, it would be desirable to compile and optimize them ahead-of-time before being installed. There can be many ways to AOTC, but we use the **AOT** module in the phoneMe Advanced.

Sun's phoneMe Advanced has an AOT option which allows compiling a list of pre-chosen methods using its JITC and saves their machine code in a file on a persistent storage (e.g., flash memory). When the JVM starts officially, it will use the compiled machine code directly without interpretation or JITC, when they are executed. A similar approach to AOTC is taken in [19,21].

The advantage of the AOT is that it can obviate the JITC overhead such as the compilation time or the interpretation time for detecting a hot spot. Since the AOT is based on JITC, the quality of the AOT-generated code is supposed to be similar to that of the JITC-generated code (which is not exactly true, as will be seen shortly). Generally, JITC would not perform any time-consuming optimizations since the compilation overhead is part of the running time. If we use an offline AOTC at the server and perform elaborate code optimizations, we might, in theory, be able to generate better code. Nonetheless, Sun's HotSpot is known to generate high-quality code, hence being used commercially for a long time from servers to embedded systems. So employing the AOT for the system/middleware classes would be useful (and we can readily use it for a commercial product without any development of a new AOTC).

Unfortunately, we found that the AOT-generated code is not exactly the same as the JITC-generated code, but worse. This is caused by static code generation using JITC, which is supposed to be used for dynamic compilation. Therefore, we need to enhance the AOT with additional optimizations. We also need to decide which methods should be compiled by the AOT. These issues are described below.

3.2.1. Exploiting AOT with Enhancements

We can perform the AOT for *all* methods of the system/middleware classes. However, this may require an unnecessarily huge space overhead since only a small portion of those methods will be executed, while only a tiny fraction of them will actually be hot. Therefore, we perform the AOT selectively based on the profile-feedback such that only those methods that are compiled by the JITC at least once during the xlet executions are compiled by the AOT. This will reduce the number of methods to be handled by the AOT, thus the space overhead, without affecting the performance much. Obviously, we can compile more, warm methods, but it includes the space overhead with a smaller performance impact, so there should be some compromise.

As to the code quality issues, the most serious problem of the AOT is method inlining. The JITC performs inlining based on the runtime behavior so as to inline only those methods that are called frequently. This is true even for the virtual methods whose callees are decided at runtime such that frequently-called target methods are inlined with a guard instruction that checks the target. On the other hand, the AOT performs inlining based on the method size without any runtime information such that only small methods are

inlined. Therefore, it can inline methods rarely called, increasing the code size unnecessarily. For virtual methods, inlining of rarely called methods can even degrade the performance since the overhead of checking the target is not likely to be offset by the benefit of inlining.

We added a profile-based inlining to the AOT. During the profiling run of xlet applications, we measure the call count of callees for each call site and save the information. During the AOT, inlining is performed based on the information, which would increase the profitability of inlining.

Another problem of the AOT is related to code patch. The code generated by the JITC is allowed to be patched later for efficient handling of class initialization, runtime resolution, or GC check. For example, the translated code for class initialization or runtime resolution does not have to be executed again once executed, so the JITC patches the code by changing the control flow so as to make it not be executed again. Similarly, if there are redundant GC check code (e.g., consecutively at the loop backedge and at the loop header), JITC deletes one of them via code patch. Unfortunately, the AOT disables code patching, so class initialization or resolution code can be executed repetitively and GC check code can be executed redundantly.

This is due to the AOT design that when the JVM starts officially, the AOT file is accessed using the *mmap()* system call and being allocated to the memory with read-only so that the AOT-generated code is accessed fast but never changed. In order to solve this problem, we change the AOT design. When the JVM starts officially, we load the machine code of the AOT file into the code cache first so that the machine code can be patched. We can now enable code patching when we do the AOT.

The third issue of the AOT is caused by relocation. The AOT process includes dumping the JITC-generated machine code in the code cache to the AOT file. When the machine code of the AOT file is loaded to the code cache at the official JVM start, the memory addresses allocated can be different from those allocated when we do the AOT. This is so since the machine code can be loaded at any arbitrary addresses in the code cache, not necessarily the same as those when we do the AOT. This disallows some JITC optimizations that are dependent on the memory addresses, and one example is the *constant pointer optimization*.

This optimization is for accelerating the access of big constants or address constants. If there are usages of big constants or address constants in a method, these constants will be located at the end of the method (constant area) and are accessed using a special register called a constant point register (CPreg). That is, the CPreg is initialized to the start address of the constant area at the beginning of the method and the access to a big constant or an address constant can be achieved via a single load instruction based on the CPreg, added with the offset. This is more efficient than constructing the constants using the LUI and ORI pairs (which sets the high and low order bits, respectively) every time they are accessed. In JITC, since the start address of the constant area will be fixed during the execution of the JITC-generated code, CPreg-based accesses work correctly. However, if this code is saved in a file during the AOT and then is loaded in the code cache later, the code might not work since the start address of the constant area can be different. This is the reason why the constant pointer optimization is disallowed in the AOT.

In order to enable the optimization in the AOT, we generate the code as follows. Instead of saving the absolute, start address of the constant area to the CPreg, we obtain the start address of the method from the method block, add the method size, and save the

(a) JITC AOT code	(b) Original AOT code	(c) Optimized AOT code
\<methodA prologue\> 0x0000: lui cp_reg, 0x0000 0x0004: ori cp_reg, 0x0100 ... \<methodA body\> ... 0x0010: ldr regA, cp_reg[0] ... **\<methodA end\>** 0x0100: 0x10000000 0x0108: memory value 0x010f: constant value ...	**\<methodA prologue\>** ... \<methodA body\> ... 0x0010: lui regA, 0x1000 0x0014: ori regA, 0x0000 ... \<methodA end\>	**\<methodA prologue\>** 0x1000: ldr cp_reg, method_info->startNPC 0x1004: addi cp_reg, 0x100 ... \<methodA body\> ... 0x1008: ldr regA, cp_reg[0] ... **\<methodA end\>** 0x1100: 0x10000000 0x1108: memory value 0x110f: constant value ...

Figure 4. Constant pointer optimization

result to the CPreg. That is, we obtain the start address of the constant area indirectly.

Figure 4 illustrates the constant pointer optimization. Figure 4 (a) shows the original code generated by the JITC, where the start address (0x0100) of the constant area at the end of method A is saved to the CP_reg using an instruction pair of LUI and ORI at the beginning of the method A. Then the access of the big constants or address constants are accessed using a single load based on the CP_reg. Figure 4 (b) shows the code generated by the AOT, where the constant pointer optimization is disabled, so all accesses to big constants and address constants should be implemented by an instruction pair of LUI and ORI. This will cause a substantial overhead if there are many such accesses. Figure 4 (c) shows the code generated by our enhanced AOT where instead of saving the start address of the constant area to CP_reg directly, we load the start address of the method A from the method block in the startNPC field, add the method size (which can be known when the AOT translates the method), and save the result to CPreg. Then, we can access big constants or address constants using the CPreg, as previously.

3.3 ITC and ITO for xlets

When the xlet application is downloaded, the TV viewer does not necessarily execute it right away. This leads the opportunities for idle-time compilation (ITC) for xlet classes and idle-time optimization (ITO) for images/texts included in the xlet applications. One issue is that for transparency they should not delay the appearance of the red-dot too noticeably. The other issue is that even if the TV viewer executes xlets in the middle of ITC or ITO, it should work correctly and efficiently, with whatever is compiled or optimized by that time. We describe our ITC and ITO below.

3.3.1 ITC for xlet Methods

If we compile xlet methods in advance, we can save the JITC overhead. The ITC is based on JITC as the AOT, so we perform the same optimizations used in our enhanced AOT. We assign a separate thread with the lowest priority for the ITC so as not to delay the main thread which displays the red-dot. Since we do not know which methods in the xlet methods will be hot, we simply compile them in an arbitrary order. If the TV viewer executes xlets in the middle of the ITC, the compiled code by that time will reside in the code cache, so there is no problem in starting the execution of xlets from that point, and the benefit of in-advance compilation is still in effect.

3.3.2. ITO for xlet Images

The xlet applications include many images for icons, menus, or charts. They are supposed to be loaded and decoded, just-in-time when they are really needed during the execution of xlets. The problem is that the loading and decoding overhead is substantial, taking almost half of the running time of xlets, (see Section 4.2). This overhead can really affect the response time. Therefore, it will be appropriate to load and decode the images in advance, and the perfect timing would be the idle time of the DTV.

Figure 5 shows the current process of image processing in the DTV. Figure 5 (a) shows the flowchart of xlet execution after it is downloaded. After the xlet is started and the red-dot is displayed, the user will execute the xlet by selecting a menu item. Figure 5 (b) shows what happens during the xlet execution, from the image processing perspectives. When an image needs to be displayed during the execution of the xlet code, it will call a system/middleware method which performs the loading and decoding of the image, saves the decoded image at the ***image cache***, and get the image object. Since an image can be used multiple times, the method actually checks first if a decoded image is already available in the image cache; if so, it is read directly into an image object.

We propose the *pre-loading/decoding* of images during the idle-time of the DTV in order to reduce the overhead of the just-in-time loading and decoding. There a couple of issues involved. The first issue is when we start the pre-loading/decoding in the xlet lifecycle and how we can incorporate it transparently. For transparency, it might be reasonable to perform it right after the red-dot displays (i.e., Started stage); otherwise, the ITO overhead might delay the display of the red-dot, affecting the user's transparency. Unfortunately, invoking startXlet() will execute the xlet code programmed by the TV station, so we cannot modify it to include pre-loading/decoding. Therefore, we should start the pre-loading/decoding earlier, before we call startXlet().

It is important to start the pre-loading/decoding as early as possible to secure a longer idle time since the user can execute xlets any time. Among the states before the Started state, the earliest candidate is "Not-loaded" state where the downloading of xlet files has started but the xlet main class is not yet loaded. However, we found that if we start it at this state, not enough image files are downloaded yet, causing a problem (explained shortly). So, we decided to start pre-loading/decoding at the Loaded state, just before we call initXlet() (we found that if we start it at the Paused state, just before we call startXlet(), both the display of the red-dot and the completion of the pre-loading/decoding are delayed by two seconds).

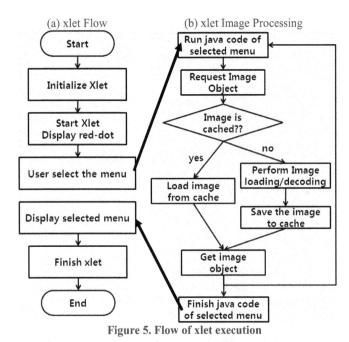

Figure 5. Flow of xlet execution

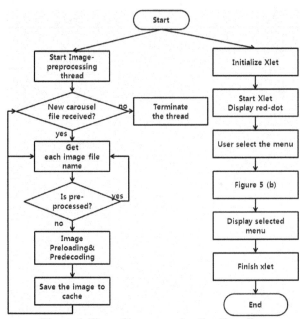

Figure 6. Flow of image pre-loading/decoding

In order to keep the transparency, we use the ITC thread for the pre-loading/decoding, which reduces the delay of displaying the red-dot. The thread performs the ITO first followed by the ITC to make all class files ready; if some class files are missing during ITC, the runtime resolution would not work correctly. Also, the ITO is more beneficial than the ITC, so performing the ITO earlier is better.

Having a separate thread for pre-loading/decoding is also useful even when the user executes an xlet menu too early before all images are processed, but remains idle after that, since the pre-loading/decoding can continue with the thread.

Figure 6 describes how the pre-loading/decoding thread works. It first checks with the object carousel file manager if there are any new files arrived. If there is none, it will finish (this is the reason why we cannot start too early, since if no image files arrived yet, the thread will finish immediately). Otherwise, it obtains the names of newly arrived image files and check if they are already pre-loaded/decoded (i.e., already in the image cache). If not, we load and decode them and save at the image cache. We repeat this process since new xlet files might have arrived in the meantime.

3.3.3. ITO for xlet Texts

The DTV displays many texts as well as many images. The downloaded texts are displayed using the Font objects, which are created during the initXlet(). Using the Font objects requires creating the MWFontMetric object as well, which includes the information on how to display the characters on the TV screen by calculating the dimension (height, width, and the area) of each character. These MWFontMetric objects are created during the execution of xlets, just in time when they are actually needed. The overhead of creating the MWFontMetric object is not trivial, though, because we first need to search the Font file, indexed by the corresponding Font object, to find the information on the font metric, and calculate the dimensions.

In order to reduce this overhead, we propose ITO of the texts by creating the MWFontMetric objects as well as the Font objects when the initXlet() is executed. During the execution of xlets, we can use the MWFontMetric objects directly without creating them, if they are already available.

4. Experimental Results

The previous section described our proposed hybrid compilation and optimization techniques for the DTV Java. This section evaluates them on a commercial DTV platform with real, on-air xlets broadcasted currently in Korea.

4.1. Experimental Environment

Our target DTV set-top box includes a 333MHz MIPS CPU with a 128MB memory. Its software platform has the Sun's phoneMe Advanced MR2 version with advanced common application platform (ACAP) middleware, running on the Linux with kernel 2.6.12. There are three terrestrial TV stations in Korea, each of which broadcasts a different xlet application. We designate them as A, B, and C in this paper. A and B xlets have news, weather, traffic, and stock menu items, while C xlets have news and weather only (other menu items of C xlets are excluded due to the difficulty of measuring the running time). We are primarily interested in the running time of displaying the chosen information on the TV screen when each menu item is selected using the remote control. Table 1 shows the size of each xlet application, which is around 2MB in total.

Table 1 Size of xlet applications (KB)

	class	image	text & etc.	Total
Station A	276	1,348	344	1,968
Station B	360	1,596	372	2,328
Station C	448	1,280	288	2,016

4.2. DTV Java behavior

We first analyze the behavior of existing DTV Java. For this experiment, we turn on the JITC only without any proposed techniques, which is the default configuration of our target DTV. Figure 7 shows the distribution of call counts among the xlet methods, the system methods, and the middleware methods. They are measured for each menu item of the three xlet applications. The graph shows that the system methods and the middleware methods are dominant for all cases, while the xlet methods take a tiny portion.

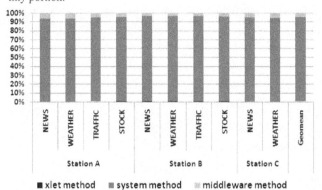

Figure 7. Distribution of method calls

We also measured the distribution of those hot methods that are compiled by the JITC, which is depicted in Figure 8. As in Figure 7, the system and the middleware methods are dominantly hot, while there is a small portion of hot xlet methods (it is higher than the portion of the call count in Figure 7, though). These results indicate that the AOTC for the system and the middleware methods will be effective, while the ITC for xlet methods will have a limited impact.

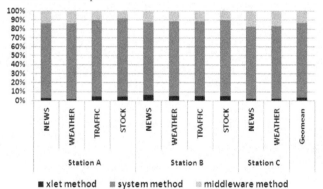

Figure 8. Distribution of JITed method

Figure 9 shows the portion of the running time that is spent for image processing. The graph shows that almost 60% of the whole running time is used for image loading and decoding on average. Therefore, we could easily expect that our proposed idle-time pre-loading/decoding can be highly effective, if there is indeed idle time.

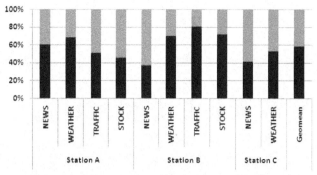

■ Image processing runtime portion ▨ others (java & native code)

Figure 9 image processing runtime portion

We also analyzed what the xlet applications really do when a menu item is chosen. A typical behavior is (1) loading and decoding images, (2) reading texts and building data structures (e.g., tables, charts) with them for displaying information, and (3) painting the data structures and images with colors, fonts, and positions programmed within the xlets. There are little computations involved with these xlets.

4.3. AOTC for the Middleware/System Classes

We experiment with AOTC for the middleware/system classes. We first compile using the original AOT of the phoneMe Advanced, for only those hot methods compiled by JITC (there are 450 methods). Then, we compile them using the enhanced AOT where our optimizations related to inlining, relocation and code patch are enabled. Other system/middleware methods and xlet methods are handled exactly as they are handled in the JITC-only environment.

Figure 10 (a) depicts the running time of JITC-only, AOT-original, and AOT-enhanced. Figure 10 (b) shows their speedups over JITC-only as 100%. The graph shows that AOT-original slightly outperforms JITC-only just for a couple of cases and it is even worse than JITC-only for A-traffic, A-stock, and B-stock. This would be due to the worse code quality than JITC's. Figure 10 (b) shows that on average there is no improvement over JITC-only, indicating that the AOT by itself is useless.

AOT-enhanced shows a running time better than AOT-original and JITC-only in most cases, especially in A-traffic and A-stock where the improvement is pronounced. The average performance improvement over JITC-only is 15%.

4.4. ITC for xlet Methods

The improvement of the running time when employing the ITC for xlet methods is little since xlet methods are called rarely (Figure 7) and are seldom hot (Figure 8). However, if we have a more substantial xlet application in the future, we can expect a tangible performance impact with the ITC.

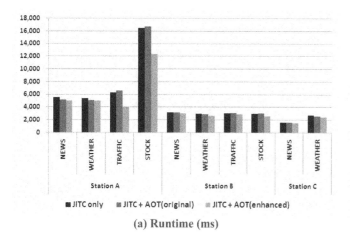

(a) Runtime (ms)

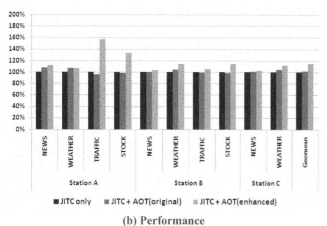

(b) Performance

Figure 10. Performance Impact of AOTC

4.5. ITO for Images and Texts

Figure 11 shows the improvement of the running time when the ITO for images is employed and when there is *enough* idle time. Since the image loading and decoding takes a significant portion of running time as seen in Figure 9, the big improvement in Figure 11 is something expected.

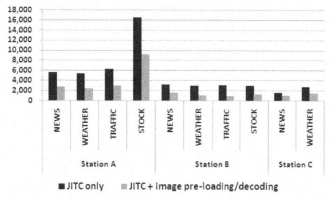

Figure 11. Runtime with image pre-loading/decoding (ms)

Figure 12 shows the improvement of the running time when the ITO for texts is employed. On average, the running time improvement is 7%. Although the runtime overhead for creating a FontMetrics object itself is small, there are 8 to 20 objects created for each xlet application, so the overall overhead is not trivial.

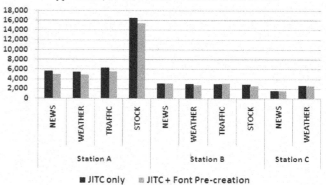

Figure 12. Runtime with text font pre-creation (ms)

4.6 Overall Performance Improvement

Figure 13 shows the overall improvement of the running time of hybrid environment compared to the JITC-only environment, which is an average of 150%.. Most of the improvement comes from the ITO of the images and texts, but the AOTC of system/middleware also improves the performance tangibly (15%). The 17-second response time of Figure 2 (d) (A-stock) is now reduced to 6 seconds.

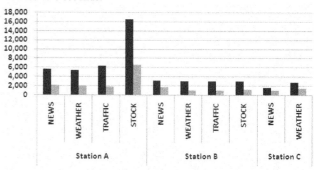

Figure 13. Runtime of xlets (ms)

4.7 Idle-Time and Red-Dot Delay

Although the ITO of the images and texts improves the performance dominantly, it is only when "enough" idle time is passed. Also, the ITO may delay the appearance of the red-dot although it is allocated to a separate thread.

In Figure 14, the black bar shows the time spent for the red-dot to display on the screen after booting the JVM, for the JITC-only environment and for the hybrid environment, respectively. On average, the hybrid environment takes 6% more time, which is relatively low and not very noticeable.

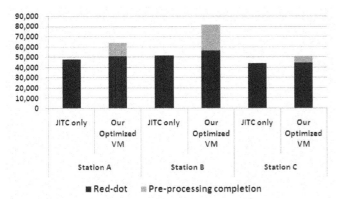

Figure 14. Red-dot delay and pre-processing completion time

Figure 14 also shows the additional time required for the preloading/decoding to complete, after the red-dot is displayed. For example, if the user is idle for at least 13 seconds after the red-dot is displayed for the channel A, we can exploit the best impact of the ITO. Of course, the user can still execute the xlet any time earlier than 13 seconds because the red-dot is already shown, and the xlet will be executed with no problem, yet with the benefit of the ITO obtained until that moment. The required idle time for the station B and C is 25 seconds and 6 seconds, respectively, which depend on the amount of images included.

5. Related Work on Hybrid Compilation

Some related work on hybrid compilation is as follows.

QuickSilver is a quasi-static compiler developed for the IBM's Jalapeno system for servers [19]. It saves all JITC methods in the files at the end of execution, and loads them directly without JITC when they are used in later execution. Therefore, it is similar to the AOT of the phoneME advanced and can work concurrently with the JITC.

Jikes RVM includes two kinds of compilers: a baseline compiler and a tiered set of optimizing compilers [20]. The baseline compiler translates the bytecode into the machine code before execution starts, while the optimizing compilers re-compile hot methods with optimizations at runtime. So, the baseline compiler and the optimizing compiler correspond to an AOTC and a JITC, respectively. However, the machine code generated by the baseline compiler corresponds more to what the interpreter does, so the relationship between the two compilers is more like the JITC-interpreter, not the JITC-AOTC.

The .NET platform of Common Language Runtime VM also employs a JITC, which translates MSIL (MS intermediate language) into machine code [21]. It is also possible to invoke the JITC offline so as to compile ahead-of-time, so it is similar to how QuickSilver works.

6. Summary

DTVs are everywhere now and will completely replace analog TVs within a few years. One of the distinguished features of DTVs is that they broadcast data using Java xlet applications and interact with TV viewers. Although Java has many benefits for a DTV platform, it has performance issues, which delay the response time of the interaction.

This paper proposes a hybrid environment of compilation and optimization for performance enhancement of the DTV Java platform by employing just-in-time, ahead-of-time, and idle-time compilations and optimizations. Our experimental results on a real DTV with real xlet applications indicate that the proposed environment can improve the performance dramatically, by as much as an average of 150%, compared to the JITC-only environment that most commercial DTVs employ currently.

Since we are still in the early stage of data broadcasting, the xlet applications are not yet substantial enough. However, we expect to see more sophisticated, killer xlet applications within a couple of years, especially due to the recently widespread IPTVs [22], and our results will be useful for improving their real-time behavior.

As to the future research, we can optimize the AOTC for the system/middleware classes further beyond the AOT, by performing an offline AOTC at the server with full code optimization enabled and install the machine code at the DTV. Translating the bytecode into C code and compiling it using gcc with would be promising [14, 15, 17], yet the call overhead between AOTC methods and interpreted/JITC methods should be reduced

References

[1] The Digital TV transition, http://www.dtv.gov/

[2] TV without Borders, http://www.interactivetvweb.org/

[3] S. Morris and A. Smith-Chaigneau, Interactive TV Standards: A Guide to Mhp, Ocap, and Javatv. ISBN 0-240-80666-2, Focal Press.

[4] Java TV, http://java.sun.com/products/javatv

[5] DVB-MHP and DVB-GEM, http://www.mhp.org/

[6] Cable Labs, http://www.cablelabs.org

[7] Advanced TV Systems Committee, http://www.atsc.org/

[8] B. Foote, Java in Digital TV update, Nov. 2005

[9] Sun Microsystems, Java ME Mobile Information Device Profile(MIDP), java.sun.com/products/midp

[10] Blu-ray Disc Association, BD-J Baseline Application and Logical Model Definition for BD-ROM, 2005.

[11] Sun Microsystems, Java ME Java Technology for the Wireless Industry (JTWI), JSR 185, java.sun.com/products/jtwi

[12] Sun Microsystems, Java ME Technology - Mobile Service Architecture, java.sun.com/javame/technology/msa

[13] J. Aycock. A Brief History of Just-in-Time, ACM Computing Surveys, 35(2), Jun 2003.

[14] T. A. Proebsting et. al, Toba: Java for Applications A Way Ahead of Time (WAT) Compiler, Proceedings of the Third USENIX Conference on Object-Oriented Technologies and Systems, Portland, Oregon, 1997.

[15] G. Muller et. al, "Harissa: a Flexible and Efficient Java Environment Mixing Bytecode and Compiled Code", Proceedings of the 3rd USENIX Conference on Object-Oriented Technologies and Systems, 1997.

[16] M. Weiss et. al, TurboJ, a Java Bytecode-to-Native Compiler, Proceedings of the ACM SIGPLAN Workshop on Languages, Compilers, and Tools for Embedded Systems (LCTES), 1998.

[17] A. Varma and S. S. Bhattacharyya, Java-through-C Compilation: An Enabling Technology for Java in Embedded Systems, Proceedings of the Design, Automation and Test in Europe Conference (DATE), 2004.

[18] phoneME project, http://phoneme.dev.java.net/

[19] M. Serrano, R. Bordawekar, S. Midkiff, M. Gupta, Quicksilver: A Quasi-Static Compiler for Java, Proceedings of ACM Conference on Object-Oriented Programming Systems, Languages, and Applications, 2000.

[20] B. Alpern et. al, "The Jikes Research Virtual Machine project: Building an open-source research community", IBM Systems Journal, 44(2), 2005.

[21] R. Wilkes, NGen Revs Up Your Performance with Powerful New Features, http://msdn.microsoft.com/msdnmag/issues/05/04/NGen

[22] Interactive TV and Mobile Devices http://www.newmediatrendwatch.com/world-overview/98-interactive-tv-and-mobile-devices

A Self-Adjusting Code Cache Manager to Balance Start-Up Time and Memory Usage

Witawas Srisa-an, Myra B. Cohen, Yu Shang, and Mithuna Soundararaj

Computer Science and Engineering
University of Nebraska-Lincoln
Lincoln, NE 68588-0115
{witty,myra,yshang,msoundar}@cse.unl.edu

Abstract

In virtual machines for embedded devices that use just-in-time compilation, the management of the code cache can significantly impact performance in terms of both memory usage and start-up time. Although improving memory usage has been a common focus for system designers, start-up time is often overlooked. In systems with constrained resources, however, these two performance metrics are often at odds and must be considered together.

In this paper, we present an adaptive self-adjusting code cache manager to improve performance with respect to both start-up time and memory usage. It balances these concerns by detecting changes in method compilation rates, resizing the cache after each pitching event. We conduct experiments to validate our proposed system and quantify the impacts that different code cache management techniques have on memory usage and start-up time through two oracle systems. Our results show that the proposed algorithm yields nearly the same start-up times as a hand-tuned oracle and shorter execution times than those of the SSCLI in eight out of ten applications. It also has lower memory usage over time in all but one application.

Categories and Subject Descriptors D.3.4 [*Programming Languages*]: code generation, compilers, memory management, runtime environments

General Terms Languages, Performance

Keywords code cache, JIT, embedded systems

1. Introduction

Just-In-Time (JIT) compilation has been used to effectively reduce the execution time of Java and .NET programs. It has been adopted in a wide range of language virtual machines from those designed for large servers (HotSpot VM) [29] to those used in small embedded devices (.NET Compact Framework and CLDC HotSpot) [28, 32]. With JIT compilation, methods represented by intermediate languages (e.g. Java bytecode) are compiled on-the-fly prior to execution. Once compiled, the methods are either stored for future reuse in a separate memory area called the code cache (the focus of this work), or intermingled with regular objects in the heap [14, 34, 35]. In desktop and server systems, compiled methods are often kept throughout a program's execution [18]; however, in memory constrained embedded devices such as cellular phones, global positioning units and medical devices, methods are periodically unloaded or *pitched* to reduce memory usage [3, 15, 18]. Once pitched, if methods are used again, they must first be re-compiled.

The pitching policy is driven by the virtual machine's *code cache management scheme* and has a large impact on system performance [33, 34, 35]. If the code cache is too small when a program starts, pitching and recompilation will occur frequently. This can cause the program to load very slowly. However, if the code cache is allowed to grow too large, start-up time is reduced, but memory is wasted and is unavailable for other applications to use. In resource constrained devices, these two goals must be balanced.

Given the fact that both start-up time and memory usage are important for embedded devices, code cache management policies should balance these concerns. One common approach to managing the code cache (or simply cache) is to "flush when full" [7, 8, 25]. In this approach, all unused methods in the cache are pitched each time the cache is full. To reduce the pitching overhead, variations of this approach also enlarge the code cache periodically. For example, the .NET Compact Framework increases the size of the code cache whenever pitching events occur too frequently [27]. In a modified version of Jikes RVM [33, 35], the initial cache size is set to 64KB, and it is enlarged by 32KB after every 10 pitching events. While these two management schemes attempt to address performance issues due to pitching, there are still three limitations that arise:

- *Untimely code cache enlargement.* In each of these schemes, the cache size is enlarged only after several pitching events have occurred, thus a large amount of effort may be spent on recompiling methods that have been unloaded. The implication is that start-up times may be slow.
- *Inefficient cache usage.* These approaches make pitching decisions based on the cache size. Both approaches start off with a small cache size, then gradually increase it, but effectively never decrease it. If the memory demand is light and the cache size is too large, memory is wasted since unused methods continue to occupy space. This may waste memory.
- *Management schemes tuned for average case performance.* Program initialization and start-up is a resource intensive period where many new methods are loaded and used for a short period of time [1, 33, 34, 35]. Unloading events during this time incurs additional compilation overhead and slows down the loading phase of a program. Although initialization occurs only once during the program's execution, it is not considered separately in these approaches, but instead only average case performance is considered. Start-up times may suffer.

In this paper, we present an adaptive, self-adjusting, code cache management scheme that considers both start-up time and memory usage. Our algorithm is driven by the rate of compilation over time rather than by the current size of the cache. This is different from most existing techniques that are based on space usage. In the proposed scheme, when the compilation demand is heavy, more cache memory is acquired without invoking any pitching event. This is to allow applications to start as quickly as possible. Once the compilation demand begins to decline, the methods are pitched to conserve memory, reducing the cache usage.

We have implemented our management scheme in the Shared Source Common Language Infrastructure (SSCLI), a research virtual machine from Microsoft [17] and conducted experiments to validate its effectiveness by comparing the results with two existing techniques and two oracles; one designed to yield optimal start-up times and one designed to yield optimal memory footprints. Our results suggest that our algorithm has lower start-up times and more efficient memory usage, resulting in shorter execution times in eight out of ten applications.

The remainder of this paper is organized as follows. Section 2 provides background information on relevant pitching mechanisms. Section 3 details the proposed algorithm. Section 4 describes the experimental environment. Section 5 compares the performance of our scheme with the existing techniques and the oracles. Section 6 discusses related work, and Section 7 concludes this paper.

2. Code Cache Management Policies

The focus of our work is comparing the performance of two "flush when full" approaches with that of our proposed dynamic policy, which can be classified as a variety of "preemptive flush" [2, 25]. Each of the two "flush when full" approaches stores compiled methods in a code cache. When the space in the code cache runs out, the methods that are not currently in used are pitched [3, 7, 8, 27]. These two approaches differ in the way that they increase the cache size to reduce pitching overhead. One approach enlarges the code cache when the pitching overhead becomes too high while the other enlarges the code cache at a fixed interval. Next, we describe the cache enlargement policies of these two approaches.

2.1 Overhead-Based Approach

This approach, used in the SSCLI, controls pitching overhead by periodically increasing the code cache size. It does so by keeping track of pitching overhead (amount of time spent on pitching). The enlargement mechanism compares this pitching overhead with a predefined threshold, and if the overhead is larger than the threshold, the manager attempts to increase the code cache size instead of invoking pitching [27].

There are two variables used in the code pitching mechanism of the SSCLI: the *reserve cache size* and the *maximum cache size*. At the start of a program, the maximum cache size is set to be very large (e.g., 2GB) to allow the most flexible growth. However, the cache may never be allowed to reach this value. The reserve cache size is the actual size the program is allowed to use. This value is re-evaluated each time the code cache grows to the reserve size. At this point, the *code cache manager* decides between increasing the reserve cache size or pitching, based on the existing pitch overhead.

Initially, the execution engine initializes the code cache by allocating small increments of memory. The default value in the SSCLI is 8KB. As program execution continues, additional heap space is allocated to the code cache in increments as is needed to store the compiled methods. The total size of the allocated heap space is called the *committed code cache size*. As the committed code cache size approaches the reserve code cache size, the allocator will decide whether to allocate more heap space beyond the current reserve cache size or pitch all compiled methods not in use. For ex-

ample, if the reserve is set to 256KB, the initial cache is 8KB and the increment used is 8KB, after 31 cache enlargements, the reserve size will be reached and the allocator must make a decision. If the reserve size is less than the maximum code cache size, and the existing pitch overhead is over the acceptable maximum (e.g., 5 ms), the manager will attempt to increase the code cache size.

We utilize these two variables, *maximum cache size* and *reserve size* to implement the proposed self-adjusting code cache management schemes (see the next section). Specifically, we set the reserve and maximum code cache sizes of the SSCLI according to the management scheme studied to force pitching on demand.

2.2 Fixed-Interval Approach

Zhang and Krintz introduced a fixed-interval approach in their study of various code-cache management schemes in Jikes RVM. This approach enlarges the cache size after a fixed interval [33]. In this scheme, the initial reserve cache size is set to 64KB. Afterward, the reserve is is enlarged by 32KB after every 10 pitching events.

3. Dynamic Self-Adjusting Code Cache Management

Instead of pitching when the cache is full, our proposed policy makes pitching decisions based on changes in the number of method compilations over time. Prior studies have shown that a large number of methods are created during application initialization [33, 34]. (We refer to this phase of execution as the *compile heavy zone*.) However, most of these methods are not used after this phase has passed, and only a small number of new methods are compiled afterward [33, 34, 35]. (We call the second phase the *compile light zone*.) By pitching compiled methods that are no longer in use at the end of the compile heavy zone, our proposed technique can reclaim a large portion of the code cache in a timely fashion. An alternative to this pitching location is to defer pitching until the beginning of the next compile heavy zone, an approach similar to the one introduced by Bala *et al.*[2]. However, this approach can waste memory by deferring the reclamation of unused methods. It also interferes with the application's execution when it is entering the next compile heavy zone.

Zhang and Krintz [33], noted that identifying the precise location to pitch and shrink the cache is not trivial and was left as an unsolved challenge. One contribution of our work is the introduction of an algorithm that dynamically detects this pitching location. We describe this next.

3.1 Resizing the Code Cache

As previously stated, both the SSCLI approach and Zhang's approach use a space-based criteria for pitching. They only consider whether or not to pitch when the cache size has been reached. The criteria used to determine whether or not to enlarge the cache is based on the pitch overhead in the SSCLI and a fixed interval in Zhang's.

On the other hand, our algorithm sets the cache size based on compilation demands. That is, the current cache size is approximately the same as the current cache usage. Furthermore, it does not use size to determine when to pitch. Instead it detects changes in the compilation rate and uses that as a pitch trigger. At the start of the program we set the cache size to be as small as possible. The cache usage increases as compiled methods are stored. When the compilation demand is high, we allow the code cache to grow unrestrained up to a predetermined maximum cache size (2MB in our experiments).

When a slow-down in the compilation rate is detected, pitching will occur and the code cache usage will be reduced. Table 1 compares the pitching and cache enlargement criteria for all of

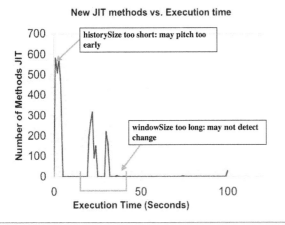

Figure 1. Window and history size considerations.

the cache management schemes discussed so far. Our technique is labeled "dynamic". We describe the last two categories (oracles) in our experimental section.

3.2 Dynamic Pitching Algorithm

To capture the changes in compilation information, we define s_{JIT} as:

$$s_{JIT} = \frac{\Delta NumMethodsCompiled}{\Delta t}$$

s_{JIT} is the slope of the line (the total method compilations or y axis over time, the x axis) in Figure 1 which graphs the number of methods compiled against execution time. Note that $\Delta NumMethodsCompiled$ can be negative if the number of methods compiled in an interval is less than the number of methods compiled in the previous interval.

Ideally, we want to capture the peaks of this graph and pitch just as the slope becomes negative. In order to make this more robust, we introduce a measurement interval and history window to supplement s_{JIT} in determining the "ideal" pitching location.

The measurement interval, (*windowSize*), defines the number of method invocations between two s_{JIT} calculations. Note that we define invocations as calls to both the compiled methods in the cache and to those that still need to be compiled. For example, if the measurement interval is set at twenty, there must be twenty method invocations between each calculation of s_{JIT}. Setting a small interval can result in a high calculation overhead, whereas setting a large interval can result in the system failing to detect changes in the compilation phase. The second issue is illustrated in Figure 1. In this situation, the window completely misses two peaks; therefore pitching may not occur, and a large amount of cache memory is potentially wasted.

The history window, (*historySize*), is used to determine the length of the list used to store s_{JIT}. This list is used to establish a compilation trend (a single negative change in the slope may not indicate an actual downturn). It defines the amount of data that must be analyzed (at a minimum) to determine if pitching should occur. If the history window size is set too small, the system may experience many false positives. That is the system may consider pitching too soon. On the other hand, if the history window size is set too large, the system may never pitch as there is no visible trend that the s_{JIT} rate has slowed down. The latter situation is similar to having too large of a window. The former is illustrated in the left part of Figure 1. In this situation, there is a small downward trend that will force pitching too soon if the history size is set too small.

Algorithm 1 Dynamic Self-Adjusting Algorithm

Input: *historySize*, *windowSize*, *error*

```
slopeDown=0
global  currentHistorySize= 0
CreateEmptyHistoryList()
invokedMethods=0
while (not ApplicationFinished){
    time= CurrentTime()
    if(JitMethodAllocation()|| ReJitMethodAllocation()) {
        invokedMethods++
        if(invokedMethods == windowSize){
            newSlope=CalculateSJIT(time)
            slopeDown=UpdateHistoryList(newSlope,slopeDown)
            if (currentHistorySize ≥ historySize) {
                if (slopeDown ≥ (historySize - error)) {
                    PitchAllMethods()
                    EmptyCodeCache()
                    ClearHistoryList()
                    invokedMethods=0
                    time=CurrentTime()
                    currentHistorySize=0
                }
            }
        }
    }
}
```

The *windowSize* and *historySize* work closely together to determine the frequency of the measurement and responsiveness of the trend detection. As an example, if the *windowSize* is set at 20 and the *historySize* is set at 10, we measure every 20 method calls and store the resulting s_{JIT}. After 10 measurements are taken (200 calls), the history list is large enough and a determination of the trend can begin. After the next measurement of s_{JIT} (220 calls), the content of the history list is examined, and a decision whether or not to pitch is made. The history list is cleared after each pitch, and this process begins again.

Our algorithm is shown as Algorithm 1. In the algorithm, each time the *windowSize* is reached, the history list is updated. The criteria for pitching is a decreasing trend in the number of newly compiled methods. When a trend of negative s_{JIT} values is seen (i.e we have at least a *historySize* of consecutive negative slopes) a downward trend is assumed and pitching occurs. The history size is allowed to be larger or smaller than the window size, but the trend is only examined when the history list is full before the s_{JIT} (i.e if the history size is 10 the trend is first examined after the 11th s_{JIT}). Provision is made to accommodate occasional deviations from the normal trend. We control this with an *error* parameter initially set to be 10% of the size of the history window.

Algorithm 2 shows the method used for updating the history list. For efficiency a running trend (*countSlopeDown*) can be maintained with only new slopes added. When the history list is full, the first slope in the list is dropped and the new slope is added onto the end. If the slope to be dropped is a negative slope then the trend is adjusted by removing its count from *countslopeDown*. When there is a consistent decrease in the number of newly compiled methods, which is indicated by *countSlopeDown* reaching the *historySize*, pitching occurs and the history list is cleared.

4. Experiments

The objective of our experiments is to determine the feasibility of our proposed algorithm and to evaluate to what extent start-up time

	Pitching Criteria	Cache Enlargement Criteria	Initial Cache Size	Increment Size	Maximum Cache Size
SSCLI [27]	cache size reached	pitch overhead too high	64KB	64KB	2MB
Zhang [33]	cache size reached	fixed intervals	64KB	32KB	2MB
Dynamic	compilation rate	demand-based	8KB	in an 8KB block as methods are stored	2MB
$Oracle_{start}$	start-up complete	none	2MB	none	2MB
$Oracle_{fp}$	cache size reached	none	application dependent (16KB to 32KB)	none	same as initial size (16KB to 32KB)

Table 1. Comparison of the different management techniques.

Algorithm 2 UpdateHistoryList()

Input: *newSlope*, *countSlopeDown*
Output: *countSlopeDown*

if *newSlope* $\leq$ 0 {
    countSlopeDown ++
}
if (*currentHistorySize* < *historySize*) {
    addSlopeToHistoryList(*newSlope*)
}
else {
    dropFirstSlope()
    addSlopeToHistoryList(newSlope)
}
currentHistorySize ++
return *countSlopeDown*

---

and memory usage are affected by different code cache management policies. Furthermore, we want to compare the performance of the proposed dynamic self-adjusting mechanism with two existing "flush when full" mechanisms. In this section, we present the virtual machine platform and benchmark applications used for our experiments; we then describe the code cache management systems and their setting. We then define and describe a set of performance metrics used in our investigation. We finish this section with the threats to experimental validity.

4.1 Virtual Machine Platform

We implemented our dynamic policy and other relevant policies on the Microsoft Shared Source Common Language Infrastructure (SSCLI) version 1.2 [17]. The SSCLI is a public implementation of the ECMA-335 standard [17] released under Microsoft's shared source license. The dynamic compilation system of the SSCLI is very similar to that used by the .NET Compact Framework, a commercial virtual machine designed for memory constrained devices. In both systems, a simple JIT compiler, instead of an optimizing compiler [6, 16], is used to ensure quick code generation [21]. The code cache management is a "flush when full" approach that also incorporates a cache enlargement mechanism based on pitching overhead. With this mechanism, the pitching effort is reduced while allowing the code cache to grow to meet the compilation demand of applications.

In terms of configuration, we set the initial cache size of the SSCLI to 64KB. The enlargement is done in a 64KB increment until the maximum cache size of 2MB is reached. We select 64KB as the increment size based on the result of our preliminary investigation indicating that 64KB is neither too coarse-grain nor fine-grain for the set of applications that we use for our experiment. We set the maximum cache size to 2MB to be representative of available memory in small embedded devices. We use 5 milliseconds, which is the SSCLI default setting, as the pitching overhead threshold.

In addition, we also extend the SSCLI to support the fixed-interval policy introduced by Zhang and Krintz [33, 35]. In this policy, we also set the initial cache size to 64KB and the increment size to 32KB, which is the same size as appeared in their paper [33]. The maximum cache size is set to 2MB.

For the dynamic approach, the code cache is initially set to 8KB. (This is the smallest cache size that still allows the SSCLI to start.) However, we set the maximum cache size to be the same as the other approaches, which is 2MB. The cache usage increases by an 8KB increment, which is the smallest unit that the SSCLI can use to commit memory. The code cache usage is controlled by pitching events when compile light zones are detected.

4.2 Applications

A standardized set of benchmark applications for the .NET Compact Framework does not exist, therefore we used a combination of programs that we have implemented in addition to some publicly available from other sources. The first three applications described below (Calendar.NET, P2P.NET, and Talk.NET) were written by us. The other five were obtained from outside sources [30, 36]. The information about each benchmark is given in Table 2.

4.3 Metrics

We define a set of metrics next that will help us to determine if we have achieved a balance between start-up time and memory usage.

Start-Up Time. A start-up time is defined as the time taken by an application to complete its initialization phase. We identify the initialization phase for each program by running it with an unconstrained heap size (i.e., no pitching occurs) and analyzing its runtime trace to detect *the initial burst of method compilations*. In order to calculate a start-up time, we *manually identify* the last method from each application that is compiled just before this phase ends. *To determine the start-up times of different code-cache management policies, we measured the time a program spends in execution prior to compiling this identified method.* That is, the policy that requires the shortest time to reach the execution location that compiles this method has the shortest start-up time.

Memory Footprint. The memory footprint of an application is the maximum memory used at any point in the program's execution. This has traditionally been used to express the maximum memory usage of an application. It also serves as a guideline for system designers to determine the amount of memory needed in a computing device. To calculate the memory footprint of an application, we analyze the trace file to find the overall maximum heap size at any point in time.

Memory Usage. The memory footprint of an application can be controlled by the management policies. For example, a policy that favors frequent pitching invocations would allow the system to operate with a modest code cache; however, the execution time of a program may be much longer. When the program takes longer to finish, it also spends more time using the memory. Therefore, the

Application	Description	LOC	Invoked Methods	Method Size		
				Maximum	Minimum	Average
P2P.NET	A non-centralized peer-to-peer file sharing application. A peer node can simultaneously function as a server and a client. (10 nodes, download 500 files/node)	876	1283	2900	52	254
Talk.NET	An instant messenger server applications. (2 clients, 500 messages/client)	429	1711	7844	52	324
Cal.NET (cli)	A calendar client program (10 messages/client).	1137	2639	7844	52	368
Cal.NET (ser)	A calendar server program (10 clients, 10 messages/client).	1137	3469	28516	52	397
LCSC	Front end of a C# compiler (using second input) [36].	12500	1322	27024	52	1199
SAT	A clause-based satisfiability solver (using second input) [36].	10900	1139	6772	52	368
JGFFFT	A Fast Fourier Transformation program from JavaGrande benchmark [30].	572	320	3496	52	276
JGFRayTracer	A ray-tracer program from JavaGrande benchmark [30].	1001	836	3701	52	295
AHCbench	A compression and decompression program using Adaptive Huffman Compression [36].	1267	723	6306	52	340
sciMark	A c# numerical benchmark measuring performance of various computation kernels [30].	2112	873	1796	52	226

Table 2. Characteristics of our benchmarks.

total memory used with a small footprint is often larger than that used when a large amount of memory is used during a single point in time. Thus, we think that it is important for the time component be factored into the memory calculation.

To take time into account we define a new metric, *memory usage* (or mem_{usage}) as the amount of actual memory used throughout a program's execution. In effect, it is the area under the graph represented as the *cache usage function*, $f(x)$. Obviously, $f(x)$ will vary depending on the code cache requirement of each application. The memory usage can be mathematically described as:

$$mem_{usage} = \int_0^t f(x)dx, \text{ where t is the execution time.}$$

In practice, we calculated mem_{usage} by interpolating time information obtained from an actual run into the cache usage information obtained from an instrumented run. It is reported in $megabytes \times seconds$.

4.4 Benchmarking with Two Oracle Systems

We also compared the results of our approach with two oracle systems implemented in the SSCLI to minimize start-up and memory footprint, respectively. We describe these two oracles in turn.

$Oracle_{start}$ is designed to represent a situation where the minimal start-up time can be achieved. We use historical runs of the program to come up with an "ideal" scenario for minimizing start-up time. We performed an analysis of the runtime trace of each application to identify the number of compile methods required to surpass the initial compile heavy phase. The information is then used by the SSCLI to precisely pitch the code cache at the end of the compile-heavy zone.

$Oracle_{fp}$ is designed to minimize the memory footprint. We again analyzed the runtime trace of each application. We identified the minimum size of the code cache that each application needs to run while still allowing it to successfully complete. This information is used to set the code cache size of the SSCLI. In this system we turn off the ability to enlarge the code cache. This oracle is created specifically for each application in our benchmark suite. Refer to Table 1 (appear in Section 3) for similarities and differences among these policies.

4.5 Tuning the Dynamic Self-Adjusting Mechanism

We conducted a set of experiments to determine "reasonable" (or baseline) values of *windowSize* and *historySize*. These are values that allow each application to invoke the first pitching event closest to that of the $Oracle_{start}$ (based on code cache size). Moreover, these values must be able to maintain reasonable performance for

the remainder of the program execution. Our experiments consisted of using the following set of values for *windowSize* and *historyWindow*: 5, 10, 20, 30, 40, 50, 100

In every application, we tried the combination 5/5 (5 for *windowSize* and 5 for *historySize*). We found this to be very sensitive to slight changes in s_{JIT}. Thus, the system pitched the code cache excessively. On the other hand, when we chose the 100/100 configuration, the system became non-responsive to changes; i.e., pitching was never invoked.

We then moved the windows in either direction to find a spot where all applications can accurately detect start-up phases. We found that the configuration that performs best in five out of ten applications is 20/20. The five exceptions were talk.NET, which performs best with 40/10 configuration; LCSC, which performs best with the 20/30 configuration; JGFFFT, which performs best with the 30/10 configuration; and JGFRayTracer and sciMark, which perform best with the 20/10 configuration. We also discovered that the five exceptions also perform well with 20/20 configuration. Given these results we used 20/20 as the baseline configuration for all applications.

4.6 Experimental Setup

We next describe the machine platform and our methodology.

Hardware Systems. Several of our benchmarks are client/server in nature (Talk.NET, P2P.NET, and Calendar.NET), therefore we initially used two computer systems to conduct our experiments: a desktop running Windows XP Professional with an AMD Athlon XP 2200 processor and 1 GB of memory and a laptop running Windows XP Professional with an Intel Pentium M 1.5 GHz processor and 1GB of memory. However, we discovered that network delays can actually result in variations in the number of invoked methods. For example, network delays can cause invocations of additional methods that deal with timeout warnings and exceptions. Such inconsistencies can result in incorrectly determining the ideal pitching location and comparing start-up time for each application. As a result, we used a single machine (the above laptop) to run the client program on one VM and the server program on another VM. In doing so, we can repeatedly reproduce the number of method invocations in all experiments. The laptop is also used to run non-networked benchmarks.

Methodology. We created several trace analysis programs written in C, PERL, and Java. For evaluation, we ran each program *five* consecutive times using five instances of VM for each code-cache management scheme. We report the average performance. Time is reported in seconds as measured during runs or derived from system traces.

4.7 Threats to Validity

We have identified several threats to validity for our experiments and have tried to control and minimize their effect. First, we have used only ten benchmark programs. These may not be representative of embedded devices, but we have used a variety of programs with different goals including interactive, non-interactive, client, and server applications. Second, in running all experiments we used the same machines, under the same configurations. We have attempted to remove as much external noise as possible (such as other running programs), but it is still possible that there were slight variations in the operating system workloads while our experiments were running.

Finally, we used the number of compiled methods to indicate the ideal pitching location for each application. We then use this location to determine the start-up time. So any changes in method compilation sequences due to exceptions and warnings can affect the start-up time. In fact, we discovered that such exceptions and warning can occur due to network delays when client and server applications are running on two different machines connected by networks. By running both client and server applications in the same machine, we improve the accuracy of our methodology to measure start-up times.

5. Results

In this section, we first evaluate the accuracy of the proposed technique in identifying a pitching location that minimizes the start-up time of each application. Then, we compare the start-up time, memory footprint, and memory usage of the proposed implementation to the two oracle systems as well as to the two existing approaches.

5.1 Pitching Accuracy

In order to determine how well the dynamic algorithm works, we compare the locations of the first pitching event of the dynamic approach with the pitching locations used to configure $Oracle_{start}$. We describe these locations using the cache size (in KB) where the first pitching event in each application occurs. We show the difference in location represented as a percentage. If the value is positive the pitching location is after that of the oracle. The result of our comparison is reported in Table 3.

Application	Pitching Location (KB)		Difference (%)
	$Oracle_{start}$	Dynamic	
P2P.NET	372.55	393.13	+5.52
Talk.NET	540.12	547.57	+1.38
Cal.NET (cli)	943.71	1047.04	+10.95
Cal.NET (ser)	640.02	696.68	+8.85
LCSC	1401.36	1288.92	-8.02
SAT	no pitching	410.79	N/A
JGFFFT	256.44	296.15	+15.49
JGFRayTracer	237.24	255.09	+7.52
AHCbench	1063.48	1262.56	+18.72
sciMark	783.45	802.50	+2.43

Table 3. Accuracy in selecting pitching locations.

In five out of ten applications (P2P.NET, Talk.NET, Cal.NET [ser], JGFRaytracer, and sciMark), our mechanisms can pitch with an accuracy of within 10% after of the ideal location. In Cal.NET (client), the pitching occurs 11% after the ideal location. For LCSC, our mechanism pitches before the ideal location is reached. For the JGFFFT and AHCbench, our system is less accurate. In SAT, the

dynamic system invokes one pitching event toward the end of the execution while $Oracle_{start}$ invokes no pitching.

Analysis: In LCSC, there is a moderate slow down in s_{JIT} just prior to the actual ideal pitching location. By setting the window sizes to 20/20, our algorithm mistakenly takes the earlier decline in s_{JIT} as the ideal pitching location. This is not surprising since LCSC is an application that performs best when the configuration is 20/30 and not 20/20. Thus, the premature pitching is caused by the *historySize* being too small. This example suggests that the next logical improvement to our proposed system is to dynamically tune *windowSize* and *historySize*. We leave this implementation for future work.

SAT is the smallest program and takes the least amount of time to execute. In this program, the methods are compiled steadily from start to finish (i.e. the entire program may be viewed as one long compile heavy zone). Since the maximum cache requirement is reached near the end of execution, $Oracle_{start}$ does not invoke pitching. The proposed scheme detects the slow down at the end and invokes one pitching event prior to the end of execution.

For JGFFFT, the configuration that can accurately detect the end of the start-up phase is 30/10. However, our baseline value is 20/20, meaning that the adopted *windowSize* is smaller than the ideal value. For AHCbench, we noticed that right after the identified start-up phase, there is another surge of method compilation activities. Because the period between the end of the start-up phase and the surge is very small, our approach pitches right after the surge instead of at the end of the start-up phase, resulting in a significant pitching lag (18%).

5.2 Start-Up Time

In this study, we compare the start-up time of the dynamic approach with $Oracle_{start}$. Note that in the dynamic approach, we measure the time from the beginning of execution to the time that the first pitching event occurs as the start-up time of each program. We use this approach for two reasons. First, the dynamic approach should only pitch after the end of the start-up phase is reached. As shown in Table 3, this is true in eight out of ten applications. Thus, the reported start-up time for the dynamic approach in each of these eight applications accounts for the time to reach the ideal pitching location, which is very similar to that of $Oracle_{start}$ and the pitching delay after the ideal location is reached. In LCSC where pitching is premature, we also report the overhead to reach the ideal pitching location. Second, we want to also show when the cache usage is reduced.

Figure 2, shows the normalized start-up times (where 100% represents the longest start-up time) and the longest start-up time (appears on top of the tallest bar) for each application. The dynamic approach and $Oracle_{start}$ are the two leftmost bars. In terms of start-up time, applications using the proposed dynamic scheme often take slightly longer to start than $Oracle_{start}$. This is due to the execution overhead to enforce the proposed policy. In terms of pitching accuracy, our technique mostly invokes pitching a short time after the ideal pitching location for each application is reached; thus, the pitching delay also introduces another time penalty that makes the start-up times of the dynamic approach longer than those of $Oracle_{start}$.

The only exception is LCSC, which appears to take less time than $Oracle_{start}$ to start. This is because our approach prematurely makes the first pitch before the ideal pitching location. However, if we measure the time to reach the ideal pitching location, LCSC takes 20.8% longer to finish the start-up phase than $Oracle_{start}$. This is due to the additional recompilation that must be done due to premature pitching.

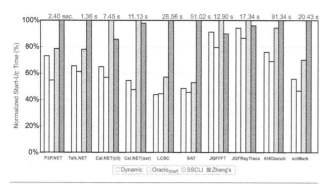

Figure 2. Comparing the normalized start-up time.

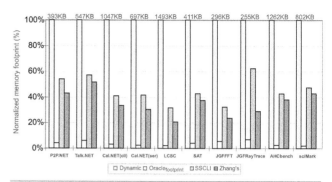

Figure 3. Comparing the memory footprint.

The proposed algorithm consistently yields shorter start-up times than the SSCLI. The proposed scheme yields speed-ups of 1.83 and 1.54 over the start-up times of the SSCLI in Calendar.NET (server) and Calendar.NET (client), respectively. Overall, the speed-ups over the SSCLI in start-up times range from 1.06 to 1.83. Zhang's approach yields the slowest start-up times in most applications.

Analysis: Because $Oracle_{start}$ and the proposed dynamic approach are designed to invoke no pitching during the initialization period, they yield the fastest start-up times. However, to understand why other techniques yield longer start-up times, we investigate the amount of pitching effort during the initialization period (see Table 4). The SSCLI invokes a significant number of pitching events during the start-up period; as a result, the SSCLI takes longer to start than the dynamic approach. Zhang's and $Oracle_{fp}$ also invoke pitching frequently during the start-up period.

Application	(# of pitching events)		
	$Oracle_{fp}$	SSCLI	Zhang's
P2P.NET	91	3	8
Talk.NET	79	7	13
Calendar.NET (cli)	157	7	42
Calendar.NET (ser)	45	4	5
LCSC	336	10	23
SAT	67	3	4
JGFFFT	51	9	17
JGFRayTracer	70	3	5
AHCbench	168	48	69
sciMark	172	4	7

Table 4. Comparing pitching events during the start-up period. The dynamic approach and $Oracle_{start}$ are not included since neither pitches during start-up.

5.3 Memory Footprint

We examine the memory footprint of our proposed scheme with the two existing techniques and $Oracle_{fp}$. The normalized and highest memory footprints are depicted in Figure 3. It is worth noting that in $Oracle_{fp}$, some applications can execute to completion with only 16KB of memory, while others require at least 32KB. However, the overall execution times using such small cache sizes can be up to 13 times slower than those of the best performing approaches.

Furthermore, the results show that our proposed scheme has the highest memory footprint. This is due to the aggressive cache size enlargement policy employed during the start-up periods. In all applications, the proposed scheme has twice to three times

larger memory footprints than that of the SSCLI. On the other hand, Zhang's approach yields the lowest footprint in all application when $Oracle_{fp}$ is not considered. The dynamic approach consistently requires anywhere from 48% to 80% more memory than Zhang's approach.

Analysis: Based on the above observation, we conclude that memory footprint alone is not sufficient to indicate memory consumption by a program. This is because in our technique, the maximum footprint is reached during the start-up period, which occurs within the first few percentage of execution in many applications. After this point is reached, our approach pitches the cache, reducing its usage once again. In each of these applications, the maximum cache usage after the start-up period ranges from 20% (JGFFFT) to 88% (LCSC) of the footprint for the remainder of execution. Note that LCSC has a large post start-up cache usage due to premature pitching in the proposed approach.

5.4 Memory Usage

As stated earlier, the memory footprint provides information about the maximum amount of memory needed by a program. However, the time spent using the entire memory footprint size can be short or long depending on the behaviors of applications. For example, the server version of Cal.NET needs nearly 700KB of code cache at one particular point in execution (around 14% completion of execution). Once this point is passed, it only needs at most 252KB for the remaining 86% of execution. In this example, using the footprint as the metric to indicate memory usage would not be representative of the actual memory usage in the program. On the other hand, applications such as AHCbench and P2P.NET usually need the cache size to be close to or at the memory footprint sizes throughout execution. In these scenarios, footprint is a good representation of memory usage throughout execution.

Instead we examine mem_{usage} as defined earlier. Figure 4 depicts the normalized mem_{usage} and the mem_{usage} of $Oracle_{fp}$ in MB x seconds. The proposed scheme has the lowest mem_{usage} in all applications except Cal.NET (client). In Cal.NET, the SSCLI has the lowest mem_{usage}, which is slightly smaller than that of the proposed dynamic approach.

Analysis: Since memory usage is calculated based on two components, cache usage and time, these factors can affect it in two ways. The first way is to provide a larger cache size throughout the execution. Both the SSCLI and Zhang's approach fit into this category since they only pitch when they reach the cache reserve (which never decreases). A larger allowable cache can reduce the overall execution time as fewer pitching events occur. Thus, it is possible for an application that is given a large code cache to have a smaller mem_{usage} because it can finish its execution more quickly. The

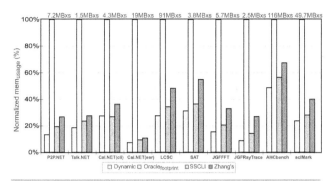

Figure 4. Comparing the memory usage.

Application	Execution time (seconds)				$\frac{SSCLI}{Dynamic}$
	Dynamic	$Oracle_{fp}$	SSCLI	Zhang's	
P2P.NET	89.15	452.43	119.33	**84.75**	1.34
Talk.NET	**12.46**	47.50	13.50	37.47	1.08
Cal.NET (cli)	**15.62**	135.60	17.60	41.36	1.13
Cal.NET (ser)	**40.36**	1208.33	43.21	132.61	1.07
LCSC	**178.43**	2845.36	184.02	235.76	1.03
SAT	**68.75**	237.45	74.34	81.68	1.08
JGFFFT	121.07	353.56	**119.35**	124.06	0.99
JGFRayTracer	35.06	157.25	36.37	**33.72**	1.04
AHCbench	**471.58**	3615.51	477.36	528.71	1.01
sciMark	**54.76**	3104.21	126.44	133.56	2.31

Table 5. Comparing execution time.

second way is to keep the cache size small and prolong the execution time. $Oracle_{fp}$ falls in to this category. Table 5 shows execution times for each method. $Oracle_{fp}$ always has the longest running times due to large numbers of pitching activities.

The proposed scheme lies somewhere between the two approaches. It can enlarge the cache quickly if the memory demand is high or keep the cache usage small if the memory demand is low. As indicated in Table 5, our approach yields the shortest overall execution times in seven out of ten benchmarks and the second shortest execution times in the remaining benchmarks.

Figure 5 shows that our technique gives larger code cache to each program during the start-up period, resulting in shorter start-up time. However, we also see that our approach often set the code cache size to be larger than those of the SSCLI or Zhang's. So it is not surprising that our technique yields the shortest execution time in seven our to ten applications. Our technique also yields lower memory usage in nine out of ten applications.

However, we also see that in applications such as Calendar.NET (client) and LCSC, the proposed technique can use significantly more cache space while yielding only modest improvement in execution time. In both of these applications, we see repetitive use of methods in phases throughout execution. In our technique, methods are discarded at the end of a phase but only to be recompiled in the next phase. Such a recompilation effort makes our proposed scheme less effective, but it still outperforms the other two approaches in terms of execution time and memory usage. This is because our scheme provides large enough space to accommodate each phase, while other techniques have to pitch within a phase. In sciMark, our technique incurs no recompilation efforts at all in while the other two approaches have to spend efforts recompiling methods. As a result, our technique can reduce execution time significantly.

6. Related Work

One of the first systems to use the "flush when full" [25] approach to manage code cache or translation cache is *Shade* — an instruction set simulator for execution profiling [7, 8]. In this system, the *translation cache* (*TC*) is a separate memory area used to store translations. When the TC is full, the system flushes all the entries in the TC. The authors claim that flushing is more advantageous than other approaches because method chaining makes selective freeing tedious. In this approach, the TC is set to a large size in order to minimize the number of flushing attempts [7].

In addition to introducing a scheme used in this paper, Zhang and Krintz [33, 34, 35] also investigate the performance of code unloading mechanisms in a virtual machine [4, 14] that stores both compiled methods and regular objects in the same heap space. Specifically, they identify "what" methods to unload and "when" to unload them. They utilize off-line and on-line profiling techniques to improve the performance. They report a code size reduction of up to 61%. Their approach triggers pitching using fixed intervals; i.e. they unload every 10 garbage collection cycles or unloading every 10 seconds.

Phase is often defined as a period of work (e.g. computation, allocation). In *phase aware* computing, phase information is used to assist with resource reclamation or program optimization. In HP Dynamo [2], a run-time dynamic optimization system, the stale transactions are flushed by detecting phase changes in a program's behavior. The optimized traces of programs are stored in a fragment cache, and most instructions are fetched from this cache during the steady state. A phase change is correlated with a sudden increase in fragment invocations, while flushing of stale fragments is triggered to accommodate new fragments. The effects of phase behavior in feedback-directed dynamic optimization systems have been observed to be important in [26].

Our proposed algorithm can be classified as an on-line dynamic feedback-directed phase detection algorithm [9, 10, 12, 13, 19, 20, 22, 23, 24]. It monitors the method compilation phases and invokes pitching at the end of a phase, instead of pitching at the beginning of the next phase [2]. Instead of profiling an entire program, our scheme uses low overhead profiling to gather the necessary information [11, 31] that enables dynamic phase detection.

Work by Bruening and Amarasinghe [5] adaptively adjusts code cache size to reflect the current working set size of an application. Their main insight, which is similar to ours, is that initialization code sequences should be evicted since they are only used during initialization. They use a FIFO policy to evict old code fragments when the cache is full. Their system records the number of newly generated fragments that have been previously evicted. If this number is large, the system doubles the cache size.

7. Conclusion

We presented and validated a self-adjusting, adaptive code-cache management algorithm that balances start-up time and memory usage in memory constrained embedded devices. The algorithm locates the region in an application where it switches from a compile-heavy to a compile-light zone and automatically adjusts the code-cache size to improve memory usage. It is unique in that (1) allows for aggressive early code-cache enlargement to improve start-up times; (2) it not only enlarges, but also effectively "reduces" the code-cache size when memory is no longer needed; and (3) it considers program start-up independently from the rest of the program.

Our algorithm provides start-up times close to that of the start-up oracle, and the reduction in start-up time when compared to that of the SSCLI ranges from 6% to 83%. However, it has a much larger memory footprint than the memory oracle and other existing schemes. This is because our technique allows cache usage to grow in an unrestricted manner when the compilation demand is high.

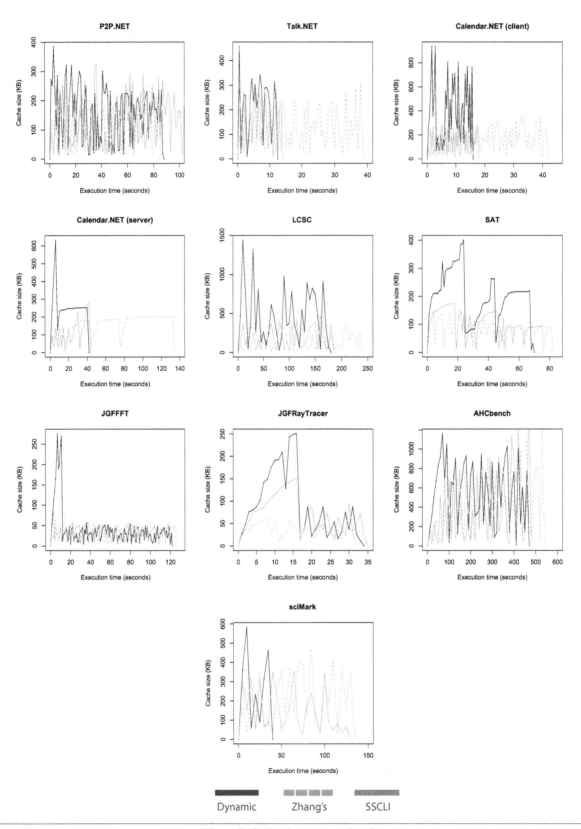

Figure 5. Cache size vs. execution time.

We have shown, however, that the memory footprint is an overestimate of memory usage representing the worst case scenario. We instead measure the actual memory usage required to complete a program's execution. The result shows that our technique yields better memory usage than those of other techniques.

For future work, we plan to develop ways to dynamically tune the window and history sizes for our algorithm. We will also conduct additional experiments that use multiple pitch criteria for computationally intensive applications.

Acknowledgments

This work is supported in part by the National Science Foundation through award CNS-0411043, CNS-0720757, and CCF-0747009, by the Air Force Office of Scientific Research through award FA9550-09-1- 0129, the Army Research Office through DURIP award W91NF- 04-1-0104, and the Office of Naval Research under contract N000140710329.

References

[1] D. Anthony, W. Srisa-an, and M. Leung. An empirical study of the code pitching mechanism in the .NET Framework. *Journal of Object Technology (Special issue: .NET Technologies 2005 Conference)*, 5:107–127, April 2006.

[2] V. Bala, E. Duesterwald, and S. Banerjia. Dynamo: A transparent dynamic optimization system. In *ACM Conference on Programming Language Design and Implementation*, pages 1–12, Vancouver, British Columbia, Canada, 2000.

[3] A. Basu. .NET code pitching. http://blogs.msdn.com/abhinaba/archive/2009/04/17/net-code-pitching.aspx, 2009.

[4] S. M. Blackburn, P. Cheng, and K. S. McKinley. Oil and Water? high performance garbage collection in Java with MMTk. In *Proceedings of the International Conference on Software Engineering*, pages 137–146, Scotland, UK, 2004.

[5] D. Bruening and S. Amarasinghe. Maintaining consistency and bounding capacity of software code caches. In *Proceedings of the International Symposium on Code Generation and Optimization*, pages 74–85, Washington, DC, USA, 2005.

[6] D. Bruening and E. Duesterwald. Exploring optimal compilation unit shapes for an embedded just-in-time compiler. In *Proceedings of the Workshop on Feedback-Directed and Dynamic Optimization (FDDO-3)*, Monterey, CA, USA, 2000.

[7] B. Cmelik and D. Keppel. Shade: a fast instruction-set simulator for execution profiling. In *Proceedings of the Conference on Measurement and Modeling of Computer Systems*, pages 128–137, Nashville, Tennessee, USA, 1994.

[8] R. F. Cmelik and D. Keppel. Shade: A fast instruction set simulator for execution profiling. Technical report, Sun Microsystems, Inc., Mountain View, CA, USA, 1993.

[9] A. S. Dhodapkar and J. E. Smith. Managing multi-configuration hardware via dynamic working set analysis. In *Proceedings of the International Symposium on Computer Architecture*, pages 233–244, Anchorage, Alaska, 2002.

[10] A. S. Dhodapkar and J. E. Smith. Comparing program phase detection techniques. In *Proceedings of the International Symposium on Microarchitecture*, pages 217–227, San Diego, CA, USA, 2003.

[11] E. Duesterwald and V. Bala. Software profiling for hot path prediction: less is more. In *Proceedings of the International Conference on Architectural Support for Programming Languages and Operating Systems*, pages 202–211, Cambridge, Massachusetts, USA, 2000.

[12] E. Duesterwald, C. Cascaval, and S. Dwarakadas. Characterizing and predicting program behavior and its variability. In *International Conference on Parallel Architecture and Compilation Techniques*, pages 220–231, New Orleans, Louisiana, USA, September 2003.

[13] M. Hind, V. Rajan, and P. Sweeney. The phase shift detection problem is non-monotonic. Technical Report Report RC23058, IBM Research, 2003.

[14] IBM. Jikes rvm. http://jikesrvm.sourceforge.net/, 2005.

[15] A. Kumar. Programming with .net compact framework 1.0 and SQL CE 2.0. http://www.c-sharpcorner.com/, 2005.

[16] D. Merrill and K. Hazelwood. Trace fragment selection within method-based jvms. In *Proceedings of the International Conference on Virtual Execution Environments*, pages 41–50, Seattle, WA, USA, 2008.

[17] Microsoft. Shared Source Common Language Infrastructure 1.2 Release. http://msdn.microsoft.com/net/sscli/, 2006.

[18] MSDN. Device memory management in the .NET Compact Framework. http://msdn.microsoft.com/en-us/library/s6x0c3a4 (VS.100).aspx, 2009.

[19] P. Nagpurkar, M. Hind, C. Krintz, P. F. Sweeney, and V. T. Rajan. Online phase detection algorithms. In *International Symposium on Code Generation and Optimization*, pages 111 – 123, NYC, NY, USA, 2006.

[20] P. Nagpurkar and C. Krintz. Visualization and analysis of phased behavior in Java programs. In *ACM International Conference on Principles and Practice of Programming in Java (PPPJ)*, Las Vegas, NV, USA, 2004.

[21] S. Pratschner. .NET CF weblog. http://weblogs.asp.net/stevenpr/archive/2005/12/12/502978.aspx, 2005.

[22] T. Sherwood, E. Perelman, and B. Calder. Basic block distribution analysis to find periodic behavior and simulation points in applications. In *International Conference on Parallel Architectures and Compilation Techniques*, Barcelona, Spain, September 2001.

[23] T. Sherwood, E. Perelman, G. Hamerly, and B. Calder. Automatically characterizing large scale program behavior. In *10th International Conference on Architectural Support for Programming Languages and Operating Systems*, San Jose, CA, USA, October 2002.

[24] T. Sherwood, S. Sair, and B. Calder. Phase tracking and prediction. In *Proceedings of the 30th International Symposium on Computer Architecture (ISCA'03)*, pages 336–349, San Diega, CA, USA, 2003.

[25] J. Smith and R. Nair. *Virtual Machines : Versatile Platforms for Systems and Processes*. Morgan Kaufmann, San Francisco, CA, USA, June 2005.

[26] M. Smith. Overcoming the challenges to feedback directed optimization. In *Proceedings of the ACM SIGPLAN Workshop on Dynamic and Adaptive Compilation and Optimization*, pages 1–11, Boston, Massachusetts, USA, 2000.

[27] D. Stutz, T. Neward, and G. Shilling. *Shared Source CLI Essentials*. O'Reilly and Associates, Sebastopol, CA, USA, 2003.

[28] Sun Microsystems. The CLDC HotSpot implementation virtual machine. http://java.sun.com/products/cldc/wp/CLDC_HI_WhitePaper.pdf, 2002.

[29] Sun Microsystems. The Java hotspot virtual machine, v1.4.1. http://java.sun.com/products/hotspot/, 2003.

[30] UC Santa Barbara RACE Lab. A Collection of Phoenix-Compatible C# Benchmarks. http://www.cs.ucsb.edu/ ckrintz/racelab/PhxCSBenchmarks/index.html, 2006.

[31] J. Whaley. A portable sampling-based profiler for java virtual machines. In *JAVA '00: Proceedings of the ACM 2000 conference on Java Grande*, pages 78–87, San Francisco, California, United States, 2000.

[32] A. Wigley and S. Wheelwright. *Microsoft .NET Compact Framework*. Microsoft Press, Redmond, WA, USA, 2003.

[33] L. Zhang and C. Krintz. Adaptive code unloading for resource-constrained JVMs. In *Proceedings of the Conference on Languages, Compilers, and Tools for Embedded Systems*, pages 155–164, Washington, DC, 2004.

[34] L. Zhang and C. Krintz. Profile-driven code unloading for resource-constrained JVMs. In *International Conference on the Principles and Practice of Programming in Java*, pages 83–90, Las Vegas, NV, USA, June 2004. ACM Press.

[35] L. Zhang and C. Krintz. The design, implementation, an evaluation of adaptive code unloading for resource-constrained environments. *ACM Transactions on Architecture and Code Optimization*, 2(2):131–164, 2005.

[36] B. Zorn. Ben's CLI benchmark. http://research.microsoft.com/~Zorn/benchmarks/default.htm, 2005.

On Improving Heap Memory Layout
by Dynamic Pool Allocation

Zhenjiang Wang[12], Chenggang Wu[1] *

[1]Key Laboratory of Computer System and Architecture,
Institute of Computing Technology, Chinese Academy
of Sciences, Beijing, China
[2]Graduate University of Chinese Academy of Sciences,
Beijing, China
{wangzhenjiang, wucg}@ict.ac.cn

Pen-Chung Yew

Department of Computer Science and Engineering,
University of Minnesota at Twin-Cities,
Minnesota, USA
Institute of Information Science, Academia Sinica,
Taiwan
yew@cs.umn.edu

Abstract

Dynamic memory allocation is widely used in modern programs. General-purpose heap allocators often focus more on reducing their run-time overhead and memory space utilization, but less on exploiting the characteristics of their allocated heap objects. This paper presents a lightweight dynamic optimizer, named *Dynamic Pool Allocation (DPA)*, which aims to exploit the affinity of the allocated heap objects and improve their layout at run-time. DPA uses an adaptive partial call chain with heuristics to aggregate affinitive heap objects into dedicated memory regions, called *memory pools*. We examine the factors that could affect the effectiveness of such layout. We have implemented DPA and measured its performance on several SPEC CPU 2000 and 2006 benchmarks that use extensive heap objects. Evaluations show that it could achieve an average speed up of 12.1% and 10.8% on two x86 commodity machines respectively using GCC -O3, and up to 82.2% for some benchmarks.

Categories and Subject Descriptors D.4.2 [*Storage Management*]: Allocation/deallocation strategies

General Terms Management, Performance

Keywords pool allocation, adaptive partial call chain, data layout, dynamic optimization

1. Introduction

The huge speed gap between modern processors and their memory has long been a main barrier that limits the performance of computer systems. The trend shows no relief in the foreseeable future. A great deal of efforts have been geared toward coping with this problem. They range from architectural support to compiler optimizations. Many try to use the cache hierarchy effectively from various aspects, including affinity-aware cache data placement on CMP, improving the data locality [7] [8] [9] [6] [10] [11] [18] [3], hiding latency using prefetching [18] [13], to name just a few.

---

* To whom correspondence should be addressed.

Improving data locality is essential to bridge the speed gap. It could reduce cache misses and thus reduce the memory bandwidth requirement. In some programs, the heap objects occupy a large portion of their work space. As a result, it is critical to improve the locality of such data objects in the heap.

Some programming languages (e.g., Lisp, Java and C#) have an automatic memory management mechanism, such as *garbage collection* (GC). *Garbage collectors* can copy some or all of the reachable objects into a new area in memory, and update all references to those objects as needed, to improve overall data locality [5]. When using garbage collectors to manage heap objects at run-time, the layout of the objects could be improved by considering their frequent access patterns [10], affinity [6], and other run-time characteristics [16].

However, there exist many applications written in languages that do not have GC support at run-time. Moving allocated objects to improve their memory layout at run-time is a great challenge because it is difficult to update all relevant pointers due to potential aliases. Hence, once data objects are allocated, their memory layout cannot be easily changed unless they are freed or moved explicitly by the programmers. Many efforts have thus been directed toward the layout of heap objects at their *allocation time* [11] [15] [2] [7] [18].

Pool allocation is a technique that aggregates heap objects at the time of their allocation into separate memory pools in order to control their layout. Lattner et al. [11] proposed a compiler technique to improve cache locality by *pool allocation*. They identify distinct data structures such as lists, graphs, or trees in the source programs using sophisticated *static* program analysis and heuristics. Such objects are then segregated into separate pools. It could gain a significant performance improvement by reducing data cache misses.

However, in many cases, source programs are not available for such analysis and optimizations. To support data layout improvement directly on the binaries at run-time, some techniques have been proposed [15] [2] [7] [3]. They collect profiling information in the prior runs, and classify objects into categories by their characteristics such as access pattern, access frequency or the lifetime of the objects. In later runs, objects in the same category are allocated in the same pool to reduce potential cache misses. Such an approach could provide a rather good estimation of the run-time behavior using a representative training input set, and hence, could be used to improve data layout for better memory performance.

In this paper, we present a *Dynamic Pool Allocation (DPA)* scheme. It analyzes the relationship among heap objects and aggregates the affinitive ones into pools guided by adaptive call chain information - all done at the run-time. It aims to eliminate the extra profiling runs and overheads, as well as the difficulty of finding representative training input sets. Experimental results show that our approach improves the performance by an average of 12.1% and 10.8% (up to 82.2%) on two x86 machines for some SPEC CPU 2000 and 2006 benchmarks that contain extensive heap objects and their usage.

Our paper makes the following contributions:

- A transparent dynamic approach to improve the performance of pointer intensive programs by controlling the layout of allocated heap memory space. It is done without the requirement of re-compilation or carrying profiling information from prior profiling runs.

- A new strategy that uses *adaptive partial call chain (APCC)* to eliminate the effect of wrappers around default system memory allocators.

- A scheme that uses heuristics based on affinity analysis to aggregate related objects in the same memory pool even if those objects are allocated at different call sites.

- A study on the multitude of factors that can impact the performance of DPA.

- A lightweight implementation of DPA that shows improvement in memory performance and running time of heap-intensive programs.

The organization of the remaining paper is as follows: Section 2 introduces the related work; Section 3 explains our approach; Section 4 illustrates our system. Section 5 contains some evaluation. Finally, section 6 concludes the paper.

2. Related Work

Since a *garbage collector* can identify all references to all objects, it has the ability to move objects safely at run-time. Many schemes aim to improve garbage collectors through exploiting data locality in the heap [6] [10] [16]. They use online object-instance sampling techniques to discover frequent access patterns. From time to time, GC rearranges data objects according to the identified access patterns. Their results show that great performance improvement could be obtained for some benchmarks.

For applications that do not have GC support, Chilimbi et al. [9] presented a semi-automatic tool, called *ccmorph*, which could reorganize the layout of homogeneous trees at run-time. It relies on annotations provided by the programmers to identify the root of a tree and to indicate whether the layout reorganization is safe. They also describe another tool, *ccmalloc*, which is a *malloc* variant that accepts hints from the programmers to allocate one object near another for better locality. Both tools require the source code and the hints from the programmers.

Lattner et al. [11] proposed a compiler framework that segregates distinct instances of heap-based data structures into separate memory pools. It is driven by their pointer analysis algorithm, called *data structure analysis (DSA)*. The approach also needs the source code.

There exist some profile-based schemes [15] [2] [7] [3] for applications without their source code. Their first step is to collect profile information. Chilimbi et al. [7] presented a profile-based analysis for co-allocating contemporaneously accessed heap objects in the same cache block. The hot data stream, i.e., a regular data access pattern that frequently repeats, is obtained through profiling. In [15], they use heuristics to predict accessing and lifetime behavior of heap objects when they are allocated. They considered a variety of information available at the time of object allocation. It includes information from stack pointer, path pointer and stack

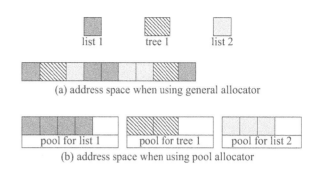

Figure 1. A typical scenario of memory space allocation

contents. Their scheme could reduce the number of page faults. A representative training input set is necessary in these approaches. However, it may not be easy to find such "representative" training input set for some real applications.

What the users prefer is a transparent mechanism that needs no extra information they have to provide, nor extra profiling work they have to do, except the application binary itself. Qin Zhao et al. [18] proposed a dynamic heap allocation scheme in DynamoRIO. They treat each static memory allocation site as a single pool, hence, the pools and the static allocation sites could be mapped one-to-one to each other. It can improve the locality for some programs, but does not work on some others as discussed in Section 3.

3. Dynamic Pool Allocation (DPA)

Most general-purpose heap allocators such as *dlmalloc* [12], a widely used memory allocator in Linux system, focus primarily on reducing the run-time overhead and enhancing the memory space utilization. An object is usually allocated in a best-fit fragment, ignoring the correlation with other objects. Figure 1 shows a scenario of heap memory layout after 3 distinct data structures are allocated.

In general-purpose allocators, only the allocation sequence and/or fragmentation status, as well as the object size are considered. Hence, objects of the same data structure could scatter around in the memory space, as Figure 1a shows. In Figure 1a, traversals of one data structure usually need to access several memory pages and several cache lines. When the working set size is large, it could cause significant TLB misses and data cache misses.

If we could design a mechanism to allocate them in 3 different pools, and form the layout as shown in Figure 1b, the locality can often be substantially improved. Component objects of each data structures are allocated in their corresponding pool next to each other, so that they are likely to reside in the same cache line and memory page. Therefore, traversals of these data structures could cause fewer cache and/or TLB misses. Moreover, hardware or software prefetching becomes easier when traversal matches the allocation sequence (the strides are regular in this case).

The key of dynamic pool allocation is deciding which pool an object should belong to. However, it is not easy to get high-level data structure information without the source code. One possible scheme is to regard all heap objects allocated at the same call site as affinitive, and put them into one object group. An object group is usually corresponding to a pool. This call-site based strategy can work well in many cases [18]. However, there exist two challenging issues that often render such schemes less effective.

The first is caused by using *wrappers* around the memory allocation routines such as *malloc*. Some programmers prefer to use *wrappers* to enhance the reliability of their programs. Figure 2 shows a typical wrapper in 300.twolf of SPEC CPU 2000.

```
char *safe_malloc(size)
unsigned size;
{
    char *p;
    extern char *malloc() ;
    if ((p = malloc(size)) == (char *) 0) {
        cleanupHandler(heap_no_mem,"safe_malloc");
    }
    return p;
}
```

Figure 2. A malloc wrapper in 300.twolf

Almost all heap objects are allocated through the wrapper routine *safe_malloc* in the program. The call sites of *malloc* inside *safe_malloc* become useless for object classification. It could trick the scheme to aggregate all heap objects into one pool. This kind of wrapper is quite common in many programs. For example, 197.vpr, 253.perlbmk and 300.twolf all have more than 80% of their heap allocation through such wrappers. What makes it worse in some cases is that some wrappers could even wrap memory allocation routines under several layers, such as those in 2.3% of heap allocations in 483.xalancbmk.

The second issue is caused by the fact that the heap objects of a data structure could be allocated through several different call sites. Using the above mentioned call-site based schemes, they will be allocated into several different pools and lose some affinity advantage. Two main reasons lead to such a phenomenon.

One is from the programmers themselves. For example, nodes of a linked list may be allocated and inserted from different code regions in a program. The other is caused by the compiler. It may cause a memory allocation call site to be duplicated several times by loop unrolling or recursive function inlining. All these duplicated call sites are from the same original call, and are supposed to build the same data structure. Again, using a call-site based strategy, objects allocated from these call sites will be put into different pools. For example, 55.4% of call sites in 197.parser are processing the same data structures with others.

A good pool allocation policy should accommodate these two challenging issues and distinguish the relationship of these heap objects correctly.

3.1 Adaptive Partial Call Chain

A call chain could be traced by the content of a dynamic call stack (stack unwinding). It starts from the current procedure, followed by its caller, caller's caller and so on. It contains useful context sensitive information. Hence, we could use it to resolve the issue caused by wrappers. An important issue here is how far back we should trace the call chain in order to identify the wrappers that have multiple layers.

One straightforward option is to use the *full call chain*. It can eliminate the problems caused by wrappers because we could use different callers of a wrapper to produce different call chains. However, using the entire call chain may make the calling context over-specialized. It could produce too many object groups with very few objects in each. This could, in turn, lead to too many pools, wasting the pool space, and making the data layout too sparse to take advantage of its spatial locality. Besides, using the entire call chain could incur large overhead at run-time, especially for those programs that have very long call chains, or functions that are recursively invoked.

Another option is to select a *partial call chain* of a fixed length n, called *n-PCC* in the rest of the paper. It has less overhead than in the *full call chain* if n could be selected appropriately. However, the

optimal chain length could vary at different call sites. For example, in our study, 1-PCC is enough for most call sites in 197.parser, while some objects need 4-PCC to eliminate the impact of wrappers in 483.xalancbmk.

In our approach, we design an *Adaptive Partial Call Chain (APCC)* strategy, which uses a *variable length* that is adaptive to the calling context. We start from the allocator's direct caller, called *procedure A* here for the ease of reference. We then analyze the data flow of the allocated memory pointer. In most cases, if procedure A does not process the allocated object or link the allocated object with other ones, but simply passes the pointer to its caller by return value or call-by-reference parameter, we could be pretty sure that procedure A is a wrapper. The length of the APCC is then increased by 1. Their analysis is repeatedly applied up the call chain until a caller does not show the behavior of a wrapper. Using the APCC strategy, we could keep enough context information to eliminate the impact of wrappers. Later, we could build an object group for each APCC.

The experimental data shows that the average length of APCC is 1.44 in our evaluated benchmarks, and the maximum length is 4 (in 483.xalancbmk). In general, it only needs to analyze dozens of instructions to recognize a wrapper on average. Moreover, after an APCC is analyzed, the result can be used for later allocations without re-analysis. Therefore, the overhead is amortized by all the allocations from the same APCC. Evaluation in Section 5.5 shows that such an overhead is quite small.

3.2 Object Group Merging

As discussed earlier, the objects allocated in several different call sites could belong to the same data structure in some cases. Call-site based schemes will put them into different object groups. To merge them back into one object group, we propose to use the *Storage Shape Graph (SSG)*

3.2.1 Storage Shape Graph

Our SSG is derived from [4] [14]. It is a tuple of the form (V, H, E). V is a set of variable nodes representing the global/stack variables. H is a set of heap nodes which represent the object groups of heap objects. $E \subseteq (V \bigcup H) \times H \times O$ is a set of graph edges, each of which abstracts a set of pointers. When a pointer points from some member field in a structure or class, O is the field offset.

Figure 3a gives a code fragment that builds a linked list, whose corresponding SSG is shown in Figure 3b. The heap nodes in the graph stand for the object groups generated by our APCC scheme. The edge $(h_1, h_2, 0)$ means that the *data* field (offset is 0) of objects in h_1 is a pointer which points to the objects in h_2.

Building an SSG needs the points-to information. The variables are extracted from the binary, and a points-to analysis, like [1] and [17], can be applied.

3.2.2 Affinity Recognition

We define two types of object affinity for objects of the same type. 1) Objects are of *type-I* affinity if they are linked to form a data structure, such as a list, a tree, or a graph. These objects are often referenced together when the data structure is being traversed. 2) The member fields in type-I affinitive objects can be pointers, which point to objects of another type. When traversing the data structure and accessing the fields, those objects are usually referenced together. We consider those objects *type-II* affinitive.

An object group consists of a number of objects. The pointers pointing to them could be kept in one of three different styles: (1) These objects may keep their pointer in some member field of themselves to form a data structure, which makes the objects type-I affinitive; (2) Sometimes the pointers of these objects are kept

```
typedef struct {
  int *data;
  struct node *next;
} node;

...
node *head;
head = (node*) malloc(sizeof(node)); // heap node h₁
head->data = (int*) malloc(sizeof(int)); // heap node h₂
head->next = NULL;
...

void foo() {
  ...
  while (...) {
    node *temp;
    node *here = head;
    ...                          // traverse "here" to a proper node
    temp = (node*) malloc(sizeof(node));  // heap node h₃
    temp->data = (int*) malloc(sizeof(int)); // heap node h₄
    temp->next = here->next;
    here->next = temp;
    ...
  }
}
```

(a) a code fragment

(b) SSG of the code fragment

Figure 3. A code fragment and its SSG

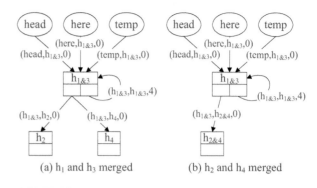

(a) h_1 and h_3 merged   (b) h_2 and h_4 merged

Figure 4. An example of object group merging

in some member field of another data structure's nodes or another array's elements. In this case, the objects are of type-II affinity; (3) Infrequently, the pointers of these objects are kept in different ways, making some objects not affinitive with the others. We cannot avoid the last style even using a full call chain, but fortunately, it seldom happens. Since object groups are usually accessed using the first two styles, we consider that the objects in an object group are always affinitive.

However, not all affinitive objects are in the same object group because they might have different APCCs due to being allocated at different call sites. The purpose of object group merging is to identify these affinitive object groups and merge them for better locality. We use an SSG to realize the merge process.

In an SSG, different heap nodes whose objects are affinitive have some key attributes. If the objects in two heap nodes are type-I affinitive, the type of these objects are the same and there is an edge connecting them. If the objects are type-II affinitive, the type of these objects are also the same, but they will have edges from the same heap node or from heap nodes whose objects are type-I affinitive, and the edges have the same offset. We merge heap nodes in an SSG using these key attributes.

Take the SSG in Figure 3b as an example. Heap nodes h_1 and h_3 are of the same type, and they have an edge $(h_1, h_3, 4)$, so they

are type-I affinitive and could be merged, as Figure 4a shows. Heap nodes h_2 and h_4 have the same type, and edge $(h_{1\&3}, h_2, 0)$ and $(h_{1\&3}, h_4, 0)$ have the same beginning heap node and offset, so h_2 and h_4 are type-II affinitive. The SSG after they are merged is shown in Figure 4b.

To recognize the affinity relationship between two heap nodes, we should first find out if their types are the same. However, type information is usually missing in executable binaries. In the experimental system we implemented, we assume that two objects of the same size will have the same type. Although this assumption may not be always true, it works reasonably well in most cases. Such errors will only affect the layout of heap objects. It will not affect the program correctness.

The merging is important when the affinity objects are left in too many object groups, or the access sequence jumps between the object groups frequently. The experimental data in Section 5.2 shows that 4 out of 12 benchmarks have distinct merging, and 2 of them have obvious speedup.

3.3 Allocate Memory Space for Merged Object Groups

After merging object groups, the next step is to allocate memory pools for them. Since we cannot predict how much memory space an object group needs, we have to find a way to allocate appropriate amount of memory space for its memory pool. A large memory space that is enough for any object group will be a waste of memory, because it uses the worst-case size for all memory pools. Our approach allocates memory space in units called *pool segments*. When the allocated segment of an object group fills up, another segment of the same size will be allocated. In our empirical study, we tested different pool segment sizes and found that a 4096-byte segment works the best, same as the virtual page size.

In the pool segment of an object group, we can use a general free-list based allocator with coalescing of adjacent free objects. This allocator aims to process objects of various sizes, so it uses object headers to keep the management information. However, in most cases (78.6% in our statistics), objects in an object group are of the same size. Therefore, we can use a lightweight allocator for these fixed size objects [18], and the object headers can be eliminated. A typical allocation/deallocation operation just needs to change a pointer or a free list. Both space and time can be saved. The effect of object header elimination is shown in Section 5.5.

However, allocating memory pools to all object groups may not be necessary and beneficial. Here, we consider two factors that could affect our decision to allocate a memory pool to an object group: number of objects in the object group and the size of the objects.

3.3.1 The Number of Objects

In many programs, some object groups have a very small number of objects, for example, a short linked list with only a few nodes allocated. We call them *small* object groups. Allocating memory pools to such small object groups is not very useful for improving locality. Besides, allocating memory pools to them will produce pool segments that are only sparsely populated. It will not only hurt the memory utilization but also the data locality.

To avoid this, we set a threshold on the number of objects in an object group before memory pools are allocated to them, and leave the allocation of memory space for the small object groups to the operating system.

A proper threshold is needed to filter out small object groups. A low threshold may allocate too many sparsely populated memory pools. Setting the threshold too high may lose too many optimization opportunities. Experiments in Section 5.3 show that a threshold of 100 is suitable for most programs on the systems we tested.

3.3.2 Object Size Threshold

The main benefit of pool allocation is from the improvement of locality. However, a large object can occupy several cache lines, which makes the same field of adjacent objects in different cache lines. A large object also makes the object header insignificant. As a result, the larger an object is, the less benefit we will gain from allocating to memory pools. Besides, for a pool segment of size s and objects of the fixed size n, since s may not be a multiple of n, a remainder of $[0, n)$ bytes may be wasted. Therefore, a larger object size may waste more memory. Our experiments in Section 5.4 show that the threshold of 128 bytes is suitable.

4. Implementation

We implemented our approach as a dynamic optimizer on Linux operating systems (IA32 ISA), named *DigitalBridge-dopt* . In this section, we present our system in detail.

The first step is to take over the memory allocation functions: the default system allocators need to be replaced with our DPA allocator at the beginning of the program execution. Several approaches are possible for this purpose. In our current implementation, we use the LD_PRELOAD environment variable [13] to intercept the main function, and modify the global offset table entries of the allocators (including *new* and *delete*). After that, the main function is resumed and the execution starts. In this way, when the program executes a memory allocation call, it will call DPA allocator instead.

The DPA allocator has the same interface as the system allocator: the request allocation size is passed to the allocator, and then the allocator returns a free memory object to the program. What DPA allocator controls is where (from which pool segment) to allocate the requested memory. As a result, DPA allocator does not affect the correctness of the program.

Figure 5a shows the basic implementation of our DPA allocator. When the DPA allocator receives an allocation request, the first step is to determine the APCC by the *APCC Generator* as described in Section 3.1. After that, the APCC is used to look up a hash table, the *APCC-OG Table*. Each entry of the table contains the analyzed APCC and its associated object group ID. If the APCC appears for the first time, it has no entry in the table. We then use the *Affinity Analyzer* to add a new heap node in the SSG and try to merge it with other heap nodes by the heuristics described in Section 3.2.2.

If the heap node is successfully merged with another heap node whose object group ID is g, a new entry <APCC, g> is inserted in the *APCC-OG Table*. If the heap node cannot be merged with other heap nodes, we build a new object group with ID g' and insert <APCC, g'> into the table. The object group ID and the request

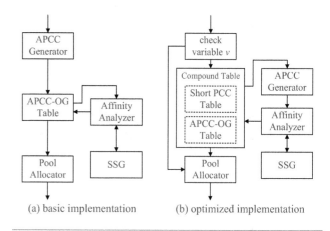

Figure 5. Structure of DPA allocator

are sent to the *Pool Allocator*, which allocates memory space as described in Section 3.3.

Note that this basic implementation has to analyze the length of APCC by the *APCC Generator* and look up the *APCC-OG Table* for *every* memory allocation request. It could incur a large overhead when the requests for allocation are frequent. Hence, we optimize it as shown in Figure 5b. The two optimizations are on the critical path to reduce the overhead.

(1) To reduce the overhead of getting APCC for each incoming request, we add an *Short PCC Table*. After *APCC Generator* gets an APCC, it can also get its corresponding shorter n-PCCs. These shorter n-PCCs are recorded in the *Short PCC Table*. When a request comes, we first look up the *Short PCC Table* with its 1-PCC. If the 1-PCC matches an entry in the table, we look up the table again with its 2-PCC. The looking up repeats until no entry is matched. In this way, we can get a PCC and check whether it is in the *APCC-OG Table*. If it does not hit, it means a new APCC appears. The *APCC Generator* is invoked to obtain the new APCC and update the *Short PCC Table*.

For incoming requests, the *Short PCC Table* can get the correct APCC so long as the APCC has been analyzed because all of its corresponding shorter n-PCCs are in the table. The overhead of looking up the *Short PCC Table* is much smaller than the overhead of the analysis using *APCC Generator*. Finally, since there is no identical n-PCC in the two tables, we combine them together as the *Compound Table*.

(2) To reduce the overhead of looking up the *Compound Table*, we instrument some code at the outermost call site of an APCC to provide its associated object group ID directly. We do this only when the next allocation (after executing the instrumented code) has surely the very APCC we want. For example, an APCC of length 2 has an outermost call site S. The call site S is not in a wrapper function, but it calls a wrapper *safe_malloc*. If the call at S is not an indirect call, and *safe_malloc* does not call any other functions before it calls the allocator, and the call to the allocator in *safe_malloc* cannot be skipped by the control flow transfer, we can conclude that when *safe_malloc* is called from S, the next allocation must have the very APCC. Hence, we instrument at the call site S to provide the associated object group ID by a global variable v. The DPA allocator first checks whether v is a valid object group ID. If so, the DPA allocator calls the *Pool Allocator* with the ID and reset v to an invalid ID. This can avoid looking up the *APCC-OG Table* in many cases.

	#1	#2
CPU Family	Intel Northwood	Intel Harpertown
Cores	1	4
Frequency	2.40GHz	2.33GHz
L1I Cache Size	32kB	32kB
L1D Cache Size	32kB	32kB
L2 Cache Size	512kB	6144kB
Memory Size	2GB	16GB
OS	Linux 2.6.27	Linux 2.6.26

Table 1. Experiment platforms

Name	Lang	Description
175.vpr	C	FPGA circuit placement and routing
197.parser	C	word Processing
253.perlbmk	C	PERL programming language
300.twolf	C	place and route simulator
197.art	C	image recognition / neural networks
183.equake	C	seismic wave propagation simulation
188.ammp	C	computational chemistry
473.astar	C++	path-finding algorithms
483.xalancbmk	C++	XML processing
447.dealII	C++	finite element analysis
453.povray	C++	image ray-tracing
482.sphinx3	C	speech recognition

Table 2. Evaluated benchmarks

5. Evaluation

In this section, we evaluate different strategies and factors discussed in Section 3. We evaluate our system on two different IA32 architectures. The hardware and operating system information are shown in Table 1. We elide some data on #2 when they are similar to those on #1. The C and C++ library on the system implements *malloc/free* using a modified *Lea allocator* [12], which is a high quality general-purpose allocator. All the runtimes shown in this section are the average time of three executions of the program.

The benchmarks we use are SPEC CPU 2000 and SPEC CPU 2006. They are compiled by GCC 4.3.2 at -O3 and with the reference input set. We select the benchmarks shown in Table 2 by the policy that their objects allocated in memory pools occupy more than 1% of all heap data in use on average. The runtimes of the other benchmarks are not affected by our optimizer. As an experiment, we replace the customized allocator in 197.parser with direct calls to *malloc/free*, because its customized allocator has semantics identical to *malloc/free*.

Our system uses APCC with object group merging. The pool segment size, object number threshold, and object size threshold are 4096 bytes, 100 and 128 bytes respectively. When analyzing the impact of one factor, the others are fixed at the above values.

5.1 Adaptive Partial Call Chain

DPA uses the Adaptive Partial Call Chain (APCC) strategy to build the object groups before object group merging. Alternative strategies include the fixed length partial call chain (n-PCC) and full call chain (FCC).

Figure 6 shows the normalized runtime of the benchmarks when using different strategy to generate object groups. The baseline is the runtime without pool allocation. The bars illustrate the performance of 1-PCC, 2-PCC, 3-PCC, 4-PCC, FCC and our APCC, respectively. The figure shows the trend that the average performance decreases when the length of PCC increases. The reason is that the

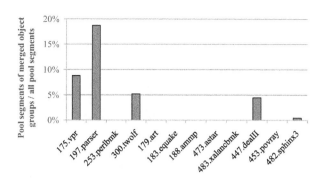

Figure 7. Pool segments of merged object groups

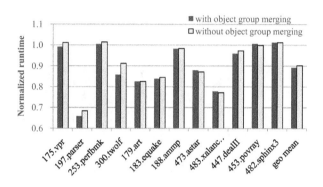

Figure 8. Normalized runtime with/without object group merging

identification of the longer call chain incurs more overhead. The trend is especially obvious for 197.parser because it has quite a few allocations (nearly one billion), and its call chain is often very long. n-PCC (n>1) is usually worse than 1-PCC, but it outperforms 1-PCC in 300.twolf and 483.xalancbmk when wrappers are used. Our APCC strategy has the best average performance (3% to 13% better than others) because it is adaptive to different call sites.

5.2 Object Group Merging

The purpose of object group merging is to aggregate affinitive objects into one object group if they have different APCCs. The pool segments of merged object groups are shown in Figure 7. The y-axis shows the percentage of these pool segments from all the pool segments. Four benchmarks are affected by the object group merging. Figure 8 shows the runtime of our approach (normalized to the runtime without pool allocation) with and without object group merging.

Two out of the four benchmarks (197.parser and 300.twolf) have a modest 3% and 6% improvement in their runtime. 175.vpr and 447.dealII have no obvious improvement because their merged object groups are used for looking up hash tables and searching in large red-black trees. The frequent access behavior is to visit some selective objects, but not traversing the entire data structures. The average runtime with object group merging has a modest 1% improvement.

5.3 Number of Objects in Object Groups

As discussed in Section 3.3.1, we set a threshold to filter out small object groups that cannot make full use of the pool segments. Figure 9 shows the impact of such filtering. The baseline is the runtime without pool allocation. When a larger threshold is selected, fewer object groups are allowed to have their pool segments. It can make the objects in the pools denser, but may lose some po-

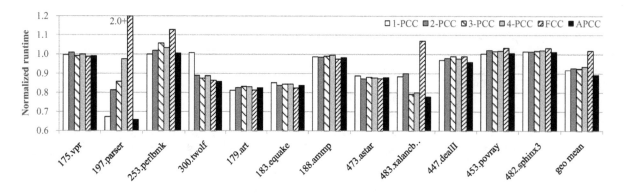

Figure 6. Normalized runtime for different strategies

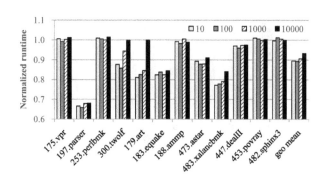

Figure 9. Normalized runtime for different object number threshold

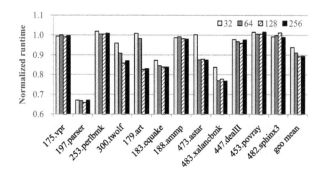

Figure 10. Normalized runtime for different maximum object size

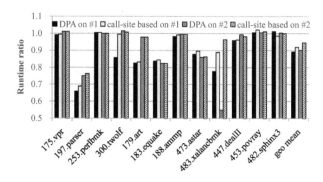

Figure 11. The runtime ratio of DPA and the call-site based approach

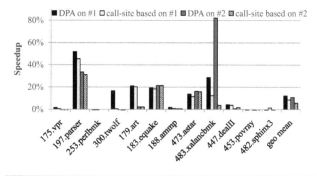

Figure 12. The speedup of DPA and the call-site based approach

tential improvement. The loss is especially obvious for 300.twolf and 179.art, because their critical object groups have only several thousand objects. In our evaluated benchmarks, a threshold of 100 makes a good trade-off and shows the best performance for almost all the benchmarks.

5.4 Object Size

A large object cannot benefit much from improved pool allocation, but may waste some space in a pool segment due to internal fragmentation. We set an object size threshold that prevents the pool allocation for large objects. As a contrast, a small threshold is too conservative and may exclude critical object groups. The impact of different thresholds is shown in Figure 10. The baseline is the runtime without pool allocation. We can see that the threshold of 32 or 64 bytes works poorly for 300.twolf, 179.art, 473.astar and

483.xalancbmk. The threshold of 128 bytes is adequate and a larger one does not help further.

5.5 Overall Performance

Now, we have explored the design space of our DPA allocator. The overall performance on the two platforms is shown in Figure 11 and Figure 12, compared with the call-site based strategy (i.e., 1-PCC without object group merging). The baseline is the runtime without pool allocation. Our approach can accelerate the benchmarks by an average of 12.1% and 10.8% on the two platforms. 483.xalancbmk shows significant speedup, 28.6% on #1 and 82.2% on #2. The reason is that several object groups in it have 188,718 small objects each, which need only 3Mb-6Mb space when using DPA allocator, but the objects are scattered in a 200M memory space when using the system allocator. For 197.parser, our approach is 1% faster than

Name	Base	DPA	Ratio
175.vpr	1370M	1365M	100%
197.parser	765M	437M	57%
253.perlbmk	139M	142M	102%
300.twolf	2304M	1863M	81%
197.art	14837M	13677M	92%
183.equake	996M	472M	47%
188.ammp	2847M	2830M	99%
473.astar	8480M	6660M	79%
483.xalancbmk	4992M	2846M	57%
447.dealII	5137M	4718M	92%
453.povray	8M	14M	169%
482.sphinx3	12623M	12840M	102%

Table 3. Cache misses on #1

Name	L2D misses			TLB misses		
	Base	DPA	Ratio	Base	DPA	Ratio
175.vpr	145M	147M	101%	1009M	998M	99%
197.parser	11M	5M	43%	1376M	1017M	74%
253.perlbmk	15M	16M	106%	162M	164M	101%
300.twolf	11K	9K	86%	815M	759M	93%
197.art	77K	15K	20%	508M	245M	48%
183.equake	188M	116M	62%	50M	39M	78%
188.ammp	56M	52M	94%	849M	846M	100%
473.astar	2584M	996M	39%	8994M	5895M	66%
483.xalancbmk	1671M	549M	33%	16920M	1472M	9%
447.dealII	770M	734M	95%	1253M	1275M	102%
453.povray	82K	56K	68%	1041M	1049M	101%
482.sphinx3	1673M	1658M	99%	2020M	2022M	100%

Table 4. Cache and TLB misses on #2

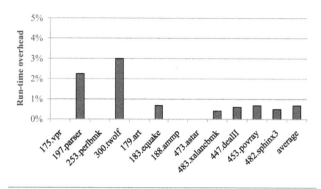

Figure 13. Run-time overhead of DPA

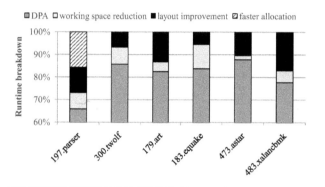

Figure 14. Breakdown of benefit

its custom allocators. Some benchmarks have a slight slow down because their benefit is less than the run-time overhead incurred.

Compared to the call-site based strategy, our approach outperforms on three benchmarks on #1 (6.6% for 197.parser, 16.1% for 300.twolf, and 16.1% for 483.xalancbmk). 100% of the memory allocation request in 300.twolf and 6.5% in 483.xalancbmk have wrappers, and APCC strategy can handle them properly. 197.parser and 300.twolf can gain benefit from object group merging, as Section 5.2 shows. 197.parser and 483.xalancbmk have similar outperform on #2. 300.twolf has no improvement on #2 because it has few cache misses (about 11K) before applying DPA, as we will show soon.

Table 3 shows the number of cache misses on platform #1 with and without applying DPA. DPA can reduce the cache misses by 15% on average. 453.povray gets more cache misses with the DPA allocator, but the total amount is quite small compared to the other benchmarks. Benchmarks with distinct cache miss reduction all have obvious speedup. We believe that the TLB misses are also reduced, but we cannot get the data because of the lack of hardware support.

Fortunately, platform #2 has more detailed performance monitors, and Table 4 shows the cache and TLB miss number on it. Due to the larger cache, the benchmarks have less cache miss number than that on #1. DPA reduces the cache misses by 37%, and TLB misses by 30% on average. The great miss reduction of 483.xalancbmk (67% and 91% respectively) leads to its significant speedup. 300.twolf and 179.art have no improvement on this machine because they have few cache misses before applying DPA.

Figure 13 shows the run-time overhead (compared to the base runtime) of our system. We evaluated the overhead by forwarding all allocation requests to the default system allocator when the objects are about to be allocated from pools. In this case the memory layout is similar to the base. The overhead includes all in our system except the pool allocator (in fact, our pool allocator has a shorter execution time than the system allocator). The graph shows that our DPA allocator has negligible overhead (0.7% on average) for most benchmarks.

Figure 14 illustrates the breakdown of the benefit gained in our system for the benchmarks that have obvious speedup. We separate the total benefit into three parts: the faster allocation/deallocation, the rearrangement of memory layout, and the reduction of working space. To measure the benefit of the first two parts, we use modified pool segments which always allocate objects with their object headers. We can get the impact from only the two parts by comparing this runtime with the base runtime. The incremental impact of working space reduction is the difference between this runtime and that of standard DPA. It is difficult to measure the benefit of faster allocation/deallocation alone, so we estimate it by small test cases. The test cases have the same number of allocation/deallocation in pools as the benchmarks, but have no data accesses to the allocated objects. This part of benefit is obvious for 197.parser because it has quite a lot of allocations. Most benchmarks (197.parser 179.art 473.astar, and 483.xalancbmk) benefit more from the improvement of layout than the working space reduction, but some benchmarks show the opposite is true (183.equake).

6. Conclusions

Accessing heap objects occupies a large portion of the workloads in many programs. It is critical to improve the locality of data in heap. An important issue is to control the heap data layout on executable binary transparently for a better performance. Existing techniques either need source code, or prior execution to collect profiling information.

In this paper, we studied the two important issues in dynamic pool allocation: widely used wrappers can group unrelated objects together, while different call sites can separate related objects into different pools. We have also studied the affinity of objects and its key attribute in the storage shape graph (SSG).

We also proposed an approach to control the layout of heap data dynamically. It eliminates the effect of wrappers using an adaptive partial call chain (APCC) strategy, and merges object groups using their key attributes in SSG. In order to reduce the waste of pool space, it uses a set of proper thresholds to filter out object groups that have a small object number or have a large object size. It also compresses the objects which have fixed size in the pool segment.

We also did a lightweight implementation of our approach, and optimized it to get the APCC and object group ID of an object with little overhead. Our approach gets a speedup of 12.1% and 10.8% on average on two commodity machines, and up to 82.2% for some benchmarks.

Acknowledgments

This paper is supported in part by the National Natural Science Foundation of China (NSFC) under the grant 60736012, the Innovation Research Group of NSFC (60921002), the National Basic Research Program of China (2005CB321602), the National High Technology Research and Development Program of China (2007AA01Z110), the National Science and Technology Major Project of China (2009ZX01036-001-002), and by the U.S. National Science Foundation under the grant CNS-0834599 and a gift grant from Intel.

References

[1] L. O. Andersen. *Program Analysis and Specialization for the C Programming Language.* PhD thesis, University of Copenhagen, 1994.

[2] D. A. Barrett and B. G. Zorn. Using lifetime predictors to improve memory allocation performance. In *Conference on Programming Language Design and Implementation*, pages 187–196, 1993.

[3] B. Calder, C. Krintz, S. John, and T. Austin. Cache-conscious data placement. In *Architectural Support for Programming Languages and Operating Systems*, pages 139–149, 1998.

[4] D. R. Chase, M. Wegman, and F. K. Zadeck. Analysis of pointers and structures. In *Conference on Programming Language Design and Implementation*, pages 296–310, 1990.

[5] C. J. Cheney. A nonrecursive list compacting algorithm. *Communications of the ACM*, 13(11):677–678, 1970.

[6] T. M. Chilimbi and J. R. Larus. Using generational garbage collection to implement cache-conscious data placement. In *International Symposium on Memory Management*, pages 37–48, 1998.

[7] T. M. Chilimbi and R. Shaham. Cache-conscious coallocation of hot data streams. In *Conference on Programming Language Design and Implementation*, pages 252–262, 2006.

[8] T. M. Chilimbi, B. Davidson, and J. R. Larus. Cache-conscious structure definition. In *Conference on Programming Language Design and Implementation*, pages 13–24, 1999.

[9] T. M. Chilimbi, M. D. Hill, and J. R. Larus. Cache-conscious structure layout. In *Conference on Programming Language Design and Implementation*, pages 1–12, 1999.

[10] X. Huang, S. M. Blackburn, K. S. McKinley, J. E. B. Moss, Z. Wang, and P. Cheng. The garbage collection advantage, improving program locality. In *Conference on Object Oriented Programming Systems Languages and Applications*, pages 69–80, 2004.

[11] C. Lattner and V. Adve. Automatic pool allocation: Improving performance by controlling data structure layout in the heap. In *Conference on Programming Language Design and Implementation*, pages 129–142, 2005.

[12] D. Lea. A memory allocator. *The C++ Report*, 1989.

[13] J. Lu, A. Das, and W. Hsu. Dynamic helper threaded prefetching on the sun ultrasparc cmp processor. In *International Symposium on Microarchitecture*, 2005.

[14] M. Marron, D. Kapur, and M. Hermenegildo. Identification of logically related heap regions. In *International Symposium on Memory Management*, pages 89–98, 2009.

[15] M. L. Seidl and B. G. Zorn. Segregating heap objects by reference behavior and lifetime. In *Architectural Support for Programming Languages and Operating Systems*, pages 12–23, 1998.

[16] M. J. Serrano and X. Zhuang. Placement optimization using data context collected during garbage collection. In *International Symposium on Memory Management*, pages 69–78, 2009.

[17] B. Steensgaard. Points-to analysis in almost linear time. In *Annual Symposium on Principles of Programming Languages*, pages 32–41, 1996.

[18] Q. Zhao, R. Rabbah, and W. Wong. Dynamic memory optimization using pool allocation and prefetching. *ACM SIGARCH Computer Architecture News*, 33(5):27–32, 2005.

An Efficient Software Transactional Memory Using Commit-Time Invalidation *

Justin E. Gottschlich, Manish Vachharajani, and Jeremy G. Siek

Department of Electrical, Computer, and Energy Engineering, University of Colorado at Boulder
{gottschl, manishv, jeremy.siek}@colorado.edu

Abstract

To improve the performance of transactional memory (TM), researchers have found many eager and lazy optimizations for *conflict detection*, the process of determining if transactions can commit. Despite these optimizations, nearly all TMs perform one aspect of lazy conflict detection in the same manner to preserve serializability. That is, they perform *commit-time validation*, where a transaction is checked for conflicts with previously committed transactions during its commit phase. While commit-time validation is efficient for workloads that exhibit limited contention, it can limit transaction throughput for contending workloads.

This paper presents an efficient implementation of *commit-time invalidation*, a strategy where transactions resolve their conflicts with in-flight (uncommitted) transactions *before* they commit. Commit-time invalidation supplies the contention manager (CM) with data that is unavailable through commit-time validation, allowing the CM to make decisions that increase transaction throughput. Commit-time invalidation also requires notably fewer operations than commit-time validation for memory-intensive transactions, uses zero commit-time operations for dynamically detected read-only transactions, and guarantees full opacity for any transaction in $O(N)$ time, an improvement over incremental validation's $O(N^2)$ time. Our experimental results show that for contending workloads, our efficient commit-time invalidating software TM (STM) is up to $3\times$ faster than TL2, a state-of-the-art validating STM.

Categories and Subject Descriptors: D.1.3 [Concurrent Programming]: Parallel Programming.

General Terms: Algorithms, Design, Performance.

Keywords: Commit-Time Invalidation, Software Transactional Memory.

1. Introduction

Transactional memory (TM) is a modern concurrency control paradigm that provides a simple parallel programming model to reduce the difficulty of writing parallel programs [15, 28]. Many

TMs use an optimistic concurrency model in which all operations are executed concurrently and the operations which violate serializability [15, 22] are undone. For TMs to provide an optimistic concurrency model such that the transaction commit order is serializable, transactions are generally atomic and isolated [17]. Unfortunately, maintaining atomicity and isolation incurs computational overhead that some researchers argue is too great for TM's practical adoption [2]. To address these concerns, researchers have found innovative ways to reduce the overhead of atomicity and isolation by optimizing conflict detection [4, 5, 18, 24, 30, 31].

Conflict detection, the process of determining if transactions can commit [30], is usually implemented as a conservative overestimation of transaction serializability. A transaction can commit when it is *consistent*; that is, it is free of transactional conflicts. A *transactional conflict* is defined as the non-null intersection between one transaction's write elements and another transaction's read and write elements [15, 19, 24]. A *true conflict* requires that at least one transaction be aborted for the TM's commit order to remain serializable. A *false conflict* exists when a specific commit order is chosen, rather than a transaction to abort, that preserves serializability. While significant work has been done in the area of conflict detection and resolution, nearly all TMs perform *commit-time validation*, a strategy where a single transaction's read elements, and sometimes its write elements, are checked for consistency at commit-time.

Commit-time validation typically uses version numbers associated with memory to track transactional conflicts [25]. In general, the version numbers of a transaction's read and write elements (also known as *read* and *write sets*) are compared against the version numbers of the same memory stored globally. If a version mismatch is found, the validating transaction is aborted since a previously committed transaction has updated the same memory. If no mismatch is found the transaction is consistent and can be committed. While commit-time validation is efficient for workloads that exhibit little contention, it limits *transaction throughput*, the number of transactions that commit per second, for contending workloads. This is because it does not determine how many in-flight transactions will be aborted due to a transaction's commit.

In this paper we consider *commit-time invalidation*, a conflict detection strategy in which transactional conflicts are found by comparing the memory of a committing transaction against the memory of in-flight transactions. Commit-time invalidation differs from commit-time validation in that all a committing transaction's conflicts with in-flight transactions are found and resolved *before* the transaction commits. Conflicts are sent to the *contention manager* (CM), the process that decides which transactions make forward progress [11, 14, 26], for resolution. The CM resolves conflicts by either (1) aborting all conflicting in-flight transactions, (2) aborting the committing transaction, or (3) stalling the committing transaction until the conflicting in-flight transactions have commit-

---

* This work was supported in part by Raytheon Company.

ted or aborted [30]. Through this mechanism, commit-time invalidation can notably increase transaction throughput when compared to commit-time validation for contending workloads.

Although invalidation is not a new idea [7, 9, 13, 14, 27, 29, 30], to the best of our knowledge, no prior work has implemented an efficient TM – i.e., a TM that is competitive with the state-of-the-art – that only uses invalidation. Inefficiencies found in prior attempts have steered TM research toward validation. In this paper we demonstrate that a TM which only uses commit-time invalidation can be implemented efficiently. In doing so, this paper presents the following contributions:

1. Full commit-time invalidation can increase transaction throughput by supplying a CM with more information than is possible using commit-time validation, allowing the CM to make informed and efficient decisions.

2. Optimized commit-time invalidation is asymptotically faster than validation for memory-intensive transactions.

3. Commit-time invalidation requires zero operations to identify conflicts in dynamically detected read-only transactions and ensures opacity[1] [12] for any transaction in $O(N)$ time, where N is the number of elements in the transaction's read set, an improvement over incremental validation's $O(N^2)$ time.

4. Our efficient commit-time invalidating software TM (STM), InvalSTM, is over $3\times$ faster than TL2 [4], a state-of-the-art validating STM, for certain contending workloads.

2. Background

In this section we present a history of invalidation and explain why prior efforts have only partially explored it, leaving many of its powerful optimizations unexplored.

Overview of Invalidation vs. Validation One of the most computationally expensive aspects of TM is the process of detecting conflicts (i.e., discovering when the commit of two or more transactions will result in an execution order that is not serializable).

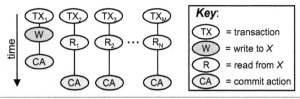

Figure 1. 1-Writer and N-Readers: A Highly Contending, Highly Concurrent Workload.

If, for a moment, we restrict ourselves to commit-time conflict detection, we can see why an invalidating TM can exploit more transaction throughput than a validating TM. Consider the scenario depicted in Figure 1 where one transaction writes to variable X and N transactions subsequently read the value of X. A TM using commit-time validation (see Figure 2 for an overview) and *lazy write acquisition*[2], will successfully validate the writer transaction at its CA (the commit action). The writer will then update X's global value and version number and commit. However, this behavior will cause all N readers to abort. When the readers reach their CA, they will be required to abort because their view of X will be inconsistent with main memory due to TX_1's commit. Thus,

---

[1] Opacity is the property where doomed transactions are identified before they can execute harmful operations [12].

[2] Lazy write acquisition is where written memory is exclusively acquired at the transaction's commit phase [17].

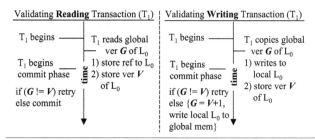

Figure 2. Transaction Using Commit-Time Validation.

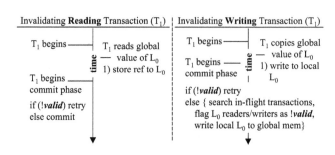

Figure 3. Transaction Using Commit-Time Invalidation.

commit-time validation effectively eliminates all concurrency between the readers and writer, a serious issue if N is large like it is in a number of workloads and systems [8, 21, 32].

Now, consider commit-time invalidation (see Figure 3 for an overview) for the scenario in Figure 1. When TX_1 reaches CA it scans all N in-flight transactions for conflicts. Each conflict is sent to the CM which, based on the number of contending *read-only transactions* (transactions that only read memory), can make an informed decision to abort TX_1 and allow the concurrent commit of the N readers. When N is large, this behavior dramatically increases transaction throughput.

Furthermore, in theory, an invalidating TM can always make the same decisions as a validating TM. Therefore, in cases when validation is efficient, such as non-contending workloads, invalidation can behave as validation does, making invalidation more powerful. Unfortunately, prior to this work, validating TMs have proven to be more efficient in practice. To understand why this is so, we must first discuss the different types of conflicts, conflict detection strategies, and the different strategies for maintaining read and write sets.

Types of Conflicts. Conflicts arise when two or more in-flight transactions access the same memory before committing and come in three varieties: *W-W*, *W-R*, and *R-W* [24]. W-W conflicts occur when two transactions write to the same memory. W-R conflicts occur when one transaction writes to a memory location and another transaction subsequently reads it (or vice versa for R-W conflicts). Without considering dependence-aware TM [23], W-W conflicts are generally classified as true conflicts [30], while W-R and R-W conflicts may be false; there may exist a serializable commit order so W-R and R-W conflicts can be resolved without transactional aborts.

Eager and Lazy Conflict Detection. Conflict detection can be performed *eagerly* or *lazily*. Eager conflict detection happens sometime before a transaction commits; lazy conflict detection happens at commit-time. TMs generally perform some conflict detection at commit-time even if the majority is handled eagerly.

Visible and Invisible Read and Write Sets. To detect conflicts, TMs maintain read and write sets (i.e., the set of locations a transaction has read and written, respectively). A transaction's read or write set is said to be *visible* if it can be seen by other transactions, otherwise it is called *invisible*. For invalidating TMs to detect W-W conflicts, write sets must be visible so that write sets from different transactions may be compared. Likewise, for invalidating TMs to detect W-R or R-W conflicts, read sets must be visible.

2.1 The Rise and Fall of Invalidating TMs

Partial invalidation is the process in which a TM performs some invalidation, either eagerly or lazily, but does not guarantee all conflicts with in-flight transactions are resolved before a transaction commits. Because of this some conflicts are missed by invalidation and subsequently require resolution through validation. Partial invalidation was first implemented in Herlihy et. al's DSTM for eager W-W conflicts, and in Harris and Fraser's WSTM for lazy W-W conflicts [13, 14]. Scott followed by proposing several invalidation techniques, which were used in Spear et al.'s *mixed invalidation* (using eager W-W and lazy W-R / R-W invalidation) in RSTM [27, 30]. Fraser and Harris's OSTM followed by implementing lazy invalidation for W-W conflicts [7].

To maximize concurrency, these TMs use *non-blocking synchronization*: they avoid the use of locks for shared data structures and instead rely on wait-free, lock-free (OSTM), or obstruction-free (DSTM, RSTM) synchronization. To maintain the visible read and write sets needed for invalidation, they use ownership records or *orecs*, which are data structures that associate memory elements with the transactions that access them [28]. On the first read or write of each memory location, the transaction is added to the orec for that location. Upon commit, the transaction is removed from all the orecs in which it was added.

In their most efficient implementation, orecs are computationally expensive. Spear et al. explain that maintaining complete visible readers per transactional memory location, necessary for W-R / R-W invalidation, incurs too much overhead for a TM to be practical [30]. They found the overhead associated with managing such readers costs more than the $O(N^2)$ overhead of *incremental validation*, the process of revalidating all of a transaction's read elements each time a new memory location is opened for reading (i.e., when a memory location is first read) [17, 30].

To gain some of the benefits of invalidation without incurring the full penalty of orecs, Spear et al.'s mixed invalidation uses one word per memory location to track readers. This reduces maintenance overhead, but limits W-R invalidation to 32 conflicts (or 64 on a 64-bit architectures) per memory location. Thus, the system must still perform version-based validation for > 32 threads.

Some *lock-based* STMs (TL2, RingSTM, and JudoSTM), those STMs which use mutual exclusion operations at their core, avoid the overhead of invalidation by not using it at all. TL2, for example, does not use invalidation, yet through its space and time optimizations, is able to perform efficient orec-based validation [4]. RingSTM and JudoSTM, on the other hand, do not use invalidation nor do they use orecs. RingSTM uses a `ring` structure to efficiently perform eager validation only against those transactions on the `ring` in which it is necessary [31], while JudoSTM uses a *value-based conflict detection* data structure to perform validation with reduced atomic instruction overhead [20]. In all three cases, invalidation is avoided entirely.

Although invalidation was proposed as early as 2003 [13, 14], implementation overhead has kept its use limited. In this paper, Section 3 explores the concurrency potential of an efficient fully invalidating TM by presenting an asymptotic analysis of version-based validation in contrast with commit-time invalidation. The section shows that invalidation provides opportunities over validation that can increase transaction throughput, making it a superior conflict detection strategy. Section 4 then shows how we efficiently

implement the data structures needed for full invalidation within InvalSTM, and Section 5 evaluates InvalSTM against TL2, a state-of-the-art validating STM.

3. The Promise of Full Invalidation

In this section we demonstrate that full invalidation offers numerous benefits over validation. We show that *any* fully invalidating TM can perform opacity and conflict detection more efficiently than a validating one. In the case of contending workloads, we illustrate how full invalidation can increase transaction throughput over validation. In addition, we demonstrate that a fully invalidating TM that uses search time optimized read and write sets can perform conflict detection for memory-intensive transactions in notably fewer operations than what is needed for the most efficient validation techniques.

Full Invalidation. For a TM to be *fully invalidating*, each transaction must resolve its conflicts before it commits. A *resolved conflict* is one that is eliminated by aborting or stalling one or more transactions to preserve serializability (as described in [22]). Therefore, when a transaction begins its commit phase in a fully invalidating TM, the TM need only check in-flight transactions for conflicts against the committing transaction. This is because fully invalidating TMs require conflicts to be resolved before transactions commit, ensuring the only unresolved conflicts are those with uncommitted, in-flight transactions. While there are numerous ways to build a fully invalidating TM, commit-time invalidation may be the least computationally expensive way. As such, for the remainder of this paper when we speak of full invalidation we mean a system that at least, and most often only, uses commit-time invalidation.

3.1 Conflict Detection and Opacity

TMs perform conflict detection to determine which transactions can commit. However, as noted by Guerraoui and Kapalka, conflict detection alone is insufficient. TMs must also ensure *opacity*, a correctness criterion that requires each transactional read return a value that is consistent with its execution, and that doomed transactions be aborted before a subsequent transactional read or write returns from its call [12]. Guerraoui and Kapalka show that even an isolated, uncommitted transaction can cause adverse program side-effects if a single transactional read is inconsistent.

To demonstrate this, consider a program invariant where variables X and Y are always one discrete value apart (+/-1). If transaction T_1 reads X as value 2, the operation X / Y will be defined, because Y will be either 3 or 1. However, if transaction T_2 performs $X = 1$, $Y = 0$ and commits after T_1 reads X but before it reads Y, the program invariant will be violated. If T_1 is permitted to read Y, the X / Y operation will result in a divide by zero exception. An opaque TM avoids this by verifying all of a transaction's reads are consistent before opening a new item for reading or writing. In this case, when T_1 opens Y for reading, the TM would identify T_1's view of X is inconsistent and force it to abort before returning the value of Y. Thus to be correct, in addition to detecting and resolving conflicts, TMs must also be opaque.

3.1.1 Validation

Many TMs ensure opacity and perform conflict detection using the same technique; they perform *incremental validation* (DSTM, RSTM, SXM, and TL2), a process in which each element in a transaction's read set is checked for consistency each time a new element is opened for reading [30]. Incremental validation performs $O(N)$ operations N times, where N is the number of elements in the transaction's read set, resulting in $O(N^2)$ operations [17]. Every validation a transaction performs prior to commit-time is an opacity check (and still results in $O(N^2)$ worst-case time because

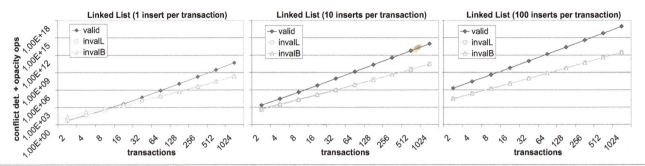

Figure 4. Conflict Detection and Opacity Overhead of Linked List for Validation and Invalidation.

$N * (N - 1) \in O(N^2)$). These eager operations are not intended to commit the transaction. Instead they ensure opacity by avoiding abnormal program behavior that would ensue from accessing stale values. The final validation operation, performed precisely once during a transaction's commit phase, is a conflict detection operation performed specifically to ensure a transaction can commit.

Given a series of M non-conflicting, committing transactions, the below equation represents the opacity and conflict detection operations sufficient for incremental validation. The variable r_i is the ith committing transaction's read set size. [3]

$$o_v(M) = \sum_{i=1}^{M} \sum_{j=1}^{r_i} j$$

The inner sum represents the number of opacity operations performed for each transaction up to and including its commit-time conflict detection operation. The outer sum includes the opacity and conflict detection operations for all M committing transactions.

3.1.2 Invalidation

Invalidation uses two different techniques for opacity and conflict detection. Invalidating TMs perform opacity by checking a boolean *valid* flag, and perform conflict detection by identifying conflicts between a committing transaction and all in-flight transactions. The invalidation processes for opacity and conflict detection are explained below.

Opacity Checks. Each transaction has a *valid* flag that is initially true. It is set to false when the TM decides to abort the transaction to resolve a conflict (Figure 3). When a transaction opens a new element for reading, the TM checks the transaction's *valid* flag – an $O(1)$ time operation. If it is false, the transaction is aborted before the new element's memory is returned. If the *valid* flag is true, the transaction continues to execute normally. Because opacity is checked incrementally, it takes $O(N)$ time to complete per transaction, an improvement over incremental validation's $O(N^2)$ time. However, to properly set each transaction's *valid* flag, the TM performs commit-time invalidation for each transaction. The commit-time invalidation algorithm behaves differently based on the type of transaction.

Conflict Detection for Writers. A *writer*, a transaction that writes to at least one memory location and reads any number of locations, must resolve its conflicts before it commits. These conflicts are limited to in-flight transactions that access memory (via read or write) that the writer has modified. When the conflicts are found the CM

can perform any one of the following actions: (1) set the committing transaction's *valid = false* and abort it, (2) set the conflicting in-flight transactions' *valid = false* so they will abort or (3) stall the committing transaction until the conflicting transactions commit or abort. A key characteristic when using commit-time invalidation is that a committing transaction's conflicts are identified (and resolved) prior to committing; this characteristic is paramount to unlocking concurrency.

Given a series of M non-conflicting, committing transactions, the below equation represents the opacity and conflict detection operations sufficient for full invalidation. The variables r_i and w_i are the ith committing transaction's read and write set size. F_i is the number of in-flight transactions at the time of the ith committing transaction. r_j and w_j are the jth in-flight transaction's read and write set sizes. s_{rj} and s_{wj} are the search time complexity associated with the jth transaction's read and write algorithms.

$$o_i(M) = \sum_{i=1}^{M} \left(r_i + \sum_{j=1}^{F_i} w_i(s_{rj}(r_j) + s_{wj}(w_j)) \right)$$

The inner sum performs conflict detection for the ith committing transaction against all in-flight transactions (F_i). The number of operations sufficient to identify conflicts with each transaction is based on the jth transaction's read and write set algorithm's worst-case search time when holding r_j and w_j number of elements, represented by $s_{rj}(r_j)$ and $s_{wj}(w_j)$. The ith transaction compares its write set for overlaps with reads and writes of in-flight transactions, resulting in $s(r_j) + s(w_j)$. Finally, w_i is multiplied by the sum of $s(r_j)$ and $s(w_j)$, because each search operation is performed w_i times, the number of elements in the committing transaction's write set. [4]

The outer sum performs the incremental opacity checks for all M committing transactions. The checks are performed with a single boolean comparison and are performed each time the ith transaction opens a new element for reading, represented by r_i.

Conflict Detection for Read-Only Transactions. Notice that read-only transactions have $w_i = 0$, which reduces the above equation to $o_i(M) = \sum_{i=1}^{M} r_i$. In other words, read-only transactions perform *zero* conflict detection operations. Furthermore, unlike prior optimizations, invalidating read-only transactions do not need to be identified as read-only before they execute to achieve this benefit. [5] Therefore, dynamically detected read-only transactions in any fully invalidating TM are guaranteed to perform zero conflict detection operations. This is a notable benefit because many trans-

---

[3] A TM using a global clock does not need to perform incremental validation if the global clock has the same value as when the transaction first began. This indicates no transaction has committed since it began [4]. However, the clock must still be read at each opacity check.

[4] This is not true for algorithms that perform set intersection in constant time, such as Bloom filters. In such cases, w_i becomes some constant C.

[5] TL2 has a space complexity optimization for read-only transactions, yet it requires the transaction be known as read-only before it is executed [4].

actions that are statically read-write may be dynamically read-only much of the time.

3.2 An Analysis of Opacity and Conflict Detection Efficiency

To demonstrate the efficiency of opacity and conflict detection using full invalidation, consider a scenario in which N transactions are appending to a linked list in which only one transaction can commit. For this scenario, each time a transaction commits all other in-flight transactions must abort and restart, regardless of the conflict detection strategy. However, as illustrated in Figure 4 full invalidation has a lower opacity cost and uses fewer conflict detection operations as transactions grow in size, resulting in a more efficient TM. Figure 4 shows the number of transactions vs. the number of operations required for conflict detection, as per the earlier equations.

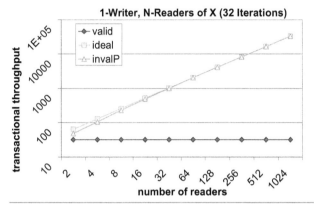

Figure 5. Transaction Throughput for 1-Writer / N-Readers of Single Variable.

Our model assumes all transactions reach their commit phase before conflicts are identified, requiring that each transaction perform incremental opacity (via version-based validation or invalidation's *valid* flag). Figure 4 demonstrates the performance of (1) incremental validation (valid), (2) commit-time invalidation using a logarithmic-time search, i.e., $s_{rj}(r_j)$ and $s_{wj}(w_j)$ at $O(logN)$ (invalL), and (3) commit-time invalidation using a constant-time search, i.e. $s_{rj}(r_j)$ and $s_{wj}(w_j)$ at $O(1)$ (invalB). While the commit-time invalidation logarithmic- and constant-time search displays little theoretical operational difference in Figure 4, their practical executions are critically different (see Section 4). In Figure 4, as the number of elements inserted per transaction grows (from 1, to 10, to 100), the performance delta between validation and invalidation widens each time by an order of magnitude (from 10^2, to 10^3, to 10^4 operational difference), illustrating our prior point that incremental validation's overhead worsens as transactions access more memory highlighting commit-time invalidation's efficiency for memory-intensive transactions.

3.3 An Analysis of Transaction Throughput

Finally, we turn our attention to highly contending, highly concurrent workloads, where concurrency can be exploited but only if the CM makes informed decisions about which transactions to commit and which to abort.

We analyze the scenario shown in Figure 1, where one transaction writes to X followed by N transactions reading X. We assume lazy write acquisition and that the writer reaches its commit phase first, followed by the N readers. Using this model, Figure 5 displays the amount of transaction throughput (y-axis) achieved as N increases (x-axis) using (1) version-based validation (valid), (2) ideal throughput or unfair commit-time invalidation (ideal), and

(3) priority-based commit-time invalidation (invalP) [10, 29]. The priority-based CM policy ensures transactions will not starve, while simultaneously promoting a high degree of transactional concurrency. It behaves in the following way. Each new transaction begins with a priority of 1. Each time a transaction is aborted, its priority is incremented by 1. Once it commits, the transaction's priority is reset to 1. For a transaction to abort other transactions, its priority must be greater than or equal to the sum of all the transactions it is attempting to abort.

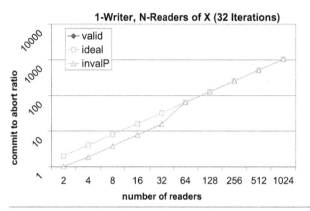

Figure 6. Commit to Abort Ratio for 1-Writer / N-Readers of Single Variable.

Figure 5 shows 32 iterations of 1-writer / N-readers, where priority-based invalidation eventually achieves $\approx 10^3 \times$ greater transaction throughput than version-based validation (for 1024 readers).[6] Figure 6 shows the commit to abort ratio of the Figure 5. Validation's commit to abort ratio ranges from 0.5 (2 transactions) to 0.000977 (1024 transactions), while priority-based invalidation ranges from 1 (a $2\times$ difference) to 1024 (a $10^6 \times$ difference).

4. InvalSTM: A Fully Invalidating STM

In this section, we explain the design of InvalSTM, our fully invalidating STM. InvalSTM uses commit-time invalidation for all conflicts (i.e., W-W, W-R, and R-W). InvalSTM also uses lazy write acquisition because it provides the CM with one-to-many conflicts at commit-time. These one-to-many conflicts are necessary for the CM to make informed decisions that can increase transaction throughput. *Eager write acquisition*, which exclusively acquires write locations as the transaction executes them, sends eager one-to-one conflicts to the CM. These one-to-one conflicts prevent the CM from seeing the entire view of conflicts and, because these conflicts are eager, force the CM to make speculative decisions that limit transaction throughput.

4.1 A Design Overview

As explained in Section 2, maintaining visible read sets through orecs can be expensive. InvalSTM addresses this in the same way JudoSTM [20], NOrec [3], and RingSTM [31] do, by avoiding orecs altogether. Instead, InvalSTM stores read and write sets inside a transaction object. In addition, because lock-based STMs have emerged with strong performance – DracoSTM [9], Ennal's STM [6], RingSTM [31], and TL2 [4] – InvalSTM uses mutual exclusion locks as its core synchronization type.

For InvalSTM to perform commit-time invalidation its transactions must be prevented from adding new memory elements to

---

[6] Our tests of up to 32,768 iterations show that priority-based invalidation remains $\approx 10^3 \times$ faster than version-based validation, although with each increased N^2 iteration invalidation grows ($\approx 1.5\times$) faster.

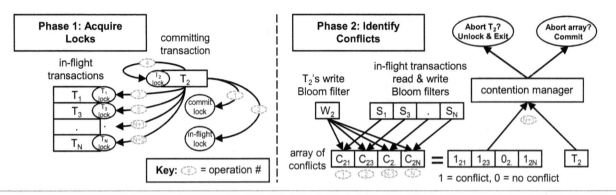

Figure 7. An Example of InvalSTM's Commit-Time Invalidation Process.

their read and write sets while a transaction commits. Without this restriction, a conflicting memory element may be added to an in-flight transaction's read or write sets after it has been found to be free of conflicts. To prevent this unwanted behavior, InvalSTM associates a lock with each transaction. Before performing commit-time invalidation, InvalSTM acquires the transactional locks of all in-flight transactions to ensure the invalidation phase will be performed without extraneous modification to the in-flight transaction's read and write sets.

While this addresses the above concern, it creates a new problem: a serialization point is created from the beginning of a transaction's commit phase until its end. To minimize the negative impact of this serialization point, InvalSTM compresses read and write sets within Bloom filters, which align with caches for fast access and constant time ($O(1)$) set intersection.

The remainder of this section discusses, in detail, the main design points summarized above. Listed below is a summary of the unique optimizations that emerge from this design.

- Full invalidation is supported, gaining all the benefits highlighted in Section 3, including boosted concurrency from informed CM decisions, zero conflict detection operations for read-only transactions and efficient conflict detection for memory-intensive transactions.

- Read sets can be stored in imprecise, compressed, and contiguous storage that reduce the time and space complexity to perform invalidation while also reducing cache line eviction rates.

- Per-memory locking (orecs) is no longer necessary. Instead, locks are associated with each transaction which can drastically reduce atomic (fenced) operations when transactions are memory-intensive [20, 31].

- Visible read sets using per-transaction storage require zero operations to cleanup, a significant savings when compared to visible read sets using per-memory (orec) storage.

4.2 A Lock-Based STM

In addition to a lock per transaction, InvalSTM uses two global locks: a commit and in-flight lock. The commit lock limits the commit phase to a single transaction. The in-flight lock is used to limit modification of the in-flight transaction list to a single thread.

Before performing commit-time invalidation, the commit lock is acquired to prevent two or more transactions from concurrently committing. InvalSTM disallows this behavior because concurrently committing transactions are not guaranteed they will have the execution time to invalidate all other concurrently committing transactions unless committing transactions are prevented from exiting the commit phase until all other committing transactions have completed their invalidation. While concurrently committing trans-

actions would increase concurrent work, it introduces livelock scenarios as new transactions enter the commit phase, creating a perpetual cycle of invalidation. This livelock cycle can decrease or even halt throughput, so InvalSTM prohibits it by limiting the commit phase to a single transaction.

The in-flight lock is acquired before commit-time invalidation is performed so new transactions cannot be put in-flight. This is needed for two reasons. First, it creates a sequential locking order based on the transactions that are currently in-flight (as seen in Figure7). Second, it prevents a livelock that could occur as invalidated transactions are removed and placed back in-flight, requiring cyclic invalidation.

While these additional locks complicate the design, their absence would reduce concurrency in the following ways. First, if only the commit lock was used, all transactions would be required to obtain it when adding elements to their read and write sets. By using the commit and transactional locks, transactions can concurrently add elements to their read and write sets, so long as no transaction is committing. Second, if the in-flight lock was removed and instead the commit lock was used to add or remove transactions from the in-flight set, transactions could not simultaneously begin the commit phase and modify the in-flight transaction list. While it is true that committing transactions generally do need to obtain the in-flight lock, they do not always need it immediately. Transactions whose *valid = false* can perform nearly all of their cleanup code prior to requiring the in-flight lock. In addition, read-only transactions only require the commit lock momentarily to identify that they are in fact read-only and to check that they are *valid*. Once checked, these transactions release the commit lock, but retain the in-flight lock to remove themselves from the list.

4.3 Serialized Commit

A downside of InvalSTM's locking design is that it creates a serialization point during a transaction's commit phase. This serialization point limits commits to one transaction at a time and prevents in-flight transactions from adding new elements to their read and write sets while a transaction commits. To minimize the negative impact of this serialization point, read and write sets are stored in Bloom filters which speed up the invalidation process by performing set intersection in constant worst-case time [1]. Below is the modified operational overhead equation ($o_{ib}(M)$ for M transactions) from Section3.1.2 when read and write sets use Bloom filters to perform full invalidation.

$$o_{ib}(M) = \sum_{i=1}^{M} r_i + (2kw * (F_i))$$

Commit-time invalidation is handled by $\sum_{i=1}^{M} 2kw * (F_i)$ where w is the number of words per bit vector, k is the number of bit vectors per Bloom filter, and F_i are the in-flight transactions

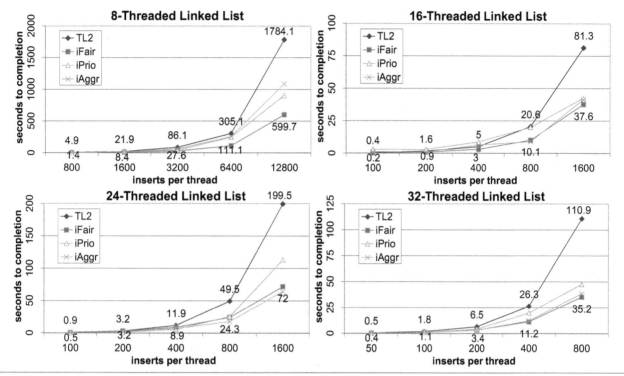

Figure 8. Linked List Benchmarks.

at the time the ith transaction is committing. The opacity checks, which are performed throughout the transaction's lifetime, add r_i (number of elements in the transaction's read set) to each summation. By using Bloom filters, the original search operations required for a single transaction is reduced from w_i to 1 (Section 3), because the conflicts between one transaction and another are found in a single set intersection. kw represents the original equation's search time of $s(w_j)$ and $s(r_j)$. Since kw must be performed twice (once per read and write set) the result is $2kw$. Because these operations must be done for each in-flight transaction, we multiply $2kw$ by F_i.

For each transaction, InvalSTM currently uses a fixed 2^{16} bits per bit vector and two bit vectors per Bloom filter. Although we experimented with a wide variety of Bloom filter configurations, our early experiments indicate the current size performs the best overall for our tested benchmarks. We expect to extend our research in this area as we analyze more benchmarks.

4.4 Transaction Implementation

In InvalSTM each transaction object contains its own read and write sets. Read sets store memory locations, while write sets store memory locations plus a copy that is used to buffer transactional writes for lazy write acquisition. The memory locations for read and write sets are stored in separate Bloom filters. This is done so different types of conflicts can be handled by the CM in different ways. For example, if a committing, writer transaction has only W-R conflicts, the CM can choose to stall the writer until the reader transactions commit. If read and write sets were not separated, the CM would only be able to resolve conflicts via abort.

Because write sets store written data along with memory locations, each transaction contains an additional map that associates written data with its memory location. This data structure is necessary in addition to the Bloom filter used for write sets, because lazy write acquisition must commit memory in such a way that false

positives are not possible [1]. Otherwise the TM could update incorrect memory locations.

Opacity Checks. In a fully invalidating TM, ensuring a transaction has no conflicts is inexpensive (an $O(1)$ operation). Therefore, InvalSTM performs opacity checks on all transaction calls, not just the ones in which it is necessary. This adds some overhead, yet, we have found it improves system performance because it can identify doomed transactions early.

Reading and Writing Transactional Memory. When a transaction accesses a memory element for reading or writing, the STM performs a read-only lookup to see if the transaction has already accessed the element. This lookup requires no locking, since the operation is not changing the read or write sets. If the lookup is successful, the appropriate value is returned. If not, the transaction's lock is acquired, the memory address (and value if necessary) is inserted into the correct set, and the transaction's lock is released.

Committing. Figure 7 provides a high-level view of the commit-time invalidation process. For brevity, some details are omitted from the diagram. Those include the priority elevation for aborted transactions, the removal of aborted transactions from the in-flight set to reduce in-flight lock contention, the CM's usage of transaction size (read + write sets) as a discriminator for the abort protocol, and the short-circuited logic used for read-only transactions.

The commit-time invalidation process, shown in Figure 7, begins with Phase I where the commit and in-flight locks are acquired. This ensures no other transaction can commit or be started while a transaction is committing. Next, the committing and in-flight transactions' associated locks are acquired in a sequential order to avoid deadlock. Phase II then identifies the conflicts the committing transaction has with the in-flight transactions. If conflicts exist, the CM is sent the batch of conflicts and allows it to make the decision on which transactions are aborted or stalled.

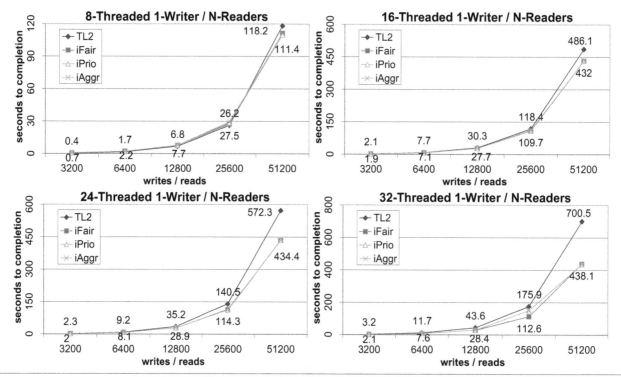

Figure 9. 1-Writer, N-Reader Benchmarks.

An important detail of InvalSTM's design is that in-flight transactions can make forward progress during the entire commit-time invalidation process. The two exceptions are (1) transactions cannot concurrently commit while another transaction is already committing and (2) they cannot add new memory elements to their read and write sets. Those limitations aside, our anecdotal experiments have shown that the forward progress of transactions while another transaction is committing significantly increases overall throughput for workloads that access a shared memory element multiple times (e.g., a head or sentinel node, a global counter, etc.).

False Positives Preventing Forward Progress. As Bloom filters can emit false positives, there is a chance these false positives will prevent forward progress. To avoid this scenario, we use a runtime threshold R that, once exceeded by our abort to commit ratio, switches our TM from using Bloom filters to using red-black trees for read and write sets, ensuring false positives are avoided. After some programmable period of time T, our system reverts back to using Bloom filters for read and write sets. In our experiments, however, this threshold is never reached.

5. Experimental Results

In this section we present the experimental results of InvalSTM, using commit-time invalidation, and TL2, the state-of-the-art validating STM. The benchmarks were run on a 1.0 GHz Sun Fire T2000 supporting 32 concurrent hardware threads with 32 GB RAM. The TL2 implementation is from RSTM.v4, University of Rochester's STM library collection. For all the graphs in this section, the y-axis shows the total execution time in seconds (lower is always better). The x-axis represents the workload executed rather than the usual threads, since, as shown in Section 3, invalidation performs more efficiently than validation as transactions access more memory. Since the number of threads is constant per graph, four graphs are used per benchmark each with a different thread count and/or workload configuration.

5.1 Contention Manager Variants

We tested three CM variants with our benchmarks: iFair (invalidation fair), iPrio (invalidation prioritized) and iAggr (invalidation aggressive). iAggr ensures the first transaction to enter the commit phase commits. It demonstrates how commit-time invalidation performs when it does not use conflict information to make informed decisions. In other words, iAggr captures the conflict detection operational difference between invalidation and validation.

iPrio associates a priority with each transaction. A transaction's priority is raised each time it aborts and is reset each time it commits. A transaction can commit if it has the highest priority of all conflicting in-flight transactions. A transaction can also commit if it has the largest read set size of all in-flight transactions or its read and write set size is larger than the average read and write set size of all conflicting transactions plus their cumulative priority.

iFair associates a priority with each transaction and raises and resets the transaction's priority in the same manner as iPrio. Unlike iPrio, a transaction can commit if its read and write set size is greater than a weighted average of the in-flight transaction's read size and their priority. A transaction can also commit if its read and write set size is greater than any of the in-flight transaction's read set size. In addition, if an in-flight transaction's read set size is $10^2 \times$ greater than the committing transaction's read set size and its priority is $2^3 \times$ greater, iFair will abort the committing transaction in favor of the higher priority, larger in-flight transaction.

Of the three CM variants, iFair performs the best overall. While iAggr and iPrio each perform well under certain conditions, iFair consistently performs as well or better and, in some cases, outperforms TL2 by more than $3\times$ (Figure 8, 32-Threaded Linked List). Based on the performance improvement as the concurrency widens from 8 to 32 threads, it seems that one can speculate that commit-time invalidation's performance will only improve over TL2 as the number of concurrent transactions grow.

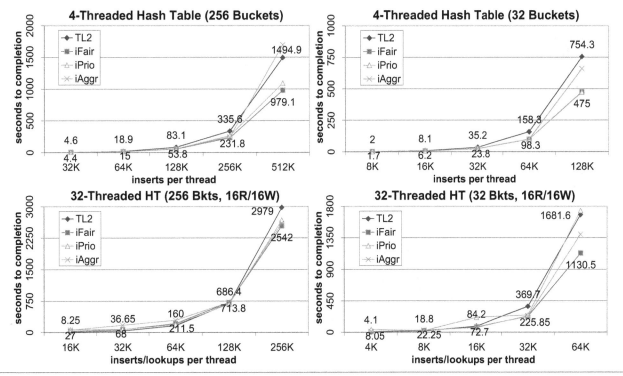

Figure 10. Hash Table Benchmarks.

5.2 Linked List

Our linked list benchmarks are shown in Figure 8. Each linked list benchmark populated a single linked list with N concurrently executing threads. Each thread inserted the same number of elements (i.e., T_1 inserts 0-99, T_2 inserts 100-199, etc.) and the insert operation was a transaction. iFair performed most consistently, especially in the 8-threaded benchmark where its CM policy drives it to outperform the other CM policies by $\approx 2\times$.

In the linked list benchmarks, InvalSTM outperforms TL2 from $\approx 2\times$ to $\approx 3\times$. At nearly all data points, as the workload increases InvalSTM improves its efficiency over TL2. For the final data point in the 32-threaded benchmark, InvalSTM's iFair is $3.15\times$ faster than TL2. It is important to note that the larger threaded benchmarks perform less work than the smaller threaded benchmarks (e.g., the 32-threaded workload inserts $<= 800$ nodes per transaction, while the 8-threaded one inserts $<= 12,800$ nodes). However, the performance difference for InvalSTM and TL2 is roughly the same for all threaded executions. This suggests that if equivalent work was executed for the 32-threaded benchmarks, the performance difference would significantly favor InvalSTM.

5.3 1-Writer / N-Readers

For highly contending but also highly concurrent workloads commit-time invalidation performs well. This is demonstrated in the 1-writer / N-reader benchmark shown in Figure 9. The 1-writer / N-reader benchmark was implemented using a linked list where the writer performs a fixed number of appends and each reader performs an iterative lookup. Both the append and lookup are transactions. While the performance difference between InvalSTM's CM strategies and TL2 for 8 and 16 threaded workloads is small, the difference between the 24 and 32 threaded workloads is notable. The 32 threaded benchmark shows iFair outperform TL2 by $\approx 1.6\times$. The reason for this is straightforward: lower threaded workloads emit fewer aborts because contention on the data is

minimal. As readers are added the contention increases as do the number of aborts. This creates a scenario where early notification of doomed transactions, a low overhead benefit of invalidation, is critical in improving performance.

Read-only Transactions. While the 1-writer / N-reader performance difference favors InvalSTM by only $\approx 1.6\times$, this margin is notable because TL2 has a space optimization for read-only transactions (though transactions must be flagged as read-only prior to executing). Commit-time invalidation has a time optimization that can defer the discovery of read-only transactions until commit-time. However, to be fair to TL2, we only leverage read-only optimizations for statically tagged read-only transactions. Since N of the transactions are read-only (where N = 7, 15, 23, and 31), both systems heavily exploit their read-only transaction optimizations for this benchmark. Although TL2's read-only optimizations are impressive, commit-time invalidation's read-only optimizations seem to have more impact on performance for this scenario.

5.4 Hash Tables

The hash table experiments are shown in Figure 10 and are implemented using N-bucketed lists (N = 32 and 256). The hash function is a modulo operation on the number of buckets. Each benchmark used a single hash table which was concurrently populated by N number of threads and used the same insert conditions as the linked list example. The performance improvement of InvalSTM over TL2 are $1.48\times$ and $1.58\times$ for the 256 and 32 bucketed hash tables, respectively. For the 32-threaded 16 reader / 16 writer benchmarks, InvalSTM is faster than TL2 by $1.17\times$ for the 256 bucketed hash table and $1.48\times$ for the 32 bucketed one.

Although these performance improvements for InvalSTM are lower than the linked list experiments, they are meaningful because a bucketed hash table is generally considered a concurrent data structure as operations are distributed across numerous, simultaneously accessible buckets [16]. However, after the buckets reach a certain threshold of size, transactions begin to contend since appending elements to densely populated buckets requires more transactional execution time. Notice that even for the 32-threaded hash table benchmarks, InvalSTM outperforms TL2 by up to $\approx 50\%$.

6. Conclusion

This paper presented an efficient implementation of commit-time invalidation, a strategy where transactions resolve all of their conflicts with in-flight transactions before they commit. We provided an early example where substantial concurrency could be exploited by invalidation, but would be missed by validation. We then explained the opportunities invalidation provides over validation such as, more complete information sent to the CM enabling it to make better decisions to increase concurrency, faster conflict detection time for memory-intensive transactions, and transactional opacity checking in $O(N)$ time instead of incremental validation's $O(N^2)$ time. We then explained InvalSTM, a new TM design that performs commit-time invalidation using transaction-based read and write sets, time and space efficient Bloom filters for read and write sets, and an orec-free design that uses transaction locks rather than memory locks to reduce atomic primitive instruction overhead. The experimental results section compared InvalSTM's commit-time invalidation to TL2's state-of-the-art validation. We presented three CM strategies for InvalSTM which outperformed TL2, in some cases by upwards of $3\times$.

Acknowledgments

We thank the University of Rochester for their TL2 implementation in RSTM. We thank the anonymous reviewers for their constructive feedback; we have tried our best to integrate their insightful suggestions. We also thank Michael F. Spear for his early support of our initial design. We are also grateful to Michael for the discussions we had with him that helped us arrive at our final design. Lastly, we thank J Smart and Jim Pastoor of Raytheon Company for their ongoing support.

References

[1] B. H. Bloom. Space/time trade-offs in hash coding with allowable errors. In *Communications of the ACM*, 1970.

[2] C. Cascaval, C. Blundell, M. Michael, H. W. Cain, P. Wu, S. Chiras, and S. Chatterjee. Software transactional memory: Why is it only a research toy? In *ACM Queue*, 2008.

[3] L. Dalessandro, M. F. Spear, and M. L. Scott. NOrec: Streamlining STM by abolishing ownership records. In *Proceedings of the Symposium on Principles and Practice of Parallel Programming*, 2010.

[4] D. Dice, O. Shalev, and N. Shavit. Transactional locking II. In *Proceedings of the Symposium on Distributed Computing*, 2006.

[5] D. Dice and N. Shavit. Understanding tradeoffs in software transactional memory. In *Proceedings of the Symposium on Code Generation and Optimization*, 2007.

[6] R. Ennals. Software transactional memory should not be obstruction free. In *Intel Research Cambridge Tech Report*, 2006.

[7] K. Fraser and T. Harris. Concurrent programming without locks. In *ACM Transactions on Computer Systems*, 2007.

[8] H. Garcia-Molina and G. Wiederhold. Read-only transactions in a distributed database. In *ACM Transactions on Database Systems*, 1982.

[9] J. E. Gottschlich and D. A. Connors. DracoSTM: A practical C++ approach to software transactional memory. In *Proceedings of the Symposium on Library-Centric Software Design*, 2007.

[10] J. E. Gottschlich and D. A. Connors. Extending contention managers for user-defined priority-based transactions. In *Proceedings of the Workshop on Exploiting Parallelism with Transactional Memory and other Hardware Assisted Methods*, 2008.

[11] R. Guerraoui, M. Herlihy, and B. Pochon. Toward a theory of transactional contention managers. In *Proceedings of the Symposium on Principles of Distributed Computing*, 2005.

[12] R. Guerraoui and M. Kapalka. On the correctness of transactional memory. In *Proceedings of the Symposium on Principles and Practice of Parallel Programming*, 2008.

[13] T. Harris and K. Fraser. Language support for lightweight transactions. In *Proceedings of the Conference on Object Oriented Programming, Systems, Languages and Applications*, 2003.

[14] M. Herlihy, V. Luchangco, M. Moir, and I. William N. Scherer. Software transactional memory for dynamic-sized data structures. In *Proceedings of the Symposium on Principles of Distributed Computing*, 2003.

[15] M. Herlihy and J. E. B. Moss. Transactional memory: Architectural support for lock-free data structures. In *Proceedings of the International Symposium on Computer Architecture*, 1993.

[16] M. Herlihy and N. Shavit. *The Art of Multiprocessor Programming*. Elsevier, Inc., 2008.

[17] J. R. Larus and R. Rajwar. *Transactional Memory*. Morgan & Claypool, 2006.

[18] V. J. Marathe and M. Moir. Toward high performance nonblocking software transactional memory. In *Proceedings of the Symposium on Principles and Practice of Parallel Programming*, 2008.

[19] K. E. Moore, J. Bobba, M. J. Moravan, M. D. Hill, and D. A. Wood. LogTM: log-based transactional memory. In *Proceedings of the Conference on High-Performance Computer Architecture*, 2006.

[20] M. Olszewski, J. Cutler, and J. G. Steffan. JudoSTM: A dynamic binary-rewriting approach to software transactional memory. In *Proceedings of the Conference on Parallel Architecture and Compilation Techniques*, 2007.

[21] J. K. Ousterhout, H. Da Costa, D. Harrison, J. A. Kunze, M. Kupfer, and J. G. Thompson. A trace-driven analysis of the UNIX 4.2BSD file system. Technical report, Berkeley, CA, 1985.

[22] C. H. Papadimitriou. Serializability of concurrent data base updates. Technical report, Cambridge, MA., 1979.

[23] H. E. Ramadan, C. J. Rossbach, and E. Witchel. Dependence-aware transactional memory for increased concurrency. In *Proceedings of the Symposium on Microarchitecture*, 2008.

[24] H. E. Ramadan, I. Roy, M. Herlihy, and E. Witchel. Committing conflicting transactions in an STM. In *Proceedings of the Symposium on Principles and Practice of Parallel Programming*, 2009.

[25] B. Saha, A.-R. Adl-Tabatabai, R. L. Hudson, C. C. Minh, and B. Hertzberg. McRT-STM: a high performance software transactional memory system for a multi-core runtime. In *Proceedings of the Symposium on Principles and Practice of Parallel Programming*, 2006.

[26] W. N. Scherer and M. L. Scott. Advanced contention management for dynamic software transactional memory. In *Proceedings of the Symposium on Principles of Distributed Computing*, 2005.

[27] M. L. Scott. Sequential specification of transactional memory semantics. In *Proceedings of the Workshop on Transactional Computing*, 2006.

[28] N. Shavit and D. Touitou. Software transactional memory. In *Proceedings of the Principles of Distributed Computing*, 1995.

[29] M. F. Spear, L. Dalessandro, V. Marathe, and M. L. Scott. A comprehensive strategy for contention management in software transactional memory. In *Proceedings of the Symposium on Principles and Practice of Parallel Programming*, 2009.

[30] M. F. Spear, V. J. Marathe, W. N. Scherer III, and M. L. Scott. Conflict detection and validation strategies for software transactional memory. In *Proceedings of the Symposium on Distributed Computing*, 2006.

[31] M. F. Spear, M. M. Michael, and C. von Praun. RingSTM: scalable transactions with a single atomic instruction. In *Proceedings of the Symposium on Parallelism in Algorithms and Architectures*, 2008.

[32] W. Vogels. File system usage in Windows NT 4.0. In *Proceedings of the Symposium on Operating Systems Principles*, 1999.

Efficient Compilation of Fine-Grained SPMD-threaded Programs for Multicore CPUs

John A. Stratton[†*] Vinod Grover[†]
Jaydeep Marathe[†] Bastiaan Aarts[†]
Mike Murphy[†] Ziang Hu[†]

[†]NVIDIA Corporation
{vgrover, jmarathe, baarts, mmurphy, zhu}
@nvidia.com

Wen-mei W. Hwu*

* University of Illinois at Urbana-Champaign,
Center for Reliable and High-Performance
Computing
{stratton, hwu}@crhc.illinois.edu

Abstract

In this paper we describe techniques for compiling fine-grained SPMD-threaded programs, expressed in programming models such as OpenCL or CUDA, to multicore execution platforms. Programs developed for manycore processors typically express finer thread-level parallelism than is appropriate for multicore platforms. We describe options for implementing fine-grained threading in software, and find that reasonable restrictions on the synchronization model enable significant optimizations and performance improvements over a baseline approach. We evaluate these techniques in a production-level compiler and runtime for the CUDA programming model targeting modern CPUs. Applications tested with our tool often showed performance parity with the compiled C version of the application for single-thread performance. With modest coarse-grained multithreading typical of today's CPU architectures, an average of $3.4\times$ speedup on 4 processors was observed across the test applications.

Categories and Subject Descriptors D.1.3 [*Concurrent Programming*]: Parallel Programming

General Terms Algorithms, Performance

Keywords CUDA, Multicore, CPU, SPMD

1. Introduction

In the coming years, commercial application developers will have a strong incentive to develop highly parallel software to take advantage of widespread parallel processors in the consumer market. However, it is unclear whether each potential user of an application will have a computing subtrate with a similar degree, granularity and style of parallelism. Even if an application is amenable to targeting a wide variety of parallel computational platforms, it is unclear whether a single expression of the application in any one programming model will be sufficient. The model must be powerful enough to effectively capture many applications, yet have enough constraints to enable a wide range of architectures to be effectively supported.

We present some initial findings of a case study testing one parallel programming model that industry is hoping will be such a portable model: fine-grained Single Program Multiple Data (SPMD) kernels, with limited thread cooperation, controlled by a centralized process. CUDA [16] and OpenCL [12], for example, are both built on an underlying programming model of fine-grained SPMD threads. For the experiments presented here, we will be working with the CUDA programming model, noting in advance that the same techniques would be applicable to OpenCL and other SPMD programming models as well.

The CUDA programming model is a hybrid of two parallel programming models initially tailored to GPU architectures. It supports bulk synchronous task parallelism [24], where each task is composed of fine-grained SPMD threads. Programmers have been using CUDA with significant success in many application fields, such as bioinformatics [19], molecular dynamics [21], machine learning [4], and medical imaging [22]. We view these successes as sufficient evidence that the fine-grained SPMD model is effective for programming a manycore architecture with explicit support for fine-grained threads. However, previously there has not been investigation of how such a model could effectively map to a more coarsely threaded architectures such as the current commodity multicore processors.

The contributions of this paper are:

- An implementation and comparison of two approaches to implementing a fine-grained SPMD programming model on a processor with coarse-grained thread-level parallelism.

- A description of programming model restrictions necessary to implement the intuitively more effective approach.

- Optimizations enabled by the serialization of a parallel model, primarily redundancy removal in both computation and data storage.

- Experimental evidence confirming the intuition, and comparing it with standard compiled C on current multicore CPUs.

The primary enabling factors for generating efficient C code from a fine-grained threading model are the restrictions

CGO '10 April 24–28, 2010, Toronto, Ontario, Canada
Copyright © 2010 ACM 978-1-60558-635-9/10/04. . . $5.00

on synchronization usage. These restrictions allow stronger reasoning in the compiler about execution semantics in the static code. The baseline microthreading approach to serializing an SPMD programming model is described in Section 4. The baseline approach represents what we believe to be the state of the art in implementing general finely-threaded programs on a system with significantly less thread-level parallelism. The second approach is summarized in our own previously published work [23] and that of Shirako et al. [20], describing a basic approach for generating structured code serializing fine-grained SPMD code. We have reimplemented and extended the functionality of these algorithms within a production-level compiler, and compile the full CUDA language without the limitations of the previous work. We show with experimental results that the structured approach enabled by restrictions on synchronization usage does indeed provide significant performance benefits over the more general baseline.

In the context of a serialized parallel model, several optimizations not available to the parallel form of the code are enabled. The optimizations detailed in Section 6 are notably analogous to existing redundancy removal optimizations in sequential programming models. However, we can leverage knowledge of explicit parallelism to reduce the burden of analysis or surpass the typical capabilities of commercial implementations.

We highlight some of the related work in cross-architecture parallel programming models in Section 2. A concise description of CUDA's execution and memory models relevant to this work is presented in Section 3. The general microthreading and structured microthreading techniques are discussed in Sections 4 and 5 respectively, followed by a description of enabled optimizations in Section 6. We describe the practical details of our compiler and runtime environment in Section 7 to provide a full context for our performance results presented in Section 8. We summarize the experiments and lessons learned in the concluding remarks of Section 9.

2. Related Work

The issue of mapping small-granularity parallel work units to CPU cores has been addressed in other programming models, such as parallel simulation frameworks [7] and dataflow or message-driven programming models [2, 3]. Such models typically implement a user-level microthreading technique similar to our baseline approach. Microthreading implementation is simplified when implemented within a single code object, as an SPMD programming model provides. OpenCL [12] is a programming model closely related to CUDA that claims such platform portability as we would like to explore. However, it has not matured to demonstrate such portability at this time. The methods and results presented here would be directly applicable to all finely-threaded SPMD programming models, including OpenCL.

Shirako et al. [20] applied many of the same transformation methodologies to serialize data-parallel loops containing barriers. We demonstrate how similar techniques can be utilized in an SPMD programming model, and demonstrate the further optimizations enabled by the application of these techniques.

Numerous other frameworks and programming models have been proposed for data-parallel applications for multiprocessor architectures. Some examples include OpenMP [17] and HPF [11]. Although widely used in a CPU symmetric multiprocessor environment, these models are yet to be proven for manycore chips. Lee et al. have described a system for compiling OpenMP programs to CUDA [13] which, if successful, could provide similar experimental benefit as extending CUDA to CPUs.

Diamos has implemented a binary translation framework from GPU binaries to x86 [10]. While binary translators have advantages in knowing statically unavailable runtime parameters, compilers have more high-level program information available to them in the structured and symbolic source code. It is unclear which of the high-level transformations we propose would be possible without high-level compiler information available, if any.

Liao et al. designed a compiler for efficiently mapping the stream programming model to a multicore CPU architecture [14]. Their implementation attempted to build into the compiler capability for removing many of the restrictions of the stream programming model. In many ways, fine-grained SPMD-threaded models remove from the stream programming model those same limitations addressed by Liao et al.'s compiler. The programmer has control over tiling and kernel merging optimizations, the range of which is potentially broader than can be discovered and applied in an automated framework.

NVIDIA has released a toolset for CUDA program emulation on a CPU, designed for debugging. In the emulation framework, each fine-grained thread is executed by a separate runtime OS thread, incurring significant thread-scheduling overhead, and performing orders of magnitude more poorly than any of our approaches in informal experiments.

3. CUDA Programming Model

CUDA as a programming model has several interacting constructs for composing parallel programs on a shared-memory system [16]. The programming model allows sequential code in the standard C language with library APIs to control and manage *grids* of parallel execution specified by *kernel* functions. The *host* portion of the code is compiled using traditional methods and tools, while the kernel code introduces constructs for expressing SPMD parallelism. This work primarily focuses on the compilation and execution of the parallel kernel functions. We will be using the example kernel function of Figure 1 throughout this paper.

Within the SPMD kernel functions, *threads* are distinguished by an implicitly defined 3-tuple index uniquely iden-

```
1   __global__ small_mm_list(float* A_list, float* B_list,
                                , const int size)
    {
2       float sum;
3       int matrix_start, col, row, out_index, i;
4       matrix_start = blockIdx.x * size * size;
5       col = matrix_start + threadIdx.x;
6       row = matrix_start + (threadIdx.y * size);

7       sum = 0.0;

8       for(i = 0; i < size; i++)
9           sum += A_list[row + i] * B_list[col + (i*size)];

        //  Barrier before overwriting input data
10      __syncthreads();

11      out_index = matrix_start +
                        (threadIdx.y * size) + threadIdx.x;
12      A_list[out_index] = sum;
```

Figure 1: Multiplying many small matrices in CUDA.

```
tid = threadIdx.x;              tid = threadIdx.x;
while(i < end)                  while(i < end)
{                               {
  x += input[i];                  x += input[i];
  if(i == end-1) {                if(i == end-1) {
    //segmented circular shift      break;
    data[(tid + 1) % shift] = x;  }
    __syncthreads();            else {
    output = data[tid];           i++;
    break;                      }
  }                             }
  else {                        //segmented circular shift
    i++;                        data[(tid + 1) % shift] = x;
  }                             __syncthreads();
}                               output = data[tid];
      (a) Incorrect Usage             (b) Correct Usage
```

Figure 2: Synchronization within control flow. (b) shows code semantically equivalent to that of (a), and obeys the synchronization usage constraints.

tifying threads within a thread *block*. Thread blocks themselves are distinguished by an implicitly defined 2-tuple variable. The ranges of these indexes are defined at runtime by the host code in special kernel invocation syntax. In the example of Figure 1, each thread block is computing one small matrix multiplication out of the list, while each thread is computing one element of the result matrix for its block.

CUDA guarantees that threads within a thread block will be live concurrently, and provides constructs for threads within a thread block to perform fast barrier synchronizations and local data sharing. Distinct thread blocks within a grid have no ordering imposed on their creation or execution. Atomic operations provide limited interblock communication.

CUDA uses textually-aligned static barrier semantics, such as those of the Titanium language [1]. For instance, it is illegal to invoke a barrier intrinsic in both paths of an if-else construct when CUDA threads may take different branches of the construct. Although all threads within a thread block will reach one of the intrinsics, they represent separate barriers, each requiring that either all or none of the threads reach it.

As a more general example, consider the constructed example of Figure 2. We assume that **end** is a function of the thread index, while the initial value of **i** is thread-invariant. Although each logical thread will hit the barrier exactly once, the code of Figure 2a will have unpredictable runtime behavior. Figure 2b shows how the code may be restructured to achieve the desired effect without violating this constraint.

CUDA is less restrictive than Titanium in that barriers can be dependent on statically thread-dependent expressions. It only requires that the dynamic evaluation of those expressions results in a uniform boolean value at runtime. For instance, if **end** and the initial value of **i** are functions of the thread index such that $(i - end)$ is thread-invariant, the code of Figure 2a will function correctly, in constrast with the restrictions of Titanium that would prohibit this case as well.

The CUDA memory model, at the highest level, separates the host and device memory spaces, such that host code and kernel code can only access their respective memory spaces directly. The device memory spaces are the *global*, *constant*, *local*, *shared*, and *texture* memory spaces. A summary of the memory spaces is given in Table 1.

```
1   __global__ small_mm_list(float* A_list, float* B_list,
                             const int size)
    {
2     float sum[];
3     int matrix_start[], col[], row[], out_index[], i[];
      int current_restart, next_restart;
      next_restart = 0;
      // Loop over barrier synchronization intervals
      while (next_restart != -1) {
        current_restart = next_restart;
        //Loop over threads within an interval
        for(each tid) {
          switch (current_restart) {
            case 0:
              goto RESTART_POINT_0;
            case 1:
              goto RESTART_POINT_1;
          }

          // Original program beginning:
          RESTART_POINT_0:
4         matrix_start[tid] = blockIdx.x * size * size;
5         col[tid] = matrix_start[tid] + tid.x;
6         row[tid] = matrix_start[tid] + (tid.y * size);

7         sum[tid] = 0.0;

8         for(i[tid] = 0; i[tid] < size; i[tid]++)
9           sum[tid] += A_list[row[tid] + i[tid]] *
                        B_list[col[tid] + (i[tid]*size)];

          // restart point induced by syncthreads()
10        next_restart = 1;
          goto end_of_thread_loop;
          RESTART_POINT_1:
11        out_index[tid] = matrix_start[tid] +
                           (tid.y * size) + tid.x;
12        A_list[out_index[tid]] = sum[tid];
          next_restart = -1; // indicates "return"
          end_of_thread_loop:
        }
      } // while
    }
```

Figure 3: Microthreaded code for our example kernel

These memory spaces follow general microarchitecture principles. Large memory spaces are expected to have long latencies and limited random-access bandwidth, while small memory spaces can reliably satisfy low-latency accesses. Efficient CUDA programs make these cost trade-offs explicitly by using localized access patterns and limiting the active working set. However, if an application is written assuming significant hardware acceleration of texture processing operations, it could lead to design choices that perform poorly on processors implementing those features in software.

4. Baseline SPMD Microthreading

The term *microthreading* describes software techniques used in contexts where parallel work units are too small to efficiently schedule individually [2, 7]. The key concept is that software emulates the execution of multiple conceptually parallel threads or computation objects in a single, sequential program. The result of applying such a microthreading technique to the kernel of Figure 1 is shown in Figure 3. Note that the implicitly defined variable **threadIdx** has been shortened to **tid** for brevity. The compiler begins by labeling each barrier with a unique number, re-

Table 1: CUDA Device Memory Spaces in GPU Execution Context

Memory Space	Permissions	Scope of an Object	Capacity	Latency	Special Features
Global	Read/Write	All threads	DRAM capacity	High	Requires aligned, contiguous simultaneous accesses for best bandwidth.
Constant	Read-Only	All threads	64KB	Low (cached)	Single-banked cache with broadcast capability to multiple threads.
Local	Read/Write	Single thread	DRAM capacity	High	Most often promoted to private registers, which are shared between threads. Values not promoted to registers have long latency access.
Shared	Read/Write	Single thread block	16KB	Low	Scratchpad memory shared between thread blocks. More shared memory used per thread block means fewer thread blocks can be simultaneously active.
Texture	Read-Only	All threads	DRAM capacity, limits per object	High	Hardware interpolation, indexable by real-valued indexes, and other features for image processing.

serving the number zero for the implicit barrier at the beginning of the program. In our example, the single barrier gets labeled with the number 1. The original code for the program is modified, with each barrier replaced by a unique label, an assignment of the `next_restart` variable with the barrier's ID, and a jump to begin executing the next conceptual thread. All exit points from the function are replaced by statements assigning an exit flag (-1) to the `next_restart` variable. The compiler then generates the microthreading iteration structures. The master while-loop iterates over the number of times the threads will synchronize, each time updating the current restart point to the place the threads synchronized. A for-loop iterates over thread indexes, and uses a switch structure to begin each thread's execution at the current restart point. For each iteration of the conceptual thread for-loop, a single conceptual thread is advanced from its previous synchronization point to its next synchronization point. The master while-loop then iterates again to emulate all conceptual threads executing the original program from the barrier statement to the next point of syncronization, unless the original program end was reached by the conceptual threads being emulated.

In our example, the master while-loop control structure will begin executing the SPMD code of the original parallel program, marked by `RESTART_POINT_0`. The program executes the original, SPMD source code until it reaches statement 10, the original synchronization point. It then marks the synchronization point it reached, and program execution continues with the next conceptual thread at the original program beginning (statement 4). When all intances of conceptual threads have been iterated over (each `tid` is exhausted), the barrier is marked as the next restart point. This corresponds to the release of all conceptual threads from the barrier, so each microthread is executed again starting at the barrier release. Each conceptual thread then writes its output and reaches the original function's end. When all conceptual thread indexes have been processed again, the master while-loop detects that all conceptual threads have completed, and exits the function.

The memory model must also be adapted to fit a monolithic shared memory system. The globally visible memory regions already fit this model, and need not be changed. The features of the texture fetching functions must be implemented in a software library. The host and device memory spaces must generally be kept distinct, implying that API functions copying between host and device memory spaces

should still operate as specified. Removing this overhead is a potential target for future work.

Local memory regions must be allocated per thread. The simplest method accomplishing this is to change each local memory object into an array of objects accessed by the CUDA thread index. The shared memory regions, private to a thread block, should be dynamically allocated for the thread blocks actively executing. For shared memory arrays of fixed size, this can be done using the program function stack. However, CUDA allows shared array of statically unspecified size, determined at kernel launch time. In C, this is most feasibly addressed by dynamically allocating a shared memory buffer of the appropriate size for each actively executing thread block. This is addressed in the runtime portion of the system.

The runtime environment is responsible for the execution of the programming model, given the adapted kernel functions generated by the compiler. Considering the thread blocks as work units, the runtime essentially implements a bulk-synchronous parallism model. It is responsible for the parallel processing of the work units within a grid, ensuring that different grids will be synchronized with each other and with the host.

5. Structured Microthreading

Consider a common case in which a kernel function has no synchronization. In this case, complex microthreading techniques are unnecessary, as the threads can be interleaved in any way we desire, including complete serialization. When barrier synchronization is present, complete serialization is not possible, but unstructured control flow caused by the added *goto* statements to and from the restart points of the previous approach is less easily analyzed by most compilers, especially for optimizations like automatic vectorization. The improved approach described in this section summarizes a variation of previous work [23] taking advantage of the synchronization restrictions to more efficiently implement microthreading.

Algorithm 1 partitions an SPMD program with textually-aligned static barriers and regular control flow into groups of statements not containing barrier synchronization. For each statement in sequence, we examine whether it is or contains a barrier statement. If not, it is included in the current partition. If it is a barrier statement, it defines a partition boundary, ending the current partition and beginning another. If it is a control-flow construct containing a barrier, then by the restrictions on the correct usage of barriers, all

Input: List of Statements F in AST representation
Output: List X of Code Partitions Free of Barriers
Begin new partition P;
while F *has next statement* S **do**
  switch *type of statement* S **do**
    case *barrier*
      | Add P to X;
      | P = new partition;
    end
    case *simple_statement*
      | Add S to P;
    end
    case *seq*
      | Prepend statements comprising S to F;
    end
    otherwise
      if S *contains a barrier statement* **then**
        | Add P to X;
        | Invoke algorithm recursively on the body
        | of S, producing a list L of partitions
        | within S; Append L to X;
        | P = new partition;
      else
        | Add S to P;
      end
    end
  end
end
if P *not empty* **then**
  | Add P to X;
end

Algorithm 1: Construction of code partitions free of barriers

```
1  __global__ small_mm_list(float* A_list, float* B_list,
                             , const int size)
   {
2    float sum[];
3    int matrix_start, col[], row[], out_index[], i[];
     for( each tid ) {

4      matrix_start = blockIdx.x * size * size;
5      col[tid] = matrix_start + tid.x;
6      row[tid] = matrix_start + (tid.y * size);

7      sum[tid] = 0.0;

8      for(i[tid] = 0; i[tid] < size; i[tid]++)
9        sum[tid] += A_list[row[tid] + i[tid]] *
                     B_list[col[tid] + (i[tid]*size)];
     }
10
     for( each tid ) {
11     out_index[tid] = matrix_start +
                        (tid.y * size) + tid.x;
12     A_list[out_index[tid]] = sum[tid];
     }
   }
```

Figure 4: Partitioned translation of our example kernel

threads must reach or not reach the construct, making it a valid partition boundary itself. The same algorithm is invoked recursively on the internal contents of the construct to partition the statements within.

These partitions define regions of code where the execution of different CUDA threads may be interleaved in any way, including complete serialization, as shown in Figure 4, where each partition is enclosed within a nested loop structure iterating through all thread indexes. Comparing Figure 4 to the previous Figure 3, we see that both perform the same sequential ordering of the original statements. However, Figure 4 does so with significantly less complex code in comparison, both inherently simpler and more easily analyzable for later optimization. For each statement of the program, the code generator also finds references to variables in the local memory space in that statement, and conservatively converts these into references to the replicated arrays.

6. Optimizations Enabled

Programmers writing parallel software make significant tradeoffs between the cost of redundant computation among parallel execution units and the cost of synchronization and communication. However, when these parallel applications are serialized to execute on a sequential processor, the cost of communication largely vanishes, and redundant computation often no longer makes sense. In sequential-program compilers, redundancy removal has been very successful, but somewhat limited by the conservative assumptions necessary to preserve sequential semantics when analysis falls short. However, when the sequential program is actually an explicitly parallel program serialized, the need for analysis is either greatly reduced or removed entirely, as interthread ordering semantics are much more loosely constrained than a typical sequential loop nest. While such optimizations should be possible within the baseline approach, it would not be possible to leverage the existing work on loop nest transformations in that context.

Variance Analysis Opportunities for redundancy removal are exposed by discovering what portions of the kernel code will produce the same value for all thread indexes. Computation that was previously performed redundantly by multiple CUDA threads now can be executed once in the single CPU thread. The core of variance analysis is the forward program slice of each element of the thread index tuple. We compute these program slices, annotating each statement with those program slices they comprise. We refer to these annotations as variance vectors. For instance, statement 9 of our example kernel has a variance vector of (x,y), because it depends on the results of statements 5 and 6 that respectively read the x and y index components. Implicitly, atomic intrinsics are considered as a use of each element of the thread index, as their return value could vary for each CUDA thread.

When no statement in a partition contains a particular element in its variance vector, the partition does not need to be executed for each value in the index range of that element. Its results are independent of that element of the conceptual thread index. In the simplest case, and perhaps the most common, a programmer could intend to only use a subset of the elements of the thread index tuple to distinguish threads, implicitly assuming that all of the other elements will have a constant value of 1. In this case, the programmer writes a kernel never using some elements of the thread index tuple. The variance analysis will not annotate any statement with an unused component, directing the code generator to not create any loops over those elements of the thread index for any partition. This is the case for our example kernel, where the z index is unused.

Adaptive Loop Nesting Even when loops over certain elements are required for a partition, perhaps not all statements in a partition require execution for all thread indexes, analogous to loop invariant removal. However, we propose a technique called *adaptive loop nesting* that is more general in that it simultaneously evaluates transformations equivalent

115

```
1   __global__ mm_list(float* A_list, float* B_list,
                                      , const int size)
    {
2     float sum[];
3     int matrix_start, col[], row[], out_index, i;

4     matrix_start = blockIdx.x * size * size;
      for(tid.x = 0; tid.x < blockDim.x; tid.x++) {
5       col[tid] = matrix_start + tid.x;

        for(tid.y = 0; tid.y < blockDim.y; tid.y++) {
6         row[tid] = matrix_start + (tid.y * size);
7         sum[tid] = 0.0;

8         for(i = 0; i < size; i++)
9           sum[tid] += A_list[row[tid] + i] *
                        B_list[col[tid] + (i*size)];
        }
      }
10
      for(tid.x = 0; tid.x < blockDim.x; tid.x++)
        for(tid.y = 0; tid.y < blockDim.y; tid.y++) {
11        out_index = matrix_start +
                                  (tid.y * size) + tid.x;
12        A_list[out_index] = sum[tid];
        }
      }
```

Figure 5: Optimized translation of our example kernel

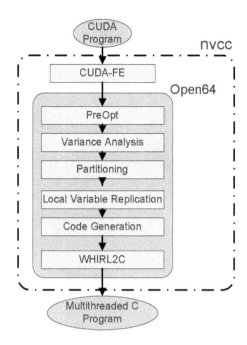

Figure 6: Compiler implementation diagram

to loop interchange, loop fission, and loop invariant removal to achieve the best redundancy removal, similar to polyhedral modeling of loop nests for sequential languages [8]. The significant distinction from typical loop-nest optimization is that all iterations can be assumed independent without analysis because of their origin from parallel threads.

The compiler may generate loops over thread index elements only around those statements that contain that element in their variance vector. To remove loop overhead, the compiler may fuse adjacent statement groups where one has a variance vector that is a subset of the other. All of the traditional cost analysis applied to loop fusion operations may apply here.

Typical cost analysis must be used to determine cases such as statements 5-9 of our example kernel. Statements 7-9 must be included in a loop nest over both x and y components of the conceptual thread index, as the computation is unique to each CUDA thread. As each of statements 5 and 6 is only dependent on one index element, either can be merged into a loop nest with statements 7-9, inside the outer loop over one component but before the inner loop of the other index. However, choosing either statement 5 or 6 to merge will lead to one of two choices for the other. We may choose to force the other into the innermost loop, causing unnecessary redundant execution, since it was independent of one of the loops now containing it. Otherwise, me must enclose it in an extra, separate loop nest for that statement alone, incurring extra control overhead. We chose a cost heuristic that in this case would determine that the extra control overhead is more costly, and would generate the control flow observed in Figure 5 that redundantly executes statement 6 for every x index.

Optimizing Local Variable Replication We note that because of the serialization of the computation in the fine-grained threads, not all data conceptually private to each thread must necessarily be instantiated as separate memory locations per thread. In particular, it is not necessary to create private memory locations for values that have a live range completely contained within a partition. In such cases, one memory location reused by all threads is

sufficient. Another case is where, even though the variable is live through multiple partitions, its value is thread-invariant. This is the case when a variable definition has an empty variance vector.

Two cases arise in which variable replication must be applied to the output value of an assignment with a nonempty variance vector. The first is if a value defined by the assignment reaches a use in another partition. As stated previous, values with a live range completely contained within a partition will never need to be saved for the same conceptual thread to use in some later partition. The second is if, in the presence of the loop over thread indexes placed around the partition, the defined value would reach a use that it previously would not have.

Assignments with an empty variance vector technically never need to write to a replicated location, such as statement 4 of Figure 5. However, we decided that for any use reachable by at least one replicated definition, all its potential definitions must write to the replicated location for simplicity.

Minimal variable replication and adaptive loop nesting share an interesting interplay in that the maximal fusing of loops over indexes can introduce additional cases requiring replication. This has been well established in work on loop fusion. The final results of these optimization algorithms would result in a generated kernel code like that shown in Figure 5.

7. Implementation

The compiler is implemented within NVIDIA's production CUDA compilation toolchain. The toolchain provides a CUDA compiler driver, called nvcc. We added a new compiler flag enabling multicore compilation. The compiler structure is shown in Figure 6. At a high level the compiler consists of two main components: a frontend (CUDAFE) and the Open64 [9] high-level backend. CUDAFE is

116

the standard CUDA production compiler front-end without modifications, just as it is used for GPU compilation.

In our implementation we generate HI-WHIRL intermediate representation (IR) for the Open64 backend infrastructure [9]. We implemented all the optimizing transformations at the HI-WHIRL level, chosen because almost all machine-independent analysis and optimization passes are available there [6]. The backend consists of five main components.

PreOpt- We use the standard Open64 optimizer to perform a few simple optimizations and, more importantly, to generate data flow information in the form of def-use chains.

Variance Analysis- The variance analysis we described earlier computes forward program slices on the thread index variables, annotating every statement with the components of the `threadIdx` variable on which that statement depends.

Partitioning- The partitioning algorithm described in Section 5 builds a list of partitions and, within each partition, collects a list of statements.

Local Variable Replication- Def-use chains restricted to the set of local variables of a function determine which variable references are read and written in multiple partitions. Each statement is annotated with the list of variable references within that statement needing to reference the expanded version of the variable.

Code Generation- This phase completes the generation of IR that is the complete, optimized transformation of the input into executable code. It traverses each partition, grouping adjacent statements if desirable given their variance vectors. It also transforms statements to use replicated versions of variables as necessary. Finally, it surrounds each grouped cluster of statements within a partition by the necessary thread loops, as required by the variance vectors of those statements.

WHIRL2C- We use the WHIRL2C [5] component from the Open64 distribution to generate C code from the transformed IR.

Thread blocks in the CUDA programming model represent independent tasks, each embodied by a sequential program following our compiler's translation. Many frameworks exist for distributing such parallel tasks to processors. Our implementation uses POSIX threads as an example. The runtime system creates several OS worker threads, the number of which can be controlled by an environment variable. At a kernel launch, the number of CUDA thread blocks in the grid to be launched is statically partitioned to the runtime threads. Each runtime thread executes its chunk sequentially and waits on a barrier. When all runtime threads reach the barrier, the grid has completed, and control is returned to the host thread.

8. Performance Evaluation

We present results on the eight CUDA benchmarks in Table 2 from application fields including fluid dynamics, astrophysics, and financial modeling. These applications were written specifically for a GPU target architecture, and have shown significant performance on that platform, some reported in previous work [18]. For benchmarking, we used an Intel Core2 Quad processor system running RedHat Enterprise Linux 4 (Update 7). We use gcc version 3.4.6 as the final C compiler, with -O3 optimization for all tests.

Table 3 shows that optimizations of the structured microthreading implementation dramatically reduced the number of replicated variables, with direct effect on reducing cache pressure. The number of references to replicated variables is also consequently reduced, intuitively leading gcc to

Benchmark	App. domain	Kernel lines	Static barriers
petrinet	stochastic models	191	5
blinn	volume rendering	155	0
blackscholes	financial models	43	0
nbody	astrophysics sim.	180	3
lbm	fluid sim.	285	1
tpacf	astronomy data processing	98	4
binoption	financial models	121	5
FDTD	electromagnetic simulation	263	6

Table 2: Benchmark summary

Benchmark	Local objects	Static local object references	Replicated local objects	Static references to replicated objects
petrinet	72	623	0	0
blinn	93	343	0	0
blackscholes	35	133	0	0
nbody	82	498	18	141
lbm	110	1269	11	51
tpacf	36	196	6	25
binoption	51	215	6	6
FDTD	46	481	13	94

Table 3: Static Results of Optimizing Transformations

promote a larger fraction of variable accesses to register accesses. The variance analysis correctly detected that, out of all of the benchmarks, only `tpacf` used two dimensions of the thread index, while all the other applications used only one.

Figure 7 shows the benefits of our optimizations over a traditional microthreaded approach. Those applications with the least performance differences, `blinn` and `blackscholes`, do not use any synchronization within the CUDA kernel. In these cases, the performance benefits of the structured implementation are primarily due to the removal of the redundant local memory objects, as the control flow structure is practically the same between the two implementations. The rest of the applications do use synchronization, and gain significant performance benefits from the structured implementation, with an average of approximately 2× performance difference between the baseline and structured implementations of microthreading.

The most extreme cases of disparity between structured and unstructured microthreading were `BinOption` and `FDTD`. These were also the applications with the most synchronization, showing that the advantage of structured microthreading and optimization generally increases with kernel program complexity.

Finally, we can see that the performance compared to a native C application varies widely. This is to be expected, as the implementation decisions were made in different programming models, although the task and general algorithm were fixed. `petrinet` and `FDTD` required the most parallel algorithm implementation overhead, reflected in the comparison with sequential execution. Some applications even saw single thread performance gains over the existing C implementation. This indicates that the optimization effort spent

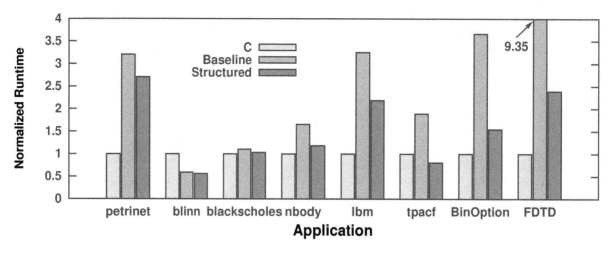

Figure 7: Translated CUDA application runtime relative to a native C implementation, each using one CPU execution thread. Only nominal programmer optimization effort was applied to either the C or CUDA versions of the code.

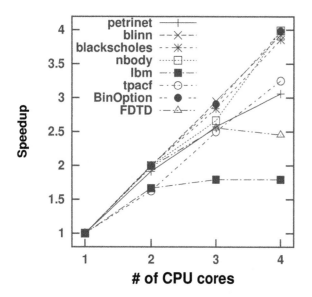

Figure 8: Application scaling from 1 to 4 threads.

on the CUDA implementation, for the GPU, was more effective for the CPU than the optimization effort spent on the C implementation.

All applications also saw significant performance gains from multithreading across the coarse-grained cores. We can see in Figure 8 that the performance scaling of the translated applications is very good, with close to ideal linear scaling for a small number of processor cores for most applications. The only application that reaches a scaling ceiling on our test system is lbm, as the application becomes bottlenecked by system memory bandwidth. Several other applications show somewhat less than ideal scaling, primarily due to load imbalance caused by our simplistic work partitioning implementation developed under the assumption of large numbers of equal-latency tasks. The two applications most affected by load imbalance are tpacf and petrinet, which have large variations in the runtimes of each block. A large existing body of work explores more effective dynamic work scheduling policies [15] applicable to our implementation

would likely move some of the applications closer to the ideal scaling curve.

9. Conclusions

We have described techniques for efficiently implementing the CUDA programming model on a conventional multiprocessor CPU architecture. We have described a baseline microthreading approach, showing that a microthreading approach based on structured control flow has significant comparative performance advantages, in part due to additional optimizations that are enabled.

We observe that a fine-grained SPMD decomposition can be translated into more coarse-grained work units effectively, but only with reasonable restrictions on the synchronization model. Fine-grained threads that may interact arbitrarily must resort to some form of unstructured microthreading, which has shown to as much as double execution times compared to the structured approach, and in no case was it better. Our results also suggest that there is a class of parallel kernels where the finely-threaded version of the code shows parity with a native C implementation in single-thread performance.

Finally, our results have shown a particular software engineering advantage for current CUDA developers requiring some CPU fallback implementation when CUDA is not installed on a particular client's system. Using these techniques, such developers could translate their CUDA code directly into multithreaded C that is almost always better than a quickly written sequential program on a small multiprocessor typical in today's systems, while still keeping a single code base.

Acknowledgments

We would like the thank NVIDIA corporation for its support, and our formal and informal reviewers for their feedback. The authors acknowledge the support of Gigascale Systems Research Center, funded under the Focus Center Research Program, a Semiconductor Research Corporation program.

References

[1] A. Aiken and D. Gay. Barrier inference. In *Proceedings of the 25th ACM Symposium on Principles of Programming Languages*, pages 342–354, 1998.

[2] H. A. Andrade and S. Kovner. Software synthesis from dataflow models for embedded software design in the G programming language and the LabVIEW development environment. In *Proceedings of the IEEE Asilomar Conference on Signals, Systems, and Computers*, pages 1705–1709, 1998.

[3] G. Bikshandi, J. G. Castanos, S. B. Kodali, V. K. Nandivada, I. Peshansky, V. A. Saraswat, S. Sur, P. Varma, and T. Wen. Efficient, portable implementation of asynchronous multiplace programs. In *PPoPP '09: Proceedings of the 14th ACM SIGPLAN symposium on Principles and practice of parallel programming*, pages 271–282, New York, NY, USA, 2009. ACM.

[4] B. Catanzaro, N. Sundaram, and K. Keutzer. Fast support vector machine training and classification on graphics processors. In *Proceedings of the 25th International Conference on Machine Learning*, pages 104–111, June 2008.

[5] W.-Y. Chen. Building a source-to-source UPC-to-C translator. Master's thesis, Department of Electrical Engineering and Computer Sciences, University of California at Berkeley, Berkeley, CA, 2004.

[6] F. Chow, S. Chan, R. Kennedy, S. ming Liu, R. Lo, and P. Tu. A new algorithm for partial redundancy elimination based on ssa form. In *Proceedings of the ACM Conference on Programming Language Design and Implementation*, pages 273–286, 1997.

[7] J. H. Cowie, D. M. Nicol, and A. T. Ogielski. Modeling the global internet. *Computing in Science and Engineering*, 1(1):42–50, 1999.

[8] P. Feautrier. Dataflow analysis of array and scalar references. *International Journal of Parallel Programming*, 20:23–53, 1991.

[9] G. Gao, J. Amaral, J. Dehnert, and R. Towle. The SGI Pro64 compiler infrastructure. Tutorial. October 2000.

[10] Gregory Diamos. The design and implementation Ocelot's dynamic binary translator from PTX to multi-core x86. Technical Report GIT-CERCS-09-18, Georgia Institute of Technology, 2009.

[11] High Performance Fortran Forum. High Performance Fortran language specification, version 1.0. Technical Report CRPC-TR92225, Rice University, May 1993.

[12] Khronos OpenCL Working Group. The OpenCL Specification, May 2009.

[13] S. Lee, S.-J. Min, and R. Eigenmann. OpenMP to GPGPU: a compiler framework for automatic translation and optimization. In *Proceedings of 14th ACM Symposium on Principles and Practice of Parallel Programming*, pages 101–110, 2008.

[14] S.-W. Liao, Z. Du, G. Wu, and G.-Y. Lueh. Data and computation transformations for Brook streaming applications on multiprocessors. In *Proceedings of the 4th International Symposium on Code Generation and Optimization*, pages 196–207, March 2006.

[15] E. P. Markatos and T. J. LeBlanc. Using processor affinity in loop scheduling on shared-memory multiprocessors. In *Proceedings of the 1992 International Conference on Supercomputing*, pages 104–113, July 1992.

[16] J. Nickolls, I. Buck, M. Garland, and K. Skadron. Scalable parallel programming with CUDA. *ACM Queue*, 6(2):40–53, 2008.

[17] OpenMP Architecture Review Board. OpenMP application program interface, May 2005.

[18] S. Ryoo, C. I. Rodrigues, S. S. Baghsorkhi, S. S. Stone, D. Kirk, and W. W. Hwu. Optimization principles and application performance evaluation of a multithreaded GPU using CUDA. In *Proceedings of the 13th ACM Symposium on Principles and Practice of Parallel Programming*, February 2008.

[19] M. Schatz, C. Trapnell, A. Delcher, and A. Varshney. High-throughput sequence alignment using graphics processing units. *BMC Bioinformatics*, 8(1):474, 2007.

[20] J. Shirako, J. M. Zhao, V. K. Nandivada, and V. N. Sarkar. Chunking parallel loops in the presence of synchronization. In *ICS '09: Proceedings of the 23rd international conference on Supercomputing*, pages 181–192, New York, NY, USA, 2009. ACM.

[21] J. E. Stone, J. C. Phillips, P. L. Freddolino, D. J. Hardy, L. G. Trabuco, and K. Schulten. Accelerating molecular modeling applications with graphics processors. *Journal of Computational Chemistry*, September 2007.

[22] S. S. Stone, J. P. Haldar, S. C. Tsao, W.-M. W. Hwu, Z.-P. Liang, and B. P. Sutton. Accelerating advanced MRI reconstructions on GPUs. In *Proceedings of the ACM International Conference on Computing Frontiers*, pages 261–272, 2008.

[23] J. A. Stratton, S. S. Stone, and W. mei W. Hwu. MCUDA: An effective implementation of CUDA kernels for multi-core CPUs. In *Proceedings of the 21st International Workshop on Languages and Compilers for Parallel Computing*, pages 16–30, July 2008.

[24] L. G. Valiant. A bridging model for parallel computation. *Communications of the ACM*, 33(8):103–111, 1990.

Keynote II

There Are At Least Two Sides to Every Heterogeneous System

Chris (CJ) Newburn

Intel

Since there are at least two sides to every heterogeneous system, optimizing for heterogeneous systems is inherently an exercise in managing complexity, balanced trade-offs and layering. Efforts to make the hardware simple may result in software complexity, unless there's an abstracting software layer involved. Different customer-driven usage models make it challenging to offer a layered but consistent programming model, a cost-effective set of performance features and a flexibly-capable systems software stack. And often, the very reasons why heterogeneous systems exist drives them to change over time, making them difficult to target from a code generation perspective.

As a company that provides hardware systems, compilers, systems software infrastructure and services, one of Intel's research and development focuses is on optimizing for heterogeneous systems, such as a mix of IA multi-cores architectures that are used for both graphics and throughput computing. This talk addresses some of the challenges we've encountered in that space, and offers some potential directions.

Primary among the case studies used in this talk is a dynamic compiler that uses Intel's Ct technology, which strives to make it easier for programmers to specify what data-parallel work needs to be accomplished, and manages extracting parallelism from the application and making use of it on multicore and many-core Intel architectures optimized for throughput computing. The set of issues that will be addressed include how to specify parallelism, safety and debugging, software infrastructure and compiler architecture, and achieving performance on heterogeneous systems.

Chris (CJ) Newburn serves as a feature architect for Intel's Intel64 platforms, and has contributed to a combination of hardware and software technologies that span heterogeneous compiler optimizations, middleware, JVM/JIT/GC optimization, acceleration hardware, ISA changes, microcode and microarchitecture over the last twelve years. Performance analysis and tuning have figured prominently in the development and production readiness work that he's done. He likes to work on projects that span the hardware-software boundary, that span organizations, and that foster collaboration across organizations. He has submitted nearly twenty patents and has numerous journal and conference publications. He helped start CGO, has served on several program committees, as a journal editor, and as an NSF panelist. He wrote a binary-optimizing, multi-grained parallelizing compiler as part of his Ph.D. at Carnegie Mellon University. Before grad school, in the 1980s, he did stints in a couple of start-ups, working on a voice recognizer and a VLIW mini-super computer. He's glad to be working on volume products that his Mom uses.

Categories and Subject Descriptors D.3.4 [**Programming Languages**]: Processors – code generation, C.1.3 [**Processor Architectures**]: Other Architecture Styles – Heterogeneous (hybrid) systems

General Terms Performance, Languages.

Keywords *Code generation*

Decoupled Software Pipelining Creates Parallelization Opportunities

Jialu Huang   Arun Raman   Thomas B. Jablin   Yun Zhang   Tzu-Han Hung   David I. August

Departments of Computer Science and Electrical Engineering
Princeton University
{jialuh,rarun,tjablin,yunzhang,thhung,august}@princeton.edu

Abstract

Decoupled Software Pipelining (DSWP) is one approach to automatically extract threads from loops. It partitions loops into long-running threads that communicate in a pipelined manner via inter-core queues. This work recognizes that DSWP can also be an *enabling transformation* for other loop parallelization techniques. This use of DSWP, called DSWP+, splits a loop into new loops with dependence patterns amenable to parallelization using techniques that were originally either inapplicable or poorly-performing. By parallelizing each stage of the DSWP+ pipeline using (potentially) different techniques, not only is the benefit of DSWP increased, but the applicability *and* performance of other parallelization techniques are enhanced. This paper evaluates DSWP+ as an enabling framework for other transformations by applying it in conjunction with DOALL, LOCALWRITE, and SpecDOALL to individual stages of the pipeline. This paper demonstrates significant performance gains on a commodity 8-core multicore machine running a variety of codes transformed with DSWP+.

Categories and Subject Descriptors D.3.4 [*Programming Languages*]: Processors—Compilers, Optimization; C.1.4 [*Processor Architectures*]: Parallel Architectures

General Terms Performance

Keywords multicore, parallelization, DSWP, speculation, enabling transformation

1. Introduction

Chip manufacturers have shifted to multicore processors to harness the raw transistor count that Moore's Law continues to provide. Unfortunately, putting multiple cores on a chip

does not directly translate into performance. The trend toward simpler cores and the increasing disparity between the growth rates of core count and off-chip bandwidth means performance may even degrade. Not only do sequential codes suffer, multi-threaded programs may too deteriorate due to smaller caches per core and lower single-threaded performance. Consequently, producing well-formulated, scalable parallel code for multicore is the biggest challenge facing the industry.

Concurrency and non-determinism pose fundamental problems for programmers looking to (re-)write parallel code, as is evident in active research in automatic tools for the identification of deadlocks, livelocks, and race conditions. Conceptually, tools to automatically identify and extract parallelism appear more attractive. Until recently, success in automatic loop parallelization was restricted to the scientific domain. If all the iterations of a loop can be executed concurrently, then the DOALL transformation can be applied to extract the parallelism [1]. If there are *inter-iteration* (or *loop-carried*) dependences in the loop, then techniques such as DOACROSS and DOPIPE may be applicable [4, 6]. The applicability of these techniques is generally limited to codes with regular, array-based memory access patterns, and regular control flow, hence their success in scientific codes.

Unfortunately, the vast majority of general-purpose applications have irregular control flow and complex memory access patterns using pointers. To parallelize such codes, *Decoupled Software Pipelining* (DSWP) was proposed [15]. An automatic parallelization technique, DSWP splits the loop body into several stages distributed across multiple threads, and executes them in a pipeline. To generate the pipeline organization, DSWP segregates dependence recurrences into separate stages. Compared to DOALL, DSWP enjoys wider applicability. Compared to DOACROSS, DSWP enjoys better performance characteristics. By keeping critical path dependences thread-local, DSWP is tolerant of long communication latencies between threads. By decoupling the execution of the threads using inter-core queues, DSWP is also tolerant of variable latency within each thread.

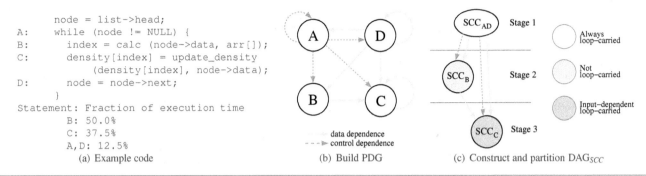

```
           node = list->head;
A:         while (node != NULL) {
B:             index = calc (node->data, arr[]);
C:             density[index] = update_density
                   (density[index], node->data);
D:             node = node->next;
           }
Statement: Fraction of execution time
       B: 50.0%
       C: 37.5%
       A,D: 12.5%
```

(a) Example code   (b) Build PDG   (c) Construct and partition DAG_{SCC}

Figure 1. Steps in the transformation of a sequential program (a) into a pipeline parallel program using DSWP. In (c), each SCC has a different loop-carried dependence pattern.

This paper looks beyond the performance benefits of DSWP, and explores DSWP as an *enabling transformation* for various loop parallelization techniques. At its core, DSWP identifies dependence cycles within a loop and isolates said cycles in stages of a pipeline. As a result, the dependence patterns of each stage tend to be much simpler. A key insight of this work is that other parallelization techniques may often be applied or applied more effectively to these simplified stages but cannot be applied to the original code.

This paper introduces DSWP+, an *enabling transformation* for other loop parallelization techniques, and evaluates DSWP+ in conjunction with several techniques such as DOALL, LOCALWRITE, and SpecDOALL [1, 10, 17]. Unlike DSWP, which tries to maximize performance by balancing the stages of the pipeline, DSWP+ tries to assign work to stages so that they can be further parallelized by other techniques. After partitioning, DSWP+ allocates enough threads to the parallelizable stages to create a balanced pipeline. DSWP+ yields more performance than DSWP and other parallelization techniques when applied separately. This paper shows how DSWP+ code partitioning can mitigate problems inherent to some parallelization techniques, such as redundant computation in LOCALWRITE.

Through manual parallelization of a variety of application loops, this paper demonstrates significant performance gains on *existing* multicore hardware. By virtue of its use of fully automatic techniques, the proposed methodology can be made fully automatic in future work.

Section 2 provides a detailed background of the DSWP transformation and then illustrates how DSWP+ uses it to create other parallelization opportunities. Section 3 discusses how various parallelization techniques are chosen and integrated with DSWP+. Section 4 provides results of experiments and analyzes factors that affect performance. Section 5 discusses related work, while Section 6 concludes the paper.

2. Motivation

The C code example in Figure 1(a) illustrates that in many applications' loops, the dependence pattern renders con-

ventional parallelization techniques either inapplicable or poorly-performing. In the example, a program traverses a linked-list list (statements A and D); the data in each node of the list indexes into an array arr in order to calculate the index (statement B), and updates the density array at index (statement C). By applying DSWP+ to this loop, the very techniques that were originally inappropriate can become applicable and well-performing. For illustrative purposes, assume that statement B accounts for 50%, statement C accounts for 37.5%, and statements A and D account for 12.5% of the total execution time of the loop.

Figure 1(b) shows the Program Dependence Graph (PDG) of the loop [7]. There are many inter-iteration dependences. The inter-iteration self-dependence in statement C arises because the index may not always be different on different iterations. It depends on the data inside each node, the contents of array arr, and the calc function.

Inter-iteration dependences prevent executing each iteration of the loop independently (as in DOALL) without costly synchronization. DOACROSS schedules entire loop iterations on different threads, while synchronizing dependences to maintain correctness. Although DOACROSS is applicable, the large amount of synchronization will severely limit the benefits of parallelization. DOACROSS communicates dependence recurrences (cycles in the PDG) from core to core, putting inter-core communication latency on the critical path [22].

Thread-Level Speculation (TLS) may speculatively remove dependences that prevent DOALL or DOACROSS from being applicable [14, 17, 20, 24]. In the example shown, speculating all loop-carried dependences to make DOALL applicable could cause excessive misspeculation since the linked-list traversal dependence manifests on every loop iteration. A better option is to synchronize these dependences as in DOACROSS and speculate only the input-dependent self-dependence in statement C. However, the problem of inter-core communication latency on the critical path persists.

In contrast to DOALL and DOACROSS which partition the iteration space across threads, DSWP partitions the loop body into stages of a pipeline, with each stage executing within a thread. DSWP's pipeline organization keeps dependence recurrences local to a thread, avoiding communication latency on the critical path. DSWP operates in four steps [15].

- First, DSWP builds the PDG of the loop [1]. The program dependence graph contains all data (both register and memory) and control dependences, both intra- and inter-iteration. Figure 1(b) shows the PDG for the loop in Figure 1(a).

- Second, DSWP finds the loop recurrences, instructions participating in a dependence cycle. DSWP groups dependence cycles into strongly-connected components (SCCs) that form an acyclic graph. Figure 1(c) shows the DAG_{SCC}. Each node in the DAG_{SCC} is a single SCC. These SCCs form the minimum scheduling units so that there are no cross-thread cyclic dependences.

- Third, DSWP allocates each SCC to a thread. Since the slowest stage in the pipeline limits overall performance, DSWP tries to balance the load on each stage when assigning SCCs to threads. This partitioning operation is shown using horizontal lines in Figure 1(c).

- Finally, DSWP inserts *produce* and *consume* operations to transmit data values in case of data dependences and branch conditions for control dependences.

While DSWP often provides noticeable performance improvement, it is limited by the number and size of the SCCs. DSWP extracts at most one thread per SCC. Further, the pipelined organization means that the throughput is limited by the slowest stage (Speedup = $1/T_{slowest\ stage}$). In the example loop, DSWP performance is limited to 2.0x (= $1/T_{Stage\ 2}$). However, as Figure 1(c) shows, the loop-carried dependence pattern in each stage is different. While the loop-carried dependences in Stage 1 *always* manifest, there are no loop-carried dependences in Stage 2 and the manifestation of the loop-carried dependence in Stage 3 depends on the input. By choosing suitable parallelization strategies for Stages 2 and 3, the execution times of SCC_B and SCC_C can be reduced to that of SCC_{AD}. The resulting pipeline is potentially balanced.

While there may be dependences inside `calc` that are carried across an inner loop, note that B does not contain any loop-carried dependences across the loop being parallelized. Consequently, DOALL may be applied to the second stage which can now be replicated across multiple threads. Stage 1 distributes the values it produces in a round-robin fashion across iterations to the multiple Stage 2 threads. By extracting a new loop with no loop-carried dependences out of the original, DSWP+ makes DOALL applicable.

After the DSWP+DOALL transformation, the obtainable speedup is limited to 2.67x (= $1/T_{Stage\ 3}$). The self-dependence in statement C inhibits parallelization. Since the `index` depends on the contents of array `arr`, `node->data`,

```
Thread i:
  if (i == owner (density[index])) {
    density[index] = update_density
      (density[index], node->data);
  }
```

Figure 2. Memory ownership checking in LOCALWRITE

and the `calc` function, it is not guaranteed to be different on different iterations; in other words, the manifestation of the dependence from statement C in one iteration to another is input-dependent. Consequently, the compiler must conservatively insert a loop-carried dependence in the PDG preventing DOALL from being applicable. However, a technique known as LOCALWRITE can be applied [10]. LOCALWRITE partitions the array into blocks and assigns ownership of each block to a different thread. Each thread only updates the array elements belonging to its block. Figure 2 shows the code for each thread: updates to the array are guarded by ownership checks. While LOCALWRITE is applicable to the original loop in Figure 1(a), it will perform poorly due to the problem of redundant computation (see Section 4.2.2 for details).

An alternative parallelization of Stage 3 is possible. Speculation can be used to remove the loop-carried dependence from statement C to itself. Hardware or software TLS memory systems can be used to detect whether the dependence manifests; if it does, then the violating iteration(s) will be rolled back and re-executed [14, 17, 20, 23]. Blindly speculating all loop-carried dependences in the original loop will cause excessive misspeculation because other loop-carried dependences (self-dependence in statement D) manifest on every iteration. The overhead of misspeculation recovery negates any benefits of parallelization. By separating out the problematic dependences, DSWP+ creates a loop with dependences that can be speculated with a much higher degree of confidence, thus getting good performance.

In summary, the example shows that DSWP+ can transform a loop with an unworkable dependence pattern into multiple loops each of which can be parallelized in (potentially) different ways using the very techniques that failed on the original loop. The following section describes the integration of specific loop parallelization techniques with DSWP+.

3. Code Transformation With DSWP+

The code example in Figure 1(a) is used to illustrate the transformations done with DSWP+. For the sake of clarity, transformations are shown at the source-code level. Although these transformations were performed manually, we emphasize that each of these techniques has been automated in parallelizing compilers. Details of the algorithms can be found in [3, 10, 15, 16]. Automation of the ensemble technique involves bringing them together into one framework and changing the optimization goal of DSWP.

```
node = list->head;                while (TRUE) {                        while (TRUE) {
while (node != NULL) {              node = consume (Q[1,2]);              node = consume (Q[1,3]);
  produce (Q[1,2], node);          if (!node) break;                     if (!node) break;
  produce (Q[1,3], node);          index = calc (node->data, arr[]);     index = consume (Q[2,3]);
  node = node->next;               produce (Q[2,3], index);             density[index] = update_density
}                                }                                         (density[index], node->data);
                                                                        }
    (a) Stage 1: SCC_AD in Figure 1(c)     (b) Stage 2: SCC_B in Figure 1(c)       (c) Stage 3: SCC_C in Figure 1(c)
```

Figure 3. DSWP applied to the loop in Figure 1(a) extracts three stages which communicate using *produce* and *consume* primitives.

3.1 DSWP+

Figure 1 shows the steps in the DSWP transformation. After building the PDG of the loop, dependence recurrences are identified, and the loop is partitioned into stages at the granularity of SCCs. DSWP+ follows the first two steps of the DSWP algorithm. In the third step, DSWP optimizes for pipeline balance. In contrast, DSWP+ tries to put as much work as possible in stages which can be subsequently parallelized by other techniques. Finally, the other techniques are performed on each stage, and threads are allocated to each stage as to achieve pipeline balance. Figure 3 shows the code for each stage. Data values and control conditions are communicated across threads using *produce* and *consume* primitives. These primitives are implemented in software using cache-aware, concurrent lock-free queues [8].

3.2 DSWP+*PAR_OPTI*

The DSWP+ transformation works in conjunction with other loop parallelization techniques. For a given parallelization technique *PAR_OPTI*, let DSWP+*PAR_OPTI* be the pipeline parallelization strategy that chooses the largest stage(s) to which *PAR_OPTI* is applicable. In this paper, we investigate DSWP+DOALL, DSWP+LOCALWRITE, and DSWP+SpecDOALL.

3.2.1 DSWP+DOALL

From Figure 1(c), the second stage is free of loop-carried dependences. DOALL may be applied to this stage. Figure 4 shows the replication of the second stage. All the threads executing the second stage share the same code. However, a logical queue between two stages is implemented as several physical queues between threads, and so the code for each stage must be parameterized to support replication (hence the thread id *i* in Figure 4). Stage 1 produces values to the Stage 2 threads in a round-robin fashion. For example, if there are two Stage 2 threads, then the values on even iterations are sent from Stage 1 to (Stage 2, Thread 1), while values on odd iterations are sent from Stage 1 to (Stage 2, Thread 2). Stage 3 consumes from (Stage 2, Thread 1) and (Stage 2, Thread 2) on alternate iterations in a corresponding fashion.

3.2.2 DSWP+LOCALWRITE

LOCALWRITE partitions an array into blocks and assigns ownership of each block to a one of several threads. Each

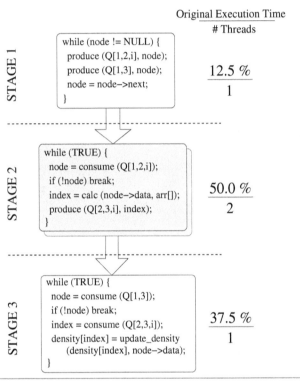

Figure 4. DSWP+ with DOALL applied to the second stage. With 2 threads assigned to the second stage, speedup can be improved to 2.67x (= $1/T_{\text{Stage 3}}$). Assigning more threads is useless because Stage 3 has become the bottleneck.

thread may only update array elements that it owns. Under this ownership discipline, array updates do not need to be synchronized. Figure 5 shows the application of LOCAL-WRITE to Stage 3 of the pipeline. Stage 1 must produce the value of node to all the Stage 3 threads. (In Figure 5, the number of Stage 3 threads is n_lw_threads.) As in DSWP+DOALL, the thread id (j in Figure 5) is used to select the physical queue between threads. Updates to global state (the density array) are guarded by the ownership check highlighted in Stage 3 in Figure 5. Typically, each thread is given ownership of a contiguous block of array elements. Figure 6 shows an example of ownership functions. The scalability of LOCALWRITE is limited by the distribution of the values of index across the array blocks; if the

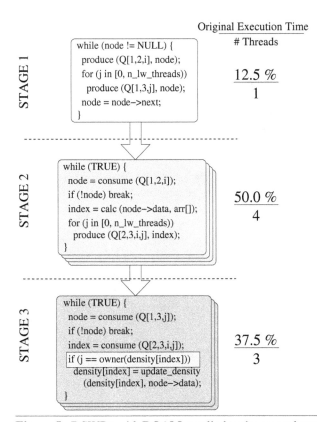

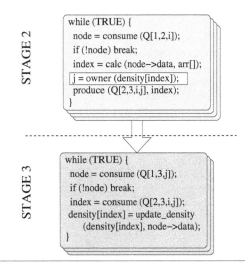

Figure 5. DSWP+ with DOALL applied to the second stage and LOCALWRITE applied to the third stage. The ownership check for LOCALWRITE in Stage 3 is highlighted. With 4 threads assigned to Stage 2 and 3 threads to Stage 3, speedup can be improved to 8x ($= 1/T_{Stage\ 1}$).

distribution is uniform, performance scales linearly with additional threads.

Referring to Figure 5, Stage 2 produces the `index` values to Stage 3. The ownership check is inserted in the consumer (Stage 3). This means that the producer (Stage 2) must produce the value of `index` on every iteration to *all* the consumer threads. Each consumer thread must perform the ownership check for every `index` value. Figure 7 shows that this redundancy can be eliminated by moving the ownership check to the producer. On each iteration, the producer uses the ownership check to determine the consumer thread that is the owner of the array element `density[index]`, and communicates the value only to that owner.

```
owner (A[i]) {
  n = number of elements in A
  block_size = n / n_lw_threads
  //n_lw_threads is the number of LOCALWRITE threads
  //Assume n is evenly divisible by n_lw_threads
  return (i / block_size)
}
```

Figure 6. Ownership function that assigns ownership of blocks of contiguous array elements to different threads

Figure 7. Moving the ownership check to Stage 2 eliminates redundancy in DSWP+LOCALWRITE.

3.2.3 DSWP+SpecDOALL

From Figures 1(a) and (c), statement C is conditionally self-dependent with respect to the contents of each `node`, the array `arr`, and the `calc` function; in other words, the probability of this dependence is a function of the input and is significantly smaller than 1. This stage can be parallelized using Speculative-DOALL. However, for the reasons mentioned in Section 2, the simplified dependence structure of the stage gives a much higher degree of confidence than the original loop.

Figure 8 shows the code transformation. Iterations of the loop in Stage 3 are executed concurrently on multiple threads. Original loads and stores become speculative loads and stores (`tx_load` and `tx_store` in Figure 8). As in DSWP+DOALL, Stage 2 is modified to produce values to the Stage 3 threads in a round-robin fashion.

DSWP+SpecDOALL allows the system to restrict speculation (and also the risk of misspeculation) to a fraction of the loop. By allowing stages to `peek` at queue entries without immediately dequeueing them, misspeculation recovery of inter-core queues has almost no cost. The queue entries that are peeked are dequeued when the iteration commits. Loop termination causes the `misspec` handler to be invoked. Conventional hardware or software TLS memory systems can be used to provide the transactional support [14, 17, 20, 24].

4. Evaluation

We evaluate DSWP+ on a dual quad-core (total of 8 cores) x86 machine. Table 1 gives the details of the evaluation platform. The results are obtained by manual application of DSWP+. The manual transformations proceeded systematically as a modern compiler would do, taking care to avoid exploiting human-level knowledge of the application's overall structure and purpose. GCC, LLVM-GCC, and LLVM

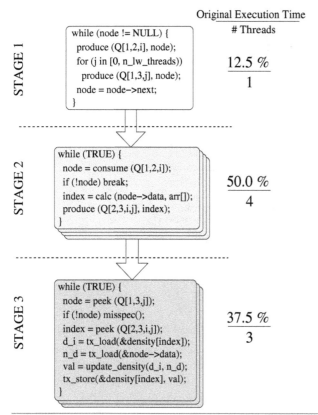

Original Execution Time / # Threads

STAGE 1
```
while (node != NULL) {
    produce (Q[1,2,i], node);
    for (j in [0, n_lw_threads))
        produce (Q[1,3,j], node);
    node = node->next;
}
```
$\underline{12.5\%}$ / 1

STAGE 2
```
while (TRUE) {
    node = consume (Q[1,2,i]);
    if (!node) break;
    index = calc (node->data, arr[]);
    produce (Q[2,3,i,j], index);
}
```
$\underline{50.0\%}$ / 4

STAGE 3
```
while (TRUE) {
    node = peek (Q[1,3,j]);
    if (!node) misspec();
    index = peek (Q[2,3,i,j]);
    d_i = tx_load(&density[index]);
    n_d = tx_load(&node->data);
    val = update_density(d_i, n_d);
    tx_store(&density[index], val);
}
```
$\underline{37.5\%}$ / 3

Figure 8. DSWP+ with DOALL applied to the second stage and SpecDOALL applied to the third stage. With 4 threads assigned to Stage 2 and 3 threads to Stage 3, speedup can be improved to 8x ($= 1/T_{\text{Stage 1}}$).

Processor	Intel Xeon®E5310
Processor Speed	1.60GHz
Processor Configuration	2 processors X 4 cores
L1 Cache size	32KB (per core)
L2 Cache size	4096KB (per 2 cores)
RAM	8GB
Operating System	Linux 2.6.24
Compiler	GCC and LLVM

Table 1. Platform details

with DSWP and DSWP+DOALL implementations assisted the parallelizations. With the exception of CG, DSWP+ parallelized the hottest loop in each benchmark. Like many scientific applications, most of the loops in CG (inside function conj_grad) are amenable to DOALL. As a result, parallelizing the remaining loop that has irregular dependence patterns becomes critical.

Table 2 gives detailed information about each benchmark including its source [2, 13, 19, 21], name of the function containing the parallelized loop, fraction of benchmark execution time constituted by the loop, and the parallelization techniques applied in conjunction with DSWP+.

4.1 Results

In Figure 9, each bar represents the *best* performance of a technique on *up to* 8 threads. For each benchmark, the first bar indicates the speedup obtained with whichever of DOALL, LOCALWRITE, and SpecDOALL is applicable. If the parallel optimization (*PAR_OPTI*) is not applicable to the unmodified code, then the speedup is shown as 1x. The second bar indicates the speedup with DSWP which tries to balance the work done by each stage. The third bar indicates the speedup with DSWP+; recall that DSWP+ creates unbalanced stages with the intent to parallelize the larger ones. By itself, the speedup with DSWP+ is worse than with DSWP. However, applying DSWP+ with one or more of DOALL, LOCALWRITE, and SpecDOALL results in significantly greater performance as indicated by the fourth bar.

Benchmark	Source Suite	Function	% of Runtime	PAR_OPTI with DSWP+
ks	Ref. Impl.	FindMaxGp-AndSwap	99.4	DOALL
otter	Ref. Impl.	find_lightest_geo_child	13.8	DOALL
052.alvinn	SPEC CFP	main	96.7	DOALL
filterbank	StreamIt	FBCore	45.6	DOALL
456.hmmer	SPEC CINT	main_loop_serial	100.0	DOALL
GTC	Ref. Impl.	chargei	58.8	DOALL, LO-CALWRITE
470.lbm	SPEC CFP	LBM_perform-StreamCollide	92.4	DOALL, LO-CALWRITE, IARD
CG	NPB3.2-SER	sparse	12.2	LOCALWRITE
ECLAT	MineBench	process_invert	24.5	LOCALWRITE
197.parser	SPEC CINT	batch_process	100.0	Spec-DOALL
256.bzip2	SPEC CINT	compressStream	98.5	Spec-DOALL

Table 2. Benchmark details

4.2 Case Studies

Factors affecting the performance of each benchmark are discussed below.

4.2.1 DSWP+DOALL

- **ks** is a graph partitioning algorithm. FindMaxGp-AndSwap's outer loop traverses a linked-list and the inner loop traverses the internal linked-lists, finding the internal linked-lists' minimum value. The linked-list traversal's loop carried dependence prevents a DOALL parallelization. DSWP+ splits the loop into two stages: the first stage traverses the outer linked-list, while the second stage traverses the internal linked-list. After min-reduction is applied, multiple traversals on the inner loop may proceed simultaneously in a DOALL-style parallelization. By spawning multiple copies of the second stage, which significantly outweighs the first, DSWP+DOALL gets much better speedup than DSWP.

- **otter** is an automated theorem prover for first-order and equational logic. The parallelized loop is similar to the one in ks. While a loop iteration in ks takes about $5\,\mu s$ on average, it takes only $0.03 - 0.22\,\mu s$ in otter.

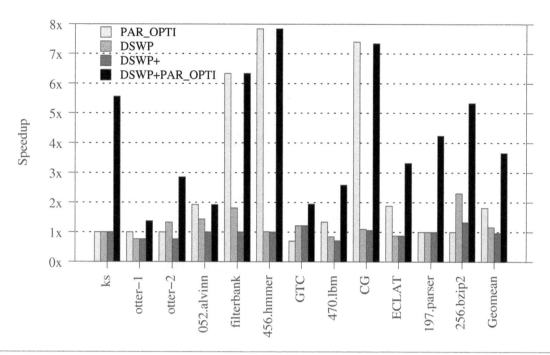

Figure 9. Loop speedup on up to 8 threads using different parallelization techniques

Consequently, the communication instructions for synchronization in the sequential stage constitute a much larger fraction of the loop iteration time, limiting the speedup. The balance between the two stages depends on the input: Figure 9 shows that DSWP achieves a much better balance and speedup on input2 (otter-2) compared to input1 (otter-1).

- **052.alvinn** is a backward-propagation-based artificial neural network. The parallelized loop is the second level loop in the loop hierarchy in main. DOALL is not directly applicable because there are loop-carried dependences on array updates. However, when combined with accumulator-expansion, DOALL yields 1.9x speedup. DSWP partitions several loops inside the parallelized loop onto different stages. By using communication queues between stages as buffers for intermediate results, DSWP performs dynamic privatization of the arrays, yielding a speedup of 1.4x with two threads. DSWP+DOALL recognizes that the loop-carried dependence in both DSWP stages can be removed using accumulator-expansion, and merges them into a single parallel stage followed by a sequential stage to perform reduction on the expanded arrays. This generates code that is equivalent to DOALL with accumulator-expansion. DSWP+DOALL also yields a speedup of 1.9x, with the sequential reduction stage limiting the performance.

- **filterbank** applies a set of filters for multirate signal processing [21]. As in 052.alvinn, the outer loop in FBCore has two major inner loops and is not amenable

to DOALL because of inter-iteration dependences on array updates. DSWP generates a pipeline with two stages, with each inner loop in one stage, yielding a speedup of 1.8x. DSWP+DOALL applies accumulator-expansion, merges the two stages into a parallel stage and performs the reduction in a sequential stage. This yields a speedup of 6.3x.

Although the structure of 052.alvinn and filterbank's parallelizations are very similar, the resulting performance results are not. The difference in the speedup of 052.alvinn and filterbank is due to the size of the reduction. In 052.alvinn, there are two arrays with a combined size of 150K bytes that need to be privatized; in filterbank, only one array of size 16K bytes needs to be privatized. With more DOALL threads, the reduction overhead soon becomes the performance bottleneck. This limits the scaling of speedup in 052.alvinn to six threads.

- **456.hmmer** is a computational biology application that searches for patterns in DNA sequences using Profile Hidden Markov Models. Scores are calculated in parallel on sequences which are randomly selected. The Commutative annotation is used to break the dependence inside the random number generator [12]. While the scores are calculated in parallel, a sequential stage computes a histogram of the scores and selects the maximum score. With the Commutative annotation and max-reduction, the loop can be parallelized using DOALL. DSWP+DOALL generates essentially the same code, and performance is

127

```
for (m=0; m<mi; m++) {
  for (n=0; n<4; n++) {
    v1 = cal_v1 (m, n);
    ... ...
    v8 = cal_v8(m, n);
    i1 = cal_i1 (m, n, A1[ ]);
    ... ...
    i8 = cal_i8 (m, n, A1[ ]);
    densityi[i1] = densityi[i1] + v1;
    ... ...
    densityi[i8] = densityi[i8] + v8;
  }
}
```

Figure 10. Example loop from `GTC`: Main dependence pattern is $A[i] = A[i] + B$

also the same. Speedup is limited by the sequential reduction phase.

4.2.2 DSWP+LOCALWRITE(+DOALL)

While LOCALWRITE is applicable to most irregular reductions, it suffers from the problem of redundant computation that significantly affects its performance potential. Referring back to Figure 1(a), applying just the LOCALWRITE transformation would result in statement C being guarded by an ownership check, and the entire loop being replicated across threads. Since the linked-list traversal and calculation of the index on each iteration is performed by every thread, performance scaling is impeded. By extracting out the common code executed by each LOCALWRITE thread into a separate stage, DSWP+ alleviates the problem of redundant computation and makes LOCALWRITE better-performing.

- **GTC** is a 3D particle-in-cell simulator that studies microturbulence in magnetically confined fusion plasma. Figure 10 shows a simplified form of the `GTC` loop. As in the example code in Figure 1, there are loop-carried dependences because of the $A[i] = A[i] + B$ irregular reduction pattern. LOCALWRITE is applicable to the loop; however, the rest of the computation in the loop is replicated in each thread. The result is a slowdown over sequential execution. DSWP+ partitions the loop into a producer stage that calculates the index and values, and a consumer stage that updates the array elements. DSWP+DOALL is applied to the producer since it does not have loop-carried dependences, while DSWP+LOCALWRITE is applied to the consumer since it has irregular reductions. This hybrid parallelization yields close to 2x speedup over sequential execution.

  `GTC`'s performance is limited by several factors. First, the producer communicates 64 values per iteration. While DSWP is tolerant of long communication latencies, the instructions executed to produce a value constitute an overhead. Second, since each consumer thread consumes values from all the producer threads, a single slow producer thread may cause a consumer thread to wait for it rather than process the values produced by the other faster producer threads. The overhead caused by the above two factors can be mitigated if each loop

```
for (i=START, i<END; i=i+ISTEP) {
  if (OBSTACLE (i)) {
    dstGrid[cal_i1(i, A[ ])] =
      srcGrid[cal_i1'(i, A[ ])];
    ... ...
    dstGrid[cal_i19(i, A[ ])] =
      srcGrid[cal_i19'(i, A[ ])];
    continue;
  }
  cal_rho (i, srcGrid, A[ ]);
  cal_ux (i, srcGrid, A[ ]);
  dstGrid[cal_j1(i, A[ ])] =
    srcGrid[cal_j1'(i, A[ ])] + cal_v1(rho, ux);
  ... ...
  dstGrid[cal_j19(i, A[ ])] =
    srcGrid[cal_j19'(i, A[ ])] + cal_v19(rho, ux);
}
```

Figure 11. Loop in `470.lbm`: Main dependence pattern is $A[i] = B$

iteration executes long enough. However, since each iteration takes only 0.55 µs, the performance improvement is limited.

- **470.lbm** implements the "Lattice Boltzmann Method" to simulate incompressible fluids in 3D. Figure 11 shows a simplified form of the parallelized loop. The main difference from `GTC` is the array update pattern which is $A[i] = B$ compared to $A[i] = A[i] + B$ in `GTC`. While the latter update to the same element can be done in any order, the former needs to respect the original sequential ordering. The iteration space is divided into chunks that are assigned to each producer in a round-robin manner. When a producer finishes an iteration chunk, it produces an "end" token to all of its queues. Each consumer thread starts from the queue holding values from the earliest iteration chunk. When it sees an "end" token, it switches to the next queue. The sequential processing of the iteration space using the "end" tokens guarantees the correct order of update of each array element. This technique yields 1.3x speedup on 8 threads, with the extra "end" token based synchronization limiting the amount of work that is done in parallel in the consumer.

  `470.lbm` shows an interesting array (dstGrid) access pattern that can be used to improve performance (see Figure 12). By using the IARD technique proposed in [18], the iterations can be partitioned into private regions and shared regions. Iterations in different private regions access non-overlapping array elements and thus can be executed concurrently, while iterations in shared regions might access the same array element and thus need synchronization. Profiling shows that the access pattern is very stable. With this information, DOALL is applied

```
Min(a): minimum updated array element index in iteration a
Max(a): maximum updated array element index in iteration a
for any two iterations x and y:
  if x is before y,
  then Min(x) <= Min(y) and Max(x) <= Max(y)
```

Figure 12. Array access pattern in `470.lbm`

to the private regions and DSWP+LOCALWRITE is applied to the shared region. This improves the speedup to 2.6x.

- **CG** from the NPB3.2-SER benchmark suite solves an unstructured sparse linear system by the conjugate gradient method [2]. The loop in CG contains the $A[i] = A[i] + B$ and $A[i] = B$ dependence patterns seen in GTC and 470.lbm respectively. Compared to the parallelization model used in those programs, the index and value computation stage in CG is very small and is executed sequentially.

Both LOCALWRITE and DSWP+LOCALWRITE are able to extract scalable speedup because there is hardly any redundant computation. LOCALWRITE is slightly better performing than DSWP+LOCALWRITE on 8 threads because DSWP+LOCALWRITE allocates one thread to the small sequential producer stage leaving 7 threads for parallel execution, whereas LOCALWRITE has all 8 threads available for parallel execution. The problem with DSWP+LOCALWRITE can be overcome by re-using the producer thread for parallel work after completing the sequential work. Speedup is limited primarily by the input size.

- **ECLAT** from MineBench is a data mining benchmark that uses a vertical database format [13]. The parallelized loop traverses a list of items and appends each item to corresponding list(s) in the database based on the item's transaction number. The loop is partitioned into two stages with the first stage calculating the item's transaction number and the second stage appending the transaction to the corresponding list(s). Transactions that do not share the same transaction number can be inserted into the database concurrently. Applying DSWP+LOCALWRITE to the second stage yields 3.32x speedup. As with GTC, LOCALWRITE is limited by the redundant computation of each item's transaction number and achieves only 1.87x speedup.

4.2.3 DSWP+SpecDOALL

- **197.parser** is a syntactic parser of the English language based on link grammar. The parsing of a sentence is grammatically independent of the parsing of others. The loop is split up into a sequential stage that reads in the sentences and determines whether it is a command or an actual sentence, and a speculatively DOALL stage that does the parsing of the sentence. Values of several global data structures need to be speculated to parse sentences in parallel. While these structures are modified inside an iteration, they are reset at the end of each iteration to the same values that they had at the beginning of that iteration. Branches that taken under special circumstances are speculated to not be taken. Loop speedup is affected primarily by the number of sentences to parse and the variability in sentence length.

- **256.bzip2** performs data compression using the Burrows-Wheeler transform. The loop is split up into three stages: The first one reads in the input, performs an initial compression, and then outputs blocks; the second stage compresses the blocks in parallel; the third serializes the blocks and outputs a bit-stream. The second stage requires privatization of the block data structure and speculation to handle error conditions while compressing the blocks. Speedup is limited by the input file's size and the level of compression.

5. Related Work

Many techniques have been proposed to extract thread-level parallelism from scientific and general-purpose applications. This paper integrates many of these techniques such as DOALL, LOCALWRITE, and SpecDOALL with DSWP [1, 10, 15].

Data Write Affinity with Loop Index Prefetching (DWA-LIP) is an optimization based on LOCALWRITE [9]. Like DSWP+LOCALWRITE, DWA-LIP also eliminates redundant computation in LOCALWRITE. It does this by prefetching loop indices, but since DWA-LIP takes the whole iteration as a parallel unit, it misses parallelism in loops that contain multiple array element updates. DSWP+LOCALWRITE can split the updates across multiple stages and provide more scalable and finer-grained parallelization.

Parallel Stage DSWP (PS-DSWP) is an automatic parallelization technique proposed by Raman et al. to improve the scalability of DSWP by applying DOALL to some stages of the DSWP pipeline[16]. DSWP+ derives its insight from this extension, and generalizes PS-DSWP by creating pipeline stages optimized for arbitrary parallelization techniques. The code transformation done by DSWP+DOALL is the same as PS-DSWP. By applying techniques like LOCALWRITE and SpecDOALL to stages with loop-carried dependences, DSWP+ can extract more parallelism than PS-DSWP.

Loop distribution isolates parts of a loop with loop-carried dependences from the the parts without these dependences [11]. Like PS-DSWP, loop distribution is used to extract a loop to which DOALL can be applied. The technique proposed in [23] is the speculative counterpart of loop distribution + DOALL, and targets loops that are almost DOALL. Other techniques such as LRPD, R-LRPD, and master/slave speculative parallelization have also been proposed to parallelize loops [5, 17, 24]. In contrast to these approaches, DSWP+ not only extracts the parts without loop-carried dependences, but also extracts parts with dependence patterns that are amenable to parallelization techniques other than (speculative) DOALL. This significantly improves both applicability and performance scalability. While loop distribution executes the sequential part of the loop *followed* by the parallel part, DSWP+ overlaps the execution of different parts of the original loop through pipeline parallelism.

6. Conclusion

This paper introduces the idea that DSWP is an *enabling transformation* that creates opportunities for various parallelization techniques to become applicable and wellperforming. By splitting up a loop with complex dependence patterns into new loops each with a dependence pattern amenable to other parallelization techniques, DSWP uncovers opportunities to extract scalable parallelism from apparently sequential code. This paper describes in detail the code transformations that occur when DSWP+ is applied in conjunction with DOALL, LOCALWRITE, and SpecDOALL. Since it leverages automatic compiler techniques, the proposed parallelization framework can be automated in future work. An evaluation of DSWP+ on a set of codes with complex dependence patterns yielded a geomean speedup of 3.69x on up to 8 threads. This surpasses the geomean speedups of DSWP (1.16x) or other parallel optimizations (1.81x) acting on their own.

Acknowledgments

We thank the entire Liberty Research Group for their support and feedback during this work. Additionally, we thank the anonymous reviewers for their insightful comments. The authors acknowledge the support of the GSRC Focus Center, one of five research centers funded under the Focus Center Research Program, a Semiconductor Research Corporation program. This material is based upon work supported by the National Science Foundation under Grant No. CCF-0811580. Any opinions, findings, and conclusions or recommendations expressed in this material are those of the authors and do not necessarily reflect the views of the National Science Foundation.

References

[1] R. Allen and K. Kennedy. *Optimizing compilers for modern architectures: A dependence-based approach.* Morgan Kaufmann Publishers Inc., 2002.

[2] D. H. Bailey, E. Barszcz, J. T. Barton, D. S. Browning, R. L. Carter, D. Dagum, R. A. Fatoohi, P. O. Frederickson, T. A. Lasinski, R. S. Schreiber, H. D. Simon, V. Venkatakrishnan, and S. K. Weeratunga. The NAS Parallel Benchmarks. *International Journal of Supercomputer Applications*, 5(3):63–73, Fall 1991.

[3] M. J. Bridges. *The VELOCITY Compiler: Extracting Efficient Multicore Execution from Legacy Sequential Codes.* PhD thesis, Department of Computer Science, Princeton University, Princeton, New Jersey, United States, November 2008.

[4] R. Cytron. DOACROSS: Beyond vectorization for multiprocessors. In *Proceedings of the International Conference on Parallel Processing*, pages 836–884, August 1986.

[5] F. H. Dang, H. Yu, and L. Rauchwerger. The R-LRPD test: Speculative parallelization of partially parallel loops. In *IPDPS '02: Proceedings of the 16th International Parallel and Distributed Processing Symposium*, page 318, 2002.

[6] J. R. B. Davies. Parallel loop constructs for multiprocessors. Master's thesis, Department of Computer Science, University of Illinois, Urbana, IL, May 1981.

[7] J. Ferrante, K. J. Ottenstein, and J. D. Warren. The program dependence graph and its use in optimization. *ACM Transactions on Programming Languages and Systems*, 9:319–349, July 1987.

[8] J. Giacomoni, T. Moseley, and M. Vachharajani. FastForward for efficient pipeline parallelism: a cache-optimized concurrent lock-free queue. In *PPoPP '08: Proceedings of the 13th ACM SIGPLAN Symposium on Principles and Practice of Parallel Programming*, pages 43–52, New York, NY, USA, February 2008.

[9] E. Gutiérrez, O. Plata, and E. L. Zapata. Improving parallel irregular reductions using partial array expansion. In *Supercomputing '01: Proceedings of the 2001 ACM/IEEE conference on Supercomputing (CDROM)*, pages 38–38, New York, NY, USA, 2001. ACM.

[10] H. Han and C.-W. Tseng. Improving compiler and run-time support for irregular reductions using local writes. In *LCPC '98: Proceedings of the 11th International Workshop on Languages and Compilers for Parallel Computing*, pages 181–196, London, UK, 1999. Springer-Verlag.

[11] K. Kennedy and K. S. McKinley. Loop distribution with arbitrary control flow. In *Proceedings of Supercomputing*, pages 407–416, November 1990.

[12] M. Kulkarni, K. Pingali, B. Walter, G. Ramanarayanan, K. Bala, and L. P. Chew. Optimistic parallelism requires abstractions. In *PLDI '07: Proceedings of the 2007 ACM SIGPLAN Conference on Programming Language Design and Implementation*, pages 211–222, New York, NY, USA, 2007. ACM.

[13] R. Narayanan, B. Ozisikyilmaz, J. Zambreno, G. Memik, and A. Choudhary. Minebench: A benchmark suite for data mining workloads. *IEEE Workload Characterization Symposium*, 0:182–188, 2006.

[14] C. E. Oancea and A. Mycroft. Software thread-level speculation: an optimistic library implementation. In *IWMSE '08: Proceedings of the 1st International Workshop on Multicore Software Engineering*, pages 23–32, New York, NY, USA, 2008. ACM.

[15] G. Ottoni, R. Rangan, A. Stoler, and D. I. August. Automatic thread extraction with decoupled software pipelining. In *Proceedings of the 38th Annual IEEE/ACM International Symposium on Microarchitecture*, pages 105–116, November 2005.

[16] E. Raman, G. Ottoni, A. Raman, M. Bridges, and D. I. August. Parallel-stage decoupled software pipelining. In *Proceedings of the 2008 International Symposium on Code Generation and Optimization*, April 2008.

[17] L. Rauchwerger and D. A. Padua. The LRPD test: Speculative runtime parallelization of loops with privatization and reduction parallelization. *IEEE Transactions on Parallel and Distributed Systems*, 10(2):160–180, 1999.

[18] D. E. Singh, M. J. Martin, and F. F. Rivera. Runtime characterisation of irregular accesses applied to parallelisation of irregular reductions. *Int. J. Comput. Sci. Eng.*, 1(1):1–14, 2005.

[19] Standard Performance Evaluation Corporation (SPEC). http://www.spec.org.

[20] J. G. Steffan, C. Colohan, A. Zhai, and T. C. Mowry. The STAMPede approach to thread-level speculation. *ACM Transactions on Computer Systems*, 23(3):253–300, February 2005.

[21] StreamIt benchmarks. http://compiler.lcs.mit.edu/streamit.

[22] N. Vachharajani, R. Rangan, E. Raman, M. J. Bridges, G. Ottoni, and D. I. August. Speculative decoupled software pipelining. In *Proceedings of the 16th International Conference on Parallel Architectures and Compilation Techniques*, September 2007.

[23] H. Zhong, M. Mehrara, S. Lieberman, and S. Mahlke. Uncovering hidden loop level parallelism in sequential applications. In *Proc. of the 14th International Symposium on High-Performance Computer Architecture*, 2008.

[24] C. Zilles and G. Sohi. Master/slave speculative parallelization. In *Proceedings of the 35th Annual IEEE/ACM International Symposium on Microarchitecture*, pages 85–96, November 2002.

Prospect: A Compiler Framework for Speculative Parallelization

Martin Süßkraut

Technische Universtät Dresden
suesskraut@se.inf.tu-dresden.de

Thomas Knauth

Technische Universtät Dresden
thomas@se.inf.tu-dresden.de

Stefan Weigert

Technische Universtät Dresden
stefan@se.inf.tu-dresden.de

Ute Schiffel

Technische Universtät Dresden
ute@se.inf.tu-dresden.de

Martin Meinhold

Kontext E GmbH
m.meinhold@kontext-e.de

Christof Fetzer

Technische Universtät Dresden
christof@se.inf.tu-dresden.de

Abstract

Making efficient use of modern multi-core and future many-core CPUs is a major challenge. We describe a new compiler-based platform, *Prospect*, that supports the parallelization of sequential applications. The underlying approach is a generalization of an existing approach to parallelize runtime checks. The basic idea is to generate two variants of the application: (1) a *fast variant* having bare bone functionality, and (2) a *slow variant* with extra functionality. The fast variant is executed sequentially. Its execution is divided into *epochs*. Each epoch is re-executed by an *executor* using the slow variant. The approach scales by running the executors on multiple cores in parallel to each other and to the fast variant. We have implemented the *Prospect* framework to evaluate this approach. *Prospect* allows custom plug-ins for generating the fast and slow variants. With the help of our novel StackLifter, a process can switch between the fast variant and the slow variant during runtime at arbitrary positions.

Categories and Subject Descriptors D.3.4 [*Processors*]: Compilers; D.3.4 [*Processors*]: Optimization

General Terms Design, Experimentation, Measurement, Performance, Security

Keywords parallelization, speculation, bounds checker, assertions, stack translation

1. Introduction

Despite many years of research, making efficient use of modern multi-core and future many-core CPUs is a major challenge. One promising approach comes from the hardware community [Zilles and Sohi 2002] which we call the *predictor/executor* approach. Two variants of an application are generated: a fast and a slow variant. The slow variant uses more CPU cycles than the fast one because the slow variant is, for example, made more robust with the help of additional error checks and error handling. The goal is to provide

the functionality of the slow variant and the runtime of the fast variant. This is achieved by running the fast variant on one core and cutting its execution into epochs. Each epoch is re-executed using the slow variant on another core. This approach scales well with the number of cores as long as the re-execution of the epochs can be decoupled from each other. The maximum speedup is determined by the ratio of the execution times of the slow and the fast version.

This approach has gained attention in the context of runtime checking [Nightingale et al. 2008; Ruwase et al. 2008; Süßkraut et al. 2009; Wallace and Hazelwood 2007]. The fast variant is the original application and the slow variant performs runtime checks that are added, as far as we know, via dynamic binary instrumentation (DBI). The parallelization reduces the user perceived overheads of the runtime checks. The use of DBI introduces, however, high runtime overheads even for simple checks. This means that one needs additional cores to hide the overheads through a higher degree of parallelization. However, gaining good speedups is not easy. For example, the parallelized taint analysis of [Nightingale et al. 2008] has a similar runtime overhead as taint analysis without parallelization [Newsome and Song 2005].

FastTrack [Kelsey et al. 2009] introduces fast-track regions. For each such region, a fast and a slow variant is given, either manually by the programmer or generated by instrumentation with a compiler plug-in. Due to the use of compile time instrumentation, FastTrack avoids the DBI-related performance issues. Most importantly, FastTrack enables additionally the instrumentation of the fast variant. But FastTrack only supports the approach on defined regions. This introduces composability problems: How should one deal with a fast-track region nested in the fast or slow path of another fast-track region? Furthermore, FastTrack does not support speculation for system calls like, for example, [Nightingale et al. 2008].

In Prospect, we combine the advantages of FastTrack with those of the predictor/executor approach. Prospect allows the integration of compiler plug-ins for generating both a fast and a slow variant from the original application. The compiler plug-ins can instrument the whole application, i.e., there are no special regions. In particular, we support system calls within the variants - similar to the approach by [Nightingale et al. 2008]. Regarding the system call speculation, the main difference to [Nightingale et al. 2008] is that the slow and the fast variant can perform different system calls. For example, to speed up the fast variant, one might execute only a subset of the system calls executed by the slow variant. In this paper, we will mainly focus on Prospect's compiler framework and not on the speculative execution of system calls.

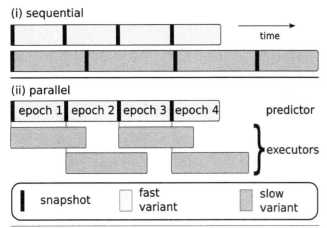

Figure 1. Our parallelization approach executes a fast variant on one core. The execution of the fast variant is partitioned into epochs. Each epoch is re-executed with a slow variant with more functionality. The re-execution happens in parallel to the fast variant on multiple cores.

Our main contribution is the Prospect StackLifter. The StackLifter is a compile time instrumentation to allow switching from the fast variant to the slow variant at given points in the application. It is required that these points are known at compile time. The StackLifter solves two major problems that need to be addressed when switching between code bases: the variants differ in (1) the machine register allocation, and (2) the stack layout. Due to the different instrumentations of the fast and the slow variant, the machine code of both variants will be different. For a given common point in both variants, machine registers may be used to hold different values / variables. For example, values held in registers in the fast variant might be temporarily stored on the stack in the slow variant. This might happen because of a higher register pressure. The slow variant executes additional code and accesses additional variables.

In Section 3, we present the StackLifter. We also describe two compiler plug-ins: (1) an out-of-bounds checker similar to [Kelsey et al. 2009] in Section 4.1, and (2) an optimizer that generates a fast variant for user-defined sanity checks in Section 4.2. We evaluate Prospect in Section 5. We describe the related work in Section 6 and Section 7 concludes the paper.

2. Prospect Overview

Prospect uses the *predictor/executor* approach of [Kelsey et al. 2009; Nightingale et al. 2008; Süßkraut et al. 2009; Zilles and Sohi 2002] to parallelize an application. Figure 1 (i) shows a *fast variant* and a *slow variant* derived from the same code base. Our goal is to provide the functionality of the slow variant while not exceeding the fast variant's runtime. To achieve this, the Prospect framework parallelizes the execution of the slow variant (see Figure 1 (ii)). At runtime, it executes the fast variant in a *predictor* process – which is used to compute future states of the slow variant. The execution of the predictor is partitioned into *epochs*. The state of the predictor at the start of an epoch is used to spawn an *executor* process. The executer re-executes an epoch using the slow code variant and the predictor state (which was obtained using the fast code variant). We can parallelize the application by running the individual executors and the predictor in parallel. The maximum possible speedup is the execution time of the slow variant divided by the execution time of the fast variant.

At each epoch boundary, Prospect takes a snapshot of the fast variant. The snapshot is similar to a UNIX `fork`. The fast variant

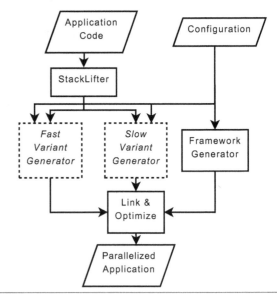

Figure 2. The Prospect work-flow: The StackLifter generates the two initial code bases for the fast and the slow variant. Both variants can be instrumented to remove or add functionality, respectively. Both variants are linked together with a generated framework code that manages the switch from the fast variant to slow variant at epoch boundaries.

continues its execution. The forked executor switches from the fast variant to the slow variant and starts executing the epoch in the slow variant. At the end of an epoch, the slow variant terminates, whereas, the fast variant forks the next epoch.

Prospect is not completely transparent for the application developer. The application developer has to ensure that the application calls `prospect_chkpnt` periodically and preferably, with a constant frequency. This function starts a new epoch and is provided by the Prospect runtime.

Prospect has two major components:

- The *Prospect compiler* which generates the fast and/or slow variant of the given application, and

- The *Prospect runtime* which provides deterministic replay for re-executing the slow variant in the executors and speculative execution for the fast variant in the predictor.

2.1 Compiler Infrastructure

The slow and fast variant are generated by the Prospect compiler from the original application. We consider three cases of variant generation:

- The original application is the fast variant. The slow variant is generated by adding additional code (like runtime security checks) to the original application [Nightingale et al. 2008].

- The original application is the slow variant. The fast variant is generated by removing code from the original application. For instance, aggressive but potential unsafe optimizations can remove code [Kelsey et al. 2009].

- The first and the second approach can by combined, i.e., both variants are generated from the original application.

Figure 2 shows the work-flow of the Prospect compiler. Our novel StackLifter (Section 3) takes the original application's code and generates the initial versions of the fast and the slow variant.

In particular, it prepares both variants in a way that it is possible to switch from the fast variant to the slow variant at epoch boundaries.

Both variants can then be instrumented, e.g., to remove existing functionality that does not affect the state or add error handling functionality (Section 4). The instrumentation must preserve the *state equivalence* property:

DEFINITION 1. *The application state of the fast variant at the end of epoch e must be equivalent to the application state of the slow variant at the end of e.*

This property ensures that from an external point of view, the parallel execution of the slow variant is equivalent to the sequential execution of the fast variant. Note, that we require neither the heap nor the stack of the fast and the slow variant to have the same values at the end of epoch e. However, there has to exist a bidirectional mapping from the state of the fast variant to the state of the slow variant. The mapping does not need to be defined. It only needs to exist. Currently, we do not enforce the state equivalence property. However, one could implement the bidirectional mapping and use the mapping to check at the end of each epoch if the state equivalence property still holds. We show in Section 4.1.2 how to partly circumvent the state equivalence property by *speculative variables*. In our experience, the instrumentation process does not need to be aware of the parallelization.

Prospect also generates framework code that connects the code bases of both variants. The framework code contains primarily a new `main` function that sets up the Prospect runtime, any additional runtime that was added for the slow variant and it starts the first epoch.

We have implemented Prospect using the LLVM compiler framework [Lattner and Adve 2004]. StackLifter and the instrumentation for the fast and slow variant are LLVM compiler passes.

2.2 Runtime Support

Prospect's runtime support consists of speculative execution and deterministic replay of system calls and speculative variables to manage additional state in the slow variant.

2.2.1 Speculative Execution and Deterministic Replay of System Calls

Prospect performs external actions of the fast variant speculatively [Nightingale et al. 2008]. For instance, `write` system calls are held back until they are re-executed by the slow variant. Hence, we ensure that external actions only become visible after the slow variant has verified them.

To support the state equivalence property, we use deterministic replay [Srinivasan et al. 2004] for re-executing the slow variant. Prospect records all non-deterministic external events that happen in epoch e for the fast variant. When the slow variant is re-executed for epoch e, Prospect replays the recorded events. For example, the time value returned by the `gettimeofday` system call in the fast variant is also returned in the slow variant for the same call to `gettimeofday`.

We have implemented the speculative execution and deterministic replay for Linux with a kernel module, similar to Speck [Nightingale et al. 2008]. Speck provides system wide speculation, i.e., external actions of the fast variant are speculative propagated to other processes. In case of an abort, all processes containing speculative state are rolled back. In contrast to Speck, our kernel module isolates multiple applications running under Prospect at the same time from each other.

Currently, to support deterministic replay we have to limit Prospect to single-threaded applications. Recording and deterministically replaying the non-deterministic scheduling decisions of the OS with a low performance overhead is still an unsolved problem.

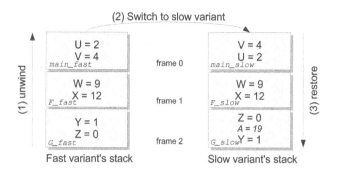

Figure 3. Translating the call stack at runtime.

However, since Prospect parallelizes the slow variant of applications, we believe that this limitation is unimportant. Any progress made in the field of deterministic replay can be incorporated into Prospect in the future. More information on speculation and deterministic replay can be found in related work [Nightingale et al. 2008; Srinivasan et al. 2004].

2.2.2 Speculative Variables

Some slow variants need to track state at runtime that does not exist in the fast variant. For instance, if the slow variant adds out-of-bounds checks, it needs to keep track of the bounds of all allocated buffers at runtime. This additional state violates the state equivalence property. There are two solution to this problem:

- One could track the state in both variants, but use it in the slow variant only. The advantage of this approach is that the state of the fast variant is exactly the same as the state of the slow variant. But, the tracking of the state slows down the fast variant. Figure 1 shows that the parallelization speedup of our approach depends on the relation between the runtimes of the fast and the slow variant. The faster the fast variant and the slower the slow variant the larger the parallelization speedup. Thus, we do not want to track any additional state in the fast variant.

- The slow variant can track the additional state in *speculative variables* previously introduced in [Süßkraut et al. 2009]. Speculative variables completely eliminate the need to track additional state in the fast variant too. We show in Section 4.1.2 how we track the state of ouf-of-bounds checks with speculative variables.

3. StackLifter

One main goal of Prospect is to enable compiler plug-ins to instrument slow and fast variants independently of each other. The issue is that we need to switch from the fast variant to the slow variant at the start of an epoch. This is difficult because, for instance, a plug-in might remove some temporary variables from the fast variant and add new temporary variables to the slow variant. The StackLifter's purpose is to instrument the application code to enable a switch from the fast to the slow variant.

A fast function `F_fast` and its slow equivalent `F_slow` may have different stack layouts. Figure 3 illustrates this for functions `main`, `F`, and `G`. After the StackLifter run, a compiler plug-in changed the order of variable definitions in `main_slow` and added a new variable `A` to `G_slow`.

After a new epoch has been spawned and before continuing execution of the slow variant, the application's call stack must be translated. To be transparent to the application, the call stack has to look like as if only slow functions had been executed. After translating the call stack, execution can continue normally. Global data and the heap do not need to be translated, as the state equivalence property requires the compiler plug-ins not to change the heap layout or the layout of global data.

Stack translation begins with setting the doUnwind flag. The call stack is traversed up to the outermost function, i.e., usually to main, saving all necessary information for each stack frame to allow reconstruction (Figure 3 step (1)). Once the top of the stack is reached (step (2)), we rebuild the call stack by calling the slow variant of each function. We use the saved information to rebuild the call stack (step (3)). When reaching the point where the stack lifting was triggered, execution resumes normally.

We use LLVM to perform the necessary modifications. All code modifications are performed statically. The input and output format is LLVM intermediate representation (IR). Therefore, our StackLifter is independent of the underlying hardware platform.

3.1 Example

For an application programmer, the main difference between Fast-Track and Prospect is the programming interface. In FastTrack, the programmer specifically starts and ends a fast-track region. This is translated to an if branch, where one branches is executed in the fast variant and the other in the slow variant.

In Prospect, we support application wide instrumentation and do not want to restrict instrumentation to a set of regions. In our current implementation, the programmer has to mark possible places where a new epoch could be spawned by calling prospect_chkpnt. Listing 1 shows an example. Like fork, a call to prospect_chkpnt from the fast variant returns twice: (1) in the fast variant, and (2) in the slow variant. When prospect_chkpnt is called from the slow variant, the re-execution of the current epoch is finished. At runtime, when prospect_chkpnt is called from the fast variant and returns into the slow variant, it needs to switch from the fast variant's code base to the slow variant's code base.

Listing 1. API example.

```
1 int foo() { ... prospect_chkpnt(); ... }
2 void bar(char* b) {
3     assert(b);
4     int i = foo();
5     return b[i];
6 }
```

For the example in Listing 1 a jump from the fast code base into the slow code base (right behind the call to prospect_chkpnt) is not enough. Consider, an instrumentation of the fast variant, that removes the assert in line 3. The slow variant b might be loaded into a machine register in line 3. When foo returns b is expected to be in this register in line 5. Whereas, in the fast variant line 3 does not exist and when foo returns b is still on the stack. That means after prospect_chkpnt returns into the slow variant b has to appear in the right register. Our approach is that both variants are prepared by the StackLifter *before* the compiler plug-ins instrument them.

3.2 Implementation Details

StackLifter clones all functions defined in a given module. Each function now comes in two flavors: (i) a fast, and (ii) a slow variant. The slow variant's name will be the original name appended with an unique suffix, e.g., originalName_slow. Hence, all functions ending in _slow belong to the set of slow functions. The predictor executes the fast variants and the executors the slow variants. An executor receives its initial state from the predictor. Hence, all stack frames on the stack belong to fast versions. Prospect needs

to replace the stack frames of the fast versions by their _slow counterparts.

StackLifter creates a new basic block for each function call. The purpose is to allow us to use the basic block as a branch label. Control flow can be diverted to any function call. This is necessary when reconstructing the call stack after an unwind. The basic block only contains an LLVM call instruction and an unconditional branch instruction. The branch will jump to the next instruction after the call as defined by the original application. Basic blocks will be given a unique name to identify them as "function call" basic blocks, e.g., call_X where X is a running number. The basic block reached via the unconditional branch instructions will carry the same name as the function call basic block plus a suffix, e.g. call_Xsucc.

The basic block of a function call in the fast variant carries two additional instructions. Upon return from each function call, the global doUnwind flag is checked. If the check fails, control flow continues as in the original program. If the check succeeds, execution continues with a *register saving* basic block (discussed in Section 3.3). Listing 2 has LLVM code for a transformed function call of the fast variant of a function.

Listing 2. Function call transformation for fast variant

```
call_1: ; name to id block as a function call site
        call void @foo()
        ; check if doing an unwind
        %doUnwind = load i8* @doUnwind
        %doUnwindCmp = icmp eq i8 %doUnwind, 0
        ; branch to register saving code or continue
        ; execution normally
        br i1 %doUnwindCmp, label %call_1succ,
                            label %save_regs_1
```

The StackLifter ensures that all slow functions only call slow functions. Once switched to slow execution, we do not want to leave the set of slow functions. Direct function calls are easily changed by simply altering the name of the called function. The target of an indirect function call, though, can only be changed at runtime. Hence, StackLifter inserts additional code before each indirect function call (see Listing 3):

Listing 3. Indirect call transformation for slow variant

```
call_3:
  %castedPtrToOrig = bitcast void ()* %orig to i8*
  ; @fp2sp translates fast function pointer
  ; to slow variant's function pointer
  %ptrToClone = call i8* @fp2sp(i8* %castedPtrToOrig)
  %castedPtrToClone = bitcast i8* %ptrToClone to void ()*
  call void %castedPtrToClone() nounwind
```

We call a function fp2sp which, given a slow/fast function's address, will return the address of the corresponding slow function. If the passed pointer already points to a slow function, fp2sp simply returns it. fp2sp will use the input function pointer as an index into a map. This map is constructed before executing the main function by code generated by the StackLifter.

3.3 Saving Registers

During a stack translation, each stack frame of a fast function must be replaced by an equivalent stack frame of its slow variant. Hence, register saving code is inserted into the fast functions. During a stack translation – when unwinding the call stack of the fast functions – for each function F, the state of F_fast is stored in a buffer. This buffer permits the reconstruction of the state in F's slow counterpart F_slow. The storing of the state is done in the *register saving* basic block.

For each function call within a fast function, there is a separate register saving basic block. In LLVM, the state of function F at instruction I is represented by the values of all live registers in F at I. After each call, different registers might be live. Hence, each function call has its own register saving basic block. We perform liveness analysis for every basic block containing at least one function call. All registers marked live on entering the function call basic block need to be preserved.

An example of a register saving basic block is shown in Listing 4. External helper functions (pushI64 and pushFloat) are called to store all live registers (%reg1 and %reg2) in a separate buffer. Additionally, a label, uniquely identifying the function call basic block, is stored too (pushLabel). This label is of importance again, when the stack frame is reconstructed. The end of each register saving basic block is marked by a simple return instruction. Stack unwinding then continues in the caller.

Listing 4. Save register block

```
save_regs_3:
        call void @pushI64(i64 %reg1)
        call void @pushFloat(float %reg2)
        call void @pushLabel(i32 1)
        ret i32 undef
```

The buffer holding live registers and labels is organized as a stack. The register saving block pushes all live registers to this stack. In the slow function all live registers are restored from the stack in reverse order.

3.4 Restoring Registers

While a fast function needs to save the live registers, its slow function needs to be able to restore the live register with the help of a *register restoring* basic block. As with register saving basic blocks, there is a restore basic block for each function call. When entering a slow function, we need to check if this is a call because of a stack reconstruction. This is done by calling the external helper function popLabel. It returns zero, if no reconstruction is going on. Otherwise, the return value is a label identifying a specific function call basic block in the current slow function. A switch statement will divert control to the correct restore basic block based upon the return value of popLabel. Listing 5 shows an example of a slow function's entry basic block.

Listing 5. New entry block

```
new_entry:
        %next_label = call i32 @popLabel()
        switch i32 %next_label, label %old_entry [
                i32 1, label %restore_regs_1
                i32 2, label %restore_regs_2
        ]
```

If no reconstruction goes on (%next_label is zero) execution continues at original entry basic block %old_entry.

Listing 6 shows an example of a register restoring basic block.

Listing 6. Restore register block

```
restore_regs_3:
        %reg2 = call i64 @popFloat()
        %reg1 = call i64 @popI64()
        br label %call2inv_3_slow
```

The basic block calls an external helper functions (popI64 and popFloat) to retrieve the value of a live register (compare with Listing 4). After all live registers have been restored, execution continues by branching to the function call basic block identified by the label pop at function entry. Restoring then continues with the function called in the function call basic block.

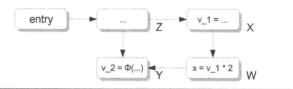

Figure 4. Sample control flow graph.

3.5 Restoring Static Single Assignment Form

LLVM uses Static Single Assignment (SSA) in its LLVM intermediate representation (IR). All modifications need to preserve SSA. Our transformations temporarily violate the SSA constraint. This section describes how the SSA form is restored.

Conceptually, we use a modified version of the algorithm described by [Cytron et al. 1991]. One assumption made in the algorithm for placing Φ nodes is that all variables are defined and initialized in the function's entry basic block [Cytron et al. 1991, pg. 25]. This, however, does not hold for programs in LLVM IR. The LLVM IR is compiled from C code, where variables can be initialized nearly anywhere in the function.

Using the unmodified algorithm proposed in [Cytron et al. 1991, pg. 25] can lead to wrongly placed Φ nodes. See Figure 4 for an example. Registers v_1 and v_2 refer to the same variable v. Variable v is defined and initialized in basic block X, and only used in basic block W. Following the algorithm in [Cytron et al. 1991], a Φ-node for v should be inserted in Y. First, v's scope is limited to basic blocks X and W. Hence, the Φ-node in Y has no uses. Second, because variable v was defined and initialized in X there is no incoming value for this Φ-node for the incoming basic block Z. If v would have been defined and initialized in basic block entry, as assumed by [Cytron et al. 1991], there would be an incoming value. However, as v's scope is limited to basic blocks X and W, the Φ-node in Y is neither possible nor needed.

Our solution is:

1. Apply the algorithm from [Cytron et al. 1991].

2. Remove any illegal Φ-nodes. We use a fix point algorithm and iteratively remove Φ-nodes. If, during one iteration, we find no Φ-nodes to remove, the algorithm terminates. We use three rules to detect an illegal Φ-node. A Φ-node is deleted if:

   (a) It is never used.

   (b) Its uses are exclusively incoming values for itself.

   (c) The definition of at-least one of its incoming values does not dominate the basic block for which the incoming value is specified.

   Rule a) is self-explanatory [Briggs et al. 1998].

   Rule b) is a special case of Rule a). A Φ-node according to Rule b) has uses (but only itself). Therefore, it cannot be removed according to Rule a). But, as the Φ-node is not used by any other instruction it is nevertheless not needed.

   Consider the control flow graph in Figure 4 as an example for Rule c). As a default incoming value for each direct predecessor of Y, the original definition of v_1 is inserted, i.e.:

   ```
   %v_2 = phi i32 [%v_1, label %W], [%v_1, label %Z])
   ```

   When updating incoming values later, the pair [%v_1, label %Z] would remain unchanged. As explained above, this Φ-node is illegal. Because of Rule c) we remove this Φ-node. The reason is that the basic block X (where the incoming value %v_1 is defined), does not dominate basic block Z (the basic block for which the incoming value is defined).

3.6 Stack-local Variables

Addresses of stack-local variables can change during stack translation because additional local variables might be present in the slow variant's function. Therefore, we put all addressable variables on a separate *alloca stack*. This stack is not changed by stack translation. Hence, the address of any variable on the alloca stack is the same for the fast and for the slow variant.

Technically, we replace all LLVM `alloca` instructions with our own implementation that allocates the variables on the alloca stack. On function entry, we store the current frame address of the alloca stack. And on each function exit, we restore the previously stored frame address.

3.7 Integration with `prospect_chkpnt`

At runtime, an application spawns a new epoch by calling `prospect_chkpnt_fast` in the fast variant. After forking the new epoch, the flag `doUnwind` is set in the executor and `prospect_chkpnt_fast` returns to its caller `func_fast`. Because `doUnwind` is set, the register saving block of `func_fast` is executed (see Sections 3.2 and 3.3). After the registers of `func_fast` are saved, `func_fast` returns to its caller. Again, the registers of `func_fast`'s caller are saved and the function returns. The process continues iteratively saving the registers of all function frames on the stack, including `main_fast`.

Function `main_fast` returns to our generated `main`. Our `main` now calls `main_slow` with the `doUnwind` flag still set. In `main_slow` the register restoring block is triggered (see Section 3.4). This restoration process continues iteratively until `func_slow` (`func_fast`'s counterpart in the slow variants code base) is reached. Function `func_slow` restores its registers and calls `prospect_chkpnt_slow`. In `prospect_chkpnt_slow` the flag `doUnwind` is cleared and it returns back into `func_slow`. Then the execution continues normally in `func_slow` in the slow variant.

4. Prospect Plug-ins

To evaluate the Prospect framework, we implemented two plug-ins: (1) *Out-of-Bounds* (OOB) instruments a slow variant with additional out-of-bounds checks for each memory access, and (2) *FastAssert* removes all `assert`s from a fast variant. We use the two plug-ins to evaluate the performance of our framework. We did not try to push the state-of-the-art of out-of-bounds checkers.

Because the plug-ins are applied after the StackLifter (see Figure 2), the StackLifter's instrumentation is visible to the plug-ins. In general, we found that these instrumentations are transparent to the plug-ins as the instrumented code is valid LLVM. It is even possible to change the restored state. In order to do so, a plug-in can wrap the restoring helper functions, e.g., `popI64` and `popFloat`).

4.1 Out-of-Bounds checks

In our experience, Prospect permits runtime checks to be added by a plug-in in almost the same way as one would add it to a sequential program. To justify this claim, we first show briefly how our simple OOB checker is implemented without Prospect and then how we adapted the OOB checker for Prospect to parallelize its runtime checks. Our goal is in both cases to detect out-of-bounds accesses to heap allocated buffers.

4.1.1 OOB without Prospect

The OOB plug-in is implemented as an LLVM pass. At compile time, the OOB plug-in adds a runtime check for every memory access. To keep track of all currently allocated buffers, our instrumentation wraps all `malloc` and `free` calls of the application.

The OOB checks fail if and only if, the checked memory access goes to the heap but not into a currently allocated buffer. In LLVM, for most memory accesses the reference of the corresponding *base addresses* (start of an allocated buffer) can be identified at compile time[1]. Our current prototype only instruments such memory accesses with checks. To do so, we keep the size and base-addresses of allocated buffers in a *hash map* at runtime. For every `malloc` call, a new entry is added to the map. Consequently, for every `free` call, the corresponding entry is removed from the map.

4.1.2 OOB with Prospect

The instrumentation for OOB with Prospect is the same as the instrumentation without Prospect except that only slow functions are instrumented. The fast variant does neither update the map nor does it perform any checks. The major problem is that the slow variant does not know which blocks are allocated. Prospect supports speculation to address this problem. For example, in Listing 7, the allocation and the memory access happen in different epochs e_i and e_{i+1}, respectively. Because, the slow variants of e_i and e_{i+1} are executed in parallel to each other, the slow variant of e_{i+1} might access variable `buf` and check its size, before e_i allocates `buf` and stores the size of `buf` in the hash map.

Listing 7. Allocation and memory access in different epochs.

```
1 char* buf = malloc(20);
2 prospect_chkpnt();
3 buf[0] = 'h';
```

Speculative Variables We solve this problem by using *speculative variables* [Süßkraut et al. 2009]. At runtime, each epoch starts with an empty hash map to store the start address and the size of each allocated buffer. When an OOB check fails, the runtime check adds a *speculative* entry into the hash map. We call this speculative entry a speculative variable. The speculative variable contains the expected buffer bounds derived from the checked memory access. For example, in Listing 7 in line 3 an entry (`&buf`, 1) is inserted into the hash-map of epoch e_{i+1}. Subsequent accesses may update the speculative variable if the expected buffer bounds have to be extended. Allocations with `malloc` create non-speculative entries. If the allocation happens before the memory access in the same epoch, no speculative variable is created. Note that the first epoch will not create speculative variables: for every memory access it must have already seen the allocation.

At the end of each epoch e_{i+1}, all speculative variables are verified against the hash map h_i of the previous epoch e_i. For each speculative variable sp in h_{i+1} there must be an entry in h_i for which the expected bounds in sp can be verified. If no such entry is found, the application is aborted. After all speculative entries are verified they become non-speculative entries. The non-speculative entries of h_i are merged into h_{i+1}. By induction, epoch e_{i+2} can than be verified against h_{i+1} of epoch e_{i+1}. We give more details about speculative variables in [Süßkraut et al. 2009].

4.2 FastAssert

Software developers are encouraged to add runtime assertions to their source code [Meyer 2000]. One of the trade-offs of runtime assertions is their runtime overhead. FastAssert (partly) mitigates the negative effects of assertions on the application runtime. The plug-in removes any assertions and functions that neither change the internal nor the external application state from the fast variant. The slow variant still contains the assertions. Hence, assertions

---

[1] In LLVM, nearly all pointer arithmetic uses the `getelementptr` instruction, which expects the base address as first operand.

Benchmark/Application	# calls to `prospect_chkpnt`
Vacation	3
Genome	4
Whetstone	6
LinPack	2
bzip2	8
BOOST's words	3

Table 1. The number of calls to `prospect_chkpnt` that we inserted into the source code per used benchmark/application.

are still checked at runtime, but their computational overhead is parallelized.

For each function f, FastAssert computes if f might change the internal or external state of the application or if f transitively calls a function that might change the internal or external state of the application. Internal state changes are identified by `store` instructions. External state changes are identified by calls to external functions. If a function f does neither, calls to f are removed from the fast variant. The external function `assert_fail` is a special case. It is used to implement the `assert` macro on our platform. Therefore, `assert_fail` is considered as not changing any state.

By removing not only assertions itself but also side-effect free computation, we also remove user defined sanity checking code. We expect that FastAssert not only mitigates the perceived performance overhead of existing assertions, but also motivates to include more (computationally expensive) assertions.

5. Evaluation

Our evaluation focuses on the speedup achieved by Prospect and the overheads introduced by Prospect's components. We performed all measurements on a DELL PowerEdge 1950 with 2x Intel XEON E5430 (8 cores) and 16 GB RAM. Each data point is the average of at least three measurements.

5.1 Parallelization Speedup

We measured the parallelization speedup on four benchmarks and two real world applications for our compiler plug-ins out-of-bounds and FastAssert. In order to make the benchmarks and applications parallelizable with Prospect we had to split them into epochs. Effectively, we had to add calls to `prospect_chkpnt` to the four benchmarks and two applications. We have two rules of thumb to place calls to `prospect_chkpnt`:

- If the benchmark or application consists of multiple stages, we place the call to `prospect_chkpnt` between stages with big workloads.

- We also added calls to `prospect_chkpnt` into loops with big workloads.

Both rules can be combined, e.g., if a stage contains a loop with big workloads.

Table 1 shows the number of calls to `prospect_chkpnt` that we inserted into the source code per used benchmark/application. We used the first five benchmarks/applications to evaluate our out-of-bounds instrumentation and BOOST's words to evaluate FastAssert.

5.1.1 Out-Of-Bounds

To measure the speedup of parallelizing the bounds checks with Prospect, we used five different benchmarks from different application domains. First, *Genome* and *Vacation* are part of the *STAMP* [Cao Minh et al. 2008] benchmark suite for transactional memory. The performance of both benchmarks is CPU and

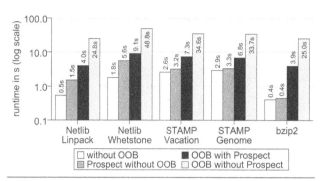

Figure 5. Runtime measurements on an 8-core Intel Xeon Server with 16GB main memory.

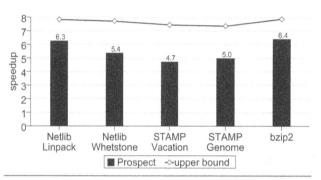

Figure 6. Speedup of out-of-bounds (OOB) with Prospect relative to OOB without Prospect.

memory-bound. All STAMP benchmarks can be executed in parallel using multiple threads. In [Süßkraut et al. 2009] we compare the scalability of the STAMP benchmarks using Prospect with parallelizing the slow variant of the STAMP benchmarks using Software Transactional Memory. We found that the parallelization with Prospect scales better. We ascribe this effect to increased contention which limits scalability. In slow variant the contention between concurrent transactions is higher than in the fast variant. For more details we refer to [Süßkraut et al. 2009].

However, for this experiments we run the STAMP benchmarks single-threaded since we want to show the parallelization with Prospect. Second, we used *Whetstone* and *LinPack*. Both come from the high performance community and are, at least in our measurements, CPU-bound only. The last application is *bzip2*, a real application and not a benchmark.

Figure 5 shows the runtime (in s) of the five benchmarks. We run all benchmarks in four configurations:

1. without out-of-bounds checks (OOB) and without Prospect to show the lower bound for the runtime,

2. without OOB but with Prospect to show the framework's overhead,

3. with OOB and with Prospect to show the runtime reduction by Prospect's parallelization, and

4. with OOB but without Prospect to show the slowdown of the OOB without parallelization.

All runs without Prospect are single-threaded, whereas with Prospect we make full use of all 8 cores. The Prospect overhead (configuration 2) is most visible for Whetstone (3.1x) and LinPack (2.8x).

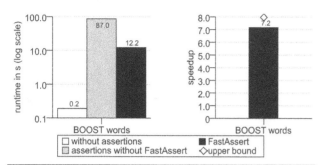

Figure 7. Runtime and Speedup with user-defined assertions in the BOOST words example.

In Figure 6 we plotted the speedup of OOB with Prospect (i.e., configuration 3) relative to OOB without Prospect (i.e., configuration 4). To estimate the maximal possible speedup on our 8 core machine, we use the following upper bound:

$$\text{slowdown} = \frac{\text{runtime configuration 4}}{\text{runtime configuration 1}}$$

$$\text{upper bound} = \frac{\text{number of cores}}{1 + \frac{1}{\text{slowdown}}}$$

This upper bound takes into account that the fast variant needs about $\frac{1}{\text{slowdown}}$ of the CPU cycles of the slow variant.

Figure 6 only presents the speedups for exactly 8 cores. In [Süßkraut et al. 2009] we also measured the scalability of our out-of-bounds checker with Prospect with a lesser number of cores to evaluate the scalability of Prospect. Our results are that Prospect scales linearly for a low number of cores. The scalability is limited by a saturation point below the theoretical upper bound. These results are confirmed by Figure 6.

5.1.2 FastAssert

We tested FastAssert with real world code. We choose the words unit-test of BOOST's multi-map implementation [Munoz 2009]. Figure 7 (left) shows the runtime of the test in three configurations:

1. without assertions and without Prospect,
2. with assertions but without Prospect, and
3. with assertions and with Prospect (FastAssert).

Configuration 1 is 458x faster than configuration 2. This is an unusual runtime overhead for assertions. FastAssert is 7.2x faster than configuration 2 (right hand side). But the runtime overhead compared to configuration 1 is still impractical 64x. Nevertheless, we believe that given more cores FastAssert would reduce the runtime of configuration 3 even more. We believe this example shows that FastAssert enables the inclusion of heavy-weight user defined sanity checks into production code.

5.2 Prospect Overhead

To analyze the runtime overheads introduced by Prospect, we measured the overhead of system call speculation, deterministic replay and the StackLifter individually. Figure 8 shows the overhead of system call speculation and deterministic replay for the Vacation benchmark with four different workloads (number of performed transactions). System call speculation and deterministic replay are implemented by our Linux Kernel module. We run Vacation only with the kernel module. The slow variant was forked right before the execution of the `main` function. Slow and fast variant share the same code. To avoid measuring overhead of the StackLifter, the

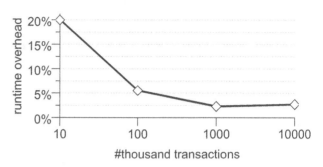

Figure 8. Overhead of the system call speculation in the fast variant and the deterministic replay in the slow variant for Vacation.

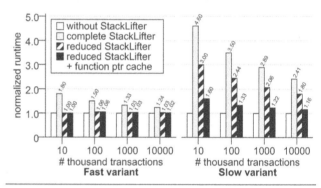

Figure 9. Overhead of the StackLifter instrumentation with three optimizations for Vacation.

whole execution took place within one epoch. No further instrumentation (especially no StackLifter) was applied. The overhead of the smaller workloads is dominated by the start-up time of our kernel module. For the two larger workloads the overhead is around 2.5%.

Figure 9 shows some overheads introduced by the StackLifter. Again, we executed Vacation with four different workloads. The StackLifter adds instrumentation to both, the fast variant and the slow variant. In this experiment, we measured the overheads introduced by this instrumentation but not the stack lifting process itself. We run both variants separately without system call speculation and deterministic replay. Applying StackLifter to all code of the fast variant increases the runtime up to 1.8x compared to vacation without Prospect. If StackLifter is restricted to functions on the path to `prospect_chkpnt`, the overhead is below 3%. The instrumentation of the slow variant introduces a higher overhead. Instrumenting all functions, the overhead is between 2.41x and 4.60x. Instrumenting only functions on the path to `prospect_chkpnt`, the StackLifter's overhead is reduced to between 1.80x and 3.0x.

The overhead of the slow variant can be further reduced by optimizing indirect function calls. Note that all function pointers (also in the slow variant) point to functions of the fast variant. Hence, before each indirect call, we need to look up the function pointer of the slow variant. A map is indexed by fast variant function pointers (see Listing 3). The last optimization is to add a one element look-up cache to `fp2cp`. This optimization is not used in the fast variant, therefore, it does not influence the overhead of the fast variant. The slow variant's overhead is reduce to 1.16x for the largest tested workload.

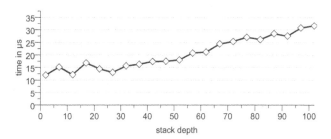

Figure 10. Time to perform a stack lifting for different stack depths.

In our experience, the time needed to switch from the fast variant to the slow variant is very small. Hence, it is difficult to get reliable measurements from our benchmarks. Therefore, we built a micro-benchmark executing a recursive function and calling `prospect_chkpnt` exactly once. Besides StackLifter, we did not apply any other instrumentation. Figure 10 shows the time needed to switch from the fast variant to the slow variant for growing stack depths. Each stack frame contains one label and three live integer registers. Unsurprisingly, it takes longer to un- and rewind from greater stack depths. A linear relation exist, indicating predictable behavior.

The runtime overhead in the slow variant is noticeable for large stack depths. However, this runtime overhead is already parallelized by Prospect.

6. Related Work

The predictor/executor approach was first introduced in the hardware community [Zilles and Sohi 2002]. A distilled program (i.e., a fast variant) is generated at compile time. The execution is similar to our approach. The main difference is on how the switch from the fast variant to the slow variant at epoch boundaries is performed. [Zilles and Sohi 2002] use a hash-map to translate program counters. States are communicated via a check-pointing unit in the memory subsystem. However, it is not clear how this approach handles different stack layouts between fast and slow variant.

FastTrack [Kelsey et al. 2009] is the system most similar to Prospect. In contrast to Prospect, FastTrack is not designed to apply the approach to the whole application. It only supports fast-track regions, which must not contain system calls. FastTrack does not need a StackLifter nor does it need speculative system calls. The other way around, we see that the StackLifter is a crucial part to apply the approach to the whole application. Additionally, FastTrack makes no use of speculation for state, added to the slow variant.

In the last few years, the predictor/executor approach has got some attention from the runtime checking community [Nightingale et al. 2008; Ruwase et al. 2008; Wallace and Hazelwood 2007]. All these projects make use of dynamic binary instrumentation with the help of the Pin tool [Luk et al. 2005]. Whereas Pin allows adding code like runtime checks, it is not suitable for efficiently removing code like user-defined assertions. A StackLifter is not needed as the state of the runtime checks are completely separated from the application state. SuperPin [Wallace and Hazelwood 2007] does not support speculation for system calls. Hence, speculative state might become visible due to unsafe optimizations or failing runtime checks. Speck's [Nightingale et al. 2008] support for system call speculation and deterministic replay is closest to ours. It is derived from Speculator [Nightingale et al. 2005]. Speculator is an operating system extension and it supports the speculative execution of one process. The speculation is propagated throughout the

system, whereas, Prospect provides isolation. Hence, it is possible to run several applications under Prospect at the same time. DIFT [Ruwase et al. 2008] uses a non-trivial hardware extension to stream data from the core, running the fast version to the slave cores. The slave cores use this data to perform runtime checks.

The StackLifter solves the on-stack replacement problem that also occurs in the dynamic software update problem. The current version of an application shall be replaced by a new version without terminating or restarting the application [Fink and Qian 2003; Makris and Bazzi 2009; Neamtiu et al. 2006]. Previous work, like Ginseng [Neamtiu et al. 2006], avoids stack rewriting by only upgrading a function that has currently no frames on the stack. Data is accessed indirectly to allow online updates. The recently published UpStare [Makris and Bazzi 2009] uses an approach similar to our StackLifter. However, UpStare works on C source code and seems to need manual intervention for mapping an old version's stack frame to a new version's stack frame, e.g., when pointers are involved. We avoid this issue by using the alloca stack and with the help of the state equivalence property. On-stack replacement (OSR) for the JVM [Fink and Qian 2003] is quite similar to the StackLifter. The goal of [Fink and Qian 2003] is to switch from the current code base *once* to another, perhaps more optimized, code base. Because the switch happens once for a code base pair, the new code base is specially prepared. The current state of the stack is explicitly inlined into the new code base as the starting state for each function. Furthermore, OSR works on Java bytecode, which is more abstract than the LLVM bytecode.

7. Conclusion

Prospect facilitates the implementation of parallelized and scalable runtime checkers. New checkers are relatively easy to program. In contrast to previous work, we even permit the parallelization of application programmer defined sanity checks. Prospect provides good speedups of instrumented programs and a low overhead compared to the sequential execution of an uninstrumented program.

We plan to extend Prospect in various ways. Currently, Prospect uses fixed-size epochs. We expect to achieve even better scalability when switching to dynamic epoch lengths. Prospect aborts the execution on a misspeculation. This is actually desirable for runtime checking and user defined sanity checks because a misspeculation always means that a check has failed. We plan to add a recovery mechanism in which an executor can spawn a new predictor in case of a misspeculation. We will therefore need to implement a "bi-directional" StackLifter, i.e., one that can also switch from the slow to the fast variant.

References

P. Briggs, K. D. Cooper, T. J. Harvey, and L. T. Simpson. Practical improvements to the construction and destruction of static single assignment form. *Softw. Pract. Exper.*, 28(8):859–881, 1998. ISSN 0038-0644. doi: http://dx.doi.org/10.1002/(SICI)1097-024X(19980710)28:8¡859::AID-SPE188¿3.0.CO;2-8.

C. Cao Minh, J. Chung, C. Kozyrakis, and K. Olukotun. Stamp: Stanford transactional applications for multi-processing. In *IISWC '08: Proceedings of The IEEE International Symposium on Workload Characterization*, September 2008.

R. Cytron, J. Ferrante, B. K. Rosen, M. N. Wegman, and F. K. Zadeck. Efficiently computing static single assignment form and the control dependence graph. *ACM Trans. Program. Lang. Syst.*, 13(4):451–490, 1991. ISSN 0164-0925. doi: http://doi.acm.org/10.1145/115372.115320.

S. J. Fink and F. Qian. Design, implementation and evaluation of adaptive recompilation with on-stack replacement. In *CGO '03: Proceedings of the international symposium on Code generation and optimization*, pages 241–252, Washington, DC, USA, 2003. IEEE Computer Society. ISBN 0-7695-1913-X.

K. Kelsey, T. Bai, C. Ding, and C. Zhang. Fast track: A software system for speculative program optimization. In *CGO '09: Proceedings of the 2009 International Symposium on Code Generation and Optimization*, pages 157–168, Washington, DC, USA, 2009. IEEE Computer Society. ISBN 978-0-7695-3576-0. doi: http://dx.doi.org/10.1109/CGO.2009.18.

C. Lattner and V. Adve. LLVM: A Compilation Framework for Lifelong Program Analysis & Transformation. In *Proceedings of the 2004 International Symposium on Code Generation and Optimization (CGO'04)*, California, 2004.

C.-K. Luk, R. Cohn, R. Muth, H. Patil, A. Klauser, G. Lowney, S. Wallace, V. J. Reddi, and K. Hazelwood. Pin: building customized program analysis tools with dynamic instrumentation. In *PLDI '05: Proceedings of the 2005 ACM SIGPLAN conference on Programming language design and implementation*, pages 190–200, New York, NY, USA, 2005. ACM. ISBN 1-59593-056-6. doi: http://doi.acm.org/10.1145/1065010.1065034.

K. Makris and R. A. Bazzi. Immediate Multi-Threaded Dynamic Software Updates Using Stack Reconstruction. In *Proceedings of the USENIX '09 Annual Technical Conference*, June 2009.

B. Meyer. *Object-Oriented Software Construction*. Prentice Hall PTR, March 2000. ISBN 0136291554.

J. M. L. Munoz. Boost.multiindex example of use of sequenced indices. http://www.boost.org/libs/multi_index, September 2009. Version 1.34.

I. Neamtiu, M. Hicks, G. Stoyle, and M. Oriol. Practical dynamic software updating for c. *SIGPLAN Not.*, 41(6):72–83, 2006. ISSN 0362-1340. doi: http://doi.acm.org/10.1145/1133255.1133991.

J. Newsome and D. Song. Dynamic taint analysis for automatic detection, analysis, and signature generation of exploits on commodity software. In *Proceedings of the Network and Distributed System Security Symposium (NDSS 2005)*, 2005.

E. B. Nightingale, P. M. Chen, and J. Flinn. Speculative execution in a distributed file system. *SIGOPS Oper. Syst. Rev.*, 39(5):191–205, 2005. ISSN 0163-5980. doi: http://doi.acm.org/10.1145/1095809.1095829.

E. B. Nightingale, D. Peek, P. M. Chen, and J. Flinn. Parallelizing security checks on commodity hardware. *SIGARCH Comput. Archit. News*, 36 (1):308–318, 2008.

O. Ruwase, P. B. Gibbons, T. C. Mowry, V. Ramachandran, S. Chen, M. Kozuch, and M. Ryan. Parallelizing dynamic information flow tracking. In *SPAA '08: Proceedings of the twentieth annual symposium on Parallelism in algorithms and architectures*, pages 35–45, New York, NY, USA, 2008. ACM. ISBN 978-1-59593-973-9. doi: http://doi.acm.org/10.1145/1378533.1378538.

S. M. Srinivasan, S. Kandula, C. R. Andrews, and Y. Zhou. Flashback: a lightweight extension for rollback and deterministic replay for software debugging. In *ATEC '04: Proceedings of the annual conference on USENIX Annual Technical Conference*, pages 3–3, Berkeley, CA, USA, 2004. USENIX Association.

M. Süßkraut, S. Weigert, U. Schiffel, T. Knauth, M. Nowack, D. Becker de Brum, and C. Fetzer. Speculation for parallelizing runtime checks. In *Proceedings of the 11th International Symposium on Stabilization, Safety, and Security of Distributed Systems (SSS 2009)*, 2009.

S. Wallace and K. Hazelwood. Superpin: Parallelizing dynamic instrumentation for real-time performance. In *CGO '07: Proceedings of the International Symposium on Code Generation and Optimization*, pages 209–220, Washington, DC, USA, 2007. IEEE Computer Society. ISBN 0-7695-2764-7. doi: http://dx.doi.org/10.1109/CGO.2007.37.

C. Zilles and G. Sohi. Master/slave speculative parallelization. In *MICRO 35: Proceedings of the 35th annual ACM/IEEE international symposium on Microarchitecture*, pages 85–96, Los Alamitos, CA, USA, 2002. IEEE Computer Society Press. ISBN 0-7695-1859-1.

Speculative Parallelization of Partial Reduction Variables

Liang Han
Dept. of Electrical and Computer Eng.
North Carolina State University
lhan@ncsu.edu

Wei Liu
Intel Corp.
wei.w.liu@intel.com

James M. Tuck
Dept. of Electrical and Computer Eng.
North Carolina State University
jtuck@ncsu.edu

Abstract

Reduction variables are an important class of cross-thread dependence that can be parallelized by exploiting the associativity and commutativity of their operation. In this paper, we define a class of shared variables called *partial reduction variables* (PRV). These variables either cannot be proven to be reductions or they violate the requirements of a reduction variable in some way.

We describe an algorithm that allows the compiler to detect PRVs, and we also discuss the necessary requirements to parallelize detected PRVs. Based on these requirements, we propose an implementation in a TLS system to parallelize PRVs that works by a combination of techniques at compile time and in the hardware. The compiler transforms the variable under the assumption that the reduction-like behavior proven statically will hold true at runtime. However, if a thread reads or updates the shared variable as a result of an alias or unlikely control path, a lightweight hardware mechanism will detect the access and synchronize it to ensure correct execution. We implement our compiler analysis and transformation in GCC, and analyze its potential on the SPEC CPU 2000 benchmarks. We find that supporting PRVs provides up to 46% performance gain over a highly optimized TLS system and on average 10.7% performance improvement.

Categories and Subject Descriptors   C.1.4 [*Processor Architectures*]: Parallel Architectures;   D.1.3 [*Programming Techniques*]: Concurrent Programming;   D.3.4 [*Processors*]: Compilers

General Terms   Algorithms, Design, Measurement, Performance

Keywords   Reduction variables, parallelization, Thread-Level Speculation, multi-core architecture

1. Introduction

Given the abundance of multi-core architectures and the relatively few programs capable of exploiting parallel architectures effectively, techniques for automatic and semi-automatic parallelization are increasingly important. Parallelizing compilers attempt to decompose a program into threads (or tasks) that can execute in parallel when there are no cross-task control or data dependences. Despite their many advances, such compilers still fail to parallelize many codes. Examples of such codes are accesses through pointers, subscripted subscripts, interprocedural dependences or input dependent access patterns. Parallelizing compilers [16, 20, 26, 39] that target architectures with support for dynamic speculation of data dependences [13, 15, 24, 25, 29, 30, 40] have shown promise

for coping with these kinds of problems. However, to move beyond the limitations of classical parallelizing optimizations, new parallelizing compilers must look to analyses and transformations that do not rely on conservative assumptions for correctness, but rather consider new ways to speculate on the likely behavior of data and control dependences at runtime. We apply this observation in the context of reduction variables.

Reduction variables are an important class of loop-carried dependences in programs. They are characterized by an expression of the following form inside a loop: $r = r \otimes expression$, where r is the reduction variable and $expression$ is a value computed independently form r. $\otimes$ is assumed to be commutative and associative. Furthermore, r is not used or defined anywhere else in the loop. Even though the computation results in a loop-carried (and likely cross-task) dependence, it can still be parallelized by exploiting the commutative and associative properties of the operation to avoid a cross-task dependence. Each thread can accumulate part of the computation privately; only when all threads are finished do they synchronize and calculate the final sum. Scientific codes exhibit these patterns in abundance and are parallelizable using this technique. However, it is harder to parallelize these patterns when they occur in highly irregular codes, pointer-intensive applications, and general purpose code with library and cross module function calls because the classical definition of reduction variable is too restrictive. However, by relaxing the definition of reduction variables and relying on additional compiler and speculation support, better parallelization is possible.

In this paper, we formulate a model for a class of dependence patterns that we call *partial reduction variables* (PRV). We call them *partial* because they do not necessarily fit the pattern or *all* of the requirements of reduction variables as defined above. They do exhibit the load-operate-update pattern on at least one path, but they may not exhibit this pattern on all paths. Furthermore, we relax the requirement that all potential uses of the reduction variable can be analyzed. This allows us to label a variable or memory location as a PRV despite must- or may-aliased references elsewhere in the code. Furthermore, we describe how to parallelize PRVs, and propose a novel architecture that supports PRV parallelization as part of a system with Thread-Level Speculation.

Overall, our work makes the following contributions:

- Defines a new class of variables called *partial reduction variables* and characterizes their presence in SPEC CPU 2000 applications.

- Describes an algorithm to detect PRVs automatically and validate manually marked PRVs to promote programmability.

- Identifies the needed hardware and software supports for PRV parallelization.

- Evaluates the impact of PRV parallelization with our proposed architectural support on SPEC CPU 2000 applications. On a set of SPEC CPU 2000 applications, we found that supporting PRVs provides up to 46% and on average 10.7% performance gain over a highly optimized TLS system.

The remainder of the article is organized as follows: Section 2 defines PRV and characterizes their occurrence in SPEC CPU 2000 applications; Section 3 describes the compiler algorithm for detecting PRVs, and Section 4 describes how to parallelize them; Section 5 discusses the architectural support added to enable PRV parallelization; Section 6 describes our experimental setup and presents result; the final section concludes.

```
for( ... ) {

    for( ... ) {
        // alias with delta_vert_cost
1 ------------> *costptr += ABS( newx - new_mean ) ... ;
    }

    ...

    // tmp_rows is global array
    rowsptr = tmp_rows[net] ;

    // rowsptr aliases with delta_vert_cost and *costptr
2 --------> for( row = 0 ; rowsptr[row] == 0 ; row++ ) ;
    ...

    // alias with *costptr and delta_vert_cost
3 --------> tmp_missing_rows[net] = -m ;

    // alias with *costptr
4 --------> delta_vert_cost += ... ;
}
```

Figure 1. The new_dbox_a function taken from 300.twolf.

2. Partial Reduction Variables

A *reduction* is kind of loop recurrence that can be parallelized on a multi-core (or multiprocessor) system easily using conventional hardware. A reduction variable has the following form inside a loop: $r = r \otimes expression$. Here, $\otimes$ is a suitable reduction operation, and expression is independent of r. There are additional constraints placed on r. It cannot be read or written in any other statement in the loop. With these restrictions in place, the computation of r can be parallelized by exploiting the associativity and commutativity of the $\otimes$ to group expressions so that there are no cross thread dependences.

Reduction variables are an important case to handle when parallelizing code, even irregular codes like SPEC CPU [19, 39]. However, the restrictions placed on a reduction variable can be prohibitive in integer or other highly irregular codes. In particular, the requirement that an RV cannot be read or written outside of the reduction operation prevents the inclusion of many variables. There are many reasons that prevent inclusion. First, conservative pointer analysis results in the appearance of possible reads or writes outside of the reduction statement that are unlikely to happen at run-time. Second, cross-module or library calls that cannot be fully analyzed must be treated conservatively as an update to any RV that may escape to that call. Finally, rarely executed code paths result in a known read or write outside of the reduction statement that will usually not occur at runtime. While the compiler is not able to parallelize these cases, they may behave like reductions at runtime. Instead of letting these opportunities pass by, we want to take advantage of the associativity and commutativity of these operations. Since they do not conform to strict definition of a reduction variable, we call them Partial Reduction Variables (PRVs).

Part of our inspiration for pursuing PRVs came from this loop in the new_dbox_a function in dimbox.c which is part of 300.twolf in the SPEC CPU 2000 suite. There are two variables (labeled 1 and 4) that have clear reduction patterns in the loop shown in Figure 1 (N.B. some code has been omitted). It would appear from inspection that they are ideal candidates for traditional RV optimization. There appear to be no other reads or writes to the variables in the loop, and the operation type is addition. However,

aliases are present in this loop (shown at 2 and 3). The aliasing write at 3 may be a definition of one of the potential RVs, and the aliasing read at 2 may use one of the potential RVs. The presence of either one is enough to disqualify both variables. However, even if 2 and 3 are removed, the problem remains since 1 and 4 may alias each other. To preserve correctness of the program at compile time, neither variable can be labeled as an RV since an alias may occur among the two RVs or with other variables in the loop.

In the remainder of this section, we will provide a definition of PRV and will characterize the frequency of PRVs in the SPEC CPU 2000 applications.

2.1 Definition of Partial Reduction Variables

To encompass the behavior shown in *twolf* we will relax some of the restrictions on an RV to create a formal definition for Partial Reduction Variable. However, first, we specify the definition of RV we will use for the remainder of the article.

A variety of techniques have been explored for detecting reduction variables [1, 4, 12, 17]. Our approach builds on the body of work that searches for specific patterns in the data dependence graph (DDG) that indicate a reduction variable. A reduction operation forms a cycle in the DDG that begins with the load of the reduction variable (*RV-load*), includes a series of true dependences that perform the operation, and updates the reduction variable (*RV-store*). The cycle is complete because the last store feeds back to the first load along a back-edge in the control flow graph (CFG). For convenience, we will call this an *RV-cycle*. For the computed *RV-cycle*, we identify a sub-graph from the *RV-load* to the *RV-store*, called the *RV-update-chain*. In order to detect a qualified *RV-cycle*, a few other properties are enforced: (1) none of the intermediate computations in the cycle can propagate to other variables, (2) there are no reads or writes of the reduction variable outside of the cycle, and (3) the chain of operations in the cycle form an associative and commutative operation. Note that this definition allows multiple *RV-update-chains* in the *RV-cycle* as long as they all must update the same variable using the same reduction operator. In addition, we tolerate *RV-update-chains* on multiple paths (in a sub-loop or in both an if-then and if-else statement) as long as all paths through the *RV-cycle* form a sequence of valid updates.

For PRVs we start with the same definition as RV, but we relax two properties, (1) and (2), of our previous definition. First, we allow both explicit and implicit references to the PRV outside of the *RV-cycle*. This means that reads or writes of the PRV are allowed that are inconsistent with the reduction operation. These reads and/or writes may come from any of the sources described earlier: aliased memory references, un-analyzed control paths that reference the PRV, or known references on analyzed paths. Even though the reads or writes may be implicit or explicit, we will refer to them all as a *PRV-may-ref*. Second, we relax the requirement that all paths through the *RV-cycle* form a sequence of valid updates. We must relax this property in order to allow a *PRV-may-ref* outside of an *RV-update-chain*. However, it also gives us considerable freedom when labeling PRVs. Instead of restricting the static control flow patterns, our definition is now flexible enough to identify reductions that may occur at runtime.

We will place some restrictions on where a *PRV-may-ref* occurs in the code. The *RV-update-chain* covers the full set of paths that begin with an *RV-load* and end with an *RV-store*. We allow a *PRV-may-ref* along any path incident with *RV-cycle* except for those in the *RV-update-chain*. These restrictions are not arbitrary, rather they are introduced to reduce the complexity of our proposed support or to improve performance. The full rationale for these restrictions may not be apparent until we describe our entire system.

Figure 2 presents several examples of our definition. In all of the charts in this figure, the outlined box represents a loop, r_u is live-in, r_d is live-out, and there exists an *RV-cycle*. Fig.2(a) shows single-statement *RV-update-chain* that makes a suitable PRV. In the case of Fig.2(b), the *RV-update-chain* is a sequence of instructions. When performing RV detection on an intermediate representation

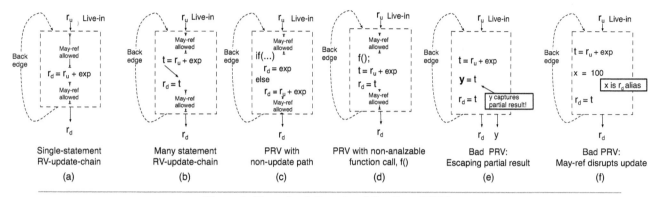

Figure 2. Example of allowed and dis-allowed PRVs.

of a program after optimization, it is more likely to find such a chain than a single statement as in Fig.2(a). Also, no *PRV-may-refs* occur inside the *RV-update-chain*, but they are allowed elsewhere in the loop. In the case of aliased references, this is reasonable since they may not actually alias dynamically. Fig.2(c) shows a case in which the *RV-update-chain* takes one control flow path but the other is just a write. This is allowed as a PRV but not as an RV. We hope to capitalize on the dynamic behavior of the PRV when its operation along the frequent path is like a reduction. Fig.2(d) has a call to a function that has not been analyzed by the compiler either because it is in a separate module or a library. If the address of *r* escapes to f, we can still mark it as a PRV in this region.

Fig.2(e,f) show cases that aren't allowed. Fig.2(e) shows the case that an intermediate result is propagated to another variable. Fig.2(f) shows the case that an aliasing or explicit write is present in the middle of the *RV-update-chain*. Neither of these cases are allowed for either RVs or PRVs.

2.2 Characterization of PRVs in SPEC CPU 2000

We implemented our definitions of RV and PRV in an analysis pass in GCC 4.3 [11] to assess the frequency of these variables in SPEC CPU 2000 applications. Table 1 shows the number of RVs and PRVs found for each application we analyzed. This is not an upper bound on the number of PRVs, but it is the number detected by our algorithm (Section 3). The second column shows the number of RVs and the third column shows the number of additional PRVs that are detected. Note that the columns are disjoint sets even though a PRV is a superset of RV.

Application	RV	PRV
crafty	26	6
gap	48	88
gzip	9	27
mcf	6	2
parser	28	12
perlbmk	14	28
twolf	45	56
ammp	8	17
art	7	2
equake	0	3
mesa	5	156
Average	18	36

Table 1. Frequency of PRVs and RVs in SPEC CPU 2000 subset.

There is considerable variation of both RV and PRV presence in these applications. Interestingly, our definition allowed us to classify significantly more variables as possible reductions than before, including the ones in *twolf* that inspired our definition. Based on the average number of RVs and PRVs, we increased the number of reduction variables considered for parallelization by a factor of 3.

3. PRV Detection

To effectively exploit PRVs in integer and irregular codes, we must first detect them. In this section, we will describe our algorithm for automatically detecting PRVs on an intermediate representation of the program. However, because our automatic detection pass occurs after many other optimizations, we also describe support for manually marking PRVs using pragmas inserted by the heroic programmer. The pragma is a hint not a mandate, and PRVs marked using the pragma must be validated by our automatic selection pass. We will describe both features, and how they work together to detect PRVs.

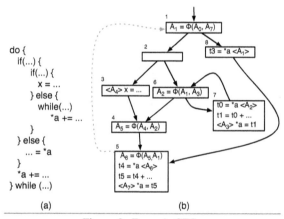

Figure 3. Example CFG.

3.1 PRV Detection Algorithm

Our PRV detection algorithm is implemented in GCC 4.3 using the Tree-SSA intermediate representation [8, 11]. This is an SSA representation that additionally annotates the SSA web with points-to set information. Each separate points-to set is given a symbolic name, and the definitions and uses of that set are converted into valid symbolic SSA form. Figure 3 illustrates such annotation. Fig.3(a) shows the original code, and Fig.3(b) shows the corresponding CFG in SSA form with the memory name A representing a points-to set. References to A in angled brackets represent a definition or use as appropriate.

The PRV detection algorithm looks for an *RV-cycle*. As described in Section 2, the *RV-cycle* is a circuit of update operations on a single variable using a single reduction operator. The example in Figure 3 has such circuit of updates if you follow the edges from $1 \rightarrow 2 \rightarrow (6, 7) \rightarrow 4 \rightarrow 5$. There is a use in block 8 and a definition in block 3 but these do not prevent classification as a PRV.

Since detecting recurrences on the CFG is well understood [1, 21], the algorithm will be described briefly. For each phi-node in a loop's header block, we will search to see if it's part of an *RV-cycle*. Figure 3 shows one such ϕ in the loop header in block 1. We recursively walk backward along the use-def chains of the SSA graph. Therefore, to begin our search, we start with the statement that defines the ϕ's argument along the backedge of the loop (definition $< A_7 >$). From here, there are a few possibilities that we must handle.

Assignment statement. If it is an assignment to the reference we are searching for, then from this statement we search for an *RV-update-chain*. Detecting the update chain involves following the dependence chains of the assignment backward until finding a PRV load. During the traversal, all dependences are searched along use-def chains until they either reach the PRV load, a constant expression, a non-aliasing memory load, or exit the basic block. On the return path after reaching a terminating condition, the algorithm collects details about the operation. By merging the results from all operands in an expression and taking the expression operators into account, we can ensure the validity of each update operation. Considering block 5 in Figure 3, it is clear that tracking back along the use-def chain will yield a valid chain quickly: $A7 \rightarrow t5 \rightarrow t4 \rightarrow A6$. After finding a chain, we continue searching backward for a complete cycle from the load operation.

If we fail to validate an *RV-update-chain* or determine the statement to be the definition of a possible alias (as is the case in block 3), we mark the store as a non-updating store and traverse back to its prior dominating definition (the one it kills) and look for an *RV-update-chain* starting there. This step is important since it allows us to overlook definitions caused by aliasing writes, un-analyzed functions, or even explicit writes that are not part of an update.

Conditional ϕ. If we find a conditional ϕ, we branch back along both paths recursively and continue searching for a statement that writes to the PRV. In order for the recursive call to return in the affirmative, one of the paths followed backward must include a valid *RV-update-chain*. From the example, the ϕ-node in block 4 would be the next statement encountered. This is a condition-ϕ, and so we search backward along both paths. Since the path through the $6 \rightarrow 7$ inner-loop includes an *RV-update-chain*, the eventual result of analyzing this statement is that a valid *RV-update-chain* was found. If *RV-update-chain* were found along both paths, then the type of reduction operations must match.

Inner-loop ϕ. If an inner-loop ϕ is encountered, the entire detection algorithm is called recursively on the inner loop and analyzed for the particular PRV of interest. In the example, we would apply the same detection mechanism described thus far, but restricted to the inner-loop $6 \rightarrow 7$. Inside the loop, the *RV-update-chain* $A3 \rightarrow t1 \rightarrow t0 \rightarrow A2$ is identified. In addition, the input argument to the inner-loop ϕ that is not from a back edge which is also searched recursively. If an *RV-update-chain* is found both in the inner-loop and along the backward use-def chain, then their operation types must match.

Header ϕ or outside region. The statement found could be the header ϕ we started from. This will not happen initially, but must eventually occur to terminate the cycle. If the header ϕ or a statement outside the loop is reached, the search terminates. As long as one path through the loop back to the header includes an *RV-update-chain*, we mark it as a potential PRV.

Final Validation. As the final step, we must verify that no *PRV-may-reference* occurs in any *RV-update-chain* in the *RV-cycle*. For each *RV-update-chain* detected during traversal, we iterate from the use to the definition and search for explicit or implicit (aliasing) references to the PRV in between. In addition, we also guarantee that each definition in the *RV-update-chain* is only consumed within the chain. This is trivially computed using the SSA graph.

3.2 Manual Detection & Auto-Validation

Manual marking of potential PRVs is done using pragmas added directly to the source code. Pragmas allow a heroic programmer the opportunity to suggest good PRVs. We found this support important in order to enable effective task selection for our automatic pass. Automatic parallelization environments often use many heuristics to decide on effective decompositions. With effective hints, these compilers can work better.

The syntax of the pragmas is very similar to OpenMP's reduction annotation. However, pragmas in our system are interpreted as a strong hint but not as a mandate. To validate PRVs marked using pragmas, we run the detection pass, as described in the previous section, on the marked loop and variable name. If it does not meet the definition, it is discarded and a warning is given to the programmer. This enables even not-so heroic programmers to suggest PRVs without breaking our system.

A key challenge in making this mechanism work is preserving the PRV until the PRV analysis pass runs. The pragma specifies the PRV using its lexical name, but these names are often lost after lowering to an intermediate representation and optimizations have been performed. To ensure that a manually marked PRV remains visible to our analysis pass, we replaced each static reference of a specified PRV (e.g. *realPRV*) with a volatile reference of equivalent type (e.g. *volaPRV*) since volatile variables are ignored by compiler optimizations that may eliminate, move, or rename memory references. We inserted assignments of '*volaPRV = realPRV;*' before and '*realPRV = volaPRV;*' after the pragma-marked region.

4. Speculative Parallelization of PRVs

In this section, we discuss the parallelization strategy for PRVs and the kinds of systems that can support it.

4.1 Parallelization Requirements

PRV parallelization involves lowering the *RV-update-chains* found in the loop to run efficiently in parallel. If the PRVs behave only like classical RVs then their parallelization can be highly efficient, and the strategies used can be similar to those that support RVs. Each reference to the PRV in an *RV-update-chain* is replaced with a reference to private variable of the same type. Before executing the parallel region, the private is initialized to a neutral value suitable for the RV operation. Either during or after the parallelized region, the private is accumulated with the PRV. Loop unrolling can be used to lengthen the region and increase the gains achieved from parallelization.

However, in the event that loads and stores to the PRV **do** occur outside of the *RV-update-chains*, the first requirement is that they have to be detected. Detection is not trivial since the compiler does not mark each PRV access. For explicit reads or writes, the compiler should handle them directly. For aliases analyzed by the compiler, runtime disambiguation tests can be used. For accesses in un-analyzed control paths, the parallelization environment must detect the access to the PRV.

Upon detection of PRV accesses outside an *RV-update-chain*, additional support is needed to ensure correct parallelization. The possible behaviors of PRVs can be divided into three cases based on the types of PRV reference that may occur: stores only, loads only, and a combination of loads and stores.

Stores only. In the case that only stores to the PRV may occur outside of the *RV-update-chain*, then care must be taken to ensure that the value of the PRV after executing the loop is equal to the last non-updating store accumulated with the private variable updates from all later iterations. This requires preserving the last store and ordering it with respect to all later iterations (and accumulations in the same thread). Fortunately, this does not require synchronization with other threads.

Loads only. In the case that only loads to the PRV may occur outside of the *RV-update-chain*, the potential overhead is much higher. When the load occurs, all private values accumulated from prior iterations must be merged with the PRV to provide the correct value. This requires that all prior iterations complete their last update to the private variable. If some of those iterations have not yet been scheduled, then the load must wait (or speculate on the loaded value).

Loads and stores. In the event that both a load and store may occur, then a combination of corrective actions are needed for both the load or store. Furthermore, the mechanisms must cooperate because a load must get the accumulated result since the last store. The overhead and efficiency of the mechanism can vary depending on the actual pattern of loads and stores in the loop. If stores frequently precede loads (especially in the same iteration), then the loads need not wait long to accumulate an up-to-date value. However, if loads and stores are far apart, then performance may appear more like the load-only case.

4.2 System for PRV Parallelization

Aspects of PRV parallelization are currently supported by some systems, but none fully support it. If PRV selection is restricted to the case of only stores occurring outside of the *RV-update-chain*, then a system like Thread-Level Speculation (TLS) [15, 24, 25, 29, 30] could support it with few modifications. The latest store to the PRV would overwrite all previous stores. When the accumulation is done after the parallel region (or as part of each iteration), the most recent store would be used. However, somehow, the accumulations from iterations prior to the store still must be discarded. Transactional Memory [14, 33] (TM) could work similarly if a partial ordering were imposed on tasks that wrote to the PRV. However, these systems cannot fully support the case of loads or stores by default.

To fully support our definition of PRV, we extend a system that implements Thread-Level Speculation to record the link between the private variable and the PRV. By exposing this link to the TLS system, we can properly correct loads and optimize the handling of stores. Since TLS naturally supports thread ordering, managing the corrective actions for all task behaviors is straightforward.

4.2.1 Thread-Level Speculation

In this section, we briefly review the key concepts of Thread-Level Speculation. A TLS compiler breaks a hard-to-analyze sequential code into tasks, and speculatively executes them in parallel, hoping not to violate sequential semantics (e.g. [2, 5, 31, 32, 36]). The control flow of the sequential code imposes a control dependence relation between the tasks. This relation establishes a total order among the tasks, and we can use the terms predecessor and successor to express this order. This ordering also determines a data dependence relation on the memory accesses issued by the different tasks that parallel execution cannot violate.

A task is *speculative* when it may perform or may have performed operations that violate data or control dependences with its predecessor tasks. When a non-speculative task finishes execution, it is ready to *commit*. The role of commit is to inform the rest of the system that the data generated by the task are now part of the safe, non-speculative program state. Among other operations, committing always involves passing the non-speculative status to a successor task. Tasks must commit in strict order from predecessor to successor. If a task reaches its end and is still speculative, it cannot commit until it acquires non-speculative status.

As tasks execute in parallel, the system must identify any violations of cross-task data dependences. Typically, this is done with special hardware support that tracks, for each individual task, the data written and the data read without first writing it. A data dependence violation is flagged when a task modifies a version of a datum that may have been loaded earlier by a successor task. At this point, the consumer task is *squashed* and all the state that it has produced is discarded. Its successor tasks are also squashed. Then, the task is re-executed. Sometimes, a task is squashed repeatedly without finishing. If this occurs, it is useful to force the thread to wait until all of its predecessors complete; this is referred to as *becoming safe*.

TLS architectures can discard the state produced by a task and re-start the task thanks to special hardware that buffers all speculative modifications, and a checkpointing mechanism that enables rollback. Note that anti and output dependences across tasks do not cause squashes.

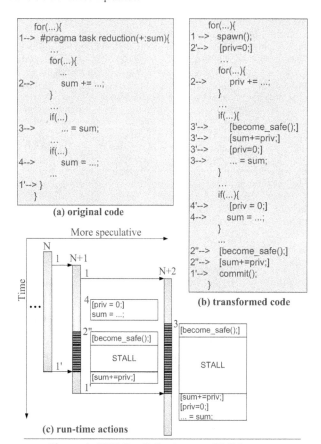

(a) original code

(b) transformed code

(c) run-time actions

Figure 4. PRV Parallelization on a TLS System.

4.2.2 Example

Figure 4 explains how we support PRV parallelization on a TLS-based system. Fig.4(a) shows the original code. The TLS compiler through heuristics or programmer hints chooses tasks for parallelization. Note that the TLS compiler can overlook any dependence due to hardware that will catch any dependence violation at runtime. The pragma at 1 in Fig.4(a) suggests to the compiler a potentially good TLS task (the region marked in between 1 and 1'), which includes a PRV named *sum* whose reduction operator is +. At location 2, *sum* operates as a traditional reduction variable, but it is read and written at locations 3 and 4 respectively, which make it a PRV.

Fig4(b) shows the transformed codes needed to create parallel tasks in TLS and support for the PRV. The *spawn()* at 1 will create a new thread beginning after the *commit()* at 1'. Similar to how a reduction is handled traditionally, *sum* is privatized as *priv* (as 2, 2', and 2" show). But in order to correctly support the load at 3 and store at 4, additional actions are inserted as 3' and 4'. In the case of the load, the first action is to prevent a squash by waiting to become safe. We do can do this explicitly using the *become_safe()* operation, and this guarantees the task will wait for the final version of sum from its predecessor task before reading it. Next, it updates sum with its accumulated value in *priv* and clears *priv*. After all this is done, it can use the value in *sum*. Also, because we cleared *priv*, additional accumulation into *priv* that could occur within the task will work correctly. In the case of the store at 4, we simply clear *priv* at 4'. At the end of the task, just before commit, *priv* is accumulated into *sum*. To ensure this does not happen prematurely, we synchronize the update using *become_safe()*.

If the compiler can fully analyze *sum* statically and make sure it has no alias, no hardware support is needed and Fig4(b) shows the transformed code added by the compiler. Otherwise, if the accesses at 3 and 4 were in fact aliases, then the instructions are not inserted by the compiler, instead hardware should detect the access to sum and take the same set of actions. This requires the hardware knowing the link between *priv* and *sum* and interpreting the read or write as occurring outside of the *RV-update-chain* (see Section 5).

Fig.4(c) shows how program correctness is guaranteed at runtime. Time proceeds down the page while tasks to the right are more speculative. Iteration N+1 contains the store at 4. The block to the right of label 4 shows the correcting actions. Note that it stalls until it can load the final accumulated value of *sum* from its predecessor. Iteration N+2 contains the load at 3 and its correcting actions. The synchronization actions needed to bring *sum* up to date do lead to stalls, but these effects are ameliorated by a couple of factors. We expect these synchronization events to be infrequent in PRV tasks selected by the TLS compiler, and even when they do occur, it is better to synchronize than pay the price of a squash.

5. Architectural Support for PRVs

We add new architectural features to a TLS system to support PRV parallelization. Figure 5 shows the key pieces of our new architecture: (1) the PRV Lookup Table (PLUT) tracks the mapping from PRV to private variable and provides key details for synchronizing updates, (2) the PRV Signature stores a hash of the addresses of all the PRV's for quick access, and the PRV Controller which implements the detection, correction, and update synchronization algorithm. The Load-Store Queue (LSQ) and Versioned Cache are assumed to be typical with no features specific to our scheme.

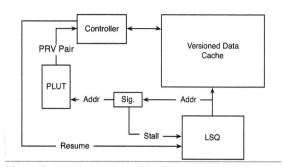

Figure 5. Architectural modifications to enable PRV parallelization.

Instruction	Description
pair_addr.op.t Rv, Rp	Pair reduction variable, whose address is in Rv, with the private variable whose address is in Rp. Op describes the operator (addition,multiplication), and *t* indicates whether the PRV is an int,float,double, or long long for proper initialization.
unpair_addr Rv	Unpair the reduction variable from any private variable.

Table 2. Description of instructions.

5.1 Support for a PRV Access

If a PRV has or may have aliases, the compiler alone cannot totally handle it. Detecting and correcting such PRV accesses occurs

at runtime when a reduction operation is in progress. Before entering a region of code with such a PRV the compiler schedules a `pair_addr` instruction to notify the hardware that a partial reduction operation is under way and links the address of the PRV to the private variable holding the partial state. Hardware keeps a record of the PRV and private variable in the PRV Lookup Table. The hardware must assume that the reduction is underway until it receives an `unpair_addr` instruction. During this window of execution, hardware monitors for illegal accesses to the PRV. It is the compiler's responsibility to insert `pair_addr` and `unpair_addr` and ensure no illegal accesses occur to the PRV outside the region. Table 2 gives the descriptions of `pair_addr` and `unpair_addr` instructions.

PRV Lookup Table Entry							
Valid	Aliased entry			int, long, float, double			
V	U	TID	A	PRV	Private	Type	Kind	Accum
Unpaired				Lookup PRV	Private Addr	add, sub, multiply		Accumulated Partial Result

Figure 6. Fields in a PLUT entry.

When a `pair_addr` instruction is executed for the first time on a PRV, a new entry is created in the PRV Lookup Table, shown in Figure 6. The `pair_addr` instruction allocates an entry in the table, sets the Valid (V) bit, clears the Unpaired (U) bit (described later), sets the Private variable address, and initializes Accumulated Partial Result. The PRV address is also added to the PRV Signature. The signature is similar to a Bloom filter [3] and provides a summary of all the addresses in the lookup table. Searching a signature is much faster than searching a modest size lookup table, so this allows the lookup to be placed off the critical path.

The `unpair_addr` instruction indicates that the pairing of PRV to the private location should be stopped, and sets the U bit in the corresponding entry indicating that the private address is no longer paired with the PRV. Also, the value currently stored in the private variable is loaded from memory and accumulated with the Accum field in the PLUT entry. Even though the PRV's address is marked as unpaired, the entry for the PRV need not be removed from the PRV Lookup Table immediately. Instead, we allow it to continue monitoring this address since the partial state is preserved in Accum. This policy optimistically delays the memory update until the end of the task when it is safe to do so without causing a squash.

5.1.1 Detecting a Conflict

If there is at least one valid entry in the PRV Lookup Table, all loads and stores will be checked against the signature for a conflict. If no conflict is found with the signature, then the table need not be checked. However, if a conflict with the signature is found, then the PRV Lookup Table is searched for a matching PRV. Upon finding a matching entry in the table, the LSQ is temporarily stalled so that the state of the PRVcan be updated as necessary. If no match is found, then no action is taken and the cache access occurs as usual.

5.1.2 Correcting the State

When a conflict on a PRV is detected, the PRV Controller will take the necessary actions to fix the program's state. These actions mirror the code inserted by the compiler when it finds a non-PRV access. We will explain correcting a load and a store separately, but note that the mechanisms also suffice for the case when both loads and stores occur.

Correcting a Load. In the case of load access to the PRV, the Controller will request the current value stored in the PRV. If the Unpaired bit is empty, it also requests the private variable. Note these requests are equivalent to memory requests made by the processor and are handled in exactly the same way as standard TLS coherence request.

Then, it will accumulate, as determined by the operation kind stored in the PLUT entry, the PRV and the Accum field in the PLUT entry. Finally, it will store the result into the PRV's location in memory and reset the private variable to the correct initial value, depending on the type of variable and reduction operator. At the end of this sequence of operations, the PRV is fully up-to-date and the private variable is reset. Now the LSQ is un-stalled and allowed to complete its load operation on the PRV. When it loads, it will find the correct value in the cache.

Finally, if after correcting a load we discover that the U-bit is set, it is safe to clear the valid bit since the entry no longer contains any partial state. The only reason the entry was still in the PLUT was to delay the PRV update as long as possible. But since the update has occurred, no reason exists to keep the entry.

Correcting a Store. The case of a store access to the PRV is somewhat simpler. In this case, we are simply updating the current value of the PRV, and we could choose not to stall that update. However, we do stall the LSQ momentarily and insert a store to the private variable to return it to its initial value, and we reset the Accum field in the PLUT entry.

Multiple PLUT entries for the same PRV The compiler may aggressively select two PRVs in the same loop that may alias. Most of the time, they will not access the same location. However, if two entries in the PLUT are added with the same PRV and a different private location, the hardware forces both into a special mode of operation, indicated by the A bit in the PLUT. Instead of monitoring for accesses to the PRV, we monitor accesses of both privates. If there is a read to the private variable, such read is automatically replaced with a PRV read. Similarly, a write to the private is treated as a write to the PRV. This will guarantee that the PRV is updated correctly with respect to both PRV chains.

5.2 Synchronizing PRV Updates

With the support already described, synchronizing updates is relatively straightforward. When a task has become safe, finished executing all its instructions, and is ready to commit, it scans its PLUT for entries that have its Task Id (TID) and that are valid. For each such entry, it is handled by using the same logic as for correcting a load. This takes care of all actions necessary to bring the PRV up-to-date.

5.3 Compiler Support

This hardware mechanism requires that the PLUT never overflow, lest a mapping between PRV and private variable be lost. To avoid unnecessary complexity in the hardware, we place two restrictions on our technique: (i) we do not allow a PRV task to be nested within another PRV task, and (ii) we require that the compiler manages the table usage to prevent overflow. In the first requirement, disallowing PRV-task nesting ensures that the compiler can determine the number of active PRVs in the PLUT through global analysis of a single subroutine. However, this does complicate task selection because this property must be enforced conservatively – even if such a nesting was unlikely to occur dynamically, if it is ever possible, such a nested task cannot be selected. Such a limitation requires selecting among alternatives, and this selection is carried out explicitly by our profiler (see Section 6).

The second requirement ensures that a task will never use more entries than available in the PLUT, and this is enforced directly through analysis of each task region. We use a compiler parameter *NumPRV* to limit the maximum static number of PRVs per task. Our empirical evidence suggests that up to 4 static PRVs finally survive for an application. So we set *NumPRV* to 4 and use 4 PLUT entries for each core in the evaluation and found this to be sufficient.

5.4 Cost Estimation

The estimated per-core hardware cost added to support PRVs for a 64-bit system includes a 4-entry PLUT (4 * 34-Byte = 136 Bytes);

1 32-bit signature (Bloom filter with single hash function derived from lower bits of address excluding the two least significant); other control logics needed to control PLUT and utilize existing ALU/FPU during accumulate; and other logics added to support the 3 new instructions (*pair_addr*, *unpair_addr*, and *become_safe*).

The main performance cost added for a store or a non-conflicting load is the delay of a 32-bit signature which is negligible since it can be done in parallel with other logic. However, the cost for a conflicting load is the stalled cycles waiting for the correct value being fed from its predecessor thread (this delay is comparable to that of a synchronization operation), plus the cycles to accumulate this value to that of the privatized variable. This may seem significant, but it is worth it compared to the squash-and-restart cycles that would otherwise occur.

6. Evaluation

We implement our system on a cycle-accurate execution-driven simulator [23]. The simulator models superscalar processors and memory subsystems in detail. The TLS architecture modeled is shown in Table 3. It is a four-processor CMP with TLS support. Each processor is a 3-issue core and has a private L1 cache that buffers the speculative data. The L1 caches are connected through a crossbar to an on-chip shared L2 cache. All communication between cores occurs through the cache coherence protocol.

Frequency	4 GHz	ROB	132
Fetch width	8	I-window	68
Issue width	3	LD/ST queue	48/42
Retire width	3	Mem/Int/Fp unit	1/2/1
Branch predictor:		Spawn Overhead	12 cycles
Mispred. Penalty	14 cycles	Squash Overhead	20 cycles
BTB	2K, 2-way		
Private L1 Cache:		Shared L2 Cache:	
Size, assoc, line	32KB, 4, 64B	Size, assoc, line	2MB, 8, 64B
Latency	3 cycles	Latency	10 cycles
		Memory:	
Lat. to remote L1	at least 8 cycles	Latency	500 cycles
		Bandwidth	10GB/s

Table 3. Core details. Cycle counts are in processor cycles.

We implement our compiler pass in a copy of the POSH [16] compiler, which has been ported to GCC 4.3 and is one of the state-of-the-art TLS compilers. We use the compiler to generate 3 different binaries for each application evaluated, shown in Table 4. The *Base* case is a sequential binary that we normalize all of our plots against. *TLS* shows the result of the POSH compiler with all of its optimizations enabled. *TLS+PRV* includes tasks automatically selected using all POSH's optimizations plus support PRV detection and parallelization. Even though a PRV may be detected and parallelized, POSH leverages a profiling stage to weed out ineffective tasks. The major criteria to evaluate a task includes its size, static and dynamic hoist distance, violation rates, prefetching effect, and costs to parallelize it. Only high quality tasks will survive to the final output.

Name	Description
Base	-O2
TLS	POSH optimizations + Base
TLS+PRV	All POSH tasks plus PRV tasks that survive optimization.

Table 4. Compile settings for each application evaluated.

We evaluate our proposal on a set of SPEC CPU 2000 applications. We exclude *vortex* and *eon* because the version of the source code we use cannot be compiled. We exclude *gcc* and *perlbmk* because the TLS infrastructure we use does not presently support them. To accurately compare the performance of the different binaries, simply timing a fixed number of instructions is incorrect. Instead, simulation markers are inserted in the code of each binary,

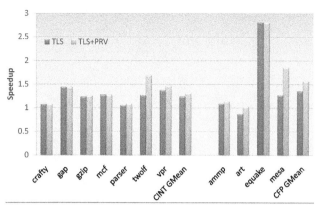

Figure 7. Speedup normalized to Base.

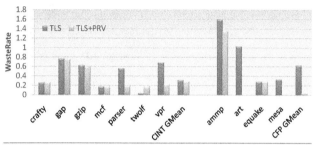

Figure 8. Fraction of wasted work. (Note, the second bars for *art* and *mesa* are too small to see.)

and simulations are run for a given number of markers. After skipping the initialization (typically 1-6 billion instructions), a certain number of markers are executed, so that the baseline binary graduates from 500 million to 1 billion instructions.

6.1 Performance

Figure 7 shows the speedup on our evaluated applications over *Base*. The geometric mean of speedup for *TLS+PRV* is 1.31 for the CINT applications and 1.57 for the CFP. Compared to *TLS*, CINT is better on our proposed system, on average, by 5.84% and, CFP is better by 15.82%. These speedups were attained mostly using a fully-automatic compiler approach and are significant.

Figure 8 shows the fraction of wasted work for *TLS* and *TLS+PRV*. This is calculated as the number of squashed instructions (due to dependence violations) out of the total number of committed instructions. Since *TLS+PRV* removes some cross-thread dependences by handling PRVs, it should have fewer dependence violations and, thus, have a lower waste rate than *TLS*. For most applications and for the average behavior for both CINT and CFP, we see such results in Fig. 8.

Table 5 provides some characterizations of the reduction variables that are included in the final speculative tasks selected by our compiler infrastructure. For each application, the reduction variables are classified as RV or PRV. Note that most reduction variables detected are *PRV* – except 2 significant *RVs* in *parser* (the 4 *RVs* in *mcf* don't speedup performance at all). That is why we did not show the speedup of *TLS+RV* in Fig. 7 – because it is almost the same as *TLS*, except that *parser* has the same speedup with that of *TLS+PRV*.

The last column of the Table 5, together with Fig. 7 and Fig. 8, explains how these reductions affect performance. Most of the gains of our approach come from PRV tasks selected in *twolf*, *vpr*, *art*, and *mesa*. Not surprisingly, these applications contain tasks that had no loop-carried dependences other than the PRVs. Once

the PRVs were optimized, the tasks were parallelizable and provided significant performance gains. The loop from *twolf* described in Section 2 is such a case. Impressively, identifying two PRVs was enough to provide the large performance gains in *twolf*. Note that the waste rates for *vpr* and *mesa* are considerably lower with *PRV* tasks. That's because the *PRVs* introduce major dependences in these tasks. Once these dependences are handled, the task selector prefers these tasks which are quite different from those of *TLS*. For *twolf*, more waste occurs on the *TLS+PRV* tasks than on the *TLS* tasks. Without PRV support, *TLS* selects a set of tasks which speculate less aggressively. For *TLS+PRV*, the additional speculation opportunities brought by PRVs brings the benefit of higher performance at the cost of higher waste.

In *parser*, *gzip*, and *mcf*, although *PRV/RV* are detected and handled, they don't boost performance much because either they are located in secondary or small tasks (*gzip*) or there still exist nontrivial cross-thread dependences other than PRVs (*mcf*). However, we can still notice the reduction in wasted work in Fig. 8 after handling the PRVs.

In *crafty*, *gap*, *ammp*, and *equake*, although many PRV/RV are detected (see Table 1), none of them survive profiling; thus, there is nearly no performance gain. However, the performance of *crafty* and *ammp* is slightly affected due to the selection of a different set of tasks. This is because the early phase of compilation handles all PRVs – this affects the behaviour of tasks in which PRVs are located and leads to a different profiling result.

The third column of Table 5 classifies the reductions from another aspect. *Local* means the RV/PRV is a locally declared variable whose address is not taken (thus has no alias); *Ptr* means it is a pointer variable; and *Global* means it is a global variable. There is another dimension not shown; it is possible for *Local* to have their address taken, but, for the tasks shown, this was never the case. From the table, note that (1) the latter 2 cases have may-aliases and need the full architectural and compiler support we proposed; (2) the *Local* PRVs are not traditional reductions and need our compiler schemes to handle them; (3) only *parser* contains significant RVs that can be handled by traditional techniques, but its performance gain is limited. Such a distribution of reductions shows the importance of handling PRVs (not just RVs) when parallelizing sequential codes.

6.2 Discussion

While many PRVs were identified by the compiler, there were many fewer tasks containing PRVs that were ultimately profitable. By examining the code that excluded these PRVs, we identified some key reasons. (1) Many PRV tasks in *gap* and *gzip* have small loop sizes and thus do not overcome the initial cost of speculation. For this reason, the compiler eliminates them during profiling. We believe that loop unrolling, if applied judiciously, can help generate some good PRV tasks by increasing the task size. (2) Some PRVs appear only on a branch which is seldom taken. Supporting these PRVs may add synchronization when not needed. Finding ways to reduce this cost and generate better PRV code help some cases found in *gzip*. (3) Some PRVs occur in tasks with other frequently occurring dependences, preventing the task from being selected. Incorporating additional techniques that target non-PRV dependences could increase the value of our mechanism.

Furthermore, some legitimate PRVs are missed by our compiler pass. Note, our algorithm requires that the update occur on a single variable. Consequently, we miss the classic array-reduction A[i]+=... if i is the induction variable for the innermost loop in the surrounding loop nest. Some preliminary analysis suggests that many such PRVs exist in this form even in SPEC applications and many of them are located in potentially good tasks. We believe that extending our techniques to support such PRVs is possible and would increase the performance of our techniques.

Benchmarks	RV	PRV	Local	Ptr	Global	Analysis
crafty	0	0				No PRV survives, but it affects task-selection a little bit and thus slows down slightly.
gap	0	0				No PRV survives. TLS and TLS+PRV select same tasks.
gzip	0	1			1	It is located in 1 task, and speedup a little bit.
mcf	4	0	4			They are located in 2 tasks, but doesn't speedup the performance due to other dependences.
parser	2	0	2			They are located in 2 tasks, from which the performance gain mostly comes
twolf	0	3		2	1	They are located in 2 tasks, from which the performance gain mostly comes. TLS doesn't select these 2 tasks due to dependences on these PRVs.
vpr	0	1	1			It is located in 1 task, from which the performance gain mostly comes
ammp	0	0				No PRV survives, but it affects task-selection a little bit and thus speedups slightly.
art	0	3	3			They are located in 3 tasks, from which the performance gain mostly comes
equake	0	0				No PRV survives. TLS and TLS+PRV select same tasks.
mesa	0	3	3			Located in 1 task, from which the performance gain mostly comes. Task selection affected

Table 5. PRV Characterization.

7. Related Work

Reductions are a type of recurrence that are easy to parallelize on multiprocessors. They have been well researched in the context of optimizing compilers. The work in this area focused on a variety of issues (loosely categorized as follows) including detection of reductions [1, 4, 12, 17], parallelization/scheduling strategies [9, 18, 22, 27, 28, 34, 35], speculative approaches [6, 7, 21, 39], and architectural support [10]. The earlier techniques were often limited to loops in which the reduction variables and operators were fully analyzable by the compiler (even if the loop bounds were unknown). However, given the frequency of array based reductions and the limitations of dependence analysis on indirect array references, many loops could be optimized with this technique.

More recent work has identified the importance of employing speculation to extract more parallelism from hard-to-analyze reductions. Rauchwerger and Padua proposed the LRPD test [21] as a way of overcoming the limitations of static analysis. Instead of requiring a complete static analysis, some disambiguation tests were delayed until runtime. Their scheme works by first creating private versions of each array participating in the reduction computation, and calculating read and write sets for each array at runtime. Their technique is able to detect if the operations were in fact reductions during the actual execution, even though static analysis could not verify it either due to control or aliasing. Refinements of the LRPD algorithm aim to increase coverage and reduce overhead of this approach [7]. Many of the arrays classified by the LRPD scheme would be classified as PRVs by our scheme. However, these mechanisms require full control-flow analysis of the code being parallelized and identification of all loads and stores that *may* participate in the reduction. Non-analyzable control flow (e.g. into libraries) with unknown reads/updates cannot be treated with this mechanism. For nested loops which dominate execution time, this limitation is reasonable, however, for many C programs, these restrictions are prohibitive. Instead, we need an approach that can cope with potentially unknown reads or writes to the reduction variable at runtime. Our proposed scheme can tolerate such reads or writes to the reduction variable by monitoring all accesses to the variable and taking corrective actions when such an update occurs. The proposed mechanism does not require the insertion of dependence tracking and tests to validate the reduction and can handle unknown paths and references never analyzed by the compiler.

Hardware support for reductions has been proposed in the past that extends beyond support for efficient synchronization primitives. Garzaran *et al.* proposed PCLR [10], hardware support for reductions that accelerates the merging phase of the reduction after the parallel region is complete. Their approach allows reductions to complete efficiently and lazily by combining the partial results of a reduction operation in hardware at the directory controller rather than in software. Our hardware support also performs merging, but that is not its primary responsibility. Our hardware support is focused on monitoring accesses to the reduction variable and taking corrective actions when needed. Our approach is largely orthogonal to PCLR and could be integrated with aspects of PCLR to support efficient merging on highly parallel codes. Past work on support for efficient synchronization primitives is also orthogonal to our scheme and could be leveraged to reduce sync time.

Our definition of PRV shares many similarities with that described by Zhang *et al* in UPAR[40]. However, UPAR only evaluates certain kinds of PRV. Our approach broadens the definition; it tolerates explicit accesses to the PRV, not just aliases. In addition, we search for PRVs in pointer-intensive integer codes, and our approach is better suited to find a wide variety of PRVs in this domain.

Compilers and systems for Thread-Level Speculation have identified the need to effectively handle reduction variables. Zhai *et al.* [39] show the benefit of reductions for SPECint applications and shows modest gains. However, this mechanism employed the strict definition of reduction variable, not the more flexible definition of PRV proposed in this paper. Also, Prabhu *et al.* [19] identifies reductions as an important transformation to unlock the potential of key loops in *vpr, mcf,* and *twolf.* Since they focused on manual techniques they transformed some reductions manually that would be classified as PRV in our approach. Finally, work in Thread-Level Speculation targeting efficient synchronization of cross-thread dependences [37, 38] is also relevant, since they are an alternative, but less direct, mechanism for supporting reduction variables.

8. Conclusion

In this work, we considered a kind of shared variable that may behave like a reduction at runtime, called partial reduction variables. PRVs differ from RVs by allowing reads and writes to the reduction variable outside of the reduction update operation. We found that PRVs are more frequently occurring than RVs in SPEC CPU 2000 applications. Given the frequency of these variables, it is important to consider hardware and software mechanisms that can exploit them.

We implemented a parallelization framework for PRVs using an automatic parallelizing compiler for Thread-Level Speculation and a new architecture with necessary supports for detecting and correcting updates to PRVs that contradict its usual reduction like behavior. On a set of SPEC 2000 applications, we found that supporting PRVs provides up to 46% and on average 10.7% performance gain over one of the state-of-the-art TLS systems.

There are still many important optimization opportunities remaining for PRVs in highly irregular and integer codes. Depending on the reference or control structure that leads to detection of a PRV instead of RV, PRVs can be further classified into a variety of types. Parallelization strategies could be tailored for each kind of PRV to enable the most parallelism. Furthermore, PRVs can also be important in a variety of other systems. For example, dynamic optimization environments are often limited in the kinds of parallelization transformations that are possible due to the limitations of dynamic analysis – both in terms of the scope of code analyzed and the quality of analysis. The flexibility of our proposed hardware mechanism may be valuable when speculatively parallelizing loops in such environments.

References

[1] Z. Ammarguellat and W. L. Harrison. Automatic Recognition of Induction Variables and Recurrence Relations by Abstract Interpretation. *SIGPLAN Not.*, 25(6):283–295, 1990.

[2] A. Bhowmik and M. Franklin. A General Compiler Framework for Speculative Multithreading. In *Proceedings of 14th ACM Symposium on Parallel Algorithms and Architectures (SPAA)*, August 2002.

[3] B. Bloom. Space/Time Trade-Offs in Hash Coding with Allowable Errors. *Communications of the ACM*, 11(7):422–426, July 1970.

[4] D. Callahan. Recognizing and Parallelizing Bounded Recurrences. In *Proceedings of the Fourth International Workshop on Languages and Compilers for Parallel Computing*, pages 169–185. Springer-Verlag, 1992.

[5] P. S. Chen, M. Y. Hung, Y. S. Hwang, R. D. Ju, and J. K. Lee. Compiler Support for Speculative Multithreading Architecture with Probabilistic Points-to Analysis. In *Proceedings of the 2003 Symposium on Principles and Practice of Parallel Programming (PPoPP'03)*, pages 25–36, June 2003.

[6] F. Dang, M. J. Garzaran, M. Prvulovic, Y. Zhang, A. Jula, H. Yu, N. Amato, L. Rauchwerger, and J. Torrellas. Smartapps, an Application Centric Approach to High Performance Computing: Compiler-Assisted Software and Hardware Support for Reduction Operations. In *Parallel and Distributed Processing Symposium., Proceedings International, IPDPS 2002, Abstracts and CD-ROM*, pages 172–181, 2002.

[7] F. Dang, H. Yu, and L. Rauchwerger. The R-LRPD Test: Speculative Parallelization of Partially Parallel Loops. Technical report, Texas A&M University, 2001.

[8] Diego Novillo. Tree SSA — A New Optimization Infrastructure for GCC. In *Proceedings of the First GCC Developers Summit*, May 2003.

[9] A. L. Fisher and A. M. Ghuloum. Parallelizing Complex Scans and Reductions. In *Proceedings of the ACM SIGPLAN 1994 Conference on Programming Language Design and Implementation*, pages 135–146, Orlando, Florida, United States, 1994. ACM.

[10] M. J. Garzaran, M. Prvulovic, Y. Zhangy, J. Torrellas, A. Jula, H. Yu, and L. Rauchwerger. Architectural Support for Parallel Reductions in Scalable Shared-Memory Multiprocessors. In *Proceedings of the 2001 International Conference on Parallel Architectures and Compilation Techniques*, page 243. IEEE Computer Society, 2001.

[11] GNU Compiler Collection. URL, 2009. http://gcc.gnu.org/.

[12] M. P. Gerlek, E. Stoltz, and M. Wolfe. Beyond Induction Variables: Detecting and Classifying Sequences Using a Demand-Driven SSA Form. *ACM Trans. Program. Lang. Syst.*, 17(1):85–122, 1995.

[13] L. Hammond, M. Willey, and K. Olukotun. Data Speculation Support for a Chip Multiprocessor. In *Proceedings of the eighth International Conference on Architectural Support for Programming Languages and Operating Systems*, pages 58–69, San Jose, California, United States, 1998. ACM.

[14] M. Herlihy and J. E. B. Moss. Transactional Memory: Architectural Support for Lock-free Data Structures. In *ISCA '93: Proceedings of the 20th Annual International Symposium on Computer Architecture*, pages 289–300, New York, NY, USA, 1993. ACM Press.

[15] V. Krishnan and J. Torrellas. A Chip-Multiprocessor Architecture with Speculative Multithreading. *IEEE Trans. on Computers*, pages 866–880, September 1999.

[16] W. Liu, J. Tuck, L. Ceze, W. Ahn, K. Strauss, J. Renau, and J. Torrellas. POSH: a TLS Compiler that Exploits Program Structure. In *Proceedings of the eleventh ACM SIGPLAN Symposium on Principles and Practice of Parallel Programming*, pages 158–167, New York, New York, USA, 2006. ACM.

[17] S. S. Pinter and R. Y. Pinter. Program Optimization and Parallelization Using Idioms. In *Proceedings of the 18th ACM SIGPLAN-SIGACT Symposium on Principles of Programming Languages*, pages 79–92, Orlando, Florida, United States, 1991. ACM.

[18] B. Pottenger and R. Eigenmann. Parallelization in the Presence of Generalized Induction and Reduction Variables. *In ACM Int. Conf. on Supercomputing (ICS95)*, 1995.

[19] M. K. Prabhu and K. Olukotun. Exposing Speculative Thread Parallelism in SPEC2000. In *Proceedings of the tenth ACM SIGPLAN Symposium on Principles and Practice of Parallel Programming*, pages 142–152, Chicago, IL, USA, 2005. ACM.

[20] C. G. Quiones, C. Madriles, J. Snchez, P. Marcuello, A. Gonzlez, and D. M. Tullsen. Mitosis Compiler: an Infrastructure for Speculative Threading Based on Pre-Computation Slices. In *Proceedings of the 2005 ACM SIGPLAN conference on Programming Language Design and Implementation*, pages 269–279, Chicago, IL, USA, 2005. ACM.

[21] L. Rauchwerger and D. Padua. The LRPD Test: Speculative Run-Time Parallelization of Loops with Privatization and Reduction Parallelization. *Parallel and Distributed Systems, IEEE Transactions on*, 10(2):160–180, 1999.

[22] X. Redon and P. Feautrier. Scheduling Reductions. In *Proceedings of the 8th International Conference on Supercomputing*, pages 117–125, Manchester, England, 1994. ACM.

[23] J. Renau, B. Fraguela, J. Tuck, W. Liu, M. Prvulovic, L. Ceze, S. Sarangi, P. Sack, K. Strauss, and P. Montesinos. SESC Simulator, January 2005. http://sesc.sourceforge.net.

[24] G. Sohi, S. Breach, and T. Vijayakumar. Multiscalar Processors. In *22nd International Symposium on Computer Architecture*, pages 414–425, June 1995.

[25] J. Steffan, C. Colohan, A. Zhai, and T. Mowry. A Scalable Approach to Thread-Level Speculation. In *Proceedings of the 27th Annual International Symposium on Computer Architecture*, pages 1–12, June 2000.

[26] J. G. Steffan, C. Colohan, A. Zhai, and T. C. Mowry. The STAMPede Approach to Thread-Level Speculation. *ACM Trans. Comput. Syst.*, 23(3):253–300, 2005.

[27] T. Suganuma, H. Komatsu, and T. Nakatani. Detection and Global Optimization of Reduction Operations for Distributed Parallel Machines. In *Proceedings of the 10th International Conference on Supercomputing*, pages 18–25, Philadelphia, Pennsylvania, United States, 1996. ACM.

[28] Y. M. Teo, W. Chin, and S. H. Tan. Deriving Efficient Parallel Programs for Complex Recurrences. In *Proceedings of the second International Symposium on Parallel Symbolic Computation*, pages 101–110, Maui, Hawaii, United States, 1997. ACM.

[29] M. Tremblay. MAJC: Microprocessor Architecture for Java Computing. Hot Chips, August 1999.

[30] J. Tsai, J. Huang, C. Amlo, D. Lilja, and P. Yew. The Superthreaded Processor Architecture. *IEEE Trans. on Computers*, 48(9):881–902, September 1999.

[31] J. Y. Tsai, Z. Jiang, and P. C. Yew. Compiler Techniques for the Superthreaded Architecture. In *International Journal of Parallel Programming*, pages 27(1):1–19, 1999.

[32] T. Vijaykumar and G. Sohi. Task Selection for a Multiscalar Processor. In *Proceedings of the 31th Annual International Symposium on Microarchitecture*, pages 81–92, November 1998.

[33] C. von Praun, L. Ceze, and C. Cacaval. Implicit Parallelism with Ordered Transactions. In *Proceedings of the 12th ACM SIGPLAN Symposium on Principles and Practice of Parallel Programming*, pages 79–89, San Jose, California, USA, 2007. ACM.

[34] J. Wu. An Interleaving Transformation for Parallelizing Reductions for Distributed-Memory Parallel Machines. *J. Supercomput.*, 15(3):321–339, 2000.

[35] H. Yu and L. Rauchwerger. Adaptive Reduction Parallelization Techniques. In *Proceedings of the 14th International Conference on Supercomputing*, pages 66–77, Santa Fe, New Mexico, United States, 2000. ACM.

[36] A. Zhai, C. Colohan, J. Steffan, and T. Mowry. Compiler Optimization of Scalar Value Communication Between Speculative Threads. In *ASPLOS X Proceedings*, San Jose, CA, October 2002.

[37] A. Zhai, C. B. Colohan, J. G. Steffan, and T. C. Mowry. Compiler Optimization of Scalar Value Communication between Speculative Threads. In *Proceedings of the 10th international conference on Architectural Support for Programming Languages and Operating Systems*, pages 171–183, San Jose, California, 2002. ACM.

[38] A. Zhai, C. B. Colohan, J. G. Steffan, and T. C. Mowry. Compiler Optimization of Memory-Resident Value Communication Between Speculative Threads. In *Proceedings of the international symposium on Code Generation and Optimization: feedback-directed and runtime optimization*, page 39, Palo Alto, California, 2004. IEEE Computer Society.

[39] A. Zhai, S. Wang, P. Yew, and G. He. Compiler Optimizations for Parallelizing General-Purpose Applications under Thread-Level Speculation. In *Proceedings of the 13th ACM SIGPLAN Symposium on Principles and Practice of Parallel Programming*, pages 271–272, Salt Lake City, UT, USA, 2008. ACM.

[40] Y. Zhang, L. Rauchwerger, and J. Torrellas. A Unified Approach to Speculative Parallelization of Loops in DSM Multiprocessors. Technical report, 1998.

Automatic Parallelization of Simulink Applications

Arquimedes Canedo   Takeo Yoshizawa   Hideaki Komatsu

IBM Research - Tokyo

{eb54189,ytakeo,komatsu}@jp.ibm.com

Abstract

The parallelization of Simulink applications is currently a responsibility of the system designer and the superscalar execution of the processors. State-of-the-art Simulink compilers excel at producing reliable and production-quality embedded code, but fail to exploit the natural concurrency available in the programs and to effectively use modern multi-core architectures. The reason may be that many Simulink applications are replete with loop-carried dependencies that inhibit most parallel computing techniques and compiler transformations.

In this paper, we introduce the concept of *strands* that allow the data dependencies to be broken while preserving the original semantics of the Simulink program. Our fully automatic compiler transformations create a concurrent representation of the program, and thread-level parallelism for multi-core systems is planned and orchestrated. To improve single processor performance, we also exploit fine grain (equation-level) parallelism by level-order scheduling inside each thread. Our strand transformation has been implemented as an automatic transformation in a proprietary compiler and with a realistic aeronautic model executed in two processors leads to an up to 1.98 times speedup over uniprocessor execution, while the existing manual parallelization method achieves a 1.75 times speedup.

Categories and Subject Descriptors D.3.4 [*Programming Languages*]: Processors-Compilers,Optimization; D.3.3 [*Programming Languages*]: Language Constructs and Features-Concurrent programming structures; D.3.2 [*Programming Languages*]: Language Classifications-Specialized application languages,Data-flow languages; I.6.2 [*Simulation and Modeling*]: Simulation Languages

General Terms Languages, Algorithms, Performance

Keywords Strands, Simulink, multi-core, compilers, coarse grain dataflow, automatic parallelization, equation-level parallelism

1. Introduction

The development of industrial embedded software is a task of enormous complexity and responsibility. Many of these applications run in safety-critical systems which human lives are depending on every day. The best practices in automotive and aeronautic software development include the use of model-based engineering tools because they increase productivity and reduce the errors introduced during development. Starting from a single high-level formalism the system under development is modeled, simulated, checked, and deployed. The automotive industry, for example, has adopted Simulink formalism [1] as the de facto standard for the development of embedded controllers. Commercial code generators are used to produce production-quality embedded code, and other tools are used to translate Simulink into other languages where formal verification methods can be applied [2]. This discipline is also economically relevant since for the €310 billion value creation in the automotive industry as projected for 2015 [3], the automotive software is estimated to be at least 40% [4] of the total.

Producing Simulink code for multi-core systems is a very promising technology to accelerate the real-time simulations that are used in the design of embedded controllers. State-of-the-art commercial code generators have concentrated on generating production-quality embedded code, but have lagged behind in automatic parallelization of Simulink applications. Although existing techniques allow Simulink applications to be compiled into multi-threaded code, the partitioning has to be done manually by the system designer [5, 6]. In most cases, the designer is not also an expert computer programmer who fully understands the complexity of the underlying architecture. Therefore, we believe, automatic parallelization of Simulink applications is a task that should be delegated to the compiler to obtain maximum performance.

Simulation code presents a challenging problem for parallelizing compilers because of the abundance of loop-carried dependencies. For example, Simulink applications describe dynamic systems and controllers that are interacting in a tightly coupled manner and their inputs and outputs are being exchanged in each iteration. Unfortunately, most parallel programming and loop optimization techniques are ineffective in the presence of loop-carried dependencies. Initially it may appear that simulation code does not have explicit parallelism due to the loop-carried dependencies created by the tightly connected simulated components. However, with a correct and faithful interpretation of their high-level semantics, Simulink models can be parallelized, as we will show in this paper.

We propose a novel concept and compilation structure called a *strand* that selectively breaks some of the data dependencies in a Simulink program. The key insight is that some of the Simulink operators are Mealy machines [7] whose outputs are a function of their internal states and the *previous* inputs. Therefore, the data dependencies on inputs to Mealy machines can be broken *during* an iteration and reestablished after the iteration finishes and before the internal states update phase begins. Using strands, our compiler breaks up the original Simulink dataflow graph and builds a concurrent program dependence graph that is planned and orchestrated for execution on parallel systems.

This paper makes the following contributions:

1. It introduces the concept of strands, which we use as the building blocks for a concurrent compiler representation of a Simulink program without violating its semantics.

2. It presents a fully automatic parallelization technique implemented in a proprietary compiler that uses strands to extract some of the thread-level parallelism from Simulink applications.

3. It gives insights into the amount of strand parallelism that is readily available in conventional and industrial Simulink applications.

4. It presents an experimental evaluation of our automatic parallelization on a realistic aeronautic application and compares its performance against existing methods.

Section 2 introduces the Simulink formalism. Section 3 introduces Strands. Section 4 presents our strand transformation that allows Simulink applications to be automatically parallelized. Section 5 presents an experimental evaluation using a realistic aeronautic application. Section 6 compares and highlights the contributions of this paper with related work. Section 7 presents some conclusions and Section 8 gives future directions.

2. Overview of Simulink Formalism

Simulink is a model-based design engineering tool that uses a block diagram notation to describe mathematical models of dynamic systems and controllers. A dynamic system is a system that varies over time and its behavior is described by a set of algebraic and differential equations. To approximate its behavior in a computer simulation, Simulink discretizes time into small time steps in which numerical integration algorithms are used to solve these equations. Several ordinary differential equation (ODE) solvers have been developed to satisfy the needs of a wide range of engineering and scientific problems. ODE solvers are classified into variable-step size solvers and fixed-step size solvers. Variable-step size solvers attempt to save computation steps by taking large steps when the local error within a threshold. For simplicity, we concentrate on fixed-step size solvers but our method is applicable to variable-step size solvers because its implementation is independent of the numerical integration method.

The size of the iteration space in a simulation is given by the simulation time divided by the step size. In each iteration, the equations are solved either by the ODE solver or algebraically. The ODE solver only cares about blocks whose outputs are a function of their inputs and their internal state. These blocks are known as Mealy machines and for the rest of the paper we will refer to them as *Mealy blocks*. Non-Mealy blocks have direct-feedthrough inputs, because their outputs directly depend on their inputs [8]. Figure 1 shows a Simulink model that includes both types of blocks. The addition block (Add) simply adds its inputs "1" and "2" and produces a constant output "3". Non-Mealy blocks are driven by their inputs. The integrator block, in contrast, receives a constant input "1" and produces a non-constant output because its result is a function of its input and its current state. In this case, its state behaves as an accumulator that is added to the constant input to produce an output of a straight line with a slope equal to 1.

3. Unbraiding Strands

Formally, Simulink enforces correct simulations by determining a block execution order. This order is given by two simple rules[1]: (1) a block must be updated *before* any non-Mealy block that is connected to its outputs, and (2) Mealy blocks, and blocks without

---

[1] For more information see "Determining Block Update Order" in [8]

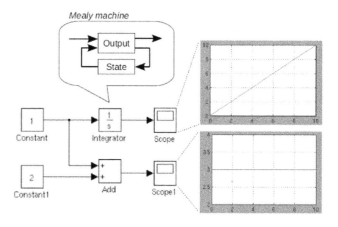

Figure 1. Outputs of Mealy blocks are a function of their inputs and internal state. The outputs of non-Mealy blocks are driven by their inputs.

inputs (feeders), can be updated in *any order* as long as they are updated before any non-Mealy blocks that are connected to their outputs. Clearly, the purpose of these rules is to ensure that Mealy blocks are updated before the blocks they drive. We use the term of *strands* to refer to these chains of data-dependent blocks that are driven by one or more Mealy blocks.

A very important observation is that Mealy blocks update their outputs as a function of their current state and the input of the *previous* iteration, and their states as a function of their current state and the input of the *current* iteration:

$$output_{new} = f(input_{prev}, state_{curr}) \qquad (1)$$

$$state_{new} = g(input_{curr}, state_{curr}) \qquad (2)$$

This means that the inputs to Mealy blocks are *broken* data dependencies that partition the dataflow graph of the program into independent strands that can be evaluated concurrently, as long as each follows the two sequencing rules. To clarify the concept, consider the closed-loop control system of a mariner-class cargo ship [9] with three subsystems connected by two feedback loops (Autopilot, Mariner-class dynamics, and Wave filter) shown in Figure 2. Beneath the subsystems, the dataflow graph consisting of primitive blocks is shown. Gray blocks represent Mealy blocks, white blocks represent non-Mealy blocks, and clouds represent a collection of non-Mealy blocks. Diagonal parallel bars placed before Mealy blocks represent the data dependencies that are broken to create three strands {S1,S2,S3}. After Equation 1 has been completed for all blocks in the model, all states are updated with Equation 2. When updating the states, the current input is required and this is the output of a strand on which the Mealy blocks are dependent. The *broken* data dependencies are restored after updating the outputs and before updating the states because the new inputs have to be forwarded among data dependent strands.

3.1 Motivation: Strand Parallelism

Strands are a powerful concept with which tightly coupled Simulink applications (typically with many loop carried dependencies) can be broken into independent fragments of operations. Table 1 summarizes the strand characteristics of ten applications including five basic, two academic, and three industrial models. On average, Mealy blocks represent about 9% of the total blocks in a model. The number of generated strands always exceeds the number of Mealy blocks because we must account for the strands that are driven by feeder blocks rather than by Mealy blocks. However, the number of strands gives an idea of how much parallelism can be exploited if every strand is mapped to one processor. For large models, the number of strands exceeds the number of cores available in current multi-core processors. Since the number of strands is about 17% of the total number of blocks, industrial Simulink models with thousands of blocks can be potentially mapped to thousands of processors. The average strand size is about 6 blocks per strand, but this metric varies greatly from program to program because it depends on the distribution of the Mealy blocks in the model and the topology of the dataflow graph. Assuming that all of the blocks have the same workload of 1, and ignoring communication and synchronization costs, then the speedup gained by executing all of the strands in parallel is proportional to the workload of the largest strand. The last column shows that on average, almost 4-fold speedups are readily available if Simulink applications are parallelized based on the strands.

4. Automatic Simulink Parallelization

In this section we present a novel code generation technique that unravels strands from Simulink models and produces multi-threaded C code. Since strands are dataflow graph fragments, we rely on conventional compiler dataflow techniques to apply our transformation. We implemented our algorithm using the BlueLink compiler infrastructure [10]. The compiler parses the MDL (Simulink source) file, and flattens the hierarchical model into a dataflow graph. The dataflow graph is then simplified and annotated by removing unnecessary input and output blocks, folding and propagating the constants, inferring the data types and the sampling times for the blocks, and detecting loops. After this, the strand transformation builds a suitable data structure to perform load-balancing, thread scheduling, communication primitives insertion, and code generation. Algorithm 1 outlines our transformation.

Algorithm 1 Strand transformation

Input: Dataflow graph of the model
Input: Number of processors, N
1: Compute broken-edge set
2: Build and annotate Concurrent Program Dependence Graph (CPDG)
3: Compute load-balanced multiprocessor schedule
4: Expose equation-level parallelism for every processor
5: Compute Message Aggregation points
6: Insert strand forwarding communication primitives
7: Emit multi-threaded code

4.1 Selecting the split-points

We first identify the set of edges in the dataflow graph that can be broken to create strands. This is done by walking the dataflow graph and recording in the broken-edge set all of the edges that are inputs to Mealy blocks. By removing the edges in the broken-edge set from the dataflow graph we can identify the strands in the Simulink model. Mealy blocks are explicit in the Simulink model and includes integrators, transfer functions, derivatives, PID controllers, unit delays, memories, and S-functions.

4.2 Concurrent Program Dependence Graph creation

The Concurrent Program Dependence Graph (CPDG) is a directed graph in which the nodes represent strands, and the edges represent the forwarding of values that occur *between* iterations. The edges in the CPDG are the edges in the broken-edge set that were removed *during* the execution of an iteration. Essentially, these edges propagate the new inputs that are needed by the Mealy blocks to update

their states according to Equation 2. Nodes in the CPDG are independent of each other and can be executed in parallel. Edges simply represent the direction and the number of values that are forwarded after their execution. An additional pass annotates the nodes of the CPDG with the total estimated workload (in cycles) and the edges with the number of values they carry between iterations. The estimated workload is computed as the sum of the estimated workloads of all of the blocks in the strand.

4.3 Load-balance and scheduling of strands

Load-balancing is critical for achieving good performance in parallel systems. Since strand scheduling for multi-core systems is an instance of the classic NP-Complete multiprocessor scheduling problem, we use a heuristic algorithm to solve the bin packing problem [11]. This approach performs load-balancing by placing strands (elements) into processors (bins) according to their estimated workload. Since our target applications are CPU-bound, we give higher priority to load-balancing than communication reduction. However, our algorithm considers the cost of inter-processor communication and attempts to pack strongly connected strands into the same processor.

For some programs, there are cases when one single strand concentrates more than 50% of the blocks or workload in a program. This typically occurs with dataflow graphs that have multiple Mealy blocks driving chains of instructions that converge to the same path. Consider the dataflow graph shown in Figure 3(a). Mealy blocks {A,B,C} drive chains of instructions that converge on the same path leading to X. Let the strand S1 have the largest portion of the program's workload. Since parallel execution is dominated by the heaviest strand, it is desirable to break S1 into smaller fragments to reduce its workload and improve the parallel performance. Figure 3(b) shows a situation in which the algorithm decides to partition S1 into strands S3 and S4. Since the merging point of the chains driven by blocks B and C is a non-Mealy block, it obeys the dataflow firing rules and it requires both of its *current* inputs to be executed. This partitioning introduces a serialization edge in the CPDG because it makes the two strands data dependent in the *current* iteration and inter-processor communication must be performed. This transformation is justified only when the inter-processor communication overhead of communicating between two strands in different processors is less than the work for computing the original fat strand in a single processor.

After the multiprocessor schedule has been computed, the algorithm maps the strands assigned to the same processor to a single worker thread. Each thread contains an identical simulation loop using a local clock that dictates the progress of the simulation. Communication code for receiving new inputs and forwarding outputs is necessary and is described in detail in the following sections. We ensure conformance to the Simulink formalism with the following code on each worker thread:

1: **while** local clock < End_of_Simulation **do**
2:     Update outputs (Equation 1)
3:     Forward strand outputs to consumers
4:     Receive new inputs from producer strands
5:     Update states (Equation 2)
6:     Compute local clock for next step
7: **end while**

4.4 Expose Equation-Level Parallelism (ELP)

Mathematically, the strands represent the right-hand sides of the algebraic and differential equations describing a dynamic system. By parallelizing the evaluation of the right-hand sides of the equations, we are exploiting the equation-level parallelism (ELP) in the system [12, 13]. On every worker thread, the execution of the independent strands is allowed to overlap by instruction-level paral-

Program	Description	Block total	Mealy total	Strands total	Strand size (blocks/strand)	Upper-bound speedup
House	Thermal model of a house	29	2	5	5.80	2.63
Cruise	Automotive cruise control	31	2	4	7.75	2.18
ABS	Automotive anti-lock brake system	34	5	7	3.78	1.62
Suspension	Automotive suspension model	35	4	9	3.50	2.18
F-14	Flight control system	43	11	14	2.53	4.30
Mariner	Naval autopilot for cargo ship	92	13	22	4.37	2.50
Induction	Electric induction motor	121	7	18	6.37	2.50
Physbe	Human circulatory system	208	17	23	9.04	4.83
SLUGS	Unmanned Air Vehicle dynamics	426	6	54	7.47	1.35
SICE	Automotive engine with 6 cylinders	1,219	75	148	7.43	12.31
Avg.		100%	9.2%	17.92%	5.84	3.67

Table 1. Strand characteristics of ten Simulink applications. Strands are related to the Mealy blocks and the topology of the dataflow graph. Substantial speedups can be obtained by parallelizing these applications via strands.

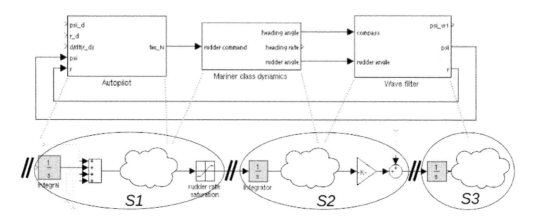

Figure 2. Simulink applications can be broken into strands. A strand is a chain of blocks that are driven by Mealy blocks. Strands are used to expose fine-grain and coarse-grain parallelism in Simulink applications.

lelism (ILP) techniques. Thus, ELP is exploited as a form of ILP by superscalar execution.

We use level-order scheduling to determine the execution order of the Simulink blocks in each thread. A level-order traversal on the strands exposes the maximum ELP that can be exploited inside each thread. Figure 4(a) shows how three strands {S1, S2, S3} are traversed in level-order from L1 to L4 by visiting all of the blocks from left to right. The numbers inside the nodes represent the position of the block in the thread. Although we do this instruction-level optimization at the block-level, it has been previously shown that the execution of closed-loop Simulink applications can be improved by about 13% [14].

4.5 Select Message Aggregation points

To minimize the overhead of inter-processor communication we use a Message Aggregation (MA) technique [6, 15]. This technique merges the forwarding of multiple values between two threads into a single communication message. We take an additional step to improve the computation of overlapping multiple threads by inserting the RECEIVE messages as late as possible, and the FORWARD messages as early as possible [16] (ALAP). Let the blocks {2, 3} in Figure 4(b) consume a value from thread X, block {8} consume a value from thread Y, block {6} produce a value for thread W, and blocks {11,12} produce a value for thread Z. Figure 4(b) shows the Message Aggregation points selected for this thread. Diamonds represent RECEIVE statements, and triangles represent FORWARD

statements. Notice that the FORWARD statement inserted between blocks {12} and {13} contains two different values consumed by thread Z. Similarly, the RECEIVE statement inserted between blocks {1} and {2} contains two values produced by thread X.

4.6 Generate multi-threaded C code

The last step consists of generating the multi-threaded C code. One thread is created per processor and its body consists of the local simulation loop enclosing the C statements that are equivalent to the algebraic and differential equations described by the strands. The order in which statements are ordered is given by the level-order schedule given by Step 4. Communication code is inserted at the computed Message Aggregation points given by Step 5. For portability we use the POSIX threads infrastructure. Mapping of threads to processors is done explicitly using the pthread_setaffinity_np function. Although communication primitives are generic, we use a custom implementation of FastForward FIFO queues to communicate with the threads [17] because it is the fastest available inter-thread communication mechanism. Using other communication mechanisms results in unacceptable performance for high-performance simulations.

5. Experimental Results

The evaluation of our technique suffers from a lack of standardized benchmarks. Most Simulink models are highly confidential indus-

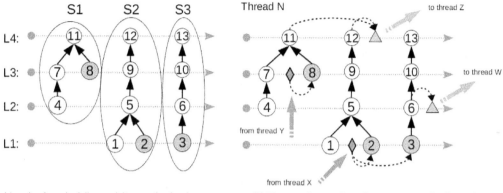

(a) Level-order scheduling exploits equation-level parallelism on every thread. This facilitates instruction-level parallelism extraction in the processor.

(b) Message Aggregation points are computed to forward values as-early-as-possible and receive values as-late-as-possible.

Figure 4. Example to illustrate (a) exploitation of equation-level parallelism, and (b) communication patterns optimization.

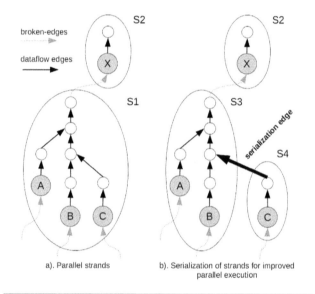

a). Parallel strands

b). Serialization of strands for improved parallel execution

Figure 3. Technique to improve load-balancing. (a) Unbalanced strands can be (b) re-balanced if serialization edges are introduced in the CPDG.

trial designs that are not published by their authors. The very few publically available models are either too small or too unrealistic. Therefore, we resorted to applying our method to a realistic six-degrees-of-freedom (6-DOF) dynamic model of an unmanned air vehicle (UAV) and present this as a case study.

5.1 Automatic Parallelization of a 6-DOF UAV Model

The Santa-Cruz Low-cost UAV GNC System (SLUGS) is an aeronautic autopilot system designed by the University of California and distributed under the MIT Open Source license [18]. The system is described entirely in Simulink and this allowed its authors to rapidly iterate the process of embedded systems design: design, simulation, testing, and deployment of the embedded software in a real aircraft. For the development of flight control systems, SLUGS provides a realistic 6-DOF aerodynamic model of an aircraft that is used in hardware-in-the-loop (HIL) simulations [19]. Using faithful software models rather than expensive and hazardous real systems, the development time and cost of embedded software can be

greatly reduced by HIL simulation. Since our technique aims at the acceleration of HIL simulations, we have selected the 6-DOF plant model as our benchmark.

Figure 5 shows the top-level Simulink diagram of the SLUGS 6-DOF plant. The system consists of five subsystems, namely *Forces & Moments*, *Engine Model*, *6-DOF EOM*, *Get GPS*, and *ISA Atmosphere & Winds*. The dynamics of these subsystems are tightly coupled as shown by the large arrows indicating the iteration-carried dependencies. After parsing, flattening, and optimizing the plant model, our compiler creates a dataflow graph that consists of 426 primitive blocks. In spite of its size, the model has only 6 Mealy blocks whose locations are indicated by the stars. One in *Forces & Moments*, one in the derivative block in the top right of the diagram, and four in *6-DOF EOM*.

Manual parallelization

Parallelization of Simulink applications has been previously proposed in [6, 5]. However, these code generators rely on manual partitioning of the program to processors done by the designer. This process can be tedious, time consuming, error-prone, and requires the system designer to make several trial-and-error attempts until the *best* partitioning for performance is found.

Two available methods are used for partitioning. The simplest and most portable is by adding annotations on top of the Simulink model that do not affect its semantics, layout, and original block configuration. These annotations are simply hints to the code generator for the proper mapping of subsystems to processors. The second method is more intrusive because it relies on custom blocks (libraries) for which some operations have been optimized for multiprocessors and can be only interpreted by the vendor's infrastructure.

Both of these methods have drawbacks in introducing communication delays whenever two processors communicate as producer and consumer. This very often violates the Simulink formalism explained in Section 2, because any edge can be broken by the partitioning. This changes the order of execution and therefore introduces numerical errors that may make the system unstable [20]. Our method, in contrast, does not induce any numerical instabilities because it honors the Simulink formalism.

The vertical dashed line in Figure 5 shows the place where a designer would be most likely to partition the model for its execution in two processors. The idea behind this partitioning is to balance the loads while assigning logical subsystems as atomic units to the two processors. Each of these subsystems represents independent

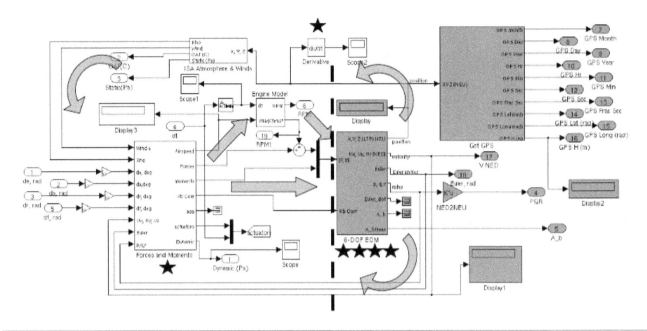

Figure 5. Top-level Simulink model of 6-DOF plant model of SLUGS UAV. Large arrows show the tightly coupled dynamics. Stars represent the location of Mealy blocks. The vertical dashed line represents the place where a designer would do manual partitioning for 2 processors.

physical components such as the engine, the airframe, the atmospheric winds, and the navigation system. In a real airplane, these are concurrent physical systems are sampling their neighbors several times per second and therefore it is more reasonable to delay one of these sampling signals than to delay a critical signal inside a physical component. Therefore, the white blocks and subsystems represent the components that are executed in one processor, and the gray blocks represent the components executed in the other processor. This manual partitioning is exactly what existing technology does and we use it as a reference point in the following sections to evaluate the characteristics and the performance of our automatic transformation.

Automatic parallelization via Strands

SLUGS 6-DOF model has several characteristics that allow us to practically demonstrate how our algorithm exposes strand parallelism from a program rich in loop-carried dependencies. The first observation about the model is that it has very few Mealy blocks, 1.4% of the total. If these Mealy blocks were evenly distributed among the model, then they would create very long strands that the compiler could naturally detect and exploit. However, four of the six Mealy blocks in the model are very close to each other and concentrated in the *6-DOF EOM*, subsystem as shown in Figure 6 by the gray blocks. The close proximity of the Mealy blocks and the loop-carried dependencies among them results in a single fat strand that contains nearly all of the blocks in the model. In Figure 6, the outputs 1,3, and 4 (dotted circles) are feedback loops that merge in the same path (R4) that eventually feeds the new inputs to all of these Mealy blocks. Naturally, a single strand is created due to the situation described in Section 4.3.

Nevertheless, the granularity of the model allows the compiler to judge whether or not the insertion of a serialization edge benefits parallel execution. Our algorithm discovers that the two Mealy blocks in region R1 (See Figure 6), and the Mealy block in R2 converge in a computation path that contains about 40% of the estimated execution time of the program. Therefore, the compiler creates a strand S1 that includes regions R1 and R2, and strand S2

including regions R3 and R4. The communication between S1 and S2 is necessarily a sequential edge where S2 blocks until it receives all of the forwarded values from S1. Despite the serialization edge, the strands execution can overlap because S1 and S2 merge in the same path near the end of the iteration (in the *Body Frame* subsystem inside *Forces and Moments*) as shown in Figure 7.

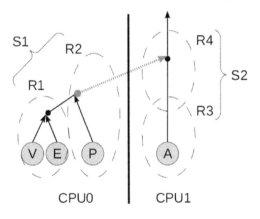

Figure 7. Two strands (S1, S2) are created out of the regions {R1,R2} and {R3, R4}.

Performance evaluation

In this section we evaluate how our automatic parallelization performs against manual parallelization methods on the 6-DOF SLUGS model. Our testbed is a 4-core Intel Xeon system with each processor running at 3.16 GHz. Each pair of processors have a shared L2 cache that we leverage to obtain maximum performance in our implementation of FastForward queues for inter-processor communication. Therefore, to obtain the best performance in both parallel versions of SLUGS, we map the program to either pair of processors that share one L2 cache. The host operating system kernel is Linux 2.6.27 and we use posix threads to encapsulate the C

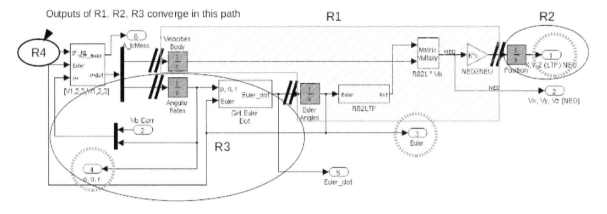

Figure 6. *6-DOF EOM* subsystem contains 4 out of the 6 Mealy blocks in the model. The close proximity and strongly connected signals creates a single fat strand. Our algorithm analyzes more deeply in an attempt to break the single strand by introducing serialization edges.

programs. All of the C programs were generated using our compiler to ensure identical numerical code. For the manual parallelization method we annotated the signals that had to be broken and our compiler inserts the communication code and the delays to couple the two halves. For the automatic parallelization, the compiler ignores these annotations and performs the strand transformation described in Section 4.

We configured the simulation time to be 500 seconds with a time step of 0.1 ms to create an iteration space of 5,000,000 iterations. To measure the raw cost of each iteration, we compiled the model using our compiler and produced uniprocessor code. On average, these 426 primitive blocks have a latency of 28,500 CPU cycles for every iteration. Considering that our fastest implementation of inter-processor communication has a latency between 200 and 300 cycles for an enqueue-dequeue operation, the computation-to-communication ratio (granularity) of this program is 57:1 if perfect load balancing is done for two processors. The rest of the programs in Table 1, except for SICE [21], have a granularity less than 5:1 and this is the main limitation when parallelizing these small models. However, it is important to note that the major limitation is the slow inter-processor communication technology currently available. Even small models could benefit from strand parallelism if fast communication mechanisms were available.

Figure 8 shows the speedup obtained with two processors by using manual parallelization and automatic parallelization in four different communication configurations described in detail in Table 2. The speedups are relative to the uniprocessor execution of the model. *Manual* parallelization achieves a speedup of 1.48 times while *Strands* is 1.42 times, and *Strands ALAP* is 1.44 times. The *Manual* version is faster because these two Strands versions have three communication channels rather than two. After Message Aggregation is applied to reduce the number of channels of S1 from 2 to 1, *Strands +MA* improves the speedup to 1.51 times. The last program, *Strands +MA ALAP*, includes the computed Message Aggregation points as described in our algorithm and this version produces the fastest simulation with a speedup of 1.53 times over the uniprocessor execution. Notice that the *Manual* program uses the Message Aggregation technique and forwarding of values as soon as they are ready and receiving of values right before they are used. Therefore, our comparison with existing methods was done fairly. With the communication configuration, Strands performs better than Manual parallelization because it achieves better load balancing. While the designer restricts the partitioning to the logical boundaries at the system level, the automatic parallelization

uses the underlying mathematical model to achieve better partitioning and better load balancing.

The previous experiment shows that Strands parallelization has the same problems that conventional parallelization techniques have, in that it is too sensitive to communication. We increased the latency of the threads by enabling the logging of signals to memory. This situation occurs in the early stages of the design when the system is being tested and signals are being monitored. Recording a signal in memory at every iteration is an expensive operation that increases the simulation time at least 5 times but improves the debugging.

Figure 9 shows that when the granularity of the threads is improved the speedups are better. *Manual* parallelization improved from 1.48 to 1.75 times. All Strands versions have the same behavior as the previous experiment but the achieved speedups are improved to 1.90, 1.93, 1.94, and 1.98 times, respectively.

It is important to notice the difference between our results and the estimated upper-bound given in Table 1. The single fat strand created by four of the six Mealy blocks that encloses most of the blocks in the model limits the upper-bound speedup to 1.35 times. This number, however, is improved by our algorithm with the insertion of a serialization edge that improves the load balance and allows the overlap of computation. As a result, from 1.45 to 1.98 speedups are possible with 2 strands.

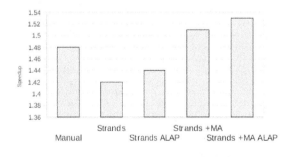

Figure 8. Speedup of manual parallelization and different configurations of Strand parallelization.

6. Related Work

Simulink is a relatively new programming formalism and therefore the related work is limited. Uniprocessor optimizations to generate production-quality code were proposed in [22]. While

Configuration	Description	Channels S1	Ch.S2
Manual	Manual parallelization with full communication optimizations	1	1
Strands	No communication optimizations	2	1
Strands ALAP	Forwarding as-late-as-possible and receiving as-early-as-possible.	2	1
Strands +MA	Message aggregation is used to merge S1 channels from 2 into 1	1	1
Strands +MA ALAP	Message aggregation ALAP/ASAP forwarding policy	1	1

Table 2. Various communication configurations to test Strands parallelization method.

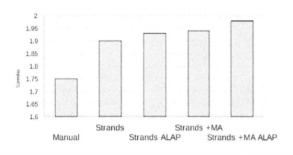

Figure 9. Speedup of manual parallelization and different configurations of Strand parallelization when communication is negligible compared to the computation cost.

uniprocessor techniques are very important for single-processor performance, we are focused on the extraction of coarse-grain parallelism. In [23], a method to optimize buffering in multitask single-processor Simulink applications was proposed. Although this method creates threads to prioritize Simulink blocks, they target single-processor implementations where a real-time operating system schedules the threads only to prioritize their execution and meet the timing requirements. In addition, their target applications are reactive Simulink models and ours are continuous dynamic Simulink models.

Our work shares the same objectives with the code generation technique proposed in [6]. In fact, we use the communication optimization the authors proposed called Message Aggregation to reduce the number of channels between two threads. However, the most important difference is that their parallelization is guided by the designer by using a modeling style called Simulink Combined Architecture Algorithm Model (CAAM). This Simulink CAAM model provides a mapping of the Simulink subsystems to processors that the compiler then reads to produce multi-threaded code. In contrast, our technique is a fully automatic parallelization method that preserves Simulink semantics. A significant advantage of our proposed method over manual parallelizations is that we comply with Simulink semantics and we do not introduce any numerical errors that may create numerically unstable simulations [20].

Modelica is a modeling language similar to Simulink in which automatic parallelization is available and well understood. In [24], a multiprocessor scheduling method that uses a Full Task Duplication Technique is demonstrated to be very effective in clusters of PCs. In [13], an automatic parallelization for multi-core systems was introduced. Their method detects opportunities for pipelining in the task-graph while exploiting the parallelism at the equation level. Unfortunately, these techniques depend greatly on the acausal (non-causal) nature of Modelica and cannot be easily applied to a causal formalism like Simulink. Nevertheless, the efforts to support automatic parallelization in the Modelica language should encourage the community for similar initiatives in visual languages such as Simulink and Scicos [25].

In this paper, we show how to leverage the high-level semantics of Simulink to break some of the data dependencies and expose DOALL parallelism in the output calculation phase. Although other parallelization techniques such as DOACROSS [26] and DSPW [27] could be applied to exploit more parallelism over the state update phase, the synchronization barrier that is necessary to advance the simulation over time create true data dependencies that inhibit this possibility. However, we acknowledge that speculative execution techniques [28, 16] open the possibility to exploit not only DOALL parallelism but also some form of pipeline parallelism in simulation codes.

7. Conclusion

This paper presents a fully automatic parallelization technique for Simulink applications. We introduced the concept of Strands and an algorithm to detect and exploit strand parallelism from tightly coupled Simulink applications. Strands break data dependencies in the Simulink models and a concurrent program representation is constructed to orchestrate coarse-grain parallelism for modern multi-core systems. We motivate our work with a study of the available strand parallelism in publically available Simulink applications where, on average, potential speedups of 3.67 times are possible. Using two processors and a realistic aeronautic model, we accelerated a version of a program suitable for high-performance simulation by 1.53 times, and a version of the program suitable for debugging by 1.98 times, compared to uniprocessor execution. Most importantly, we demonstrated that our method can automatically perform better partitioning and load balancing than a manual parallelization done by an experienced system designer, without altering the original semantics.

8. Future Work

The use of strands is a sound concept that allows Simulink applications to be partitioned for parallel execution without altering their original semantics and therefore without introducing numerical errors. We will continue exploring in this direction and we plan to enhance strand parallelism with other technologies. Speculative execution is a promising technique to break more data dependencies in Simulink programs because continuous signals vary by very small amounts over the iteration space. Combining strand parallelism with speculative execution would be a solid combination for large-scale simulations of complex dynamic systems in future multi-core systems and supercomputers. The study of parallel ODE solvers will become much more tractable, since Strands are well formed entities. Solving ordinary differential equations is the heart of simulation code and Strands can be used as the formalism to explore new solvers that run concurrently. In the future, we will use Strands to implement parallel ODE solvers that are able to handle stiff dynamic systems. We also plan to use Strands for code generation for distributed embedded systems.

Acknowledgments

The authors would like to thank Mariano Lizarraga from the University of California for facilitating the access to and providing information related to the SLUGS UAV Simulink model. The authors would also like to thank Ju Lei for his valuable comments during the preparation of this paper.

References

[1] Mathworks, "Simulink." http://www.mathworks.com/products/simulink/.

[2] T. Stavros, S. Christos, C. Paul, and C. Adrian, "Translating Discrete-time Simulink to Lustre," *Trans. on Embedded Computing Sys.*, vol. 4, no. 4, pp. 779–818, 2005.

[3] J. Dannenberg and C. Kleinhans, "The Coming Age of Collaboration in the Automotive Industry," *Mercer Manage. J.*, vol. 18, pp. 88–94, 2004.

[4] B. Hardung, T. Kölzow, and A. Krüger, "Reuse of Software in Distributed Embedded Automotive Systems," in *EMSOFT '04*, pp. 203–210, ACM, 2004.

[5] dSPACE, "RTI-MP dSPACE." http://www.dspaceinc.com/ww/en/inc/home/products/sw/impsw/rtimpblo.cfm.

[6] L. Brisolara, S.-i. Han, X. Guerin, L. Carro, R. Reis, S.-I. Chae, and A. Jerraya, "Reducing Fine-Grain Communication Overhead in Multithread Code Generation for Heterogeneous MPSoC," in *SCOPES '07*, pp. 81–89, ACM, 2007.

[7] G. H. Mealy, "A Method for Synthesizing Sequential Circuits," *Bell System Technical Journal*, vol. 34, pp. 1045–1079, 1955.

[8] Mathworks, "Simulink User's Guide." http://www.mathworks.com/access/helpdesk/help/toolbox/simulink/ug/bqchgnk.html.

[9] T. Fossen and T. Perez, "Marine Systems Simulator (MSS)." http://www.marinecontrol.org/.

[10] IBM, "BlueLink Compiler." http://domino.research.ibm.com/comm/research_projects.nsf/pages/bluelink.index.html.

[11] M. R. Garey and D. S. Johnson, *Computers and Intractability: A guide to the Theory of NP-Completeness*. W H Freeman & Co, 1979.

[12] N. Andersson and P. Fritzson, "Generating Parallel Code from Object Oriented Mathematical Models," in *POPP '95*, pp. 48–57, ACM, 1995.

[13] H. Lundvall, K. Stavåker, P. Fritzson, and C. Kessler, "Automatic Parallelization of Simulation Code for Equation-based Models with Software Pipelining and Measurements on Three Platforms," *SIGARCH Comput. Archit. News*, vol. 36, no. 5, pp. 46–55, 2008.

[14] A. Canedo, "Leveraging Equation-Level Parallelism in Simulink Compilation," *IBM Research Report RT0848*, 2009.

[15] S. P. Amarasinghe and M. S. Lam, "Communication Optimization and Code Generation for Distributed Memory Machines," in *PLDI '93: Proceedings of the ACM SIGPLAN 1993 conference on Programming language design and implementation*, (New York, NY, USA), pp. 126–138, ACM, 1993.

[16] A. Zhai, J. G. Steffan, C. B. Colohan, and T. C. Mowry, "Compiler and Hardware Support for Reducing the Synchronization of Speculative Threads," *ACM Trans. Archit. Code Optim.*, vol. 5, no. 1, pp. 1–33, 2008.

[17] J. Giacomoni, T. Moseley, and M. Vachharajani, "FastForward for Efficient Pipeline Parallelism," in *PACT '07*, p. 407, IEEE Computer Society, 2007.

[18] U. of California, "SLUGS." http://slugsuav.soe.ucsc.edu/.

[19] M. I. Lizarraga, V. Dobrokhodov, G. H. Elkaim, R. Curry, and I. Kaminer, "Simulink Based Hardware-in-the-Loop Simulator for Rapid Prototyping of UAV Control Algorithms," *Americal Institute of Aeronautics and Astronautics*, 2009.

[20] D. Word, J. J. Zenor, R. Bednar, R. E. Crosbie, and N. G. Hingorani, "Multi-rate Real-time Simulation Techniques," in *SCSC: Proc. of 2007 summer computer simulation conference*, pp. 195–198, Society for Computer Simulation International, 2007.

[21] A. Ohata, J. Kako, T. Shen, and K. Ito, "Introduction to the Benchmark Challenge on SICE Engine Start Control Problem," in *Proc. of the 17th World Congress*, pp. 1048–1053, The Intl. Federation of Automatic Control, 2008.

[22] H. Hanselmann, U. Kiffmeier, L. Koster, M. Meyer, and A. Rukgauer, "Production Quality Code Generation from Simulink Block Diagrams," *IEEE CACSD '99*, pp. 213–218, 1999.

[23] M. D. Natale and V. Pappalardo, "Buffer Optimization in Multitask Implementations of Simulink Models," *ACM Trans. Embed. Comput. Syst.*, vol. 7, no. 3, pp. 1–32, 2008.

[24] P. Aronsson, P. Fritzson, and F. M. Models, "Multiprocessor Scheduling of Simulation Code from Modelica Models," 2002.

[25] INRIA, "Scicos: Block diagram modeler/simulator." http://www.scicos.org/.

[26] R. Cytron, "Doacross: Beyond Vectorization for Multiprocessors," in *ICPP*, pp. 836–844, 1986.

[27] G. Ottoni, R. Rangan, A. Stoler, and D. I. August, "Automatic thread extraction with decoupled software pipelining," in *MICRO*, pp. 105–118, 2005.

[28] N. Vachharajani, R. Rangan, E. Raman, M. J. Bridges, G. Ottoni, and D. I. August, "Speculative Decoupled Software Pipelining," in *PACT '07*, pp. 49–59, IEEE Computer Society, 2007.

Coloring-based Coalescing for
Graph Coloring Register Allocation

Rei Odaira, Takuya Nakaike, Tatsushi Inagaki, Hideaki Komatsu, Toshio Nakatani

IBM Research – Tokyo

1623-14, Shimotsuruma, Yamato-shi, Kanagawa-ken, 242-8502, Japan

{ odaira, nakaike, e29253, komatsu, nakatani } @jp.ibm.com

Abstract

Graph coloring register allocation tries to minimize the total cost of spilled live ranges of variables. Live-range splitting and coalescing are often performed before the coloring to further reduce the total cost. Coalescing of split live ranges, called sub-ranges, can decrease the total cost by lowering the interference degrees of their common interference neighbors. However, it can also increase the total cost because the coalesced sub-ranges can become uncolorable. In this paper, we propose coloring-based coalescing, which first performs trial coloring and next coalesces all copy-related sub-ranges that were assigned the same color. The coalesced graph is then colored again with the graph coloring register allocation. The rationale is that coalescing of differently colored sub-ranges could result in spilling because there are some interference neighbors that prevent them from being assigned the same color. Experiments on Java programs show that the combination of live-range splitting and coloring-based coalescing reduces the static spill cost by more than 6% on average, comparing to the baseline coloring without splitting. In contrast, well-known iterated and optimistic coalescing algorithms, when combined with splitting, increase the cost by more than 20%. Coloring-based coalescing improves the execution time by up to 15% and 3% on average, while the existing algorithms improve by up to 12% and 1% on average.

Categories and Subject Descriptors D.3.4 [**Programming Languages**]: Processor – Compilers.

General Terms Algorithms, Performance, Experimentation.

Keywords Register allocation; register coalescing.

1. Introduction

Global register allocation was formalized by Chaitin et al. [7][8] as a vertex coloring problem on an interference graph, where a node represents the live range of a variable, an edge between nodes indicates the interference between the live ranges, and a color corresponds to a physical register. The goal of the graph coloring register allocation is to minimize the total cost of uncol-

ored nodes. The cost of a node is the sum of the execution costs of the uses and definitions in the corresponding live range. Chaitin's coloring algorithm heuristically determines the coloring order for the nodes based on the degree of interference in addition to the spill cost of each node. The larger the degree is, the lower the node is in the coloring order because it restricts the coloring of many interference neighbors.

Since the graph coloring register allocation is a simple formalization, it can only determine whether the entire live range can be assigned to a single register or must be spilled out to memory. This is because the graph does not contain any further details about the live range. When a live-range is spilled, spill-out (store) instructions are inserted after every definition and spill-in (load) instructions before every use [7]. However, it is often the case that the total cost of spill instructions can be further reduced by assigning only some parts of a live range to a register and by assigning different parts of a live range to different registers [5].

For this reason, various live-range splitting approaches have been proposed [1][5][16]. They split live ranges into shorter ranges, which we call *sub-ranges*, before the graph coloring register allocation. The sub-ranges derived from the same live range are connected by copy instructions at splitting points, and thus they are called *copy-related* sub-ranges. These live-range splitting approaches then exploit Chaitin's coloring algorithm, which is expected to determine a good coloring order of the sub-ranges to minimize the total cost of spill instructions.

In fact, it is well known that coalescing of copy-related sub-ranges is necessary between live-range splitting and register allocation to reduce the total spill cost [14][19][20]. This is because coalescing decreases the degree of the common interference neighbors of coalesced sub-ranges. If copy-related sub-ranges X1 and X2 interfere with a sub-range Y, coalescing X1 and X2 will decrease the interference degree of Y by one. The lower the degree is, the more likely the node will be assigned a color. On the other hand, coalescing can also increase the total spill cost because if the coalesced sub-ranges are spilled, we might have to pay as much as the sum of the spill costs of the sub-ranges. Although various coalescing algorithms have been proposed, none of them can effectively reduce the total spill cost. They are either too conservative [6][10] or too aggressive [7][19] in coalescing criteria.

In this paper, we propose a simple but powerful coalescing algorithm called *coloring-based coalescing*. The key idea is to perform trial coloring of the sub-ranges. We coalesce the copy-related sub-ranges that are assigned the same color together, which we call *companion* sub-ranges. After the coalescing, all of the colors are cleared, and the actual graph coloring register allocation is performed in the usual manner. The rationale is that the more interference neighbors a group of copy-related sub-ranges share, the more often such sub-ranges are assigned the same color together. This is because the coloring of the sub-ranges is restricted by their common interference neighbors. More importantly, if sub-ranges are assigned different colors, there are some interference neighbors that prevent them from being assigned the same color. That means if we forced them to be coalesced, they would be spilled in the actual coloring. Therefore we should coalesce companion sub-ranges and let non-companion sub-ranges remain split.

The benefits of coloring-based coalescing are twofold:

- It is effective in reducing the total cost of spill instructions. To the best of our knowledge, this is the first work to reveal the combined power of live-range splitting and graph coloring register allocation by coalescing companion sub-ranges.
- It is simple in its design because it can utilize the existing coloring algorithm for register allocation. All that is needed is to perform coloring twice. After the first coloring, we do not generate the actual spills but only coalesce copy-related sub-ranges with the same color.

Here is the structure of the rest of this paper. Section 2 covers graph coloring register allocation and live-range splitting. Section 3 clarifies and exemplifies our target problems. Section 4 describes our coloring-based coalescing algorithm. Section 5 explains our implementation and gives experimental results. Section 6 discusses related research in register allocation. Section 7 concludes the paper.

2. Background

In this section, we first describe the algorithm of Briggs-style graph coloring register allocation [6]. Next we show how live-range splitting transforms a program.

2.1 Graph Coloring Register Allocation

Chaitin et al. [7][8] invented the original algorithm for graph coloring register allocation that was later found to be too pessimistic. Briggs et al. [6] improved the algorithm by using the optimistic approach shown in Figure 1(a).

1. **Renumber**: Each disjoint live range is given a unique name.
2. **Build**: An interference graph is built.
3. **Spill costs**: A spill cost $Cost(lr)$ is calculated for each live range lr. The cost is the total number of accesses to the live range weighted by instruction cost and by loop nesting level. If an execution profile is available, the cost is the total execution frequency of accesses.
4. **Simplify**: Nodes are removed from the interference graph and pushed into a coloring stack. For nodes whose interference degrees are larger than or equal to the number of physical registers, the one with the minimum value of $Cost(lr) / Degree(lr)$ is removed first. Here, $Degree(lr)$ is the interference degree of live range lr. Thus the smaller the degree of a node is, the more likely it is that the node is assigned a color.
5. **Select**: A node is repeatedly popped from the coloring stack and assigned a color if possible. If no color is available for the node, it is marked for spilling.
6. **Spill code**: If any node is marked for spilling, spill instructions are inserted. Because a spill instruction requires a temporary register to hold a spilled-in or spilled-out value, the whole register allocation process has to be iterated after clearing all of the assigned colors.

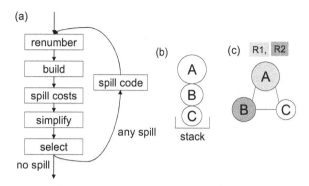

Figure 1. (a) Briggs-style graph coloring allocation. (b) Results of the simplify phase for the example in Figure 2(a). (c) Results of the select phase on the interference graph.

(a)
```
1:    A = ...
2:    B = ...
3:    while (true) {
4:        C = ...
5:        ...= A + ...
6:
7:        ...= C + ...
8:
9:        if (...) {
10:           A = ...
11:           B = C + ...
12:       } else {
13:
14:
15:           if (B) {
16:               A = ...
17:               ...= B + ...
18:
19:           } else {
20:
21:               if (A > 0) break
22:           }
23:       }
24:       A = A + ...
25:       B = B + ...
26: }
```

(b)
```
1:    A1 = ...
2:    B1 = ...
3:    while (true) {
4:        C1 = ...
5:        ... = A1 + ...
6:        A2 = A1
7:        ... = C1 + ...
8:        C2 = C1
9:        if (...) {
10:           A3 = ...
11:           B2 = C2 + ...
12:       } else {
13:           B2 = B1
14:           B3 = B1
15:           if (B1) {
16:               A3 = ...
17:               ... = B3 + ...
18:               B2 = B3
19:           } else {
20:               A3 = A2
21:               if (A2 > 0) break
22:           }
23:       }
24:       A1 = A3 + ...
25:       B1 = B2 + ...
26: }
```

Figure 2. Before (a) and after (b) live-range splitting based on load-range analysis.

In Figure 2(a), suppose there are two physical registers, R1 and R2, available for three variables A, B, and C. Figure 1(c) shows the interference graph. Since these variables interfere with one another and C has the minimum number of accesses in the loop, we spill C. Figure 1(b) is the coloring stack after the simplify phase, where C is pushed first, and Figure 1(c) is the results of the select phase, where A is assigned R1 first and then B R2. As a result, we generate one spill-out and two spill-in instructions at statements 4, 7, and 11. Actually, an additional variable needs to be spilled to allocate registers to the temporary variables used by the spill instructions.

2.2 Live-range Splitting

Live-range splitting takes place before graph coloring register allocation with the expectation that graph coloring can choose the best parts of live ranges to assign to registers. Researchers have proposed various splitting algorithms such as the load-range analysis [16] and the forward-and-reverse-SSA approach [5]. In this paper, we do not assume any particular type of live-range splitting, although the performance of each coalescing algorithm described later can depend on the type used.

After splitting the live range, each part is given a unique name and copy instructions are inserted at the splitting points. We call each short part of a live range a *sub-range*. A pair of sub-ranges is *copy-related* if they are connected by a copy instruction. A copy instruction can be eliminated after register allocation if both its source and target are assigned to the same register. In this paper, we mainly focus on reducing spill instructions rather than copy instructions, because spills have larger execution costs than copies in modern CPU architectures. However, it is still important not to increase copy instructions too much while reducing spill instructions.

Figure 2(b) shows an example of live-range splitting based on load-range analysis [16], which splits the live ranges of A, B, and C at every use point. Each sub-range originates from a use and extends up to the most recent accesses to the variable. For example, B2 corresponds to the use of B at statement 25 and extends up to the uses at 17 and 15 and the definition at 11. Thus new copying definitions of B2 are inserted around 15 and 17, and the target of 11 is modified to B2. The sub-ranges A1 and A2, A2 and A3, B1 and B2, B2 and B3, B3 and B1, and C1 and C2 are all copy related.

3. Problems

In this section, we show that coalescing is necessary to reduce the total spill cost after live-range splitting. We then explain why existing coalescing algorithms are not able to decrease the cost effectively.

3.1 Biased Coloring

When used with live-range splitting, the graph coloring register allocation normally uses a biased coloring [6], where copy-related sub-ranges are assigned to the same color as often as possible. Figure 3(a) shows the interference graph of the program in Figure 2(b) and the results of biased coloring using two registers, R1 and R2. Thick lines connect copy-related nodes in the graph. All of the sub-ranges in this example are considered to have the same spill cost because each load range corresponds to a single use. In this example, A1 and A2 are spilled, so that one spill-out at statement 24 and two spill-ins at 5 and 20 are generated in the loop. The copy at statement 6 is removed. Note that no spill-in instruction is generated for the use at statement 21 because it can refer to a register that was just loaded at its previous statements. In summary, we do not benefit from live-range splitting in this example because without splitting we generate the same number of spills in the loop as described in Section 2.1.

However, if we somehow spilled B1, we could assign A1 and A2 to R2 and would generate only one spill-out at statement 25 and one spill-in at 13 in the loop. Note that the uses at 14 and 15 can refer to a register loaded by the spill-in at 13. Unfortunately, biased coloring does not offer any heuristic to choose B1 for spilling. A2 is pushed onto the coloring stack before B1 because it has a larger degree of five. After pushing A2 and B3, when the trian-

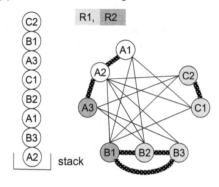

(a) Results of biased coloring

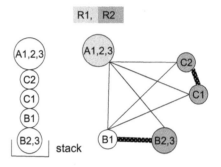

(b) Results of biased coloring after ideal coalescing of A1, A2, and A3; and B2 and B3

Figure 3. (a) Results of biased coloring on the interference graph of the example program in Figure 2(b). (b) Results of biased coloring after ideal coalescing. Note that neither iterated nor optimistic coalescing can generate these results.

gle of A1, B1, and C1 remains, the coloring algorithm does not have any reason to prefer B1 to A1 for spilling.

3.2 Coalescing of Sub-ranges

Coalescing of sub-ranges can reduce the total spill cost because it can lower the degree of the common interference neighbors of the coalesced sub-ranges. Coalescing was proposed to remove copies, but is nowadays important for reducing spills, which take longer execution cycles.

Apparently, we should coalesce copy-related sub-ranges that have many common interference neighbors. In Figure 3(a), the neighbors of A1 and A3 are totally included in those of A2, and the same is true for B2 and B3. If we coalesce A1, A2, and A3, and B2 and B3, we will have the graph in Figure 3(b). The number of spilled nodes is successfully reduced from two to one.

However, further coalescing will increase the total spill cost. In Figure 3(a), B1 and B2 share two interference neighbors, and the same is true for C1 and C2. If we decide to coalesce those copy-related sub-ranges that have more than one common neighbor, we will have a graph that is the same as the one before splitting. Therefore we cannot reduce the total spill cost. In general, it is not clear to what extent we should coalesce sub-ranges if we solely use the information about the sharing of interference neighbors.

3.3 Iterated and Optimistic Coalescing

George et al. proposed iterated coalescing [10], which coalesces copy-related nodes during the simplify phase only when the coalesced nodes will not become uncolorable. It uses two criteria for coalescing: the Briggs test for non-precolored nodes and the George test for precolored nodes. A node is precolored before the graph coloring when it must be assigned to a certain physical register because of an architectural reason, for example because it is used as an argument to a function call. Under the Briggs test, two copy-related nodes can be coalesced if the node after the coalescing has fewer significant interference neighbors than the number of physical registers. A node is called significant when the number of its neighbors is equal to or greater than the number of physical registers. In fact, this is the "full" Briggs test named by Hailperin [14], which is more powerful than the one described in [10]. In the example, after pushing A2, B3, and A1 into the stack, iterated coalescing merges C1 and C2 by using the Briggs test. Iterated coalescing cannot coalesce other nodes because the resultant node might become uncolorable. Thus it does not produce better results than simple biased coloring. In general, the criteria in iterated coalescing are too conservative.

Park et al. proposed optimistic coalescing [19], which first merges all of the coalescable nodes. It then splits a merged node back into separate nodes when the node is found to be uncolorable in the select phase. In the example, optimistic coalescing first reverts the interference graph back to the original one before splitting, and then splits C again into C1 and C2 during the select phase. Unfortunately, at that point, it is too late to color any of them, because each of them interferes with nodes A and B, which are already colored. This consequence is due to the aggressiveness of optimistic coalescing.

4. Coloring-based Coalescing

So far we have shown that existing coalescing approaches can be either too conservative or too aggressive to reduce spill instructions. Our experimental results in Section 5 confirm this fact. We need new coalescing criteria with which we can coalesce as many copy-related nodes that share interference neighbors as possible without making too many coalesced nodes uncolorable.

4.1 Basic Concept

We propose a simple but powerful coalescing algorithm called coloring-based coalescing. Coloring-based coalescing first attempts to color a graph using the same coloring algorithm as the register allocation, and then coalesces all copy-related nodes that are assigned the same color. We call such nodes *companion* nodes. During the trial coloring, it uses more colors than the number of physical registers to color all of the nodes.

Coloring-based coalescing is based on our assumption that the results of the coloring reflect the essential structure of the graph: the more interference neighbors a group of nodes share, the more often such nodes are assigned the same color in the trial coloring. This is because the common neighbors impose a similar set of restrictions on the coloring of the nodes. Thus we can infer the sharing of interference neighbors from the coloring. More importantly, coalescing of differently colored nodes could result in spilling because there are some interference neighbors that prevent them from being assigned the same color. Therefore, we should not coalesce non-companion nodes.

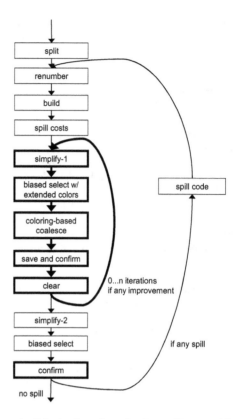

Figure 4. Coloring-based coalescing. Boxes with thick borders are our extension to the biased coloring.

4.2 Algorithm

Figure 4 shows the five main phases of the coloring-based coalescing algorithm. Those boxes with thick borders are our extension to the biased coloring:

1. **Simplify-1**: This is exactly the same as the simplify phase in the graph coloring register allocation. Simplify-2 in Figure 4 also does the same thing. We can also use iterated coalescing in this phase.

2. **Biased select with extended colors**: We extend the select phase by using more colors than the number of physical registers. Otherwise, we would not assign any color to spilled nodes, so that we could not coalesce them. The purpose of this trial coloring is not to allocate registers but to analyze the structure of the interference graph. Therefore, we need to apply the coloring algorithm to all the nodes. The algorithm is as follows, where the colors corresponding to physical registers are called real colors, while the other colors are called extended colors. Steps 1 to 4 are the same as the existing biased coloring, while Steps 5 to 7 are our extension:

   1. If the coloring stack is empty, then stop.
   2. Pop a node X from the stack.
   3. If there is a real color that is not allocated to any of its interference neighbors and is allocated to any of its copy-related nodes, then assign X to that real color and go back to Step 1.
   4. If there is a real color that is not allocated to any of its interference neighbors, then assign X to that real color and go back to Step 1.

5. If there is an extended color that is not allocated to any of its interference neighbors and is allocated to any of its copy-related nodes, then assign X to that extended color and go back to Step 1.

6. If there is an extended color that is not allocated to any of its interference neighbors, then assign X to that extended color and go back to Step 1.

7. Otherwise, introduce a new extended color, assign X to that extended color, and go back to Step 1.

It is important not to introduce extended colors at the beginning but to add them on demand. We first try to allocate real colors whenever possible because the trial coloring should resemble the actual graph coloring register allocation. We also try to reuse existing extended colors as much as possible. Otherwise, too many spilled nodes could be assigned to the same extended color.

3. **Coloring-based coalesce**: We coalesce all of the copy-related nodes that are assigned the same color, real or extended.

4. **Save and confirm**: With more iterations of coalescing, we can expect that the total spill cost will be further reduced. However, too many iterations might promote too much coalescing and increase the number of spilled nodes. Therefore, we save the results of this iteration and compare them with that of the previous iteration. Only when we confirm an improvement in the total spill cost, we go back to the simplify-1 phase. Otherwise we restore the results of the previous iteration and exit the loop. Practically, we should limit the maximum number of iterations because of the increase in the compilation time. We also confirm the improvement at the end of the graph coloring register allocation as shown in the bottom of Figure 4. Although this method does not guarantee to find the best number of iterations, it allows coloring-based coalescing to always succeed in coloring a graph that is colorable by the original graph coloring algorithm.

5. **Clear**: Before exiting or continuing the loop, we clear the colors of the nodes because the colors themselves do not matter on the changed interference graph.

Coloring-based coalescing does not distinguish a precolored node from a non-precolored one. We coalesce non-precolored and precolored nodes when they are copy-related and when the former is assigned the same color as the latter by the trial coloring.

The algorithm of coloring-based coalescing is simple. Although we illustrate the first trial coloring and the next graph coloring register allocation as separate phases, in fact we only need to iterate coloring. Except for the last iteration, after the coloring we coalesce the copy-related nodes that are assigned the same color. In the last iteration, we generate the spill instructions for any nodes that are assigned to extended colors. Our implementation of coloring-based coalescing is based on a Briggs-style allocator, but the rationale behind coloring-based coalescing is effective for other graph coloring register allocators whose heuristics are based on interference degrees.

The spatial complexity of our coalescing is the same as that of iterated coalescing. It requires a list of the coalescable pairs of copy-related nodes. The temporal complexity is the sum of the time to scan the list for coalescing and the complexity of graph coloring register allocation. The overhead of using extended colors is negligible in practice.

4.3 Example

Figure 5(a) shows the results of the trial coloring using real colors R1 and R2 plus an extended color R101. This is the same as the result in Figure 3 except for the use of the extended color. Based

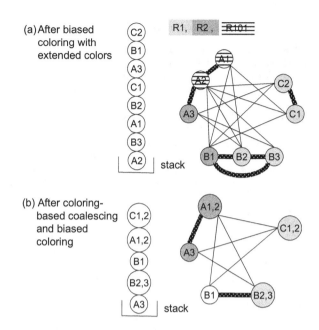

Figure 5. Results of coloring-based coalescing

on this trial coloring, we coalesce three groups of copy-related nodes that are assigned the same color: A1 and A2; B2 and B3; and C1 and C2. Thus they are companion nodes. The new nodes have the sum of the spill costs of the coalesced nodes because each node before coalescing corresponds to a single use and thus each new node represents two uses in the original program shown in Figure 2(a). Note that in general the cost of a new node may not be the sum of the costs of the coalesced nodes but depends on the splitting algorithm used. Figure 5(b) shows the final results of the register allocation. A3 or B1 is randomly chosen first to be pushed onto the stack because they have the same spill cost and the same interference degree. Whichever is chosen first, we reach the same results, which are the optimal coloring of the graph.

This example shows how coloring-based coalescing reveals sub-ranges to be coalesced. The key to obtaining a good coloring in this example is to coalesce A1 and A2 and not to coalesce B1 with B2 or B3. Iterated coalescing cannot do anything here because it must guarantee the colorability of the coalesced nodes by taking account of their degrees. In contrast, coloring-based coalescing discovers that A1 and A2 share common interference neighbors and no other neighbors prevent them from being assigned the same color. For B1, B2, and B3, although they share a common neighbor A2, other neighbors force them to be assigned different colors. That is, B1 interferes with C2, C2 with A3, and A3 with B2 and B3. This interference chain means that coalescing of B1 with B2 or B3 creates a new triangle, which is not two-colorable. Coloring-based coalescing can sense the danger of the coalescing from the fact that they are assigned different colors.

In summary, coloring-based coalescing is more powerful than iterated coalescing because it can perform coalescing regardless of the interference degrees. When compared with optimistic coalescing, coloring-based coalescing is more effective because it can optimize the shape of an interference graph before the simplify-2 phase. It is often too late to optimize coloring in the final select phase.

Program	Number of frequently executed methods	Without live-range splitting			With forward-and-reverse-SSA live-range splitting
		Total number of nodes in frequently executed methods	Total number of spilled nodes with 8 registers (percentage of spill)	Total number of spilled nodes with 16 registers (percentage of spill)	Total number of nodes in frequently executed methods
_201_compress	4	603	131 (21.7%)	36 (6.0%)	1345
_202_jess	8	1608	223 (13.9%)	96 (6.0%)	5711
_209_db	5	309	65 (21.0%)	20 (6.5%)	1198
_213_javac	10	1423	207 (14.6%)	62 (4.4%)	5641
_222_mpegaudio	12	1307	390 (29.8%)	195 (14.9%)	2500
_227_mtrt	13	2224	341 (15.3%)	194 (8.7%)	10878
_228_jack	32	2878	29 (1.0%)	10 (0.3%)	4147
hsqldb	127	7496	784 (10.5%)	205 (2.7%)	21598
luindex	38	2623	465 (17.7%)	137 (5.2%)	7589

Table 1. Characteristics of the benchmark programs

4.4 Conservativeness of Coloring-based Coalescing

We calculate the upper bound of the chromatic number of the coalesced graph to show the worst case for our algorithm.

THEOREM 1. *The chromatic number of the graph G″ that results from coalescing companion nodes of the graph G′ that was generated by splitting nodes in a graph G is less than or equal to the chromatic number of G or the number of colors used in the trial coloring of G′, whichever is smaller.*

PROOF. We use the fact that splitting never increases the chromatic number. Since we limit coalescing to copy-related nodes, we can reach G″ from G by splitting. Thus the chromatic number of G″ is less than or equal to that of G. Let H be the graph that results from coalescing into one node all of the nodes that are assigned the same color by the trial coloring. The chromatic number of H is less than or equal to the number of colors used in the trial coloring. Since we can reach G″ from H by splitting, the chromatic number of G″ is less than or equal to the number of colors used in the trial coloring. Q.E.D.

The theoretical effectiveness of the algorithm is an open question: on what kind of graphs does the coalescing of companion nodes definitely reduce the total spill cost?

5. Experiments

5.1 Implementation

We implemented coloring-based coalescing in IBM J9/TR 2.4 [11], a Java™ VM with an advanced Just-In-Time (JIT) compiler. Note that our algorithm was not designed specifically for use in a JIT compiler. We used the JIT compiler mainly because it is our compiler infrastructure. In order to get stable results from run to run, we did not use the execution frequency profile of basic blocks in the compiler. For spill cost calculations, we multiplied the spill costs of definitions and uses in a loop by ten. This is common heuristics as in [2][7]. In addition, the cost was set to zero if a definition or a use was on a path that is statically regarded as a rare path, such as backup code for a devirtualized method call. We call the cost calculated in this way a *static cost*.

Our JIT compiler performs aggressive inlining first and then eliminates redundancy by value numbering and partial redundancy elimination. It also unrolls frequently executed loops. In-

struction scheduling is performed twice, before and after the register allocation.

We implemented a Briggs-style graph coloring register allocator as our baseline register allocator. It is equipped with biased coloring and iterated coalescing with the full Briggs and George tests [14]. Therefore, our coloring-based coalescing uses iterated coalescing both in the trial coloring and in the actual register allocation. The baseline allocator performs spill coalescing and spill propagation [17] as post optimizations. We also implemented optimistic coalescing including copy graph optimization [19], which has a function similar to spill propagation.

We mainly show the results of using forward-and-reverse-SSA live range splitting [5] because it can effectively split live ranges around a loop. We also implemented splitting at every basic block boundary to present the effectiveness of our algorithm. Our coalescing implementations do not distinguish copies introduced by the splitting from the other copies. Even when live-range splitting is turned off, our baseline register allocator uses iterated coalescing to remove copies that exist in an original program or that are introduced by other compiler optimizations.

5.2 Evaluation

We used all seven programs in SPECjvm98 [21] and two larger programs in the DaCapo [9] benchmarks. We ran the benchmarks on an IBM System z9 2094 [15] with four 64-bit processors and 8 GB of RAM. We used a 1-GB Java heap. The machine has sixteen integer registers and sixteen floating-point registers. We also simulated an eight-register architecture by using only eight integer and eight floating point registers. Since three integer registers are reserved for special purposes, thirteen out of sixteen and five out of eight integer registers can be used for register allocation.

For execution performance, we ran each program (e.g. _201_compress) sequentially twenty times in a Java VM process and chose the run with the shortest execution time. We used the shortest time to exclude JIT compilation time from the execution time. We confirmed that JIT compilation ended early in the sequential runs. We invoked the sequential runs four times for each program and report the averages of the shortest execution times.

We summarize the characteristics about the benchmark programs in Table 1. The second column shows the number of frequently executed methods in each program. In the following results except for execution performance, we show the total statistics for these hot methods alone rather than the entire program, because a Java program executes many non-application methods during initialization. The third column is the total numbers of

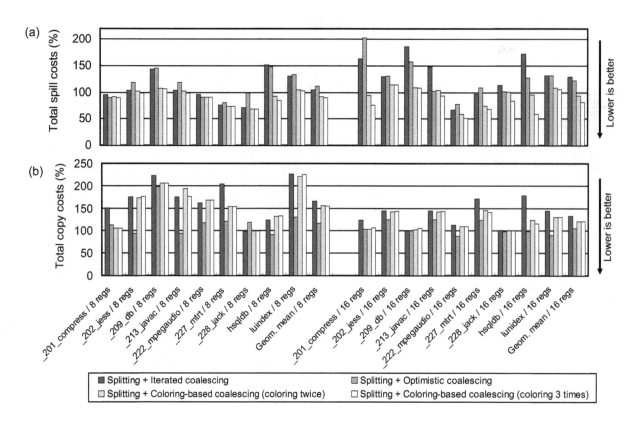

Figure 6. Comparison of (a) total static spill costs and (b) total static copy costs
for frequently executed methods in the benchmark programs (100% = Register allocation w/o splitting)

nodes (including precolored ones) when live-range splitting is not used. Note that the spill costs of these nodes significantly differ from one another, depending on where and how many times the corresponding variables appear in the methods. The fourth and fifth columns show the total numbers of spilled nodes when eight and sixteen registers are used, respectively. We also include in parentheses the percentages of the spilled nodes among all of the nodes. The numbers of frequently executed methods for _208_jack, hsqldb, and luindex are larger than for the other programs, but they mostly exhibit low register pressure because they contain few computationally complex methods in their frequently executed paths. The sixth column is the numbers of nodes when the forward-and-reverse-SSA live range splitting is used. The splitting results in 2.9 times more nodes on average than the case without splitting.

In the following results, the baseline is the graph coloring register allocation without live-range splitting. With forward-and-reverse-SSA live-range splitting turned on, we compared iterated coalescing, optimistic coalescing, and our coloring-based coalescing. All the results are normalized to the results of the graph coloring allocation without splitting. For coloring-based coalescing, we experimented with no iteration and the maximum iteration of one for the inner loop of Figure 4. Note that the no iteration and one iteration actually execute coloring twice (one for coalescing and the other for actual register allocation) and 3 times at maximum, respectively. Thus we name them "coloring-based coalescing (coloring twice)" and "coloring-based coalescing (coloring 3 times)."

We first show the total static costs of spill instructions. Figure 6(a) is the results for the eight-register case on the left hand side and for sixteen registers. Note that a spill instruction in a loop is weighted by ten in the spill cost calculation. The combination of live-range splitting and our coloring-based coalescing (coloring twice) successfully reduced the total static spill costs on average by 8% with eight registers and by 6% with sixteen registers, compared with the baseline register allocation. Coloring-based coalescing (coloring 3 times) reduced the costs on average by 10% and by 18%, respectively. The large reductions are mostly due to removing spill instructions from loops. Iterated coalescing and optimistic coalescing did not reduce the total static spill costs on average, when combined with the live-range splitting. In several methods, they increased the cost by more than 50%. In contrast, coloring-based coalescing increased the cost by up to 14%. Contrary to our expectations, optimistic coalescing did not perform well in combination with live-range splitting, because it can assign only one color to sub-ranges of a spilled live range.

When we increased the maximum times for coloring, we observed consistently better results for the total static spill costs as shown in Figure 6(a). However, we found that even coloring 3 times was sometimes more than needed for some methods. These results indicate that we do not need to iterate coloring-based coalescing many times to get reasonable improvements.

Even when we used basic-block-based splitting instead of SSA-based splitting, coloring-based coalescing (coloring twice) achieved 31% reduction in the total static spill costs on sixteen registers compared with iterated coalescing, and 22% with opti-

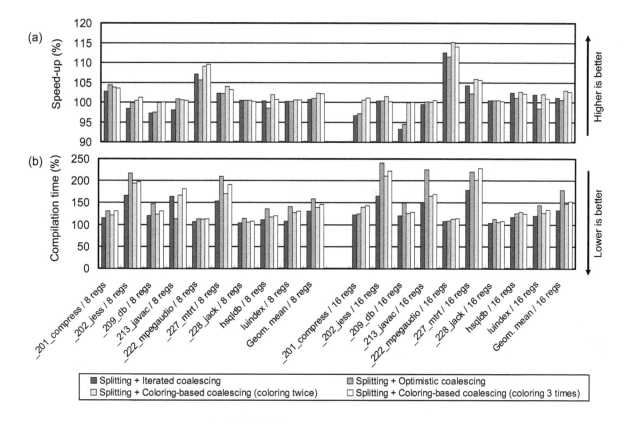

Figure 7. Comparison of (a) execution time speed-up for the benchmark programs (not including compilation time) and (b) compilation time for frequently executed methods in the benchmark programs. (100% = Register allocation w/o splitting)

mistic coalescing. Thus coloring-based coalescing is effective for different splitting algorithms.

When comparing the eight-register and sixteen-register results in Figure 6(a), we saw smaller increases or decreases in the relative costs with eight registers. This is because when only eight registers are available, there are many inevitable spill instructions that none of the coalescing algorithms can remove.

Figure 6(b) shows the total static costs of copy instructions. The copies include those from splitting, from other compiler optimizations, and from the original program source code. The combination of live-range splitting and coloring-based coalescing increased the copy cost by 56% and 21% on average with eight and sixteen registers, respectively. Coloring-based coalescing generally worked better than iterated coalescing. Optimistic coalescing is an effective technique to reduce copies, but it cannot effectively reduce the spills as shown in Figure 6(a). In general, more copies remained unremoved with eight registers than with sixteen registers because the registers were more restricted.

Figure 7(a) is the execution performance results. Coloring-based coalescing (coloring twice) achieved 2.5% speed-up on average and 9% speed-up at maximum, compared with the eight-register baseline. With sixteen registers, the speed-up was 3% on average and 15% at maximum. The speed-up in _222_mpegaudio resulted from the reduction in spill instructions in the innermost loop of hot methods. For most of these programs, it delivered better performance than iterated and optimistic coalescing. The average speed-up over the best of the existing algorithms was 1.5% with eight registers and 2% with sixteen registers. The existing algorithms degraded performance by more than 2% in several

programs, while coloring-based coalescing showed at least the same performance as the baseline without splitting. Coloring-based coalescing (coloring 3 times) did not always perform better than coloring twice, because we did not use execution profile to estimate spill costs. The fact that the increase or decrease in the static costs in Figure 6(a) was not always reflected in the execution time in Figure 7(a) indicates that we need more sophisticated methods to predict runtime costs. Overall, coloring-based coalescing performs well with both eight and sixteen registers.

Figure 7(b) shows the compilation time for each program, including time spent in live-range splitting, coalescing, and register allocation. The combination of live-range splitting and coloring-based coalescing (coloring twice) increased the compilation time by 39% and 47% over the baseline when using eight and sixteen registers, respectively. To evaluate the overhead of the iterations of graph coloring, one should note the difference between coloring-based coalescing and iterated coalescing, which is 8% to 14% on average. In _202_jess and _227_mtrt, there were a few methods for which the number of nodes exploded due to splitting, causing the compilation time to increase regardless of the coalescing algorithms. The compilation time also depended on how many times the coloring algorithm iterated the loop in Figure 1(a) or the outer loop in Figure 4. For example in hsqldb with 16 registers, coloring-based coalescing with coloring 3 times took slightly less compilation time than with coloring twice, because it iterated the outer loop a fewer number of times in some methods.

6. Related Work

Hack et al. [13] proved that the colorability of a program in SSA form can be determined by the maximum number of simultaneously live variables. They also presented a quadratic-time optimal coloring algorithm for a SSA-program. This means that SSA-based live-range splitting leads to optimal register allocation for a colorable SSA-program. However, if the program is not colorable, they only provided greedy heuristics for spilling. Among the 249 hot methods we described in Section 5, 125 methods have the number of simultaneously live variables larger than five, which is the number of available physical registers in the eight-register configuration. Even in the sixteen-register configuration, 63 methods including most of the SPECjvm98 methods (except for _228_jack) have more than thirteen simultaneously live variables. Thus coloring-based coalescing can help reduce spills in these methods. Hack et al. [12] also proposed a safe coalescing algorithm for their SSA-based register allocation. The purpose of their algorithm is not to reduce spills but to reduce register-to-register copies at splitting points.

Vegdahl [20] proposed node merging to improve graph coloring register allocation. The technique maintains a pair-score for each pair of nodes, which is the ratio of the number of common interference neighbors to the total number of neighbors in the smaller-degree node. It coalesces high-pair-score nodes when there remain only significant-degree nodes in the simplify phase. It has a similarity to coloring-based coalescing in that it focuses on a node pair that has many common interference neighbors. However, it often results in overly aggressive coalescing because it does not reflect the colorability of the coalesced nodes. In contrast, coloring-based coalescing takes advantage of the trial coloring and takes account of factors that can prevent the pair from receiving the same color.

Nakaike et al. [18] proposed two-phase register allocation to be used after live-range splitting. The first phase is to spill subranges in high-register-pressure regions and also to coalesce subranges on hot paths. The second phase is the graph coloring register allocation. It is similar to coloring-based coalescing in that it performs pre-allocation and coalescing before the actual register allocation. However, it heavily relies on an execution profile, while coloring-based coalescing does not.

Appel et al. [1] used integer linear programming to find out optimal splitting points. Their approach spills variables to make no more than K variables simultaneously live at any point, where K is the number of physical registers. It does not necessarily compute a globally optimal solution, despite the fact that it requires an ILP solver in a compiler. Our coloring-based coalescing provides a reasonable reduction in spill costs by taking advantage of the existing coloring algorithm in a register allocator.

Bouchez et al. pointed out [4] that the power of iterated coalescing is limited because they can only coalesce pairs of nodes at one time. It is often the case that a better interference graph cannot be reached without coalescing a group of nodes at once. Coloring-based coalescing is effective because it can coalesce all of the copy-related nodes with the same color at one step. Bouchez et al. also proposed [3] advanced conservative and optimistic coalescing algorithms. Their purpose is to reduce register-to-register copies when coloring a greedy-k-colorable graph. Specifically, they proposed chordal-based incremental coalescing, which can merge a group of nodes at once along a "path" of non-interfering nodes in an interval graph. However, it is not clear whether or not those algorithms help reduce spills in a general non-k-colorable graph.

7. Conclusions

In this paper, we proposed a new coalescing algorithm called coloring-based coalescing. It first performs a trial coloring with an extended number of colors and then coalesces all of the copy-related nodes that are assigned the same color, which we call companion nodes. After the coalescing, all colors are cleared, and the actual graph coloring register allocation is performed. Companion nodes are worth coalescing because they share common interference neighbors and do not have other neighbors that would make the coalesced nodes uncolorable. To the best of our knowledge, this is the first coalescing alogrithm to strengthen the combined power of live-range splitting and graph coloring register allocation by focusing on companion nodes. It is simple because it utilizes the existing graph coloring function of a register allocator. Experiments on Java programs using sixteen registers showed that the combination of live-range splitting and coloring-based coalescing reduced the total static cost of spill instructions by more than 6% on average, comparing to the baseline coloring allocation without splitting. On the other hand, well-known iterated and optimistic coalescing algorithms increased the total static cost by more than 20%, when combined with splitting. Coloring-based coalescing improved the execution time by up to 15% and 3% on average, whereas iterated and optimistic coalescing improved by up to 12% and 1% on average. We also conducted experiments using only eight registers. Coloring-based coalescing provided up to 9% and on average 2.5% speed-up, which were larger than 7% maximum and 1% average speed-up by the existing coalescing algorithms.

Acknowledgments

We thank the members of the Systems group in IBM Research - Tokyo, who gave us valuable suggestions. We are also grateful to anonymous reviewers for providing us with helpful comments.

References

[1] Appel, A. W. and George, L. Optimal spilling for CISC machines with few registers. In *Proceedings of the ACM SIGPLAN 2001 Conference on Programming Language Design and Implementation*, pages 243-253, June 2001.

[2] Bernstein, D., Golumbic, M. C., Mansour, Y., Pinter, R. Y., Goldin, D. Q., Krawczyk, H., and Nahshon, I. Spill code minimization techniques for optimizing compilers, In *Proceedings of the ACM SIGPLAN 1989 Conference on Programming Language Design and Implementation*, pages 258-263, July 1989

[3] Bouchez, F., Darte, A., and Rastello, F. Advanced conservative and optimistic register coalescing. In *Proceedings of the 2008 International Conference on Compilers, Architectures and Synthesis for Embedded Systems*, pages 147-156, 2008.

[4] Bouchez, F., Darte, A., and Rastello, F. On the complexity of register coalescing. In *Proceedings of the International Symposium on Code Generation and Optimization* 2007, pages 102-114, March 2007.

[5] Briggs, P. Register Allocation via Graph Coloring. PhD thesis, Rice University, April 1992.

[6] Briggs, P., Cooper, K. D., and Torczon, L. Improvements to graph coloring register allocation. *ACM Transactions on Programming Languages and Systems*, Vol. 16, No. 3, pages 428- 455, May 1994.

[7] Chaitin, G. J. Register allocation and spilling via graph coloring. In *Proceedings of the ACM SIGPLAN 1982 Symposium on Compiler Construction*, pages 201-207, SIGPLAN Notices Vol. 17, No. 6, pages 98-105, June 1982.

[8] Chaitin, G. J., Auslander, M. A., Chandra, A. K., Cocke, J., Hopkins, M. E., and Markstein, P. W. Register allocation via coloring. *Computer Languages*, Vol. 6, No. 1, pages 47-57, January 1981.

[9] DaCapo Benchmarks, http://dacapobench.org/.

[10] George, L. and Appel, A. W. Iterated register coalescing. *ACM Transactions on Programming Languages and System*s, Vol. 18, No. 3, pages 300-324, May 1996.

[11] Grcevski, N., Kilstra, A., Stoodley, K., Stoodley, M., and Sundaresan, V. Java just-in-time compiler and virtual machine improvements for server and middleware applications. In *Proceedings of the 3rd Virtual Machine Research and Technology Symposium*, pages 151-162, May, 2004.

[12] Hack, S. and Goos, G. Copy coalescing by graph recoloring. In *Proceedings of the ACM SIGPLAN 2008 Conference on Programming Language Design and Implementation*, pages 227-237, June 2008.

[13] Hack, S., Grund, D., and Goos, G. Register allocation for programs in SSA-form. In *International Conference on Compiler Construction (CC'06)*, Vol. 3923 of LNCS, pages 247-262, Springer Verlag, 2006.

[14] Hailperin, M. Comparing conservative coalescing criteria. *ACM Transactions on Programming Languages and Systems*, Vol. 27, No. 3, pages 571-582, May 2005.

[15] IBM System z9. IBM Journal of Research and Development Vol. 51, Number 1/2, 2007.

[16] Kolte, P. and Harrold, M. J. Load/store range analysis for global register allocation. In *Proceedings of the ACM SIGPLAN 1994 Conference on Programming Language Design and Implementation*, pages 268-277, June 1993.

[17] Leung, A. and George, L. A new MLRISC register allocator. *Standard ML of New Jersey compiler implementation notes*, 1998.

[18] Nakaike, T., Inagaki, T., Komatsu, H., and Nakatani, T. Profile-based global live-range splitting. In *Proceedings the ACM SIGPLAN 2006 Conference on Programming Language Design and Implementation*, pages 216-227, June 2006.

[19] Park, J. and Moon, S. Optimistic Register Coalescing. *ACM Transactions on Programming Languages and Systems*, Vol. 26, No. 4, pages 735-765, July 2004.

[20] Vegdahl, S. R. Using node merging to enhance graph coloring. In *Proceedings of the ACM SIGPLAN 1999 Conference on Programming Language Design and Implementation*, pages150-154, May 1999.

[21] Standard Performance Evaluation Corporation. SPECjvm98 Benchmarks, http://www.spec.org/osg/jvm98/.

Linear Scan Register Allocation on SSA Form

Christian Wimmer   Michael Franz

Department of Computer Science
University of California, Irvine
{cwimmer, franz}@uci.edu

Abstract

The linear scan algorithm for register allocation provides a good register assignment with a low compilation overhead and is thus frequently used for just-in-time compilers. Although most of these compilers use static single assignment (SSA) form, the algorithm has not yet been applied on SSA form, i.e., SSA form is usually deconstructed before register allocation. However, the structural properties of SSA form can be used to simplify the algorithm.

With only one definition per variable, lifetime intervals (the main data structure) can be constructed without data flow analysis. During allocation, some tests of interval intersection can be skipped because SSA form guarantees non-intersection. Finally, deconstruction of SSA form after register allocation can be integrated into the resolution phase of the register allocator without much additional code.

We modified the linear scan register allocator of the Java HotSpot™ client compiler so that it operates on SSA form. The evaluation shows that our simpler and faster version generates equally good or slightly better machine code.

Categories and Subject Descriptors   D.3.4 [*Programming Languages*]: Processors—Compilers, Optimization, Code generation

General Terms   Algorithms, Languages, Performance

Keywords   Java, just-in-time compilation, register allocation, linear scan, SSA form, lifetime analysis, SSA form deconstruction

1.   Introduction

Register allocation, i.e., the task of assigning processor registers to local variables and temporary values, is one of the most important compiler optimizations. A vast amount of research has led to algorithms ranging from simple and fast heuristics to optimal algorithms with exponential time complexity. Because the problem is known to be NP-complete [8], algorithms must balance the time necessary for allocation against the resulting code quality. Two common algorithms in modern compilers are *graph coloring* (see for example [5, 8]), which is suitable when compilation time is not a major concern, and *linear scan* [22, 28], which is faster and therefore frequently used for just-in-time compilers where compilation time adds to run time.

Static single assignment (SSA) form [9] is a type of intermediate representation that simplifies many compiler optimizations. All variables have only a single point of definition. At control flow joins, *phi functions* are used to merge different variables of the predecessor blocks. Because processors cannot execute phi functions, it is necessary to replace them with move instructions during code generation (*SSA form deconstruction*).

Traditionally, SSA form deconstruction was performed before register allocation. Only recently has it been observed that register allocation on SSA form has several advantages due to additional guarantees on variable lifetime. Lifetime information is essential for register allocation because two variables that interfere, i.e., that are live at the same time, must not have the same register assigned. The interference graph of a program in SSA form is *chordal* (every cycle with four or more edges has an edge connecting two vertices of the cycle, leading to a triangulated structure).

Many graph algorithms are simpler on chordal graphs, e.g., graph coloring can be performed in polynomial time. These properties were used to simplify register allocators based on graph coloring [14]. When the maximum register pressure is below or equal to the number of available registers, allocation is guaranteed to succeed. This allows to split the algorithms for spilling and register assignment. Traditionally, spilling and register assignment were interleaved, i.e., a variable was spilled when the graph turned out to be not colorable. This led to a time-consuming repeated execution of the graph coloring algorithm.

This paper explores the impact of SSA form on linear scan register allocation. The *lifetime intervals*, which are the basic data structure of the algorithm, are easier to construct and have a simpler structure. Additionally, infrastructure already present in the linear scan algorithm can be used to perform SSA form deconstruction after register allocation, thus making a separate SSA form deconstruction algorithm unnecessary.

Our implementation for the Java HotSpot™ client compiler shows that SSA form leads to a simpler and faster linear scan algorithm. It generates the same or even better code than the current product version that deconstructs SSA form before register allocation. In summary, this paper contributes the following:

- We show how SSA form affects the lifetime intervals used by the linear scan algorithm.

- We present an algorithm for constructing lifetime intervals that does not require data flow analysis. The algorithm can also be adapted to construct the interference graph for graph coloring register allocation.

- We show how to use SSA form properties during allocation.

- We integrate SSA form deconstruction into the resolution phase of the linear scan algorithm.

- We evaluate the algorithm using the Java HotSpot™ client compiler.

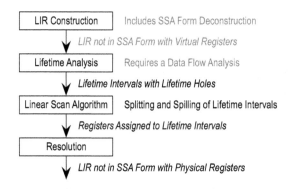

Figure 1. Linear scan register allocation not on SSA form.

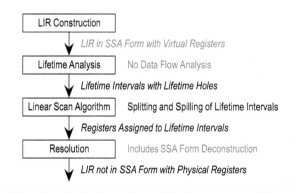

Figure 2. Linear scan register allocation on SSA form.

2. Overview

The linear scan algorithm is used for register allocation in many major compilers, e.g., the client compiler of the Java HotSpot™ VM [11, 16], the optimizing compiler of the Jikes RVM [1], and the compiler of the Low Level Virtual Machine (LLVM) [17]. All implementations use different heuristics to make the algorithm fast and to produce good machine code, but none operate on SSA form. However, all three compilers use SSA form for global optimizations, so all provide the necessary infrastructure for SSA-form-based register allocation.

We use our previous work on linear scan register allocation for the Java HotSpot™ client compiler [30] as the baseline for this study. The client compiler is a production-quality just-in-time compiler and thus highly tuned both for compilation speed and code quality. Its source code is available as open source from the OpenJDK project [27]. Implementation details of the linear scan register allocator are available from [29].

The front end of the client compiler first parses Java bytecodes [18] and constructs the high-level intermediate representation (HIR), which is in SSA form. Several optimizations are performed on the HIR, including constant folding, global value numbering, method inlining, and null-check elimination. The back end translates the HIR into the low-level intermediate representation (LIR). It is not in SSA form in the current product version, so the translation includes SSA form deconstruction.

The LIR is register based. At first, most operands are virtual registers. Only register constraints of the target architecture are modeled using physical registers in the initial LIR. Before register allocation, the control flow graph is flattened to a list of blocks. The register allocator replaces all virtual registers with physical registers, thereby inserting code for spilling registers to the stack if more values are simultaneously live than registers are available. This is accomplished by splitting lifetime intervals, which requires a resolution phase after register allocation to insert move instructions at control flow edges. There is no distinction between local variables and temporary values, they are all uniformly represented as virtual registers. After register allocation, each LIR operation is translated to one or more machine instructions, whereby most LIR operations require only one machine instruction. Figure 1 shows the compiler phases of the current product version that are relevant for register allocation.

Figure 2 illustrates the changes necessary for SSA-form-based register allocation. SSA form is no longer deconstructed before register allocation. Additionally, construction of lifetime intervals is simplified because no data flow analysis is necessary. The main linear scan algorithm remains mostly unchanged, but still benefits from some SSA form properties. If SSA form is no longer required after register allocation, as in our implementation, SSA form de-

construction can be easily integrated into the already existing resolution phase.

Moving out of SSA form after register allocation is reasonable because register allocation is usually one of the last global optimizations, so SSA form would not be beneficial afterwards. However, it would also be possible to maintain SSA form, which requires the insertion of new phi functions for variables whose lifetime intervals were split. The standard algorithm for SSA form construction [9] can be used for this.

3. Lifetime Intervals and SSA Form

Our variant of the linear scan algorithm requires exact lifetime information: The lifetime interval of a virtual register must cover all parts where this register is needed, with lifetime holes in between. Lifetime holes occur because the control flow graph is reduced to a list of blocks before register allocation. If a register flows into an `else`-block, but not into the corresponding `if`-block, the lifetime interval has a hole for the `if`-block. In contrast, a register defined before a loop and used inside the loop must be live in all blocks of the loop, even blocks after the last use.

The lifetime intervals resulting from phi functions have characteristic patterns. When SSA form is deconstructed before register allocation, move instructions are inserted at the end of a phi function's predecessor blocks. This leads to a lifetime interval with multiple definition points and lifetime holes before these definitions. SSA form deconstruction inserts the moves in a certain order. While there are some constraints for the order in cases where the same register is both used and defined by phi functions of the same block, the order is mostly arbitrary.

Figure 3(c) shows the lifetime intervals for the LIR fragment (computing the factorial of a number) shown in Figure 3(a). Four blocks B1 to B4 use six virtual registers R10 to R15. Assume that R10 and R11 are defined in B1, and that R10 and R12 are used in B4. R10 represents a long-living value that is infrequently used but still alive, e.g., the `this` pointer of a Java method. The LIR operations 20 to 42 (numbers are incremented by two for technical reasons) are arithmetic and control flow operations that use up to two input operands (either virtual registers or constants) and define up to one output operand (a virtual register).

The registers R12 and R13 represent the original phi functions, and the registers R14 and R15 represent the new values assigned to the phi functions at the end of the loop. Therefore, R12 and R13 have the characteristic lifetime intervals i12 and i13 in Figure 3(c) (virtual registers and intervals use matching numbers). Interval i12 is defined by the operations 20 and 36. Because the definition at 36 overwrites the previous value without using it, there is a lifetime hole before this operation, starting at the last use at operation 32. The intervals i12 and i13 have a similar structure, only i12 ex-

```
       define R10 and R11
20: move 1 -> R12
22: move R11 -> R13                  define R10 and R11
24: label B2                     20: label B2
26: cmp R13, 1                       phi [1, R14] -> R12
28: branch lessThan B4               phi [R11, R15] -> R13
                                 22: cmp R13, 1
30: label B3                     24: branch lessThan B4
32: mul R12, R13 -> R14
34: sub R13, 1 -> R15            26: label B3
36: move R14 -> R12             28: mul R12, R13 -> R14
38: move R15 -> R13             30: sub R13, 1 -> R15
40: jump B2                      32: jump B2
42: label B4                     34: label B4
      use R10 and R12                  use R10 and R12
```

(a) LIR without SSA form   (b) LIR with SSA form

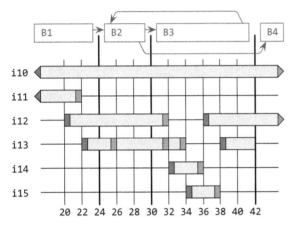

(c) Lifetime intervals without SSA form

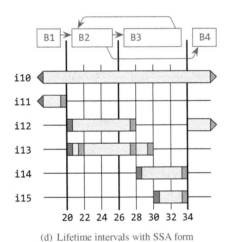

(d) Lifetime intervals with SSA form

Figure 3. Example of LIR and lifetime intervals.

tends after operation 42 because R12 is used somewhere later in block B4. Note that although the interval i12 is contiguous from B3 to B4, there is no direct control flow possible between these two blocks.

Building lifetime intervals directly from LIR in SSA form changes the pattern of the intervals. All phi functions at the beginning of a block have *parallel copy* semantics, i.e., they are not

ordered. All phi functions together specify a permutation of registers and not a list of copies. Therefore, it would be counterproductive to assign individual operation numbers to them; we just attach them to the block label. The lifetime interval for the virtual register defined by a phi function starts directly at the beginning of the block. The lifetime intervals for the virtual registers used by a phi function end at the end of the corresponding predecessor blocks (as long as the virtual registers are not used by other operations after the phi function).

Figure 3(b) and Figure 3(d) show the LIR and the lifetime intervals of our example when using SSA form. The two phi functions of block B2 are attached to operation 20. Therefore, the lifetime intervals i12 and i13 both start at position 20. The linear scan algorithm, which processes intervals ordered by their start position, can freely decide which interval to process first, i.e., in cases of high register pressure it can better decide which intervals to spill at this position. Interval i13 no longer has a lifetime hole. Interval i12 still requires a lifetime hole because the value is live at the beginning of B4 but not at the end of B3, however the lifetime hole ends at a block boundary.

These patterns of lifetime intervals show two advantages when performing linear scan register allocation on SSA form: (1) No artificial order is imposed for moves resulting from phi functions, resulting in more freedom for the register allocator. (2) The lifetime intervals for phi functions have fewer lifetime holes, leading to less state changes of the intervals during allocation.

Note that both with and without SSA form, no coalescing of non-overlapping lifetime intervals is performed. Without SSA form, i.e., in the current product version, it would be too slow and complicated. With SSA form, it is not allowed because it would violate SSA form. In both cases, *register hints* are used as a lightweight replacement. Intervals that should be assigned the same physical register are connected via a register hint. The linear scan allocator honors this hint if possible, but is still allowed to assign different registers. The source and target of a move are connected with such a hint. With SSA form, the input and result operands of a phi function are also connected. In our example, the intervals i11, i13, and i15 are connected, as well as the intervals i12 and i14. In this small example, the register hints lead to machine code without any move instructions, both with and without SSA form.

4. Lifetime Analysis

Traditionally, lifetime information has been computed using an iterative data flow analysis that is repeated until a stable fixed-point is reached. Using properties guaranteed by SSA form in combination with a special block order allows us to eliminate the data flow analysis. With SSA form, each virtual register has a single point of definition. This definition is "before" all uses, i.e., the definition dominates all uses [7]. If the definition and a use are in different blocks, this means that the block of the definition is a dominator of the block of the use.

The linear scan algorithm does not operate on a structured control flow graph, but on a linear list of blocks. The block order has a high impact on the quality and speed of linear scan: A good block order leads to short lifetime intervals with few holes. Our block order guarantees the following properties: First, all predecessors of a block are located before this block, with the exception of backward edges of loops. This implies that all dominators of a block are located before this block. Secondly, all blocks that are part of the same loop are contiguous, i.e., there is no non-loop block between two loop blocks. Even though the current product version of the client compiler's linear scan algorithm could operate on any block order, this order turned out to be best.

BUILDINTERVALS
```
for each block b in reverse order do
    live = union of successor.liveIn for each successor of b

    for each phi function phi of successors of b do
        live.add(phi.inputOf(b))

    for each opd in live do
        intervals[opd].addRange(b.from, b.to)

    for each operation op of b in reverse order do
        for each output operand opd of op do
            intervals[opd].setFrom(op.id)
            live.remove(opd)
        for each input operand opd of op do
            intervals[opd].addRange(b.from, op.id)
            live.add(opd)

    for each phi function phi of b do
        live.remove(phi.output)

    if b is loop header then
        loopEnd = last block of the loop starting at b
        for each opd in live do
            intervals[opd].addRange(b.from, loopEnd.to)

    b.liveIn = live
```

Figure 4. Algorithm for construction of lifetime intervals.

4.1 Algorithm

Input of the algorithm:

1. Intermediate representation in SSA form. An operation has input and output operands. Only virtual register operands are relevant for the algorithm.

2. A linear block order where all dominators of a block are before this block, and where all blocks belonging to the same loop are contiguous. All operations of all blocks are numbered using this order.

Output of the algorithm: One lifetime interval for each virtual register, covering operation numbers where this register is alive, and with lifetime holes in between. Thus, a lifetime interval consists of one or more *ranges* of operation numbers.

Figure 4 shows the algorithm. In addition to the input and output data structures, it requires a set of virtual registers, called *liveIn*, for each block. It is used to propagate the virtual registers that are live at the beginning of a block to the block's predecessors. The algorithm requires one linear iteration of all blocks and all operations of each block. The iteration is in reverse order so that all uses of a virtual register are seen before its definition. Therefore, successors of a block are processed before this block. Only for loops, the loop header (which is a successor of the loop end) cannot be processed before the loop end, so loops are handled as a special case.

The initial set of virtual registers that are live at the end of block b is the union of all registers live at the beginning of the successors of b. Additionally, phi functions of the successors contribute to the initial live set. For each phi function, the input operand corresponding to b is added to the live set. For each live register, an initial live range covering the entire block is added. This live range might be shortened later if the definition of the register is encountered.

Next, all operations of b are processed in reverse order. An output operand, i.e., a definition of a virtual register, shortens the current range of the register's lifetime interval; the start position of the first range is set to the current operation. Additionally, the register

is removed from the set of live registers. An input operand, i.e., a use of a virtual register, adds a new range to the lifetime interval (the new range is merged if an overlapping range is present). The new live range starts at the beginning of the block, and again might be shortened later. Additionally, the register is added to the set of live registers.

Phi functions are not processed during this iteration of operations, instead they are iterated separately. Because the live range of a phi function starts at the beginning of the block, it is not necessary to shorten the range for its output operand. The operand is only removed from the set of live registers. The input operands of the phi function are not handled here, because this is done independently when the different predecessors are processed. Thus, neither an input operand nor the output operand of a phi function is live at the beginning of the phi function's block.

The steps described so far are sufficient to create the lifetime intervals for methods without loops. With loops, the intervals are incomplete: When a loop's end block is processed, the loop header has not been processed, so its *liveIn* set is still empty. Therefore, registers that are alive for the entire loop are missing at this time. These registers are known at the time the loop header is processed: All registers live at the beginning of the loop header must be live for the entire loop, because they are defined before the loop and used inside or after it. Using the property that all blocks of a loop are contiguous in the linear block order, it is sufficient to add one live range, spanning the entire loop, for each register that is live at the beginning of the loop header.

Finally, the current set of live registers is saved in the *liveIn* field of the block. Note that *liveIn* is only a temporary data structure. Because the loop handling adds live ranges but does not update *liveIn* sets, they remain incomplete. If the *liveIn* sets were needed by a later compiler phase, a fixup would also be necessary. However, we do not need them later.

4.2 Example

The example shown in Figure 3(b) and Figure 3(d) uses the virtual registers R10 to R15. The algorithm processes the blocks in the order B4, B3, B2, and B1. At the beginning of B4, the registers R10 and R12 are live and therefore in the *liveIn* set of B4. The live ranges of these values for B4 have been added.

The first complete block of the example is B3. The *liveIn* set of its successor B2 is empty since B2 has not been processed yet. B2 has two phi functions, whose operands relevant for B3 are R14 and R15. They are added to the live set, and the initial ranges spanning the entire block B3 are added. When the definitions of R14 and R15 are encountered at operation 28 and 30, respectively, the ranges are shortened to their final starting points. Ranges for R12 and R13 are added, and these two registers are in the *liveIn* set of B3. Note that the live range of R10 for B3 is not yet present.

The initial live set of B2 is the union of *liveIn* of B3 and B4, i.e., it contains R10, R12, and R13. These three registers are live for the entire block. Because R12 and R13 are defined by phi functions of B3, they are removed from the live set when the phi functions are processed, so R10 is the only register live at the beginning of B2. Because B2 is a loop header, the special handling for loops is performed: The *loopEnd* block is B3, so a live range spanning from the beginning of B2 to the end of B3 is added to the interval of R10. This live range is merged with the existing one, resulting in R10 being live contiguously.

Finally, B1 is processed. The register R10 is initially live because it is in the *liveIn* set of the successor B2, and R11 is live because it is the relevant operand for a phi function. Live ranges are added to the intervals of these two registers. The remaining handling of B1 is outside the scope of this example. Figure 3(d) shows the final intervals for the example.

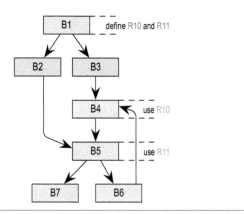

Figure 5. CFG with irreducible loop.

4.3 Irreducible Control Flow

The algorithm presented in the previous sections does not work properly for irreducible loops, i.e., for loops with multiple entry points. Java bytecodes are usually created from structured languages like Java, so irreducible loops do not occur normally. However, since Java bytecodes themselves are unstructured, they are possible with handcrafted bytecodes.

Figure 5 shows such a loop: it can be entered via the blocks B4 and B5. The figure shows definitions and uses of the registers R10 and R11. For R11, the algorithm works correctly: the register is in the *liveIn* sets of B4 and B5 and thus the liveness information is correctly propagated to the blocks B3 and B2. However, the register R10 is only in the *liveIn* set of B4, since it was not yet regarded as live when B5 was processed. It is therefore not considered live in B2, which is erroneous. There are two solutions to handle this problem:

1. Perform a precise loop analysis for irreducible loops that correctly detects all entry blocks. Irreducible loops must be contiguous, i.e., all non-loop blocks leading to a loop entry must be placed before the first loop entry. After all blocks of a loop have been processed by our algorithm, the *liveIn* of all loop headers must be set to the union of the registers flowing into the loop. This solution requires a more complicated loop analysis as well as modifications to our algorithm.

2. Make sure that *no* values flow into an irreducible loop, i.e., that the *liveIn* set of all loop headers is empty. This can be achieved by inserting phi functions at the loop headers for variables that are not modified inside the loop. These phi functions serve as explicit definitions of virtual registers inside the loop.

We use the second solution because the necessary preconditions, the additional phi functions, are already fulfilled by the client compiler. The client compiler uses a conservative SSA form construction algorithm where phi functions are created when they *might* be needed, and unnecessary phi functions are eliminated later. However, they are not eliminated for irreducible loops because this would complicate the elimination algorithm and the additional phi functions are not harmful. This is a good example how the conservative handling of corner cases in multiple parts of the compiler play nicely together.

One special case where irreducible loops occur in practice are methods compiled for *on-stack replacement* (OSR) [10, 15]. In order to switch from the interpreter to compiled code in the middle of a long-running loop, the method is compiled with a special entry point that jumps directly into the middle of the method. This leads to a loop with two entry points. However, since values flowing into

the loop from the normal pre-loop code and from the OSR entry point are completely disjoint, phi functions must always be present. Therefore, OSR methods need no special handling in our register allocator.

4.4 Analogy with Interference Graphs

Our algorithm to build lifetime intervals can be modified to build the interference graph for a graph coloring register allocator in a single pass over the operations. The live sets are managed in the same way. Whenever a definition of a register is encountered, this register interferes with all registers that are currently in the live set. It is sufficient to look at the definition points because SSA form guarantees that two registers that interfere somewhere also interfere at the definition of one of the registers [7]. Again, a special handling is necessary at the loop header: A register live at the loop header interferes with all registers defined inside the loop. It is straightforward to collect all registers defined inside the loop during the iteration of the operations, and to add the interference edges with all registers live at the loop header.

5. Linear Scan Algorithm

The main linear scan algorithm needs no modifications to work on SSA form. Because the algorithm is extensively described in [30], we give only a short summary here. It processes the lifetime intervals sorted by their start position and assigns a register or stack slot to each interval. For this, four sets of intervals are managed: *unhandled* contains the intervals that start after the current position and are therefore not yet of interest; *active* contains the intervals that are live at the current position; *inactive* contains the intervals that start before and end after the current position, but that have a lifetime hole at the current position; and *handled* contains the intervals that end before the current position and are therefore no longer of interest. An interval can switch several times between *active* and *inactive* until it is finally moved to *handled*. If a register is not available for the entire lifetime of an interval, this or another interval is split and spilled to a stack slot, leading to new intervals added to the *unhandled* set during the run of the algorithm. However, the algorithm never backtracks, i.e., all added intervals always start after the current position.

The main part of the linear scan algorithm is the selection of a free register if one is available, or the selection of an interval to be split and spilled if no register is available. Figure 6 shows fragments of these two algorithms. While the original linear scan algorithm [22] was designed to have linear runtime complexity,

---

TRYALLOCATEFREEREG
set *freeUntilPos* of all physical registers to *maxInt*
for each interval *it* in *active* **do**
    freeUntilPos[it.reg] = 0
for each interval *it* in *inactive* intersecting with *current* **do**
    freeUntilPos[it.reg] = next intersection of *it* with *current*
reg = register with highest *freeUntilPos*
...

ALLOCATEBLOCKEDREG
set *nextUsePos* of all physical registers to *maxInt*
for each interval *it* in *active* **do**
    nextUsePos[it.reg] = next use of *it* after start of *current*
for each interval *it* in *inactive* intersecting with *current* **do**
    nextUsePos[it.reg] = next use of *it* after start of *current*
reg = register with highest *nextUsePos*
...

Figure 6. Algorithm for register selection (from [30]).

```
RESOLVE
for each control flow edge from predecessor to successor do
    for each interval it live at begin of successor do
        if it starts at begin of successor then
            phi = phi function defining it
            opd = phi.inputOf(predecessor)
            if opd is a constant then
                moveFrom = opd
            else
                moveFrom = location of intervals[opd] at end of predecessor
        else
            moveFrom = location of it at end of predecessor
        moveTo = location of it at begin of successor
        if moveFrom ≠ moveTo then
            mapping.add(moveFrom, moveTo)

    mapping.orderAndInsertMoves()
```

Figure 7. Algorithm for resolution and SSA form deconstruction.

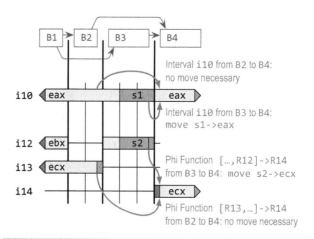

Figure 8. Example for resolution and SSA form deconstruction.

the extensions to support lifetime holes and interval splitting [28, 30] introduced non-linear parts. Two of them are highlighted in Figure 6 where the set of inactive intervals is iterated. The set can contain an arbitrary number of intervals since it is not bound by the number of physical registers. Testing the current interval for intersection with all of them can therefore be expensive.

When the lifetime intervals are created from code in SSA form, this test is not necessary anymore: All intervals in *inactive* start before the current interval, so they do not intersect with the current interval at their definition. They are inactive and thus have a lifetime hole at the current position, so they do not intersect with the current interval at its definition. SSA form therefore guarantees that they never intersect [7], making the entire loop that tests for intersection unnecessary.

Unfortunately, splitting of intervals leads to intervals that no longer adhere to the SSA form properties because it destroys SSA form. Therefore, the intersection test cannot be omitted completely; it must be performed if the current interval has been split off from another interval. In summary, the highlighted parts of Figure 6 can be guarded by a check whether *current* is the result of an interval split, and need not be executed otherwise. For our set of Java benchmarks, this still saves 59% to 79% of all intersection tests.

6. Resolution and SSA Form Deconstruction

Linear scan register allocation with splitting of lifetime intervals requires a *resolution* phase after the actual allocation. Because the control flow graph is reduced to a list of blocks, control flow is possible between blocks that are not adjacent in the list. When the location of an interval is different at the end of the predecessor and at the start of the successor, a move instruction must be inserted to resolve the conflict. The resolving moves for a control flow edge have the same semantics as the moves necessary to resolve phi functions: They must be treated as parallel copies, i.e., a mapping from source to target locations. The only difference is that moves resulting from interval splitting originate from a single interval, while moves resulting from phi functions have different intervals for the source and the target. In both cases, the moves must be ordered properly so that registers holding incoming values are not overwritten with outgoing values.

Adding SSA form deconstruction requires only small extensions to the existing resolution algorithm. Figure 7 shows the entire algorithm. It visits every edge of the control flow graph, connecting a block *predecessor* with a block *successor*, and iterates all intervals that are live at the beginning of *successor*. The algorithm compares the location of the interval at the end of *predecessor* and

the beginning of *successor*. If they are different, a move operation is inserted. Because all moves must be ordered properly, they are first added to a mapping and then ordered and inserted afterwards. This part of the algorithm is not shown because it requires no SSA form specific changes.

Intervals of phi functions of *successor* are live at the beginning of *successor*, but not at the end of *predecessor*. SSA form properties and the block order guarantee that these intervals start at the beginning of *successor*. This guarantee allows for a simple check whether an interval is defined by a phi function. Three steps are necessary to compute the source operand of the move operation that resolves the phi function:

1. the phi function that defined the interval is retrieved,

2. the input operand of the phi function that belongs to block *predecessor* is retrieved, and

3. the interval of this operand is used to add the move operation.

If the input operand is a constant, no interval is present because constants can be directly used as the source of move operations.

Figure 8 shows an example for resolution that is necessary at the edges to block B4. Block B4 has two predecessors, B2 and B3. Two intervals are live at the beginning of B4: i10 and i14. Interval i10 is defined before the beginning of B4 (actually it is defined outside the scope of our example). During register allocation, i10 was split twice. At first, the location is the register eax. In the middle of block B3, it was spilled and thus the location changes to stack slot s1. At the beginning of block B4, it is reloaded to register eax.

Interval i14 (with the assigned register ecx) is defined at the beginning of block B4 by a phi function. Assume that the operands of the phi function are R12 (when coming from block B3) and R13 (when coming from block B2). The according intervals are i12 and i13, respectively. Interval i12 was split in block B3 and thus changes the location there from register ebx to stack slot s2, while interval i13 is always in register ecx. The scenario depicted is realistic in that a method call inside block B3 requires all intervals to be spilled.

First, we look at the control flow edge from B2 to B4. The location of interval i10 at the end of B2 is eax, and at the beginning of B4 is also eax. Thus, no resolving move is necessary. Interval i14 starts at B4. Accessing the corresponding phi function, its input operand for block B2, and the interval for this operand, yields the interval i13. Because the location of i13 and i14 are both ecx, again no resolving move is necessary, and the mapping for this control flow edge remains empty.

175

	SPECjvm2008			SPECjbb2005			DaCapo			SciMark		
	Baseline	SSA Form		Baseline	SSA Form		Baseline	SSA Form		Baseline	SSA Form	
Compilation Statistics												
Compiled Methods	6,788	6,813		521	520		8,242	8,242		23	24	
Compiled Bytecodes [KByte]	1,094	1,098		78	78		2,272	2,275		3.64	3.65	
Avg. Method Size [Byte/Method]	165	165		153	153		282	283		162	156	
Compilation Time [msec.]	4,250	4,080	-4%	287	275	-4%	13,390	12,700	-5%	14.8	13.6	-8%
Back End Time [msec.]	1,170	1,020	-13%	82	71	-13%	2,930	2,460	-16%	4.8	3.9	-19%
Machine Code Size [KByte]	4,581	4,563	-0%	404	401	-1%	11,760	11,719	-0%	14.5	14.3	-1%
Memory Allocation												
Lifetime Analysis [KByte]	65,248	58,877	-10%	5,047	4,559	-10%	171,650	129,794	-24%	270	246	-9%
Allocation and Resolution [KByte]	48,171	48,169	-0%	3,255	3,239	-0%	89,144	88,879	-0%	180	168	-7%
LIR Before Register Allocation												
Moves	203,671	180,640	-11%	15,797	13,644	-14%	402,678	355,936	-12%	908	593	-35%
Phi Functions	0	10,689		0	973		0	20,542		0	168	
LIR After Register Allocation												
Moves Register to Register	55,592	53,856	-3%	4,473	4,245	-5%	127,318	124,351	-2%	193	177	-8%
Moves Constant to Register	35,348	34,612	-2%	3,129	3,028	-3%	71,967	70,663	-2%	99	98	-1%
Moves Stack to Register	4,537	4,550	+0%	335	335	-0%	3,718	3,722	+0%	12	12	0%
Moves Register to Stack	38,715	33,650	-13%	2,636	2,187	-17%	65,973	56,639	-14%	166	158	-5%
Moves Constant to Stack	0	926		0	105		0	1,386		0	1	
Moves Stack to Stack	0	294		0	22		0	647		0	0	

Figure 9. Comparison of compilation statistics.

The same steps are performed for the control flow edge from B3 to B4. The location of interval i10 is s1 at the end of B2 and eax at the beginning of B4, so a move from s1 to eax is added. The phi function requires a resolving move from interval i12 to i14, i.e., from the location s2 to ecx. Because the operands of the two moves are not overlapping, they can be emitted in any order, and resolving the mapping is trivial in this case.

Both the source and target operand of a move can be a stack slot. Because one interval is assigned only one stack slot even when it is split and spilled multiple times, moves between two different stack slots can only occur with our added handling for phi functions. Stack-to-stack moves are not supported by most architectures and must be emulated with either a load and a store to a register currently not in use, or a push and a pop of a memory location if no register is free. Our implementation for the Intel x86 architecture does not reserve a scratch register that is always available for such moves. However, the register allocator has exact knowledge if there is a register that is currently unused, and it is also possible to use a floating point register for an integer value because no computations need to be performed. Therefore, a register is available in nearly all cases. Still, a stack-to-stack moves requires two machine instructions, so we try to assign the same stack slot to the source and target of a phi function when the according intervals do not overlap.

7. Evaluation

We modified the client compiler of Sun Microsystems' Java HotSpot™ VM, using an early snapshot version of the upcoming JDK 7 available from the OpenJDK project [27]. All benchmarks are executed on a system with two Intel Xeon X5140 2.33 GHz processors, 4 cores, and 32 GByte main memory, running Ubuntu Linux with kernel version 2.6.28. The results are obtained using 32-bit VMs.

We compare our modified linear scan algorithm that operates on SSA form with the unmodified baseline version of the JDK. We evaluate using the following groups of benchmarks: (1) SPECjvm2008 [26] excluding the startup benchmarks (because each of these runs in a new VM but we want to accumulate compilation counters of one VM run) and the SciMark benchmarks (because we evaluate them separately), (2) SPECjbb2005 [25], (3) the DaCapo benchmarks [2] version 2006-10-MR2, and (4) SciMark 2.0 [23]. SciMark is available both standalone and as part of SPECjvm2008. It consists of scientific kernels that require only few methods to be compiled. We use the standalone version because the framework infrastructure of SPECjvm2008 would significantly increase the number of compiled methods.

7.1 Impact on Compile Time

Measuring the compile time is complicated because compilation is done in parallel with execution and thus subject to random noise. In particular, the Java HotSpot™ VM does not allow the recording and replaying of a certain set of compiled methods. Therefore, a slightly different set of methods is compiled when repeatedly executing the same benchmark. To reduce this noise, we limit the benchmarks to one benchmark thread if possible, disable compilation in a separate thread, and report the average of 20 executions. The standard deviation of the number of compiled methods and the size of compiled bytecodes is less than 0.8% (relative to the reported mean) for all benchmarks. Nevertheless, Figure 9 shows slightly different numbers when comparing the baseline and our modified version of the client compiler.

The first group of rows in Figure 9 shows the basic compilation statistics. SPECjvm2008 and DaCapo are large benchmark suites

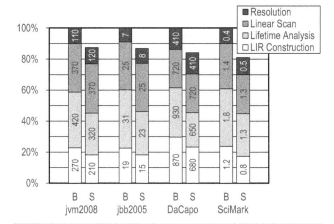

Figure 10. Compilation time of baseline (*B*) and SSA form (*S*) version of linear scan.

where several thousand methods are compiled, SPECjbb2005 is of medium size, and SciMark is small and requires only few methods to be compiled. The average method size of the DaCapo benchmarks is significantly larger than for the other benchmarks. The lower compilation speed indicates that the overall compilation time does not scale linearly with the method size, which is reasonable because some optimizations of the client compiler do not run in linear time. The average method size of SciMark is comparable to SPECjvm2008 and SPECjvm2005, however SciMark consists only of methods with several nested loops. This leads to a higher density of phi functions and thus a different behavior of the compiler. SPECjvm2008 and SPECjbb2005 show roughly the same behavior for all aspects of the compiler that we measured.

Our new register allocator decreases the overall compilation time by 4% to 8%. The percentage for SciMark is larger compared to the other benchmarks because the compiler spends less time optimizing the HIR in the front end. The time spent in the back end optimized by our changes (LIR construction, lifetime analysis, linear scan register allocation, and resolution) is reduced by 13% to 19%.

Figure 10 shows the detailed numbers for these four compiler phases. For each benchmark, the first bar (*B*) shows the baseline and the second bar (*S*) our modified SSA form version of linear scan. The sizes of the bars are normalized to the baseline of the according benchmark. The numbers shown inside the bars are the total time in milliseconds spent in this phase, so they sum up to the *back end time* row of Figure 9. LIR construction is 19% to 27% faster because SSA form deconstruction is no longer performed. The lifetime analysis is 25% to 31% faster because the algorithm described in Section 4 needs no global data flow analysis. The time necessary for the linear scan algorithm is mostly unchanged because our changes are minor. Only SciMark shows a 13% speedup due to a high density of phi functions, whose intervals are simpler now. The elimination of interval intersection checks described in Section 5 does not gain a measurable speedup. The resolution phase is 1% to 10% slower because it now includes SSA form deconstruction. However, the additional time for the resolution phase is much smaller than the time saved during LIR construction, because SSA form deconstruction is only a small addition to the resolution algorithm while it was a complex algorithm during LIR construction.

The reduced compilation time is also accompanied by a reduced memory consumption. Because no intermediate data structures for the data flow analysis are necessary, and the lifetime intervals for phi functions have fewer lifetime holes, the total memory allocated during lifetime analysis is reduced by 9% to 24%. The memory allocated during the linear scan algorithm and resolution is mostly unchanged, only SciMark requires 7% less memory for these phases.

The bottom half of Figure 9 shows how our changes affect the number of move operations. Before register allocation, the number of moves is 11% to 35% lower because phi functions are not yet resolved with moves. But even the sum of the number of moves and phi functions is lower than the original number of moves because one phi function needs to be resolved to at least two moves.

After register allocation, when all phi functions are already resolved, the number of moves is still lower, especially the moves from a register to the stack. This benefit is partially alleviated by two new categories of moves introduced by our changes: (1) moves from a constant to the stack, and (2) moves between two stack slots. These moves are introduced because the lifetime interval of a phi function can have a stack slot assigned at the point of definition. If a block has more phi functions than the processor has physical registers, this assignment is inevitable because the intervals for the phi functions all start at the same position. In the old implementation, the phi functions were already resolved by a series of moves, and spill decisions could be made after each move. This resulted in cases where, for example, a constant was loaded to a register and then the register was immediately spilled to a stack slot. Now, the constant is stored directly into the stack slot, leading to fewer moves in total. Because of the lower number of moves, the overall machine code size is also reduced, however this change is rather insignificant (1% or less).

7.2 Impact on Run Time

The impact of our changes on the run time of the benchmarks are low. Because the main allocation algorithm of linear scan is unchanged, mostly the same allocation and spilling decisions are made with and without SSA form. The speedups are generally below the random noise and therefore not statistically significant. The only exception is the FFT benchmark of SciMark with a speedup of 1%, which is statistically significant because of the low variance of SciMark results. It is caused by fewer moves in the heavily executed innermost computation loop of the benchmark. There is no slowdown for any benchmark.

7.3 Impact on Compiler Code Size

Our modifications simplify the code of the client compiler and reduce its code size. We measure the impact on the lines of C++ code, not counting empty lines, comments, assertions, verification code, debug outputs, and any other code excluded from product builds. The old code for SSA form deconstruction before register allocation is completely unnecessary, eliminating about 180 lines. Only about 20 lines are added to perform SSA form deconstruction during resolution. The old code for initializing the data structures and performing the global data flow analysis required about 150 lines and is now unnecessary. Our new algorithm for building lifetime intervals, which is an extension of code that was already present, added about 100 lines. Additionally, a number of smaller changes both removed and added some lines. In total, the new code is about 200 lines shorter than the old code.

8. Related Work

Poletto et al. introduced the linear scan algorithm [22]. Their variant does not use lifetime holes and is not able to split intervals, i.e., an interval has either one register assigned or is spilled for its entire lifetime. This restricts the allocator but allows for a fast allocation because it does not require a resolution phase. They already mentioned that building the lifetime intervals consumes a considerable amount of the allocation time, and experimented with conservative heuristics for fast building of intervals. However, note that it is not possible to do without a lifetime analysis. The *second chance binpacking* algorithm of Traub et al. added lifetime holes and interval splitting [28]. This makes the linear scan algorithm suitable for architectures with a low number of registers and few or even no callee-saved registers.

In previous work, we presented additional optimizations that improve the quality of linear scan register allocation without impacting compile time overly much [30]. We use register hints as a lightweight alternative to coalescing of intervals, move spill stores and loads out of loops, and eliminate redundant spill stores. The implementation for the Java HotSpot™ client compiler is part of the product version since Java 6 and the baseline for this implementation.

Sarkar et al. claim that their *extended linear scan* algorithm produces better code than graph coloring algorithms [24]. They show that the abstraction of graph coloring introduces unnecessary constraints that can be avoided by a linear scan algorithm with aggressive splitting of lifetime intervals. However, they only cover spill free register allocation as well as register allocation with total spills where entire lifetime intervals are spilled. This is a severe restriction especially for register constrained architectures. None of the previously mentioned versions of linear scan operates on SSA form.

Mössenböck et al. provide an early approach to perform linear scan register allocation directly on SSA form [19]. However, they still deconstruct SSA form before register allocation during the construction of the lifetime intervals: They insert move instructions into predecessor blocks for phi functions, leading to intervals that start in the predecessor blocks and extending into the successor. They only keep the phi functions in the successor block as a placeholder to start a new interval. They use data flow analysis to construct the lifetime intervals, pre-order the moves and phi functions instead of using the parallel copy semantics of the phi functions, and use no structural properties guaranteed by SSA form.

The original graph coloring register allocators (see for example [5, 8]) are not based on SSA form. Only recently, the properties guaranteed by SSA form were found to be beneficial [6, 12]. The same properties that we use to simplify linear scan register allocation, namely that the definition of every value dominates all uses and that it is enough to check interference at the definition points of values [7], simplify the construction of the interference graph and allow spilling decisions to be decoupled from the actual coloring phase. Hack et al. present an implementation for the libFirm library [14]. Copy coalescing of phi functions and their arguments is performed via graph recoloring [13].

Pereira et al. use the even more specialized *static single information* (SSI) form for their register allocation based on puzzle solving [20]. SSI form requires not only phi functions for all variables at every join point, but also *pi* functions at every point where control flow splits. They claim to be faster and better than linear scan register allocation, however their comparison is performed with a linear scan variant not based on SSA form such as our implementation.

Boissinot et al. present a fast algorithm for liveness checking of SSA form programs, using the structural properties guaranteed by SSA form [4]. Their algorithm performs only few precomputations, but still allows fast answers to the question whether a certain value is live at a certain point in a method. It is not designed to allow fast answers for *all* points in the program, therefore it is not suitable for building lifetime intervals. Our algorithm to build lifetime intervals requires more time than their pre-computation, but then the intervals contain information about the lifetime of all values for the entire method.

Boissinot et al. present an algorithm for SSA form deconstruction that is provably correct [3]. The complications they describe where previous algorithms failed only arise when critical edges of the control flow graph cannot be split. However, this is always possible when compiling from Java bytecodes, so this is not a concern for our simple integration of SSA form deconstruction into the resolution phase of the linear scan algorithm.

Pereira et al. provide an algorithm for SSA form deconstruction after register allocation [21]. It requires the input program to be in *conventional SSA* (CSSA) form. Additionally to the normal SSA form properties, CSSA form requires that all variables of a phi function do not interfere. For example, the lifetime intervals of a phi function's input parameters must neither overlap the lifetime interval of the phi function, nor themselves. CSSA form can be obtained from SSA form by splitting life ranges that violate this property, leading to a higher number of variables. However, it is then always safe to assign the same stack slot to a phi function and all its input parameters when spilling is necessary. This avoids moves between two different stack slots, which sometimes occur with our algorithm.

9. Conclusions

Linear scan is a fast algorithm for register allocation especially used by just-in-time compilers. This paper explored how the algorithm benefits from an intermediate representation in SSA form. The dominance property guaranteed by SSA form allows for a simple construction of lifetime intervals and eliminates checks for interval intersection during allocation. Additionally, SSA form deconstruction can be easily integrated into the resolution phase of the register allocator. Our implementation for the Java HotSpot™ client compiler shows that the resulting algorithm is both simpler and faster.

Acknowledgments

Parts of this effort have been sponsored by the California MICRO Program and industrial sponsor Sun Microsystems under Project No. 07-127, as well as by the National Science Foundation (NSF) under grants CNS-0615443 and CNS-0627747. Further support has come from generous unrestricted gifts from Sun Microsystems, Google, and Mozilla, for which the authors are immensely grateful.

The U.S. Government is authorized to reproduce and distribute reprints for Governmental purposes notwithstanding any copyright annotation thereon. Any opinions, findings, and conclusions or recommendations expressed here are those of the authors and should not be interpreted as necessarily representing the official views, policies, or endorsements, either expressed or implied, of the NSF, any other agency of the U.S. Government, or any of the companies mentioned above.

References

[1] B. Alpern, C. R. Attanasio, J. J. Barton, M. G. Burke, P.Cheng, J.-D. Choi, A. Cocchi, S. J. Fink, D. Grove, M. Hind, S. F. Hummel, D. Lieber, V. Litvinov, M. F. Mergen, T. Ngo, J. R. Russell, V. Sarkar, M. J. Serrano, J. C. Shepherd, S. E. Smith, V. C. Sreedhar, H. Srinivasan, and J. Whaley. The Jalapeño virtual machine. *IBM Systems Journal*, 39(1):211–238, 2000.

[2] S. M. Blackburn, R. Garner, C. Hoffman, A. M. Khan, K. S. McKinley, R. Bentzur, A. Diwan, D. Feinberg, D. Frampton, S. Z. Guyer, M. Hirzel, A. Hosking, M. Jump, H. Lee, J. E. B. Moss, A. Phansalkar, D. Stefanović, T. VanDrunen, D. von Dincklage, and B. Wiedermann. The DaCapo benchmarks: Java benchmarking development and analysis. In *Proceedings of the ACM SIGPLAN Conference on Object-Oriented Programming Systems, Languages, and Applications*, pages 169–190. ACM Press, 2006.

[3] B. Boissinot, A. Darte, F. Rastello, B. D. de Dinechin, and C. Guillon. Revisiting out-of-SSA translation for correctness, code quality and efficiency. In *Proceedings of the International Symposium on Code Generation and Optimization*, pages 114–125. IEEE Computer Society, 2009.

[4] B. Boissinot, S. Hack, D. Grund, B. Dupont de Dinechin, and F. Rastello. Fast liveness checking for SSA-form programs. In *Proceedings of the International Symposium on Code Generation and Optimization*, pages 35–44. ACM Press, 2008.

[5] P. Briggs, K. D. Cooper, and L. Torczon. Improvements to graph coloring register allocation. *ACM Transactions on Programming Languages and Systems*, 16(3):428–455, 1994.

[6] P. Brisk, F. Dabiri, R. Jafari, and M. Sarrafzadeh. Optimal register sharing for high-level synthesis of SSA form programs. *IEEE Transactions on Computer-Aided Design of Integrated Circuits and Systems*, 25(5):772–779, 2006.

[7] Z. Budimlic, K. D. Cooper, T. J. Harvey, K. Kennedy, T. S. Oberg, and S. W. Reeves. Fast copy coalescing and live-range identification. In *Proceedings of the ACM SIGPLAN Conference on Programming Language Design and Implementation*, pages 25–32. ACM Press, 2002.

[8] G. J. Chaitin, M. A. Auslander, A. K. Chandra, J. Cocke, M. E. Hopkins, and P. W. Markstein. Register allocation via coloring. *Computer Languages*, 6:47–57, 1981.

[9] R. Cytron, J. Ferrante, B. K. Rosen, M. N. Wegman, and F. K. Zadeck. Efficiently computing static single assignment form and the control dependence graph. *ACM Transactions on Programming Languages and Systems*, 13(4):451–490, 1991.

[10] S. J. Fink and F. Qian. Design, implementation and evaluation of adaptive recompilation with on-stack replacement. In *Proceedings of the International Symposium on Code Generation and Optimization*, pages 241–252. IEEE Computer Society, 2003.

[11] R. Griesemer and S. Mitrovic. A compiler for the Java HotSpot[TM] virtual machine. In *The School of Niklaus Wirth: The Art of Simplicity*, pages 133–152. dpunkt.verlag, 2000.

[12] S. Hack and G. Goos. Optimal register allocation for SSA-form programs in polynomial time. *Information Processing Letters*, 98(4):150–155, 2006.

[13] S. Hack and G. Goos. Copy coalescing by graph recoloring. In *Proceedings of the ACM SIGPLAN Conference on Programming Language Design and Implementation*, pages 227–237. ACM Press, 2008.

[14] S. Hack, D. Grund, and G. Goos. Register allocation for programs in SSA-form. In *Proceedings of the International Conference on Compiler Construction*, pages 247–262. LNCS 3923, Springer Verlag, 2006.

[15] U. Hölzle and D. Ungar. Optimizing dynamically-dispatched calls with run-time type feedback. In *Proceedings of the ACM SIGPLAN Conference on Programming Language Design and Implementation*, pages 326–336. ACM Press, 1994.

[16] T. Kotzmann, C. Wimmer, H. Mössenböck, T. Rodriguez, K. Russell, and D. Cox. Design of the Java HotSpot[TM] client compiler for Java 6. *ACM Transactions on Architecture and Code Optimization*, 5(1):Article 7, 2008.

[17] C. Lattner and V. Adve. LLVM: A compilation framework for lifelong program analysis & transformation. In *Proceedings of the International Symposium on Code Generation and Optimization*, pages 75–88. IEEE Computer Society, 2004.

[18] T. Lindholm and F. Yellin. *The Java[TM] Virtual Machine Specification*. Addison-Wesley, 2nd edition, 1999.

[19] H. Mössenböck and M. Pfeiffer. Linear scan register allocation in the context of SSA form and register constraints. In *Proceedings of the International Conference on Compiler Construction*, pages 229–246. LNCS 2304, Springer-Verlag, 2002.

[20] F. M. Q. Pereira and J. Palsberg. Register allocation by puzzle solving. In *Proceedings of the ACM SIGPLAN Conference on Programming Language Design and Implementation*, pages 216–226. ACM Press, 2008.

[21] F. M. Q. Pereira and J. Palsberg. SSA elimination after register allocation. In *Proceedings of the International Conference on Compiler Construction*, pages 158–173. LNCS 5501, Springer Verlag, 2009.

[22] M. Poletto and V. Sarkar. Linear scan register allocation. *ACM Transactions on Programming Languages and Systems*, 21(5):895–913, 1999.

[23] R. Pozo and B. Miller. *SciMark 2.0*, 1999. http://math.nist.gov/scimark2/.

[24] V. Sarkar and R. Barik. Extended linear scan: An alternate foundation for global register allocation. In *Proceedings of the International Conference on Compiler Construction*, pages 141–155. LNCS 4420, Springer Verlag, 2007.

[25] Standard Performance Evaluation Corporation. *SPECjbb2005*, 2005. http://www.spec.org/jbb2005/.

[26] Standard Performance Evaluation Corporation. *SPECjvm2008*, 2008. http://www.spec.org/jvm2008/.

[27] Sun Microsystems, Inc. *OpenJDK*, 2009. http://openjdk.java.net/.

[28] O. Traub, G. Holloway, and M. D. Smith. Quality and speed in linear-scan register allocation. In *Proceedings of the ACM SIGPLAN Conference on Programming Language Design and Implementation*, pages 142–151. ACM Press, 1998.

[29] C. Wimmer. Linear scan register allocation for the Java HotSpot[TM] client compiler. Master's thesis, Johannes Kepler University Linz, 2004.

[30] C. Wimmer and H. Mössenböck. Optimized interval splitting in a linear scan register allocator. In *Proceedings of the ACM/USENIX International Conference on Virtual Execution Environments*, pages 132–141. ACM Press, 2005.

Integrated Instruction Selection and Register Allocation for Compact Code Generation Exploiting Freeform Mixing of 16- and 32-bit Instructions

Tobias J.K. Edler von Koch   Igor Böhm   Björn Franke

Institute for Computing Systems Architecture
School of Informatics, University of Edinburgh
Informatics Forum, 10 Crichton Street, Edinburgh, EH8 9AB, United Kingdom
T.J.K.Edler-Von-Koch@sms.ed.ac.uk, I.Bohm@sms.ed.ac.uk, bfranke@inf.ed.ac.uk

Abstract

For memory constrained embedded systems code size is at least as important as performance. One way of increasing code density is to exploit compact instruction formats, e.g. ARM Thumb, where the processor either operates in standard or compact instruction mode. The ARCompact ISA considered in this paper is different in that it allows freeform mixing of 16- and 32-bit instructions without a mode switch. Compact 16-bit instructions can be used anywhere in the code given that additional register constraints are satisfied. In this paper we present an integrated instruction selection and register allocation methodology and develop two approaches for mixed-mode code generation: a simple opportunistic scheme and a more advanced feedback-guided instruction selection scheme. We have implemented a code generator targeting the ARCompact ISA and evaluated its effectiveness against the ARC750D embedded processor and the EEMBC benchmark suite. On average, we achieve a code size reduction of 16.7% across all benchmarks whilst at the same time improving performance by on average 17.7%.

Categories and Subject Descriptors   D.3 [*Programming Languages*]: Processors—Code Generation;   D.3 [*Programming Languages*]: Processors—Compilers

General Terms   Algorithms, experimentation, measurement, performance

Keywords   Instruction selection, register allocation, code size, dual instruction set architecture, variable-length instructions, ARCompact

1. Introduction

A large number of embedded processors are deployed in cost-sensitive, but high-volume markets where even modest savings of unit cost can lead to a substantial overall cost reduction. Highly integrated systems-on-chip (SoC) serve these markets and provide embedded processors as part of a more complex system integrated with other components such as memories and various peripheral devices on the same chip. Of all components, memories typically occupy the largest fraction of the chip area and, hence, contribute most to the overall cost. Among embedded memories, flash storage plays a prominent role as non-volatile memory that needs to be large enough to store the full image of the binary executable. As a consequence, any reduction in code size translates directly to equivalent savings of die area and, eventually, unit cost. For example, 128-Mbit of NOR flash (two bits per cell) fabricated with $0.13\mu m$ design rules using a multilevel-charge (MLC) storage scheme occupy a chip area of $27.3mm^2$ [6] whereas an ARM Cortex-M3 processor (CM3Core core) only occupies $0.43mm^2$ at the same technology node [3].

One popular architectural approach to code size reduction is the provision of a compact instruction set architecture (ISA) alongside the standard, full-width RISC ISA. For example, some ARM processors (e.g. ARM7TDMI) implement the compact Thumb instruction set whereas MIPS has a similar offering called MIPS16e. Common to these compact 16-bit ISAs is that the processor either operates in 16-bit or 32-bit mode and switching between modes of operation is done through mode change operations which add a certain runtime and code size overhead. Furthermore, not all registers available in 32-bit mode are also accessible in 16-bit mode. Compilers seeking to take full advantage of compact instruction formats need to analyse the code and identify regions where the benefits of a compact instruction format outweigh its disadvantages (i.e. mode switching overhead and increased register pressure on the restricted register set). Significant care needs to be taken as performance degradation by up to 98% as a result of an overly aggressive use of compact instructions has been reported in e.g. [11].

In this paper we consider the ARCompact [2] ISA implemented by the ARC 600 & 700 series of embedded processors. The ARCompact, ARM Thumb-2 [14] and also the recently introduced microMIPS [13] ISAs are different from other compact ISAs in that they allow freeform mixing of 16- and 32-bit instructions *without a mode switch*. This enables the compiler to generate a fine-grained interleaving of 16- and 32-bit instructions, thus potentially leading to greater code density without performance loss. However, at the same time the compiler needs to decide for *every* instruction that has a compact counterpart whether to emit the full-width or compact version. This decision does not only depend on the availability of an equivalent compact instruction, but additional register constraints need to be obeyed. Due to fewer instruction bits, 16-bit instructions comprise shorter register fields, and can only address eight rather than 32 registers for the standard 32-bit instructions in case of the ARCompact ISA. These register constraints demand an integrated approach where instruction selection and register allocation are considered simultaneously. Failure to do so may lead to missed opportunities or, even worse, to code bloat and performance loss due to excessive register-to-register data movement and, thus, negate the intended code size reduction effect.

1.1 Motivating Example

Before we discuss the proposed code generation approach in detail, we provide a motivating example that highlights some of the issues encountered in the selection of compact instructions.

Consider the small basic block in the first column of table 1. Suppose that in this block only registers *r2..r4* are available for use while all other registers contain values whose live ranges begin before and end after this basic block.

32-Bit Only	**Mixed Mode** (Aggressive)	**Mixed Mode** (Integrated)
`ld r2,[sp,0]`	`ld_s r2,[sp,0]`	`ld_s r2,[sp,0]`
`ld r3,[sp,4]`	`ld_s r3,[sp,4]`	`ld_s r3,[sp,4]`
	`mov r4,r1`	
`ld r4,[sp,8]`	`ld_s r1,[sp,8]`	`ld r4,[sp,8]`
`add r2,r2,r3`	`add_s r2,r2,r3`	`add_s r2,r2,r3`
`asl r2,r2,2`	`asl_s r2,r2,2`	`asl_s r2,r2,2`
`sub r2,r2,r4`	`sub_s r2,r2,r1`	`sub r2,r2,r4`
	`mov r1,r4`	
24 bytes	**20** bytes	**16** bytes

Table 1. Three versions of a sample basic block: 32-bit instructions only; aggressive use of 16-bit instructions; integrated instruction selection and register allocation avoiding register-to-register data movement.

Of these, *r2* and *r3* can be accessed by 16-bit instructions whereas *r4* cannot. We give three different versions of the basic block. The first one uses 32-bit instructions only (left column), this results in a code size of $6 \times 4 = 24$ bytes. For the second version (second column), we instructed the code generator to use 16-bit instructions – denoted by the suffix "_s" – wherever possible. This clearly leads to a problem: since these compact instructions can only operate on a limited set of registers, the register allocator has to insert additional move instructions to "spill" the value currently stored in *r1*, which is 16-bit accessible, to *r4* so it can use three 16-bit accessible registers, *r1..r3*. The aggressive use of compact instructions has increased the overall instruction count and the resulting code size is $6 \times 2 + 2 \times 4 = 20$ bytes. A better solution is presented in the third version of the basic block (third column). In that version, only some of the instructions have been replaced by their 16-bit counterparts. Those instructions operating on register *r4* remain 32-bit instructions. As a result "spilling" from the limited 16-bit accessible registers into the general-purpose registers is avoided and, thus, the instruction count remains constant while the code size is further reduced to $4 \times 2 + 2 \times 4 = 16$ bytes. This example demonstrates that instruction selection and register allocation need to be considered simultaneously to avoid excessive register traffic and to fully exploit the benefits of a compact ISA.

1.2 Contributions

Among the contributions of this paper are:

1. The development of an integrated instruction selection and register allocation framework targeting freely interleavable compact and standard RISC instructions for code size reduction,

2. the investigation of an opportunistic instruction selection procedure that obeys the stricter register constraints of the compact instruction format, but does not actively seek to maximise the usage of compact instructions,

3. the development of a more sophisticated instruction selection scheme that uses feedback information obtained from standard instruction selection and register allocation for improved compact code generation,

4. a demonstration of the practical integration of both schemes in a CoSy-based compiler targeting the ARCompact ISA,

5. an extensive evaluation against the industry standard EEMBC benchmark suite and a cycle-accurate simulator of the ARC750D processor, and

6. a comparison with GCC 4.2.1 targeting the ARCompact ISA on the same platform.

1.3 Overview

The remainder of this paper is structured as follows. In Section 2 we provide background information on the ARCompact instruction set architecture and its particular ability of freeform mixing of 16- and 32-bit instructions without a mode switch as well as on the CoSy compiler development system [1]. This is followed by an in-depth description of our code generation approach in Section 3 where we develop two schemes for the selection of compact instructions under register constraints. In Section 4 we evaluate the effectiveness of our methodology and present extensive benchmarking results. The context of related work is established in section 5, before we summarise and conclude in section 6.

2. Background

In this section, we give an overview of the ARC750D processor and its instruction set architecture. This is followed by a brief presentation of those features of the CoSy compiler construction framework that are relevant to the work presented in this paper.

2.1 ARC750D and the ARCompact ISA

The ARC750D processor [2] is a configurable implementation of the ARCompact instruction-set architecture with the particular goal of creating an energy-efficient and easily extensible embedded microprocessor. ARCompact is a 32-bit RISC ISA supporting both 32-bit-wide and 16-bit-wide instructions. Both types of instructions can be intermixed freely without additional overhead as no mode-switch or decompression stage is required. A 32-bit memory value may contain either one 32-bit instruction, two 16-bit instructions or even a combination of half a 32-bit instruction and one 16-bit instruction. Thus, the frequent use of 16-bit instructions could reduce code size up to a theoretical maximum of 50%. In practice, this value is lower as not all instructions have a compact counterpart. ARC claim up to 40% code size reduction on their web site [2]. Obviously, compact instructions have certain limitations when compared to their 32-bit counterparts: in most cases, they only have access to a limited subset of the 32 core registers, namely the eight registers r0..r3 (callee-saved) and r12..r15 (caller-saved); the range for immediate operands is generally limited; and flags, such as carry, overflow, zero-result etc. are not set, to name a few. In table 2, we give examples of a few of the 32-bit *add* and the corresponding 16-bit *add_s* instructions to illustrate these limitations.

2.2 CoSy Compiler Construction Framework

Having seen the opportunities for code size reduction provided by 16-bit instructions, we will now describe the CoSy compiler framework [1] that has been used in the implementation of the proposed compact code generator.

CoSy provides a multi-pass compiler architecture where the compiler back-end operates on a *mid-level intermediate representation* (MIR), produced by the compiler's front- and mid-end. The code generator executes three principal passes, namely *Match/Cover*, *Register Allocation* and *Code Emis-*

Instruction	dest	src1	src2
add a,b,c	any reg	any reg	any reg
add a,b,u6	any reg	any reg	6-bit unsig. imm.
add a,b,limm	any reg	any reg	long immediate
add_s a,b,c	16bit reg	16bit reg	16bit reg
add_s a,b,u3	16bit reg	16bit reg	3-bit unsig. imm.
add_s a,a,limm	16bit reg	(dest)	long immediate

Table 2. Comparison of 32-bit and 16-bit formats for the *add dest,src1,src2* instruction.

sion. The *Match/Cover* pass computes a cost minimal covering of the MIR given the usual tree-pattern rewrite rules mapping IR nodes onto processor instructions. Each rule is associated with a – possibly dynamic – cost. According to the selected rules the MIR is transformed into a directed acyclic graph (DAG) *low-level intermediate representation* (LIR) that is annotated with pointers to the original MIR nodes. Later passes maintain and extend these annotations such that the user is able to trace back the creation point of any LIR node. We make use of this feature in Section 3.2 to implement feedback-guided instruction selection. A graph colouring-based register allocator maps pseudo-registers to actual registers or memory and is responsible for inserting spill code. The register allocator provided with CoSy can handle several overlapping register classes and we use this feature for the implementation of separate, but non-disjoint registers classes for 16-bit accessible and globally accessible registers, respectively. Finally, assembly code is emitted for each LIR node using code emission rules for each type of LIR node.

2.3 Naïve ARCompact Code Generation using CoSy

The obvious approach to add support for 16-bit instructions to the CoSy compiler framework would be to add new tree-pattern rules for this class of instructions with lower costs than their 32-bit counterparts. The compiler would then select 16-bit instructions wherever possible and we would hope that this measure has the desired effect on code size. Such a naïve scheme, however, has serious shortcomings that are due to register allocation occurring after the *Match/Cover* pass and register access constraints of 16-bit instructions as described above. By using 16-bit instructions almost exclusively, we effectively reduce the size of the available register set to just a small subset of the general-purpose registers available to 32-bit instructions. This inevitably leads to higher register pressure and results in an increased number of register-to-register data moves or even spills to memory. Thus, even though we might be able to reduce code size initially, these additional instructions will negate the benefits from using a compact instruction format. In addition, extra data moves and spills will most certainly degrade performance and are therefore highly undesirable.

182

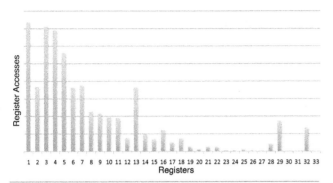

Figure 1. Typical distribution of dynamic register accesses.

3. Methodology

From our discussion in Section 2.3 it becomes evident that we need to balance the use of 16-bit instructions against the increase in register pressure resulting from their restricted register addressing capabilities. Keeping in mind our goal of reducing code size as much as possible, we therefore want to maximise the use of 16-bit instructions while minimising the amount of move and spill instructions inserted at the register allocation stage solely because of the use of 16-bit instructions. In the following sections, we propose two methods to achieve this. The first one, the opportunistic use of 16-bit instructions, is implemented purely at the code emission stage and requires no further changes to the compiler framework. The second one, the selective use of 16-bit instructions directed by MIR annotations using code generator feedback, is more involved but less dependent on specific traits of the ARCompact ISA and expected to produce better results.

3.1 Opportunistic Instruction Selection

Our first compact instruction selection scheme is motivated by the non-uniform distribution of register accesses that favours registers with lower ID over those with higher ID. An example distribution is shown in Figure 1. It is clearly visible that the lower part of the register set is accessed much more frequently than the upper part. This is partly due to the fact that the standard graph colouring register allocator always selects the register with the lowest ID of the set of possible registers for a value. In addition, calling conventions dictate that arguments are passed in registers r0..r7 and the result is returned in register r0. Finally, immediate values tend to be small and often fall within the limited bounds 16-bit instructions can operate on.

We exploit the fact that 16-bit accessible registers are already frequently used in standard 32-bit code and construct an *opportunistic* instruction selector that does not aim to specifically identify compact instructions in the match/cover stage, but delays this decision until after standard 32-bit instruction selection and register allocation. Only at the code emission stage do we check if an instruction that possesses a 16-bit counterpart *incidentally* satisfies the stricter register constraints of that compact instruction. If this is the case

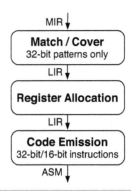

Figure 2. Sequence of stages of the *opportunistic* scheme for mixed-mode instruction selection.

we emit a short 16-bit instruction, otherwise we emit a standard 32-bit instruction. In either case, we leave the register allocation intact as only the type of instruction is affected. Figure 2 summarises this approach schematically. Certainly, this approach will only work because of the coincidental match between frequently used registers and those registers accessible by 16-bit ARCompact instructions. Still, this opportunistic scheme avoids the main drawback of the naïve solution from Section 2.2, namely the introduction of additional register moves and spilling. In addition, this compact code generation scheme has low implementation complexity and only requires local changes to the code emission pass.

3.2 Feedback-Guided Instruction Selection

The opportunistic instruction selection scheme presented in the previous section has a number of shortcomings. First, we rely on the coincidence that standard graph colouring results in code that frequently satisfies the stricter register constraints of the 16-bit ARCompact instructions. Other architectures may embed registers accessible by short instructions elsewhere in the register set and our simple opportunistic approach will become less effective. Second, it seems conceptually unsound that 16-bit instructions are handled outside the cost framework of the match/cover stage and defy standard instruction selection and register allocation. For this reason, it appears likely that we may miss further opportunities for the use of 16-bit instructions.

We therefore propose an improved approach based on code generator feedback, which is illustrated in Figure 3. In summary, we run two iterations over the match/cover and register allocation stages. The purpose of the first iteration is to attempt aggressive 16-bit code generation including instruction selection and register allocation. At the end of this first iteration feedback is gathered and made available to the second iteration of code generation. During the second code generation stage the feedback is then used to determine and annotate register pressure points in the MIR where 16-bit instructions should be avoided. This allows for the feedback-guided, selective use of 16-bit instructions in the second iteration and, thus, avoids the introduction of register pressure related register-to-register move operations.

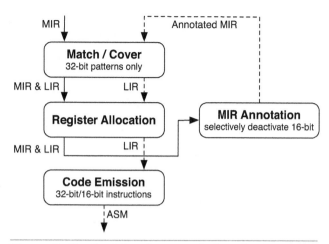

Figure 3. Feedback-based approach for mixed-mode instruction selection.

In the following paragraphs we explain the two phases – IR *Annotation* and *Feedback-guided Code Generation* – in detail:

I. IR Annotation.

1. **Match/Cover.** In contrast to the opportunistic approach, we add all 16-bit instructions as separate tree-pattern matching rules to the match/cover stage with costs lower than those of the corresponding 32-bit instructions, i.e. we use both 16- and 32-bit rules with a preference for the 16-bit ones due to their lower cost.

2. **Register Allocation.** The aggressive use of 16-bit instructions will most likely introduce a large number of additional register moves and spills during register allocation. When such additional instructions are inserted into the LIR, the register allocator inserts backpointers to the MIR nodes that "caused" them. For example, suppose that one of the operands for a 16-bit *add* instruction is originally located in a register that is not 16-bit accessible. In this case, the register allocator will insert an additional register move operation to place the value in a register accessible by short instructions. This may result in more *move* operations to be inserted to free the temporary space in the 16-bit accessible register set. All of these move operations will be inserted before the actual *add* instruction node and links will be set up pointing to the newly created auxiliary *move* nodes. After register allocation, we can then trace back exactly which MIR nodes were at the origin of additional moves or spills.

3. **MIR Annotation.** In this pass we iterate over all LIR nodes and identify those moves and spills that were directly caused by 16-bit instructions based on a number of simple tree patterns. Whenever such a node is found, we use the backpointer inserted during the previous register allocation pass and determine the 16-bit instruc-

tion node it relates to. This in turn allows us to locate the MIR node that gave rise to it using the MIR-LIR links inserted at the match/cover stage (see Section 2.2). We can then annotate this MIR node with an additional "no 16-bit" flag indicating that the node should not be covered with a 16-bit instruction rule so as to avoid additional move or spill instructions. Finally, the LIR produced in this iteration is discarded.

II. Feedback-guided Code Generation.

1. **Match/Cover.** In the second iteration, the match/cover stage uses MIR annotations to selectively disable the use of 16-bit instruction rules for nodes flagged in the previous IR annotation stage. This is achieved by specifying special CONDITION clauses available in the code generator description language that should hold for rules to be applied.

2. **Register Allocation.** We expect that the register allocator will insert significantly fewer, if any, additional moves and spills caused by 16-bit instructions in this second iteration. While it is possible that new moves or spills will appear in different places, this is unlikely since most of the register pressure actually results from temporary variables that have short live ranges within a basic block.

3. **Code Emission.** In this stage, we perform standard code emission targeting 16- and 32-bit rules. As before in the opportunistic scheme, we may find that even for some 32-bit instruction nodes marked with the "no 16-bit" flag the stricter register constraints for the use with 16-bit instructions are incidentally satisfied. Thus, we additionally employ the opportunistic scheme and use 16-bit instructions wherever possible as doing so does not incur any extra cost.

For the example shown in Table 1 we would initially generate the code in the second column, however, without actually emitting this code (see Figure 4). Next, we would identify the two inserted `mov` instructions as ones that have been introduced by the register allocator to free space in the 16-bit accessible register range for the `ld_s r1,[sp,8]` and `sub_s r2,r2,r1` instructions, respectively. We mark these two short instructions with the "no 16-bit" flag, before entering the actual feedback-guided code generation stage. When we encounter the two instructions again, we check for the "no 16-bit" flag and decide not to emit compact instructions, but to resort to their standard 32-bit versions. Finally, after the subsequent run of the register allocator the shorter code sequence shown in the third column of Table 1 is emitted.

It is important to note that although we are using feedback to guide instruction selection in our compact code generation methodology, this feedback information is generated statically within the compiler and unlike [10, 11, 12] does not require any profiling.

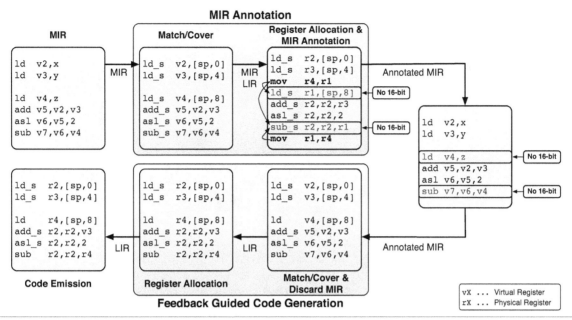

Figure 4. Feedback-guided compact code generation for the example in Table 1.

4. Empirical Evaluation

We have extensively evaluated our integrated code generation approach and in this section we describe our experimental setup and methodology before we present and discuss our results.

4.1 Experimental Setup and Methodology

We have evaluated our compact code generation approach against the EEMBC 1.1 benchmark suite [7] that comprises applications from the automotive, consumer, networking, office and telecom domains. All codes have been built with our highly optimising compiler based on the commercial CoSy compiler development system [1]. Our main interest has been on code size, therefore we have measured code size, i.e. the total `size` of the `.text` segments of all object files forming a single benchmark (except for the benchmark harness), using the UNIX tool size. In addition, we have measured the performance impact resulting from our code generation methodology using a verified, cycle-accurate simulator of the ARC750D processor. Table 3 lists the configuration details of our target processor.

Finally, we have also compiled the full set of benchmarks with the ARC port of the GCC 4.2.1 compiler with full optimisation and mixed code generation enabled (*'-mA7 -O3 -mmixed-code'*) in order to compare the benefits of exploiting the compact instruction format of the ARCompact ISA with GCC to our approach.

Throughout this section, plain 32-bit code (featuring 32-bit instructions exclusively) serves as the baseline. This code is generated by our CoSy-based compiler for the discussion of our compact code generation schemes, and by GCC for the evaluation of GCC's approach so that relative improvements

Core	ARC750D
Pipeline	7-stage (interlocked)
Execution Order	In-Order
Branch Prediction	Yes
ISA	ARCompact
Floating-Point	Hardware
Memory System	
L1 Cache	
Instruction	8k/2-way associative
Data	8k/2-way associative
L2 Cache	None
Bus Width/Latency/Clock Divisor	32-bit/16 cycles/2
Simulation	
Simulator	Full-system, cycle-accurate
Options	Default
I/O & System Calls	Emulated

Table 3. Configuration of the ARC750D simulator.

due to mixed-mode code generation become comparable for both compilers.

4.2 Code Size

We initially discuss code size reduction due to the selection of compact instructions as this has been the primary motivation for our work. Our overall code size results are summarised in the diagram shown in Figure 5. For each of the EEMBC benchmarks from the automotive, consumer, networking, office and telecommunication domains we present three results relating to the percentages of code size improvements resulting from (a) our opportunistic scheme, (b) our feedback-guided instruction selection scheme, and (c)

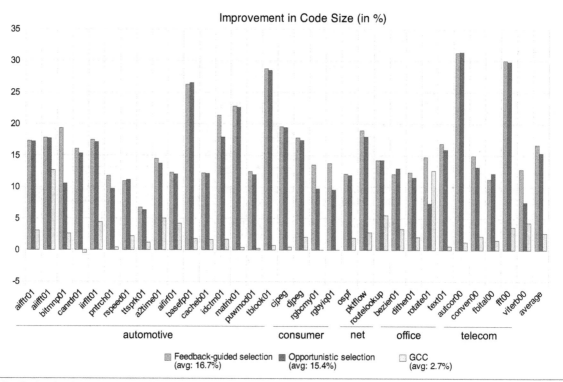

Figure 5. Code size improvements due to compact code generation for the EEMBC 1.1 benchmarks (baseline: 32-bit only).

the ARC port of the GCC 4.2.1 compiler. We will discuss the GCC results separately in Section 4.4.

For the opportunistic scheme code size reductions between 6.4% and 31.4% are achieved, with an average improvement of 15.4%. For individual programs (fft00 and autocor00) code size improvements of 30% are reached (30.0%) or exceeded (31.4%). This result is slightly surprising given that the opportunistic scheme does not actively seek to maximise the use of 16-bit instructions, but only identifies and converts 32-bit instructions that already satisfy the stricter register constraints of the corresponding 16-bit instructions. Only 6 out of 32 applications fail to deliver code size reductions of more than 10% for this simple scheme, while 14 benchmarks are improved by more than 15%. This suggests that our initial assumption, namely that in standard 32-bit code most register traffic is already handled in 16-bit accessible registers, holds in general (see Figure 1). Any scheme trying to improve on this would need to identify further opportunities among the few remaining instructions that operate on non-16-bit accessible registers whilst the 16-bit accessible registers are not fully utilised.

With this information it is not surprising that our feedback-guided instruction selection scheme performs only slightly better than the simpler opportunistic scheme. We observe that although the average improvement (16.7%) is not much higher than for the simple scheme (15.4%) feedback-guided instruction selection provides *more consistent* improvements across the range of benchmarks and reduces the standard deviation from the mean from 6.45% to 5.86%. In partic-

ular, our more advanced scheme produces denser code for benchmarks such as bitmnp01, pntrch01, rgbcmy01, rgbyiq01 and viterb00 where the simple scheme does not perform too well. Still, both schemes perform similarly on those applications that provide the greatest opportunities for code size reductions (autocor00, fft00, tblook01, basefp01).

It is important to note that for both of our compact code generation schemes there is not a single case where the code size has been increased as this is impossible for either of the two algorithms.

ARC claims up to 40% code size reduction for the extensive use of compact instructions [2], however, this represents a theoretical upper bound only achievable if compact instructions are used for virtually all operations and all live data fits into the small 16-bit accessible register subset. In practice, our code generation methodology comes close to this theoretical limit for a number of applications (e.g. autocor00 and fft00) while for the majority of codes we reach about 45% of the hypothetical peak code size savings.

4.3 Performance

Next we evaluate the performance impact of our compact code generation methodology. A summary of our results is shown in the diagram in Figure 6.

Across the range of benchmarks the opportunistic scheme reduces the cycle count by 16.6% on average. For individual applications (conven00 and viterb00) performance im-

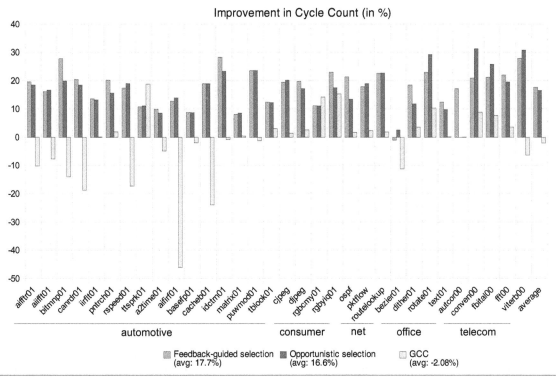

Figure 6. Performance improvements due to compact code generation for the EEMBC 1.1 benchmarks (baseline: 32-bit only).

provements in excess of 30% can be observed. Only 5 out of 32 applications are improved by less than 10%, whereas 7 programs are sped up by more than 20%. Not a single program suffers from performance degradation as a result of opportunistic compact code generation.

Similar to the code size evaluation in the previous Section, feedback-guided instruction selection gives a slight improvement over the simpler opportunistic scheme. On average, performance is improved by 17.7%. Unlike the case with code size, feedback-guided instruction selection does not perform better across the entire set of applications, but there are benchmarks where one of the two schemes clearly outperforms the other. For example, the opportunistic scheme produces faster code for the `rotate01`, `conven00`, `fbittal00` and `viterb00` benchmarks whereas the feedback-guided scheme takes a lead on the `bitmnp01`, `pntrch01`, `idctrn01`, `rgbyiq01`, `ospf` and `autocor00` codes. For a single program (`bezier01`) the feedback-guided scheme results in a negligible performance loss of 1.06%.

We have investigated the origin of the performance gains observed in our experiments and found that these largely result from improved instruction cache behaviour due to increased code density of the mixed-mode code. With 8kB the size of the level-1 instruction cache in our processor is relatively small, but representative for typical low-power and low-cost embedded processor cores. Any code size reduction technique will inevitably lead to higher instruction

cache hit rates for any non-trivial application. For the one application where we see a minor performance degradation we have found that this is caused by an increased number of instruction cache conflicts. The conflicts can be avoided if we configure the ARC750D processor to contain a 4-way associative instruction cache rather than the 2-way associative cache that has been used in our experiments.

The reason why most of the prior work in this field [9, 10, 11, 12, 16] has reported performance losses or, at best, the same level of performance for mixed-mode code is that the mode switching overhead associated with the Thumb, Thumb-2 and MIPS16e ISAs exceeds the performance gains from a reduced number of instruction cache misses. Due to the ability to freely interleave compact and standard instructions without mode switch the ARCompact ISA does not suffer this penalty.

4.4 Comparison to GCC

The diagrams in figures 5 and 6 contain additional data points for the official ARC port of the GCC 4.2.1 compiler targeting the ARCompact ISA and ARC750D processor.

The comparison of code size improvements when going from plain 32-bit code to mixed-mode code reveals that GCC performs significantly worse than either of our two schemes. On average, mixed-mode code generation in the GCC compiler results in a modest 2.7% reduction in code size over the 32-bit baseline. For two programs the code size reduction exceeds 10%, however, for the majority of programs code size savings of less than 5% are the norm. The poor performance

Publication	Comment	Platform (Architecture/ISA)	Compiler	Benchmarks (Name/Number)	Code Size Red. (Avg./Range)	Performance Gain (Avg./Range)
[9]	Repeated instruction selection, no caches, 1-cycle mem. access	Custom MIPS4000/ Modified MIPS16	EXPRESS	Livermore Loops/22	38%/ 31%-49%	-6%/ up to -24% (=loss)
[10, 11]	Profile-guided IS, SimpleScalar	StrongARM SA-110/ ARM-Thumb	XScale GCC 2.9	MediaBench/12	28.2%/ 22.8%-31.9%	-2.03%/ up to -14.5% (=loss)
[12]	Profile-guided IS, code size levels	Intel Xscale PXA250	Zephyr/VPO	MiBench & MediaBench/4	34.5%/ up to 42.1%	0% to -49% (=loss)
[16]	ISA not fixed, but app.-specific	UniCore (proprietary)	GCC 3.2.1 (Post-pass)	MediaBench/15	16%/ 14%-18%	0%/ up to -2% (=loss)

Table 4. Comparison to other published results for mixed-mode code generation.

of the GCC compiler is due to the non-integrated instruction selection and register allocation stages where 16-bit instructions are generated without taking into consideration the increased register pressure on the restricted, 16-bit accessible register subset.

The performance results for the GCC compiler shown in Figure 6 are even more disappointing. On average, mixed-mode applications generated by GCC perform 2.08% *worse* than their 32-bit counterparts. 13 out of 32 programs suffer from performance degradation with individual benchmarks (aifirf01) taking 46.1% *more* cycles to execute. At the same time the possible performance gains that can be observed for the remaining programs are limited and do not come close to those resulting from our proposed techniques. For only two programs (ttsprk01 and rgbcmy01) GCC delivers higher speed improvements than either of our two schemes. Overall, we feel the very modest code size improvements achieved by GCC do not justify the potentially large drop in performance. This may present a serious obstacle to the widespread adoption of mixed-mode GCC code generation by code size and performance aware users.

5. Related Work

Compact instruction sets are supported by a number of commercial embedded processors and code size aware compilation techniques targeting these short instruction formats have found significant interest in the scientific community [9, 10, 11, 12, 16]. All of these papers address mixed mode code generation where there is an overhead associated with switching between compact and standard instruction sets. In this paper, however, we are concerned with an ISA that allows freeform mixing of 16- and 32-bit instructions and to the best of our knowledge this problem has not yet been addressed in the academic literature.

A direct comparison of our results to those published elsewhere is difficult due to different choices of benchmarks, compiler frameworks and not least instruction set architectures. Nonetheless, we juxtapose the available results on code size reduction and performance impact along with relevant details relating to the architectures and ISAs, compilers, and benchmarks in Table 4.

In [9] a modified MIPS16 ISA is targeted and a compiler flow with repeated instruction selection passes is proposed. After the first instruction selection stage targeting a generic 3-address ISA a profitability analysis is performed that guides the second instruction selection stage in its selection of compact instructions. In a final step register allocation takes place. This work is similar to our approach in that compiler feedback is used to improve compact code generation, however, the main difference is that register allocation is not taken into account and, as a consequence, excessive spilling may occur. The single-cycle memory access model, however, almost eliminates the spilling cost. This and the trivial Livermore loops benchmarks may lead to overly optimistic performance results, which still show an overall slowdown. The reported code size reduction, however, is impressive, but requires further evaluation on more representative benchmarks.

Feedback information is used in [10, 11] for the selection of ARM and Thumb instructions. Frequently executed functions are identified via profiling before a heuristic based on expected performance and relative code size is used to choose between 32-bit ARM and 16-bit Thumb instructions. In contrast, our approach does not require this expensive profiling stage and operates on purely static information available in the compiler. Overall, code size reduction is good, but the higher code density does not translate to performance gains resulting from improved instruction cache behaviour.

Instruction set assignment is determined on a per-basic-block basis in [12]. This requires a profile-guided control flow analysis to determine the program points where the processor's execution mode should be switched. An effort level is chosen depending on a code size budget set by the user. In order to avoid excessive mode switching overhead a detailed profitability analysis that estimates the cost and benefit of using different instruction sets for different parts of a given program is required. As a secondary goal the impact of using a compact instruction format on the worst-case execution time is analysed. Again, we do not rely on profiling, but employ static feedback information within the compiler. While the overall code size reduction is good for four small applications and the most aggressive code size budget, the performance penalty can be drastic. For more relaxed settings, the performance loss can be compensated, but at the same time code size savings drop sharply.

A slightly unconventional approach to compact code generation is taken in [16] where mixed mode code generation is performed as a post pass to the actual compiler. In addition, the semantics of the chosen compact ISA is changed in order to efficiently encode mode changing operations. This results in good code size reductions without incurring any significant performance loss. In contrast, we target a fixed ISA requiring no architectural changes whilst reducing code size and, at the same time, *improving* performance across the entire range of benchmarks.

In summary, those techniques in [9, 10, 11, 12, 16] that achieve higher code size reductions than our approach result in significant performance losses. For [16] the code size gains are comparable, but we generate faster code and do not rely on hardware modifications.

The method in patent [8] describes a compilation technique targeting compact instructions of the ARCompact instruction set where a block of code is compiled for *both* standard 32-bit and compact 16-bit instruction sets. Eventually, whichever version is "better" gets chosen. In this scheme compact code generation is aggressive, however, whenever spilling occurs a "clean up" operation is performed to offload memory references to the general-purpose register set. This scheme is largely identical to the aggressive scheme shown in Table 1 with all its disadvantages.

MIPS and ARM state code size savings up to 35% and 26%, respectively, for their microMIPS [13] and Thumb-2 [14] ISAs while performance drops by 2%. A direct comparison of the Thumb, Thumb-2, MIPS16e and ARCompact ISAs is given in [15]. Design trade-offs for microprocessors with variable length instructions are subject of [5] and general code-size reduction methods are surveyed in [4].

6. Summary and Conclusions

We have developed an integrated instruction selection and register allocation methodology for a compact ISA with freely interleavable 16- and 32-bit instructions. We have presented a simple, yet powerful opportunistic instruction selection scheme and a more general, feedback-guided scheme that is more portable and does not, unlike the first scheme, depend on a particular distribution of register accesses. Experimental results based on our highly optimising CoSy compiler targeting the ARC750D processor demonstrate that an average code size reduction of 16.7% can be achieved across the industry standard EEMBC benchmarks whilst at the same time improving performance by on average 17.7%. This result is encouraging and shows that code size reduction and optimisation for performance are not mutually exclusive, but can be obtained simultaneously.

Future work will include the power/energy evaluation of our compact code generation methodology.

References

[1] ACE Associated Computer Experts bv. CoSy compiler development system. http://www.ace.nl, retrieved 12 August 2009.

[2] ARC International. ARC750D Core. http://www.arc.com, retrieved 12 August 2009.

[3] ARM Ltd. ARM Cortex-M3. http://www.arm.com, retrieved 12 August 2009.

[4] Árpád Beszédes, Rudolf Ferenc, Tibor Gyimóthy, André Dolenc, and Karsisto, Konsta. Survey of code-size reduction methods. ACM Computing Surveys, Vol. 35, No. 3, pp. 223–267, 2003.

[5] John Bunda, Don Fussell, W.C. Athas, and Roy Jenevein. 16-bit vs. 32-bit instructions for pipelined microprocessors. SIGARCH Computer Architecture News, Vol. 21, No. 2, pp. 237–246, 1993.

[6] Dave Bursky. Nonvolatile Memory: More Than A Flash In The Pan. In *electronic design*, http://electronicdesign.com, ED Online ID 5267, July 2003.

[7] The Embedded Microprocessor Benchmark Consortium. EEMBC Benchmark Suite. http://www.eembc.org, retrieved 12 August 2009.

[8] Richard A. Fuhler, Thomas J. Pennello, Michael Lee Jalkut, and Peter Warnes. Method and Apparatus for Compiling Instructions for a Data Processor. United States Patent US 7278137B1, Oct. 2, 2007.

[9] A. Halambi, A. Shrivastava, P. Biswas, N. Dutt, A. Nicolau. An Efficient Compiler Technique for Code Size Reduction Using Reduced Bit-Width ISAs. In *Proceedings of the Conference on Design, Automation and Test in Europe (DATE)*, p. 402, 2002.

[10] Arvind Krishnaswamy and Rajiv Gupta. Profile guided selection of ARM and Thumb instructions. ACM SIGPLAN Notices, Vol. 32, No. 7, pp. 56–64, 2002.

[11] Arvind Krishnaswamy and Rajiv Gupta. Mixed-width instruction sets. Communications of the ACM, Vol. 46, No. 8, pp. 47–52, 2003.

[12] Sheayun Lee, Jaejin Lee, Chang Park, Sang Min. Selective code transformation for dual instruction set processors. ACM Transactions on Embedded Computing Systems, Vol. 6, No. 2, 2007.

[13] MIPS Technologies. microMIPS Instruction Set Architecture. MD00690, Revision 01.00, October 2009.

[14] Richard Phelan. Improving ARM Code Density and Performance – New Thumb Extensions to the ARM Architecture. ARM Thumb-2 Core Technology Whitepaper, June 2003.

[15] Jim Turley. Code compression under the microscope. In *Embedded Systems Design*, http://www.embedded.com, retrieved 12 August 2009.

[16] Liu Xianhua, Zhang Jiyu, Cheng Xu. Efficient code size reduction without performance loss. In *Proceedings of the ACM Symposium on Applied Computing (SAC)*, pp. 666–672, 2007.

Automatic Creation of Tile Size Selection Models *

Tomofumi Yuki

Colorado State University

yuki@cs.colostate.edu

Lakshminarayanan
Renganarayanan

IBM T.J. Watson Research Center

lrengan@us.ibm.com

Sanjay Rajopadhye

Colorado State University

Sanjay.Rajopadhye@cs.colostate.edu

Charles Anderson

Colorado State University

anderson@cs.colostate.edu

Alexandre E. Eichenberger

IBM T.J. Watson Research Center

alexe@us.ibm.com

Kevin O'Brien

IBM T.J. Watson Research Center

caomhin@us.ibm.com

Abstract

Tiling is a widely used loop transformation for exposing/exploiting parallelism and data locality. Effective use of tiling requires selection and tuning of the tile sizes. This is usually achieved by hand-crafting tile size selection (TSS) models that characterize the performance of the tiled program as a function of tile sizes. The best tile sizes are selected by either directly using the TSS model or by using the TSS model together with an empirical search. Hand-crafting accurate TSS models is hard, and adapting them to different architecture/compiler, or even keeping them up-to-date with respect to the evolution of a single compiler is often just as hard.

Instead of hand-crafting TSS models, can we automatically learn or create them? In this paper, we show that for a specific class of programs fairly accurate TSS models can be automatically created by using a combination of simple program features, synthetic kernels, and standard machine learning techniques. The automatic TSS model generation scheme can also be directly used for adapting the model and/or keeping it up-to-date. We evaluate our scheme on six different architecture-compiler combinations (chosen from three different architectures and four different compilers). The models learned by our method have consistently shown near-optimal performance (within 5% of the optimal on average) across all architecture-compiler combinations.

Categories and Subject Descriptors D.3.4 [*Programming Languages*]: Processors—Optimization; Compilers

General Terms Performance, Algorithms, Languages

Keywords Tiling, Neural Network, Performance Modeling, Machine Learning

---

* This material is partly based upon work supported by the Defense Advanced Research Projects Agency under its Agreement No. HR0011-07-9-0002

1. Introduction

The compute and data intensive kernels of several important applications are loops. Tiling [16, 35, 22, 41] restructures loop computations to exploit parallelism and/or data locality by matching the program characteristics (e.g., locality and parallelism) to those of the execution environment (e.g., memory hierarchy, registers, and number of processors). Effective use of tiling requires techniques for tile shape/size selection and tiled code generation. In this paper we focus on the key step of *tile size selection* (TSS).

TSS is an important step in the effective use of tiling. The importance is evident from the vast literature available on this topic, and is also highlighted in the performance chart shown in Figure 1. There is a 5x and 2.5x difference in performance between the best and worst tile sizes for Power5 and Opteron, respectively. TSS involves the development of a (cost) model, which is used to characterize and select the best tile sizes for a given combination of program, architecture, and compiler. For an overview of TSS models, see [31, 25].

TSS solutions can be broadly classified into two categories, viz., static model based [21, 35, 9, 15, 7, 34, 25, 42, 12, 33] and model-driven empirical search based [39, 10, 20, 8, 13, 30]. In the static model based approach, the compiler uses a pre-designed TSS model to pick the best tile sizes for a given program-architecture pair. In the model-driven empirical search approach, the TSS model is used to characterize and prune the space of good tile sizes. For each tile size in the pruned search space, a version of the program is generated and run on the target architecture, and the tile sizes with the least execution time is selected. Due to the large space of valid tile sizes an exhaustive search, without using any TSS model to prune the space, is often not feasible.

Both the static model and model-driven empirical search approaches require a well designed TSS model. Constructing a good TSS model is hard. The extensive literature on the TSS problem is evidence of the importance as well as the difficulty of the problem. The problem of creating accurate TSS models is further exacerbated by (i) the complexity of the memory hierarchy in multi-core processor architectures and (ii) the highly intertwined optimization phases of a compiler. For example, Yotov et al. [42, 43] show the level of detailed understanding of the architecture and compiler optimization required to construct effective TSS models.

In addition to the effort involved in creating a TSS model, adapting it to a different architecture and/or compiler requires significant effort. Further, keeping a TSS model up-to-date with respect to the evolution of optimizations in a single compiler is in itself a significant task. In fact, the recognition of this difficulty in constructing

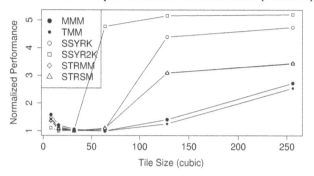

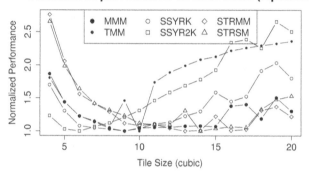

Figure 1. Variation in execution time of tiled code for six scientific kernels. The execution time is normalized to the best (lowest) running time of the points shown in the figure. Note that two processors show a very different behavior, and scale of x-axis is quite different in the two figures.

and maintaining accurate TSS models led to the wide spread use of empirical search techniques. Unfortunately, to be efficient and fast enough empirical search techniques also require TSS models to (at least) prune the search space, and these models themselves are also non-trivial to construct and adapt.

In summary, accurate TSS models are needed to select the best tile sizes and constructing and adapting them are becoming more and more difficult.

Previous approaches to TSS have used hand-crafted TSS models to either directly select the tile sizes [21, 35, 9, 15, 7, 34, 25, 42] or as a part of an empirical search to prune the search space [39, 10, 20, 8, 13, 30]. There are also TSS methods where hand-crafted TSS models are used to define a space of valid/good tile sizes and then machine learning techniques are used to efficiently search the space for the best tile sizes [38, 23, 11, 29]. As discussed earlier, the hand-crafted models used in these approaches are difficult to create, adapt, and maintain.

Instead of hand-crafting TSS models, can we automatically learn or create them? If so, we can use the same techniques to automatically adapt or keep them up-to-date with respect to changes in architectures and compilers. In this paper, we show, for a specific class of programs (3D loop nest with 2D data), that by using a combination of simple program features, synthetic kernels and standard machine learning techniques, highly effective and accurate TSS models can be learned with little or no human involvement. The two key ideas behind our approach are (i) the use of six simple program features that capture the effects of spatial and tem-

poral locality of tiled programs and (ii) the use of synthetic and automatically generated programs to learn the TSS models.

We consider the problem of selecting tile sizes for a single level of tiling for caches. For validation, we use scientific computation kernels that are known to benefit from cache tiling. We report extensive validation of our scheme on three different architectures (Intel Core2Duo, AMD Opteron, Power5) and four different compilers (gcc, IBM xlc, PathScale pathcc, and Intel icc). We show that fairly accurate TSS models can be automatically created on all the six different architecture-compiler combinations. The tile sizes predicted by our machine-crafted models, trained separately for each architecture-compiler combination, consistently show near-optimal performance on a variety of scientific kernels. The training of the machine-crafted models involves a couple of days of data collection and very little effort to tune the neural network parameters. The resulting TSS model can be directly used by a compiler to compute the best tile sizes for a given program, or can be used by an auto-tuner to perform a model-driven empirical search.

The paper makes the following contributions:

- We identify a set of six simple program features that characterize the spatial and temporal locality benefits of a tiled program.

- We show that the simple structure of the program features can be exploited to generate synthetic tiled programs which can be used for learning the TSS models.

- We formulate a machine learning scheme which models the optimal tile sizes as a continuous function of the program features.

- We report extensive validation of our technique on six different compiler-architecture combinations. We show that very effective TSS models, which predict the near-optimal tile sizes across all the six platforms can be automatically learned for our target class of programs.

To the best of our knowledge, our work is the first one to use a combination of a simple set of features and synthetic programs to automatically create TSS models.

The rest of the sections are organized as follows. Section 2 introduces loop tiling for caches and the architectural features that affect the performance of tiled programs. Section 3 introduces the program features, predicted outputs, and the use of artificial neural networks to learn TSS models. In Section 4, we outline the different stages of our scheme and in Section 5 we present experimental evaluation. Section 6 compares the performance of the machine-crafted TSS models with two well known hand-crafted TSS models from the literature. Section 7 presents some conclusions and pointers to future work.

2. Loop Tiling For Cache Locality

Cache tiling, also called cache blocking, transforms a set of loops into another set of loops, which performs the same computation but in a different order so that the program has better cache locality. Tiling is used to maximize reuse and avoid costly accesses to lower levels in the memory hierarchy. For example, consider the loop nest in Figure 2, which is the symmetric rank k update (SSYRK) kernel. If you consider the access to the C matrix, the entire matrix is accessed in each iteration of the outer-most i loop. If the cache is large enough to store the entire C matrix, the program will read the matrix from the main memory when it was first used, and then the remaining accesses only needs to wait for the cache. With the original code, we need enough cache to hold N^2 elements of the C array, and additional $2N$ for the A array to maximize reuse. However, L1 data caches of modern processors are around 32KB to 128KB, and are often not enough to store the entire matrix for large problem instances.

```
for (i=0; i<N; i++)
  for (j=0; j<N; j++)
    for (k=j; k<N; k++)
      C[j][k] += A[i][j] * A[i][k];
```

Figure 2. SSYRK

```
for (Tj = 0; Tj < N; Tj+=tSize)
  for (Tk = Tj; Tk < N; Tk+=tSize)
    for (i=0; i<N; i++)
      for (j=Tj; j<min(Tj+tsize,N); j++)
        for (k=j; k<min(Tk+tsize,N); k++)
          C[j][k] += A[i][j] * A[i][k];
```

Figure 3. Tiled SSYRK

```
for(i=0; i<N; i++)
  for(j=0; j<N; j++)
    for(k=0; k<=j; k++)
      if (k <= j-1)
        B[j][i]=B[j][i]-L[j][k]*B[k][i];
      if (k == j)
        B[j][i]=B[j][i]/L[j][j];
```

Figure 4. TRISOLV

MMM	Matrix Matrix Multiplication
TMM	Triangular MM ($C = AB$)
SSYRK	Symmetric Rank K Update
SSYR2K	Symmetric Rank 2K Update
STRMM	In-place TMM ($B = AB$)
STRSM	Solve Triangular Matrix ($AX = \alpha B$)
TRISOLV	Solve Triangles ($Ax = b$)
LUD	LU Decomposition
SSYMM	Symmetric MMM

Table 1. Nine real kernels used for validation

Tiling partitions the iteration space and changes the order of execution so that data will be reused while still performing the same computation. A possible application of tiling to the SSYRK kernel is shown in Figure 3. New loops with indices Tj and Tk control the memory requirement by the tile size parameter $tSize$ so that $tSize^2$ elements fit in the available cache.

Tiling has been studied extensively and is an important optimization in highly tuned linear algebra libraries such as BLAS or ATLAS [40, 43]. The above example only shows the use of tiling to maximize L1 cache reuse, but tiling can be applied simultaneously to other memory hierarchies such as registers, and other levels of caches. In addition, multiple levels of tiling can be applied to optimize for multiple levels of the memory system.

2.1 Cache Tiling and Hardware Prefetching

Let us consider a hardware prefetcher that can prefetch subsequent cache lines to L1 cache when cache lines are accessed sequentially, such as the one in Power5 processor. On such a processor, all the references in Figure 2 can be prefetched, because all of them are along the cache line (assuming row-major layout). With hardware prefetching, the untiled code performs slightly better than tiled code with best tile size, since it does not suffer from loop control overhead associated with tiling.

However, not all programs have prefetcher-friendly structure. Consider Figure 4. Because the k loop is dependent on the outer j loop, simple loop permutation cannot make the reference B[k][i] prefetcher-friendly. Also, multiple computations may be fused in practice, which may result in a prefetcher-unfriendly code segment. Again by loop fusion, the total number of references in a loop nest may increase beyond the number of prefetcher streams available, which again limits the benefit of hardware prefetching.

It has been shown by Kamil et al. [17] that cache blocking may not be effective for stencil computations with 2D data. Stencil computations have uniform accesses that can be easily prefetched . Combined with large on-chip memories available on modern hardware, the level of reuse already achieved without transforming the loop is comparable with tiled code. We therefore exclude stencil computations from the target class of programs in this paper.

Some of the recent architectures have even better hardware prefetchers that start prefetching when constant-stride accesses are observed in addition to the unit-stride accesses. With constant-stride prefetcher, references that access by columns (not along the cache line) can also be prefetched if the access pattern is regular. However, recent Intel processor series, which were the only processors with constant-stride hardware prefetchers, cannot prefetch if the stride crosses 4KB page boundaries [1]. Because of this constraint, constant-stride prefetcher in the Intel processors cannot do any better than unit-stride prefetchers when the problem instance is large enough so that each row is more than 4KB (512 doubles).

When optimizing for multi-core, tiling is used to expose parallelism and improve cache locality [3]. Some loop permutations that would make a loop nest prefetcher-friendly might not be the best transformation for parallelism. Consider SSYRK in Figure 2. Permuting the loops to make i loop the innermost loop can reduce the synchronization overhead when this code is parallelized for a shared memory environment. If this code were to be parallelized using OpenMP, one would prefer reordering the loops so that the j loop is outermost, and mark the outermost loop as the parallel loop. The number of synchronization is now reduced from N to 1, compared to inserting the parallelization pragma before the i loop in the original code (Figure 2). However, the new loop ordering (j, k, i) makes the two references to array a are prefetcher-unfriendly, and tiling could be used for better locality.

2.2 Target Class of Programs

In this paper, we focus on a class of scientific computations, such as linear algebra, which are known to benefit from tiling. Tiled code generators, such as TLoG [32], Pluto [3], PrimeTile [14], and D-tiling [18], are available for these class of programs, which make it easier to use our TSS learning approach. Although there are highly tuned libraries available for common kernels like matrix multiplication, computations that are not covered by the libraries may still come up by trying to use a specific loop ordering or as a result of other transformations, such as fusing multiple kernel computations. The nine kernels we use in this paper are summarized in Table 1.

Among this class of programs, we consider the programs that have three dimensional loops with two dimensional data. Many scientific kernels, like matrix multiplication, fit in to this subset of programs. Also programs with more than three dimensional loops can be still handled in our model by only tiling the inner three dimensions. We consider cubic tiles only to reduce data collection time. Allowing all three dimensions to have different tile sizes significantly increases the number of possible tile sizes. Our approach can be directly extended to predict rectangular tile sizes by increasing the data collection time, which will be described later in more detail. We do not consider data padding or copy optimization, since available code generators do not handle these optimizations.

```
for (i=0; i<N; i++)
  for (j=0; j<N; j++)
    for (k=0; k<N; k++)
      C[i][j] += A[i][k] * B[k][j];
```

Figure 5. Matrix Matrix Multiplication

3. Learning TSS Models

In this section we describe the basic components of TSS model learning; the inputs to and outputs of the model, and the machine learning technique we use.

3.1 Input Program Features

In order to use a model to predict optimal tile sizes for different programs, the model needs to be provided with inputs that distinguish different programs. The inputs to our model are features of the programs. Previous methods that use machine learning techniques for compiler optimizations have often used syntactic features such as the number of operands or the number of loop nests [36, 27, 6]. After experimenting with a variety of features that capture the spatial and temporal locality effects of loop tiling, we arrived at a set of six features.

The features are based on the number of references in the innermost statements, classified into three different types of references. Then each type of reference is further classified into reads and writes for a total of six features. The three types of references are *non-prefetched* references, *prefetched* references, and references that are constant in the innermost loop (*invariant*). The *invariant* reference captures those references that are reused for all the iterations of the innermost loop. The *prefetched* reference captures references that enjoy spatial locality given by the prefetcher, and *non-prefetched* references are those that need temporal locality for good performance. Read and write references are distinguished because of the possible differences in how they are treated especially in multi-core processors where L2 cache is commonly shared among the cores.

For example, in matrix multiplication shown in Figure 5, the reference to array c is *write-invariant* (WI), because it is written to the same location by all iterations of the innermost loop. Reference to array a is *read-prefetched* (RP), because the innermost loop index k is used to index the columns of the array, and such accesses are prefetched by unit-stride prefetcher. Reference to array b is *read-non-prefetched* (RNP), since k is used to index the rows, and we are assuming row-major layout. These features can easily be extracted by looking at the loop orderings used to reference arrays. The compiler needs to be aware of the type of hardware prefetcher is used on each architecture to calculate these values, but we believe this is a simple requirement. Detailed information about the prefetcher is not required, the compiler only needs to know if unit-stride access is prefetched. With the current hardware prefetching technology, even a constant-stride prefetcher works effectively as an unit-stride prefetcher as discussed earlier. More information may become necessary with significant advance in hardware prefetching.

3.2 Predicted Outputs

There are multiple possible outputs for a TSS model. One possibility is to model the performance of tiled code itself and search the learned function for tile sizes that optimize performance given a specific program. However, this approach requires searching the function after modeling. In the case of analytical models, the function may be smooth and the optimal is easy to find using some kind of optimization method. With functions learned by neural networks, the function may not be smooth and optimization methods can get trapped in one of many local minima. Finding global minima in such functions is itself a separate and difficult problem, which we would like to avoid.

Another possible output is the optimal tile size itself. Classifying programs to optimal tile sizes allows skipping the step of searching the function and directly gives tile size as an output. Classifiers can be also learned by neural networks or other machine learning techniques such as support vector machines. However, simple classification is only capable of classifying programs into predefined set of optimal tile sizes. Thus, it does not suit our goal of predicting optimal tile sizes of unseen programs, unless we have enough training data to cover all possible tile sizes, which is unlikely.

We used a solution between the two ways described above. We use the optimal tile size as the output, but we do not learn classifiers. Instead, we formulate the TSS model to be learned as a continuous function from the six program features (described earlier in 3.1) to the optimal tile sizes. The following example gives an intuitive motivation for formulating the TSS model to be a continuous function. Consider three programs with identical program features except for number of RNP references. Program A has optimal tile size of 100 with RNP=1, program B has optimal tile size of 50 with RNP=3. It is reasonable to think that program C with RNP=2 has optimal tile size somewhere between 50 and 100, since it requires more data per iteration compared to program A, but less compared to B.

3.3 Using ANN to Learn TSS Model

We used artificial neural networks (ANN), a supervised learning method, to learn tile size prediction model. Supervised learning methods require pairs of input and desired output, and learn some function to minimize error between the output of the function and the desired output. The neural network we used is a back-propagation neural network and was trained with Scaled Conjugate Gradient method [26].

We use multi-layered neural networks [2]. The number of nodes in the output layer is equal to the number of outputs to be produced by the neural network. Each hidden layer can have any number of nodes. The inputs to the ANN is given to the first hidden layer, and outputs from each layer is given to the next layer. The outputs from hidden layers is a function of weighted sum of the inputs to that layer, where the function is the hyperbolic tangent. The output layer performs weighted sum of the outputs from the last hidden layer, but does not apply the hyperbolic tangent function. Given output layer weights w, output from the last hidden layer h, desired output b, and number of training data N, each output layer node tries to minimize the error calculated using the equation below.

$$\Sigma_{n=1}^{N} \left((h.w)_n - b_n \right)^2$$

The neural network starts with random values as initial weights in each node, and then iteratively updates the weights to minimize the error. The scaled conjugate gradient method is a type of gradient method that approximates the second order derivative to allow faster convergence to the local minimum, and hence accelerate training of ANN compared to standard back-propagation with gradient descent.

Models learned using neural networks return real valued numbers as optimal tile size. Since tile sizes are integers, we simply round the given value to a closest integer and use that as the predicted optimal tile size.

4. Our Approach

Our approach has the following four different stages

1. Synthetic program generation

2. Data Collection

3. Learning TSS models using ANN

4. Use of ANN based TSS model

Stages 1 through 3 are part of the TSS model creation phase and are done offline. Stage 4 represents the use of the learned TSS model and is done on-line during the compilation of a program to select the tile sizes.

4.1 Synthetic Program Generation

We need to collect training data to train neural networks. Data gathered from real applications or kernels are commonly used as the training data for machine learning based modeling. However, using real applications limits the training data to the real applications available at the time of training. The neural network cannot be expected to perform well on programs with features that are significantly different from any program in the training data. With real applications as training data, there is not much control over the range of programs that is covered by the neural network. In addition, some of the real applications need to be separated out from the training data for validation. Also, if multiple applications have the same program feature, the neural networks may become overtrained to better suit that program feature more than others.

We use synthetic programs to overcome these limitations. The synthetic programs we use are programs that fit in our class of interest (three dimensional loops and two dimensional data), with statements in the innermost loop that are generated to have the specified number of references for each type. We exhaustively search for optimal tile sizes of the generated programs to create the training data set. We used the open source tiled code generator, TLoG [32], to generate codes with all three dimensions tiled.

With synthetic programs, we have better control over training data, and the ability to train using a large number of training data points. We believe these benefits given by synthetic programs are one of the main reasons that lead to well performing models.

The use of synthetic programs was only possible because we have simple program features. If a large number of program features were used, then it becomes infeasible to try a large range of possible programs with synthetic programs. Even if real programs were used, the coverage of programs that can be represented by complex program features is going to be sparse.

We selected a range of values of program features, and hence programs, that cover all the kernels we used, but also includes many others so that the model is not specialized to just those kernels. Table 2 shows the range of values we used to bound the feature space. Column names represent the type of reference, prefetched (P), non-prefetched (NP), invariant(I) for read (R) and write (W). These bounds were constructed so that the space is not too large, but still captures a wide variety of programs. The number of reads are usually more than the writes, so we only have a small number of writes. RNP is always greater than 0, to ensure the program stays in the class of interest (at least one reference is not prefetched). There are a total of 2835 program instances in this space with at least one write.

The range of program features to be covered can be changed to better suit expected programs. If you know that the compiler is going to see a small subset of the possible feature space beforehand, the model can be specialized for that range of programs.

From the bounded feature space, we collected optimal tile sizes for a number of points in the feature space. Table 3 shows the points used for the training data. We also exclude from the training data,

	RP	RNP	RI	WP	WNP	WI
Range	0-8	1-5	0-8	0-1	0-1	0-1

Table 2. Bounds on feature space for the model as number of references of each type

	RP	RNP	RI	WP	WNP	WI
Range	0,2,4,8	1-5	0,2,4,8	0-1	0-1	0-1

Table 3. Data points used for training

programs with features identical to features of real kernels, so that real kernels we used to test our model remain unseen during the training.

4.2 Data Collection

Collecting training data is time consuming, but can be done without much human effort. The use of a parameterized tiled code generator helped our data collection by avoiding compilation for each tile size explored for a program.

Data collection took between 20-40 hours for each compiler-architecture combination. We used problem sizes that take around 10 seconds of execution time for each synthetic program instance. Because the number of references in a program affects its running time, using the same problem sizes would cause the running time of some synthetic program instances to be much larger than 10 seconds. We used a very simple linear function of number of references to adjust the problem size. This adjustment was only for avoiding long execution times during data collection, and the accuracy of the adjustment was not an issue.

4.3 Learning TSS Models Using ANN

There are many parameters in the training process, including the range of programs to target, the range of training data, and parameters of the neural network. The former two can be made larger and larger if time permits, since we want the model to cover a larger range of programs, and having more training data always helps learning.

The parameters of the neural network are not as simple. There are many parameters for a neural network, the important ones being the number of hidden layers, the number of nodes in each layer, how initial weights are selected, and the termination condition. In addition, we can train multiple neural networks individually for more stable output. Averaging the output of multiple neural networks helps stabilize the output, because neural networks learned are heavily influenced by the initial weights. The number of neural networks to be trained for averaging in the end is also another parameter. We do not try to optimize the neural network parameters. Instead we manually tune the neural network parameters based on our intuition and testing on small data sets. We hope to develop an automated approach to optimize neural network parameters in the future.

We used three-layered (two hidden layers) neural networks with 30 hidden nodes per hidden layer, and weights randomly initialized to values between 1 and -1. The termination condition was slightly different for each architecture-compiler combination based on how easy it was to fit the training data for a particular combination. These parameters are picked by trying out multiple combinations of parameters and looking at the rate of convergence and root mean square errors, a measure of how far the predicted outputs are away from the desired outputs.

It took about two hours of initial tuning to get a good basic design of the neural network, and then the SAME basic neural network configuration was applied to all architecture-compiler combinations. Note that this design time is a one-time effort. After the basic design, for each architecture-compiler combination, a slight tuning of the termination condition was needed. We tuned the termination condition using the collected training data, by looking at how the error between predicted and desired output changes between iterations. Where the improvement starts to flatten could be different for each training data, and we selected a condition to terminate when it starts to flatten. This tuning is pretty standard and can be automated.

With the above configuration, training of each neural network completes within a minute for a total of at most five minutes for five different neural networks trained for each architecture-compiler combination.

4.4 Use of ANN Based TSS Model

Once we have the trained TSS model, it can be used as a part of the compiler to predict the optimal tile sizes, or used as a part of a model-driven search method to find the optimal tile sizes. The first step is to extract the program features, which should not take much time due to its simplicity. Then the six program features are used as an input to the learned model to produce the output, which can be directly used as the tile size selected for that program. When the model is used as a part of a model-driven search method, the tile sizes in the neighborhood of the predicted tile sizes can be empirically tested for the best performance. It is also possible to alter the neural network to output expected performance of a program with a given tile size, which may be a better model for mode-driven search.

The only on-line cost associated with the use of our model in a compiler is the use of the neural network and extraction of the six program features. The use of neural networks is computationally close to two matrix-vector products of size 31x6, which is trivial with modern compute power.

4.5 Extension to Rectangular Tiles

Our approach can be directly extended to predict rectangular tile sizes as well. The flow described above does not change at all. The only pieces that need to be changed is the outputs of the neural network, and the data collection. The outputs from the neural network needs to be increased from one to two or three, depending on whether two or three dimensions are tiled, because tile size in each dimension can be now different. The data collection phase needs to be adjusted accordingly to find the optimal tile sizes including rectangular tiles. Because neural networks naturally handle more than one outputs, no other change is required.

5. Experimental Validation of Machine-Crafted Models

We have used our approach to learn tile size selection models on the six architecture-compiler combinations summarized in Table 4. We used the nine kernels previously summarized in 1 with problem sizes adjusted for each architecture to run for about a minute. We chose a longer target execution time compared to the 10 seconds of the synthetic programs so that the problem sizes used were significantly different from the problem sizes used during validation. The problem sizes used for real kernels were around 3000, where as the problem sizes used during training was around 1000.

Feature extraction was done manually, but it can be easily done in a compiler. We used the same set of program features on all architectures, because even the constant-stride prefetcher on Core2Duo effectively worked only as a unit-stride prefetcher due to its constraint on access distance.

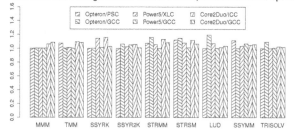

Figure 6. Execution time normalized to the true optimal of kernels with tile sizes selected by machine-crafted models for each combination of architecture-compilers.

5.1 Performance

For each architecture-compiler combination, we compare the execution time of kernels with the true optimal (found by exhaustive search) and the predicted optimal tile sizes. Figure 6 shows the normalized execution time of nine kernels with tile sizes selected by machine-crafted models learned for each architecture-compiler combination. The performance given by tile sizes predicted by our machine-crafted models is consistently near the optimal. The performance is only 20% off the optimal even in the worst case, which is significantly small compared to the slowdown one would get with a poor tile size (recall Figure 1). This supports our claim that well performing TSS models can be learned from simple features and training data collected through synthetic programs for different architecture and compilers. Although we do not have results for different versions of the same compiler, we have shown results for different compilers, which is just as hard if not harder. This indicates that the learned TSS models can be easily updated (re-trained) with respect to the evolution of a single compiler.

5.2 Performance with Local Search

The focus of this paper is on learning TSS models that can predict good tile sizes for different architecture and compilers without much human effort. In this section we quantify its potential when used as a part of model-driven empirical search approaches. We show how close the predicted tile sizes is to the optimal by simply looking at neighboring tile sizes within a certain distance. Here, distance is the difference between the predicted tile size and the tile sizes actually explored.

Table 5 shows the mean slowdown over all nine kernels when the best tile size within a certain distance of the predicted tile size were used. Only by looking at immediate neighbors of distance ten, the model can give the exact optimal performance for all kernels on Opteron, and for eight out of the nine kernels for Power5. The performance improvement on Core2Duo is relatively small compared to other architectures, but notable improvement can be observed.

We think the cause of relatively small improvement on Core2Duo is due to the very high set-associativity (8-way). There is a very wide range of good tile sizes, and the automated training data col-

Architecture	Compilers	L1 Cache	Options
Opteron	PSC, GCC	64KB 2-way	-O3, -O3
Power5	XLC, GCC	32KB 4-way	-O5, -O3
Core2Duo	ICC, GCC	32KB 8-way	-O3, -O3

Table 4. Architecture and compilers used

	Predicted	Distance 10	Distance 20
Opteron/PSC	4.3%	0%	0%
Opteron/GCC	6.3%	0%	0%
Power5/XLC	4.6%	0.4%	0%
Power5/GCC	1.7%	0.2%	0%
Core2Duo/ICC	7.8%	4.0%	1.9%
Core2Duo/GCC	5.1%	4.0%	1.9%

Table 5. Mean slowdown over all kernels when the best tile size within some distance from the predicted tile size is used.

	Machine-Crafted	LRW	EUC	Yotov et al.
Opteron/PSC	4%	178%	217%	169%
Opteron/gcc	6%	100%	147%	139%
Power5/XLC	5%	168%	268%	9%
Power5/gcc	2%	77%	133%	3%
Core2Duo/ICC	8%	6%	246%	5%
Core2Duo/gcc	5%	3%	128%	4%

Table 6. Mean of slowdowns with tile sizes predicted by each model over all nine kernels on each architecture-compiler combination

lection is likely to have more noise compared to others. The optimal on a flat surface can be easily affected by small noises from the operating system or other environment not necessarily connected to the program being executed. We believe this noise can be suppressed by increasing the problem size and/or running each instance of the synthetic program a number of times and taking the minimum (or mean) execution time

Another reason is that with GCC on Core2Duo, two kernels, MMM and TMM, are showing optimal performance with a tile size that is far from the tile size predicted by our model. We suspect that this is due to some optimization applied by the compiler only for the standard matrix multiplication, since by changing the compiler option from -O3 to -O2, the tile size predicted by our model shows identical performance with the true optimal.

How good are the models created by our approach, compared to randomly picking points in the search space, when local search is performed is a question that the readers may have. It has also been shown by Kisuki et al. [19] that random search takes large number of iterations (100+) to reach within 5% of the optimal for most of the benchmarks they used, which included dense linear algebra computations as well.

Even a naive local search around the tile sizes predicted by the machine-crafted models show significant improvements. This demonstrates its potential to perform better when combined with the more sophisticated search methods proposed in the literature.

6. Comparison with Hand-Crafted Models

Many static models have been previously developed to maximize performance of tiled code, and those models are analyzed in detail by Hsu and Kremer [15]. We have taken two models that were reported to perform well [15], and another model by Yotov et. al [42] used in ATLAS for comparison. First, we briefly describe the logic behind the three models, LRW [21], EUC [9] and the model-driven ATLAS model [42]. Then these models are evaluated in the same manner as in the previous section. The goal of this section is to show that our approach can generate models that are at least as good as the previous models for all architecture-compiler combinations.

LRW [21] is an analytical model developed by closely studying the performance of tiled matrix multiplication. It chooses square tiles for a given program using an estimate of cache misses based on memory footprint and self-interference. EUC [9] is also an analytical model with similar considerations used as in LRW, but it predicts rectangular tile sizes instead of square. EUC takes cross-interference into account as well as self-interference. Both of these models take problem sizes as an input, where as our model does not. Yotov et al. [42] uses multiple models to compute many parameters including tile sizes for cache tiling with cubic tiles. Their model for tile size selection assumes fully associative caches and does not consider conflict misses. We would like to clarify that when we refer to Yotov et al. in the following, we did not use the ATLAS auto-tuned kernels. We only used the analytical model for predicting square tile sizes for cache locality in [42].

6.1 Tailoring Hand-Crafted Models to Modern Architectures

We made a small but necessary modification to all the hand-crafted models to adapt to the current architecture. Since some of the hand-crafted models were developed when hardware prefetcher was not commonly available, they treat all references as non-prefetched. However, it is obvious that prefetched references do not have to stay in the cache, and they can be excluded when calculating the tile size so that the cache is utilized well. Because it is straight-forward and it would not take much effort to modify the model to take the prefetching into account, we modified all of the models so that prefetched references are excluded from calculation. Further, for programs that has more than one references that is not prefetched, we give smaller cache sizes to the model. Also, in [21], they briefly mention extension of their algorithm to set associative caches, we have used their modification so that larger tile sizes are selected when compared to assuming direct mapped cache.

6.2 Performance of Hand-Crafted Models

Figure 7 shows the normalized execution time of nine kernels using tile sizes given by hand-crafted static models. The same problem sizes used for measuring execution time using machine-crafted models were used. Although the hand-crafted models have predicted near optimal tile sizes for some of the kernels, the performance is not as consistent as what was observed with our machine-crafted models. LRW and Yotov et al. model performs relatively worse on Opteron compared to the other architectures. Opteron has smaller set associativity, which seems to make the performance more sensitive to small changes in tile size, leading to greater performance hit. LRW does perform more than 2x slower on Opteron with matrix multiplication that was used to develop the model.

EUC was unable to give good tile sizes for some kernels across all architecture-compiler combinations. It is interesting to note that EUC had predicted a tile size that performs better than the optimal cubic tile found for SSYR2K on Opteron with PSC. The optimal cubic tile size found for SSYR2K was 6x6x6, but it was not the optimal when rectangular tiles were considered. EUC was able to find a very thin tile that has better memory utilization for this case.

Table 6 summarizes the effectiveness of each model by showing the percentage of slowdown when compared to the optimal using cubic tile sizes. LRW and Yotov et al. model show comparable performance on some combinations, but overall the machine-crafted model provides consistently near-optimal performance across all architectures. We believe the reason for LRW and Yotov et al. model showing comparable performance on Core2Duo and Power5 is also due to the fact that these processors have very wide ranges of good tile sizes, as previously discussed in Section 5.2. In addition relatively high set associativity of these processors are closer to the assumption of Yotov et al. that caches are fully associative.

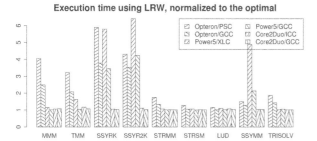

Execution time using LRW, normalized to the optimal

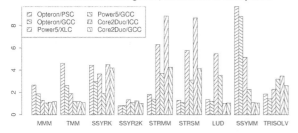

Execution time using EUC, normalized to the optimal

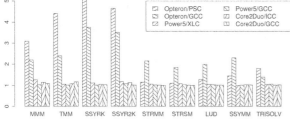

Execution time using the model by Yotov et al. normalized to the true optimal

Figure 7. Execution time of kernels with tile sizes selected by hand-crafted models for each combination of architecture-compilers, normalized to the optimal.

7. Related Work

Many analytical models have been proposed in the past for TSS [21, 35, 9, 15, 7, 34, 25, 42, 12, 33]. These models are constructed by carefully observing the performance of a small set of kernels and modeling the performance using detailed hardware and software characteristics. Although developing analytical models can give greater insight into how the hardware and software interacts, the cost of development is quite high. Our work focuses on creating good tile size selection models with little human effort.

Another class of tile size selection techniques is the model-driven empirical search methods [39, 10, 20, 8, 13, 30, 19, 38, 29]. Empirical tuning with global search may be a feasible solution for optimizing libraries of commonly used kernels [39], but is not feasible for optimization during compilation. Model-driven approaches share the same motivation of achieving performance close to what can be obtained by global empirical search, but with less overhead. Replacing the hand-crafted models currently used in these approaches is a possible application of our work.

Recently, machine learning techniques have been successfully used in compiler optimization. Many of the applications were toward deriving models and heuristics to accurately predict the behavior of modern complex architectures. The wide range of applications include branch prediction [4], instruction scheduling within

basic blocks [28, 24], and deciding if certain optimization should be applied [5, 6, 37, 27]. Some of the hand-crafted tile size selection approaches have also used some form of machine learning methods [38, 23, 11, 29, 36]. We use machine learning techniques to automatically learn TSS models.

8. Conclusions and Future Work

Tile size selection is an important step in the profitable use of loop tiling. Hand-crafting effective TSS models is hard and adapting or maintaining them is often harder. We have shown that highly effective TSS models can be automatically created using a small set of program features, synthetic programs and standard machine learning techniques. We have shown that the machine-crafted TSS models consistently predict near-optimal (on the average, within 5% of optimal) tile sizes across six different compiler-architecture combinations. We have also shown that, a naive search within a small neighborhood of the predicted tile sizes can find the true optimal tile sizes in some cases, and in other cases find tile sizes that are very close to the optimal. This clearly indicates the strong potential of machine-crafted TSS models in a model-driven empirical search scheme.

Several directions of future work are promising. The proposed approach can be directly extended to construct TSS models for multiple levels (cache and register) tiling. We have described how our approach can be extended to rectangular tile sizes with little change, which is also a possible direct extension. Another direct extension is to construct TSS models where tiling is used to expose coarse-grain parallelism [3]. Another promising direction is the use of machine-crafted TSS models together with sophisticated search techniques to develop an efficient model-driven empirical search technique for use in auto-tuners. Our approach in itself is quite flexible and with appropriate interpretation of program features, it can be extended to other class of programs. Extending to programs with irregular array references is another interesting direction.

There are some possible future work on the neural network side of our approach as well. As mentioned previously, automatic selection of neural network parameters is the only part that is not automated in our approach. There are well known approaches for selecting neural network structure, which may be applied to fully automate our approach. Our model cannot provide any insight about the underlying architecture, where the process of developing analytical models by hand tend to increase the understanding of the underlying architecture and programs as a sub-product. It would be useful if we could extract some insight from the trained neural network.

References

[1] *Intel 64 and IA-32 Architectures Optimization Reference Manual.*

[2] C.M. Bishop et al. *Pattern recognition and machine learning.* Springer New York:, 2006.

[3] Uday Bondhugula, Albert Hartono, J. Ramanujam, and P. Sadayappan. A practical automatic polyhedral program optimization system. In *ACM SIGPLAN Conference on Programming Language Design and Implementation (PLDI)*, June 2008.

[4] Brad Calder, Dirk Grunwald, Michael Jones, Donald Lindsay, James Martin, Michael Mozer, and Benjamin Zoren. Evidence-based static branch prediction using machine learning. *ACM Transactions on Programming Languages and Systems*, 19(1):188–222, January 1997.

[5] J. Cavazos and J.E.B. Moss. Inducing heuristics to decide whether to schedule. In *Proceedings of the ACM SIGPLAN 2004 conference on Programming language design and implementation*, pages 183–194, 2004.

[6] J. Cavazos and M.F.P. O'Boyle. Method-specific dynamic compilation using logistic regression. In *Proceedings of the 21st annual ACM*

SIGPLAN conference on Object-oriented programming languages, systems, and applications, pages 229–240, 2006.

[7] Jacqueline Chame and Sungdo Moon. A tile selection algorithm for data locality and cache interference. In *1999 ACM International Conference on Supercomputing*, pages 492–499. ACM Press, 1999.

[8] Chun Chen, Jacqueline Chame, and Mary Hall. Combining models and guided empirical search to optimize for multiple levels of the memory hierarchy. In *CGO '05: Proceedings of the international symposium on Code generation and optimization*, pages 111–122, Washington, DC, USA, 2005. IEEE Computer Society.

[9] S. Coleman and K.S. McKinley. Tile size selection using cache organization and data layout. In *Proceedings of the ACM SIGPLAN 1995 conference on Programming language design and implementation*, pages 279–290. ACM New York, NY, USA, 1995.

[10] J. Demmel, J. Dongarra, V. Eijkhout, E. Fuentes, A. Petitet, R. Vuduc, R.C. Whaley, and K. Yelick. Self-Adapting Linear Algebra Algorithms and Software. In *Proceedings of the IEEE*, 93(2):293, 2005.

[11] Arkady Epshteyn, María Jesús Garzarán, Gerald DeJong, David A. Padua, Gang Ren, Xiaoming Li, Kamen Yotov, and Keshav Pingali. Analytic models and empirical search: A hybrid approach to code optimization. In *Proceedings of the International Workshop on Languages and Compilers for Parallel Computing*, pages 259–273, 2005.

[12] K. Esseghir. Improving data locality for caches. Master's thesis, Rice University, 1993.

[13] Basilio B. Fraguela, M. G. Carmueja, and Diego Andrade. Optimal tile size selection guided by analytical models. In *PARCO*, pages 565–572, 2005.

[14] A. Hartono, M.M. Baskaran, C. Bastoul, A. Cohen, S. Krishnamoorthy, B. Norris, J. Ramanujam, and P. Sadayappan. Parametric multi-level tiling of imperfectly nested loops. In *Proceedings of the 23rd international conference on Conference on Supercomputing*, pages 147–157. ACM New York, NY, USA, 2009.

[15] Chung-Hsing Hsu and Ulrich Kremer. A quantitative analysis of tile size selection algorithms. *J. Supercomput.*, 27(3):279–294, 2004.

[16] F. Irigoin and R. Triolet. Supernode partitioning. In *15th ACM Symposium on Principles of Programming Languages*, pages 319–328. ACM, Jan 1988.

[17] Shoaib Kamil, Parry Husbands, Leonid Oliker, John Shalf, and Katherine Yelick. Impact of modern memory subsystems on cache optimizations for stencil computations. In *Proceedings of the Workshop on Memory System Performance*, pages 36–43, New York, NY, USA, 2005. ACM Press.

[18] DaeGon Kim and Sanjay Rajopadhye. Efficient tiled loop generation: D-tiling. In *The 22nd International Workshop on Languages and Compilers for Parallel Computing*, 2009.

[19] T. Kisuki, P.M.W. Knijnenburg, and MFP O' Boyle. Combined selection of tile sizes and unroll factors using iterative compilation. In *Proceedings of the 2000 International Conference on Parallel Architectures and Compilation Techniques*, page 237. Citeseer, 2000.

[20] P. M. W. Knijnenburg, T. Kisuki, K. Gallivan, and M. F. P. O'Boyle. The effect of cache models on iterative compilation for combined tiling and unrolling. *Concurr. Comput. : Pract. Exper.*, 16(2-3):247–270, 2004.

[21] M.D. Lam, E.E. Rothberg, and M.E. Wolf. The cache performance and optimizations of blocked algorithms. *Proceedings of the 4th international conference on architectural support for programming languages and operating systems*, 25:63–74, 1991.

[22] Monica S. Lam and Michael E. Wolf. A data locality optimizing algorithm (with retrospective). In *Best of PLDI*, pages 442–459, 1991.

[23] Xiaoming Li and María Jesús Garzarán. Optimizing matrix multiplication with a classifier learning system. *Workshop on Languages and Compilers for Parallel Computing*, pages 121–135, 2005.

[24] A. McGovern, E. Moss, and A. Barto. Scheduling straight-line code using reinforcement learning and rollouts. (UM-CS-1999-023), , 1999.

[25] N. Mitchell, N. Hogstedt, L. Carter, and J. Ferrante. Quantifying the multi-level nature of tiling interactions. *International Journal of Parallel Programming*, 26(6):641–670, 1998.

[26] Martin F. Møller. A scaled conjugate gradient algorithm for fast supervised learning. *Neural Networks*, 6:525–533, 1993.

[27] A. Monsifrot, F. Bodin, and R. Quiniou. A machine learning approach to automatic production of compiler heuristics. *Lecture notes in computer science*, pages 41–50, 2002.

[28] Eliot Moss, Paul Utgoff, John Cavazos, Doina Precup, Darko Stefanovic, Carla Brodley, and David Scheeff. Learning to schedule straight-line code. In *Proceedings of Neural Information Processing Symposium*, pages 929–935. MIT Press, 1997.

[29] Saeed Parsa and Shahriar Lotfi. A new genetic algorithm for loop tiling. *The Journal of Supercomputing*, 37(3):249–269, 2006.

[30] Apan Qasem and Ken Kennedy. Profitable loop fusion and tiling using model-driven empirical search. In *ICS '06: Proceedings of the 20th annual international conference on Supercomputing*, pages 249–258, New York, NY, USA, 2006. ACM.

[31] Lakshminarayanan Renganarayana and Sanjay Rajopadhye. Positivity, posynomials and tile size selection. In *SC '08: Proceedings of the 2008 ACM/IEEE conference on Supercomputing*, pages 1–12, Piscataway, NJ, USA, 2008. IEEE Press.

[32] Lakshminarayanan Renganarayanan, DaeGon Kim, Sanjay Rajopadhye, and Michelle Mills Strout. Parameterized tiled loops for free. In *PLDI '07: Proceedings of the 2007 ACM SIGPLAN conference on Programming language design and implementation*, pages 405–414, New York, NY, USA, 2007. ACM.

[33] Gabriel Rivera and Chau wen Tseng. A comparison of compiler tiling algorithms. In *Proceedings of the 8th International Conference on Compiler Construction (CC'99*, pages 168–182, 1999.

[34] V. Sarkar, N. Megiddo, I.B.M.T.J.W.R. Center, and Y. Heights. An analytical model for loop tiling and its solution. *Performance Analysis of Systems and Software, 2000. ISPASS. 2000 IEEE International Symposium on*, pages 146–153, 2000.

[35] R. Schreiber and J. Dongarra. Automatic blocking of nested loops. Technical Report 90.38, RIACS, NASA Ames Research Center, Aug 1990.

[36] M. Stephenson and S. Amarasinghe. Predicting unroll factors using supervised classification. In *Proceedings of International Symposium on Code Generation and Optimization (CGO)*, pages 123–134, 2005.

[37] Mark Stephenson, Saman Amarasinghe, Martin Martin, and Una-May O'Reilly. Meta optimization: Improving compiler heuristics with machine learning. In *Proceedings of the ACM SIGPLAN '03 Conference on Programming Language Design and Implementation*, pages 77–90. ACM Press, 2002.

[38] Xavier Vera, Jaume Abella, Antonio González, and Josep Llosa. Optimizing program locality through cmes and gas. In *PACT '03: Proceedings of the 12th International Conference on Parallel Architectures and Compilation Techniques*, page 68, Washington, DC, USA, 2003. IEEE Computer Society.

[39] R. Clint Whaley and Jack J. Dongarra. Automatically tuned linear algebra software. In *Proceedings of the 1998 ACM/IEEE conference on Supercomputing (CDROM)*, pages 1–27. IEEE Computer Society, 1998.

[40] R. Clint Whaley and Antoine Petitet. Minimizing development and maintenance costs in supporting persistently optimized BLAS. *Software: Practice and Experience*, 35(2):101–121, February 2005.

[41] Jingling Xue. *Loop Tiling For Parallelism*. Kluwer Academic Publishers, 2000.

[42] K. Yotov, Xiaoming Li, Gang Ren, M. J. S. Garzaran, D. Padua, K. Pingali, and P. Stodghill. Is search really necessary to generate high-performance BLAS? In *Proceedings of the IEEE*, 93:358–386, 2005.

[43] Kamen Yotov, Keshav Pingali, and Paul Stodghill. Think globally, search locally. In *ICS '05: Proceedings of the 19th annual international conference on Supercomputing*, pages 141–150, New York, NY, USA, 2005. ACM.

Parameterized Tiling Revisited

Muthu Manikandan Baskaran[1]   Albert Hartono[1]   Sanket Tavarageri[1]   Tom Henretty[1]
J. Ramanujam[2]   P. Sadayappan[1]

[1]Dept. of Computer Science and Engineering
The Ohio State University
2015 Neil Ave. Columbus, OH, USA
{baskaran,hartonoa,tavarage,henretty,saday}@cse.ohio-state.edu

[2]Dept. of Electrical & Computer Engineering
Louisiana State University
Baton Rouge, LA, USA
jxr@ece.lsu.edu

Abstract

Tiling, a key transformation for optimizing programs, has been widely studied in literature. Parameterized tiled code is important for auto-tuning systems since they often execute a large number of runs with dynamically varied tile sizes. Previous work on tiled code generation has addressed parameterized tiling for the sequential context, and the parallel case with fixed compile-time constants for tile sizes. In this paper, we revisit the problem of generating tiled code using parametric tile sizes. We develop a systematic approach to formulate tiling transformations through manipulation of linear inequalities and develop a novel approach to overcoming the fundamental obstacle faced by previous approaches regarding generation of parallel parameterized tiled code. To the best of our knowledge, the approach proposed in this paper is the first compile-time solution to the problem of parallel parameterized code generation for affine imperfectly nested loops. Experimental results demonstrate the effectiveness of the implemented system.

Categories and Subject Descriptors D.3.4 [*Programming Languages*]: Processors—Code generation, Compilers, Optimization

General Terms Algorithms, Performance

Keywords Code generation, Tiling, Compile-time optimization

1. Introduction

Tiling is a crucial loop transformation, both for data locality enhancement as well as coarse-grained parallel execution on multicore processors. Although tiling [14] has received considerable attention in the computer science research community, [6, 26, 27, 22, 3, 32, 13, 25], the state-of-practice in production compilers is still limited. Consider the following example.

```
for (i=0; i<=N−1; i++)
  for (j=i; j<=N−1; j++)
    for (k=0; k<=N−1; k++)
      C[i][j] = beta*C[i][j] + alpha*A[i][k]*A[k][j];
```

Figure 1. DSYRK kernel

This code was run through the Intel's icc 10.0 compiler and gcc 4.2.3; neither compiler was able to generate tiled code.

Compiler	Run Time	Tiled Run Time	Tiled Speedup
gcc	14.48s	3.56s	4.07
icc	15.37s	3.69s	4.17

Table 1. Normal vs. tiled run times of DSYRK

Although production compilers today have limited tiling capability, there have been significant advances in code generation for tiling [1, 8, 9, 16, 15, 24, 29, 18, 12, 23, 2, 20, 10, 21]. Over the last few years, a number of source-to-source tiling transformation systems have been developed and made publicly available - TLOG and HITLOG [29, 24, 12, 18], PrimeTile [10, 21], and Pluto [2, 20]. TLOG was the first system to generate parametrically tiled code (where tile sizes are runtime parameters) for arbitrary perfectly nested loops with affine loop bounds (where inner loop bounds depend on outer loop indices) and HITLOG enhanced TLOG to perform efficient multi-level tiling. Pluto is a source-to-source automatic parallelization system that performs tiling. Pluto is more general than HITLOG in that imperfectly nested affine loops can be tiled. Also, Pluto can generate parallel tiled code for multicore/SMP systems. However, a limitation of Pluto is that tile sizes must be constant, specified as an input to the transformation system. Parameterized tiled code is preferable since it can be used in auto-tuning systems like ATLAS [30, 31] that repeatedly run the code on the target platform for many combinations of tile sizes. PrimeTile is a system that can generate parameterized tiled code for imperfectly nested loops. However, unlike Pluto, PrimeTile does not address parallelism.

In this paper we develop an approach to generating parameterized parallel tiled code for imperfectly nested affine loops. The developed system combines all the positive attributes of the previous tiling systems: allows parameterized tile sizes, handles imperfectly nested loops, and generates parallel code. The primary contributions of this work include:

- an approach to overcoming a fundamental problem faced by previous "polyhedral" code generation approaches in handling parametric tile sizes.

- development of the first system to generate tiled parallel code with parameterized tile sizes for affine imperfectly nested loops.

The paper is organized as follows. Section 2 presents an overview of the approach to parameterized tiling. In Section 3, we describe the techniques and details for parallel tiled code generation. In Section 4, we discuss some preprocessing steps that are performed before tiled code generation. Experimental results on a number of benchmarks are presented in Section 5. Related work is discussed in Section 6. We conclude the paper with a discussion in Section 7.

2. Approach to Code Generation for Parameterized Tiling

We first discuss the approach to parameterized tiling for the sequential case. Our approach considers affine programs that are suitably transformed for rectangular tiling as input programs. The developed system for parallel parametric tiling can generate code for arbitrary imperfectly nested affine codes, with different statements having possibly different dimensionality. However, the key ideas are easier to present using the model of a single statement domain. Hence for most of the presentation in this paper, we use a system of inequalities that represents a single statement domain. In Sec. 4, we elaborate on the preprocessing steps and handling of multi-statement programs.

The domain of the input affine program is expressed as a system of affine inequalities. We show how we formulate parameterized tiling using the system of inequalities and later generate tiled code using them.

2.1 Parameterized Single Level Sequential Tiles

Let $v_1, v_2, \ldots, v_n$ represent the loop variables of the given program, which has a n depth loop nest (v_1 representing the outermost loop and v_n representing the innermost loop). Let $p_1, p_2, \ldots, p_k$ represent the parameters (such as problem sizes) involved in the program. The system S (of m inequalities) representing the domain of the program is given by

$$S : \sum_{j=1}^{n} B_{ij}.v_j + \sum_{j=1}^{k} P_{ij}.p_j + c_i \geq 0, \qquad i \in [1..m]$$

where each B_{ij} and P_{ij} represent the coefficients of the corresponding loop variable and parameter, respectively, and c_i represents a constant in an inequality.

The m inequalities represent the lower and upper bounds of all loop variables. Hence the system S is in a specific form in which the inequalities expressing the loop bounds of a variable v_i has coefficient 0 for all variables $v_j : i < j \leq n$. In other words, the bounds of a loop variable v_i are expressed as a function of its outer loop variables ($v_j : 1 \leq j < i$), parameters and constants. The loop bounds would look like:

$$max(f_{11}(\vec{p}, c), \ldots, f_{1k}(\vec{p}, c)) \leq v_1 \leq$$
$$min(g_{11}(\vec{p}, c), \ldots g_{1l}(\vec{p}, c))$$
$$max(f_{21}(v_1, \vec{p}, c), \ldots, f_{2q}(v_1, \vec{p}, c)) \leq v_2$$
$$\leq min(g_{21}(v_1, \vec{p}, c), \ldots g_{2r}(v_1, \vec{p}, c))$$
$$\ddots$$
$$max(f_{n1}(v_1, \ldots, v_{n-1}, \vec{p}, c), \ldots, f_{ny}(v_1, \ldots, v_{n-1}, \vec{p}, c)) \leq$$
$$v_n \leq min(g_{n1}(v_1, \ldots, v_{n-1}, \vec{p}, c), \ldots g_{nz}(v_1, \ldots, v_{n-1}, \vec{p}, c))$$

We further refer to this form in which a loop variable is expressed in terms of the outer loop variables (and parameters and constants) as *row echelon* form.

Lemma 1. *Given a system of inequalities in row echelon form, loops generated with bounds for each loop variable derived directly from the system (in row echelon form) scan all valid integer points represented by the system.*

Proof. We need to prove that any point scanned by the generated loops is valid and that all valid points are scanned by the loops and no valid point is missed. Let us prove the first part that any scanned point is valid. This is straightforward. Assume the loop nest to be n-depth. Any point is represented by an n-tuple $\langle i_1, i_2 \ldots, i_n \rangle$. Since the point is scanned by the loops, each $i_j, 1 \leq j \leq n$ satisfies the bounds of the corresponding loop variable j and hence the point is

valid. Let us now prove the second part, namely, all valid points are scanned. Let us assume that there exists a valid point $\langle i_1, i_2 \ldots, i_n \rangle$ that is not scanned by the loops. Let us go level by level from 1 through n to see at which level this point might have been missed by the loops generated. The point has a value i_1 at level 1. If this point is missed by the scanning, then either the loops don't scan any point that has value i_1 at level 1 or the point is missed at some inner level, $2 \ldots n$. The loop at level 1 runs through all points that is defined by the lower bound and upper bound inequalities in the system and hence the point could not have been missed at level 1. The same reasoning applies at all levels. Hence the point $\langle i_1, i_2, \ldots, i_n \rangle$ is not a valid point and hence it is not scanned. Thus no valid point is missed by the loops generated. □

Our approach to parameterized tiling relies on the above Lemma for generating code from a system of inequalities in row echelon form and the fact that a system with tiling transformation (equivalent to the original system) can be derived. When the program is tiled, each statement instance of the program is represented with respect to the tile it belongs to and a point within the tile. Each tile can be represented either by its origin in terms of points in the original iteration space or by its coordinates in the tile space. In our approach we chose the later for representing tiles. Each variable v_j in the domain (which in turn represents each dimension in the domain) can be expressed in terms of tile coordinates t_j, tile sizes s_j, and intra-tile coordinates u_j as: $v_j = s_j.t_j + u_j \wedge 0 \leq u_j \leq s_j - 1$. The system S can now be (equivalently) represented as:

$$S' : \sum_{j=1}^{n} B_{ij}.s_j.t_j + \sum_{j=1}^{n} B_{ij}.u_j + \sum_{j=1}^{k} P_{ij}.p_j + c_i \geq 0,$$
$$i \in [1..m] \quad \wedge \quad 0 \leq u_j \leq s_j - 1, \ j \in [1..n]$$

We derive a new system S_T from S' such that the solutions to S' satisfy S_T. In the new system S_T, the intra-tile coordinates are eliminated through a relaxed projection. S_T is as follows:

$$S_T : \sum_{j=1}^{n} B_{ij}.s_j.t_j + \sum_{j=1}^{n} B_{ij}^{+}.(s_j - 1) + \sum_{j=1}^{k} P_{ij}.p_j + c_i \geq 0, \quad i \in [1..m]$$

We prove two important properties of S_T, namely, (1) the solutions to S' still satisfy S_T and (2) S_T is in row echelon form so that scanning S_T will generate the tile loops (loops with tile coordinates). The first property is easier to observe from the way S_T is constructed. The term $\sum_{j=1}^{n} B_{ij}.u_j$ is substituted with $\sum_{j=1}^{n} B_{ij}^{+}.(s_j - 1)$. This means that in any inequality in which $B_{ij} \leq 0$, the term corresponding to $B_{ij}.u_j$ is zeroed and in any inequality in which the $B_{ij} > 0$, the term corresponding to $B_{ij}.u_j$ is substituted with the maximum possible value for the term, i.e., $B_{ij}.(s_j - 1)$, since u_j can at most be $s_j - 1$. Hence any solution to S' that satisfies all inequalities (≥ 0) will satisfy the system S_T. We need to bring forth the fact that S_T is in a form that is suitable to generate tile loops. It is to be noted in the system S, the parameters are $p_1, p_2, \ldots, p_k$. In the system S_T, in addition to the parameters of S, the tile sizes $s_1, s_2, \ldots, s_n$ are also treated as parameters. To see if S_T is suited for generating tile loops, we need to see if the bounds of any tile loop variable t_i are expressed as a function of its outer tile loop variables ($t_j : 1 \leq j < i$), parameters and constants. By carefully observing the inequalities of S_T, it can be noted that except the term $\sum_{j=1}^{n} B_{ij}.s_j.t_j$, all other terms involve only constants or parameters. Hence if the term $\sum_{j=1}^{n} B_{ij}.s_j.t_j$ involving tile loop variables appears in row echelon form, we can state that S_T is in a form that is suitable to generate tile loops. We know that the coefficients B_{ij} in the inequalities in the original system S are in row echelon form. The coefficients $B_{ij}.s_j$ in S_T have the same sign (positive, zero or negative) as B_{ij} in S, as they are just scaled by a positive quantity (tile size) s_j. Hence the term $\sum_{j=1}^{n} B_{ij}.s_j.t_j$ involving tile loop variables appears in row echelon form. The constraints expressed by S_T together with that expressed by S' represent the complete set of inequalities characterizing the loop structure of sequential tiled code. Scanning S_T generates the tile loops as discussed above. Scanning S' generates the intra-tile loops in terms of tile coordinates, tile sizes, and intra-tile coordinates.

2.2 Example

We explain the approach to parameterized tiling using an illustrative example, namely, Jacobi-2D. The original code looks like:

```
for (t=0;t<T;t++) {
 for (i=2;i<N-1;i++)
  for (j=2;j<N-1;j++)
   S1(t,i,j): B[i][j] = (A[i][j]+A[i][j-1]+
      A[i][j+1]+A[i-1][j]+A[i+1][j])/5;
 for (i=2;i<N-1;i++)
  for (j=2;j<N-1;j++)
   S2(t,i,j): A[i][j] = B[i][j];
}
```

The code that is generated after applying skewing transformation to enable rectangular tiling is shown below.

```
for (v1=0;  v1 <= T-1;v1++)
 for (v2=2*v1+2; v2 <= 2*v1+N-1;v2++)
  for (v3=max(2*v1+2,v2-N+4) ;
      v3 <=min(2*v1+N-1,v2+N-4) ;v3++)
   if (v1 >= max(⌈(v2-N+2)/2⌉,⌈(v3-N+2)/2⌉))
     S1(v1,-2*v1+v2,-2*v1+v3) ;
   if (v1 <= min(⌊(v2-3)/2⌋,⌊(v3-3)/2⌋))
     S2(v1,-2*v1+v2-1,-2*v1+v3-1) ;
```

For better understanding, we explain the tiling of the nested loop structure (involving v_1, v_2, and v_3) enclosing both the statements, ignoring the inequalities in the *if* conditions. The system S of inequalities from the nested loop structure is:

$$
\begin{aligned}
v_1 &\geq 0 \\
-v_1 + T - 1 &\geq 0 \\
-2v_1 + v_2 - 2 &\geq 0 \\
2v_1 - v_2 + N - 1 &\geq 0 \\
-2v_1 + v_3 - 2 &\geq 0 \\
2v_1 - v_3 + N - 1 &\geq 0 \\
-v_2 + v_3 + N - 4 &\geq 0 \\
v_2 - v_3 + N - 4 &\geq 0
\end{aligned}
$$

Now expressing the original iteration variables as functions of tile coordinate variables, intra-tile variables and tile sizes, we rewrite each $v_i, 1 \leq i \leq 3$ as $v_i = s_i.t_i + u_i$. Now the new system S' is derived by adding the constraints of S, where $v_i, 1 \leq i \leq 3$ is replaced as expressed above, and also adding the constraints on $u_i, 1 \leq i \leq 3$,

namely, $0 \leq u_i \leq s_i - 1, 1 \leq i \leq 3$. The system S' is as follows.

$$
\begin{aligned}
s_1.t_1 + u_1 &\geq 0 \\
-s_1.t_1 - u_1 + T - 1 &\geq 0 \\
-2s_1.t_1 - 2u_1 + s_2.t_2 + u_2 - 2 &\geq 0 \\
2s_1.t_1 + 2u_1 - s_2.t_2 - u_2 + N - 1 &\geq 0 \\
-2s_1.t_1 - 2u_1 + s_3.t_3 + u_3 - 2 &\geq 0 \\
2s_1.t_1 + 2u_1 - s_3.t_3 - u_3 + N - 1 &\geq 0 \\
-s_2.t_2 - u_2 + s_3.t_3 + u_3 + N - 4 &\geq 0 \\
s_2.t_2 + u_2 - s_3.t_3 - u_3 + N - 4 &\geq 0
\end{aligned}
$$

As discussed in Section 2.1, from system S' where we have tile coordinate variables t_i and intra-tile variables u_i, we derive S_T a system with only tile coordinate variables and parameters (including tile sizes as parameters) in row echelon form that can be scanned to generate tile loops. The system S_T is as shown below.

$$
\begin{aligned}
s_1.t_1 + s_1 - 1 &\geq 0 \\
-s_1.t_1 + T - 1 &\geq 0 \\
-2s_1.t_1 + s_2.t_2 + s_2 - 1 - 2 &\geq 0 \\
2s_1.t_1 - s_2.t_2 + 2s_1 - 2 + N - 1 &\geq 0 \\
-2s_1.t_1 + s_3.t_3 + s_3 - 1 - 2 &\geq 0 \\
2s_1.t_1 - s_3.t_3 + 2s_1 - 2 + N - 1 &\geq 0 \\
-s_2.t_2 + s_3.t_3 + s_3 - 1 + N - 4 &\geq 0 \\
s_2.t_2 - s_3.t_3 + s_2 - 1 + N - 4 &\geq 0
\end{aligned}
$$

The generated tile loops are shown below.

```
for (t1 = ⌈(-s1+1)/s1⌉;t1 <= ⌊(T-1)/s1⌋;t1++)
 for (t2 = ⌈(2*s1*t1-s2+3)/s2⌉;t2 <= ⌊(2*s1*t1+2*s1+N-3)/s2⌋;t2++)
  for (t3 =max(⌈(2*s1*t1-s3+3)/s3⌉,⌈(s2*t2-s3-N+5)/s3⌉);
      t3 <=min(⌊(2*s1*t1+2*s1+N-3)/s3⌋,⌊(s2*t2+s2+N-5)/s3⌋);t3++)
```

2.3 Multi-level Tiling

The approach that we have detailed above can be clearly applied to multiple levels of parameterized tiling. In the case of multi-level tiling, a variable in the original domain is expressed in terms of the tile coordinates and tile sizes at all levels, and intratile coordinates. We begin with the system S (of m inequalities) representing the domain of the program

$$
S : \sum_{j=1}^{n} B_{ij}.v_j + \sum_{j=1}^{k} P_{ij}.p_j + c_i \geq 0, \qquad i \in [1..m]
$$

Let us consider two levels of tiling for better understanding of the technique. Each variable v_j in the domain can now be expressed in terms of tile coordinates at outer level t_j^1, tile sizes at outer level s_j^1, tile coordinates at inner level t_j^2, tile sizes at inner level s_j^2, and intra-tile coordinates u_j as:

$$
v_j = s_j^1.t_j^1 + s_j^2.t_j^2 + u_j \qquad \text{where } 0 \leq u_j \leq s_j^2 - 1.
$$

The system S can now be represented as:

$$
\begin{aligned}
S' : \quad &\sum_{j=1}^{n} B_{ij}.s_j^1.t_j^1 + \sum_{j=1}^{n} B_{ij}.s_j^2.t_j^2 + \sum_{j=1}^{n} B_{ij}.u_j + \sum_{j=1}^{k} P_{ij}.p_j \\
&+ \ c_i \geq 0 \quad i \in [1..m] \ \wedge \ 0 \leq u_j \leq s_j^2 - 1, \ j \in [1..n]
\end{aligned}
$$

We perform multiple (here, two) levels of relaxed projection to first eliminate intra-tile variables and then to eliminate inner level tile coordinates. The system S_T^2 that has intra-tile coordinates eliminated is as follows:

$$S_T^2 : \qquad \sum_{j=1}^{n} B_{ij}.s_j^1.t_j^1 + \sum_{j=1}^{n} B_{ij}.s_j^2.t_j^2 + \sum_{j=1}^{n} B_{ij}^{+}.(s_j^2 - 1)$$

$$+ \quad \sum_{j=1}^{k} P_{ij}.p_j + c_i \geq 0, \qquad i \in [1..m]$$

The system S_T^1 that has inner level tile coordinates eliminated is as follows:

$$S_T^1 : \qquad \sum_{j=1}^{n} B_{ij}.s_j^1.t_j^1 + \sum_{j=1}^{n} B_{ij}^{+}.s_j^2.\left(\lceil \frac{s_j^1}{s_j^2} \rceil - 1 \right) + \sum_{j=1}^{n} B_{ij}^{+}.(s_j^2 - 1)$$

$$+ \quad \sum_{j=1}^{k} P_{ij}.p_j + c_i \geq 0, \qquad i \in [1..m]$$

The constraints expressed by S_T^1 and S_T^2 together with that expressed by S' represent the complete set of inequalities characterizing the loop structure of sequential tiled code. Scanning S_T^1 generates the outer tile loops. Scanning S_T^2 generates the inner tile loops. Scanning S' generates the intra-tile loops in terms of tile coordinates, tile sizes, and intra-tile coordinates.

3. Generation of Parallel Tiled Code

After tiling as described in the previous section, if any of the tiling loops is parallel (i.e. has no loop carried dependences), coarse-grained parallel tiled execution is directly possible. However, even if none of the tiling loops is parallel, wavefront parallelism is always feasible among the tiles. This is because the loop system to be tiled has been pre-processed for rectangular tilability, i.e. all dependences have only positive components/directions. We first describe how wavefront-parallel tiled execution is achieved by the Pluto transformation system and discuss why the approach is not extensible for parameterized tile sizes. We then describe a novel approach to overcome this limitation - by viewing the n-dimensional tiled iteration space as a sparse $(n+1)$ dimensional space by introducing an additional wavefront iterator and then optimizing the scanning of the tiled iteration space in wavefront order for parallel execution.

3.1 Parallel Non-parametric Tiling in Pluto

Pluto generates parallel tiled code with fixed tile sizes. If $t_1, t_2, \ldots, t_n$ are the outer tile loop iterators, then $t_1 + t_2 + \cdots + t_n$ represents a wavefront such that all points (in this case, tiles) in the wavefront are independent of each other and hence can be executed in parallel. The approach to wavefront-parallel code generation in Pluto is explained below.

Let a tile space with tile variables $t_1, t_2, \ldots, t_n$ be described as a set of lower-bound and upper-bound inequalities in row-echelon form. In order to execute the tiles in wavefront-parallel order, a new iterator w is introduced with $w = t_1 + t_2 + \cdots + t_n$. Wavefront-parallel execution can be achieved via a unimodular transformation from the original tile iteration space to a new space with iterators $w, t_1, t_2, \ldots, t_{n-1}$, outermost to innermost. The system of inequalities involving t_n are now rewritten in terms of $w, t_1, t_2, \ldots, t_{n-1}$, using the equality $t_n = w - (t_1 + t_2 + \cdots + t_{n-1})$.

Fourier-Motzkin elimination is used to derive a system in row-echelon form for the nesting order $w, t_1, t_2, \ldots, t_{n-1}$. The last set of inequalities in $w, t_1, t_2, \ldots, t_{n-1}$ is already in row-echelon form. But there are no inequalities for w in row-echelon form. In order to generate such inequalities, n steps of Fourier-Motzkin elimination are performed, where in $step_i$ (i from n to 1), new sets of inequalities are generated by matching each lower-bound row-echelon form inequality for t_i with each upper-bound inequality for t_i. These new

inequalities eliminate t_i and are added to the set of row-echelon inequalities for t_{i-1}. By proceeding in this fashion, inequalities are generated for w.

The above process becomes intractable when symbolic tile sizes are used. The Fourier-Motzkin steps create new inequalities where coefficients for a variable t_i are obtained by adding coefficients for t_i from pairs of inequalities. When symbolic terms with opposite signs are combined, the sign of the resulting coefficient in the new inequality is indeterminate. This is problematic since the Fourier-Motzkin procedure at $step_i$ matches upper-bound inequalities (positive coefficient for t_i) with lower-bound inequalities (negative coefficient for t_i). If the sign of a coefficient depends on the values of parametric tile sizes, it is not possible to determine whether the inequality is a lower-bound or upper-bound inequality.

3.2 Parallel Parametric Tiling

We next develop a novel method to overcome the problems in extending the above described approach for wavefront-parallel tiled code generation to handle parameterized tile sizes. Instead of viewing wavefront-parallel tile execution as involving a unimodular transformation from one n-dimensional space (nesting order $t_1, t_2, \ldots, t_n$ of sequential tiled execution) to another n-dimensional space (nesting order $w, t_1, t_2, \ldots, t_{n-1}$), we view wavefront-parallel execution in terms of a sparse $n+1$ dimensional space with nesting order $w, t_1, t_2, \ldots, t_n$. While this might seem very wasteful, by optimizing the scanning of this higher dimensional space, we achieve parameterized parallel tiled execution with negligible overhead of scanning empty tiles. The primary problem of generating loop bounds for the outermost w loop via Symbolic Fourier Motzkin elimination is eliminated by generating the lowest and highest numbered wavefronts in the untiled form of the loops (which can be generated as a parametric expression in the problem parameters by use of an integer linear programming solver such as PIP [7, 19]) and then generating bounds for the lowest and highest numbered tiled wavefront loop. No explicit "skewing" of the tile space is done; the $t_1, t_2, \ldots, t_n$ loops are executed in original lexicographic order but constrained to include only those tiles that actually belong in the current tile wavefront w. The $n + 1$ dimensional loop nest $w, t_1, t_2, \ldots, t_n$ is optimized by addition of constraints derived from the wavefront inequalities.

From the formulation explained in 2.1, we derive the system S_T that would generate the tile loops for sequential tiled execution. Now to the system S_T we add the equality $w = \sum_{j=1}^{n} t_j$ representing the relation between the tile loop variables and the wavefront number. We add the equality in the form of the following two inequalities:

$$w - \sum_{j=1}^{n} t_j \quad \geq \quad 0$$

$$-w + \sum_{j=1}^{n} t_j \quad \geq \quad 0$$

If the additional inequalities are only considered for the innermost tile loop t_n bounds, the new system, say S_T', remains in row echelon form and can be scanned to generate tile loops wherein the innermost tile loop has additional loop bound constraints with respect to the wavefront. This would still result in correct code, but the generated code visits unnecessary iterations in the outer tile loops before pruning them out at the innermost level. Hence we develop techniques to use the additional wavefront inequalities to tighten the bounds for all tile loops. Considering the wavefront inequalities for all tile loop bounds makes the system S_T' non-row-echelon. This is because the bounds for a tile loop variable t_j, $1 \leq j \leq n$ will be a function of all tile loop variables t_i, $1 \leq i \leq n \land j \neq i$. However the bounds for a tile loop variable t_j should only be a function of the

```
for  ( it = lbit ; it <=ubit; it ++)
 for  ( jt = lbjt ; jt <=ubjt; jt ++)
  for  (kt=lbkt; kt<=ubkt; kt++)
   for  ( lt = lblt ; lt <=ublt; lt ++)
    //  ...  Intratile  loops  i, j, k, l  (omitted)  ...
```

(a) Tiled sequential loop structure (a 4D loop)

```
for  (w=wmin; w<=wmax; w++) // sequential
 for  ( it = lbit ; it <=ubit; it ++)    // parallel
  for  ( jt = lbjt ; jt <=ubjt; jt ++)    // parallel
   for  (kt=lbkt; kt<=ubkt; kt++) {    // parallel
    lt = w−it−jt−kt;
    if  ( lblt <=lt && lt<=ublt)
     //  ...  Intratile  loops  i, j, k, l  (omitted)  ...
   }
```

(b) Optimizing innermost iterator using wavefront inequalities

```
for  (w=wmin; w<=wmax; w++) // sequential
 for  ( it =max(lbit, w−jtmax−ktmax−ltmax);
        it <=min(ubit, w−jtmin−ktmin−ltmin);
        it ++)          // parallel
  for  ( jt =max(lbjt, w−it−ktmax−ltmax);
        jt <=min(ubjt, w−it−ktmin−ltmin);
        jt ++)          // parallel
   for  (kt=max(lbkt, w−it−jt−ltmax);
        kt<=min(ubkt, w−it−jt−ltmin);
        kt++)           // parallel
    lt = w−it−jt−kt;
    if  ( lblt <=lt && lt<=ublt)
     //  ...  Intratile  loops  i, j, k, l  (omitted)  ...
  }
```

(c) Tiled parallel loop structure optimized by bounded wavefront inequalities

Figure 2. Parallel tiling of a multidimensional loop nest

RSFME: To eliminate one variable from a given set of constraints and generate new wavefront constraints for outer-level loops. This procedure is successively called from innermost loop to outermost loop. The output of each RSFME call (i.e., $\mathcal{L}_n$ and $\mathcal{U}_n$) is given as input to the next RSFME call (i.e., $\mathcal{L}_w$ and $\mathcal{U}_w$). Initially, the set of lower-bound wavefront constraints ($\mathcal{L}_w$) of the innermost loop is $w - i_1 - \ldots - i_n \leq 0$, whereas the set of upper-bound wavefront constraints ($\mathcal{U}_w$) of the innermost loop is $w - i_1 - \ldots - i_n \geq 0$.

Input: Lower-bound original rows: $\mathcal{L}_o$; Upper-bound original rows: $\mathcal{U}_o$; Lower-bound wavefront rows: $\mathcal{L}_w$; Upper-bound wavefront rows: $\mathcal{U}_w$. Each row has $3n + k + 1$ columns, where n is the total number of loop iterators, k is the total number of global parameters, and the last column is used for constant. The first n columns are used for the coefficients of the loop iterators t_j for $1 \leq j \leq n$, and the following $2n$ columns are used for the coefficients of the parametric bounded values t_j^{min} and t_j^{max} for $1 \leq j \leq n$.
Output: New lower-bound wavefront rows: $\mathcal{L}_n$; New upper-bound wavefront rows: $\mathcal{U}_n$.

1. Initialize new wavefront constraints: $\mathcal{L}_n \leftarrow \emptyset$ and $\mathcal{U}_n \leftarrow \emptyset$.
2. For each pair of rows $l \in \mathcal{L}_w$ and $u \in \mathcal{U}_o$:
   (a) Add the two rows: $r \leftarrow \mathbf{ADD}(l, u)$.
   (b) $c_i \leftarrow$ the symbolic coefficient of the rightmost loop iterator t_i that has a non-zero coefficient (for $i \in [1..n]$).
   (c) *Relaxation step*: If the sign of the symbolic coefficient c_i is *indeterminate*:
      i. Split the symbolic coefficient c_i into two groups of coefficients with the same sign: $c_i^+ \leftarrow \mathbf{POSITIVE}(c_i)$ and $c_i^- \leftarrow \mathbf{NEGATIVE}(c_i)$.
      ii. Create a new relaxed lower-bound wavefront constraint: $r_l \leftarrow r$ with c_i^+ as the coefficient of t_i and c_i^- as the coefficient of t_i^{min}.
      iii. Create a new relaxed upper-bound wavefront constraint: $r_u \leftarrow r$ with c_i^- as the coefficient of t_i and c_i^+ as the coefficient of t_i^{max}.
      iv. Scale r_l using the reciprocal of the symbolic coefficient c_i^+: $r_l \leftarrow \mathbf{SCALE}(x^+, r_l)$, where x^+ is the reciprocal of c_i^+.
      v. Scale r_u using the reciprocal of the symbolic coefficient c_i^-: $r_u \leftarrow \mathbf{SCALE}(x^-, r_u)$, where x^- is the reciprocal of c_i^-.
      vi. Add the new lower-bound row r_l to $\mathcal{L}_n$, and add the new upper-bound row r_u to $\mathcal{U}_n$.
      vii. Continue with the next loop iteration (Step 2).
   (d) Scale r using the reciprocal of the symbolic coefficient c_i: $r \leftarrow \mathbf{SCALE}(x, r)$, where x is the reciprocal of c_i.
   (e) Add the new row r to $\mathcal{L}_n$.
3. Repeat Step 2 for each pair of rows $l \in \mathcal{L}_o$ and $u \in \mathcal{U}_w$, to generate new upper-bound wavefront constraints for $\mathcal{U}_n$.
4. Return $(\mathcal{L}_n, \mathcal{U}_n)$.

Figure 3. Algorithm for Relaxed Symbolic Fourier Motzkin Elimination (RSFME)

---

outer tile loop variables $t_i, 1 \leq i < j$. We address this problem by constructing a system S_T' from the system S_T by adding $2n$ inequalities as follows:

$$w - \left(\sum_{j=1}^{i-1} t_j\right) - t_i - \left(\sum_{j=i+1}^{n} t_j^{min}\right) \geq 0, \quad i \in [1..n]$$

$$-w + \left(\sum_{j=1}^{i-1} t_j\right) + t_i + \left(\sum_{j=i+1}^{n} t_j^{max}\right) \geq 0, \quad i \in [1..n]$$

The above inequalities represent the following: for a tile loop variable t_i, retain the tile loop variables $t_j, 1 \leq j < i$ in the original wavefront inequality and replace the tile loop variables $t_j, i < j \leq n$ with parametric bounds (t_j^{min} or t_j^{max}) derived from the system S_T. This construction makes the new system S_T' to be in row echelon form and hence makes it feasible to generate tile loops (with parametric bounds) that would be placed inner to the wavefront loop.

Fig. 2 shows an example to illustrate the loop code structure of parallel tiled code generated using bounded wavefront inequalities.

3.2.1 Relaxed Symbolic Fourier Motzkin Elimination

The approach discussed above to generate parallel tiled code with bounded wavefront inequalities generates less scanning overhead in iterating through useless iterations at the outer tiling loops that are pruned at the innermost tiling loop. We now discuss a technique to further tighten the bounds of the tiling loops with respect to the wavefront inequalities. We use a specialized *relaxed* symbolic Fourier Motzkin Elimination (RSFME) procedure (outlined in Fig. 3) in this approach.

We first detail how we represent and handle the symbolic coefficients in the symbolic Fourier Motzkin Elimination procedure.

The coefficient of a loop iterator in the loop bound expressions is a symbolic fraction whose numerator and denominator are a sum of products, where each product is a *polynomial* term constructed from global parameters and tile size variables. The symbolic coefficient of each loop iterator in the bound expression can be represented as

$$\frac{\sum_{i=1}^{p} c_i x_1^{e_{1,i}} \cdots x_n^{e_{n,i}}}{\sum_{i=p+1}^{q} c_i x_1^{e_{1,i}} \cdots x_n^{e_{n,i}}}$$

where coefficient c_i are integers, and variables $x_1, \ldots, x_n$ are global parameters and tile size variables (whose values are positive integers), and the exponents $e_{1,i}, \ldots, e_{n,i}$ are either zero or positive integers. p is the total number of polynomial terms in the numerator, whereas $q - p$ is the total number of polynomial terms in the denominator. Each polynomial term is abstracted using an integer scalar (to represent the coefficient c_i) an array of integers (to represent $e_{1,i}, \ldots, e_{n,i}$ corresponding to variables $x_1, \ldots, x_n$). As an example, assuming that there are four tile size variables s_1, s_2, s_3, s_4 and one global parameter N, the polynomial term $2 * s_1 * s_3^2 * s_4 * N$ can be represented using integer 2 (for the coefficient) and array $[1,0,2,1,1]$ where the last column is used for storing the exponent of N. Such representation enables simple application of arithmetic operations on polynomial terms and therefore, symbolic coefficients. Multiplying two polynomial terms is done by adding the two arrays and multiplying the two coefficients of the polynomial terms. Redundant polynomial terms may appear in a symbolic coefficient and they have identical exponents (hence, identical array structure). Such redundancy can be eliminated by retaining only one of the redundant terms and adding the coefficients of these redundant terms.

Consider the system S_T for generating sequential tile loops (as discussed earlier) and the wavefront inequalities representing $w = \sum_{j=1}^{n} t_j$. The RSFME procedure starts by combining the lower bound inequalities of t_n from S_T with the wavefront inequality $w - \sum_{j=1}^{n-1} t_j - t_n \geq 0$ and upper bound inequalities of t_n from S_T with the wavefront inequality $-w + \sum_{j=1}^{n-1} t_j + t_n \geq 0$, to eliminate t_n and hence derive new lower and upper bound inequalities for t_{n-1}. However while combining the bounds, there is a possibility that we might need to add symbolic coefficients of two terms with opposite signs and the resulting sign may be indeterminate at compile-time. At this point, we replace the tile loop variables with their parametric bounded values (t_j^{min} or t_j^{max}) and use relaxed bound inequalities. At any level k of the RSFME procedure, we combine new wavefront inequalities added at level k with the existing lower bound and upper bound inequalities at level k to eliminate the tile loop variable at level k and derive new lower and upper bound inequalities for level $k - 1$.

Consider the system S_T for generating sequential tile loops (as discussed earlier) and the wavefront inequalities representing

$$w = \sum_{j=1}^{n} t_j.$$ The RSFME procedure starts by combining the lower bound inequalities of t_n from S_T with the wavefront inequality

$$w - \sum_{j=1}^{n-1} t_j - t_n \geq 0$$ and upper bound inequalities of t_n from S_T

with the wavefront inequality $-w + \sum_{j=1}^{n-1} t_j + t_n \geq 0$, to eliminate t_n and hence derive new lower and upper bound inequalities for t_{n-1}. However while combining the bounds, there is a possibility that we might need to add symbolic coefficients of two terms with opposite signs and the resulting sign may be indeterminate at compile-time. At this point, we replace the tile loop variables with their parametric bounded values (t_j^{min} or t_j^{max}) and use relaxed bound inequalities. At any level k of the RSFME procedure, we combine new wavefront inequalities added at level k with the existing lower bound and

upper bound inequalities at level k to eliminate the tile loop variable at level k and derive new lower and upper bound inequalities for level $k - 1$.

Fig. 4 illustrates an example of applying RSFME on a non-rectangular tiled loop nest. The example shows that tighter bounds can be generated for the tile loops with the wavefront inequalities using the RSFME procedure.

4. Preprocessing Steps

In this section, we describe the pre-processing steps that an input affine code is subjected to. Like all previous work on parametric tiling, the PTile system takes rectangularly tileable code as input. The pre-processing approach used here is identical to that we developed in PrimeTile [10, 21]. PrimeTile uses the Pluto tool to first perform any transformations (such as skewing) to ensure that all dependences at all loop levels are always in the positive direction. Bands of such loops are amenable to rectangular tiling by PTile. We illustrate the needed pre-processing steps in Fig. 5.

Fig. 5(a) shows an example input code (the same Jacobi code seen earlier) and Fig. 5(b) shows the affine transformation (generated by Pluto) to make the code rectangularly tileable – by ensuring that all dependence vector components are non-negative. Fig. 5(c) shows the code obtained by transforming the original code using the transformation shown in Fig. 5(b). A key additional step of preprocessing is the generation of a version of the code where each statement is surrounded by exactly the same number of loops. This can be done through the introduction of semantics preserving one-time loops that have identical lower and upper bounds. The reason for doing this is so that all statements of an imperfectly nested loop can be viewed as embedded in a common embedding iteration space. The convex hull of the individual statement iteration spaces is generated and PTile tiles that space. The convex hull of the multiple statements' iteration spaces can be viewed as a relaxation of the boundary constraints of each of the the individual statements - any point in the actual iteration space of a statement will also be a solution to the relaxed system of inequalities representing the convex hull.

The process of code generation for an imperfectly nested loop containing statement iteration spaces of different dimensionalities is very homogeneous - since all statements have exactly the same number of surrounding loops (including the dummy one-time loops). Fig. 5(e) shows the parametrically tiled code generated.

5. Experimental Evaluation

The experiments were run on a multicore Intel Xeon workstation with dual quad-core E5462 Xeon processors (a total of 8 cores) clocked at 2.8 GHz (1600 MHz FSB), with 32 KB L1 cache, 12 MB of L2 cache (6 MB shared per core pair), 16 GB of DDR2 FBDIMM RAM, running Linux kernel version 2.6.25 (x86-64). The tiled parallel codes were generated using two compilers: (i) GCC 4.2.4 (with "-O3 -fopenmp" flags), and (ii) ICC 10.1 (with "-fast -openmp" flags).

The parallel parameterized tiling system developed in this paper (*PTile*) was evaluated on a set of benchmarks previously used to evaluate the PrimeTile system [10, 21]. Performance was compared over a range of tile sizes with parallel tiled code generated by Pluto. The benchmarks are listed in Table 2 along with the problem sizes used in the experiments; Table 2(a) lists the benchmarks with imperfect loop nests and Table 2(b) lists benchmarks that are perfectly nested.

We generated tiled code using one and two levels of tiling for various tile sizes. For one-level tiling, we considered tile sizes of the form 2^n for n ranging from 2 to 10. For two-level tiling, the evaluated outer tile sizes (T_{outer}) were 128, 256, 512, 768, and

	Lower-bound constraint	Upper-bound constraint
Outermost wavefront loop:	(1a): wmin $\leq$ w	(1b): w $\leq$ wmax
Loop it:	(2a): (1-Ti+1)/Ti $\leq$ it	(2b): it $\leq$ N/Ti
Loop jt:	(3a): (1-Tj+1)/Tj $\leq$ jt	(3b): jt $\leq$ (N-it.Ti)/Tj
Loop kt:	(4a): (it.Ti-Tk+1)/Tk $\leq$ kt	(4b): kt $\leq$ N/Tk
Wavefront constraints:	(5a): w-it-jt $\leq$ kt	(5b): kt $\leq$ w-it-jt
Eliminate variable kt to derive new wavefront constraints for loop jt:	(6a): Combine (5a) and (4b) w-it-jt $\leq$ N/Tk w-it-N/Tk $\leq$ jt (w.Tk-it.Tk-N)/Tk $\leq$ jt	(6b): Combine (5b) and (4a) (it.Ti-Tk+1)/Tk $\leq$ w-it-jt jt $\leq$ w-it-it.Ti/Tk+1-1/Tk jt $\leq$ (w.Tk-it.Tk-it.Ti+Tk-1)/Tk
Eliminate variable jt to derive new wavefront constraints for loop it:	(7a): Combine (6a) and (3b) w-it-N/Tk $\leq$ N/Tj-it.Ti/Tj w-N/Tj-N/Tk $\leq$ it-it.Ti/Tj *(ambiguous sign encountered)* $\rightarrow$ (i) Relaxation to obtain a new lower-bound constraint: w-N/Tj-N/Tk+itmin.Ti/Tj $\leq$ it (w.Tj.Tk-N.Tj-N.Tk+itmin.Ti.Tk)/(Tj.Tk) $\leq$ it $\rightarrow$ (ii) Relaxation to obtain a new upper-bound constraint: it.Ti/Tj $\leq$ itmax-w+N/Tj+N/Tk it $\leq$ (itmax.Tj.Tk-w.Tj.Tk+N.Tj+N.Tk)/(Ti.Tk)	(7b): Combine (6b) and (3a) 2/Tj-1 $\leq$ w-it-it.Ti/Tk+1-1/Tk it+it.Ti/Tk $\leq$ w+2-2/Tj-1/Tk it $\leq$ (w.Tj.Tk^2+2.Tj.Tk^2-Tj.Tk-2.Tk^2)/(Ti.Tj.Tk+Tj.Tk^2)

Figure 4. Example of application of Relaxed Symbolic Fourier Motzkin Elimination (RSFME) on a non-rectangular tiled loop nest

```
for (t=0;t<=T−1;t++) {
  for (i=1;i<=N−2;i++)
    B[i]=(A[i−1]+A[i]+A[i+1])/3; /*S1*/
  for (i=1;i<=N−2;i++)
    A[i]=B[i]; /*S2*/
}
```

(a) Original code

$S1 : (t', i') = (t, 2*t+i)$
$S2 : (t', i') = (t, 2*t+i+1)$

(b) Affine transformation (skewing)

```
for (t=0;t<=T−1;t++) {
  B[1]=(A[1+1]+A[1]+A[1−1])/3;
  for (i=2*t+2;i<=2*t+N−2;i++) {
    B[−2*t+i]=(A[1+−2*t+i]+A[−2*t+i]
        +A[−2*t+i−1])/3;
    A[−2*t+i−1]=B[−2*t+i−1];
  }
  A[N−2]=B[N−2];
}
```

(c) Skewed code

```
for (t=0;t<=T−1;t++) {
  for (i=2*t+1;i<=2*t+1;i++)
    B[1]=(A[1+1]+A[1]+A[1−1])/3;
  for (i=2*t+2;i<=2*t+N−2;i++) {
    B[−2*t+i]=(A[1+−2*t+i]+A[−2*t+i]
        +A[−2*t+i−1])/3;
    A[−2*t+i−1]=B[−2*t+i−1];
  }
  for (i=2*t+N−1;i<=2*t+N−1;i++)
    A[N−2]=B[N−2];
}
```

(d) Skewed code with one-time loops

```
for (tt1=ceil((0−T1t+1)/T1t);
     tt1 <=floor((T−1)/T1t);
     tt1 ++)
for (it1=ceil((2*tt1*T1t+1−T1i+1)/T1i);
     it1 <=floor((2*(tt1*T1t+T1t−1)+N−1)/T1i);
     it1 ++)
for (t=max(0,tt1*T1t);
     t<=min(T−1,tt1*T1t+T1t−1);t++) {
  for (i=max(2*t+1,it1*T1i);
       i<=min(2*t+1,it1*T1i+T1i−1);i++)
    B[1]=(A[1+1]+A[1]+A[1−1])/3;
  for (i=max(2*t+2,it1*T1i);
       i<=min(2*t+N−2,it1*T1i+T1i−1);i++) {
    B[−2*t+i]=(A[1+−2*t+i]+A[−2*t+i]
        +A[−2*t+i−1])/3;
    A[−2*t+i−1]=B[−2*t+i−1];
  }
  for (i=max(2*t+N−1,it1*T1i);
       i<=min(2*t+N−1,it1*T1i+T1i−1);i++)
    A[N−2]=B[N−2];
}
```

(e) One-level tiled sequential code

Figure 5. Example to illustrate pre-processing steps: 1D Jacobi

1024, and the inner tile sizes ranged from 4 to ($\frac{T_{outer}}{2}$). We used square tiles in our experiments. We generated tiled code using Pluto and *PTile* and measured the execution time for all combinations of tile sizes, and report the best performance. Table 3 shows the execution times of the best-performing parallel codes from *PTile* and Pluto.

From Table 3, it may be seen that with gcc, the single core performance of the *PTile*-generated code is close to that of Pluto-generated code. However, the parallel performance of *PTile*-generated code is better than that of Pluto-generated code for six of the eight benchmarks, in some instances almost 60% better. With icc, for four of the benchmarks, *PTile*-generated code outperforms Pluto-generated code, while for two of the benchmarks, the *PTile*-generated code is worse.

Table 4 compares the code generation time for *PTile* and Pluto. Pluto generates code only for fixed (not parameterized) tile sizes. Therefore, Pluto had to be repeatedly used to generate code for each tile size. In contrast, *PTile* generated parameterized tiled code;

therefore, the code was generated once using *PTile* and then used for all tile size combinations. The code generation times shown in Table 4 are for one instance in the case of Pluto and therefore must be multiplied by the number of tile size combinations to determine the total Pluto code generation time for the experiments. The Pluto system works for up to two levels of tiling (therefor only two columns are sown under Pluto), where as *PTile* can generate code for multiple levels of tiling. The highest code generation time for *PTile* was 0.97 seconds among the eight benchmarks evaluated. Also, the code generation times for *PTile* remained almost the same irrespective of the number of levels of tiling. In contrast, the code generation time for Pluto increases significantly for many benchmarks when going from one to two levels of tiling. For one level of tiling, the primary reason for the higher compile times with PTile is that the system is implemented in Python while Pluto is implemented in C.

The experimental data from these benchmarks show that *PTile* is effective in code generation for parameterized tiling for the

Table 2. Benchmarks used in the experiments
(a) Imperfect loop nests

Name	Description	Max. loop depth	Problem sizes
1D Jacobi	1D Jacobi method	2	$T = 2000, N = 6 \times 10^6$
2D FDTD	2D Finite Difference Time Domain method	3	$T = 2000, N = 2000$
TriSolver	Triangular solver	3	$N = 3000$
LU	LU factorization	3	$N = 2500$
Cholesky	Cholesky factorization	3	$N = 5000$

(b) Perfect loop nests

Name	Description	Max. loop depth	Problem sizes
Seidel	3D Gauss Seidel	3	$T = 2000, N = 2000$
DSYRK	Symmetric rank k update	3	$N = 3000$
DTRMM	Triangular matrix multiplication	3	$N = 3000$

Table 3. Execution times of best-performing tiled parallel codes (in seconds)

			Number of cores							
			1	2	3	4	5	6	7	8
GCC	1D Jacobi	Pluto	28.73	15.02	11.46	8.11	8.27	8.50	8.43	4.95
		PTile	26.82	14.56	10.94	7.74	7.82	7.64	7.70	4.60
	2D FDTD	Pluto	71.44	38.13	26.86	20.39	17.56	15.38	13.47	11.95
		PTile	73.59	40.17	27.91	21.22	17.80	15.24	13.37	11.48
	TriSolver	Pluto	36.07	18.09	12.32	9.26	7.32	6.16	5.39	4.65
		PTile	32.69	16.89	11.42	8.71	7.08	6.04	5.24	4.68
	LU	Pluto	13.24	7.44	5.01	3.85	3.23	2.77	2.45	2.32
		PTile	13.33	7.35	5.04	3.90	3.19	2.75	2.44	2.18
	Cholesky	Pluto	41.61	30.86	22.18	16.76	13.72	12.03	11.00	10.00
		PTile	40.52	21.30	14.48	11.12	9.12	7.83	6.89	6.10
	Seidel	Pluto	116.50	59.29	39.83	30.44	24.83	21.51	18.00	16.69
		PTile	103.17	52.28	35.21	27.01	22.00	18.59	15.64	13.99
	DSYRK	Pluto	36.64	27.91	20.76	16.35	13.96	11.48	11.44	8.79
		PTile	37.01	19.10	13.01	9.94	8.15	6.94	6.09	5.44
	DTRMM	Pluto	39.15	19.83	13.23	9.87	7.94	6.71	5.73	4.98
		PTile	37.19	19.68	13.25	10.17	8.17	7.02	6.03	5.33
ICC	1D Jacobi	Pluto	15.24	7.84	5.96	4.04	4.07	4.07	3.62	2.28
		PTile	18.46	9.92	7.31	5.16	5.07	4.91	4.45	2.67
	2D FDTD	Pluto	49.39	26.40	19.13	14.42	12.88	10.84	10.15	8.63
		PTile	40.50	21.17	14.93	11.36	9.87	8.59	8.06	6.47
	TriSolver	Pluto	19.29	9.89	7.02	4.98	4.17	3.36	2.95	2.63
		PTile	25.12	12.66	8.58	6.58	5.35	4.54	3.96	3.46
	LU	Pluto	8.46	4.66	3.25	2.56	2.19	1.92	1.74	1.58
		PTile	8.45	4.66	3.25	2.60	2.28	1.95	1.79	1.62
	Cholesky	Pluto	32.96	24.23	17.41	13.30	10.79	9.19	8.00	7.19
		PTile	28.63	14.79	10.29	8.06	6.75	5.83	5.21	4.80
	Seidel	Pluto	68.47	34.52	23.16	17.57	14.08	11.86	10.28	9.13
		PTile	56.56	29.21	19.76	15.22	12.23	10.33	9.05	7.82
	DSYRK	Pluto	16.82	12.82	9.54	7.52	6.43	5.28	5.26	4.04
		PTile	20.15	10.60	7.23	5.53	4.54	3.88	3.40	3.05
	DTRMM	Pluto	21.78	11.17	7.44	5.58	4.72	3.76	3.74	2.85
		PTile	20.13	10.32	7.05	5.45	4.50	3.85	3.40	3.07

sequential and parallel cases. In addition, the code generation time remains constant with increasing number of levels of tiling.

6. Related Work

Much work exists in the area of tiling (with fixed tile sizes) of perfectly nested loops for both the sequential and parallel case [14, 6, 26, 27, 22, 3, 32, 13, 25]. Goumas et al. [9] presented a code generation technique for fixed-size parallel tiling of perfectly nested loops.

Parameterized sequential tiling has received much attention recently. Renganarayana et al. [24, 29] developed an effective code generation technique for parameterized tiling of perfectly nested loops , based on enumerating tile origins using a method called the "outset method." Later Kim et al. [18, 12] extended the approach to multi-level parameterized tiling of perfectly nested loops. Both these systems generate sequential tile code. Renganarayana [23] also developed an approach to parameterized sequential tiling using a symbolic extension of Fourier-Motzkin elimination. However, that approach (which relies upon the *bilinear set* property) does not

Table 4. Tiled code generation times (in seconds)

Levels of Tiling ⟶	PTile				Pluto	
	1	2	3	4	1	2
1D Jacobi	0.53	0.57	0.57	0.57	0.03	0.06
2D FDTD	0.93	0.94	0.95	0.97	0.25	3.02
TriSolver	0.53	0.55	0.58	0.59	0.08	1.77
LU	0.53	0.55	0.56	0.56	0.03	0.20
Cholesky	0.62	0.62	0.63	0.65	0.07	0.74
Seidel	0.49	0.54	0.55	0.55	0.02	0.07
DSYRK	0.48	0.53	0.53	0.54	0.02	0.05
DTRMM	0.49	0.53	0.53	0.55	0.02	0.10

extend to parallel tiling, e.g., enumeration of tiles in wavefront order. Kim and Rajopadhye [17] recently developed a non-polyhedral approach to sequential parametric tiling of loop nests. Jimenez et al. [15] developed techniques for register tiling of non-rectangular iteration spaces. In a later paper, they [16] also developed a code generation technique for parameterized multi-level tiling of perfectly nested loops.

A script-based compositional transformation framework has been developed by Chen et al. [5]; their framework can be used for fixed-size tiling of imperfectly nested loops. Specialized frameworks [4, 28, 33] have been developed for fixed-size tiling of particular classes of imperfectly nested loops. Parallel tiling of general imperfectly nested loops was developed by Bondhugula et al. [2] in the Pluto [20] system, but tile sizes are restricted to be compile-time constants. Recently, we developed PrimeTile in which we employ a non-polyhedral approach to parameterized sequential tiling of imperfectly nested loops [21, 10]. Parallel execution of parametrically tiled code has also been addressed using a dynamic scheduling approach [11] in which tiles are scheduled at runtime to different processor cores in the system.

The PTile system developed in this paper uses the same preprocessing approach as PrimeTile, to ensure rectangular tilability of imperfectly nested multi-statement affine programs and uses a modified version of CLooG to generate rectangularly tileable loop structures with preserved embedding information in the target space. To the best of our knowledge, it is the first system to generate parallel parametrically tiled code for affine imperfectly nested loops.

7. Conclusions

Loop tiling is an important optimization for exploiting coarse-grained parallelism and enhancing data locality. Tiled codes with variable tile size parameters are important for empirical tuning systems. Previous work has addressed the generation of sequential parametric tiled code or parallel code with fixed tile sizes. In this paper we have developed *PTile*, an effective system for generating parametrically tiled parallel code from sequential untiled input code. The developed system combines all the positive attributes of previous tiling systems: allows parameterized tile sizes, handles imperfectly nested loops, and generates parallel code. The effectiveness of the *PTile* system has been demonstrated through experimental results on several benchmarks.

Acknowledgments This work was supported in part by the U.S. National Science Foundation through awards 0403342, 0541409, 0811457, 0811781, 0926687 and 0926688, and by Army through contract W911NF-10-1-0004.

References

[1] C. Ancourt and F. Irigoin. Scanning polyhedra with do loops. In *PPoPP'91*, pages 39–50, 1991.

[2] U. Bondhugula, A. Hartono, J. Ramanujam, and P. Sadayappan. A practical automatic polyhedral program optimization system. In *PLDI'08*, 2008.

[3] P. Boulet, A. Darte, T. Risset, and Y. Robert. (Pen)-ultimate tiling? *Integration, the VLSI Journal*, 17(1):33–51, 1994.

[4] S. Carr and K. Kennedy. Compiler blockability of numerical algorithms. In *Proc. Supercomputing '92*, pages 114–124, 1992.

[5] C. Chen, J. Chame, and M. Hall. Chill: A framework for composing high-level loop transformations. Technical Report 08-897, USC Computer Science Technical Report, June 2008.

[6] S. Coleman and K. McKinley. Tile Size Selection Using Cache Organization and Data Layout. In *PLDI'95*, pages 279–290, 1995.

[7] P. Feautrier. Parametric integer programming. *Operationnelle/Operations Research*, 22(3):243–268, 1988.

[8] G. Goumas, M. Athanasaki, and N. Koziris. An Efficient Code Generation Technique for Tiled Iteration Spaces. *IEEE Trans. Parallel Distrib. Syst.*, 14(10):1021–1034, 2003.

[9] G. I. Goumas, N. Drosinos, M. Athanasaki, and N. Koziris. Automatic parallel code generation for tiled nested loops. In *Symposium on Applied Computing*, pages 1412–1419, 2004.

[10] A. Hartono, M. M. Baskaran, C. Bastoul, A. Cohen, S. Krishnamoorthy, B. Norris, J. Ramanujam, and P. Sadayappan. Parametric multilevel tiling of imperfectly nested loops. In *ACM International Conference on Supercomputing (ICS)*, 2009.

[11] A. Hartono, M. M. Baskaran, J. Ramanujam, and P. Sadayappan. Parametric tiled loop generation for effective parallel execution on multicore processors. In *IPDPS '10: Proceedings of the 2010 IEEE International Symposium on Parallel & Distributed Processing*, 2010.

[12] HiTLoG: Hierarchical Tiled Loop Generator. http://www.cs.colostate.edu/MMAlpha/tiling/.

[13] K. Hogstedt, L. Carter, and J. Ferrante. Selecting tile shape for minimal execution time. In *SPAA*, pages 201–211, 1999.

[14] F. Irigoin and R. Triolet. Supernode partitioning. In *ACM SIGPLAN Principles of Programming Languages*, pages 319–329, 1988.

[15] M. Jiménez, J. Llabería, and A. Fernández. Register tiling in nonrectangular iteration spaces. *ACM Trans. Program. Lang. Syst.*, 24(4):409–453, 2002.

[16] M. Jiménez, J. Llabería, and A. Fernández. A cost-effective implementation of multilevel tiling. *IEEE Trans. Parallel Distrib. Syst.*, 14(10):1006–1020, 2003.

[17] D. Kim and S. Rajopadhye. Parameterized tiling for imperfectly nested loops. Technical Report CS-09-101, Colorado State University, Department of Computer Science, February 2009.

[18] D. Kim, L. Renganarayanan, M. Strout, and S. Rajopadhye. Multilevel tiling: 'm' for the price of one. In *SC*, 2007.

[19] PIP: The Parametric Integer Programming Library. http://www.piplib.org.

[20] Pluto: A polyhedral automatic parallelizer and locality optimizer for multicores. http://pluto-compiler.sourceforge.net.

[21] PrimeTile: A Parametric Multi-Level Tiler for Imperfect Loop Nests. http://www.cse.ohio-state.edu/~hartonoa/primetile/.

[22] J. Ramanujam and P. Sadayappan. Tiling multidimensional iteration spaces for multicomputers. *JPDC*, 16(2):108–230, 1992.

[23] L. Renganarayana. *Scalable and Efficient Tools for Multi-level Tiling*. PhD thesis, Colorado State University, Fort Collins, CO, February 2008.

[24] L. Renganarayana, D. Kim, S. Rajopadhye, and M. Strout. Parameterized tiled loops for free. In *PLDI'07*, pages 405–414, 2007.

[25] L. Renganarayana and S. Rajopadhye. A geometric programming framework for optimal multi-level tiling. In *SC*, 2004.

[26] G. Rivera and C. Tseng. Locality optimizations for multi-level caches. In *Supercomputing '99*, page 2, 1999.

[27] R. Schreiber and J. Dongarra. Automatic blocking of nested loops. Tech. Report 90.38, RIACS, NASA Ames Research Center, 1990.

[28] Y. Song and Z. Li. New tiling techniques to improve cache temporal locality. In *PLDI*, pages 215–228, 1999.

[29] TLoG: A Parametrized Tiled Loop Generator. http://www.cs.colostate.edu/MMAlpha/tiling/.

[30] R. C. Whaley and J. J. Dongarra. Automatically tuned linear algebra software. In *Proceedings of the ACM/IEEE SC98 Conference*, pages 1–27. IEEE Computer Society, 1998.

[31] R. C. Whaley, A. Petitet, and J. J. Dongarra. Automated empirical optimization of software and the ATLAS project. *Parallel Computing*, 27(1–2):3–35, 2001.

[32] J. Xue. *Loop tiling for parallelism*. Kluwer Academic Publishers, Norwell, MA, USA, 2000.

[33] Q. Yi, K. Kennedy, and V. Adve. Transforming complex loop nests for locality. *J. Supercomput.*, 27(3):219–264, 2004.

Minimizing Communication in Rate-Optimal Software Pipelining for Stream Programs

Haitao Wei, Junqing Yu[+], Huafei Yu

School of Computer Science and Technology
HuaZhong University of Science and Technology,
Wuhan, 430074, China

whtaohust@gmail.com, yhfei2008@gmail.com
+Corresponding author: yjqing@hust.edu.cn

Guang R. Gao

Department of Electrical and Computer Engineering
University of Delaware
Newark, DE 19711

ggao@capsl.udel.edu

Abstract

Stream programming model has been productively applied to a number of important applications domains. Software pipelining is an important code scheduling technique for stream programs. However, the multi-/many-core evolution has presented a new dimension of challenges: that is while searching a best software pipelining schedule how to ensure the communications between processing cores are also minimized? In this paper, we proposed a new solution methodology to address the above problem. Our main contributions include the following. A *unified* formulation has been proposed that *combines* the requirement of both rate-optimal software pipelining and the minimization of inter-core communication overhead. This formulation has been developed based on a synchronized dataflow graph model, and is expressed as an integer linear programming problem. A solution testbed has been implemented for the proposed problem formulation on the IBM Cell architecture. This has been realized by extending the Brook stream programming environment with our software pipelining support -- named DFBrook. An experimental study has been conducted to verify the effectiveness of the proposed solution. And a comparison of other scheduling methods has demonstrated the performance superiority of our proposed method.

Categories and Subject Descriptors D.3.4 [**Programming Languages**]: Processors Compilers

General Terms Languages, Algorithms, Performance, Theory.

Keywords Multi-core, Stream programs, DFBrook, Software pipelining, Cell processor

1. Introduction

Multi-core architectures have become the mainstream solution and industry standard from servers to desktop platforms and handheld devices. Many chip vendors have produced their own multi-core processors. For example, the Sony/Toshiba/IBM cell has 9 cores [1], the Sun Niagara2 has 8 cores [2], the Nvidia GeForce 8800 GPU consists of 16 stream processors each with 8 processing units [3], and Intel and AMD x86 have quad-core processors. Multi-core processor increases the computation ability,

but it pushes the performance burden to the compiler and programmer to effectively exploit the coarse-gained parallelism across the cores. Traditional programming model like C, C++ and Fortran are poorly suited to multi-core architectures because of the assumed single instruction stream execution model and centralized memory structure.

The stream programming model offers a promising approach for exploring parallelism for multi-core architecture. Stream languages like StreamIt [4], Brook [5], CUDA [3], SPUR [6] and Cg [7] are motivated by the prevalent application in media processing domains like video/image processing, graphics, signal and networking. Stream languages are generally based on synchronous dataflow (SDF) [8] or regular stream flow graphs (RSFG) [9] where each node represents a computation task (actor) and each arc represents the communication (flow of data) between them. During program execution, each actor must fire repeatedly in a periodic schedule to satisfy the balancing condition [8] [9]. Each actor has independent instruction stream and address space and the dependences between actors can be made through communication channels. These characteristics offer compiler an opportunity to orchestrate parallel execution.

Software pipelining is an efficient method to exploit the coarse-grained parallelism in stream programs [10] [11]. It takes the whole program as a loop and takes periodic schedule as iteration of the loop. Actors' firings in successive iterations can be overlapped. On the other hand, stream programs can be easily and naturally mapped to communication-exposed multi-core architecture. However the gains obtained through parallel execution can be overshadowed by the costs of communication and synchronization. Resource limitations of the system including processor capability, memory associated with each processor element, interconnect bandwidth and direct memory access (DMA) latency are another impact on performance. Therefore, the challenging problem is how to construct an efficient software pipelining schedule which takes the tradeoff decision between computation rate and communication cost under resource constraint system.

In other words, *how does one construct an efficient software pipelining schedule which minimizes the communication cost while still executing stream program at optimal computation rate under the resource constraint communication-exposed architecture?* Minimizing communication is at the prerequisite of optimal computation rate. Hence we refer this problem as Minimum Communication at Rate-Optimal (MCRO) scheduling problem.

In this paper we formulate this problem as a *unified* Integer Linear Programming (ILP) problem. It is based on the synchronized dataflow graph model and combines the requirement of both rate-optimal and the minimization of inter-core communication overhead. We implement the software pipelining scheduling solution to the problem formulation for DFBrook stream language programs on accelerator-based multi-core architecture like Cell. DFBrook is derived from Brook stream language with the extension to represent data flow programming paradigm. It is designed for accelerator-based architecture and some actors are restricted to run in control core. We improve our formulation scheduling to model this category programming model which has *special* constraints. We also compare our scheduling framework with heuristic list schedule (List) in traditional software pipelining, periodic admissible parallel schedules (PAPS) and rate optimal ILP formulation schedule (RO) to verify the effectiveness.

Software pipelining schedule using ILP formulation for communication-exposed architecture is proposed by M. Kudlur and S. Mahlke [11]. The scheduler consists of two steps. First an integrated actor fission and partitioning step is performed to ensure maximum work balance. Actors are selectively replicated and split to increase the even work distribution. The second step is a stage assignment algorithm wherein each actor is assigned to a pipeline stage for execution. Data communication is assigned to satisfy the data dependences.

Our work differs from the above as following. First, the objective in our schedule is minimizing communication at rate-optimal requirements not only the rate-optimal. Second, communication time is always assumed shorter than actor's execution time and can be overlapped with computation. It is not always the case. Our work eliminates this assumption and formulates it in our schedule. Third, we formulate actor assignment, data transform and stage assignment as a unified integer linear programming rather than two separating steps.

This paper offers following contributions.

• We proposed a unified formulation that combines the requirement of both rate-optimal software pipelining and the minimization of inter-core communication overhead. It achieves optimal computation rate while minimizing the communication.

• This formulation has been developed based on a synchronized dataflow graph model, and is expressed as an integer linear programming problem.

• A solution testbed has been implemented for the proposed problem formulation on the IBM Cell architecture. This has been realized for DFBrook stream programming environment with software pipelining support.

• We implement our scheduling scheme and demonstrate an average 47% improvement in computation rate over PAPS method and up to 24% improvement over List method. The improvement in communication cost is 7.0%-40.9% with respect to RO method, and 8.5%-40.7% with respect to List method.

The rest of this paper is organized as following: section 2 provides an overview of the DFBrook language and compilation. Section 3 illustrates the MCRO scheduling problem by an example. Section 4 details the ILP formulations for dataflow graph and DFBrook program on Cell. In Section 5 we report the experimental results. Section 6 discusses related work and section 7 concludes the paper.

2. DFBrook Stream Language

DFBrook is a stream programming language that modifies the syntactics and semantics of Brook language [12] to implement synchronous data flow (SDF) [8] programming model. It is designed for programming accelerator-based architecture. A DFBrook program consists of legal C code plus stream code. Stream code is composed of *streams* declaration, *kernels* definition and *stream Operator*. Figure 1 illustrates a DFBrook program and corresponding SDF graph.

Each actor is represented as a kernel function. The *stream rates* namely, number of tokens (values) produced and consumed by each invocation of the kernel function is represented as the length of stream data type arguments. The kernel currently only supports a fixed stream rate. The input and output streams are distinguished by the keyword *out*. The input stream argument is restricted to read-only and the output stream is restricted to write-only. *Stream data type* (annotated by "<>") is a new data type which can only be processed in the kernel function. In figure 1(a), the kernel function *mul* has two input streams and one output stream. For each invocation, mul function respectively consumes 10 tokens from two input streams *vec_a* and *vec_b* and produces 10 tokens to the output stream *vec_result*. In the mul kernel, stream vec_a and vec_b are read-only and stream vec_result is write-only.

```
kernel void mul(float vec_a<10>, float
vec_b<10>,out float vec_result<10>)
{…}
kernel void sum(float vec<10>,out float
result<1>)
{…}
main(){
…
float data_matrix[100];
float data_vector[10];
float matrix<>, vector<>;
float tempmv<>, result<>;
streamfor(…){
streamRead(matrix, data_matrix,100);
streamRead(vector,data_vector,10);
mul(matrix,vector,tempmv);
sum(tempmv,result);
streamWrite(result, data_result,10);
}
…}
```

(a)

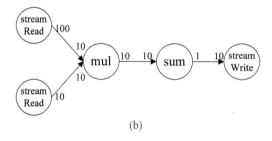

(b)

Figure 1. (a) An Example DFBrook Program and (b) corresponding middle representation synchronous data flow graph.

In the main function the body of *streamfor* statement corresponds to the dataflow program (stream code) or stream graph of the system. Kernel function calls are only allowed in the body of streamfor statement. Streaming data are transferred from one kernel functions to another by passing stream arguments between them. For now, we only support one streamfor statement for a program. *StreamRead* and *streamWrite* referred to as stream Operator are two special functions. streamRead fills stream from outside data of C code. It offers data source to the dataflow program, hence only has output stream rate which is specified by the third argument. streamWrite dumps stream to the outside data of C code when the dataflow program is done. Hence, it only has input stream rate which also specified by the calling argument. In figure 1, streamRead reads the source data from array *data_matrix* and *data_vector* to the streams which are passed to kernel mul as input streams to produce output stream *tempmv*. The tempmv is consumed by *sum* kernel to produce stream *result* which at last is written back to array *data_result*. These streams passed between kernels are implemented as FIFO communication channels. The lengths are determined by the compiler.

Kernels in DFBrook are all *stateless* for now. The kernel carries no state across firings and the output of it only depends on its input. Different invocations of the same kernel can be parallelized. *Stateful* kernels have some internal state persistent across firings and contain dependence edge between successive invocations. They must be executed in sequential.

Our DFBrook compiler for now only consists of frontend translator from DFBrook language to dataflow graph and software pipelining scheduler. The frontend does the data flow analysis for the application program to build dataflow graph as illustrated in figure 1 (b). A node is corresponding to a kernel function call. Each edge denotes a data transfer between two kernel function calls. Stream rates on each edge are annotated by the arguments of kernel functions. In this paper, node, actor and kernel function have the same meaning and are used discriminately.

The scheduler takes the dataflow graph as input, assigns each node in the stream graph to a processor and generates DMA for nodes on different processors in the target platform. It also assigns a software pipelining stage to each node and each edge. The details will be discussed in Section 4. The target architecture in our work is accelerator-based multi-core platform that has a control processor (CP) and multiple data processors (DP). We use Cell as our target architecture. Cell has one control processor PPE and a number of data processor SPEs. Each SPE has its own local memory and DMA engine. Ordinary C code is executed on PPE, and codes and data of kernel functions are scheduled to SPEs. Specially, to streamRead and streamWrite, the interfaces between C code and stream code are restricted to PPE.

3. A Motivating Example

In this section we first introduce the concept of software pipelining for SDF model. Subsequently, we will motivate our work on minimizing communication cost in rate-optimal schedule with the help of a simple example.

We adopt the concepts from paper [8, 14] to describe SDF model. A schedule is a sequence of actor firings (executing). A schedule ensuring that stream graph can execute infinite number of times with finite buffer is called *steady state schedule*. We call each firing of some kernel an *instance* of that kernel in the schedule. The minimum numbers of times that each actor must execute in a steady state schedule is presented as *repetition vector* or *firing rates*. It can be computed by solving the steady state balance equations or steady state rate equations.

Figure 2(a) shows a stream graph where kernel A produces three tokens and kernel B consumes two tokens each firing. The dependencies between various instances of kernel A and B are illustrated in figure 2(b). Figure 3 shows two kinds of software pipelining schedules – two-step schedule in [11] and minimum communication in rate-optimal schedule for the example in figure 2. The amount of work done by each instance is presented as the

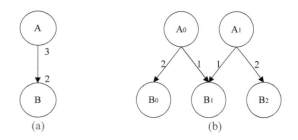

Figure 2. (a) An example stream graph. Kernel A produces 3 tokens each firing and kernel B consumes 2 tokens each firing. (b) The data dependence graph on each instance of each kernel. The edge indicates the number of tokens transmitted with the dependence.

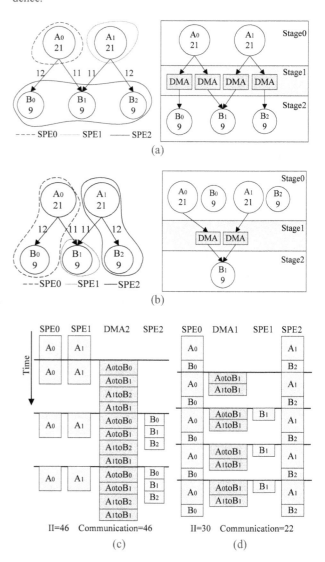

Figure 3: Two kinds of software pipelining schedules for the example in figure 2. (a) Processor, DMA and stage assignments of two-step schedule. (b) Processor, DMA and stage assignments in minimizing communication in rate-optimal schedule. (c) Software pipelining schedule for (a). (d) Software pipelining schedule for (b).

number in the node. The different instances of the same kernel have the same amount of work. The number beside each edge presents the communication. In our work each instance of the kernel is considered as the fundamental schedule unit.

Given three processors and each processor equipped with a DMA engine, the two-step schedule in figure 3(a) firstly assigns instance A0 to SPE0 and instance A1 to SPE1. Three instances of kernel B – B0, B1 and B2 are all assigned to SPE2. Subsequently, the scheduler checks each edge the instances of which are assigned to different processors, and assigns it to a DMA engine. Finally, stages are assigned to each instance and edge. Instance A0 and A1 are assigned to stage 0, instance B0, B1 and B2 are assigned to stage 2 and four DMA are assigned to stage 1. Minimum communication in rate-optimal schedule in figure 3(b) takes processor, DMA and stage assignments as a whole considering. Instance A0 and B0 are assigned to SPE0, instance B1 is assigned to SPE1 and instance A1 and B2 are assigned to SPE2. Hence, the communication costs between A0 and B0 as well as A1 and B2 are eliminated. Only two DMAs that transmit data from A0 to B1 and from A1 to B1 are needed. Instance A0, B0, A1 and B2 are assigned to stage 0, B1 is assigned to stage 2 and two DMAs are assigned to stage1. Figure 3(c) and 3(d) compares the result of two kinds of software pipelining schedules. The two-step schedule attains the *Initiation Interval (II)* of 46 units with 46 units communication cost. Compared to the two-step schedule, the minimum communication in rate-optimal schedule achieves the *II* of 30 units with 22 units communication cost. It reduces the communication cost while keeping a high computation rate.

The motivating example indicates the MCRO problem introduced in section 1. Given a stream graph, how to choose the schedule that attains the optimal rate while keeping the minimum communication cost. We answer the question by formulating it in our ILP schedule framework.

4. Minimizing Communication in Rate-Optimal Schedule Formulation

In this section, we first formulate the minimizing communication in rate-optimal schedule problem as an ILP problem. Then we extend the ILP formulation for DFBrook on accelerator based architecture. Each instance of the stateless kernel is considered as the basic schedule unit. For stateful kernel, the basic schedule unit is the total workload of the kernel in one iteration.

4.1. ILP Formulation

Consider a stream graph $G = (V, E)$ corresponding to a stream program. V denotes the set of nodes and E denotes the set of edges in stream graph. Let the repetition vector be r, where r_v represents the number of times $v \in V$ executed in a steady state schedule. $G_d = (V_d, E_d)$ is the data dependence graph (DDG) corresponding to stream graph G. V_d is the set of instances of all nodes (kernels) in G. Each node in DDG is denoted by $v_j, v \in V, 0 \leq j < r_v$ and each edge is denoted by $(u_i, v_j) \in E_d$, where $u \in V, 0 \leq i < r_u$. Let DP be the set of all DPs, denoted by 0, 1, ..., P_{max}-1.

We introduce 0-1 variable $a_{v,j,p}$ for each instance v_j to denote if the jth instance of the kernel v is assigned to DP p. We model the processor constraints as following.

$$\sum_{p=0}^{P_{max}-1} a_{v,j,p} = 1 \quad \forall v \in V, 0 \leq j < r_v \quad (1)$$

Equation (1) ensures that each instance of each kernel is assigned to exactly one DP. Let $work(v)$ represents the execution time of kernel v. The *II* is the initiation interval of the software pipelining schedule.

$$\sum_{v \in V} \sum_{j=0}^{r_v-1} a_{v,j,p} \times work(v) \leq II \quad 0 \leq p < P_{max} \quad (2)$$

Equation (2) models the fact that all the workload assigned to a DP is constrained to be completed in a specified *II*.

The processor assignment only provides information for maximizing processor workload balance without taking data precedence constraints, namely edges into consideration. If two connected instances are assigned to different DPs, a DMA transfer must be needed. For each edge $(u_i, v_j) \in E_d$, we define 0-1 variable $d_{u,i,v,j,p}$ to denote if the edge (u_i, v_j) is assigned to DMA p. The variable will be 1 if v_j is assigned to DP p while u_i is assigned to a different DP. The following inequalities (3) ensure that a DMA transfer is not introduced between two connected instances if they are on the same DP.

$$\begin{cases} d_{u,i,v,j,p} \geq a_{v,j,p} - a_{u,i,p} \\ d_{u,i,v,j,p} \leq a_{v,j,p} \\ d_{u,i,v,j,p} \leq 1 - a_{u,i,p} \end{cases}$$
$$\forall (u_i, v_j) \in E_d, 0 \leq p < P_{max} \quad (3)$$

In the schedule, it is always assumed that the DMA transfer between a pair of connected instances is located on the DP on which the destination instance is running. Let $Communication(u_i, v_j)$ represents the data transfer workload between u_i and v_j. The computation rate is also decided by the data transfer workload across all DPs. The following constraint (4) ensures all data transfer workload assigned to a DMA will not larger than *II* specified.

$$\sum_{(u_i, v_j) \in E_d} d_{u,i,v,j,p} \times Communication(u_i, v_j) \leq II$$
$$0 \leq p < P_{max} \quad (4)$$

The formulation above only provides the information about how instances are executing overlapped across DPs and how data transfer are assigned to DMAs. Namely it only specifies the information in space dimension for software pipelining schedule. To schedule instances and edges in time dimension, we use the concept *stage* in traditional modulo scheduling [13]. We define integer variable $sv_{v,j}$ for each instance v_j to denote the *stage number* which is assigned to the jth instance of the kernel v. And we define integer variable $se_{u,i,v,j}$ to represent the stage number which is assigned to each edge $(u_i, v_j) \in E_d$. The stage assignment constraints are modeled as following.

$$se_{u,i,v,j} \geq sv_{u,i} + \sum_{p=0}^{P_{max}-1} d_{u,i,v,j,p}$$
$$\forall (u_i, v_j) \in E_d, \quad se_{u,i,v,j} \geq 0, \quad sv_{u,i} \geq 0 \quad (5)$$

$$sv_{v,j} \geq se_{u,i,v,j} + \sum_{p=0}^{P_{max}-1} d_{u,i,v,j,p}$$
$$\forall (u_i, v_j) \in E_d, \quad se_{u,i,v,j} \geq 0, \quad sv_{v,j} \geq 0 \quad (6)$$

213

For a given edge (u_i, v_j), the stage number of destination instance should come after the source instance, namely $sv_{v,j} \geq sv_{u,i}$ to preserve data dependence. If u_i and v_j are assigned to different DPs, a DMA operation must be performed to transfer data. The DMA transfer from u_i to v_j is given a separate stage number $se_{u,i,v,j}$. As shown in figure 3, the inequality $sv_{u,i} < se_{u,i,v,j} < sv_{v,j}$ is enforced between the stages of two instances and the DMA transfer. Each instance of it can only be assigned to exactly one DP. From inequality (3) it is concluded that given an edge, either only one DMA it will be assigned to or none of DMA it will be assigned to. The sum equation $\sum_{p=0}^{P_{max}-1} d_{u,i,v,j,p}$ equates to 1 when instance u_i and v_j are assigned to different DPs and 0 when two instances are assigned to the same DPs. Equation (5) ensures that the DMA transfer is separated from the source instance u_i by at least one stage, and similarly equation (6) ensures that the destination instance v_j is separated from DMA transfer by one stage when instance u_i and v_j are assigned to different DPs. The inequality $sv_{v,j} \geq sv_{u,i}$ is retained when instance u_i and v_j are assigned to the same DP and variable $d_{u,i,v,j,p}$ will be useless.

$$Min \sum_{p=0}^{P_{max}-1} \sum_{(u_i,v_j) \in E_d} d_{u,i,v,j,p} \times Communication(u_i, v_j) \quad (7)$$

Equation (7) formulates all the communication between different instances. The objective in our ILP formulation is minimizing all the communication cost. Equations (1)-(7) constitute an ILP formulation for the software scheduling for minimum communication in rate-optimal schedule problem.

4.2 ILP Formulation for DFBrook on Accelerator based Architecture

In order to formulate schedule for DFBrook programs, we define $G' = (V', E')$ to represent the stream graph of DFBrook programming and $G_d' = (V_d', E_d')$ to denote corresponding data dependency graph. $V' = V \cup V_r \cup V_w$, V denotes the set of user defined kernels, V_r denotes the set of *streamRead* and V_w denotes the set of *streamWrite*. Let CP_{max} be the number of all CPs, denoted by P_{max}, $P_{max}+1$, ..., $P_{max}+CP_{max}-1$.

We redefine 0-1 variables $a_{v,j,p}$ to represent the assignment of instance v_j in G_d' to P_{max} data processors and CP_{max} control processors. In order to ensure each instance is assigned to exactly one processor, equation (1) is remodel to (8).

$$\sum_{p=0}^{P_{max}+CP_{max}-1} a_{v,j,p} = 1 \quad \forall v \in V', 0 \leq j < r_v \quad (8)$$

In our schedule, each instance of kernel $v \in V$ is only assigned to data processor. Equation (9) ensures that each instance of kernel v in V can never be assigned to any control processor. Equation (10) ensures that each instance of streamRead or streamWrite in $V_r \cup V_w$ can only be assigned to control processor. Equation (11) is improved from equation (2) to model the workloads of data processors and control processors to be completed in II.

$$\sum_{v \in V} \sum_{j=0}^{r_v-1} a_{v,j,p} = 0$$
$$Pmax \leq p < Pmax + CPmax - 1 \quad (9)$$

$$\sum_{v \in V_r \cup V_w} \sum_{j=0}^{r_v-1} \sum_{p=P_{max}}^{P_{max}+CP_{max}-1} a_{v,j,p} = \sum_{v \in V_r \cup V_w} r_v \quad (10)$$

$$\sum_{v \in V} \sum_{j=0}^{r_v-1} a_{v,j,p} \times work(v) \leq II$$
$$0 \leq p < P_{max} + CP_{max} - 1 \quad (11)$$

We also redefine 0-1 and $d_{u,i,v,j,p}$ to denote the assignment of edge (u_i, v_j) in E_d' to P_{max} DMA engines in data processors. StreamWrite is constrained to be assigned to control processor, hence the DMA transfer from some source instance u_i to streamWrite should be launched by the data processor that instance u_i is assigned to. We improve constraints from equation (3) to equation (12).

$$
\begin{aligned}
d_{u,i,v,j,p} &\geq \begin{cases} a_{v,j,p} - a_{u,i,p} & if \ v \in V \\ a_{u,i,p} - a_{v,j,p} & if \ v \in V_w \end{cases} \\
d_{u,i,v,j,p} &\leq \begin{cases} a_{v,j,p} & if \ v \in V \\ a_{u,i,p} & if \ v \in V_w \end{cases} \\
d_{u,i,v,j,p} &\geq \begin{cases} 1 - a_{u,i,p} & if \ v \in V \\ 1 - a_{v,j,p} & if \ v \in V_w \end{cases}
\end{aligned}
\quad (12)
$$

By substituting set E_d with E_d' in equation (5) (6) and (7), the formulations of stage assignments for instances and edges as well as the objective of minimizing communication can work for DFBrook programs. Equations (8)-(12) and the three new equations generated from (5)-(7) constitute an ILP formulation for DFBrook on accelerator based architecture.

4.3 A Solution Method

In this ILP formulation of MCRO problem, for a given II, each variable (i.e. $a_{v,j,p}$, $d_{u,i,v,j,p}$, $sv_{u,i}$ and $se_{u,i,v,j}$) is only multiplied by a constant factor; thus an integer linear programming solver (IP solver) can be used to find a solution. However, since the primary objective is rate-optimal, we need to iteratively solve the MCRO problem, until the smallest II with a feasible solution is found. First, the low bound of II is computed and II is set to the low bound. Second the IP solver is used to solve the MCRO problem to minimize the second objective of communication. If the IP solver fails to find a feasible solution, the II is incremented, and the second step is repeated; otherwise, the optimal solution is found. Binary search can also be used to find the smallest II.

5. Experiments and Evaluation

We have implemented our software pipelining scheduling for DFBrook language. In this section, we demonstrate the effectiveness of our MCRO formulation methodology and compare it with three other existing schedule methods.

5.1 Experimental Infrastructure and Methodology

The scheduler for DFBrook language is implemented based on the Brcc compiler [5] of BrookGPU. We modify the Brcc compiler front-end to parse the DFBrook language, to apply dependency analysis on stream variables and to construct stream graph for our scheduler. There are three kinds of communication modes in DFBrook program, streamRead to kernel, kernel to kernel and kernel to streamWrite corresponding to PPE to SPE, SPE to SPE and SPE to PPE. 1 PPE and 2 SPEs were used to measure the running time of each kernel and the communication time of each data transfer. The timing profile was collected using the UNIX syscall gettimeofday and used by our scheduler that generates for DFBrook program. The scheduler uses the CPLEX mixed integer programming solver to solve the ILP and produces the result of our software pipelining schedule. We evaluate our scheme on a PlayStation3 equipped with a Cell processor (6 SPEs available). IBM's Cell SDK 3.0 and the gcc compilers for SPE and PPE were used to compile the program.

We use the set of benchmarks in Table 1 to evaluate the schedule methods. The details of each benchmark such as the number of kernel instances, streamRead/streamWrite (R.W.) and communication arcs (Comm. Arcs) are illustrated in the table. Most benchmarks are from image processing domain. Gausslaplacian implements image edge detection using Gaussian Laplacian. Histogram is a parallel histogram algorithm. shortEnergy implements a streaming short energy feature extracting algorithm for audio. averageMotion implements a parallel motion vector feature extracting algorithm for video.

5.2 Experimental Results and Comparisons

Figure 4 shows the *II* ratio obtained by our MCRO schedule over single SPE on 1-6 SPEs for the benchmarks. Our scheduler achieves near linear *II* ratio for most benchmarks. The benchmarks of FFT and histogram obtain no more improvement beyond 4 and 5 SPEs. This is because they don't have enough kernel instances to span all processors. It can be improved by unfolding the stream graph to increase parallelism. As shown in Table 1, FFT only have 10 kernel instances (The kernel instance number plus R.W. instance number equals to the instance number.) and histogram only have 9 kernel instances. DCT and MatrixMult with 33 and 21 kernel instances both achieve the linear improvement.

We compare the schedule generated by the MCRO formulation with those generated by three other schedule methods: (i) heuristic list (List) method schedule in traditional software pipelining, (ii) the periodic admissible parallel schedules (PAPS) method [8] and (iii) rate optimal integer linear programming based formulation schedule (RO). Table 2 shows the schedule results of comparison between MCRO and three other methods above for the benchmarks in Table 1. It is tested on 6 SPEs. For each benchmark, we report the optimal iteration period *II*, the iteration period of PASP schedule and communication cost for various schedules. We also report the improvement in iteration period compared with List and PAPS schedules, and the improvement in communication cost attained by MCRO schedule compared to the three other methods.

Comparison with List Schedule. List schedule method is a popular schedule in traditional modulo schedule software pipelining [15, 16]. We modify classic prior-level based list schedule algorithm [17] to construct software pipelining as following. For each node, we use list schedule to assign processor and stage assignment algorithm proposed by M. Kudlur and S. Mahlke [11] to assign stage. From Table 2, it is observed that for benchmarks that have large computation such as DCT, shortEnergy and averageMotion, MCRO schedule achieves 17.8%-24.7% improvement in computation rate. For benchmarks that have large communication such as FFT, and mergesort, 31.8%-40.7% improvements are achieved in communication cost. This is because the program that have larger stream graph offers more schedule opportunity for MCRO schedule to improve the performance. The average improvement in communication is 23%.

Comparison with PAPS Schedule. Periodic admissible parallel schedules (PAPS) proposed by Lee [8] is a well known block schedule. In PAPS schedule, the executions of instances from different iterations are not overlapped. We use list schedule algorithm to implement PAPS schedule. The experimental result in Table 2 illustrates that MCRO schedule performs 47% improvement in computation rate compared to PAPS schedule. For benchmarks of FFT and mergesort, MCRO schedule achieves as high as 58.9% and 53.9% improvement. The minimum improvement for imagesmooth is 38.4%. For most benchmarks, MCRO schedule performs 10%-20% improvement in communication. For benchmarks like histogram, the communication costs of MCRO schedule are a little higher than that of PAPS schedule. This is due to the fact that the data transfer in histogram can be overlapped by the computation in the same iteration in PAPS schedule. On the other side, MCRO schedule need first solve the ILP to get the optimal rate, and communication in the rate-optimal is not totally overlapped by the computation in the different iterations.

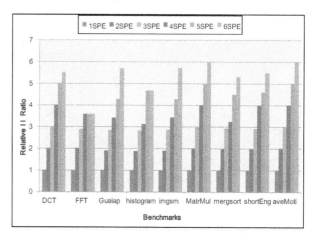

Figure 4. MCRO schedule *II* ratio normalized to single SPE

Comparison with RO Schedule. Rate optimal (RO) schedule is a rate optimal integer linear programming formulation schedule method [11]. The objective of RO schedule is minimizing computation rate or II. We construct RO schedule by simply modifying the objective of equation (7) in our MCRO formulation schedule. As mentioned in section 4.3, we generate MCRO schedule by increasing II until the smallest II with a feasible solution is found, thus MCRO schedule has the same optimal computation rate as RO schedule. In fact, the solution for MCRO is a subset of that for RO schedule. The experiments show that the MCRO schedule performs 7%-40.9% improvement in communication cost compared to RO schedule. The average improvement is 21.7%. Only histogram benchmark has the same communication cost as RO schedule. This is because that the workload of communication is much less than computation and it is overlapped by computation workload in the program.

We conclude the discussion with a mention of the time of solving MCRO formulation. We use binary search to find the minimum II with a feasible solution. The low bound of II can be obtained by the minimum initiation interval (MII), MII=max(ResMII, RecMII). ResMII is 0 for all the benchmarks, since we only considered the DFBrook programs which have no loops. The up bound is estimated by max($\sum$ work, $\sum$ Communication). The solver is allotted 30 seconds to attempt a solution with this II. If it fails to find a solution in 30 seconds, the low bound is set by this II and the new II is computed. Most benchmarks take less than 30 seconds to solve, except DCT, averageMotion and MatrixMult which take about 100 seconds. Thus, this is quite efficient.

Table 1: Benchmark characteristics

Benchmark	Instances	R.W. Instances	Comm. Arcs	Description
DCT	35	2	48	8x8 Discrete Cosine Transform
FFT	12	2	14	8x8 Fast Fourier Transform
Gausslaplacian	28	6	54	Image edge detection using Gaussian Laplacian
histogram	11	2	15	Image histogram
imagesmooth	28	6	54	Image smooth using 3x3 template
MatrixMult	24	3	37	Blocked matrix multiply
mergesort	17	2	24	Parallel merge sort for 16 floats
shortEnergy	20	2	26	Short energy feature extracting for audio
averageMotion	28	3	43	Average motion vector feature extracting for video

Table 2: Comparisons of Schedule methods on Benchmarks

Benchmark	Iteration Period (100ns)			% Improvement in Iteration Period		Communication Cost (100ns)				% Improvement in Communication Cost		
	MCRO	List	PAPS	Over List	Over PAPS	MCRO	List	PAPS	RO	Over List	Over PAPS	Over RO
DCT	6600	8028	12905	17.8	48.9	5514	6828	6974	7120	19.2	20.9	22.5
FFT	3254	3354	7923	3.0	58.9	1259	1845	1406	1992	31.8	10.5	36.7
Gausslaplacian	24500	27017	39891	9.3	38.6	7025	9317	8023	7554	24.6	12.4	7.0
histogram	9406	10937	16205	13.9	41.9	2892	2745	2701	2892	-5.4	-7.1	0
imagesmooth	14379	16738	23349	14.1	38.4	7021	9313	7447	8696	24.6	5.7	19.2
MatrixMult	3548	4014	6741	11.6	47.4	3596	4918	4391	4771	26.9	18.1	24.6
mergesort	3665	4140	7960	11.4	53.9	2142	3611	2289	3624	40.7	6.4	40.9
shortEnergy	15077	19011	31827	20.7	52.6	3149	3443	3488	3590	8.5	9.7	12.3
averageMotion	14449	19199	27975	24.7	48.4	4758	7219	5719	7025	34.1	16.8	32.3

6. Related Works

There have been numerous works discussing the scheduling problem of stream graph. Early work from Ptolemy project has focused on Synchronization Data Flow (SDF) model of computation and scheduling [8, 18] .Some of their scheduling techniques [20, 21] have focused on scheduling stream graphs to multiprocessor systems. Gao, et al have defined a set of rules for stream graph to construct Regular Stream Flow Graphs (RSFG) [9] which can be statically scheduled at compiler time.

Stream compilation based on programming paradigms for multi-core systems has been widely researched. Coarse-grained task, data, and pipeline parallelism have been exploited for StreamIt programs on raw architecture [10]. A linear analysis and optimization for stream programs has been studied in [22]. Gummaraju et al maps StreamC to a multithreaded processor [23]. Affine partitioning techniques are used to map Brook to multicore processor [24]. Das et al proposed the technology to compile the stream program on Imagine Stream Architecture [25].

Software pipelining a well known technology for loop optimization recently has been used to schedule stream programs. Govindarajan et al use a linear programming formulation framework to study the minimum buffer requirements of rate optimal software pipelining of RSFGs [26]. There is an extension to above method to implement software pipelining for StreamIt on GPUs [14]. The schedule method mainly focuses on the share memory model architecture. Kudlur and Mahlke propose a stream graph modulo scheduling algorithm for StreamIt applications on multi-core systems [11]. An unfolding and partitioning step based on integer linear programming is used to balance workload and then a stage assignment algorithm is used to assign pipelining stage. A code generation method is also proposed. Choi et al represent a module scheduling for stream programs on real-time constrain multi-core architecture [27]. It uses ILP to formulate the memory and real-time constraints. Hormati et al uses an adaptive static and dynamic hybrid compilation for stream programs [28]. It constructs an initial schedule for virtualized resources at compilation time, and then an adaption system dynamically modifies the initial schedule according to current resource of systems.

Our work is distinctly different from theirs in that, we target the communication exposed architecture with distributed memory model, and use a unified integer programming formulation to construct an optimal software pipelining scheduling. It integrates resource assignments and stage assignments into a unified ILP framework and achieves optimal computation rate while minimizing communication overhead.

7. Conclusion

In this paper, we have proposed a unified ILP formulation that combines the requirement of both rate-optimal software pipelining and the minimization of inter-core communication overhead. Also, we improve and implement the formulation method for DFBrook stream language on the Cell architecture. Compared to traditional list schedule, PAPS schedule and RO schedule, our scheme achieves a good performance improvement. The schedule method proposed in the paper can also be used to architectures with hierarchical memory. Our future work will mainly focus on handing for memory constraints and improving the DFBrook language to support split and join syntactic structures as in StreamIt.

Acknowledgments

This paper is financially supported by the National Natural Science Foundation of China under Grant No.60703049; Intel grant for a study of multi-core programming environment.

References

[1] H. P. Hofstee. Power efficient processor design and the Cell processor. In *Proc. of the 11th International Symposium on High-Performance Computer Architecture*, pages 258–262, February 2005.

[2] P. Kongetira, K. Aingaran, and K. Olukotun. Niagara: A 32-way multithreaded SPARC processor. *IEEE Micro*, 25(2):21-29, February 2005.

[3] J. Nickolls and I. Buck. NVIDIA CUDA software and GPU parallel computing architecture. In *Microprocessor Forum*, May 2007.

[4] W. Thies, M. Karczmarek, and S. P. Amarasinghe. StreamIt: A language for streaming applications. In *Proc. of the 2002 International Conference on Compiler Construction*, pages 179–196, 2002.

[5] I. Buck et al. Brook for GPUs: Stream computing on graphics hardware. *ACM Transactions on Graphics*, 23(3):777–786, August 2004.

[6] D. Zhang, Z. Li, H. Song, and L Liu. A programming model for an embedded media processing architecture. In *Proc. of the 5thInternational Symposium on Systems, Architectures, Modeling, and Simulation*, volume 3553 of Lecture Notes in Computer Science, pages 251–261, July 2005.

[7] W. Mark, R. Glanville, K. Akeley, and J. Kilgard. Cg: A system for programming graphics hardware in a C-like language. In *Proc. of the 30thInternational Conference on Computer Graphics and Interactive Techniques*, pages 893–907, July 2003.

[8] E. A. Lee and D. G. Messerschmitt. Static Scheduling of Synchronous Data Flow Programs for Digital Signal Processing. *IEEE Trans. Computers.*, 36(1):24–35, 1987.

[9] G. Gao, R. Govindarajan, and P. Panangaden. Well-Behaved Dataflow Programs for DSP Computation. *ICASSP-92: IEEE International Conference on Acoustics, Speech, and Signal Processing*, 1992., vol. 5, pp. 561–564 vol.5, Mar 1992.

[10] Michael I. Gordon, William Thies, and Saman Amarasinghe. Exploiting coarse-grained task, data, and pipeline parallelism in stream programs. In *14th International Conference on Architectural Support for Programming Languages and Operating Systems*, pages 151–162, New York, NY, USA, 2006.

[11] M. Kudlur and S. Mahlke. Orchestrating the Execution of Stream Programs on Multicore Platforms. In *Proceedings of the 2008 ACM SIGPLAN Conference on Programming Language Design and Implementation*, 2008, pp. 114–124.

[12] Ian Buck. Brook Spec v0.2 http://merrimac.stanford.edu/brook/brookspec-v0.2.pdf. 2003

[13] B. R. Rau, M. S. Schlansker, and P. P. Tirumalai. Code generation for modulo scheduled loops. In *Proc. of the 25th Annual International Symposium on Microarchitecture*, pages 158–169, November 1992.

[14] Abhishek Udupa, R. Govindarajan and Matthew J. Thazhuthaveetil. Software Pipelined Execution of Stream Programs on GPUs. In *Proc. of 2009 International Symposium on Code Generation and Optimization*, pages 200-209, 2009.

[15] B. R. Rau. Iterative Modulo Scheduling: An Algorithm for Software Pipelined Loops. In *Proc. of the 27th Annual International Symposium on Microarchitecture*, pages 63–74, November 1994.

[16] M. Lam. Software pipelining: An effective scheduling technique for VLIW machines. In *Proc. of the SIGPALN'88 Conf. on Programming Language Design and Implementation*, pages 318-328, 1988.

[17] Oliver Sinnen. Task Scheduling for Parallel Systems, *Wiley*, 2007.

[18] S. S. Bhattacharyya, P. K. Murthy and Edward A. Lee. Synthesis of Embedded Software from Synchronous Dataflow Specifications. *Journal of VLSI Signal Processing* vol. 21, pages 151–166, 1999.

[19] Praveen K. Murthy, Shuvra Bhattacharyya, and Edward A. Lee. Joint Minimization of Code and Data for Synchronous Dataflow Programs. *Journal of Formal Methods in System Design*, 11(1): 41-70, July 1997.

[20] Jose Luis Pino, Shuvra S. Bhattacharyya, and Edward A. Lee. A hierarchical multiprocessor scheduling framework for synchronous dataflow graphs. Technical Report UCB/ERL M95/36, University of California, Berkeley, May 1995.

[21] Soonhoi Ha and Edward A. Lee. Compile-time scheduling and assignment of data-flow program graphs with data dependent iteration. *IEEE Transactions on Computers*, 40(11):1225–1238, 1991.

[22] Andrew A. Lamb, William Thies and Saman Amarasinghe. Linear Analysis and Optimization of Stream Programs. In *Proceedings of the 2003 ACM SIGPLAN Conference on Programming Language Design and Implementation*, pp. 12-25, 2003.

[23] Jayanth Gummaraju and Mendel Rosenblum. Stream programming on general-purpose processors. In *Proc. of the 38th Annual International Symposium on Microarchitecture*, pages 343–354, Washington, DC, USA, 2005. IEEE Computer Society.

[24] Shih wei Liao, Zhaohui Du, GanshaWu, and Guei-Yuan Lueh. Data and computation transformations for brook streaming applications on multiprocessors. In *Proc. of the 2006 International Symposium on Code Generation and Optimization*, 0(1):196–207, 2006.

[25] A. Das, W. Dally, and P. Mattson. Compiling for Stream Processing. In *Proceedings of Parallel Architectures and Compilation Techniques (PACT)*, pages 33-42, Sep. 2006.

[26] R. Govindarajan, G. Gao, and P. Desai. Minimizing Memory Requirements in Rate-optimal Schedules. In *ASAP '94: Proceedings of the 1994 International Conference on Application Specific Array Processors*, pages 75–86, Aug 1994.

[27] Yoonseo Choi, Yuan Lin, Nathan Chong, Scott Mahlke and Trevor Mudge. Stream Compilation for Real-time Embedded Multicore Systems. In *Proc. of 2009 International Symposium on Code Generation and Optimization*, pages 210-220, 2009.

[28] Amir H. Hormati, Yoonseo Choi, Manjunath Kudlur, Rodric Rabbah, Trevor Mudge and Scott Mahlke. Flextream: Adaptive Compilation of Streaming Applications for Heterogeneous Architectures. In *Proceedings of Parallel Architectures and Compilation Techniques (PACT)*, 2009.

Level by Level: Making Flow- and Context-Sensitive Pointer Analysis Scalable for Millions of Lines of Code

Hongtao Yu [*][$]   Jingling Xue [†]   Wei Huo [*][$]   Xiaobing Feng [*]   Zhaoqing Zhang [*]

[*]Institute of Computing Technology
Chinese Academy of Sciences, China

[$]Graduate School
Chinese Academy of Sciences, China

[†]School of Computer Science and Engineering
University of New South Wales, Australia
jingling@cse.unsw.edu.au

{htyu, huowei, fxb, zqzhang}@ict.ac.cn

Abstract

We present a practical and scalable method for flow- and context-sensitive (FSCS) pointer analysis for C programs. Our method analyzes the pointers in a program level by level in terms of their *points-to levels*, allowing the points-to relations of the pointers at a particular level to be discovered based on the points-to relations of the pointers at this level and higher levels. This level-by-level strategy can enhance the scalability of the FSCS pointer analysis in two fundamental ways, by enabling (1) fast and accurate flow-sensitive analysis on full sparse SSA form using a flow-insensitive algorithm and (2) fast and accurate context-sensitive analysis using a full transfer function and a meet function for each procedure. Our level-by-level algorithm, LevPA, gives rises to (1) a precise and compact SSA representation for subsequent program analysis and optimization tasks and (2) a flow- and context-sensitive MAY / MUST mod (modification) set and read set for each procedure. Our preliminary results show that LevPA can analyze some programs with over a million lines of C code in minutes, faster than the state-of-the-art FSCS methods.

Categories and Subject Descriptors   D.3.4 [*Processors*]: Compilers; F.3.2 [*Semantics of Programming Languages*]: Program Analysis

General Terms   Algorithms, Languages, Performance

Keywords   Pointer Analysis, Alias Analysis

1. Introduction

Pointer analysis is the basis of most other static program analyses and many compiler optimizations, especially for C programs. The motivation to enhance the scalability of flow- and context-sensitive (FSCS) pointer analysis is that the increased precision thus obtained is crucial for many security-related program analysis and verification tasks and may also open up new opportunities for future compiler optimizations in the multi-core era. However, none of the existing FSCS pointer analysis algorithms [10, 13, 14, 17, 20, 25, 28] can analyze beyond a million of lines of code efficiently. In this paper, we introduce a FSCS (and also field-sensitive) pointer analysis that can analyze some of these programs in minutes.

Flow-sensitive pointer analysis provides the points-to information in the form of points-to sets [1] or graphs [3], which is often used by def-use analysis. Conversely, def-use analysis provides the def/use information useful for flow-sensitive pointer analysis. For example, assignments to a pointer through dereferences of other pointers can alter the points-to information of that pointer. To facilitate def-use analysis, the static single assignment (SSA) form [8] is widely used. As a result, many flow-sensitive analysis problems can be sped up on SSA by using flow-insensitive algorithms.

In this paper, we present a FSCS pointer analysis, LevPA, that analyzes the pointers in a C program level by level according to their points-to levels. This level-by-level strategy may significantly enhance the scalability of the FSCS pointer analysis. On one hand, the time and space efficiency of flow-sensitive pointer analysis can be improved by applying a flow-insensitive algorithm on full-sparse SSA. On the other hand, the precise and compact SSA form enables precise alias relations to be exploited to eliminate spurious def/use points, sharpening the precision of def-use analysis.

The feasibility of binding full-sparse SSA and pointer analysis together comes from a simple observation. If all the def (definition) and use sites (either direct or indirect) of a pointer variable have been determined, we can build the SSA form for all accesses to the pointer and then analyze them flow-sensitively (by using a flow-insensitive algorithm). A variable can be referenced directly or indirectly through dereferences of another pointer. If we want to know all the indirect references of a variable, we need to analyze all the pointers possibly pointing to it first. To guarantee this, we assign a property, *points-to level*, to each variable and analyze the variables in a program in decreasing order of their levels.

Hardekopf and Lin [11] have recently proposed a flow-sensitive pointer analysis on SSA. However, their method is semi-sparse in the sense that it only builds the SSA form for the *top-level* pointer variables, i.e., those that cannot be referenced indirectly, in a program. In contrast, LevPA is fully sparse. By going beyond just the *top-level* pointer variables, LevPA reaps the full benefits of performing pointer analysis on SSA for all pointers at all levels.

Context-sensitive pointer analysis also benefits from a level-by-level approach. The key in achieving context-sensitivity is to obtain the output of a procedure according to a given input. Some methods accomplish this by distinguishing different calling paths for a procedure, and consequently, have to analyze the entire program on an exploded call graph [24, 28]. Instead, LevPA builds a full transfer function for a procedure and applies it in all its calling contexts.

A transfer function for a procedure is a description of the relations between its *formal-out* parameters and its *formal-in* parameters. The *formal-in* parameters of a procedure *proc* include not only the declared formal parameters but also the global variables, escaped local variables (into this procedure) and dynamic allocated objects whose values may be accessed by *proc* or the procedures that *proc* invokes. Similarly, the *formal-out* parameters of a procedure *proc* include not only its return value but also the global variables, escaped local variables (from this procedure) and dynamic allocated objects whose values may be modified by *proc* or the procedures that *proc* invokes.

If the higher-level formal-in parameters of a procedure have been analyzed, the pointers of a particular level in the procedure body can be analyzed succinctly. Therefore, we make use of the points-to sets of formal-in parameters at higher levels (and possibly at the same level due to the presence of points-to cycles) to distinguish the calling contexts for a procedure and encode them in its transfer function. Our transfer functions can precisely describe the modification side effects of procedures while keeping their space requirements and function application costs to a minimum. This is mostly achieved by representing for the first time the points-to relations with context-sensitive conditions using BDDs [2].

We do the same for the interprocedural read side effects for a procedure by using a so-called meet function to describe the read side effects of the procedure on all its formal-ins.

In summary, the paper contributes a fully flow- and context-sensitive, and also field-sensitive pointer analysis that

- is the first to carry out a level-by-level FSCS pointer analysis that is different from the summary-based algorithm in [14];

- performs a full-sparse flow-sensitive analysis on SSA flow-insensitively with significantly reduced time and space costs;

- performs a context-sensitive analysis efficiently with a precise full transfer function and a meet function for each procedure;

- yields flow- and context-sensitive interprocedural MAY/MUST modification and read side effects on a compact SSA form; and

- analyzes million lines of code in minutes, faster than the state-of-the art FSCS pointer analysis algorithms.

The rest of the paper is organized as follows. Section 2 introduces the LevPA framework and describes how to compute the points-to levels of variables. Section 3 discusses the pointer analysis performed by LevPA for a particular level. Section 4 presents and discusses our experimental results. Section 5 introduces the related work, and finally, Section 6 concludes the paper.

2. The LevPA Framework

Our method can cover full C features. As in [1], it suffices to consider only four types of assignments: (1) $x = y$, (2) $x = \&y$, (3) $*x = y$, and (4) $x = *y$. Arrays are treated as monolithic scalar objects. Heap objects are modeled by representing an allocation site at a program point loc by a statement of the form $p = \&alloc_{loc}$. A memory deallocation statement for p is replaced by $p = NULL$. All memory operations on structs are flattened into memory operations on scalar fields. Function pointers are handled as in [5]. Pointer arithmetic operations are handled by assigning the union of the points-to sets of all pointer operands in a pointer-related assignment to the resulting pointer [22]. Type casting is handled by inferring the locations accessed by the pointer being cast.

Suppose we have computed a property, *points-to level*, for every abstract memory location, such as a scalar variable or a dynamic allocated object (with all such abstract locations being called variables henceforth). The points-to level of a variable v, denoted $ptl(v)$, satisfies the two conditions stated below.

Condition 1. *If a variable x is possibly pointed to by a pointer y during an execution of the program, then $ptl(x) \leqslant ptl(y)$.*

Condition 2. *If a variable x is possibly modified by assigning the value of y to x during an execution of the program, through*

Algorithm 1 The LevPA pointer analysis.

```
 1: Compute the points-to levels for all variables;
 2: Build the procedure call graph, denoted PCG;
 3: Reduce PCG to a SCC-DAG, denoted AVG;
 4: repeat
 5:     for lev from highest to lowest do
 6:         Bottom-up_analysis(AVG, lev)
 7:         Top-down_analysis(AVG, lev)
 8:     end for
 9:     Update PCG and AVG due to resolved indirect calls;
10: until PCG does not change;
```

---

direct or indirect references to x and y, then $ptl(x) \leqslant ptl(y)$. (The modification can happen due to (1) $x = y$, (2) $*p = y$, where p may point to x or (3) $x = *q$, where q may point to y.)

Our LevPA framework is summarized in Algorithm 1. We start by computing the points-to levels for all variables in a program. We then build its procedure call graph (PCG), where no function pointer is resolved yet. To handle recursive calls, PCG is partitioned into strongly connected components (SCC) to form a directed acyclic graph (a SCC-DAG), denoted AVG. The procedures in the same SCC form a recursion cycle. We then start analyzing the pointers of the same level together from highest to lowest. When working at a level, only the points-to sets of the pointers at this level are computed. The points-to sets of higher-levels pointers are used while the pointers at the lower level are ignored. Conditions 1 and 2 guarantee that whenever a variable is analyzed, all the other variables that may have an impact on its value either have been analyzed earlier or are being analyzed at the same time. The analysis at each level typically entails traversing AVG twice, first bottom-up (by Algorithm 3) and then top-down (by Algorithm 6), but iterations (not shown in Algorithm 1 explicitly) may be required as described in the next paragraph. During the bottom-up phase, we construct the (extended) SSA form for the pointers of the current level and perform the pointer inference to compute the points-to set for every pointer at the current level that may be possibly expressed in terms of the points-to sets of some formal-ins. In addition, we also build a full transfer function (and also a meet function) for each procedure. During the top-down phase, we propagate the points-to sets of the formal-in pointers of the level being analyzed to their use sites, and at the same time, expand the dereferences for the pointers at the current level to prepare for the analysis of the pointers at the next level (and lower levels). In actuality, the pointer dereference expansion performed signals the beginning of the SSA form construction for the pointers at the next and lower levels but this step can be moved into the bottom-up phase at the level below.

The pointer analysis at a level may involve two types of iterations. First, on detecting some cyclic points-to relations during the pointer dereference expansion performed in the top-down phase for a level, the pointers at this level are analyzed iteratively until their points-to sets are fully resolved (as discussed in Section 3.1.6). Second, in the presence of recursion, iterations are required to analyze the pointers in the procedures in each recursion cycle in PCG. In addition, in the presence of function pointers, PCG is built incrementally, causing iterations to be performed in order to accommodate both the modification and read side effects introduced by the newly resolved procedure calls on the program being analyzed.

As shown in Algorithm 2, we compute the points-to level of a variable based on the points-to graph built by a Steensgaard-styled pointer analysis [21, 22, 26] (line 1), which runs in almost linear time. Steensgaard-styled pointer analysis is an equivalence-based analysis. If there is an assignment between two variables x and y, both must point to the same object in the underlying points-

Algorithm 2 Computing points-to levels.

1: Perform the Steensgaard-styled pointer analysis;
2: Add pair-wise points-to edges for all predecessors of a node in the points-to graph thus obtained;
3: Reduce the points-to graph to a SCC-DAG;
4: Set $ptl(r) = 0$ for every leaf node r;
5: **for** each non-leaf node r such that the points-to levels of all its successors have already been computed **do**
6:     Let $s_1, \ldots, s_n$ be all the successors of r;
7:     Set $ptl(r) = \max\{ptl(s_1), \ldots, ptl(s_n)\} + 1$;
8: **end for**

```
int   obj, t;

main()
{
    L1:     int **x, **y;
    L2:     int *a, *b, *c, *d, *e;
    L3:     x = &a;        y = &b;
    L4:     foo(x, y);
    L5:     *b = 5;
    L6:     if (t)    { x = &c;  y = &e; }
    L7:     else      { x = &d;  y = &d; }
    L8:     c = &t;
    L9:     foo(x, y);
    L10:    *e = 10;
}

void   foo(int **p, int **q)
{
    L11:    int *tmp = *q;
    L12:    *p = tmp;
    L13:    tmp = &obj;
    L14:    *q = tmp;
}
```

Figure 1. A motivating example.

to graph. In line 2, we ensure conservatively that Condition 2 is always satisfied. Otherwise, if x and y point to the same object in the points-to graph when y participates in a cycle that does not contain x, then $ptl(x) > ptl(y)$ would be possible. In this case, an assignment like $x = y$ would be rendered unanalyzable. In lines 3 – 8, the points-to level of a variable is computed as the longest distance from the node containing the variable to a leaf node.

Theorem 1. *Conditions 1 and 2 are satisfied by the points-to levels of variables computed by Algorithm 2 for a program.*

Proof. If a variable x is possibly pointed to by a pointer y, there must be a points-to edge from the node representing y to the node representing x in the Steensgaard-styled points-to graph. After line 3, x and y may be in the same SCC. In any case, $ptl(x) \leqslant ptl(y)$ always holds. So Condition 1 is guaranteed to be satisfied. Due to line 2, if a variable x is possibly modified by assigning the value of y to x, then x and y must be in the same SCC. Again $ptl(x) \leqslant ptl(y)$ holds. Condition 2 is satisfied, too. $\square$

Our motivating example is given in Figure 1. For convenience, all assignments have already been put into the form supported in the LevPA framework. By applying Algorithm 2, we find that the pointers are organized in three levels: $ptl(x) = ptl(y) = ptl(p) = ptl(q) = 2$, $ptl(a) = ptl(b) = ptl(c) = ptl(d) = ptl(e) = ptl(tmp) = 1$ and $ptl(t) = ptl(obj) = 0$. LevPA will compute the points-to sets first for the pointers in $\{x, y, p, q\}$, then the pointers in $\{a, b, c, d, e, tmp\}$, and finally, the pointers in $\{t, obj\}$.

Algorithm 3 Bottom-up analysis.

1: **procedure** Bottom-up_analysis(AVG, lev)
2: **begin**
3:   **for** each node scc in reverse topological order of AVG **do**
4:     **for** each procedure $proc$ of scc **do**
5:       (a) Create_μ_χ_for_callsites($proc, lev$);
6:       (b) Build the extended SSA form;
7:       (c) Perform pointer inference;
8:     **end for**
9:   **end for**
10: **end**

---

3. Analyzing a Level

Analyzing a level amounts to computing the points-to sets for the pointers at this level. LevPA proceeds in two phases, first bottom-up and then top-down. Both phases are inter-related. The bottom-up phase determines the points-to set for a pointer at the level being analyzed possibly in terms of the points-to sets of some formal-ins. All these points-to sets will be fully resolved subsequently in the top-down phase by propagating the points-to sets of formals-in to their use sites (with the actual parameters of a procedure call being bound to their corresponding formal parameters).

In this section, we focus on discussing how to analyze the pointers of a specific level on the assumption that the pointers of higher levels have already been analyzed. We first look at the bottom-up phase and then the top-down phase.

3.1 Bottom-Up Analysis

Algorithm 3 gives the key steps performed for a given level, lev. In this phase, we process the nodes in AVG in reverse topological order. Step 3(a) collects the flow- and context-sensitive read and modification side effects of all call sites in a procedure in terms of the μ and χ operators, respectively [7]. The μ and χ operators for the dereferencing operations on the pointers of level $lev+1$ are introduced earlier during the top-down analysis for $lev+1$. Step 3(b) builds the extended SSA form [7, 8] for the pointers of level lev. Step 3(c) performs the pointer inference to compute the points-to set for every pointer of level lev, which may be expressed in terms of some formal-ins at lev or higher. In this last step, we also obtain a full transfer function for each procedure that encodes its flow- and context-sensitive MAY/MUST modification side effects for its formal-outs and a meet function that gives its flow- and context-sensitive read side effects for its formal-ins.

In Algorithm 3, a node scc may represent multiple procedures contained in a recursion cycle. As a result, the bottom-up analysis for each procedure may have to be done iteratively using a work list in a demand-driven fashion. Whenever the transfer or meet function of a procedure has changed, the procedure is inserted into the work list, causing more iterations for its callers and indirect callers until a fixed point has been reached (i.e., when the work list is empty).

Section 3.1.1 introduces the full transfer functions used for specifying the interprocedural MAY/MUST modification side effects of procedures. Section 3.1.2 introduces the meet functions used for specifying the interprocedural read side effects of procedures. Section 3.1.3 introduces the extended SSA form used in the LevPA framework. Sections 3.1.4 - 3.1.6 describe Steps 3(a) - 3(c) of Algorithm 3, respectively, and illustrate them by examples.

3.1.1 Full Transfer Functions

To obtain high scalability while maintaining context-sensitivity, we build a single full transfer function for a procedure that can describe the modification side effect of the procedure independently of its inputs. Wilson and Lam [25] use partial transfer functions (PTFs) in their flow- and context-sensitive pointer analysis. PTFs are built for a procedure according to different alias inputs. This may result in analyzing a procedure more than once. For example, in Figure 1, the call sites L4 and L9 provide different alias inputs to foo. The formal parameters p and q do not alias with each other at L4 but may both point to d at L9. They thus analyze foo to build two different PTFs. Our method may also analyze a procedure multiple times, once for each level. However, the analysis at one level does not overlap with the analysis of another level. Furthermore, their parameterized representations of PTFs may result in precision loss. In Figure 1, their method employs so-called extended parameters 1_p and 1_q to represent all the variables pointed to by p and q, respectively. As 1_p and 1_q are aliases at L9, foo is regarded as having the same side effect on 1_p and 1_q, leading to the spurious points-to relation that c may point to obj after L9. Perhaps the major advantage of PTFs is that they summarize the side effects of a procedure only for those aliases that may actually occur in the program. However, by proceeding level by level, LevPA also eliminates unrealized alias relations according to calling contexts. Once the full transfer function for a procedure is available, we can apply it to different call sites accurately and efficiently.

We do not use full calling paths to distinguish calling contexts of a procedure when working at a particular level lev. Instead, we use the points-to sets of formal-in parameters at higher levels (and possibly at lev due to the existence of points-to cycles) to distinguish the calling contexts for the pointer accesses to the pointers at level lev and encode them into the transfer function for the procedure. We have designed a new points-to representation that not only describes the objects pointed to but also under which conditions the objects are pointed to. These context conditions are used to distinguish the calling contexts of a procedure so that its transfer function can be used in any calling context.

Definition 1 (Points-to Set). *Given a variable p of level lev, its points-to set, $Ptr(p)$ is $\{\langle v, M \rangle \mid v$ is an abstract memory location and $M \in \{may, must\}\}$. For convenience, we write $p \Rightarrow v$ ($p \to v$) to highlight the fact that p must (may) point to v.*

Definition 2 (Context Condition). *When working at a level lev, a context condition $\mathbb{C}(c_1, \ldots, c_k)$ is a Boolean function such that c_i evaluates to true (false) if the points-to relation that it represents for a pointer at lev or a higher level evaluates to true (false).*

As one of the contributions in this work, context conditions are implemented using BDDs [2], thereby greatly reducing the costs for representing and applying transfer functions. With BDDs, we can not only compactly represent context conditions but also enable Boolean operations to be evaluated efficiently. For example, Figure 2 shows how the context condition $\mathbb{C} = (p \to a \land q \to a) \lor p \to b$ is represented by a BDD. Each variable node in the BDD represents a points-to relation. We allocate a unique id for each points-to relation by organizing all points-to relations of all levels in a vector. This vector is filled up incrementally during the level-by-level analysis. The unique id of a points-to relation is just the index of the vector. For example, if only the points-to relation $p \to b$ holds at a call site, we can evaluate the context condition by writing $\mathbb{C}|_{x1=0, x2=0, x3=1}$ to see whether $\mathbb{C}$ holds at the call site or not. (The formal parameters of a procedure in $\mathbb{C}$ will be mapped to their corresponding actual parameters at the call site.)

Due to the inter-phase dependency between the top-down and bottom-up phases conducted at a level lev, the points-to-set $Ptr(p)$ of a variable p may not be explicitly computed until only after both phases are finished. Specifically, $Ptr(p)$ can be deduced from the following two sets given in Definitions 3 and 4, respectively.

Definition 3 (Local Points-to Set). *Given a variable p of level lev, $Loc(p)$ yields a so-called points-to set that is computed explicitly*

variable   *x1* represents $p \to a$

variable   *x2* represents $q \to a$

variable   *x3* represents $p \to b$

Figure 2. The BDD for $\mathbb{C} = (p \to a \land q \to a) \lor p \to b$.

during the bottom-up phase and that may be included in $Ptr(p)$. It is recorded as a map $\{\langle v, \mathbb{C}(c_1, \ldots, c_k) \rangle \mid v$ is an abstract memory location and $\mathbb{C}(c_1, \ldots, c_k)$ is a context condition$\}$, meaning that p may/must point to v if and only if $\mathbb{C}(c_1, \ldots, c_k)$ holds. (Whether p may or must point to v at a particular point depends on the objects possibly pointed to by p, given by $Loc(p)$ and $Dep(p)$, at the point.)

For example, if x = $\&y$ is analyzed during the bottom-up phase at a level lev, then $\langle y, true \rangle$ will be included in $Loc(x)$.

Definition 4 (Dependence Set). *Given a variable p of level lev, the dependence set $Dep(p)$ specifies the set of formal-ins f whose points-to sets may be included in $Ptr(p)$, i.e., are dependent on by $Ptr(p)$. It is is recorded as a map $\{\langle q, \mathbb{C}(c_1, \ldots, c_k) \rangle \mid q$ is a formal-in parameter of level lev and $\mathbb{C}(c_1, \ldots, c_k)$ is a context condition$\}$, meaning that for every $(q, \mathbb{C}(c_1, \ldots, c_k)) \in Dep(p)$, $Ptr(p)$ includes $Ptr(q)$ if and only if $\mathbb{C}(c_1, \ldots, c_k)$ holds.*

The dependence set $Dep(p)$ of a variable p at a level lev is used to record the data dependency between p and some formal-in parameters at the same level, since the points-to sets of p and the formal-ins will have to be determined together during the top-down phase. For example, a pointer may point to whatever a formal parameter points to when both are analyzed at the same level. The points-to set of the pointer can be determined as soon as the points-to set of the formal-in parameter is (propagated top-down).

The transfer function of a procedure is a combination of the transfer functions of all its formal-out parameters.

Definition 5 (Transfer Function). *Given a formal-out v at level lev of a procedure $proc$, its transfer function $Trans(proc, v)$ is a quadruple $\langle Loc(v), Dep(v), \mathbb{C}(c_1, \ldots, c_k), M \rangle$, where $\mathbb{C}(c_1, \ldots, c_k)$ is a context condition and $M \in \{may, must\}$, meaning that v may (must) be modified at a call site invoking $proc$ if M = "may" (M = "must") provided that $\mathbb{C}(c_1, \ldots, c_k)$ (with all formal parameters of $proc$ being mapped to their actual parameters) holds at the call site. The transfer function $Trans(proc, lev)$ of $proc$ at level lev is a combination of the individual transfer functions $Trans(proc, v)$ for all formal-out parameters v at lev.*

Let us understand the transfer functions thus defined using the example given in Figure 1. We start with the bottom-up analysis at level 2 first. The procedure foo does not modify any variable of level 2. So its transfer function at level 2 is empty:

$$Trans(foo, p) = Trans(foo, q) = \{\} \qquad (1)$$

The procedure $main$ modifies x and y, but these two variables are local. So its transfer function at level 2 is also empty:

$$Trans(main, x) = Trans(main, y) = \{\} \qquad (2)$$

A top-down analysis that follows immediately propagates the points-to sets of the actuals x and y of foo to their corresponding formal-ins p and q, respectively. In this case, LevPA finds that

$$Ptr(p) = \{\langle a, must \rangle, \langle c, may \rangle, \langle d, may \rangle\}$$
$$Ptr(q) = \{\langle b, must \rangle, \langle d, may \rangle, \langle e, may \rangle\} \qquad (3)$$

221

Next, we start the bottom-up analysis for a, b, c, d, e and tmp at level 1, where the first five variables are formal-outs (and also formal-ins) of foo. The transfer function $Trans(foo, 1)$ is thus a combination of the following five individual transfer functions:

$$Trans(foo, a) = \langle \{\}, \{\langle b, q \Rightarrow b\rangle, \langle d, q \to d\rangle, \langle e, q \to e\rangle, \\ p \Rightarrow a, must\rangle$$
$$Trans(foo, c) = \langle \{\}, \{\langle b, q \Rightarrow b\rangle, \langle d, q \to d\rangle, \langle e, q \to e\rangle, \\ p \to c, may\rangle$$
$$Trans(foo, b) = \langle \{\langle obj, q \Rightarrow b\rangle\}, \{\}, q \Rightarrow b, must\rangle \quad (4)$$
$$Trans(foo, e) = \langle \{\langle obj, q \to e\rangle\}, \{\langle e, q \to e\rangle\}, q \to e, may\rangle$$
$$Trans(foo, d) = \langle \{\langle obj, q \to d\rangle\}, \{\langle b, p \to d \wedge q \Rightarrow b\rangle, \\ \langle d, p \to d\rangle, \langle e, p \to d \wedge q \to e\rangle\}, \\ p \to d \vee q \to d, may\rangle$$

As can be observed from the transfer functions given above, $Trans(foo, a)$ and $Trans(foo, c)$ are structurally identical, and similarly for $Trans(foo, b)$ and $Trans(foo, e)$. When analyzing a procedure at a level lev during the top-down phase, LevPA tries to allocate a common parameterized space to a set of its formal-out parameters at the level below (i.e., $lev - 1$) to merge their transfer functions by merging the side effects on them. Thus, $Trans(foo, 1)$ is simplified to be a combination of the following three transfer functions:

$$Trans(foo, V^p) = \langle \{\}, \{\langle V^q, true\rangle\}, true, must\rangle$$
$$Trans(foo, V^q) = \langle \{\langle obj, true\rangle\}, \{\}, true, must\rangle$$
$$Trans(foo, d) = \langle \{\langle obj, q \to d\rangle\}, \{\langle V^q, true\rangle, \langle d, p \to d\rangle\}, \quad (5) \\ p \to d \vee q \to d, may\rangle$$

where the formal-out parameters a and c are parameterized by V^p, and b and e by V^q but d is not parameterized (during the top-down analysis at level 2). Unlike [25], the way we merge the side effects on formal-outs in a procedure by using a parameterized space (in Algorithm 7) never loses precision because the formal-ins parameterized together have exactly the same def/use points in the procedure except they may differ in their MAY/MUST modification effects. (This is why d is not parameterized as either part of V^p or V^q.) Such differences are distinguished at a calling context when the transfer function of the procedure is applied (lines 36 and 39 of Algorithm 4).

3.1.2 Meet Functions

We also need to define a meet function for a procedure that merges the inputs to the procedure at different calling contexts, specifying essentially its interprocedural read side effects.

Definition 6 (Meet Function). *Given a formal-in parameter v of level lev read (referenced) in a procedure proc, its meet function $Meet(proc, v)$ is a tuple $\langle Ptr(v), \mathbb{C}(c_1, \ldots, c_k)\rangle$, meaning that v (or the corresponding actual parameter of v if v is a formal parameter of proc) may/must be read at a call site invoking proc only when $\mathbb{C}(c_1, \ldots, c_k)$ (with the formal parameters of proc being mapped to their actual parameters) holds at the call site. The meet function $Meet(proc, lev)$ of proc is a combination of all such individual meet functions $Meet(proc, v, lev)$ for all its formal-ins v at lev.*

The level-wise meet functions for our example are:

$$Meet(foo, p) = \langle \{\langle a, must\rangle, \langle c, may\rangle, \langle d, may\rangle\}, true\rangle$$
$$Meet(foo, q) = \langle \{\langle b, must\rangle, \langle d, may\rangle, \langle e, may\rangle\}, true\rangle$$
$$Meet(foo, V^q) = \langle \{\}, true\rangle \quad (6)$$
$$Meet(foo, d) = \langle \{\}, q \to d\rangle$$

In each meet function, the pointed-to objects (if any) are the read side effects. Note that V^p is not read (referenced) in foo.

3.1.3 Extended SSA Form

The SSA form on which our pointer analysis operates is an extended SSA form [7] that can effectively represent aliases and indirect memory operations in the SSA. We employ and further extend the μ and χ operators to precisely characterize aliasing effects.

In the extended SSA form [7], the μ and χ operators are introduced to specify the aliasing effects for indirect memory operations and call statements. A μ operator for an indirect memory operation is used to specify which variables may be read by the operation. In $\mu(v_i)$, μ takes as its operand the version i of v that may be read and produces no result. In our extension, we append a context condition $\mathbb{C}(c_1, \ldots, c_k)$ to μ to indicate the calling context that the variable can be read. Thus, a μ operator has the form $\mu(v_i, \mathbb{C}(c_1, \ldots, c_k))$.

A χ operator for an operation is used to model which variables the operation may modify. The operand of a χ operation is the last version of a variable and its result is the version after this potential definition. So χ links up the use-def edges through a may-definition. We add a context condition $\mathbb{C}(c_1, \ldots, c_k)$ to χ to model under which calling context the variable can be modified. We also add a MAY/MUST modification field $M \in \{may, must\}$ to χ to distinguish between the two types of modifications of a variable. So a χ operation has the form $v_{i+1} = \chi(v_i, \mathbb{C}(c_1, \ldots, c_k), M)$.

The μ and χ operators for the variables read and modified at a call site are created in Step 3(a) of Algorithm 3. The μ and χ operators for the variables read and modified by a pointer dereferencing operation is created during the top-down phase (in Algorithm 6).

Property 1 (Context Condition for a Meet Function). *The context condition of a meet function $Meet(proc, p)$ for a formal-in p of proc at level lev is a disjunction of the context conditions of all its use sites, including all its μ statements.*

Property 2 (Context Condition for a Transfer Function). *The context condition of a transfer function $Trans(proc, p)$ for a formal-out p of proc at level lev is a disjunction of the context conditions of all its def sites, including all its χ statements.*

3.1.4 Step 3(a): Create the μ and χ Lists for a Call site

For every call site in a procedure $proc$, the μ and χ lists are created at the call site for all variables of level lev that may be read (referenced) and modified, respectively, by all the procedures that may be invoked at the call site, as shown in Algorithm 4. In lines 5 – 22, all the variables read at a call site in $proc$ are appended to the μ list of the call site. In lines 23 – 46, all the variables modified at a call site in $proc$ are appended to the χ list of the call site.

For the sake of time and space efficiency (as discussed earlier in Section 3.1.1), some parameterized spaces may be created for lev during the top-down phase at the preceding level, i.e., at $lev + 1$ (as shown in Algorithms 6 and 7). Such parameterized spaces are handled by the if statements in lines 10 and 29. In line 6, we need to know the context condition of the meet function for each callee. This is available at this phase but the associated points-to set, which is not used here, is not known until after the top-down analysis at the same level is finished (Property 1). In line 24, the transfer function of each callee is known since it has just been built in the bottom-up phase for lev (Property 2). In lines 9 and 28, $\mathbb{C}''$ is simplified from $\mathbb{C}'(c_1, \ldots, c_k)$ to include only the points-to relations that hold at the entry of $proc$. It is then used to build the context conditions required for the μ and χ operators created. When creating a parameterized space for a set of formal-ins, their *may* and *must* fields are also "merged" due to the fact they are collectively represented by the MAY/MUST field of the parameterized space (lines 32 – 36 in Algorithm 6). As a result, in lines 31 – 35, the MAY/MUST field for a parameterized space is refined at a calling context. In lines 37 and 40, the meet operator $\sqcap$ on $\{may, must\}$

222

```
f()
{
    L1:    p₁ = &a;
    L2:    g1();
               p₂=χ(p₁, true, may)
               q₂=χ(q₁, true, may)
               r₂=χ(r₁, true, may)

               μ(r₂, true)
    L3:    g2();
               s₂=χ(s₁, true, may)

    L4:    g3();
               s₃=χ(s₂, true, may)
               t₂=χ(t₁, true, may)

    L5:    g4();
               t₃=χ(t₂, true, must)
}
```

Figure 3. χ optimization (with redundant ones striken through).

---

has the standard meaning: $may \sqcap e = e \sqcap may = may$, for $e \in \{may, must\}$, and $must \sqcap must = must$.

However, creating many μ and χ variables this way at each call site can sometimes introduce many constraints to be resolved at the pointer inference stage performed in Step 3(c). Some of these variables at a call site may not directly impact the points-to relations of the caller if they are not accessed in any way in the body of the caller; they only serve to transfer the modification or read side effects upwards through the caller. In this case, we can directly deduce their modification and read side effects on these variables from the transfer and meet functions at each call site.

In our implementation, we only create explicitly χ operators at all call sites for a variable v in a procedure $proc$ if one of the following three conditions is satisfied:

W1. v may be read or modified by some non-call statement(s) in the body of $proc$, explicitly or implicitly;

W2. v may be modified at a call site and may also be read at another call site that may or may not be different; and

W3. v must be modified at a call site that must be called by $proc$.

In the case of μ operations, there are two conditions instead:

R1. v may be modified by some non-call statement(s) in the body of $proc$, explicitly or implicitly; and

R2. v may be modified at a call site and may also be read at another call site that may or may not be different.

This optimization looks simple but computationally significant. By eliminating redundant μ and χ operators this way, we have observed a ten-fold analysis time reduction in some benchmarks.

We use the example given in Figure 3 to illustrate the three conditions for the χ optimization. The χ for q can be removed since it is possibly modified by $g1$ but not anywhere else. However, due to Condition W1, the χ for p must be kept. Note that s is possibly modified by $g2$ and $g3$. However, the points-to set of s at the exit of f is the union of the points-to sets of s_2 and s_3 since neither of the two definitions can be killed. In this case, the χ operations are not created at L3 and L4. Instead, $Trans(f, s)$ can be directly deduced from $Trans(g2, s)$ and $Trans(g3, s)$ without losing any precision. However, due to Condition W2, r is possibly modified by $g1$ and possibly read by $g2$. The χ for L2 and the μ for L3 must be created in order not to miss any points-to relations. Finally, t is definitely modified by $g4$. Due to Condition W3, we cannot merge the side

---

Algorithm 4 Creating μ and χ for the call sites in a procedure.

1: **procedure** Create_μ_χ_for_callsites($proc, lev$)
2: **begin**
3: **for** each $callsite$ of $proc$ **do**
4: **for** each $callee$ of $callsite$ **do**
5:   **for** each formal-in f of $callee$, where $ptl(f) = lev$ **do**
6:    Let $\mathbb{C}'(c_1, \ldots, c_k)$ be the context condition $\mathbb{C}(c_1, \ldots, c_k)$ of $Meet(callee, f)$ with all the formal parameters of $callee$ being replaced by their corresponding actual parameters at $callsite$;
7:    Let c_i' be 1 if c_i holds at $callsite$ and 0 otherwise;
8:    **if** $\mathbb{C}'(c_1', \ldots, c_k')$ evaluates to $true$ **then**
9:     Let $\mathbb{C}''$ include all and only the points-to relations in $\mathbb{C}'(c_1, \ldots, c_k)$ that hold at the entry of $proc$;
10:     **if** f is a parameterized space V^p **then**
11:      Map p to an actual parameter q at $callsite$;
12:      **for** each $\langle v, \mathbb{C}_v \rangle$ of $Loc(q)$ **do**
13:       Insert $\mu(v, \mathbb{C}'' \wedge \mathbb{C}_v)$ to μ list of $callsite$;
14:      **end for**
15:      **for** each $\langle w, \mathbb{C}_w \rangle$ of $Dep(q)$ **do**
16:       Insert $\mu(V^w, \mathbb{C}'' \wedge \mathbb{C}_w)$ to μ list of $callsite$;
17:      **end for**
18:     **else if** f is not a formal parameter of $callee$ **then**
19:      Insert $\mu(f, \mathbb{C}'')$ to μ list of $callsite$;
20:     **end if**
21:    **end if**
22:   **end for**
23:   **for** each formal-out f of $callee$, where $ptl(f) = lev$ **do**
24:    Let the transfer function $Trans(callee, f) = \langle Loc(f), Dep(f), \mathbb{C}(c_1, \ldots, c_k), M \rangle$ be given;
25:    Let $\mathbb{C}'(c_1, \ldots, c_k)$ be obtained from $\mathbb{C}(c_1, \ldots, c_k)$ with all the formal parameters of $callee$ being replaced by their corresponding actual parameters at $callsite$;
26:    Let c_i' be 1 if c_i holds at $callsite$ and 0 otherwise;
27:    **if** $\mathbb{C}'(c_1', \ldots, c_k')$ evaluates to $true$ **then**
28:     Let $\mathbb{C}''$ include all and only the points-to relations in $\mathbb{C}'(c_1, \ldots, c_k)$ that hold at the entry of $proc$;
29:     **if** f is a parameterized space V^p **then**
30:      Map p to an actual parameter q at $callsite$;
31:      **if** $(|Loc(q)| == 1 \;\&\&\; Dep(q) == \{\}) \;||\; (Loc(q) == \{\} \;\&\&\; |Dep(q)| == 1)$ **then**
32:       $M' = $ "must";
33:      **else**
34:       $M' = $ "may";
35:      **end if**
36:      **for** each $\langle v, \mathbb{C}_v \rangle$ of $Loc(q)$ **do**
37:       Insert $\chi(v, \mathbb{C}'' \wedge \mathbb{C}_v, M \sqcap M')$ to χ list of $callsite$;
38:      **end for**
39:      **for** each $\langle w, \mathbb{C}_w \rangle$ of $Dep(q)$ **do**
40:       Insert $\chi(V^w, \mathbb{C}'' \wedge \mathbb{C}_w, M \sqcap M')$ to χ list of $callsite$;
41:      **end for**
42:     **else if** f is not the return vale of $callee$ **then**
43:      Insert $\chi(f, \mathbb{C}'', M)$ to χ list of $callsite$;
44:     **end if**
45:    **end if**
46:   **end for**
47: **end for**
48: **end for**
49: **end**

$\mu(b_1, true)$
L4:   foo(x, y);
        $a_2 = \chi(a_1, true, must)$
        $b_2 = \chi(b_1, true, must)$

        $\mu(d_1, true)$
        $\mu(e_1, true)$
L9:   foo(x, y);
        $c_2 = \chi(c_1, true, may)$
        $d_2 = \chi(d_1, true, may)$
        $e_2 = \chi(e_1, true, may)$

Figure 4. $main$ with the μ and χ operations introduced for its two call sites at level 2. Other statements are not shown.

effects of t_2 and t_3 since t_3 must kill the definition of t_2. So the χ operations for t must be kept.

3.1.5 Step 3(b): Build the Extended SSA Form

In applying the SSA creation algorithm described in [8], the variable operands of μ and χ are treated as uses and the results of χ as additional assignments. The variables in the μ and χ operations are then renamed together with the rest of the program variables.

3.1.6 Step 3(c): Pointer Inference

After the extended SSA form has been created, we perform a flow-sensitive pointer analysis on SSA using a flow-insensitive algorithm. Each SSA variable is treated as an independent variable. The flow-insensitive algorithm used is set-constraint-based, like the Andersen-styled pointer analysis [1]. Therefore, there are two stages: constraint generation and constraint resolution.

Constraint Generation In this first stage, we set up a constraint system for the relevant statements including those with μ, χ and ϕ operators, as shown in Table 1. Rule Init does the initialization for a formal-in parameter, assuming that its first version in the SSA form is 0. Rules Base and Simple are self-explanatory. Rules Mu and Chi are applicable to pointer dereferencing operations. In particular, a Mu constraint is introduced for a read access while a Chi constraint for a write access. The operator $\supseteq_{\mathbb{C}}$ is the conditional set inclusion. Phi applies to a ϕ operation in the standard SSA form.

When encountering a call statement for a callee, the transfer function of the callee is applied by calling Algorithm 5 to generate the constraints required at the call site.

Consider the program given in Figure 1. Suppose that we have already analyzed level 2. We are now working on the pointers at level 1, a, b, c, d, e, and tmp, during the bottom-up phase. Suppose that we have just finished analyzing foo. Its transfer function $Trans(foo, 1)$ is a combination of the three individual transfer functions $Trans(foo, V^p)$, $Trans(foo, V^q)$ and $Trans(foo, d)$ given earlier in (5). During the bottom-up analysis of $main$ at level 1, we have created the μ and χ lists for its two call sites, L4 and L9, as shown in Figure 4. To generate the constraints at the two call sites, $Trans(foo, 1)$ is applied at L4 and L9, respectively, by calling Algorithm 5. At L4, $a_2 \supseteq b_1$ and $b_2 \supseteq \{obj\}$ are generated. At L9, $c_2 \supseteq d_1$, $c_2 \supseteq e_1$, $c_2 \supseteq c_1$, $e_2 \supseteq \{obj\}$, $e_2 \supseteq e_1$, $d_2 \supseteq \{obj\}$, $d_2 \supseteq e_1$ and $d_2 \supseteq d_1$ are generated.

Constraint Resolution In this second stage, we obtain the points-to relations by computing the transitive closure of the constraint graph representing the constraints generated during the constraint generation stage. When propagating the value from a node to a successor, a guarded set union operation $\supseteq_{\mathbb{C}}$ is used. So $\supseteq$ is a special case of $\supseteq_{\mathbb{C}}$ with its context condition being $true$.

Some operations on local points-to sets are introduced below.

Algorithm 5 Applying a full transfer function at a call site.

```
 1: procedure Apply_FTF(callsite, lev)
 2: begin
 3: for each v_m = χ(v_n, ℂ_v, M) generated for callsite do
 4:     for each callee of callsite do
 5:         Map v to a formal-out parameter f of callee;
 6:         Let Trans(callee, f) = ⟨Loc(f), Dep(f), ℂ_f, M⟩;
 7:         for each ⟨p, ℂ(c_1, ..., c_k)⟩ of Loc(f) do
 8:             Let ℂ'(c_1, ..., c_k) be obtained from ℂ(c_1, ..., c_k)
                 with all the formal parameters of callee being replaced
                 by their corresponding actual parameters at callsite;
 9:             Let c'_i be 1 if c_i holds at callsite and 0 otherwise;
10:             if ℂ'(c'_1, ..., c'_k) evaluates to true then
11:                 Let ℂ'' include all and only the points-to relations
                     in ℂ'(c_1, ..., c_k) that hold at the entry of the caller;
12:                 Generate a constraint v_m ⊇_ℂ'' {p}
13:             end if
14:         end for
15:         for each ⟨q, ℂ(c_1, ..., c_k)⟩ of Dep(f) do
16:             Let ℂ'(c_1, ..., c_k) be obtained from ℂ(c_1, ..., c_k)
                 with all the formal parameters of callee being replaced
                 by their corresponding actual parameters at callsite;
17:             Let c'_i be 1 if c_i holds at callsite and 0 otherwise;
18:             if ℂ'(c'_1, ..., c'_k) evaluates to true then
19:                 Let ℂ'' include all and only the points-to relations
                     in ℂ'(c_1, ..., c_k) that hold at the entry of the caller;
20:                 Map q to a list of actual parameters, actuals
21:                 for each a_i in actuals do
22:                     Generate a constraint v_m ⊇_ℂ'' a_i
23:                 end for
24:             end if
25:         end for
26:     end for
27:     if M == "may" then
28:         Generate a constraint v_m ⊇_ℂ_v v_n
29:     else
30:         Generate a constraint v_m ⊇_~ℂ_v v_n
31:     end if
32: end for
33: end
```

Definition 7 (Union for Local Points-to Sets). $Loc(p) \cup Loc(q)$ is a new points-to set that contains $\langle v, \mathbb{C} \rangle$ if $\langle v, \mathbb{C} \rangle$ is either contained in $Loc(p)$ or $Loc(q)$ exclusively or satisfies the property that if $\langle v, \mathbb{C}_1 \rangle \in Loc(p)$ and $\langle v, \mathbb{C}_2 \rangle \in Loc(q)$, then $\mathbb{C} = \mathbb{C}_1 \vee \mathbb{C}_2$.

Definition 8 (Guarded Assignments for Local Points-to Sets). $Loc(p) \times \mathbb{C} = \{\langle v, \mathbb{C} \wedge \mathbb{C}' \rangle \mid \langle v, \mathbb{C}' \rangle \in Loc(p)\}$.

These operations on dependence sets are similarly defined. During the resolution process, a cycle in the constraint graph needs to be resolved iteratively until a fixed point has been reached.

Transfer and Meet Functions For the meet function of a formal-in v of a procedure foo, $Meet(foo, v) = \langle Ptr(v), \mathbb{C} \rangle$, $Ptr(v)$ is fully resolved in lines $8 - 19$ in Algorithm 6 (but its points-to relations are determined during the bottom-up phase) and $\mathbb{C}$ is computed based on Property 1.

For the transfer function of a formal-out v of a procedure foo, $Trans(foo, v) = \langle Loc(v), Dep(v), \mathbb{C}, M \rangle$, $Loc(v)$ and $Dep(v)$ are computed during the bottom-up phase and $\mathbb{C}$ by Property 2. The M field is computed by solving a constraint propagation problem together with the pointer inference. Each SSA variable is associated with a property, named $mod \in \{may, must\}$, to indicate how the

Rule	Statement	Constraint(s)	Meaning
Init	$a_1 = \chi(a_0, true, must)$ $ptl(a_1) = lev$	$a_1 \supseteq a_0$	$Loc(a_1) = \{\}$ $Dep(a_1) = \{\langle a, true \rangle\}$
Base	$a_i = \&b$ $ptl(a_i) = lev$	$a_i \supseteq \{b\}$	$Loc(a_i) = \{\langle b, true \rangle\}$ $Dep(a_i) = \{\}$
Simple	$a_i = b_j$ $ptl(a_i) = lev$	$a_i \supseteq b_j$	$Loc(a_i) = Loc(b_j)$ $Dep(a_i) = Dep(b_j)$
Mu	$\mu(v_k, \mathbb{C}_v)$ $a_i = *b_j$ $ptl(a_i) = lev$	$a_i \supseteq_{\mathbb{C}_v} v_k$	$Loc(a_i) = Loc(a_i) \cup Loc(v_k) \times \mathbb{C}_v$ $Dep(a_i) = Dep(a_i) \cup Dep(v_k) \times \mathbb{C}_v$
Chi	$*a_i = b_j$ $v_m = \chi(v_n, \mathbb{C}_v, M)$ $ptl(v_m) = lev$	$v_m \supseteq_{\mathbb{C}_v} b_i$ if $M ==$ "may" $v_m \supseteq_{\mathbb{C}_v} v_n$ else $v_m \supseteq_{\sim \mathbb{C}_v} v_n$	$Loc(v_m) = Loc(b_j) \times \mathbb{C}_v$ $Dep(v_m) = Dep(b_j) \times \mathbb{C}_v$ if $M ==$ "may" $\quad Loc(v_m) = Loc(v_m) \cup Loc(v_n) \times \mathbb{C}_v$ $\quad Dep(v_m) = Dep(v_m) \cup Dep(v_n) \times \mathbb{C}_v$ else $\quad Loc(v_m) = Loc(v_m) \cup Loc(v_n) \times (\sim \mathbb{C}_v)$ $\quad Dep(v_m) = Dep(v_m) \cup Dep(v_n) \times (\sim \mathbb{C}_v)$
Phi	$a_i = \phi(a_j, a_k)$ $ptl(a_i) = lev$	$a_i \supseteq a_j$ $a_i \supseteq a_k$	$Loc(a_i) = Loc(a_j) \cup Loc(a_k)$ $Dep(a_i) = Dep(a_j) \cup Dep(a_k)$
Call	$callsite\ c$	Call Apply_FTF(c, lev) given in Algorithm 5	

Table 1. Constraint generation for the pointer inference at level lev.

variable is defined. Initially, for an SSA variable defined by a direct (Base) assignment or a χ (Chi) assignment whose M field is *must*, its *mod* is initialized to be "*must*". For every other SSA variable, its *mod* is initialized to be "*may*". When resolving the points-to constraints, we propagate the value of *mod* from node to node along the constraint edges corresponding to ϕ assignments in the constraint graph. The left-hand side variable of a ϕ operation is *must*-defined if and only if all its operands are.

3.2 Top-Down Analysis

The top-down analysis traverses ACG and processes each of its nodes in topological order, as shown in Algorithm 6. We propagate the points-to sets of formal-ins to their use sites at each call site with actual parameters being bound to formal parameters (lines 6 – 20). Again, due to the presence of recursion cycles, the computation of $Ptr(f)$ for a formal-in may have to be carried out iteratively. Recall that the points-to set of a pointer computed during pointer inference in the bottom-up phase may depend on the points-to sets of some formal-ins. As a result of this points-to set propagation, the points-to sets of all pointers at the level being analyzed are fully resolved. In addition, we expand the pointer dereferences of the variables at the level being analyzed by inserting the μ or χ operators for them to expose the def/use points for the pointed-to variables so that they can be analyzed at the next level and lower levels (lines 24 – 54).

For the program in Figure 1, we perform the top-down analysis for level 2 immediately after the bottom-up analysis for this level is finished. In the top-down phase analyzing $main$, we know that at L4, x must point to a and y must point to b. At L9, x may point to $\{c, d\}$ and y may point to $\{d, e\}$. We propagate the points-to sets of x and y to p and q, respectively, so that p points to $\{a, c, d\}$ and q points to $\{b, d, e\}$ as given in (3). Since $main$ has no pointer dereferences, we proceed to analyze foo in the top-down phase. By expanding the pointer dereferences $*p$ and $*q$, we obtain the code in Figure 5 with the newly introduced μ and χ operators, which are used in analyzing the pointers at the next level, i.e., level 1.

```
void foo( int **p, int **q)
{
                μ(b, q ⇒ b)
                μ(d, q → d)
                μ(e, q → e)
L11:    tmp₁ = *q₁;

L12:    *p₁ = tmp₁;
                a=χ(a, p ⇒ a, must)
                c=χ(c, p → c, may)
                d=χ(d, p → d, may)

L13:    tmp₂ = &obj;

L14:    *q₁ = tmp₂;
                b=χ(b, q ⇒ b, must)
                d=χ(d, q → d, may)
                e=χ(e, q → e, may)
}
```

Figure 5. foo with the μ and χ operations introduced during top-down analysis at level 1 (without using parameterized spaces).

Let us revisit the notion of parameterized spaces discussed earlier. Many variables accessed in a procedure do not explicitly appear in its body since they only appear implicitly in some μ or χ operators, either through pointer dereferences or call statements. If we use a unique variable to represent the variables that have the same def-use chains, we can save a lot of space and reduce the analysis time as well. For the program in Figure 5, a and c have the same def/use points, and similarly for b and e. In a program, a formal-in parameter may point-to many variables at different call sites. So a dereference of a formal-in parameter may produce a lot of μ or χ operators, resulting in space pressure. We merge the side effects on such formal-ins by using a unique variable, called a parameterized

Algorithm 6 Top-Down Analysis.

```
 1: procedure Top-down_analysis(AVG, lev)
 2: begin
 3:   for each node scc in topological order of AVG do
 4:     for each procedure proc of scc do
 5:       for each callsite of proc do
 6:         for each actual v or μ(v, ℂ) associated with callsite,
              where ptl(v) = lev do
 7:           for each callee of callsite do
 8:             Map v to a formal-in f of callee;
 9:             if |Loc(v)| == 1 && Dep(v) == {} then
10:               M == "must";
11:             else
12:               M == "may";
13:             end if
14:             for each ⟨p, ℂ_p⟩ of Loc(v) do
15:               Ptr(f) = Ptr(f) ∪ {⟨p, M⟩};
16:             end for
17:             for each ⟨p, ℂ_p⟩ of Dep(v) do
18:               Ptr(f) = Ptr(f) ∪ Ptr(p);
19:             end for
20:           end for
21:         end for
22:       end for
23:       ComVars = Alloc_Parameterized_Spaces(proc, lev);
24:       for each assignment S :=_{def} a = *b of proc do
25:         if ptl(b) == lev then
26:           for each ⟨v, ℂ⟩ of Loc(b) do
27:             Insert μ(v, ℂ) to μ list of S
28:           end for
29:           for each ⟨p, ℂ⟩ of Dep(b) do
30:             Insert μ(V^p, ℂ) to μ list of S
31:             for each ⟨v, ℂ', M⟩ of ComVars(p) do
32:               Insert μ(v, ℂ ∧ ℂ') to μ list of S
33:             end for
34:           end for
35:         end if
36:       end for
37:       for each assignment S :=_{def} *b = a of proc do
38:         if ptl(b) == lev then
39:           if (|Loc(b)| == 1 && Dep(b) == {}) || (Loc(b)
              == {} && |Dep(b)| == 1) then
40:             M' = "must"
41:           else
42:             M' = "may"
43:           end if
44:           for each ⟨v, ℂ⟩ of Loc(b) do
45:             Insert χ(v, ℂ, M') to χ list of S
46:           end for
47:           for each ⟨p, ℂ⟩ of Dep(b) do
48:             Insert χ(V^p, ℂ, M') to χ list of S
49:             for each ⟨v, ℂ', M⟩ of ComVars(p) do
50:               Insert χ(v, ℂ ∧ ℂ', M ⊓ M') to χ list of S
51:             end for
52:           end for
53:         end if
54:       end for
55:     end for
56:   end for
57: end
```

Algorithm 7 Allocating Parameterized Spaces (for $lev - 1$).

```
 1: procedure Alloc_Parameterized_Spaces(proc, lev);
 2: begin
 3:   for each formal-in p of proc, where ptl(p) = lev do
 4:     Let Meet(proc, lev) = ⟨Ptr(p), ℂ_p⟩,
 5:     Let V^p be a parameterized space representing a subset of
        the pointed-to objects in Ptr(p) such that if v is explicitly
        accessed in proc, where ⟨v, M⟩ ∈ Ptr(p), then v ∉ V^p;
 6:   end for
 7:   Refine all parameterized spaces thus obtained so that they are
      pair-wise disjoint and as large as possible;
 8:   for each formal-in p of proc, where ptl(p) = lev do
 9:     for each ⟨v, M⟩ ∈ Ptr(p) such that v ∉ V^p do
10:       Let ℂ_v be q ⇒ v(q → v) if M is "must" ("may");
11:       ComVars(p) = ComVars(p) ∪ {⟨v, ℂ_v, M⟩}
12:     end for
13:   end for
14: end
```

space, to represent the dereference of a formal-in parameter. This is done by calling Algorithm 7 in line 23 of Algorithm 6. However, care must be taken to avoid losing any precision. If two formal-in parameters may point-to a common variable v, then v must not be parameterized (unlike [9, 23]). These unparameterized formal-ins are collected in *ComVars* in Algorithm 7. If a variable v appears in the procedure body directly, then v is not represented by any parameterized space. By using parameterized spaces, the code in Figure 5 becomes as shown in Figure 6.

```
void foo( int **p, int **q)
{
            μ(V^q, true)
            μ(d, q → d)
L11:    tmp = *q;

L12:    *p = tmp;
            V^p = χ(V^p, true, must)
            d = χ(d, may, p → d)

L13:    tmp = &obj;

L14:    *q = tmp;
            V^q = χ(V^q, true, must)
            d = χ(d, may, q → d)
}
```

Figure 6. Code of foo in Figure 5 using parameterized spaces.

Finally, the pointer analysis at a level lev may have to be performed iteratively in the presence of points-to cycles formed by some pointers at lev. During pointer dereferencing, if a pointed-to variable introduced as an operand of a μ or χ operation happens to be at lev, a points-to cycle has been detected. Whenever this happens, the pointer analysis for the same level is repeated so that more points-to relations for the pointers at lev may be discovered, resulting in potentially more μ and χ statements to be introduced. This iterative process stops as soon as all pointed-to variables discovered in the last iteration are at a lower level than lev.

4. Experiments

We have implemented our LevPA algorithm in the Open64 compiler using the BDD library cudd-2.4.2. Our current implementation consists of over 20,000 lines of C++ code. We have measured

Benchmark	KLOC	#Pointers	#Callsites	#Indirect Callsites	#Recursion Cycles	#Proc in Largest Recursion Cycle	#Points-to Relations in BDDs
icecast-2.3.1	22	1618	877	40	14	1	350
sendmail	115	31004	19578	364	40	28	176640
httpd	128	20162	8992	270	23	6	4360
445.gombk	197	16076	10078	44	26	22	17433
wine-0.9.24	1905	336591	393689	24376	264	113	159149
wireshark-1.2.2	2383	333654	245278	2230	123	30	75899

Table 2. Benchmark characteristics.

Benchmark	LevPA: 64 Bit / 32 Bit (secs)				Mem (MB)	Bootstrapping [14]
	Points-to Levels	Recursion	Function Pointers	Total		
icecast-2.3.1	0.30 / 0.40	0.07 / 0.10	0.26 / 0.68	2.18 / 5.73	30	- / 29
sendmail	2.91 / 7.15	4.27 / 11.00	22.26 / 35.30	72.63 / 143.68	568	- / 939
httpd	0.23 / 0.53	0.50 / 1.70	2.30 / 5.39	16.32 / 35.42	136	- / 161
445.gombk	1.93 / 4.47	0.30 / 0.69	3.72 / 6.67	21.37 / 40.78	691	-
wine-0.9.24	45.79 / 120.75	15.10 / 27.32	35.66 / 76.8	502.29 / 891.16	2526	-
wireshark-1.2.2	17.86 / 52.31	11.97 / 24.63	17.36 / 56.26	366.63 / 845.23	2288	-

Table 3. Analysis statistics.

its performance by using the six benchmarks listed in Table 2. The first three benchmarks are taken from Kahlon's paper [14] in order to compare the efficiency between the two methods. To our best knowledge, Kahlon's method is one of the latest FSCS pointer analysis techniques. Of these three benchmarks, `icecast`, `sendmail` and `httpd`, `httpd` is the largest used in his experiments. To evaluate the ultimate performance of our method on larger benchmarks, we have also selected three more benchmarks, `gombk`, `wine` and `wireshark`. The characteristics of these benchmarks are summarized in Table 2, including the numbers of lines, pointers, call sites, indirect call sites, recursion cycles and procedures contained in the largest recursion cycle (Columns 2 – 7). The last column gives the number of points-to relations used for building the context conditions in terms of BBDs (as discussed in Section 3.1.1).

We conducted our experiments on two computer platforms: an Intel 64-bit 2.66GHz Xeon system with 16GB RAM and an Intel 3.0GHz Pentium 4 with 2GB RAM. To compare with Kahlon's method, we have selected our 32-bit Intel 3.0GHz Pentium4 with 2GB RAM purposely to analyze the first three benchmarks given in Table 2 since Kahlon conducted his experiments on a slightly faster Intel 3.2GHz Pentium4 system with the same amount of RAM as our 32-bit system. Table 3 gives the analysis times of the three benchmarks by LevPA. In the last column, the times for the first three benchmarks consumed by Kahlon's method are taken directly from his paper [14]. For all the three benchmarks, our method is a few times faster.

Looking again at Table 3, Column 5 gives the times taken by LevPA for analyzing all the six benchmarks on each platform. In addition, Columns 2 – 4 give the times consumed by some internal phases of our method. In particular, Column 2 gives the time spent computing the points-to levels for each benchmark on both platforms, including the time elapsed in the Steensgaard-styled pointer analysis. Column 3 gives the time due to the iterative analysis for

handling recursive calls for each benchmark. Column 4 gives the time taken due to the iterative analysis required for resolving function pointers. Due to the existence of recursion or indirect calls, we need to re-analyze pointers iteratively. As discussed in Section 3.1, we have adopted a demand-driven strategy to re-analyze the procedures in a cycle only when they may need to be analyzed. Of the six benchmarks, `wireshark` has more than two million lines of code. To our knowledge, this paper is the first to run a FSCS pointer analysis on benchmarks of this scale in minutes.

This level of scalability of LevPA is attributed to the facts that LevPA conducts its pointer analysis on the full-sparse SSA form, level by level, by avoiding redundant μ and χ operators at call sites and pointer dereferences and by making use of BDDs to produce a full transfer function and a meet function for a procedure that are precise as well as efficiently applicable to all calling contexts.

5. Related Work

There are many flow- and context-sensitive pointer analysis techniques reported during the last two decades, such as [4, 6, 9, 10, 14–17, 20, 25, 28] and some references therein.

Landi and Ryder [16] give a method that performs an iterative dataflow analysis on the CFG of a program while maintaining an alias relation set at each program point. Their method is not fully flow-sensitive because it cannot perform indirect strong updates. When encountering a procedure call, it enters into the body of a callee and recomputes the alias set at its exit. So this method can be classified a cloned-based context-sensitive analysis.

Choi *et al.* [6] present a method that performs an iterative dataflow analysis on a Sparse Evaluation Graph (SEG) rather on a CFG. SEG is a simplified CFG with the nodes that do not manipulate pointer information omitted. Their interprocedural algorithm is summary-based but not fully context-sensitive because it only considers one level of calling contexts.

Emani *et al.*'s method [9] is an interval analysis. The algorithm has an exponential time complexity since it is clone-based.

As discussed earlier in Section 3.1.1, Wilson and Lam [25] use partial transfer functions to summarize the behavior of already analyzed procedures. Unlike full transfer functions, partial transfer functions describe the output of a procedure based on a specific input. Their method is an iterative dataflow analysis and is fully flow-sensitive. It can scale up to 20 KLOC of C code.

Chatterjee *et al.* [9] use unknown initial values for parameters and global variables so that the summaries about a procedure can be computed by flow-sensitive alias analysis. They use a two-phase interprocedural analysis framework to compute flow- and context-sensitive alias information. Their analysis is not sparse since it needs to maintain a points-to graph at each program point. In addition, their strategy for handling function pointers is conservative. They use an over-approximated call graph. For an indirect call site, all functions with names taken and identical signatures are considered as possible callees.

Zhu [28] proposes a flow- and context-sensitive pointer analysis by using BDDs. His analysis is symbolic but not fully flow-sensitive because the kill information can only come from direct assignments. His method can scale to 200 KLOC of C code.

Zheng and Yew [27] is the first to propose the idea of performing the FSCS pointer analysis level by level. However, their method relies on type declarations to determine points-to levels and does not handle recursive data structures well. In addition, it does not use SSA form to optimize the analysis, and uses a different form of context-sensitivity.

Kahlon [14] proposes a bootstrapping algorithm that partitions a program into small subsets and uses a divide-and-conquer strategy to concurrently find solutions in these subsets. A summary-based approach is used for scalable context-sensitive alias analysis. His work is also based on the level-by-level strategy but his definition of points-to level (called depth) does not go all the way as ours. Furthermore, his approach to analyzing a level, by first computing flow- and context-insensitive alias summary and then analyzing pointers flow- and context-sensitively differs from ours. His algorithm can scale up to 128 KLOC of C code.

Kang *et al.* [15] propose a bottom-up flow- and context-sensitive pointer analysis. It is based on a new modular pointer analysis domain called the update history that can abstract memory states of a procedure independently of the information on aliases between memory locations and keep the information on the order of side effects performed. However, their method is not very efficient since for a 20 KLOC program, the elapsed analysis time is 213 seconds.

Chase *et al.* [3] present a flow-sensitive but context-insensitive pointer analysis. There are no experimental results reported. Tok *et al.* [23] give a similar method that also binds the def-use analysis and the pointer analysis together. Their method can scale up to 70 KLOC of C code. Hasti *et al.* [12], Lundberg *et al.* [18], Naeem *et al.* [19] and Hardekopf *et al.* [11] use SSA form to optimize a flow-sensitive but context-insensitive pointer analysis. Of these methods, Hardekopf and Lin's [11] is semi-sparse because in the sense tha it only builds the SSA form for the top-level pointer variables.

6. Conclusion

We have proposed a practical and scalable flow- and context-sensitive (FSCS) pointer analysis for C programs. We analyze the pointers level by level according to their points-to levels on the points-to graph in order to perform fast and accurate full sparse flow-sensitive analysis in a flow-insensitive style. This level-by-level strategy also facilitates a fast and accurate summary-based context-sensitive analysis. Our pointer analysis results in 1) a pre-cise and compact SSA form for subsequent program analyses and optimizations, and 2) a flow- and context-sensitive mod/ref set for each procedure. We have implemented our algorithm in Open64 and our preliminary results show our new approach can analyze some large benchmarks with over a million lines of C code in minutes.

Acknowledgments

Thanks to Zhaowei Ding who for building the whole environment for our experiments. This work is supported in part by a Chinese National Basic Research Grant (2005CB321602), a Chinese National High Technology Research and Development Grant (2008AA01Z115), a Chinese National Science and Technology Major Project (2009ZX01036-001-002), a NSFC Innovation Research Group Project (60921002), a Chinese National Science Fund for Distinguished Young Scholars (60925009), and an Australian Research Council Grant (DP0987236).

References

[1] ANDERSEN, L. O. Program analysis and specialization for the c programming language, 1994.

[2] BRYANT, R. E. Graph-based algorithms for boolean function manipulation. *IEEE Trans. Comput. 35*, 8 (1986), 677–691.

[3] CHASE, D. R., WEGMAN, M., AND ZADECK, F. K. Analysis of pointers and structures. In *PLDI '90: Proceedings of the ACM SIGPLAN 1990 Conference on Programming Language Design and Implementation* (New York, NY, USA, 1990), ACM, pp. 296–310.

[4] CHATTERJEE, R., RYDER, B. G., AND LANDI, W. A. Relevant context inference. In *POPL '99: Proceedings of the 26th ACM SIGPLAN-SIGACT symposium on Principles of programming languages* (New York, NY, USA, 1999), ACM, pp. 133–146.

[5] CHENG, B.-C., AND HWU, W.-M. W. Modular interprocedural pointer analysis using access paths: design, implementation, and evaluation. In *PLDI '00: Proceedings of the ACM SIGPLAN 2000 conference on Programming language design and implementation* (New York, NY, USA, 2000), ACM, pp. 57–69.

[6] CHOI, J.-D., BURKE, M., AND CARINI, P. Efficient flow-sensitive interprocedural computation of pointer-induced aliases and side effects. In *POPL '93: Proceedings of the 20th ACM SIGPLAN-SIGACT symposium on Principles of programming languages* (New York, NY, USA, 1993), ACM, pp. 232–245.

[7] CHOW, F. C., CHAN, S., LIU, S.-M., LO, R., AND STREICH, M. Effective representation of aliases and indirect memory operations in ssa form. In *CC '96: Proceedings of the 6th International Conference on Compiler Construction* (London, UK, 1996), Springer-Verlag, pp. 253–267.

[8] CYTRON, R., FERRANTE, J., ROSEN, B. K., WEGMAN, M. N., AND ZADECK, K. F. Efficiently computing static single assignment form and the control dependence graph. *ACM Transactions on Programming Languages and Systems 13* (1991), 451–490.

[9] EMAMI, M., GHIYA, R., AND HENDREN, L. J. Context-sensitive interprocedural points-to analysis in the presence of function pointers. In *PLDI '94: Proceedings of the ACM SIGPLAN 1994 conference on Programming language design and implementation* (New York, NY, USA, 1994), ACM, pp. 242–256.

[10] HACKETT, B., AND AIKEN, A. How is aliasing used in systems software? In *SIGSOFT '06/FSE-14: Proceedings of the 14th ACM SIGSOFT international symposium on Foundations of software engineering* (New York, NY, USA, 2006), ACM, pp. 69–80.

[11] HARDEKOPF, B., AND LIN, C. Semi-sparse flow-sensitive pointer analysis. In *POPL '09: Proceedings of the 36th annual ACM SIGPLAN-SIGACT symposium on Principles of programming languages* (New York, NY, USA, 2009), ACM, pp. 226–238.

[12] HASTI, R., AND HORWITZ, S. Using static single assignment form to improve flow-insensitive pointer analysis. In *PLDI '98: Proceedings*

of the ACM SIGPLAN 1998 conference on Programming language design and implementation (New York, NY, USA, 1998), ACM, pp. 97–105.

[13] HIND, M., BURKE, M., CARINI, P., AND CHOI, J.-D. Interprocedural pointer alias analysis. *ACM Trans. Program. Lang. Syst. 21*, 4 (1999), 848–894.

[14] KAHLON, V. Bootstrapping: a technique for scalable flow and context-sensitive pointer alias analysis. In *PLDI '08: Proceedings of the 2008 ACM SIGPLAN conference on Programming language design and implementation* (New York, NY, USA, 2008), ACM, pp. 249–259.

[15] KANG, H.-G., AND HAN, T. A bottom-up pointer analysis using the update history. *Inf. Softw. Technol. 51*, 4 (2009), 691–707.

[16] LANDI, W., AND RYDER, B. G. A safe approximate algorithm for interprocedural aliasing. *SIGPLAN Not. 27*, 7 (1992), 235–248.

[17] LIVSHITS, V. B., AND LAM, M. S. Tracking pointers with path and context sensitivity for bug detection in c programs. In *ESEC/FSE-11: Proceedings of the 9th European software engineering conference held jointly with 11th ACM SIGSOFT international symposium on Foundations of software engineering* (New York, NY, USA, 2003), ACM, pp. 317–326.

[18] LUNDBERG, J., AND LÖWE, W. A scalable flow-sensitive points-to analysis. In *Compiler Construction - Advances and Applications, Festschrift on the occasion of the retirement of Prof. Dr. Dr. h.c. Gerhard Goos* (2007), Springer Verlag. accepted.

[19] NAEEM, N. A., AND LHOTÁK, O. Efficient alias set analysis using ssa form. In *ISMM '09: Proceedings of the 2009 international symposium on Memory management* (New York, NY, USA, 2009), ACM, pp. 79–88.

[20] RYDER, B. G., LANDI, W. A., STOCKS, P. A., ZHANG, S., AND ALTUCHER, R. A schema for interprocedural modification side-effect analysis with pointer aliasing. *ACM Trans. Program. Lang. Syst. 23*, 2 (2001), 105–186.

[21] STEENSGAARD, B. Points-to analysis by type inference of programs with structures and unions. In *CC '96: Proceedings of the 6th International Conference on Compiler Construction* (London, UK, 1996), Springer-Verlag, pp. 136–150.

[22] STEENSGAARD, B. Points-to analysis in almost linear time. In *POPL '96: Proceedings of the 23rd ACM SIGPLAN-SIGACT symposium on Principles of programming languages* (New York, NY, USA, 1996), ACM, pp. 32–41.

[23] TOK, T., GUYER, S., AND LIN, C. Efficient Flow-Sensitive Interprocedural Data-Flow Analysis in the Presence of Pointers. In *Compiler construction: 15th international conference, CC 2006, held as part of the Joint European Conferences on Theory and Practice of Software, ETAPS 2006, Vienna, Austria, March 30-31, 2006: proceedings* (2006), Springer-Verlag New York Inc, p. 17.

[24] WHALEY, J., AND LAM, M. Cloning-based context-sensitive pointer alias analysis using binary decision diagrams. In *Proceedings of the ACM SIGPLAN 2004 conference on Programming language design and implementation* (2004), ACM New York, NY, USA, pp. 131–144.

[25] WILSON, R. P., AND LAM, M. S. Efficient context-sensitive pointer analysis for c programs. In *PLDI '95: Proceedings of the ACM SIGPLAN 1995 conference on Programming language design and implementation* (New York, NY, USA, 1995), ACM, pp. 1–12.

[26] YU, H., AND ZHANG, Z. An Aggressive field-sensitive unification-based pointer analysis. *Chinese Journal of Computers 32*, 9 (2009).

[27] ZHENG, B., AND CHUNG YEW, P. A hierarchical approach to context-sensitive interprocedural alias analysis, 1999.

[28] ZHU, J. Towards scalable flow and context sensitive pointer analysis. In *DAC '05: Proceedings of the 42nd annual Design Automation Conference* (New York, NY, USA, 2005), ACM, pp. 831–836.

Towards Program Optimization through Automated Analysis of Numerical Precision

Michael D. Linderman   Matthew Ho
David L. Dill   Teresa H. Meng

Computer Systems Laboratory
Stanford University
Stanford, CA, USA
{mlinderm, matthew.ho, thm}@stanford.edu,
dill@cs.stanford.edu

Garry P. Nolan

Microbiology & Immunology
Stanford University
Stanford, CA, USA
gnolan@stanford.edu

Abstract

Reducing the arithmetic precision of a computation has real performance implications, including increased speed, decreased power consumption, and a smaller memory footprint. For some architectures, e.g., GPUs, there can be such a large performance difference that using reduced precision is effectively a requirement. The trade-off is that the accuracy of the computation will be compromised. In this paper we describe a proof assistant and associated static analysis techniques for efficiently bounding numerical and precision-related errors. The programmer/compiler can use these bounds to numerically verify and optimize an application for different input and machine configurations. We present several case study applications that demonstrate the effectiveness of these techniques and the performance benefits that can be achieved with rigorous precision analysis.

Categories and Subject Descriptors   D.2.4 [*Software Engineering*]: Program Verification–Validation;   D.3.4 [*Programming Languages*]: Processors–Optimization;   G.1.0 [*Mathematics of Computing*]: Numerical Analysis–Computer Arithmetic

General Terms   Design, Performance, Verification

Keywords   Numerical Precision, Static Error Analysis, Floating-Point Numbers, Fixed-Point Numbers

1. Introduction

For many programmers numerical precision is an afterthought; developers choose the numerical type with the maximum practical precision for their variables (typically `double`) and treat these operands as real numbers. Floating and fixed point numbers are only an approximation to the real numbers. In the worst case this approximation manifests itself in subtle bugs [17]. And so programmers over-provision, using a more precise representation than is necessary, with the goal of preventing numerical precision errors. The choice of numerical types has real impacts on application performance, though, and should not be made casually.

The absence of tools for program-driven analysis of numerical errors makes it difficult for programmers to rigorously evaluate performance-accuracy trade-offs. We encountered this absence first-hand when re-implementing a Bayesian network inference application [1] (described in Section 4) that targets modern general purpose processors (GPPs), graphics processing units (GPUs) and programmable logic (FPGAs). This work grew out of efforts to verify and optimize this application for the different kinds of fixed and floating arithmetic available on those platforms.

On GPPs, GPUs and FPGAs reducing precision can improve application performance. When targeting FPGAs, or designing custom application-specific hardware (ASICs), reduced precision directly translates to fewer gates and narrower datapaths, and thus potentially to reduced energy consumption and increased maximum clock rate [14]. On GPPs, reduced precision can reduce functional unit latency, e.g. division, and improve memory and arithmetic throughput [13]. Switching from 64 to 32-bit floating point potentially improves memory bandwidth and cache utilization (measured in operands per time or volume) by $2\times$ and the throughput of the 128-bit SIMD SSE unit by $2\times$ as well. The difference is even more striking for GPUs: 32-bit arithmetic throughput is 933 GigaFLOPs peak vs. 78 GigaFLOPs for 64-bit floating point on the 2009 NVIDIA Tesla C1060.

The challenge is to determine when precision reduction is possible. Detailed simulation and testing, along with hand analysis, is the most commonly used technique. However simulation is time consuming, requires both working "ideal" and test implementations, and does not guarantee the absence of problems in cases not tested. Compile-time program-driven *static analysis*, which can efficiently and accurately bound numerical errors in a computation without considering a potentially unbounded set of inputs, offers a desirable alternative. In contrast to simulation, static analysis provides comprehensive coverage and guaranteed bounds on rounding errors. These bounds will by definition be pessimistic; our goal is to ensure that they are accurate enough to be useful for program verification and optimization.

In this paper we introduce Gappa++, an enhanced version of the Gappa proof assistant[1] [6], and a set of accompanying techniques that enable automated analysis of numerical errors in fixed and floating point, linear and non-linear, computations. Gappa++ extends Gappa's interval arithmetic (IA)-based proof engine with an affine arithmetic (AA)-based engine that can more accurately

---

[1] We obtained Gappa 0.11.3 from http://lipforge.ens-lyon.fr/www/gappa/, our modified version along with case study inputs can be obtained from http://merge.stanford.edu/gappa

bound linear computations with correlated errors. Using Gappa++ we verify the correctness and optimize the performance for several real-world applications.

This paper makes the following contributions:

- We describe Gappa++, a novel static precision analysis tool that enhances the Gappa proof assistant with: 1) an AA-based extension that computes more accurate bounds for linear computations; 2) better support for transcendental functions; and 3) support for rounding modes on NVIDIA GPUs.

- We present analysis techniques for verifying and optimizing applications using the proof assistant for GPPs, FPGAs and GPUs. We detail the GPU assembly-to-Gappa transformations used to accurately model the GPU's hardware intrinsics.

- We present three representative application case studies: Bayesian network inference [1], neural prosthetics [25], and Black-Scholes stock option pricing [2], that demonstrate the effectiveness of the proof assistant, and the performance benefits that can be achieved with rigorous precision analysis.

The remainder of the paper is organized as follows: Section 2 provides relevant background on fixed and floating point arithmetic, IA and AA; Section 3 describes the Gappa++ proof assistant; Section 4 presents several application case studies; and finally Section 5 concludes.

2. Background and Related Work

2.1 Floating and Fixed Point Error

Evaluating a computation includes two primary sources of error: 1) approximation errors (often termed methodical errors), such as approximating e^x as 0 for $x \ll 0$; and 2) rounding errors, produced when using an insufficiently precise numerical representation.

Rounding errors result from having only finite precision to represent real numbers. Fixed point numbers are represented as $m \cdot 2^e$, where m is the signed mantissa and 2^e is an implicit, constant scaling factor determined by the format. Floating point numbers (following the IEEE 754 standard [21]) are implemented as $sign \cdot 1.m \cdot 2^{(e-bias)}$, where m is the unsigned mantissa and e is the variable exponent[2].

The maximum fixed point rounding error is a function of the format and independent of the magnitude of the number. The floating point rounding error is dependent on both the format and magnitude of the number. An approximate error model for round-nearest-even (RNE) is given by:

$$
\begin{aligned}
x_f &= x + x \cdot 2^{-(t+1)} \cdot \epsilon \\
x_f \circ y_f &= (x_f \bullet y_f) + (x_f \bullet y_f) \cdot (2^{-(t+1)} \cdot \epsilon) \quad (1)
\end{aligned}
$$

where x_f is the floating point representation of a real number x, $\circ$ is the floating point implementation of the operation $\bullet$, t is the mantissa bit width, and $\epsilon \in [-1, 1]$ is the error term [24] ($2^{-(t+1)}$ corresponds to .5 ULPs, or unit in the last place, which is the difference between adjacent floating point numbers). Note that not all floating point conversions or arithmetic operations introduce rounding errors. Some numbers, e.g. .5, and operations, e.g., subtraction of numbers of similar magnitude [24], can be represented exactly.

To bound numerical errors programmers can run exhaustive simulations comparing different implementations to an "ideal" version. However, as discussed earlier, these simulations can be difficult and time-consuming to prepare and run and provide limited test coverage. While simulation will continue to be a part of the ver-

ification workflow, we would like to reserve that effort for the end of the design process, where we test an implementation already optimized and checked by other means. Static analysis bounds errors at compile time using the application source code, user-supplied bounds on the inputs, and error models similar to Equation (1). Unlike simulation, static analysis can produce provable error bounds, and since these approaches require much less effort by the programmer, can be used to efficiently and even automatically explore the design space. The trade-off is that by their nature static analysis techniques are conservative, often overly so.

Static analysis tools seem to be split between those used for program verification [3, 15, 10, 4], and those designed for program optimization [19, 7, 8, 23, 14, 16, 5]. There are numerous techniques for static analysis. In general, these techniques attempt to construct a transfer function for the computation [19, 3, 15], use a form of range-based arithmetic [7, 8, 14], e.g, interval or affine, through which errors are propagated, or both [5]. Often, the static analysis is combined with simulation in hybrid static-dynamic approaches [23]. In this work, we propose a static analysis approach using a combination of range arithmetic and algebraic rewriting that provides high accuracy, i.e., tight error bounds, efficient evaluation, and is suitable for integration into the compiler.

The most similar work is the Caduceus static analyzer for C programs [4]. Caduceus integrates Gappa (along with other tools) into its back-end proof infrastructure for proving assertions about C applications. The focus of Caduceus is verification, while the focus of this work is program optimization, and extending Gappa to support a broader set of computations.

2.2 Interval and Affine Arithmetic

Interval arithmetic (IA) [18] represents a number, $\bar{x}$, by an inclusive interval, $[x.lo, x.hi]$ such that $x.lo \leq x \leq x.hi$. For each operation there is a corresponding IA implementation, e.g. IA addition is given as

$$
\bar{z} = \bar{x} + \bar{y} = [x.lo + y.lo, x.hi + y.hi].
$$

Similar formulas can be derived for other common mathematical operations. The primary weakness of IA is overestimation, particularly in the presence of correlated variables. In the simplest example, if $\bar{x} = [-1, 1]$, $\bar{x} - \bar{x}$ will result in $[-2, 2]$ instead of 0. Overestimation accumulates throughout the computation, potentially resulting in an exponential growth in the range estimates.

Affine arithmetic (AA) [9] is a refinement to IA that addresses the above problem by keeping track of correlations between variables. Instead of an interval, a number, x, is represented by an affine expression, given as

$$
\hat{x} = x_0 + x_1\varepsilon_1 + x_2\varepsilon_2 + \ldots + x_n\varepsilon_n \text{ where } \varepsilon_i = [-1, 1]. \quad (2)
$$

Each ε_i is an independent source of uncertainty, and may contribute to the uncertainty of more than one variable. Thus correlations are preserved. In the simple example above, if $\hat{x} = x_0 + x_1\varepsilon_1$, the expression $\hat{x} - \hat{x}$ will return 0.

As a more complex example, consider the fixed-point expression $y = c \cdot x_1 + (x_2 - x_1)$ adapted from [7], where $x_1 = [-10, 10]$ RNE with 3 fractional bits, $x_2 = [-5, 5]$ RNE with 2 fractional bits and all operations are RNE with 3 fractional bits. The AA expression for o is

$$
\begin{aligned}
\hat{x_1} &= 10\varepsilon_1 + 2^{-4}\varepsilon_{e1} \\
\hat{x_2} &= 5\varepsilon_2 + 2^{-3}\varepsilon_{e2} \\
\widehat{c \cdot x_1} &= 5\varepsilon_1 + 2^{-5}\varepsilon_{e1} + 2^{-4}\varepsilon_{e3} \\
\widehat{x_2 - x_1} &= -10\varepsilon_1 + 5\varepsilon_2 - 2^{-4}\varepsilon_{e1} + 2^{-3}\varepsilon_{e2} \\
\hat{y} &= -5\varepsilon_1 + 5\varepsilon_2 - 2^{-5}\varepsilon_{e1} + 2^{-3}\varepsilon_{e2} + 2^{-4}\varepsilon_{e3}
\end{aligned}
$$

---

[2] Fully IEEE-compliant implementations also provide subnormal numbers. Gappa supports subnormal numbers, but for brevity they are not discussed here.

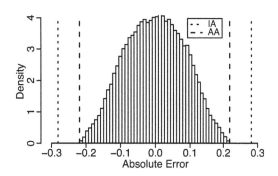

Figure 1. IA and AA bounds, along with a histogram of simulated errors for $c \cdot x_1 + (x_2 - x_1)$

```
c_m     = 0.5;
o_m     = (c_m*x1_m)+(x2_m-x1_m);
c_fx    = fixed<-1,ne>(c_m);
x1_fx   = fixed<-3,ne>(x1_m);
x2_fx   = fixed<-2,ne>(x2_m);
o_fx fixed<-3,ne> = (c_fx*x1_fx)+(x2_fx-x1_fx);
{ x1_m in [-10,10] /\ x2_m in [-5,5] ->
  o_fx-o_m in ? }
```

Figure 2. Gappa input script for bounding the rounding error in the expression from Figure 1. A note about syntax and convention: the rounding operator on the left-hand side of the equals is applied to all operations, but not variables, on the right-hand side; we use the suffixes _m, _f, and _fx to represent mathematically ideal, floating and fixed point variables, respectively.

where $\varepsilon_{e1}, \varepsilon_{e2}, \varepsilon_{e3}$ are the rounding errors in $x_1, x_2, c \cdot x_1$ respectively. Figure 1, shows both the IA bound on the rounding error (as computed with Gappa), the AA bounds, and a histogram of simulated errors for 100,000 trials[3]. IA does not capture the correlated error in x_1 and as a result produces less accurate bounds.

For affine, i.e., linear, operations, the resulting affine forms can be derived from Equation (2). The results of a non-linear operation, $f(\ldots)$, are no longer affine. To obtain an affine expression, f is replaced with a linear approximation f^*, and a new ε term is added to the expression to capture the approximation error. Many AA implementations use Chebyshev approximations, $f(x) = Ax + B + \delta\varepsilon$ for non-affine operations [9]. For large input ranges, the added error term $\delta\varepsilon$ can be larger than the numerical errors we are trying to analyze. Thus IA or AA alone are often ill suited for non-linear computations; in these cases alternative techniques, such as algebraic rewriting (described in Section 3), are needed.

3. Gappa++ Proof Assistant

Gappa++ extends the Gappa proof assistant [6] to better support transcendental functions and linear computations. This section describes both Gappa and our extensions.

3.1 Gappa

Gappa proves the validity of logical properties involving the bounds of mathematical expressions. The initial application for Gappa was verifying libm implementations of elementary functions.

Gappa only manipulates expressions on real numbers. Floating or fixed point arithmetic is expressed with separate "rounding operators", functions that map a real number x to its rounded value $\diamond(x)$. Rounding is captured explicitly and specifically for each operand. Bounds on the rounding or numerical error are computed from $\diamond(x) - x$, the enclosure of the difference of the approximate and ideal value.

The Gappa input script for the computation in Figure 1 is shown in Figure 2. Each script has four parts: 1) the code segment with rounding operators of the form

`[fixed|float]<precision,direction>`

2) a set of hypotheses, e.g., `x1_m in [-10,10]`; 3) a set of enclosures to be proved, e.g., `o_fx-o_m in ?`; and 4) an optional set of hints (not shown). Using this script Gappa computes the bounds on absolute error in `o_fx - o_m` = [-.28125,.28125], given the hypotheses on `x1_m`, `x2_m`.

All values within Gappa are expressed as intervals, and IA plays a key role in ensuring that Gappa proofs are machine checkable.

Enclosures are only one type of predicate. Floating and fixed point numbers are actually discrete sets; Gappa includes FIX and FLT predicates, which indicate a number is uniquely representable at a given precision. These predicates are to identify situations, cited in Section 2, in which numbers or expressions are uniquely representable, and thus no rounding errors are introduced. This capability separates Gappa from other tools that use a simpler error model.

As discussed previously, IA fails to capture correlations between expressions with shared terms. Gappa uses algebraic rewriting to expose correlated errors. For example, $\diamond(a) - b$ can be rewritten as $(\diamond(a) - a) + (a - b)$, which separates the rounding error from the difference of a and b. IA without rewriting would compute the enclosures of $\diamond(a)$ and b separately, then subtract them, potentially leading to a much larger bound on the difference. In contrast to AA, which also captures correlations, algebraic rewriting can be used to generate tight bounds over large input ranges for non-linear operations, such as log, that have well-known algebraic properties. Adding additional support for transcendental functions to Gappa was a key part successfully applying Gappa++ to the applications in Section 4.

3.2 Operator, Rewriting and Rounding Extensions

Several of the case study applications make use of log and exp functions. We added these operators, along with their base-2 variants, exp2 and log2 to Gappa.

We incorporated new rewriting rules for these operations, including

$$
\begin{aligned}
\log(a) - \log(b) &\rightarrow \log(1 + (a-b)/b) \\
\exp(a) - \exp(b) &\rightarrow \exp(b) \cdot (\exp(a-b) - 1) \\
a + \log(b) &\rightarrow \log(\exp(a) \cdot b)
\end{aligned}
$$

and many similar variants. These rewriting rules help isolate the rounding errors in expressions with transcendental functions, even when using large input ranges.

Along with new operators and rewriting rules, we also added a new rounding operator, cuda_32, which implements the semantics of 32-bit floating point arithmetic on NVIDIA GPUs. cuda_32 is similar to ieee_32, but without subnormal numbers [20].

3.3 Affine Extension

In theory, algebraic rewriting should be sufficient to capture correlated errors. As practical matter, however, Gappa often does not rewrite aggressively enough, as shown by the loose bounds in Figure 1. For linear expressions, AA is more effective at capturing correlated errors, and so we developed an AA extension to the Gappa proof engine to improve accuracy in these cases. The AA engine is invoked with a hint in the input script. At each invocation Gappa++ passes to the AA extension hypotheses on input variables

---

[3] Unless otherwise noted all simulated errors in this paper are computed using an extended precision (60-bit mantissa) implementation as the "ideal" reference

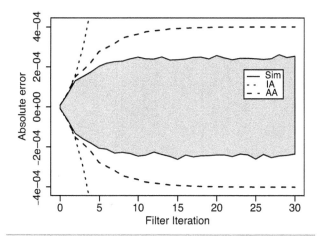

Figure 3. AA and IA error bounds along with simulated error (gray region) for simple IIR filter in Equation (3)

and rounding errors; the AA extension returns a new bound for the expression, computed with AA, that is added to Gappa++ as a hypothesis. The AA result is one of several potential bounds computed within Gappa++; if the AA engine fails to return a tighter bound, it is ignored by Gappa++. Thus there is no risk, other than to execution time, for using the AA hint.

The AA extension only supports addition, subtraction and multiplication (with both single and dual variable terms); expressions with other operators are ignored by the AA extension. The above operations are implemented as suggested in [9], using the MPFR multiple precision floating point library [11] to implement the coefficients with the same extended precision used within Gappa++ itself.

At creation, the AA engine reports to Gappa++ dependencies on the enclosures of all input, e.g., $x1\_m$, and on the magnitude of all rounding errors, e.g.,

```
fixed<ne,-16>(x1_m)-x1_m
```

The latter information is used to generate the error epsilons for rounding operations. Thus the AA extension can leverage Gappa++'s best bounds on the error (and its predicate system, etc.) Sometimes, however, the AA extension has more accurate information about the magnitude of variables than Gappa++, and so separate AA-based error bounds are computed. The tighter of these two errors bounds is chosen for each rounding operator.

Using the affine extension in Gappa++, we can calculate more accurate bounds for linear expressions. For example, for the script in Figure 2, Gappa++ computes more accurate bounds of [-.21875,.21875]. The difference in accuracy is even more pronounced for more complex computations, particularly those with feedback. Figure 3 shows the IA, AA and simulated errors for the simple filter

$$y_n = x_n + c_1 y_{n-1} + c_2 y_{n-2} \qquad (3)$$

where $c_1 = \frac{1}{\sqrt{2}}, c_2 = .5, x_n = [-64, 64]$ and all computations and operands are RNE with 16 fractional bits (adapted from [7]). As the simulation shows, since the filter is stable, the error is also stable (after some number of iterations). The AA error is also stable, while the IA error is not. The IA error, computed with an unmodified version of Gappa, grows exponentially and is too large to be usable.

The trade-off for using the AA extension is execution time. AA maintains significantly more information for each variable, and is thus slower to compute enclosures than IA methods. However, computing bounds for 30 filter iterations took only .38s using

Gappa++ vs. .35s for plain Gappa[4]. For contrast the corresponding simulation took 130s.

In general, the affine extension increased the execution time of Gappa++ by up to $12\times$ and memory usage by up to $10\times$. However, even the largest affine problem we ran (Section 4.2) completed in less than 125s, and most took less than a minute. So even with the AA extension, the static analysis techniques are still faster than simulation. We are working to improve the performance of the AA extension and believe significant reductions in execution time can be made by reducing the number of times Gappa invokes the affine engine.

4. Case Studies

The development of Gappa++ was motivated by several informatics applications, presented as case studies in this section. Each application demonstrates a different Gappa++ usage model, including: optimizing numerical approximations (network inference, Section 4.1); comparing different sources of error (neural prosthetics, Section 4.2); and verifying that an application satisfies an absolute error bound (option pricing, Section 4.3).

4.1 Bayesian Inference

The inside of a cell is a complex dynamical environment in which proteins interact in complex causal networks. Understanding the causal structures of these networks on a per-individual basis is important for advancing both basic biological and clinical knowledge. The structure of these networks can be inferred using Bayesian techniques; however, the algorithm is extremely computationally demanding [1].

Previous efforts have achieved $> 10\times$ speedups using specialized accelerators, such as GPUs and FPGAs. Porting this application to these platforms is challenging. Incorporating rigorous precision analysis into our workflow helped us improve the performance of the FPGA version by 33% plus $4\times$ better precision, and speedup the baseline CPU implementation by 15% without reducing overall accuracy.

The algorithm uses Monte-Carlo Markov Chain sampling to explore the space of potential graphs. Inside the inner-most loop is the accumulation of local scores, ls_n, which represent the log probabilities of particular parent-child relationships. The accumulation is implemented as

```
acc += log(1+exp(ls[i]-acc));
```

The $\log(1 + \exp(x))$ expression is only non-linear over a small region around 0 and can be approximated as 0 or x for $x \ll 0$ and $x \gg 0$ respectively. The approximations are much faster than the actual computation, and so it is beneficial to set the boundaries within which we actually do the computation as tight as possible.

The original implementation used [-30,30] as the approximation boundary, chosen to be conservative with respect to accuracy. However, using Gappa++ we can show that those bounds are too conservative, and do not actually improve overall accuracy. The baseline implementation already used **float** precision; however, that does not mean that 32-bit computations are being performed. GCC with optimization level 3 (-O3) actually emits double precision operations for $\log(1 + \exp(x))$, only rounding to 32-bits at the end. Our Gappa++ analysis (an example script is shown in Figure 4a) is driven from the assembly, and accurately models the actual precision in use.

Figure 4b compares the error in the positive and negative approximations, i.e. $x - \log(1 + \exp(x))$, and the rounding error in-

---

[4] These and all other performance results in this paper are measured using wall clock time on a 2.66 GHz Core 2 Quad with 8 GB of RAM, having been compiled with GCC -O3 unless otherwise noted

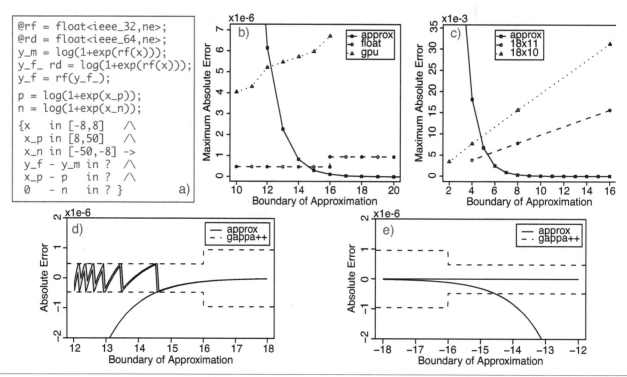

Figure 4. Gappa++ and simulation-based analysis of the approximation of score accumulation in inference algorithm: a) Gappa++ script used in panel b; b), c) absolute error vs. boundary of approximation for CPU, GPU (b) and FPGA-based (c) implementation; negative and positive approximations overlap and are represented by a single line; d), e) simulation and Gappa++-computed errors at the positive (d) and negative (e) approximation boundaries.

troduced in the $\log(1+\exp(x))$ computation for both "float" implementation on the CPU and the same code compiled for an NVIDIA GPU (Gappa++ analysis of GPU applications is described in more detail in Section 4.3). The "crossover" point where the rounding error exceeds that of the approximation is much less than 30. Continuing to perform the actual computation beyond the cross-over point only reduces performance. Setting the boundary to a still conservative [-16,16] improves GPP performance on our benchmark platform by 15%. Tightening the approximation boundary only requires modifying a single constant, making this an effort-efficient optimization in an already heavily optimized application.

The above results are verified with detailed simulation. Figure 4d,e shows simulated errors (gray region) vs. the approximation vs. the Gappa++ estimates. Note that the Gappa++ estimate is computed over the entire non-approximated range, i.e. [-12,12], and thus represents the maximum error over that space. Gappa++ accurately captures the error at the positive boundary. The analytical "crossover" point matches the simulated convergence of the computation and approximation errors. Interestingly, this convergence occurs when there is insufficient precision to capture the effect of the 1+ operation. Above this threshold the computation effectively simplifies to the approximation.

At the negative boundary, where the result is near 0 and floating point numbers are much more precise, the absolute errors are very small and the actual computation and approximation only converge for very negative inputs. Although the actual computation is more precise in the region, that additional precision does not necessarily improve overall accuracy (which is set by the positive boundary) and so maintaining the more conservative boundary only slows the application (small, subnormal, numbers are slower on modern x86 processors).

A second interesting feature is the step function increase at 16 in the Gappa++ error bounds. This results from a limitation in the range-based analysis being performed. The bulk of the Gappa++ error results from the double-to-single rounding operation occurring at the end of the computation. At large x, however, because the input x is rounded to single precision, the output of $\log(1 + \exp(x))$ is effectively rounded to single precision; a fact that Gappa++ does not capture in its predicates and rewriting. This is a subtle effect, and one that we are actively working to handle in future iterations of Gappa++.

Precision analysis plays an even larger role in the FPGA porting effort. On the FPGA, the algorithm is implemented using fixed point arithmetic and block RAM-implemented lookup tables (LUT) for the $\log(1 + \exp(x))$ accumulation. Our goal is to maximize performance and accuracy (compared to baseline CPU implementation). Performance on the FPGA is a direct function of the amount of aggregate bandwidth we can extract from the block RAM (BRAM) macros distributed throughout the chip. Specifically, the peak FPGA performance can be modeled as

$$\frac{\text{Number of RAMs}}{0.5 + \text{RAMs per LUT}} \cdot \text{Clock Rate} \qquad (4)$$

and thus we need to minimize the RAMs per LUT we use.

The Xilinx Virtex5 FPGAs we are using for this application have several BRAM configurations: 36x10 (10 bits of address, 36-bit words); 18x11; and $2\times$ 18x10. The original implementation used 36x9 with a boundary of -12,16, which translates to .5 BRAM per LUT (each BRAM is dual ported). This configuration truncates the input to the LUT to 4 fractional bits to form the address (5 integer bits, 4 integer bits). The truncation is the dominant source of error in the FPGA implementation, since the actual accumulation is performed with 16+ fractional bits.

Table 1. Difference equations for filter second-order sections used in neural prosthetic system

DF I	$y_n = b_0 x_n + b_1 x_{n-1} + b_2 x_{n-2} - a_1 y_{n-1} - a_2 y_{n-2}$
DF II	$w_n = x_n - a_1 w_{n-1} - a_2 w_{n-2}$ $y_n = b_0 w_n - b_1 w_{n-1} - b_2 w_{n-2}$

Table 2. Summary of Gappa++ (above) and simulated (below) error bounds for IIR filter. Uniformly distributed [0,1] input rounded to model data from 12-bit ADC.

DF I	Actual	Ideal Coeffs.	Ideal Arith.
32-bit float	±9.77e-4 ±2.02e-5	±9.71e-4	±1.10e-5
16-bit fix	±5.77e-2 ±3.15e-3	±5.51e-2	±2.76e-3
DF II	**Actual**	**Ideal Coeffs.**	**Ideal Arith.**
32-bit float	±9.70e-4 ±6.15e-5	±9.64e-4	±1.10e-5
16-bit fix	±2.94e-3 ±6.42e-4	±2.61e-4	±2.76e-3

The first optimization is to use the entire address to pick up an additional factional bit. Using Gappa++ we can do better. Since the error is dominated by the truncation, we can use the narrower 18 bit configurations to get more address space (18x11) or more ports ($2\times$ 18x10). Shrinking the range over which we use the LUT reduces the number of integer bits needed, and thus increases the precision of the truncation. Figure 4c shows the error for different boundaries and BRAM configurations; the optimal boundaries are [-8,8] for both configurations. The latter trades away an additional fractional bit for a 33% increases in performance (.25 RAM per LUT vs. .5 RAM per LUT). Since we already have increased precision over the original, we choose the faster 18x10 configuration. Thus as a result of this analysis, the performance of the FPGA implementation improves 33% over the original 36x9 configuration, with 2 bits ($4\times$) more precision, all within the same resource usage.

This case study helps demonstrate Gappa++'s effectiveness as a backend analysis tool for performance optimization. We identified a join (ϕ node) in the dataflow graph with unequal error incoming on each branch. Using Gappa++ we are able to optimize the boundary of the approximation to equalize the error on each branch. Similar analyses and optimizations could be performed in situations where the same variable is being computed in different ways on different branches.

4.2 Neural Prosthetics

Neural prosthetics systems seek to restore lost movement or communication functionality to patients with neural deficits [25]. These systems translate the electrical messages sent between neurons, recorded with electrodes implanted in the brain, into commands for the prosthetic device. Reducing the power consumption of a future implantable prosthetic processor (IPP) is a key challenge. Previous estimates show that the IPP can be built within the allotted power budget if implemented with energy-efficient fixed point arithmetic [25]. Our goal is to use static analysis to help verify and optimize that implementation.

One of largest power consumers is the front-end digital filter (4th order high-pass infinite impulse response (IIR) filter with $f_c = 250$ Hz implemented as two second-order-sections in series; difference equations for direct form (DF) I and II implementations are shown in Table 1). Using Gappa++ we can explore the effects of rounding on the noise properties of the filter. Table 2 summarizes the Gappa++ and simulated errors for both 32-bit floating point and fixed point with 16 fractional bits, RNE, for DF I and II implementations. The Gappa++ results are obtained by unrolling the loop into straight-line code until the errors stabilize (300 iterations in this case).

Published results indicate that the root mean square (RMS) electrical noise observed in the filtered signal would be $\sim \pm 3.9\text{e-}3$ in the above scenario [22]. The results in Table 2 suggest that a 16-bit fixed point DF II implementation would be sufficient. Further, for the DF II filter, the arithmetic appears to be a lesser source of error than coefficient quantization. If the user is comfortable with the filter performance with quantized coefficients, the arithmetic precision could potentially be further optimized to improve performance and energy-efficiency.

Our goal in this initial work is not to perform optimized float-to-fixed (F2F) translation, but instead just to demonstrate that

Gappa++ can accurately bound errors for non-trivial linear *and* non-linear computations. And thus could serve as the back-end analysis tool for an optimizing F2F translator. Although not shown here, Gappa++ can compute enclosures for individual variables (not just differences) and thus can also be used to set the number of integer bits to avoid overflow (a key part of F2F translation).

The difference between the DF I and II implementations is an example of how otherwise functionally equivalent code can have different numerical properties. The compiler could play a role in helping the programmer smartly select among different implementations for the same computation. In this case it is among variants that have similar performance; in the next case study, Black-Scholes, it is among variants with very different performance characteristics.

4.3 Black-Scholes Stock Option Pricing

The Black-Scholes [2] algorithm, defined in Figure 5, analytically computes the value of European-style stock options. Each option can be computed independently and in parallel, and so Black-Scholes is often used as a performance benchmark for different processors, particularly x86 SSE extensions and GPUs. As described earlier, GPUs can provide a $10\times$ boost in computing power – if – the application can be implemented using 32-bit floating point. In the case of Black-Scholes, the programmer would like to verify without time-consuming simulation that the GPU implementation, for example, is accurate to less than one cent.

Using Gappa++ we verified that 64 and 32-bit IEEE-compliant and 32-bit GPU-based implementations all are accurate to much less than one cent relative to a mathematically ideal implementation. The Gappa++ and simulated error bounds are summarized in Table 3. The analytical bounds are typically 1-3 orders of magnitude larger than the simulated enclosures; however, in all cases, Gappa++ produces sufficiently accurate bounds to verify that the different implementations meet the penny threshold.

In the case of `float` and `double` the Gappa++ scripts are purposely conservative. When compiled for sequential execution, the compiler will often produce 64-bit floating point instructions for the "float" implementation. When compiled for SSE units, however, most of the operations will be performed at 32-bit precision. Thus by using a uniform `ieee_32` rounding operator in the Gappa++ script we can ensure the application meets the required error bounds even if all operations were computed using the SSE unit.

Switching to 32-bit arithmetic can yield real performance benefits. Table 4 summarizes the execution time for various implementations of Black-Scholes, including sequential `float` and `double`, SSE `float` and `double` [12], and a NVIDIA 9800 GTX GPU [20]. Note that all implementations were compiled with `icc -fast`.

$$call = SN(d_1) - X\exp(-rT)N(d_2)$$
$$put = X\exp(-rT)N(-d_2) - SN(-d_1)$$

where

$$d_1 = \frac{\log(S/X) + (r + \sigma^2/2)T}{\sigma\sqrt{T}}$$
$$d_2 = d_1 - \sigma\sqrt{T}$$

Figure 5. Definition of Black-Scholes algorithm where S: stock price, X: strike price, r: risk-free interest rate, T: time to expiration, σ: voltatility, and $N(x)$: fifth-order approximation of the cumulative normal distribution function.

Table 3. Summary of Gappa++ and simulated error bounds for Black-Scholes. Inputs: stock price = [5,30]; strike price = [1,100]; time = [.25,10]; R = .02; and volatility = .3.

Puts	Gappa++	Simulation
double	[-1.202e-12, 1.187e-12]	[-3.064e-15, 2.998e-14]
float	[-6.585e-4, 6.738e-4]	[-1.286e-5, 1.349e-5]
gpu	[-2.990e-3, 3.090e-3]	[-2.196e-5, 1.367e-5]

Calls	Gappa++	Simulation
double	[-1.198e-12, 1.183e-12]	[-1.399e-15, 1.323e-14]
float	[-6.572e-4, 6.816e-4]	[-6.335e-6, 6.246e-6]
gpu	[-3.0e-3, 3.1e-3]	[-8.319e-6, 1.093e-5]

Table 4. Execution for different Black-Scholes implementations pricing 1,000,000 put and call options

	Time (ms)	Speedup
double	118	1.0
float	125	0.95
double SSE	104	1.13
float SSE	66	1.8
GPU	14	8.4

The `float` and `double` Gappa++ scripts are direct translations of the application source code to Gappa syntax and rounding operators. The `GPU` script is the product of a separate translation pass, taking CUDA PTX assembly as input, that introduces additional error terms and rounding operators to faithfully model GPU operations.

The most relevant operations for Black-Scholes are multiply-add (MAD), log and exp. The GPU's MAD operator truncates the intermediate result, and thus must be modeled as

```
float<cuda_32,ne>(a+float<cuda_32,zr>(b*x))
```

The GPU provides hardware support for the elementary functions `exp2` and `log2`, among others. "Fast" versions of `exp` and `log` are synthesized from these intrinsic by multiplying the input or output by the appropriate constant. The intrinsics have an additional error compared to the correctly rounded single precision result (2 ULPs for `exp2`, 3 ULPs for `log2`). We model this additional error by introducing additional hypotheses that express the actual result as an approximation of the correctly rounded result. Specifically, y=exp2(x) is modeled as

```
y_ = float<cuda_32,ne>(exp2(x));
...
{(y-y_)/y_ in [-2b-23,2b-23] /\ ...
```

`log2` and other intrinsics are modeled similarly, using the errors reported in the CUDA programming guide [20].

Although mostly straight-line code, the Black-Scholes implementation has two branches that require dataflow-style analysis. At each branch we "decouple" the analysis by computing magnitude and error enclosures for all live variables. These enclosures are modified by the conditional statement and used as hypotheses for two new scripts (one for each branch). The enclosures computed by the branch scripts are merged together with a $\cup$ operation at the dataflow join.

In computing the bounds in Table 3 we made extensive use of Gappa's bisection feature. Bisection attempts to produce more accurate error bounds by splitting the input ranges into disjoint sub-ranges, computing the bounds on each sub-range, and merging the results with the $\cup$ operator. The trade-off is increased runtime. We bisected the ranges before the control flow decoupling into 500 uniform sub-ranges, and 100 sub-ranges after the decoupling. For `ieee_32` bisection improved the bounds from $\sim \pm2.6$e-2 to $\sim \pm6.8$e-4 with the total runtime increasing from $\sim$1s to $\sim$90s. Analyses at other precisions showed similar trade-offs.

The Black-Scholes case study demonstrates Gappa++'s effectiveness in bounding the error in complex, non-linear computations, and the performance benefits that result from being able to confidently reduce the arithmetic precision.

5. Conclusion

In this paper we have presented Gappa++, an enhanced version of the Gappa proof assistant, and a set of techniques for using Gappa++ to analyze numerical and precision-related errors in real informatics applications. In a series of case studies we demonstrated the effectiveness of Gappa++ across a range of applications and hardware platforms, and showed the kinds of performance improvements that can be achieved with rigorous precision analysis.

Motivated by these results we argue that precision analysis should be a more regular part of a programmer's workflow. Although Gappa++ was not directly integrated with the compiler in this initial work, both the tool and analysis techniques described in this work could be readily used as part of a compiler-based static analysis suite. Gappa is already in use as a back-end in the Caduceus static analyzer [4]. And none of the analysis performed in this work required Gappa's interactive features, such as hints; the scripts were direct translation of the source code-under-test and thus could be generated and invoked automatically.

Much of the precision analysis and optimization is effectively dataflow-based, and could be integrated alongside similar passes in an optimizing compiler. For example, in the Bayesian Inference case study we used Gappa++ to equalize the error on the different incoming branches at a join in the dataflow graph. The compiler could readily notify the programmer that such situations might present optimization opportunities. With annotations to indicate functional equivalence and acceptable error bounds, the compiler could automatically compare and contrast different implementations and or verify correctness, as was done in the neural prosthetic and Black-Scholes case studies.

We imagine and are actively working towards a future in which the compiler helps the programmer verify and optimize the numerical aspects of their application.

Both short and long-term hardware trends will make this kind of tool support increasingly important. For example, GPUs have already begun to support 64-bit floating point operations, although, as discussed, with 2-10$\times$ less throughput than 32-bit arithmetic. Selectively making use of 64-bit operations may enable additional applications to use GPUs that for precision reasons were not able to do so previously. A key challenge for the programmer and the compiler is to identify the minimum set of operations that must be performed at increased precision, so as to maximize performance.

Long-term, more and more applications will be implemented on high-performance heterogeneous systems (CPUs plus SSE, GPUs, FPGAs, etc.) and high-efficiency embedded platforms; all of which introduce non-trivial accuracy-performance trade-offs. As a result, there will be a growing need to help developers automatically verify and optimize the numerical behavior of their applications for these new and different platforms.

Acknowledgments

The authors would like to sincerely thank Guillaume Melquiond, the developer of Gappa, for making his software publicly available and patiently answering our many questions. In addition we would like to thank James Balfour, and the anonymous reviewers whose valuable feedback has helped the authors greatly improve the quality of this paper. This work was partially supported by the C2S2 Focus Center, one of six research centers funded under the Focus Center Research Program (FCRP), a Semiconductor Research Corporation subsidiary; and NIH grant R01 CA130826-01.

References

[1] Narges Bani Asadi, Teresa H. Meng, and Wing H. Wong. Reconfigurable computing for learning bayesian networks. In *Proc. of FPGA*, pages 203–211, 2008.

[2] Fischer Black and Myron Scholes. The pricing of options and corporate liabilities. *Journal of Political Economy*, 81(3):637–654, 1973.

[3] B. Blanchet, P. Cousot, R. Cousot, J. Feret, L. Mauborgne, L. Miné, D. Monniaux, and X. Rival. A static analyzer for large safety-critical software. In *Proc. of PLDI*, pages 196–207, 2003.

[4] Sylvie Boldo, J. C. Filliâtre, and Guillaume Melquiond. Combining Coq and Gappa for certifying floating-point programs. In *Proc. of Symp. on Integration of Symbolic Comp. and Mech. Reasoning*, 2009.

[5] J. Cong, K. Gururaj, B. Liu, C. Liu, Z. Zhang, S. Zhou, and Y. Zou. Evaluation of static analysis techniques for fixed-point precision optimization. In *Proc. of FCCM*, pages 231–234, 2009.

[6] Florent de Dinechin, Christoph Quirin Lauter, and Guillaume Melquiond. Assisted verification of elementary functions using gappa. In *Proc. of Symp. on Applied Computing*, pages 1318–1322, 2006.

[7] F. Fang, Claire, Rob A. Rutenbar, and T. Chen. Fast, accurate static analysis for fixed-point finite-precision effects in dsp designs. In *Proc. of Conf. on Computer-aided Design*, page 275, 2003.

[8] F. Fang, Claire, Rob A. Rutenbar, M. Püschel, and T. Chen. Toward efficient static analysis of finite precision effects in dsp applications. In *Proc. of DAC*, pages 496–501, 2003.

[9] Liuz H. de Figueiredo and Jorge Stolfi. *Self-Validated Numerical Methods and Applications*. Brazilian Mathematics Colloquium monographs. IMPA/CNPq, Rio de Janeiro, Brazil, 1997.

[10] J. C. Filliâtre and S. Boldo. Formal verification of floating-point programs. In *Proc. of ARITH*, 2007.

[11] Laurent Fousse, Guillaume Hanrot, Vincent Lefèvre, Patrick Pélissier, and Paul Zimmermann. Mpfr: A multiple-precision binary floating-point library with correct rounding. *ACM Trans. Math. Softw.*, 33(2):13, 2007.

[12] Anwar Ghuloum, Gansha Wu, Xin Zhou, Peng Guo, and Jesse Fang. Programming option pricing financial models with Ct. Technical report, Intel Corporation, 2007.

[13] *Intel 64 and IA-32 Architectures Optimization Reference Manual*. Intel Corporation, 2009.

[14] D.-U. Lee, A. A. Gaffar, R. C. C. Chueng, O. Mencer, W. Luk, and G. A. Constantinides. Accuracy-guaranteed bit-width optimization. *IEEE Tran. on Computer-Aided Design of Integrated Circuits and Systems*, 25(10):1990–2000, 2006.

[15] Matthieu Martel. Semantics of roundoff error propagation in finite precision calculations. *Higher Order Symbol. Comput.*, 19(1):7–30, 2006.

[16] Matthieu Martel. Program transformation for numerical precision. In *Proc. of PEPM*, pages 101–110, 2009.

[17] David Monniaux. The pitfalls of verifying floating-point computations. *ACM Trans. Program. Lang. Syst.*, 30(3):1–41, 2008.

[18] R. E. Moore. *Interval Analysis*. Prentice Hall, 1966.

[19] A. Nayak, M. Haldar, A. Choudhary, and P. Banerjee. Precision and error analysis of matlab applications during automated hardware synthesis for FPGAs. In *Proc. of DATE*, pages 722–728, 2001.

[20] *NVIDIA CUDA Compute Unified Device Architecture Programming Guide*. NVIDIA, 2.0 edition, 2008.

[21] IEEE Task P754. *ANSI/IEEE 754-1985, Standard for Binary Floating Point Arithmetic*. IEEE, 1985.

[22] Gopal Santhanam, Michael D Linderman, Vikash Gilja, Afsheen Afshar, Stephen I Ryu, Teresa H Meng, and Krishna V Shenoy. Hermesb: a continuous neural recording system for freely behaving primates. *IEEE Trans Biomed Eng*, 54(11): 2037–50, Nov 2007. doi: 10.1109/TBME.2007.895753.

[23] C. Shi and R. Broderson. Automated fixed-point data-type optimization tool for signal processing and communications systems. In *Proc. of DAC*, pages 478–483, 2004.

[24] P. H. Sterbenz. *Floating Point Computation*. Prentice Hall, 1974.

[25] Z. S Zumsteg, C. Kemere, S. O'Driscoll, G. Santhanam, R. E. Ahmed, K. V. Shenoy, and T. H. Meng. Power feasibility of implantable digital spike sorting circuits for neural prosthetic systems. *IEEE Trans Neural Syst Rehabil Eng*, 13(3):272–279, 2005. ISSN 1534-4320 (Print).

Statistically Regulating Program Behavior via Mainstream Computing

Mark Stephenson

IBM Austin Research Lab

mstephen@us.ibm.com

Ram Rangan *

NVIDIA

rrangan@nvidia.com

Emmanuel Yashchin

IBM Watson Research Center

yashchi@us.ibm.com

Eric Van Hensbergen

IBM Austin Research Lab

ericvanhensbergen@us.ibm.com

Abstract

We introduce *mainstream computing*, a collaborative system that dynamically checks a program—via runtime assertion checks—to ensure that it is running according to expectation. Rather than enforcing strict, statically-defined assertions, our system allows users to run with a set of assertions that are *statistically guaranteed* to fail at a rate bounded by a user-defined probability, p_{fail}. For example, a user can request a set of assertions that will fail at most 0.5% of the times the application is invoked. Users who believe their usage of an application is mainstream can use relatively large settings for p_{fail}. Higher values of p_{fail} provide stricter regulation of the application which likely enhances security, but will also inhibit some legitimate program behaviors; in contrast, program behavior is unregulated when $p_{fail} = 0$, leaving the user vulnerable to attack. We show that our prototype is able to detect denial of service attacks, integer overflows, frees of uninitialized memory, boundary violations, and an injection attack. In addition we perform experiments with a mainstream computing system designed to protect against soft errors.

Categories and Subject Descriptors D. Software [*D.2. Software Engineering*]: D.2.4. Program Verification

General Terms Reliability, Security

1. Introduction

A variety of issues threaten the stability of today's systems: code vulnerabilities, soft errors, insider threats, race conditions, hardware aging, etc. While there is no doubt that these threats are dangerous, we are fortunate that they rarely present themselves. The vast majority of the time, code running on modern systems executes in a manner consistent with user and programmer expectations.

Current protection mechanisms tend to be designed for a *specific* vulnerability (*e.g.*, buffer overruns, or illegal control-flow transfers). In this paper we introduce *mainstream computing*, which by simply detecting and enforcing *likely* program properties, naturally provides some level of protection against a wide variety of systems liabilities.

---

* Contributed to this paper while employed at IBM Austin Research Lab.

Mainstream computing is a collaborative methodology that leverages the rarity of unanticipated system state in order to protect users. At a high level, our approach allows a user to say, "ensure that my program's behavior conforms with at least 99.9% (or some other user-defined percentage) of the usage patterns for this program." Put another way, we ask users to specify a tolerance for failure, p_{fail}, which bounds the rate at which the system will flag anomalies (which can be due to system liabilities, or can simply be benign *false positives* on legitimate executions). Statistically then, the more mainstream, or "normal" a user's usage is, the less likely it is for the user to encounter an anomaly for a given setting of p_{fail}.

Mainstream computing tracks program-level runtime statistics for an application across a community of users. Similar to other invariant tracking systems, mainstream computing constantly profiles applications in an effort to determine likely invariants for a program's operands and control flow. Unlike prior art, our system provides statistical bounds on false positive rates, and we ask the user to set the bounds appropriately. This approach is analogous to the "privacy" slider bar present in some web browsers that allows users to easily trade functionality of the browser for potential loss of privacy.

It is the mainstream computing server's responsibility to generate, with statistical guarantees, the set of constraints that satisfy a user's requests. As with prior art on collaborative infrastructures, the server collects data from multiple clients, creating a large corpus of data from which it can create constraints. Unlike previous work, however, we show that mainstream computing can create valuable models by only consulting a small portion of the corpus. We argue that this property of mainstream computing is crucial because it limits the influence rogue users may have on constraint creation.

The novel contributions of this paper are as follows:

- We introduce mainstream computing.

- We show that mainstream computing will likely generate untainted constraints, even when malicious users are part of the collaborative community.

- We show that mainstream computing systems can protect against buffer overruns, integer overflows, memory free bugs, denial of service attacks, and injection attacks.

- We show that mainstream computing systems can be used to recover from many soft errors.

2. Mainstream Computing

At the conceptual level, mainstream computing attempts to automatically *whitelist* common behavior, and log, reject, sandbox, or repair abnormal behavior. This section describes the many components of a mainstream computing system. We begin with a high-

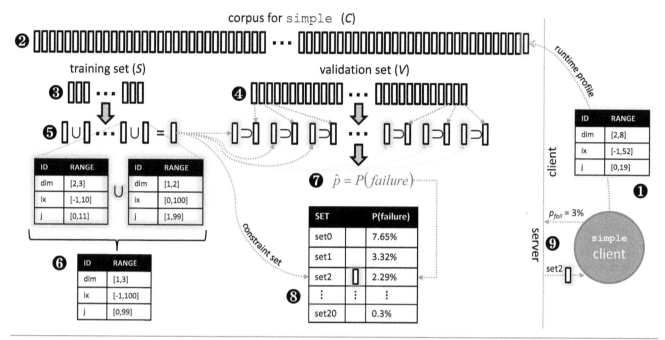

Figure 1. A high-level depiction of mainstream computing. A *mainstream client*, which is simply an application that has been instrumented with a mainstream compiler, submits a *runtime profile* of its execution to a centralized server upon exiting (❶). The server maintains a corpus of such runtime profiles (❷) which it uses to generate a table of *constraint sets* (❽). The table associates a constraint set with the likelihood that one or more of its constraints, or assertion checks, will fail during an execution of a client. A client can request a suitable constraint set for a given *tolerance for failure* (❾). Please see text for a description of our constraint-generation strategy. Best viewed in color.

level description of mainstream computing, and then subsequently fill in many details.

At the highest level, a mainstream computing system takes a collaborative, data-driven approach to finding constraints that regulate program behavior. Thus, one or more *mainstream clients* share summaries of program behavior with a centralized server. Here, a mainstream client is merely an application that was compiled with a mainstream compiler. The compiler augments the application with a runtime system that monitors and records low-level details of the application's execution. As Figure 1❶ shows, when a mainstream client exits, the client sends a record of its execution, which we call a *runtime profile*, to the centralized server.

The runtime profile contains a distillation of values assigned to the application's variables, program paths that were traversed, and properties of the application's dynamic call graph. For clarity, the figure only shows information related to the *range* of the values assigned to each program variable. Sections 2.1.1 through 2.1.3 detail the full suite of information our runtime system extracts.

We refer to each entry in the runtime profile as an *aspect*, and each aspect is comprised of one or more *features*. For example, the runtime profile in ❶ contains three aspects, each of which have a single feature (the data range). The feature associated with dim summarizes the values that a program variable named dim assumed during that invocation of the application.

Every time a mainstream client runs it eventually deposits a runtime profile in the server's corpus of runtime profiles. As Figure 1❷ shows, a typical centralized server maintains an enormous corpus of runtime profiles, collected from one or more mainstream clients. For clarity, we assume that the server in this figure is responsible only for one application, say a program called simple. Thus, all of the runtime profiles in the corpus are from simple mainstream clients.

The goal of mainstream computing is to regulate program behavior so that it conforms to a user-defined percentage of *all* historical executions of the program. To that end, the server uses the runtime profiles in its corpus to generate *constraint sets* that regulate program behavior. We will shortly describe the form of a constraint set, but for now it should suffice to say that constraint sets contain zero or more constraints (or equivalently assertions) that clients use to restrict program behavior. For example, a constraint in a constraint set could specify that the variable dim cannot assume values less than one or greater than eight.

Our strategy for generating constraint sets is straightforward. We first create two *disjoint* sets of runtime profiles by randomly choosing (without replacement) runtime profiles from the corpus: one is a comparatively small set called the *training set* (❸), and the other is a large set called the *validation set* (❹). We use the runtime profiles in the training set to generate a constraint set; and we use the runtime profiles in the validation set to estimate the *failure rate* of the constraint set.

As we illustrate in Figure 1❺—and expound upon later—we can *merge* (∪) together the runtime profiles in the training set to create a constraint set. Remember that each runtime profile in the training set corresponds to an actual execution of a mainstream client. If we take the features in a single runtime profile and use them to generate a set of constraints for regulating a program's behavior, the constraints would be specific to a *single* instantiation of the program and would therefore likely have an extremely high failure rate when applied to other invocations of the application. However, by merging multiple runtime profiles together, we can *loosen* constraints such that they become more generic: in ❻ we see how the server merges two profiles together, essentially loosening the features associated with dim, ix, and j. For example, in one profile dim's data range is $[2, 3]$, and in the other its range is $[1, 2]$.

239

The server combines the two features to generate a constraint for `dim` of $[1, 3]$.

At the end of the merging process, we are left with the minimal constraint set that subsumes every runtime profile in the training set. In other words, the constraint set does not contain superfluous constraints, each of the constraints is only "loose" enough to contain all of the training set profiles, and none of the constraints in the constraint set would have been violated during the executions associated with the runtime profiles.[1] In general, it is preferable to limit the size of the training set so that we can tolerate having malicious runtime profiles in the corpora. The algorithms we present later in this section effectively limit the size of the training set.

In ❼ the server then determines the likelihood that the newly-created constraint set will cause program executions to *fail*. To do so, the server simply determines the fraction of runtime profiles in the validation set in which the constraint set created in ❺ would have been violated. As a concrete example, assume the aforementioned constraint for `dim` of $[1, 3]$ is in the constraint set. If a validation runtime profile also had the feature `dim`, but with range $[2, 8]$, the constraint would fail (because in this case the feature is not subsumed by the constraint). The failure rate, $\hat{p}$, is then simply the percentage of runtime profiles in the validation set for which one or more constraints in the constraint set failed. In section 2.2 we discuss the statistical guarantees mainstream computing provides regarding $\hat{p}$.

When the server has determined the failure rate for the constraint set, it enters the set in a table sorted by failure rate, as in ❽. This allows the server to quickly respond to incoming client requests, which we show in ❾. When the mainstream computing client begins execution, it requests a constraint set that will bound its failure rate, p_{fail}, essentially ensuring that its execution conforms to some percentage $(1 - p_{fail})$ of all historical invocations of `simple`. The client continually checks its execution against the constraints in the constraint set.

In the subsequent subsections we describe each component of a mainstream computing system, including the client instrumentation, the runtime libraries, details of the server's constraint-generation algorithms, and possible recourse when constraints fail. Throughout the remainder of the paper we refer to a *runtime profile* as a set of *aspects*; each aspect contains one or more *features* which describe a facet of the execution for a given instance of a client's execution. Finally, a *constraint set* is a set of constraints that regulates program behavior.

2.1 Client Instrumentation

While the server creates constraint sets, the clients are responsible for two main tasks: collecting the features for the runtime profiles that make up the server's corpora, and ensuring that execution does not violate any of the constraints in the supplied constraint set.

For our prototype we consider three types of features and their associated constraints: features that summarize the values assigned to variables, features that summarize the traversal of control flow, and features that summarize caller-callee relationships. We now describe each type in turn.

2.1.1 Value-Based Features and Constraints

Value-based features capture high-level information about the set of values assigned to a particular *variable* in the compiler's inter-

---

[1] Because clients continually inspect their execution, our approach assumes that a constraint will fail on a validation runtime profile *iff* the constraint would have failed during the actual invocation of the application that generated the runtime profile. In other words, we assume that if we were to generate a constraint set from a single runtime profile, the resulting constraint set would not fail in a client running in an identical environment to that in which the runtime profile was generated.

Value	Data-Range	Popcount	Bit-Lattice
-	$[\infty, -\infty]$	$[\infty, -\infty]$	$(\perp\ \perp\ \perp\ \perp\ \perp\ \perp\ \perp\ \perp)$
32	$[32, 32]$	$[1, 1]$	$(0\ \ 0\ \ 1\ \ 0\ \ 0\ \ 0\ \ 0\ \ 0)$
33	$[32, 33]$	$[1, 2]$	$(0\ \ 0\ \ 1\ \ 0\ \ 0\ \ 0\ \ 0\ \ \top)$
64	$[32, 64]$	$[1, 2]$	$(0\ \ \top\ \ \top\ \ 0\ \ 0\ \ 0\ \ 0\ \ \top)$
7	$[7, 64]$	$[1, 3]$	$(0\ \ \top\ \ \top\ \ 0\ \ 0\ \ \top\ \ \top\ \ \top)$

Figure 2. The value-based features for a variable over time.

$$
\begin{array}{ccc}
 & \top & \\
 \diagup & & \diagdown \\
 0 & & 1 \\
 \diagdown & & \diagup \\
 & \bot & \\
\end{array}
\qquad
\begin{array}{ccccc}
0 & \cup & 0 & = & 0 \\
1 & \cup & 1 & = & 1 \\
0 & \cup & 1 & = & \top \\
\top & \cup & X & = & \top \\
\bot & \cup & X & = & X \\
\end{array}
$$

Figure 3. A bit in the bit-lattice and its associated union operation.

mediate representation. One simple, but extremely effective feature that we have already mentioned is the *data-range feature*, which records the minimum and maximum values assigned to a variable. We define the data-range union operation $(\cup)$ to be the union over the single connected subrange of the integers where, $[a_l, a_h] \cup [b_l, b_h] = [min(a_l, b_l), max(a_h, b_h)]$. Figure 2 shows the value-based features associated with a hypothetical variable over time. Each row corresponds to a subsequent assignment to the variable during the execution of the client. The "value" column shows the value that is assigned to the variable, and the "data-range" column shows how the data-range feature changes. In this example we see that subsequent assignments cause the data-range feature to widen.

The *data-range constraint* then is simply an assertion check that signals if a variable's value is outside the range specified by the constraint. Intuitively, data-range constraints are useful for catching boundary violations, integer overflows and underflows, and improper loop exit conditions.

We also use the *constant-bit feature*, which identifies bits in a variable's representation that are constant (*i.e.*, are always '1' or '0'). The runtime system does this according to the lattice and rules shown in Figure 3. We use $\bot$ to refer to an uninitialized bit, '0' and '1' to refer to bit values of '0' and '1' respectively, and $\top$ to refer to an unconstrained bit. As with data ranges, we define a commutative and associative union operation $(\cup)$ that allows us to merge two bit-lattices according to the rules in Figure 3. In the figure, X designates any of the four possible values in the lattice. The purpose of this operation is to identify constant bits, and hence we see that merging a '0' and '1' bit together saturates the bit at $\top$. The "lattice" column in Figure 2 shows how this feature changes with subsequent assignments to the hypothetical variable.

The *constant-bit constraint* dictates the bit-values that a variable can assume during execution. For instance, assume the server creates the following constant-bit constraint for an 8-bit variable: $(\top\top 1\top 00\top 1)$. This constraint would not allow the variable to assume values that have anything other than '1' in bit positions 0 and 5, and '0' in bit positions 2 and 3. The other bits are unconstrained.

Finally, we consider the *population-count feature*. Population count refers to the number of bits in a binary value that are '1' at any given time. For instance, thirteen has binary representation $1101b$, and therefore its population count is three. The "popcount" column in Figure 2 shows how the population count feature changes as assignments are made to the hypothetical variable. Because our prototype maintains population count features as ranges, we use the same union operation $(\cup)$ to merge population-count features as we do for data-range features. The *population-count constraint* ensures that the population count of a value assigned to variable is within the bounds specified by the server. Population count can identify power-of-two series among other properties.

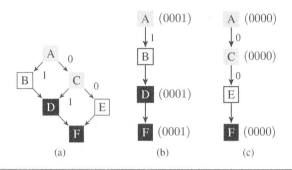

Figure 4. Sampling for control flow features.

As we can see from the example in Figure 2, the three different features we consider offer complementary information content. Value-based constraints are extremely useful for identifying rare behavior. As we later describe, value-based constraints were able to identify exploits in several of our benchmarks (`libvorbis`, `libpoppler`, `libtiff`, `bc`, `man`, and `gzip`).

2.1.2 Control Flow Features and Constraints

Our system also considers *control flow features*. At control flow graph (CFG) diverge points the compiler inserts instrumentation code that maintains a simple global history vector (GHV) that records the outcomes of the last 64 diverge points. Our compiler samples the value of the GHV at confluence points. In Figure 4(b) we show the lower four elements of the GHV for the path traversal $ABDF$ through the CFG in part (a); in this example we start with a GHV value of (0000) for clarity. In block A, which is a diverge point, the instrumentation code shifts a '1' into the GHV because the condition specifies that the branch should be taken. The GHV is not modified in block B because it is neither a diverge point nor a confluence point. Blocks D and F are confluence points, and thus our runtime system will sample the value of the GHV at these points. The value that is sampled in block F, for instance is (0001), which indicates that the outcome of the last conditional branch was '1'. The runtime system treats the GHV as a bit-lattice and uses the union operator shown in Figure 3 to merge samples.

Figure 4(c) shows another path traversal through the CFG, again starting with a GHV of (0000) for clarity. During the execution of $ACEF$, the GHV's value that is sampled at basic block F is still (0000) because the outcomes of the last two conditional branches were both '0'. *Control flow constraints* ensure for a given diverge or confluence point, that the value of the GHV agrees with the server-provided constraint.

Control flow features allow a mainstream system to determine the likely paths of execution of a client. This can be useful to protect against malicious attacks that force a program down an unanticipated path of control flow, as we later show with the benchmarks `grep` and `gzip`.

2.1.3 Call-Set Features and Constraints

The last mechanism we consider relates to the set of callers for a particular callee. A mainstream compiler assigns a (probably unique) 64-bit identification number to each method in a program. The runtime system employs a *single* global variable for the entire program, called the CSV, that is maintained in callee headers and is used to keep track of the current method being executed. More specifically, the compiler inserts instrumentation code at method entry points that samples (with the same bit-lattice and rules described in Figure 3) the current value of the CSV, and then immediately assigns the current method's hash identification value to the CSV. In this way, our system can efficiently (though with

information loss) keep track of the set of callers for a particular callee. Of course, if a callee is called by dozens of callers, the call-set feature for the callee will contain many ⊤ elements. Nevertheless, the call-set constraint can in some cases flag anomalous call stacks; call-set constraints effectively identified exploits in `xterm`, and `libpoppler`.

2.2 Server Aggregation

This subsection discusses what the centralized server does with the runtime profiles it receives. However, before describing our aggregation methodology, we define the following terms: we use C to designate the corpus of runtime profiles that the server has received (for a given application), and $|C|$ to specify its size. We assume C is very large. We define p_{fail} to be the user-defined tolerance level, which again is simply an upper bound for the probability that a constraint will be violated for any given instance of the client.

To quickly serve client requests, the server constructs a table of constraint sets which associates each constraint set with a probability of failure $\hat{p}$. The construction of this table is an iterative process that begins by randomly selecting a small subset S of runtime profiles from C. In our prototype implementation, the server begins with $|S| = 100$. The server then straightforwardly creates a constraint set that subsumes all of the runtime profiles in S. This is done by merging together all of the runtime profiles according to the union operations we have defined. For instance, consider the following two aspects from disparate runtime profiles:

ID	Data-Range	Bit-Lattice	Popcount
dim	$[4, 5]$	$(0000010\top)$	$[1, 2]$
dim	$[6, 7]$	$(0000011\top)$	$[2, 3]$

The union ($\cup$) operators that merge these aspects produce:

dim	$[4, 7]$	$(000001\top\top)$	$[1, 3]$

After the server has created a constraint set by merging the runtime profiles in S, it determines the frequency with which the constraint set *fails* on a separate validation set, $V \subset C$, where V and S are disjoint. If at least one constraint in the constraint set does not totally subsume its associated feature in a validation runtime profile, it is a failure. The failure rate for the constraint set then, $\hat{p}$ is the number of failed runtime profiles in V divided by $|V|$.

It is very important to point out that *this failure rate is only an estimate*—an estimate whose accuracy depends on $|V|$. The larger $|V|$ is, the better our estimate $\hat{p}$ is to the *true* probability of failure, p, for the community. To provide statistical guarantees about $\hat{p}$, we turn to the well-known solution to the *polling problem*. The polling problem is used to randomly sample a population of voters, who can vote for one of two candidates, to determine with statistical bounds on error, the frequency with which voters prefer a particular candidate [6]. Cast to our problem, we randomly sample runtime profiles from C, which can either fail on the constraint set or succeed, to determine with statistical bounds on error, the frequency with which the runtime profiles fail.

More precisely, using $|V|$, the system computes the maximum error margin, ϵ, between the server's estimate $\hat{p}$ and the true probability p for a fixed confidence interval α:

$$P(|\hat{p} - p| \geq \epsilon) \leq \alpha. \qquad (1)$$

For an ϵ of 0.001 and an α of 0.05 (*i.e.*, a 95% confidence level), we would need to include 960,000 runtime profiles in our validation set. For large communities, collecting this number of runtime profiles would not be difficult [21]; for smaller communities, larger error margins would suffice for many users (*e.g.*, just 9,604 sam-

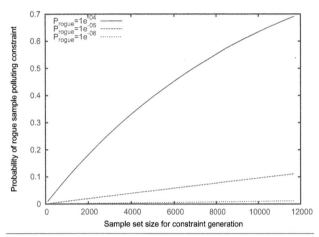

Figure 5. Probability of including a rogue runtime profile in S when generating a constraint set.

ples are required for $\epsilon = 0.01$). Though we can't precisely know p, we can now statistically bound it to lie within $\hat{p} \pm \epsilon$, and therefore, for a given constraint set we ensure that the true failure rate will exceed $\hat{p} + \epsilon$ with low probability.

After this process the server enters the constraint set and $\hat{p} + \epsilon$ in the table. It then chooses another, *larger* random subset S for training and repeats the process. In our prototype we increase the size of the training set by 100 after each iteration. By the end of the process the table contains several constraint sets and their associated $\hat{p} + \epsilon$. When a client requests a constraint set for a given p_{fail}, the server can simply return the constraint set with largest $\hat{p} + \epsilon$ such that $\hat{p} + \epsilon \leq p_{fail}$; if the user's tolerance level cannot be satisfied, then client execution will not be regulated.

A major difference between our approach and prior art on automatic likely invariant detection [17, 18] is mainstream computing's ability to tolerate runtime profiles from rogue users. In a real system, runtime profiles from rogue users are likely to be present in the corpora; and therefore a single rogue input would effectively loosen the constraints checked by the clients, allowing an opportunity for a hacker to compromise the system.

Mainstream computing's robustness against malicious behavior stems from the fact that, although the size of V can be enormous, the size of the training set $N = |S|$ from which the server generates constraint sets, is generally quite small! We can compute the probability, p_{pwned}, of including a rogue runtime profile when generating constraints:

$$p_{pwned} = 1 - \frac{\binom{|C| \cdot (1 - p_{rogue})}{N}}{\binom{|C|}{N}} \qquad (2)$$

Here, p_{rogue} is the probability of any given runtime profile coming from a rogue user. Figure 5 plots p_{pwned} for various N, with $|C| = 1,000,000$. As we can see from the figure, the probability of including a tainted runtime profile in the training set (and hence, in the constraint set) drops as N decreases. We expect rogue runtime profiles to be rare, but the figure shows that even for p_{rogue} rates as high as $1/10,000$, an N of over $6,000$ still reduces the risk of generating a tainted constraint set to below chance. As we show in the results section, for many applications we can provide very low probabilities of failure with much smaller N.

2.2.1 Filtering Volatile Features

Some applications contain variables that can often, or worse yet, *always* cause client constraints to fail. For instance, the series of

values assigned to timing-based variables such as timestamps is often monotonic. By definition future values of such variables will be outside the range of previously assigned values. We use a simple approach to prune such volatile variables from constraint sets. Our approach can provide low client failure rates, even for relatively small training sets.

Our approach leverages the *cross validation* technique commonly employed by machine learning practitioners [16]. The motivation for using cross validation is to determine how well a model can generalize to unseen data. The high-level idea is to repeatedly and randomly subdivide the *training set S* into two disjoint sets. Similar to the approach we have already presented, we use one set to create a set of constraints, and the other set to validate how well those constraints are satisfied. To significantly reduce the element of chance, this approach is repeated multiple times using different random subsets for generating constraints and validating the constraints [16]. After iteratively repeating this process multiple times (we iterate 100 times for our experiments), the server knows the observed failure rate for each feature in the training set. Variables associated with volatile features have high failure rates and can be removed from the resulting constraint set. The server currently removes features that failed one or more times during cross validation. Future work will consider smarter filtering methodologies.

2.3 Recourse for "Flagged" Applications

The user is able to adjust p_{fail} to effectively bound the percentage of time that a constraint will be violated. However, even for cases in which the user specifies p_{fail} near zero, the constraints still may fail with legitimate program usage. These cases arise when processing truly novel inputs. For example, a calendar application may spawn false positives when passing into a new year. Although our prototype automatically removes most volatile variables and can effectively bound a client's probability of failure, successfully dealing with flagged applications—including false positives—is crucial for mainstream computing. When our runtime system flags a constraint violation, it currently launches a GTK+ GUI dialog that presents the user with several options: 1) trust the application and continue running, 2) abort execution, 3) log the behavior, and 4) continue running failure obliviously [13, 29]. The failure oblivious methodology we employ forces an offending operand to be constrained according to its guarding constraint, and then continues running. Other possible options include sandboxing a flagged application, or taking a checkpoint-restart approach such as Software Rx [28].

3. Infrastructure and Methodology

This section describes the infrastructure and methodology we employ for collecting results.

3.1 Compiler Implementation

Our prototype system relies on a static compiler to instrument client binaries. Our prototype is implemented in GCC (version 4.2), which we chose because it is the de facto standard for compiling Linux applications. Our compiler inserts calls to a runtime library to perform both constraint checking and feature collection. In Figure 6, which shows an instrumented region of code in GCC's intermediate representation, our sampling library calls have the "__gcov" prefix. Notice that these calls take two arguments: the variable being sampled, and a pointer to a dedicated statically allocated region of memory for that variable. Calls to the sampling library use this memory to record features. For value-based features, the cumulative range, bit-lattice, and population count features are stored in this memory; for control flow and call-set features, the memory is used to record the cumulative bit-lattice.

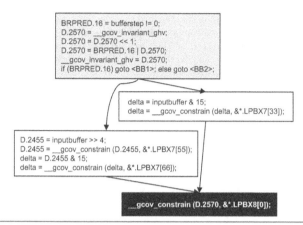

```
BRPRED.16 = bufferstep != 0;
D.2570 = __gcov_invariant_ghv;
D.2570 = D.2570 << 1;
D.2570 = BRPRED.16 | D.2570;
__gcov_invariant_ghv = D.2570;
if (BRPRED.16) goto <BB1>; else goto <BB2>;
```

```
delta = inputbuffer & 15;
delta = __gcov_constrain (delta, &*.LPBX7[33]);
```

```
D.2455 = inputbuffer >> 4;
D.2455 = __gcov_constrain (D.2455, &*.LPBX7[55]);
delta = D.2455 & 15;
delta = __gcov_constrain (delta, &*.LPBX7[66]);
```

```
__gcov_constrain (D.2570, &*.LPBX8[0]);
```

Figure 6. Profiling instrumentation.

Benchmark	Version	Vulnerability	Description
grep	2.5.4	DOS [15]	Text searching utility.
libvorbis	1.2.0	DOS [1]	Audio codec for Ogg files.
libpoppler	0.6.4	UPF/BV [4]	PDF rendering library.
xterm	229	INJ [3]	X Windows terminal emulator.
libtiff	3.6.1	OVF [2]	Tag Image File Format library.
bc	1.0.6	BV [25]	GNU interactive calculator.
compress	4.2.4	BV [25]	Compression/decompression.
gzip	1.2.4	BV [25]	Compression/decompression.
man	1.5h1	BV [25]	Online reference manual.
tar	1.20		GNU tar archiving utility.
bzip2	1.0.4		Block sorting file compressor.
jpeg	[20]		JPEG decoding
wc	6.10		Word count.

Table 1. Benchmarks surveyed in this paper. The abbreviations in the "vulnerability" column indicate what type of vulnerability the application has. DOS indicates denial of service, BV indicates a boundary violation, OVF specifies an integer overflow, UPF is an uninitialized pointer free, and INJ designates a command injection.

In addition, the server-provided constraints are stored in this dedicated memory. Depending on how this dedicated memory for a particular constraint is initialized, the runtime system will either just collect features, or it will collect features *and* enforce server-attained constraints. Our compiler creates an object file constructor that initializes the memory according to the server-acquired constraint set before the application starts.

The gray basic block in Figure 6 shows how the condition for the branch associated with the block is shifted into the global history vector (__gcov_invariant_ghv); The black basic block, which is a confluence point, is instrumented to call a function in our library to sample the value of the global history vector.

To handle `fork` variants, our prototype assigns mainstream clients a unique string during client initialization; when the program—or a forked copy of the program—exits, this string is sent to the server along with the client's runtime profile. Because this string is copied to the forked process, a runtime profile from a forked copy of the original process will transmit the same string to the server. The server then merges together runtime profiles with matching strings to prevent double counting. Our compiler replaces `exec` variants with a call to our sampling library that sends a runtime profile to the server before executing `exec`.

3.2 Benchmarks

Table 1 lists the benchmarks that we survey in this paper. For each application in the table, we also indicate the version we use, and whether there is a known vulnerability. In general, we chose benchmarks for which we could readily collect a large corpus of runtime profiles ($> 4,000$) in order to fulfill requests for $p_{fail} \approx 0$ with reasonably small ϵ. Many of the applications and libraries we consider contain known exploits.

Most of the benchmarks in the table are common Linux applications, and as such, it was not difficult to populate the server's corpora with runtime profiles. For `grep`, `libvorbis`, and `xterm` we were able to mostly use real-world runs, supplemented with some simulated runs, to collect runtime profiles. For `libtiff`, `libpoppler`, and `jpeg` we used a web crawler to gather a diverse set of input files. For `tar`, in addition to day-to-day usage, we collected additional runtime profiles by tarring inputs comprised of Linux kernel directories, tarballs of several open source projects, artificially created directories with only symbolic links, and degenerate inputs formed by directories with two or fewer entries. The runtime profiles for the compression applications come from real-world usage, and from processing several tarballs of various sizes, C and Java source code, image files, and some binaries and libraries. It was straightforward to obtain a diverse set of inputs for

`man` from a regular Linux workstation. Real-world usage along with several randomly chosen text and code files formed the input sets of `wc`. We tried in earnest to simulate a diverse user community by gathering varied inputs and varying the command line options to the benchmarks.

3.3 The Host Platform

We currently have clients running on two platforms. One is a 3 Ghz Intel® Xeon 5160 CPU with 16 gigabytes of memory running Linux version 2.6.24, and the other is a 2.16 Ghz Intel Core Duo CPU with 2 gigabytes of memory. When a client constraint fails, the client communicates with a locally running daemon, which prompts user interaction via a GTK+ GUI.

4. Results

This section discusses the effectiveness of a mainstream computing system. We first describe the system's ability to limit the failure rate, and we then provide two case studies that highlight the system's ability to flag anomalous behavior.

4.1 False Positive Study

Figure 7 shows the estimate $\hat{p}$ for various training set sizes on our benchmarks. Since, to our knowledge, none of the runtime profiles are the product of hacker exploits, $\hat{p}$ can be seen as the false positive rate. For these experiments, the minimum validation set size we use is $2,000$, leading to $\epsilon \leq 0.022.$[2] The x-axis shows the number of runtime profiles used to create constraint sets, and the y-axis shows the observed failure rates. For the applications that have volatile variables (*e.g.*, timestamps, process id-related variables) our filtering methodology is able to quickly drive failure rates well below $0.01 + \epsilon$ for many of these applications. That low settings of p_{fail} ($< 0.005 + \epsilon$) can be satisfied with small $|S|$ for most of these applications is an exciting result. Refer to Figure 5 to see the likelihood of including a rogue input with various $|S|$.

4.2 Case Study I: Detecting Exploits

The first usage of mainstream computing that we consider is identifying suspicious inputs that may exploit program bugs. For each of the applications that we consider in this section we use a constraint set that has been generated such that the failure rate $\hat{p} < 0.01 + \epsilon$. The two notable exceptions are `xterm` and `libpoppler`, which

---

[2] For `xterm` we do not have enough samples to provide tight bounds for ϵ. Instead, we resort to cross validation to better estimate $\hat{p}$ for this benchmark [16].

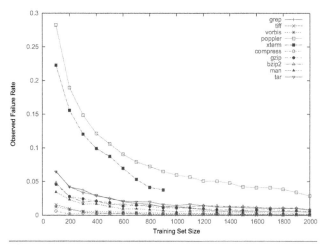

Figure 7. False-positive rates of constraints for different training set sizes, N. Here the server filters out volatile variables.

have $\hat{p}$ of $0.04 + \epsilon$ and $0.03 + \epsilon$ respectively. As an interesting exercise, for each exploitable application, we also employ a failure oblivious execution methodology and observe the output.

A recently exposed bug in `xterm` allows a hacker to construct a specially crafted file, that when printed to the screen, injects arbitrary commands into the terminal [3]. The exploit in `xterm` is part of a method that handles device control strings. We have several features related to the method in question in our corpus of data, indicating that several of our prior `xterm` instantiations executed this method (for font coloration and when we accidentally dumped binary files to the screen). However, when we `cat` the malicious file, the mainstream computing system flags the execution as anomalous. The sequence of calls to the method `unparseputc1` is inconsistent with the pattern specified by the call-set constraint. Mainstream computing is able to identify the malicious attempt as non-mainstream behavior. Because the violated constraint is based on unanticipated control flow, failure oblivious computing cannot thwart the attack.

For `libvorbis` we crafted a file that exploits a DOS bug. Here the programmer does not check for the nonsensical value of zero for the codec's codebook dimension [1]. Our system quickly reacts to the malicious input, flagging an integer overflow, and an anomalous `for` loop exit condition. Failure oblivious execution renders this input less harmful, as the library breaks out of the `for` loop and gracefully exits after about 10 seconds of "processing."

There is a documented "uninitialized pointer free" bug in `libpoppler` in which a crafted file can cause the library to throttle the CPU for several minutes before segfaulting [4]. Our system flags numerous call-set constraint violations before finally segfaulting. In addition to the documented memory bug, our system also flagged a previously unknown boundary violation in `pdftops` that occurs when a user tries to write a file to a directory in which he does not have permissions.

The string searching utility `grep` allows a user to concisely specify extremely complex patterns. In particular, the user can exponentiate patterns, which can lead to memory exhaustion and CPU throttling. For example, as discussed in [15], the simple query, `grep -E 'a{100}{100}{100}' /etc/password`, very quickly crashed our testing platform. Even using a constraint set with a failure rate as low as $0.004 + \epsilon$ our system flagged an anomalous control flow path in the method `dfainit` in `dfa.c`. That this execution was flagged is no fluke. This method was instantiated in most `grep` executions, and the path profiles therein are all different than this outlier. The authors of [15] recommended *whitelisting* regular expression patterns to prevent against such common attacks; and in a sense, this is what mainstream computing has automatically done.

We have just seen how our system can effectively protect against injection attacks, integer overflows, and denial of service attacks. A mainstream system can also detect array boundary violations. While we acknowledge that there are more precise mechanisms available for detecting buffer overflows—such as SoftBound [26], CCured [9], CRED [30], and DynamoRio [19]—our system has the advantage that in many cases anomalous behavior is flagged far in advance of the overrun even occurring.

We gathered a file that exploits an overflow in a string table in `libtiff` version 3.6.1 [2]. When we process the file with a non-mainstream version of the library with `tiff2bw`, a utility that converts a color image to black and white, the application segfaults due to an overflowed index. The mainstream version easily catches this bug—and long before the actual buffer overrun occurs—by noticing that several of the key fields extracted from the tiff file are well outside the ranges seen in previous tiff images. When we apply a failure oblivious approach, our system patches the key fields such that they satisfy the server-supplied constraints and continues running. Rather than inducing the overflow and segfaulting, the application gracefully exits with the following warning: "Warning, badinput.tif: invalid TIFF directory; tags are not sorted in ascending order."

There is a bug in BugBench's version of `bc` that allows a heap buffer overflow. The cause of the overflow is that the programmer mistakenly used the wrong global variable to limit the tripcount of a loop that copies data into memory. Running with an estimated $\hat{p}$ of $0.003 + \epsilon$, mainstream computing flags the malformed input long before the actual buffer overflow occurs. It is able to do so when the wrongly used global variable is set to a value outside the upper bound of the range-constraint. Before the segmentation fault occurs, many subsequent flags are raised as the array index into the buffer where the actual overflow occurs continues to march into uncharted territory.

A similar bug exists in BugBench's version of `man`. Again, the programmer used the wrong loop exit condition, which allows certain inputs to overflow a static array. When the application is passed command line arguments with at least 100 ':' characters preceding the man page to look at (BugBench's supplied input requests the `ls` page), the stack buffer overflows. The array bounds are $[0, 99]$, and at all values of $\hat{p}$ for which we tested, the observed ranges of indices into the array were much smaller. With failure oblivious execution, the overflow does not happen and the application simply prints, "No manual entry for ls."

For the input to `gzip` that exposes its buffer overrun, our system flags anomalous path behavior after the buffer overrun occurs, but before a return from the current stack frame happens. We see numerous path violations handling error conditions that had not been previously seen in a population of $2,000$ test cases. Furthermore, if the input string is modified such that the program does not crash, before the return from the overflowed stack frame some of the constraints in stack variables that were modified by the overflow are flagged. In this case, mainstream computing mimicked the operation of StackGuard [12]. The overrun occurs in an uninstrumented library, so failure oblivious computing cannot repair execution.

Our system does not catch the bug in BugBench's `compress`. This stack overflow occurs because a command line argument is passed *directly* to `strcpy` in the C library. We did not instrument the C library, and the instrumentation code that our compiler inserted in `compress` collected no data that could have identified an attack. Because the overflow occurs in uninstrumented library code, other static compilation approaches—such as SoftBound [26] and CRED [30]—would have similarly missed the overflow.

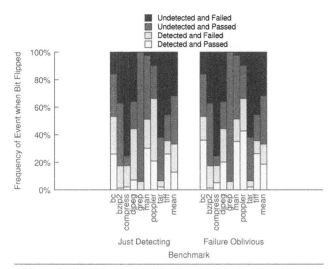

Figure 8. Breakdown of results from bit-flipping experiments.

4.3 Case Study II: Detecting Soft Errors

This section presents mainstream computing's ability to flag soft errors. We have added special hooks in our runtime library that allow us to inject single bit-flips with a parametrized probability p_{flip}. For these experiments we sample features for *all* GCC intermediate representation variables. All variables—even those for which the server does not generate a constraint—have an equal chance of being perturbed. For the purposes of this evaluation, we operate under the assumption that the memory used to store constraints is immune to soft errors.

For these experiments we take a single input that does not generate false positives, and we run the input $1{,}000$ times, randomly flipping bits with probability p_{flip}. We adjust p_{flip} so that on average we generate one flip per run, though sometimes we generate no flips and other times we generate multiple flips. For each run in which we flip at least one bit we note whether our system flagged the violation, and whether the application generated the correct output. In some cases the bit-flip introduces serious instability that leads to either an infinite loop or a segmentation violation.

The left portion of Figure 8 shows the results of our bit-flipping experiments. For each of the benchmarks we use the constraint set that yielded the lowest failure rate. The stacked bars contain four segments, each of which represents a combination of the application's output being correct, and whether our runtime system flagged the bit-flip. The black section of each stacked bar (the top-most section) shows the percentage of time that mainstream computing is not able to detect an error *and* the result of the run was an invalid output; this is the most serious situation. The remainder of the time our prototype was either able to detect the error, or the bit-flip did not manifest itself in the output. On average over 68% of the cases were either flagged, or the bit-flip was unimportant to the computation. On average our system flags 35% of the flips, considerably more for some of the applications. While there are other effective mechanisms for detecting soft errors, this case study is exciting because it highlights mainstream computing's potential for identifying system instability.

Instead of merely detecting a soft error, we also experiment with failure obliviously "repairing" the error [13, 29]. When the runtime system detects a violation, it attempts to tweak the offending violation such that it passes the constraint, and then it allows the client to continue running. The repair algorithm is straightforward: it repeatedly randomly flips a single bit of the value in question, and then

tests to see whether the new value satisfies the constraint. Our algorithm currently returns the first value that satisfies the constraint.

We show the results of these experiments in the right portion of Figure 8. The whitest bar in each stack corresponds to the frequency of time that our system detected the error yet the results of the computation were correct. Using the failure oblivious methodology, on average the system was able to increase the frequency of this event from 12% to 19%. In djpeg, the failure oblivious methodology allowed the computation to break out of some infinite loops, and allowed the percentage of "detected" runs that passed to increase from 7% to over 20%. Interestingly, for libpoppler while the failure oblivious methodology increased the percentage of detected runs that passed from 21% to 43%, it also induced many infinite loops. For bzip2 and tar, all detections come from failed path-constraints, and therefore the failure oblivious approach does nothing.

For these experiments we ensured that the input file on which we tested contained no false positives. In a real world mainstream system to guard against soft errors there would be no guarantees that a violated constraint would be due to a bit-flip. In fact, the probability of a soft error is far lower than that of seeing a false positive. A checkpoint-and-restart system could be used to determine whether the constraint violation corresponds to a soft error: if the constraint failure vanishes upon a restart, then the failure was likely because of a soft error; otherwise, the system would assume that it is an ordinary constraint failure. While these experiments are provided as a proof of concept, the results are exciting because they showcase the information content contained in server-provided constraint sets.

4.4 Overhead of Mainstream Computing

Our prototype system was engineered to be flexible, which allowed us to explore many different constraint-checking schemes. Constraint checks and sampling are part of a runtime library, which requires that every check perform a function call, and this flexible methodology incurs large slowdowns. Table 2 shows the overhead of our prototype when considering all features (*Full*). Here, in addition to performing control flow and call-set instrumentation, the system collects features for *every* variable in the program. The table also shows the overhead when we consider only control flow features (*CF*), only call-set features (*CS*), and only value-based features (*VB*). The overheads in the table include the time required to communicate with a local server.

We can effectively reduce runtime overheads with two techniques: The first approach only instruments critical variables such as those used to compute loop exit conditions, indices into arrays, type conversions, and denominators of divide statements. These checks would have allowed us to flag nearly the same set of exploits that full instrumentation did. The second approach only considers data-ranges and constant-bits for value-based features. The population count constraint is expensive to compute, and our studies have not shown it to be useful.

As shown in the *Selective* column of Table 2, these recommendations allow us to significantly reduce the overhead, even with our library-based approach. This overhead is on par with other state-of-the-art approaches for securing software systems [8, 9, 11, 30]. Hardware support for sampling and constraint checking can further drive down the overhead; however a discussion of such support is beyond the scope of this paper.

5. Related Work

Mainstream computing uses a distributed collaborative data collection methodology similar to that introduced by Liblit et al. [21–23]. These systems collaboratively collect sparsely sampled program *predicates* which capture runtime relationships between program

Benchmark	Overhead (factor over -O1)				
	Full	*CF*	*CS*	*VB*	*Selective*
bc	10.8	2.5	1.0	8.6	3.2
bzip2	21.4	3.4	1.0	19.0	4.3
compress	8.5	2.2	0.9	7.5	4.4
grep	4.2	1.3	1.0	4.0	1.7
gzip	16.4	4.1	1.0	13.1	7.2
jpeg	29.8	3.1	1.0	27.7	4.2
libpoppler	9.8	0.8	1.0	9.2	0.9
libtiff	15.0	1.3	1.0	15.0	4.5
libvorbis	15.0	1.5	1.0	14.8	5.6
tar	1.1	1.0	1.0	1.1	1.0
wc	4.3	1.9	1.0	4.4	1.9

Table 2. Prototype instrumentation overhead.

variables (*e.g.* is variable a less than variable b?). Statistical data mining techniques are then employed to identify the predicates that are best able to predict program crashes. While these systems help software developers pinpoint probable causes for critical software failures, they cannot protect against undiscovered vulnerabilities.

Our work also leverages the software invariant detection ideas pioneered in Daikon [17] and Diduce [18], and in later hardware-based solutions [14]. While in some sense systems like Daikon and Diduce identify mainstream behavior, the goals of our systems are very different. In systems like Daikon, Diduce, and mainstream computing, a user will encounter false positives. Because mainstream computing is meant to protect *deployed* applications, we allow users to specify a tolerance for failure with which they will be comfortable. This aspect of mainstream computing uniquely allows it to cope with malicious users.

"Taint analyses" of various forms have been proposed and used to prevent untrusted data from affecting program execution (*e.g.*, [8, 11, 31]). Similarly, Castro et al. propose a (necessarily conservative) approach for detecting situations where the runtime flow of data does not agree with the static data-flow graph [7].

Recently many promising approaches for tolerating software bugs have arisen. Bouncer is a system that generates and uses filters to drop messages with malicious payloads before they can be processed by a vulnerable program [10]. Rx is a checkpointing system in which a program that encounters a failure is restored to a previous checkpoint and rerun in the context of a different environment [28]. Locasto et al. use a reactionary approach to immunizing an application community against software failures [24]. Once an application instance detects an error, it communicates information about the error to other application instances, which then use emulation for the program methods involved in the failure.

Failure oblivious computing is an approach in which failures are ignored, and values that directly led to the failure are set such that computation can resume [29]. The Die Hard system probabilistically manages memory, which greatly increases the chances that programs with memory errors will execute properly [5]. These systems often convert catastrophic errors into correct executions, or executions with relatively benign issues.

ClearView is a collaborative system that relies on "monitors" to detect buffer overruns and illegal control transfers [27]; and similar to statistical bug isolation [21], ClearView maintains likely invariants which it mines to automatically generate software patches when a monitor is triggered. Because ClearView relies on monitors to tell the system when a failure has occurred, it does not detect arbitrary failures (such as injection and denial of service attacks).

Philosophically, mainstream computing is fundamentally different than all of these works. It makes no assumptions about error types, their root causes, or their implications. It simply enforces mainstream behavior at runtime. This simplicity makes it a powerful, generic tool, enabling it to detect a wide variety of software failures (and often, long before actual data corruption happens).

A direct extension to failure oblivious computing that inspired our work is presented in [13]. Demsky et al. use the Daikon invariant system to determine invariants for the fields of critical program structures. Upon violation of an invariant, the system will failure-obliviously "repair" the error according to the invariants specified for the offending field. The major differences between our work and [13] are three-fold: 1) we allow users to bound false positive rates based on their needs; 2) we demonstrate the ability of a mainstream system to tolerate soft errors and several different kinds of attacks; and 3) we describe a methodology for automatically extracting the invariants by leveraging a community of users.

6. Future Work

While we are encouraged by our prototype's initial success, there are still many open questions that must be answered before mainstream computing is viable. First and foremost, it remains to be seen how our prototype system would behave in a real deployment. Though we went to great lengths to simulate a real user community, our setup is limited in scope, and therefore our runtime profiles may be biased. In order to collect unbiased data, future work will consider larger scale deployments. That said, in some cases belonging to a biased community may have significant security advantages. At the extreme, future work will consider personalized servers that cater constraint sets to an individual user.

In addition, work is already underway to broaden the types of applications we consider. In particular, future work will consider "server" applications which potentially run for weeks at a time. Such applications may require periodically submitting partial runtime profiles to the server, while simultaneously updating the client's constraint sets.

We will also investigate smarter merging and filtering methodologies to reduce $\hat{p}$ for a given training set size. While a 1% tolerance for failure would be perfectly acceptable for many users (*e.g.*, one-per-day usage would only prompt the user once every several months), other users would find such tolerances unacceptable. In addition, some users may object that mainstream computing's statistical guarantees are not with respect to a single user, but with respect to the collaborative community: a "unique" user in a homogeneous community may be frustrated by the mainstream computing approach.

Finally our prototype was not engineered to have low runtime overheads. We will explore incorporating our ideas into a dynamic code generation system. Inlining our instrumentation code and completely omitting unnecessary constraint checks would allow us to drastically reduce the overhead of the runtime system. Furthermore, we will investigate the potential of sparse sampling to reduce the overhead of collecting features. Liblit et al. show that their approach reduces the overhead of sampling to a marginal amount ($< .05$) for equally heavy weight instrumentation [23].[3]

7. Conclusion

This paper explores a novel approach to increasing security and reliability. By enforcing mainstream behavior—the level of which is user definable—we show that a mainstream computing system can effectively identify unanticipated and potentially malicious computation. To our knowledge, our system is the first that allows users to specify the failure rates that they are willing to tolerate. Higher tolerances for failure may provide more protection through stricter regulation. Our approach allows mainstream computing to effec-

---

[3] Such an approach would destroy the property that a constraint would fail on a runtime profile *iff* it would have failed during the actual execution; sparse sampling would therefore require reworking our constraint generation and validation approach.

tively limit the number of runtime profiles that it uses for constraint creation. This is a very important property as it allows our system to tolerate rogue runtime profiles, which will almost certainly be part of a large corpora.

We show that mainstream computing can identify a variety of attacks, including command injections, buffer overruns, integer overflows and underflows, and denial of service. Furthermore, to highlight the information content stored in a constraint set, we show that a mainstream computing system can effectively be used to identify soft errors. We believe that mainstream computing also has the potential to identify and protect against Trojan Horses and rarely seen race conditions.

In a manner akin to the privacy and security mechanisms in web browsers and virus scanners, our mainstream computing runtime library allows a user to continue running a flagged application provided that he or she trusts the input. While our field is making tremendous progress in automatically finding liabilities, we believe that systems will continue to exhibit (exploitable) liabilities. Mainstream computing has exciting potential to limit the damage caused by unexpected execution.

References

[1] *Advisory CVE-2008-1419.*

[2] *Advisory CVE-2008-2327.*

[3] *Advisory CVE-2008-2383.*

[4] *Advisory CVE-2008-2950.*

[5] E. D. Berger and B. G. Zorn. DieHard: Probabilistic Memory Safety for Unsafe Languages. In *PLDI '06: Proceedings of the 2006 ACM SIGPLAN Conference on Programming Language Design and Implementation*, pages 158–168, New York, NY, USA, 2006. ACM.

[6] D. P. Bertsekas and J. N. Tsitsiklis. *Introduction to Probability*. Athena Scientific, 2002.

[7] M. Castro, M. Costa, and T. Harris. Securing Software by Enforcing Data-Flow Integrity. In *OSDI '06: Proceedings of the 7th Symposium on Operating Systems Design and Implementation*, pages 147–160, Berkeley, CA, USA, 2006. USENIX Association.

[8] J. Clause, W. Li, and A. Orso. Dytan: A Generic Dynamic Taint Analysis Framework. In *ISSTA '07: Proceedings of the 2007 International Symposium on Software Testing and Analysis*, pages 196–206, New York, NY, USA, 2007. ACM.

[9] J. Condit, M. Harren, S. Mcpeak, G. C. Necula, and W. Weimer. CCured in the Real World. In *Proceedings of the ACM SIGPLAN 2003 Conference on Programming Language Design and Implementation*, pages 232–244. ACM Press, 2003.

[10] M. Costa, M. Castro, L. Zhou, L. Zhang, and M. Peinado. Bouncer: Securing Software by Blocking Bad Input. In *SOSP '07: Proceedings of Twenty-First ACM SIGOPS Symposium on Operating Systems Principles*, pages 117–130, New York, NY, USA, 2007. ACM.

[11] M. Costa, J. Crowcroft, M. Castro, A. Rowstron, L. Zhou, L. Zhang, and P. Barham. Vigilante: End-to-End Containment of Internet Worms. In *SOSP '05: Proceedings of the Twentieth ACM Symposium on Operating Systems Principles*, pages 133–147, New York, NY, USA, 2005. ACM.

[12] C. Cowan, C. Pu, D. Maier, J. Walpole, P. Bakke, S. Beattie, A. Grier, P. Wagle, Q. Zhang, and H. Hinton. StackGuard: Automatic Adaptive Detection and Prevention of Buffer-Overflow Attacks. In *Proc. 7th USENIX Security Conference*, pages 63–78, San Antonio, Texas, jan 1998.

[13] B. Demsky, M. D. Ernst, P. J. Guo, S. McCamant, J. H. Perkins, and M. Rinard. Inference and Enforcement of Data Structure Consistency Specifications. In *ISSTA '06: Proceedings of the 2006 International Symposium on Software Testing and Analysis*, pages 233–244, New York, NY, USA, 2006. ACM.

[14] M. Dimitrov and H. Zhou. Anomaly-Based Bug Prediction, Isolation, and Validation: An Automated Approach for Software Debugging. In *ASPLOS '09: Proceedings of the 2009 International Conference on Architectural Support for Programming Languages and Operating Systems*. ACM, 2009.

[15] W. Drewry and T. Ormandy. Insecure Context Switching: Inoculating Regular Expressions for Survivability. In *WOOT'08: Proceedings of the 2nd USENIX Workshop on Offensive Technologies*, pages 1–10, Berkeley, CA, USA, 2008. USENIX Association.

[16] R. Duda, P. Hart, and D. Stork. *Pattern Classification*. Wiley-Interscience, 2001.

[17] M. D. Ernst, J. H. Perkins, P. J. Guo, S. McCamant, C. Pacheco, M. S. Tschantz, and C. Xiao. The Daikon System for Dynamic Detection of Likely Invariants. *Sci. Comput. Program.*, 69(1-3):35–45, 2007.

[18] S. Hangal and M. S. Lam. Tracking Down Software Bugs using Automatic Anomaly Detection. In *ICSE '02: Proceedings of the 24th International Conference on Software Engineering*, pages 291–301, New York, NY, USA, 2002. ACM.

[19] V. Kiriansky, D. Bruening, and S. Amarasinghe. Secure Execution via Program Shepherding. In *Proceedings of the 11th USENIX Security Symposium*, pages 191–206, Berkeley, CA, USA, 2002. USENIX Association.

[20] C. Lee, M. Potkonjak, and W. H. Mangione-Smith. MediaBench: A Tool for Evaluating and Synthesizing Multimedia and Communication Systems. In *International Symposium on Microarchitecture*, volume 30, pages 330–335, 1997.

[21] B. Liblit, A. Aiken, and A. Zheng. Distributed Program Sampling. In *Proceedings of the ACM SIGPLAN 2003 Conference on Programming Language Design and Implementation*, San Diego, California, June 9–11 2003.

[22] B. Liblit, A. Aiken, A. X. Zheng, and M. I. Jordan. Bug Isolation via Remote Program Sampling. In *Proceedings of the ACM SIGPLAN 2003 Conference on Programming Language Design and Implementation*, San Diego, California, June 9–11 2003.

[23] B. Liblit, M. Naik, A. X. Zheng, A. Aiken, and M. I. Jordan. Scalable Statistical Bug Isolation. In *Proceedings of the ACM SIGPLAN 2005 Conference on Programming Language Design and Implementation*, Chicago, Illinois, June 12–15 2005.

[24] M. E. Locasto, S. Sidiroglou, and A. D. Keromytis. Software Self-Healing Using Collaborative Application Communities. In *Proceedings of the 13th Annual Symposium on Network and Distributed System Security (SNDSS)*, February 2006.

[25] S. Lu, Z. Li, F. Qin, L. Tan, P. Zhou, and Y. Zhou. Bugbench: Benchmarks for Evaluating Bug Detection Tools. In *PLDI Workshop on the Evaluation of Software Defect Detection Tools*, June 2005.

[26] S. Nagarakatte, J. Zhao, M. M. Martin, and S. Zdancewic. SoftBound: Highly Compatible and Complete Spatial Memory Safety for C. *SIGPLAN Not.*, 44(6):245–258, 2009.

[27] J. H. Perkins, S. Kim, S. Larsen, S. Amarasinghe, J. Bachrach, M. Carbin, C. Pacheco, F. Sherwood, S. Sidiroglou, G. Sullivan, W.-F. Wong, Y. Zibin, M. D. Ernst, and M. Rinard. Automatically Patching Errors in Deployed Software. In *Proceedings of the 22nd Symposium on Operating Systems Principles*. ACM, 2009.

[28] F. Qin, J. Tucek, Y. Zhou, and J. Sundaresan. Rx: Treating Bugs as Allergies— a Safe Method to Survive Software Failures. *ACM Trans. Comput. Syst.*, 25(3), 2007.

[29] M. Rinard, C. Cadar, D. Dumitran, D. M. Roy, T. Leu, and W. S. Beebee. Enhancing Server Availability and Security Through Failure-Oblivious Computing. In *Proceedings of the 6th Symposium on Operating Systems Design and Implementation (OSDI)*, pages 303–316, 2004.

[30] O. Ruwase and M. S. Lam. A Practical Dynamic Buffer Overflow Detector. In *Proceedings of the 11th Annual Network and Distributed System Security Symposium*, pages 159–169, 2004.

[31] G. E. Suh, J. W. Lee, D. Zhang, and S. Devadas. Secure Program Execution via Dynamic Information Flow Tracking. In *ASPLOS-XI: Proceedings of the 11th International Conference on Architectural Support for Programming Languages and Operating Systems*, pages 85–96, New York, NY, USA, 2004. ACM.

Exploiting Statistical Correlations for Proactive Prediction of Program Behaviors

Yunlian Jiang

Computer Science Department
The College of William and May
Williamsburg VA
jiang@cs.wm.edu

Eddy Z Zhang

Computer Science Department
The College of William and May
Williamsburg VA
eddy@cs.wm.edu

Kai Tian

Computer Science Department
The College of William and May
Williamsburg VA
ktian@cs.wm.edu

Feng Mao

Computer Science Department
The College of William and May
Williamsburg VA
fmao@cs.wm.edu

Malcom Gethers

Computer Science Department
The College of William and May
Williamsburg VA
mgethers@cs.wm.edu

Xipeng Shen

Computer Science Department
The College of William and May
Williamsburg VA
xshen@cs.wm.edu

Yaoqing Gao

IBM Toronto Lab
ygao@ca.ibm.com

Abstract

This paper presents a finding and a technique on program behavior prediction. The finding is that surprisingly strong statistical correlations exist among the behaviors of different program components (e.g., loops) and among different types of program-level behaviors (e.g., loop trip-counts versus data values). Furthermore, the correlations can be beneficially exploited: They help resolve the proactivity-adaptivity dilemma faced by existing program behavior predictions, making it possible to gain the strengths of both approaches—the large scope and earliness of offline-profiling–based predictions, and the cross-input adaptivity of runtime sampling-based predictions.

The main technique contributed by this paper centers on a new concept, seminal behaviors. Enlightened by the existence of strong correlations among program behaviors, we propose a regression-based framework to automatically identify a small set of behaviors that can lead to accurate prediction of other behaviors in a program. We call these seminal behaviors. By applying statistical learning techniques, the framework constructs predictive models that map from seminal behaviors to other behaviors, enabling proactive and cross-input adaptive prediction of program behaviors. The prediction helps a commercial compiler, the IBM XL C compiler, generate code that runs up to 45% faster (5%–13% on average), demonstrating the large potential of correlation-based techniques for program optimizations.

Categories and Subject Descriptors D.3.4 [*Programming Languages*]: Processors—optimization, compilers

General Terms Performance, Measurement

Keywords Program behavior prediction, Dynamic optimizations, Seminal behaviors, Feedback directed optimizations, Program behavior correlations

1. Introduction

Accurate prediction of program behaviors is the basis of various program optimizations. Program behaviors in this paper refer to the operations of a program and the ensuing activities of the computing system, in relation to the input and running environment. Examples include memory references, data values, function calling frequencies, and so on. The prediction of program behaviors critically determines how optimizers transform a program and the resulting performance. As the complexity in modern hardware and software continuously grows, accurate behavior prediction becomes both more important and more challenging than before.

Besides accuracy, two other properties of behavior prediction are essential for optimizations: scope and timing. The scope of a prediction may be a small execution interval, a loop, a procedure, or the entire program. The larger the scope is, the more likely the optimizer is able to avoid local-optimum traps when making optimization decisions. The third property, the timing of prediction, refers to when a prediction can occur. The earlier the prediction occurs, the earlier an optimization can happen, and the larger the portion of the execution that may benefit from the resulting code. We also call the earliness the *proactivity* of a prediction.

In existing program optimizers, behavior predictions are based on either training runs (in profiling-based optimizers) or runtime sampling (in runtime optimizers). Their strategies are essentially the same: using the behaviors of a program component (e.g., a procedure or loop) observed previously (in either a training run or the earlier part of the current execution) to predict the future behaviors of the *same* component. This strategy, although effective for many programs, can lead to a *proactivity-adaptivity dilemma*: Predictions based on training runs have a large scope and good proactivity, but cannot adapt to input changes, whereas, predictions based on runtime sampling have good adaptivity but limited scope and proactivity.

Recent studies show that prediction based on program inputs may gain the strengths of both approaches, improving optimizations significantly. For instance, improvements of 7%–21% have been observed on a variety of Java programs [13]. However, that approach relies on programmers' manual specifications on program inputs. An automatic solution to the proactivity-adaptivity dilemma remains an open question.

In this paper, we attack the problem by exploiting the correlations among the behaviors of program components. The intuition is simple. Consider the trip-counts (number of iterations) of two loops, L1 and L2. Suppose that they strongly correlate with each other (e.g., the trip-counts of L1 are always about double those of L2). Then, as soon as the trip-counts of one of them become known in an execution, the trip-count of the other will be easily predicted.

A set of questions must be answered for using those correlations for behavior prediction. How common are such correlations in programs? How can they be identified? And how can they be exploited?

This paper presents our explorations in answering those questions. It first reports a systematic measurement (Section 2), showing that strong statistical correlations exist not only among the behaviors of different program components commonly, but also among different types of program-level behaviors (e.g., loop trip-counts versus data values).

It then introduces a technique to exploit the correlations for program behavior prediction and optimizations. The technique centers on a new concept (Section 3.1), *seminal behaviors*, which refers to a small set of behaviors that strongly correlate with most other behaviors in the program, and meanwhile, expose their values early in typical executions. Section 3.2 presents a framework for identifying seminal behaviors and building predictive models that map from seminal behaviors to other behaviors. Section 3.3 and Section 3.4 discuss how to use seminal behaviors for behavior prediction and program optimizations, respectively. Experimental results in Section 4 show that seminal behaviors can lead to accurate prediction of several types of program behaviors. The prediction is distinctive in being both cross-input adaptive and proactive—the whole-program behaviors can be predicted as soon as the values of the seminal behaviors get exposed (no later than 10% of the execution). The prediction helps a commercial compiler, IBM XL C/C++ Enterprise Edition 10.1, generate code that runs up to 45% faster (5%–13% on average).

In summary, this work makes three main contributions.

- To the best of our knowledge, this work is the first study that systematically explores and exploits the statistical correlations among different types of program-level behaviors for dynamic program optimizations.

- This work introduces the concept of seminal behaviors and their identification, laying the foundation for correlation-based behavior prediction.

- The proposed seminal-behavior-based prediction offers an automatic way to predict program behaviors proactively and cross-input adaptively, resolving the proactivity-adaptivity dilemma in existing techniques.

2. Correlations Among Program-Level Behaviors

In this section, we first present a qualitative view of the behavior correlations, using an example to illustrate the intuition behind in. We then report the measurement of the correlations in 14 programs, quantitatively examining the properties and strength of the correlations.

2.1 A Qualitative View

Formally, we define *behavior correlations* as follows. The behaviors of two program components are correlated if, when the inputs to the program change, their values vary together in a way not expected on the basis of chance alone.

The existence of behavior correlations is due to the connections inherent in program code. Take Figure 1 as an example. It outlines a simplified code for mesh generation. The "main" function invokes a recursive function "genMesh" to create a mesh for the vertices listed in an input file. Before the creation, it reads vertices and a reference mesh in the function "mesh_init" in preparation; after the creation, it verifies the generated mesh in the function "verify".

The example illustrates both deterministic and non-deterministic connections among program behaviors. A deterministic example is the relation between the value of "vN" and the trip-counts of the two "for" loops in "mesh_init". Once the value of "vN" is known, the numbers of the iterations are easily determined. Similar relations exist between "vN" and the number of times the recursive function "genMesh" is invoked, and the size of the vertex array "v". A non-deterministic connection exists between the "while" loop in the function "mesh_init"and the "for" loop in the function "verify". Although these two loops tend to have the same trip-counts, they may differ with each other when the generated mesh is wrong. Some of these relations may be detectable by compilers, but many of them are undetectable because of the complexities in pointer analysis, alias analysis, and interprocedure analysis.

The existence of the correlations can be explained from another perspective. For a given program in a given environment, all the behaviors essentially stem from the same entity–the inputs to the program. They are hence likely to correlate with one another (although do not necessarily correlate, if two behaviors stem from the different parts or features of an input) .

2.2 Quantitative Measurements

2.2.1 Methodology

Behaviors under Study In this experiment, we concentrate on the following program-level dynamic behaviors: loop trip-counts (numbers of iterations), procedure calling frequencies, the number of times a basic block is accessed (*data profiles*), the counts of certain values from some special expressions, referenced by the nodes and edges in the control flow graph, (*edge profiles* and *node profiles*, respectively), which are important for program optimizations (judged by the IBM XL C/C++ compiler v10.1). We choose these types of behaviors because of their importance for program optimizations. In fact, the final three kinds of profiles compose the entire feedback the IBM XL compiler uses for its profiling-directed compilation. The other two kinds of behaviors are important for loop optimizations and function inlining.

We collect the loop trip-counts through a modified GCC (v4.3.1), and obtain the calling frequencies through GNU gprof (v2.19). The machine is equipped with Intel Xeon 5310 quad-core processors running the Linux 2.6.22 operating system. We get the other three kinds of profiles using IBM XL C/C++ Enterprise Edition 10.1 on IBM Power5 processors (with the IBM AIX 5.3.8 operating system installed). The compiler is the primary commodity compiler on AIX platforms. The use of two different platforms offers the

```
main(int argc, char * argv){
    ...
    mesh_init (dataFile,mesh,refMesh);
    genMesh (mesh,0,mesh->vN);
    verify (mesh, refMesh);
}


// recursive mesh generation
void genMesh (Mesh *m, int left, int right){
    if (right>3+left){
        genMesh (m, left, (left+right)/2);
        genMesh (m, (left+right)/2+1, right);
        ...}
    ...
}


void verify (Mesh *m, Mesh *mRef){
    ...
    for (i=0; i< m->edgesN; i++){
        ...
    }
}
```

```
Mesh * mesh_init
(char * initInfoF, Mesh* mesh, Mesh* refMesh)
{
    FILE * fdata = fopen (initInfoF, "r");
    fscanf(fdata, "%d\n", &vN );
    mesh->vN = vN;
    v = (vertex*) malloc (vN*sizeof(vertex));
    // read positions of vertices
    for (i=0; i<vN; i++) {
        fscanf(fdata, "%f %f\n", &v[i].x, &v[i].y);
    ...}
    // sort vertices by x and y values
    for (i=1; i< vN; i++){
        for (j=vN-1; j>=i; j--){
            ...}
    }
    while (!feof(fd)){
        ...
        /* read edges into refMesh for
            later verification */
    }
}
```

Figure 1. A simplified mesh generation program.

opportunity for studying the correlations between the behaviors of a program on different platforms.

Programs   Table 1 lists the programs used in our experiments. They include 14 C programs in SPEC CPU2000 and SPEC CPU2006. We include no C++ or Fortran programs because the instrumentor we implement (the modified GCC) currently works only for C programs. We exclude those programs that are either similar to the ones included (e.g., bzip2 versus gzip) or have special requirements on their inputs and make the creation of extra inputs (which are essential for this study) very difficult.

Although each benchmark comes with several sets of inputs by default, more inputs are necessary for a systematic study of statistical correlations. We collect more inputs as shown in the fourth column of Table 1. During the collection, we try to ensure that the inputs are typical in the normal executions of the benchmarks. Specifically, we collect those inputs by either searching the real uses of the corresponding applications or deriving the inputs after gaining enough understanding of the benchmark through reading its source code and example inputs. Some of those inputs come from Amaral's research group [Berube et al.]. The sixth column of Table 1 shows the changes that different inputs brought to the loop trip-counts, reflecting the large differences among those inputs.

2.2.2   Calculation of Correlations

We use the standard way in statistics, the Pearson product-moment correlation coefficient [9], to quantify the correlations. Let X and Y represent two behaviors of a program, such as the trip-counts of two different loops. Suppose we run the program for n times, each time on a different input data set. We get n measurements of both X and Y, written as x_i, y_i where $i = 1, 2, \ldots, n$. The correlation coefficient of X and Y is calculated as follows:

$$r_{XY} = \frac{\sum (x_i - \bar{x})(y_i - \bar{y})}{(n-1)s_X s_Y},$$

where, $\bar{x}$ and $\bar{y}$ are, respectively, the mean values of X and Y, and s_X and s_Y are the sample standard deviation of X and Y.

The value range of correlation coefficients is [-1,1]. The absolute value of a correlation coefficient indicates the strength of a *linear* relationship between two random variables. The higher the absolute value is, the stronger the relationship is.

Correlation coefficients cannot directly reflect the non-linear relationship between behaviors. (The regression to be presented in

Section 3 captures some of those relationships.) But that limitation does not affect the conclusion of the experiment: The observed correlations already confirm the common existence of strong correlations among program behaviors, as shown next.

2.2.3   Measurement Results

In this section, we first report the correlation coefficients among the trip-counts of different loops and then describe the coefficients from loops to other types of behaviors. The concentration on loops is because of their importance in programs and their critical roles in the exploitation of correlations, as Section 3 will describe. In all measurements, we ignore the behaviors that have never occurred in any of the executions (correlations among them are trivially 1).

Inter-Loop Coefficients   In the study of correlations among loops, we compute the correlation coefficients between the trip-counts of every pair of loops. For each loop, we find the highest correlation coefficient between this loop's trip-counts and all the other loops'. We refer to such coefficient as the *inter-loop coefficient* of this loop. If its inter-loop coefficient is high, this loop's trip-count is likely to be able to be predicted accurately as soon as the trip-count of the other loop is known. The seventh column in Table 1 shows the average of the absolute values of such coefficients across all loops in each program. All numbers are greater than 0.98 except 0.94 for *mcf*. Since the maximal correlation coefficient is 1, the inter-loop correlations are remarkably strong.

More detailed information on the correlations appears in the first column of Figure 2. Each pie shows the distribution of the values of the correlation coefficients. The dominance of the high coefficients further confirms the common existence of strong correlations between loop trip-counts.

Loops and Others   We measure the correlation coefficients between loop trip-counts and each of the four other types of behaviors: procedure calling frequencies, edge, node, and data profiles. The corresponding correlations are respectively denoted as loopcall, loop-edge, loop-node, and loop-data.

For each target behavior (e.g., the calling frequency of a procedure), we compute the correlation coefficients between the tripcounts of every loop and this target behavior. The highest value is taken as the coefficient from loops to this target behavior. It (partially) reflects the possibility to predict the value of the target behavior from a loop.

Table 1. Benchmarks

Program		lines	inputs	loops	Factor of changes caused by inputs	Mean corr coef from loop to				
name	description					loop	call	edge	node	data
ammp	Computational Chemistry	13263	20	425	9.9×10^1	1.00	0.97	0.97	0.91	1.00
art	Image Recognition / Neural Networks	1270	108	101	4.0×10^4	1.00	1.00	0.99	0.88	0.70
crafty	Game Playing: Chess	19478	14	425	4.6×10^8	0.99	0.97	1.00	0.99	0.98
equake	Seismic Wave Propagation Simulation	1513	100	106	1.0×10^2	1.00	1.00	0.99	0.15	1.00
gap	Group Theory, Interpreter	59482	12	1887	1.1×10^8	0.99	0.98	0.93	0.77	0.91
gcc	C Compiler	484930	72	7615	1.1×10^6	0.98	0.98	0.97	0.94	0.92
gzip	Compression	7760	100	223	4.3×10^7	0.98	0.94	0.95	0.86	0.98
h264ref	Video Compression	46152	20	2074	2.1×10^9	1.00	1.00	1.00	0.98	1.00
lbm	Fluid Dynamics	875	120	27	6.0×10^6	1.00	0.93	1.00	1.00	1.00
mcf	Combinatorial Optimization	1909	64	76	1.4×10^5	0.94	0.99	0.99	0.30	1.00
mesa	3D Graphics Library	50230	20	995	2.0×10^1	1.00	1.00	1.00	0.28	1.00
milc	Physics / Quantum Chromodynamics	12837	10	473	2.1×10^9	0.98	0.98	1.00	0.70	1.00
parser	Word Processing	10924	20	1350	2.1×10^6	0.99	1.00	0.99	0.97	0.98
vpr	FPGA Circuit Placement and Routing	16976	20	435	3.9×10^6	0.99	0.98	0.99	0.84	0.64

The rightmost four columns in Table 1 report the average of such coefficients for each type of behaviors. The loop-call and loop-edge coefficients are all greater than 0.93. The loop-node coefficients are the lowest among the four, smaller than 0.84 for five programs. The main reason is the many conditional statements in their source code. The loop-data coefficients are higher than 0.92 for most of the programs. The two exceptions are programs, *art* and *vpr*, 0.7 and 0.64 respectively. The rightmost four columns of Figure 2 reveal the distribution of those coefficients.

Summary and Implications This section shows that even though conditional branches in a program sometimes weaken the correlations between loops and basic block execution frequencies, overall, strong statistical correlations exist between loop trip-counts, and from loop trip-counts to other types of behaviors. It suggests the possibility of using the correlations for runtime behavior prediction. When the values of certain types of behaviors of some program components (e.g., a set of loop trip-counts) are exposed in an execution, we may use them as the predictors of the behaviors of other (to-be-executed) components in the program. This kind of prediction is both proactive, occurring before the execution of the other program components, and adaptive, being specific to the current input data set.

The usefulness of the prediction is determined by its accuracy and how early the predictors expose their values. The next section describes a framework for identifying the appropriate set of predictors and the use of them for program optimizations.

3. Exploitation of Behavior Correlations

In this section, we describe a framework and a set of techniques for exploiting the correlations revealed in the previous section. The framework has two functions: 1) to find the small set of behaviors that expose their values early in an execution and strongly correlate with other behaviors in the execution; 2) to build predictive models that capture the correlations among program behaviors. At the center of the framework is the concept of seminal behaviors.

3.1 Concept of Seminal Behaviors

Roughly speaking, seminal behaviors are those behaviors that are suitable to be used for predicting other behaviors. Before presenting the formal definition, we need to introduce two concepts.

DEFINITION 1. *For a given set of behaviors B and a threshold r, a set of behaviors S is a predictor set of B if there is a mapping function f from S to B such that the average Euclidean distance*

between $f(V_S)$ and V_B is less than r, where V_S and V_B are the values of S and B.

DEFINITION 2. *Let S be a predictor set of a given set of behaviors B of a program G. In an execution of G, let B' represent the subset of B whose values are exposed after the exposure of the values of S. The earliness of S in that execution is defined as $|B'|/|B|$.*

In these two terms, we express the definition of seminal behaviors as follows.

DEFINITION 3. *For a given set of behaviors B of a program G, a seminal behavior set, S, is a predictor set of B whose earliness, averaged across all executions of G, is the highest among all the predictor sets of B. Each member of S is called a seminal behavior.*

The definition suggests two properties of a seminal behavior set. First, it leads to accurate prediction of other behaviors. Second, it enables the earliest (on average) prediction among all B's behavior-predictor sets. These two properties make a seminal behavior set desirable for the uses in proactive and cross-input adaptive prediction of program dynamic behaviors.

3.2 Identification of Seminal Behaviors

The concept of seminal behaviors suggests that whether a behavior is a seminal behavior depends on B, the behaviors to be predicted. In this work, we concentrate on those five types of behaviors (loop trip-counts, calling frequencies, edge, node, data profiles) listed in Section 2.2.1.

A brute-force way to identify seminal behavior sets is to enumerate every possible subset of the program's behaviors, try all kinds of mapping functions, and consider all executions of the program. The high complexity suggests the need for heuristics and approximations. We employ a heuristics-based framework as described next.

Candidate Behaviors Rather than consider all kinds of behaviors, we select two types of behaviors as the candidates for seminal behaviors. The first is program *interface behaviors*, which mainly include the values directly obtained from program inputs. Specifically, this type of behaviors include the values obtained directly from command lines[1] and file operations. We ignore the content of

---

[1] In this work, we assume that the applications are C programs with inputs coming from command lines. The analysis can be applicable to other programs with interactive features; details are out of the scope.

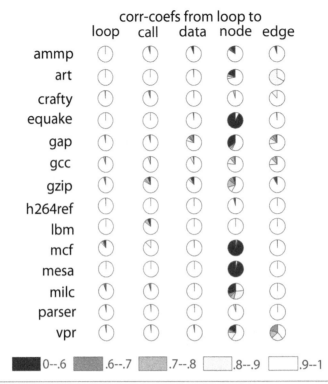

Figure 2. Distribution of values of correlation coefficients.

a file if the corresponding file operations are within a loop whose trip-count is either large (greater than 10 in our experiments) or unknown during compile time. Those data are likely to be a massive data set for processing; their values may not influence the coarse-grained behaviors much, but including them may significantly inflate the candidate behavior set and complicate the recognition of seminal behaviors. Instead, we include the trip-counts of those surrounding loops as they often reflect the size of the data set. We also record the size of input files, obtained through file descriptors, as another clue of the size of data. All these behaviors together form a set called the *interface behavior set*.

The second type of behaviors we include are the trip-counts of all the loops (beside those that are already counted as interface behaviors) in the program. This inclusion is due to the importance of loops and the correlations the previous section shows.

Computation of Predictive Capability From the definition of seminal behaviors, we know that they must be able to lead to accurate prediction of other behaviors. For a given set of behaviors B, we define *predictive capability* of a set S as the number of behaviors in the set $B - S$ that can be predicted from S with an accuracy above a predefined threshold (80% in this study).

For the reduction of complexity, we take a simplification as follows. We limit B to loop trip-counts during the examination of the predictive capability of different candidate behavior sets. The intuition is that because there are strong correlations between loops and other types of behaviors, the sets selected in this way are likely to show good predictive capability on other types of behaviors as well. The results in Section 4 confirm this intuition.

The computation of predictive capabilities in our experiments is based on the standard 10-fold cross-validation [9]. It works iteratively. Suppose we did N profiling runs of a program, and obtained N instances of S and B. In each iteration, 9/10 of the N instances are used to construct predictive models from S to B, and the other 1/10 are used to test the model for prediction accuracy.

Next, we describe the framework for seminal behavior identification first, and then explain the construction of predictive models.

Identification Framework A brute-force way to identify seminal behaviors is to compute the predictive capability and earliness of every subset of candidate behaviors and choose the best one. To circumvent the exponential complexity, we take an incremental approach, which gradually builds a number of affinity lists. *An affinity list* is a list consisting of two sets of behaviors, a header set and a body set, such that the values of the behaviors in the header can lead to accurate prediction of the values of those behaviors in the body.

The construction of affinity lists proceeds as follows. It starts with the set of interface behaviors, because of their earliness and direct connections with program inputs. It ignores those interface behaviors that have constant values across all training runs as they are irrelevant to behavior variances among different runs. It then uses the remaining interface behaviors as predictors, builds predictive models from them to each loop trip-count. The loop trip-counts that can be predicted accurately are put into the body of the first affinity list. All the interface behaviors that appear in the predictive models are put into the header of that affinity list. The first column in Figure 3 illustrates the result of this step on a program *mcf*.

The construction process then selects, in an order shown next, one of the remaining candidate behaviors as the header of the second affinity list, computes the predictive capability of this header on the remaining behaviors, and adds the predictable ones into the body of the second affinity list. This process continues until no candidate behaviors are left. For the program *mcf* shown in Figure 3, the process constructs 6 affinity lists; the last one has an empty body. An affinity list with an empty body means no behaviors are predictable from its header.

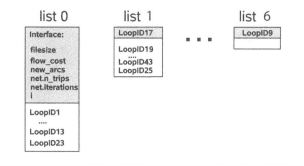

Figure 3. The affinity lists of program *mcf*.

In our experiment, the order, in which loop behaviors are selected, is the order of the time when the trip-counts of the loops get exposed. (The average order is used when there are two or more training runs.) This is to maximize the earliness of the resulting seminal behavior set.

The union of the headers of the affinity lists forms a possible seminal behavior set as all other candidate behaviors are predictable from it. These header sets may be ranked in a descending order of the sizes of their bodies. The exclusion of the low-rank header sets may have little influence on the prediction of most behaviors. Section 4 examines the trade-off of the size and the predictive capability of those sets.

We note that the headers of the affinity lists essentially embody a kind of characterization of program inputs: Each of the headers reflects some aspects or attributes of the inputs; together they determine most of the program's behaviors.

Predictive Models   In this part, we describe some details of the construction of the predictive models used during the identification process. We employ two standard regression techniques, namely LMS linear regression and Regression Trees [9]. The former handles linear relations among behaviors, the latter for non-linear relations. The construction process applies Regression Trees only if the linear regression results are not good enough (automatically assessed through cross-validation). During the construction of the first affinity list, the standard forward stepwise feature selection [9] is used so that only important interface behaviors are stored in the header.

Both LMS and Regression Trees models are efficient to build and use. The resulting models are represented by only a small number of coefficients (for linear models) and questions (for Regression Trees). (We limit the tree size to be no greater than 10.) A specially appealing feature of Regression Trees is that it handles both numerical and categorical values smoothly.

Discussions   There are several points worth mentioning. First, as we mentioned earlier, static analysis cannot capture many relations because of the complexities in the program, and difficulties in pointers and aliases analysis. But its integration into our framework may help reduce certain overhead by revealing some definite connections.

Second, the accuracy threshold used in the construction of affinity list determines the number of resulting affinity lists. The appropriate value depends on the ultimate use of the prediction. We take 80% as the threshold for our experimental exploration.

Finally, using multiple behaviors rather than a single behavior as the header in each affinity list (besides the first list) may improve the prediction accuracy. However, the large number of possible combinations of behaviors would significantly increase the training cost. Detailed explorations are out of the scope of this paper.

3.3   Uses for Behavior Prediction

Using seminal behaviors for behavior prediction is straightforward. It just needs to build a predictive model mapping from the values of the seminal behaviors to those of the target behaviors. We employ the same regression techniques as described in the previous paragraph for the model construction. In a new execution, as soon as the values of the seminal behaviors are exposed, the models will be able to immediately predict the values of the target behaviors, hence enabling proactive, cross-input adaptive prediction, opening new opportunities for dynamic optimizations.

3.4   Uses in Program Optimizations

As shown in the previous sections, a small set of seminal behaviors are enough to produce reasonably accurate prediction for various types of behaviors, suggesting the potential of seminal behaviors for input-specific program optimizations. This section discusses the uses.

For programs running in a managed environment, such as Java Virtual Machines (JVMs), the seminal behaviors-based prediction may help the Just-In-Time (JIT) compilers make better decisions on the timing and parameters in method optimizations. During an offline profiling process, the seminal behaviors of an application and the predictive models for certain kinds of program behaviors can be determined using the approach described in Section 3.2. After that, when a new run of the application launches on a new input, the runtime system can use the predictive models to predict how the application will behave in the rest of this run as soon as the values of the seminal behaviors get exposed in the current execution. The JIT compiler can then optimize the application in a way that best suits the predicted behaviors. This process is similar to many dynamic optimization systems (such as JVMs), except that the knowledge of seminal behaviors makes the optimization *proactive* to the major part of the execution. As showed by previous studies [5, 13], proactive dynamic optimizations may outperform traditional reactive schemes significantly.

For programs written in imperative languages, such as C, seminal behaviors may boost the effectiveness of dynamic code version selection for performance improvement. Dynamic code version selection is a technique for enabling the adaptation of program optimizations on input data sets [8]. The default scheme works in this way. For each function, the compiler generates several versions using different optimization parameters. At run time, those versions are used and timed in the first certain number of invocations of a function; the version taking the shortest time to run is selected for the rest of the execution. The reliance on runtime trials of different versions makes the technique hard to apply to the functions that have very few invocations in a run. (Such functions could contain major loops and be important for the program execution.) If we can build a mapping from the values of seminal behaviors to the suitable versions during training time, we can immediately predict the best version to use for a real run as soon as the values of seminal behaviors get exposed in that run. In this way, we do not need the trials of the different versions in real runs, hence circumventing the limitations the default scheme has.

4.   Evaluation

This section first reports the identified seminal behaviors and their effectiveness in predicting other behaviors, and then examines the potential of the prediction for performance improvement through profile-directed-feedback (PDF) compilation by the IBM XL compiler. (Section 2.2.1 has described the platforms and programs we use.)

Seminal Behaviors and Prediction Accuracy   Table 2 reports the accuracy of seminal-behavior–based behavior prediction. The data in the table are organized in four sections. The first (leftmost) section corresponds to the case when only the interface behaviors are taken as seminal behaviors, the second and third sections correspond to the cases when the seminal behavior sets also include the other affinity headers (all are loop trip-counts) whose earlinesses are over 90% and 80%, respectively. The rightmost section corresponds to the case when the headers of all affinity lists are included in seminal behavior sets.

In each section, the column "num" lists the sizes of the seminal behavior sets, and the other columns show the average accuracy when we use the seminal behaviors to predict each of the five types of behaviors. The standard 10-fold cross-validation [9] is used so that each time the testing and training data have no overlap.

We first discuss the overall average. With just interface values, the loop and data behaviors can be predicted with an over 92% accuracy, while the accuracies on the other three types of behaviors are from 69% to 82%. Because the values of all interface behaviors get exposed in the first 1%–3% portion of every execution, this case has very high earliness. When we sacrifice some earliness to allow certain loop behaviors get exposed and used along with the interface values for prediction (the 90% case), the accuracies improve by about 3% for loop trip-counts and data profiles, 7% for function invocations and node profiles, and 10% for edge profiles. However, when more loops are used for prediction, the prediction accuracies increase only a little. For some programs, the accuracies even become worse. The diminishing benefits are due to the well-known *curse of dimensionality* in statistical learning—too many predictors cause overfitting to the models.

We now concentrate on the "earliness ≥ 90%" section in Table 2. All programs show high prediction accuracies on loop trip-counts and data profiles. Several programs show modest accuracies on the other three types of behaviors, mainly because of the large numbers of conditional statements in those programs. An extreme example is *mesa*. Its two largest files are *get.c* and *eval.c*. There are 5 switch-case statements with 1008 cases in *get.c*, and 231 cases and 108 "if" statements in *eval.c*. So many branches make it hard to predict the execution paths to a given node in control flow, which explains the low prediction accuracy of its node profiles. It is consistent with the low correlations between loops and node profiles shown in Table 1.

Not all prediction accuracies are consistent with the correlations in Table 1. For example, *mcf* has very low correlations between loops and node profiles, but shows 90% prediction accuracy for node profiles. This inconsistency is because as mentioned earlier, correlation coefficients cannot capture non-linear relations, whereas the prediction models can. On the other hand, even though *crafty* shows high correlation coefficients between loops and node profiles, the prediction accuracy of node profiles is only 45%. One reason for the inconsistency is that some important loops are missing in the seminal behavior set because their trip-counts get exposed late. When all headers of the affinity lists are used, the accuracy boosts to 61%. Another reason for the modest accuracy is the small number of inputs *crafty* has. More inputs and improved seminal behavior identification can possibly improve the prediction accuracy.

As one of the most complex benchmarks, the program *gcc* is worth a detailed examination. This GNU general-purpose compiler includes hundreds of command-line options, 130 files, 484,930 lines of code. Besides the complexity of its code, its inputs—C programs—are also very difficult to characterize, as shown in previous work [11].

In our work, the seminal behavior identification process marks 48 interface behaviors, from which, four are identified as seminal behaviors because of their strong correlations with loop trip-counts. Among the 7,615 loops of *gcc*, the process constructs 129 affinity

lists with one loop in each list header. The values of 50 out of the 129 headers get exposed in the first 10% portion of each *gcc* execution. After they are added into the seminal behavior set, the prediction accuracy for almost all types of behaviors jumps to over 93% (except 86% for function invocations). Given the complexity of *gcc*, these results offer an especially strong evidence of the feasibility of seminal behaviors for proactive, cross-input adaptive prediction of program behaviors.

As to the overhead, the main time is on the training process, including the identification of seminal behaviors and the construction of predictive models. But since the training happens during offline, the overhead is not critical. The prediction of a behavior using the predictive models takes little time, as it only requires the computation of a linear expression and possibly several conditional checks (for Regression Trees). In our experiments, the prediction of the 7,615 loops of *gcc* takes the longest time, but still finishes within 11 milliseconds. The next section demonstrates the practical usefulness of seminal behaviors in program optimizations.

Potential for Performance Improvement. We examine the potential of seminal behaviors for performance improvement through the PDF (profile-directed-feedback) compilation offered by the IBM XL C compiler.

The default PDF compilation works in two steps. For a given application, the compiler first instruments it (through the option "-qpdf1") and lets users run it on a training input. That run generates a file, containing three sections that correspond to the node, edge, and data profiles mentioned in Section 2.2.1. The compiler then recompiles the application using the profiling results as feedback (through the option "-qpdf2").

To examine the usefulness of seminal behaviors, we let the XL compiler do PDF compilation using those predicted profiles. We compare the performance of the resulting code with that of the static compilation (on the highest optimization level) and the PDF compilation on real profiles. Figure 4 shows the results (average of 5 repetitions; negligible variances observed). Because the speedup of a program varies across inputs, we show the range of speedup, with the performance of static compilation as the baseline, on all inputs in each bar.

It is worth mentioning that unlike the predicted profiles, the real profiles are typically not usable by the compiler in production runs as they are not available until the finish of the execution. So the right bars in Figure 4 essentially show the speedup in the ideal case. The occasional better performance from predicted profiles than that from real profiles is due to the imperfect design of the compiler. It is no surprise given the extreme complexity in compiler construction.

On average, the programs produced by predicted profiles achieve 6%–15% speedup, within 2% distance from the speedup real profiles can bring (the right bars). The up to 14% speedup of GCC specially demonstrates the potential of seminal behaviors for input characterization.

5. Discussions

Seminal-behavior-based prediction may occasionally exhibit low accuracies. It would be desirable to prevent such predictions from negative affecting program optimizations. One option is to check the prediction accuracy by observing the behaviors exposed during an execution and either correct or disable the predictions for other behaviors accordingly. The other option is to adopt the discriminative scheme [13], which assesses the predictive capability of a seminal behavior set through history runs and use the set for prediction only if its assessment result passes some confidence threshold.

We note that proactive behavior prediction complements rather than conflicts with reactive prediction and program phase detections. Program phases can be treated as a special kind of behaviors

Table 2. Numbers of Seminal Behaviors and Prediction Accuracies

Prog	interface values						earliness ≥ 90%						earliness ≥ 80%						all headers					
	num	accuracy					num	accuracy					num	accuracy					num	accuracy				
		loop	call	edge	node	data		loop	call	edge	node	data		loop	call	edge	node	data		loop	call	edge	node	data
ammp	1	99.5	96.7	100	91.1	99.7	1	99.5	96.7	100	91.1	99.7	1	99.5	96.7	100	91.1	99.7	1	99.5	96.7	100	91.1	99.7
art	4	91.0	96.8	100	82.0	96.8	4	91.1	96.8	100	80.0	96.1	4	89.7	93.4	100	80.1	96.2	5	90.4	88.1	100	85.2	96.3
crafty	1	89.9	58.9	88.2	35.5	76.0	2	91.1	63.0	90.8	44.5	79.3	4	93.0	70.8	90.5	58.2	84.7	6	93.6	72.6	89.7	61.3	85.6
equake	1	98.0	100	100	96.3	99.3	1	98.0	100	100	96.3	99.3	1	98.0	100	100	96.3	99.3	1	98.0	100	100	96.3	99.3
gap	2	97.5	44.9	11.9	44.2	76.6	7	99.5	78.7	56.3	69.7	88.5	8	99.6	79.7	59.0	71.6	89.2	8	99.6	79.7	59.0	71.6	89.2
gcc	4	82.9	38.9	56.2	61.0	78.5	54	97.0	86.1	93.6	95.4	95.6	92	99.2	94.9	98.8	100	99.1	133	99.3	94.9	97.8	100	99.4
gzip	3	92.2	87.0	84.1	67.5	94.5	6	91.6	87.6	83.5	69.0	94.5	6	91.6	87.6	83.5	69.0	94.5	6	91.6	87.6	83.5	69.0	94.5
h264ref	3	99.8	99.8	98.7	98.8	99.8	4	99.8	99.7	97.0	97.8	99.7	4	99.8	99.7	97.0	97.8	99.7	5	99.8	99.5	98.0	97.9	99.7
lbm	3	99.8	90.1	100	100	100	3	99.8	90.1	100	100	100	3	99.8	90.1	100	100	100	3	99.8	90.1	100	100	100
mcf	5	87.3	87.7	100	92.2	97.8	10	92.2	91.0	100	89.5	97.5	10	92.2	91.0	100	89.5	97.5	10	92.2	91.0	100	89.5	97.5
mesa	1	100	100	99.5	12.2	100	1	100	100	99.5	12.2	100	1	100	100	99.5	12.2	100	1	100	100	99.5	12.2	100
milc	2	79.2	72.1	37.1	27.4	93.9	18	83.0	72.8	100	52.0	99.7	21	78.1	66.8	100	52.1	99.7	21	78.1	66.8	100	52.1	99.7
parser	1	90.2	85.4	73.8	75.9	87.6	2	91.8	88.0	79.2	78.0	90.8	18	94.0	87.8	79.5	81.9	91.0	23	93.4	86.1	79.3	79.5	88.9
vpr	3	93.3	95.1	60.4	81.9	94.6	9	95.2	95.5	64.0	82.2	95.8	9	95.2	95.5	64.0	82.2	95.8	10	95.1	95.1	65.4	82.2	95.7
Average	2.4	92.9	82.4	79.3	69.0	92.5	8.7	95.0	89.0	90.3	75.5	95.5	13.0	95.0	89.6	90.8	77.3	96.2	16.6	95.0	89.2	90.9	77.7	96.1

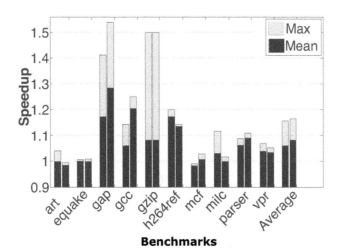

Figure 4. Speedups from profile-directed-feedback compilation using predicted profiles (left bars), and real profiles (right bars). The baseline is the performance by IBM XL compiler with the highest optimization level.

to be modeled and predicted by the framework. A system with both proactive and reactive schemes may predict large-scope behaviors early, and meanwhile, adapt to program or environment changes quickly.

6. Related Work

This work makes the following main contributions: the uncovering of the strong correlations among the behaviors of different program components and among different types of program behaviors, and the introduction of seminal behaviors and the uses of them for cross-input proactive prediction of large-scope program behaviors. This section summarizes the previous studies related to each of them.

Correlations between Program Components We are not aware of any prior studies on systematically exploring and exploiting statistical correlations between the behaviors of different program components. Previous explorations on the connections between program components mainly concentrate on static analysis [1, 2], including data-flow analysis, symbolic analysis, and so on. The connections revealed in those analyses typically have a limited scope, because of the difficulties in pointer analysis and alias analysis.

Correlations between Different Types of Behaviors Previous studies (e.g., [3, 14]) have observed strong correlations between program control flow signatures and hardware-level performance (instructions per cycle, branch miss rates, cache misses, etc.). Our work shows that strong correlations also exist between different types of *program-level* behaviors. The correlations observed in previous work are mainly used for performance prediction and phase detection. The correlations revealed in this current work are important for guiding program optimizations.

Seminal Behaviors for Cross-Input Adaptation Seminal behavior is a new concept introduced in this work. It allows the proactive prediction of a large scope of behaviors, while also supporting cross-input adaptation.

Previous work in cross-input adaptation mainly falls into two categories. The first category treats program inputs explicitly; those studies manually specify a set of input features that are important for the execution of the application, and then use search or machine learning techniques to derive a model to help the execution of the application adapt to those features in an arbitrary input. Examples include the parametric analysis for computation offloading [16], machine learning-based compilation [11], adaptive sorting [12]. Because of the required manual efforts, those explorations have been focused on some particular applications. A recent work [13] proposes the use of specification languages for alleviating the efforts for general programs, but it still needs certain manual specifications. Seminal behaviors offer a way to automatic cross-input adaptation.

The second category of prior work includes the large body of runtime adaptive optimizations (e.g., [4, 6, 7, 10, 15, 17]). These techniques deal with input-sensitive behaviors implicitly through runtime sampling-based reactive behavior prediction. In contrast, seminal behaviors offer proactive predictions. The comparison has been discussed in Section 1.

7. Conclusion

In this paper, we have described a systematic exploration on the correlations among program-level behaviors, and introduced the concept of seminal behaviors for program behavior prediction. By employing a set of statistical learning techniques, we empirically demonstrate the existence of seminal behaviors for a variety of benchmarks. We evaluate the effectiveness of seminal behaviors in predicting a set of other kinds of program behaviors on both code and data levels. The results suggest that seminal behaviors are promising in automating input-based behavior prediction, offering new opportunities for the advancement of dynamic program optimizations.

Acknowledgments

We owe the anonymous reviewers our gratitude for their helpful comments on the paper. This material is based upon work supported by the National Science Foundation under Grant No. 0720499 and 0811791 and IBM CAS Fellowship. Any opinions, findings, and conclusions or recommendations expressed in this material are those of the authors and do not necessarily reflect the views of the National Science Foundation or IBM Corporation.

References

[1] A. V. Aho, M. S. Lam, R. Sethi, and J. D. Ullman. *Compilers: Principles, Techniques, and Tools*. Addison Wesley, 2nd edition, August 2006.

[2] R. Allen and K. Kennedy. *Optimizing Compilers for Modern Architectures: A Dependence-based Approach*. Morgan Kaufmann Publishers, 2001.

[3] M. Annavaram, R. Rakvic, M. Polito, J. Bouguet, R. Hankins, and B. Davies. The fuzzy correlation between code and performance predictability. In *Proceedings of the 37th Annual IEEE/ACM International Symposium on Microarchitecture*, pages 407–420, 2004.

[4] M. Arnold, S. Fink, D. Grove, M. Hind, and P.F. Sweeney. Adaptive optimization in the Jalapeno JVM. In *Proceedings of ACM SIGPLAN Conference on Object-Oriented Programming Systems, Languages and Applications*, Minneapolis, MN, October 2000.

[5] M. Arnold, A. Welc, and V.T. Rajan. Improving virtual machine performance using a cross-run profile repository. In *the Conference on Object-Oriented Systems, Languages, and Applications*, 2005.

[Berube et al.] P. Berube and J. N. Amaral. Additional inputs for SPEC CPU2000. http://www.cs.ualberta.ca/Ёberube/compiler/fdo/inputs.shtml.

[6] W. Chen, S. Bhansali, T. M. Chilimbi, X. Gao, and W. Chuang. Profile-guided proactive garbage collection for locality optimization. In *Proceedings of PLDI*, 2006.

[7] B. Childers, J. Davidson, and M. L. Soffa. Continuous compilation: A new approach to aggressive and adaptive code transformation. In *Proceedings of NSF Next Generation Software Workshop*, 2003.

[8] P. Chuang, H. Chen, G. Hoflehner, D. Lavery, and W. Hsu. Dynamic profile driven code version selection. In *Proceedings of the 11th Annual Workshop on the Interaction between Compilers and Computer Architecture*, 2007.

[9] T. Hastie, R. Tibshirani, and J. Friedman. *The elements of statistical learning*. Springer, 2001.

[10] J. Lau, M. Arnold, M. Hind, and B. Calder. Online performance auditing: Using hot optimizations without getting burned. In *Proceedings of PLDI*, 2006.

[11] H. Leather, E. Bonilla, and M. O'Boyle. Automatic feature generation for machine learning based optimizing compilation. In *Proceedings of the International Symposium on Code Generation and Optimization (CGO)*, 2009.

[12] X. Li, M. J. Garzaran, and D. Padua. A dynamically tuned sorting library. In *Proceedings of the International Symposium on Code Generation and Optimization*, 2004.

[13] F. Mao and X. Shen. Cross-input learning and discriminative prediction in evolvable virtual machine. In *Proceedings of the International Symposium on Code Generation and Optimization (CGO)*, 2009.

[14] T. Sherwood, E. Perelman, G. Hamerly, and B. Calder. Automatically characterizing large scale program behavior. In *Proceedings of International Conference on Architectural Support for Programming Languages and Operating Systems*, pages 45–57, 2002.

[15] M. Voss and R. Eigenmann. High-level adaptive program optimization with ADAPT. In *Proceedings of ACM Symposium on Principles and Practice of Parallel Programming*, pages 93–102, Snowbird, Utah, June 2001.

[16] C. Wang and Z. Li. Parametric analysis for adaptive computation offloading. In *Proceedings of ACM SIGPLAN Conference on Programming Languages Design and Implementation*, pages 119–130, 2004.

[17] R. W. Wisniewski, P. F. Sweeney, K. Sudeep, M. Hauswirth, E. Duesterwald, C. Cascaval, and R. Azimi. Performance and environment monitoring for whole-system characterization and optimization. In *PAC2 Conference on Power/Performance Interaction with Architecture, Circuits, and Compilers*, 2004.

Contention Aware Execution: Online Contention Detection and Response

Jason Mars

University of Virginia
jom5x@cs.virginia.edu

Neil Vachharajani   Robert Hundt

Google, Mountain View, California
{nvachhar, rhundt}@google.com

Mary Lou Soffa

University of Virginia
soffa@cs.virginia.edu

Abstract

Cross-core application interference due to contention for shared on-chip and off-chip resources pose a significant challenge to providing application level quality of service (QoS) guarantees on commodity multicore micro-architectures. Unexpected cross-core interference is especially problematic when considering latency-sensitive applications that are present in the web service data center application domains, such as web-search. The commonly used solution is to simply disallow the co-location of latency-sensitive applications and throughput-oriented batch applications on a single chip, leaving much of the processing capabilities of multicore micro-architectures underutilized. In this work we present a **Contention Aware Execution Runtime (CAER)** environment that provides a lightweight runtime solution that minimizes cross-core interference due to contention, while maximizing utilization. CAER leverages the ubiquitous performance monitoring capabilities present in current multicore processors to infer and respond to contention and requires no added hardware support. We present the design and implementation of the CAER environment, two separate contention detection heuristics, and approaches to respond to contention online. We evaluate our solution using the SPEC2006 benchmark suite. Our experiments show that when allowing co-location with CAER, as opposed to disallowing co-location, we are able to increase the utilization of the multicore CPU by 58% on average. Meanwhile CAER brings the overhead due to allowing co-location from 17% down to just 4% on average.

Categories and Subject Descriptors   D.1.3 [*Programming Techniques*]: Concurrent Programming—parallel programming;   D.3.4 [*Programming Languages*]: Processors—code generation, runtime environments, compilers, optimization; D.4.8 [*Operating Systems*]: Performance—measurements, monitors

General Terms   Performance, Algorithms, Measurement

Keywords   contention, multicore, cross-core interference, dynamic techniques, online adaptation, execution runtimes

1.   Introduction

Multicore architectures are ubiquitous and have become the norm in computing systems today. These architectures dominate in many domains, including those with quality of service (QoS) and low latency requirements. Multicore architectures are composed of a number of processing cores, each with a private cache(s), and typically larger caches that are shared among many cores [13]. Other shared system resources include the bus, main memory, disk, and other I/O devices. When processes and threads are executing in parallel on a single multicore CPU we say they are *co-located*. Co-located processes and threads place varying amounts of demand on these resources; this demand can often lead to *contention* for these resources. Resource contention directly impacts application performance. When an application's performance is negatively affected by another application executing on a separate core, we call this *cross-core interference*.

Application priority and quality of service requirements often cannot withstand unexpected cross-core interference. For example, applications commonly found in the web service data center domain such as search, maps, image search, email and other user facing web applications are *latency-sensitive* [4, 7]. These applications must respond to the user with minimal latency, as having high latency displeases the user. Data centers for web services classify applications as either being *latency-sensitive* or as throughput-oriented *batch* applications, where latency is not important [4]. To avoid cross-core interference between latency-sensitive and batch applications, web service companies simply disallow the co-location of these applications on a single multicore CPU. Using this solution may leave the CPU severely underutilized, and is a contributing reason to the server utilization of these data centers often being 15% or less [18]. Low utilization results in wasted power, and lost cost saving opportunities.

Much research effort has been spent developing QoS and fairness mechanisms [5, 11, 14, 15, 17, 21], simulated approaches for cache resource management [23–25, 27] , and to better understand the algorithmic and theoretical characteristics of cache contention [2, 3, 6, 16]. However to date, there is no readily deployable approach to both minimize cross-core interference due to contention, and maximize utilization, for existing commodity multicore architectures.

In this work we propose such a solution. We present an execution environment, the **Contention Aware Execution Runtime (CAER)** environment, which is capable of online contention detection and response on current commodity hardware. The insight and opportunity that drives the design of CAER comes from the ubiquitous availability of performance monitoring capabilities in today's hardware. These performance monitors are capable of collecting information about dynamic application behavior in hardware without added overhead to the application. In this work we exploit the available performance information to gain information about cross-core interference due to application contention. Using this information we are able to detect and respond to this cross-core interference.

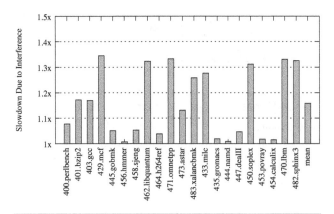

Figure 1. Performance degradation due to contention for shared last level cache on Core i7 (Nehalem) while running alongside lbm.

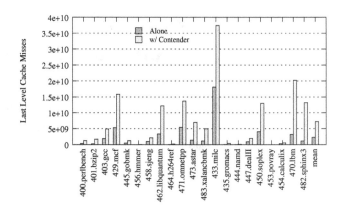

Figure 2. Increase in last level cache misses when running with contender.

CAER is composed of a lightweight runtime on which all applications of interest run. This runtime classifies these applications into the *latency-sensitive* and *batch* categories mentioned earlier. CAER dynamically probes the hardware *performance monitoring unit* (PMU) to collect information about the applications it hosts. This information is continually collected and analyzed throughout the lifetime of all applications running on CAER.

We have designed and evaluated two contention detection heuristics: **Burst Shutter**, and **Rule Based** techniques. These two heuristics are used by CAER to detect contention online. When contention is detected, CAER dynamically adapts the batch applications to minimize the contention. In our current prototype, we adapt by throttling down the execution of the batch applications to relieve the pressure on the contended resource. If no/low contention is detected, CAER allows the application to run more aggressively to maximize utilization.

To evaluate our approach we developed a working prototype of CAER including implementations of the two contention detection and response heuristics, and deployed CAER on current multicore architecture. Using the SPEC2006 benchmark suite we co-located multiple instances of different benchmarks simultaneously executing on a Intel Core i7 (Nehalem) Quad Core machine. Allowing co-location with CAER, as opposed to disallowing co-location, we are able to increase the utilization of the multicore CPU by 58% on average. Meanwhile CAER brings the overhead due to allowing co-location from 17% down to just 4% on average.

The contributions of this work include:

- A framework and runtime environment that addresses the problem of cross-core interference that can be deployed on current multicore architecture.

- The design and analysis of two online contention detection heuristics, their algorithms, and an evaluation of each.

- A thorough evaluation of the CAER runtime system on commodity hardware with the SPEC2006 benchmark suite.

Next in Section 2 we explore the problem of cross-core interference and motivate our work. We then discuss the design and architecture of CAER in Section 3. In Section 4 we describe the design of our two online contention detection heuristics and discuss responses to detection in Section 5. We describe our experimental setup and present results in Section 6, present related work in Section 7, and finally conclude in Section 8.

2. Problem and Motivation

Current multicore chip design in commodity hardware is composed of unshared and shared caches. For example, Intel's Core 2 Duo architecture has 2 cores, each with a private L1 cache and a single L2 of 4mb shared between the two cores. Intel's new Core i7 (Nehalem) architecture has 4 cores, each with private L1 and L2 caches and a single 8mb shared L3 cache for all 4 cores [13]. These types of shared memory multicore architectures are common in the data center space. When the workload of the individual application processes and threads executing on these multicore processors fits neatly into private caches, there is no cross-core interference (assuming coherence traffic is at a minimum). When the size of an application's working set exceeds the size of the private cache, the working set spills over into the larger shared caches. The shared last level cache presents the first level of possible contention. Contention can also exist later in the memory subsystem such as contention on the bus, in the memory controller, for shared memory, disk, etc. However much of the contention in these levels manifest themselves as traffic off-chip and thus show up as misses in the last level cache on the chip.

In this work, our strategy is to monitor activity in the last level of cache to detect contention and focus on minimizing contention in this level of the cache. When more than one application is using the shared last level of cache heavily, and the data is not shared, contention occurs. One way to address this problem is to increase the size and associativity of the cache. However, although cache sizes have been increasing with every generation of processors, we are still far behind the demands of today's application workloads. Figure 1 shows the degradation in performance of a set of applications due to cross-core interference caused by cache contention. This experiment was run on a state of the art general purpose processor (Intel Core i7 920 Quad Core), and demonstrates the impact of just two applications contending on a multicore chip for a large 8mb, 16way associative, shared, last level cache. The applications shown come from the SPEC2006 benchmark suite. Each application was first run alone on the quad core chip, then with the lbm benchmark running alongside on a neighboring core. The bars in Figure 1 shows the slowdown of each benchmark running alongside lbm. Lbm is an example of an application with aggressive cache usage. An application that is more affected by lbm implies that that application is also aggressive with its cache usage. Remember this data shows just two applications running on a quad core machine with a large cache designed to handle the load from four cores simultaneously doing work. In many cases we see a performance degradation exceeding 30%.

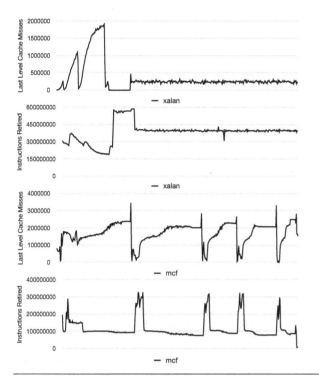

Figure 3. Correlating last level shared cache misses, and reduction in instruction retirement rate.

Figure 2 shows the increase in last level cache misses when running with a contender. It is important to notice the delta in cache misses between the application running alone and when it is running with the contender. It is also important to get a sense of the absolute number of misses for each and how that impacts its sensitivity to contention. Having a 150% increase in cache misses impacts performance much less as the absolute number of misses goes down. From this graph it is clear that the more last level cache misses an application experiences, the more sensitive it is to cross-core interference.

For the remainder of this work we define *utilization* of a multi-core processor as

$$U = \frac{\sum_{i=1}^{N} \frac{R_i}{R_i + I_i}}{N} \quad (1)$$

for some time, where N is the number of cores on the chip, R_i is the amount of time spent running on core i, and I_i is the amount of time idle on core i.

3. A Solution with CAER

Our goal is to address the contention in the shared caches of current multicore chip design by minimizing the cross-core interference penalty on latency-sensitive applications while maximizing chip utilization. To do so we have developed CAER, a *contention aware execution runtime* environment.

3.1 Inferring Contention

Hardware performance monitoring capabilities are ubiquitous in today's chip micro-architectures [13]. These hardware performance monitors provide realtime micro-architectural information about the applications currently running on chip. As the counters record this information, the program executes uninterrupted, and thus recording this online profiling information presents no instrumentation overhead. These capabilities enable new opportunities for

online and reactive approaches, and can be leveraged with one of the many software APIs, such as PAPI [19] or Perfmon2 [9]. To build our solution, we use Perfmon2 as it is one of the most robust and flexible PMU interfaces, and supports a wide range of micro-architectures.

The basic premise of our solution is that information from PMUs can be used in a low/no overhead way to infer contention. In this work we focus on the shared last level cache (LLC) miss behavior. Last level cache misses directly (and negatively) impact the instruction retirement rate (i.e. IPC). Figure 3 illustrates this phenomenon with two SPEC2006 benchmarks that exhibit clear LLC miss phases. These benchmarks were run on their `ref` inputs to completion. The x-axis represents time from beginning of the application run to the end in all four of the graphs presented. Figure 3 shows two pairs of graphs, each pair correlating the LLC miss rate over time to the instruction retirement rate over time. We can see clear and compelling evidence of the inverse relationship between the number of LLC misses and the retirement rate.

CAER is based on the hypothesis that if two or more applications are simultaneously missing heavily in the last level shared cache of the micro architecture, they are both making heavy usage of the cache and probably evicting each others data (i.e. contending). This contention then leads to increased cache misses in both applications, which is evident in Figure 2. We believe that if we can dynamically monitor and analyze the chip wide information about thread/core specific impact on the last level cache misses we should be able to detect contention and thusly respond to this contention.

3.2 Architecture of CAER

The design and architecture of the CAER execution environment is presented in Figure 4. To the left of the diagram we present the overall design vision of the CAER environment, and to the right we present the actual working prototype we have implemented for this study. In the scenario presented on the left of the diagram we have two latency-sensitive applications or threads, and two batch applications or threads. In order to monitor and collect thread/core specific performance information on current hardware, we must issue the performance monitoring unit (PMU) configuration and collection directives on the particular core hosting the application of interest. For this reason a virtual layer must be present beneath all application threads of interest. These CAER virtual layers are cooperative and must share information, respond, and adapt to each other.

CAER's cooperation is accomplished via shared memory using a communication table as is shown in Figure 4 (arrows pointing into the table). Notice that the virtual layer (CAER M) beneath the latency-sensitive applications appear thinner in Figure 4. These (monitor) virtual layers are more light weight than the main CAER engines and only are responsible for collecting PMU data and placing this data in the communication table. The main CAER engines that lie underneath the throughput-oriented batch applications processes this information and perform the contention detection and response heuristics. CAER only applies any dynamic adaption or modifications on the batch application. The latency applications always remain untouched.

The CAER runtime employs a *periodic probing* approach [20], meaning information is gathered and analyzed by the virtual layer intermittently. Using a timer interrupt the environment periodically reads and restarts the PMU counters. Periodic probing has shown to be an extremely low overhead approach to perform lightweight online application monitoring.

In this work the CAER runtime uses a period of one millisecond. Every millisecond each CAER runtime probes their relevant performance monitoring units and reports last level cache information to the communication table. This table records a window of

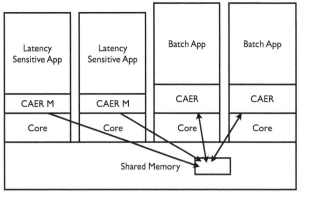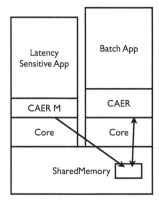

Figure 4. Architecture of our Contention Aware Execution Runtime

sample points, which allows us to observe trends of many samples. The main CAER engines that lie under the batch processes detect and react to contention. Note that all of the batch processes/threads must react together. Reaction directives are also recorded in the table, and all batch processes must adhere to the reaction directives. In the current design of CAER, these directive include pausing and staggering execution.

Our prototype is shown to the right of Figure 4. This instance of CAER supports two applications, one running atop CAER M, and the other on the main CAER engine. The CAER runtime is statically linked into the binary. Our prototype is fully functional and, as it is shown in Section 6, effective on real commodity hardware.

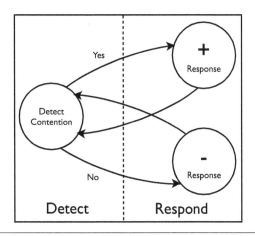

Figure 5. Basic Detection Response

The diagram in Figure 5 shows the contention detection and response phases used in the CAER runtime that lies under the batch applications. Throughout execution CAER resides in one of these states and continually transitions among these states. After CAER performs its contention detection heuristic, either contention, or the absence of contention is asserted, and we enter into the relevant response state as shown with the `yes` and `no` transitions in Figure 5. We call the state where contention is asserted the *c-positive* response, and the state where the absence contention is detected the *c-negative* response. The next section explores the heuristics and methods by which we detect contention corresponding to the

left side of Figure 5, and the subsequent section explores CAER's contention responses corresponding to the right side.

4. Detecting Contention with CAER

Before CAER can react to contention in the shared cache, it must first detect that the applications are indeed contending. We have developed two heuristics for this task: a *burst shutter* approach and a *rule based* approach. These heuristics run continuously throughout the lifetime of CAER to detect and respond to contention.

4.1 Burst-Shutter Approach

If our batch application's execution is going to increase the last level cache misses in the neighboring latency-sensitive application, we should be able to see that spike in misses when the batch application has a burst of execution. That is, if the latency-sensitive application is running alone while the batch application is halted, when the batch application then has a burst of execution, we should see a sharp increase in the last level cache misses of the latency-sensitive application. We perform this analysis online as follows:

1. We have a number of periods where we halt the execution of the batch application and collect samples of the last level cache misses of the latency-sensitive application.

2. We then record the average last level cache miss rate.

3. We then have a number of periods where we execute the batch at full force (i.e. burst) and record the misses of the latency-sensitive application.

4. We calculate the average miss rate for these periods.

5. If the number of cache misses are significantly higher in the burst case, we assert the batch application is impacting the miss rate of the latency-sensitive application and report contention, else we report no contention.

The corresponding algorithm is presented in Algorithm 1. There are a number of parameters that can be tuned. We must determine how long (as in how many periods) we would like to halt the batch process's execution, how long the burst should last, and how high the sharp increase should be before asserting contention. In Algorithm 1 these parameters correspond to setting the `switch_point`, `end_point` and `impact_factor`.

4.2 Rule-Based Approach

Our rule based approach is more closely based on the premise of our hypothesis. Remember our hypothesis is that if two or more

260

Algorithm 1: CAER Shutter Burst Algorithm

Description: This main loop is executed throughout the lifetime of the host application. (pause_self is used to signal whether to pause execution for the next period)

$count \leftarrow 0$;
while *application running* **do**
    update l_window with llc_misses;
    update r_window with $neighbors\_llc\_misses$;
    $count$++;
    $pause\_self \leftarrow true$;
    if $count$ equals $switch\_point$ **then**
        foreach e in r_window until $switch\_point$ **do**
            $steady\_average \leftarrow steady\_average +$
            $(e/(\text{Size}(r\_window) - switch\_point))$
        end
        $pause\_self \leftarrow false$;
    end
    if $(count > switch\_point)$ and $(count < end\_point)$ **then**
        $pause\_self \leftarrow false$;
    end
    if $count$ equals end_point **then**
        foreach e in r_window from $switch\_point$ to end_point **do**
            $burst\_average \leftarrow$
            $burst\_average + (e/(end\_point - switch\_point))$
        end
        if $((burst\_average - steady\_average) >$
        $noise\_thresh)$ and $(burst\_average >$
        $(steady\_average * (1 + impact\_factor)))$ **then**
            $contending \leftarrow true$;
        end
        else
            $contending \leftarrow false$;
        end
    end
end

Algorithm 2: CAER Rule Based Algorithm

while *application running* **do**
    update l_window with llc_misses;
    update r_window with $neighbors\_llc\_misses$;
    $contending \leftarrow true$;
    foreach e in l_window **do**
        $average \leftarrow average + (e/\text{Size}(l\_window))$
    end
    if $average < usage\_thresh$ **then**
        $contending \leftarrow false$
    end
    $average \leftarrow 0$;
    foreach e in r_window **do**
        $average \leftarrow average + (e/\text{Size}(r\_window))$
    end
    if $average < usage\_thresh$ **then**
        $contending \leftarrow false$
    end
end

---

running average of the last level cache miss windows for both the latency-sensitive, and batch applications. When this average for either application dips below a particular threshold, we assert that we are not contending, otherwise we report contention. Algorithm 2 presents the corresponding algorithm. In this heuristic the parameters include the size of the window and defining what missing heavily means. In the algorithm these correspond to `window` and `usage_thresh`.

5. Responding to Contention with CAER

As Figure 5 shows, after detecting contention we transition into one of the response states, either *c-negative* or *c-positive*. In these states the CAER runtime environment can respond by dynamically modifying and adapting the batch application under which it runs. In this work CAER reacts to contention by enforcing a fine grained throttling of the execution of the batch application to relieve pressure in the shared cache.

Our CAER runtime environment currently employs two throttling based dynamic contention response mechanisms: a *red-light green-light* approach, and a *soft locking* approach. Our red-light green-light approach, as the name implies stops or allows execution for a fixed or adaptive number of periods, based on the outcome of our contention detection phase. The red-light part of this response technique correlates to the c-positive result, the green-light correlates to the c-negative result. An adaptive approach can be applied, increasing the length if the detection phase is consistently producing the same result. In our CAER runtime environment we use this *red-light green-light* response with our burst shutter approach.

Our soft locking response technique applies a *soft lock* on the shared last level cache until the cache is no longer being used heavily by the latency-sensitive application. The amount of pressure placed on the cache by the latency-sensitive application is measured using the same performance monitoring information used for the contention detection phase. The batch application is allowed to fully resume execution when the pressure on the cache subsides. In our CAER runtime environment we use this response technique with our rule based approach.

6. Evaluation

The goals of this work is to provide a contention aware execution runtime environment that can dynamically detect and respond to contention on today's commodity multicore processors. We aim to minimize the cross-core interference penalty (overhead of the latency-sensitive application due to contention) and maximize the utilization of the chip. We demonstrate the effectiveness of our CAER environment by showing a considerable reduction in this cross-core interference penalty when allowing co-location, while achieving a significant increase of chip utilization compared to disallowing co-location.

6.1 Experimental Design

Our CAER prototype supports two applications, one deemed latency-sensitive and the other a throughput-oriented batch application. We use the SPEC2006 benchmark (C/C++ only) and run all programs to completion using their reference inputs. We use the Intel Core i7 (Nehalem) 920 Quad Core architecture to perform our experimentation. This processor has three levels of cache, the first two private to each core, the third shared across all cores. The sizes of the L1 and L2 caches are 16kb and 256kb respectively. The L3 cache is 8mb and inclusive to the L1 and L2. The system used has 4gb of main memory, and runs Linux 2.6.29.

In the experiments shown here, the `lbm` benchmark served as our batch application and was co-located on a neighboring core. The main benchmark is assumed to be the latency-sensitive appli-

applications are simultaneously missing heavily in the last level shared cache of the micro architecture, they are both making heavy usage of the cache and probably evicting each others data (i.e. contending). The rule based heuristic tries to test this directly. The basic intuition says, if the latency-sensitive application is not missing in the cache heavily, it is probably not suffering from cache contention, and also if the batch application is not missing heavily in the cache, it is probably not using or at least not contending in the cache very much. This heuristic works by maintaining a

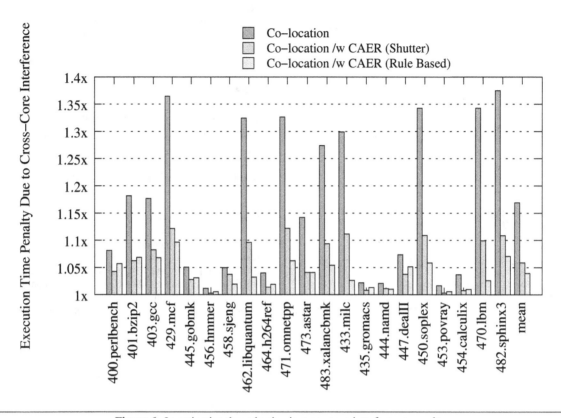

Figure 6. Investigating the reduction in cross-core interference penalty.

cation. Lbm was chosen as our batch application because it presents an interesting adversary as it makes heavy usage of the L3 cache. We have performed complete runs using other benchmarks such as libquantum and milc and produced very similar results. Note that adversaries that make light usage of the L3 cache present more trivial scenarios; contention occurs when two or more applications are making heavy usage of the last level cache. As presented shortly, our experimentation covers cases where the latency-sensitive application make both light and heavy usage of the shared cache.

We have scripted our SPEC runs to launch the latency-sensitive application shortly after the batch is launched. As our applications run, CAER logs the decisions it makes and wall clock execution time of our latency-sensitive application running on CAER M. In the few cases the lbm (batch) benchmark completes before the latency-sensitive we automatically and immediately relaunch it and aggregate logs.

6.2 Minimizing Contention and Maximizing Utilization

First we evaluate the reduction in cross-core interference penalty due to contention when running on our CAER environment. In Figure 6 we show the slowdown in execution time due to contention when we co-locate the latency-sensitive and batch applications. The first bars show the cross-core interference penalty when co-locating the native applications directly on multicore chip. The second bars shows the cross-core interference penalty when co-locating the native applications on CAER with the *burst shutter* heuristic. The last bars show this co-location on CAER with the *rule based* approach.

As Figure 6 shows we significantly reduce the cross-core interference penalty for the wide range of SPEC2006 benchmarks.

Our *burst shutter* contention detection technique uses the *red-light green-light* response with a response length of 10 periods. The impact threshold in Algorithm 1 for the burst shutter detection is set to 5%, meaning if the batch application burst causes a spike of 5% or more in last level cache misses of the latency-sensitive application we assert contention. Using this approach CAER brings the overhead due to contention from 17% down to 6% on average, while gaining close to 60% more utilization of the processor over running the latency-sensitive application alone, which can be seen in Figure 7.

Our *rule based* contention detection technique uses the *soft locking* response and the usage threshold found in Algorithm 2 is set to 1500, meaning we have to see an average of 1500 or more last level cache misses per period (1 ms) to assert heavy usage of the cache. Using this approach CAER brings the overhead due to contention from 17% down to 4% on average, while gaining 58% more utilization of the processor over running the latency-sensitive application alone, as show in Figure 7.

Our *rule based* CAER contention detection approach slightly outperforms our *shutter based* approach on average. However the *shutter based* approach has some desirable characteristics. The *burst shutter* approach is highly tunable to the QoS requirements of the application. The impact threshold determines how much cross-core interference the latency application is willing to withstand; this provides a "knob" which intuitively sets the sensitivity of detection. Here we use "sensitivity" to mean the amount of impact needed to trigger a *c-positive* response. Although the *rule based* approach is also tunable as to how conservative or liberal the definition of "heavy usage" of the cache is, it provides a less intuitive abstraction. As the goal of this evaluation is to demonstrate the ef-

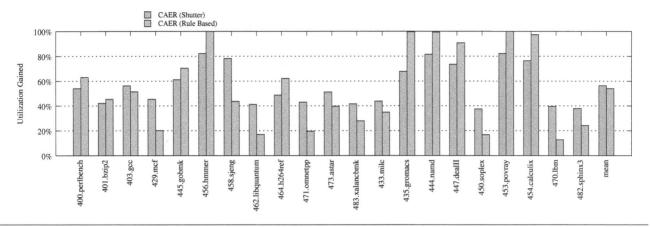

Figure 7. Maximizing Utilization (Higher is Better)

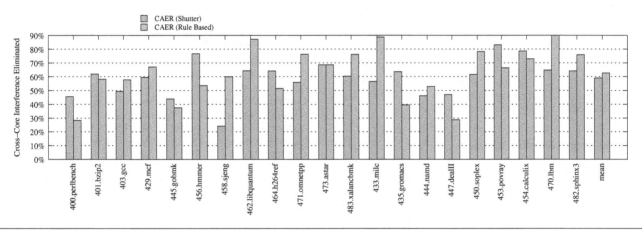

Figure 8. Minimizing Cross-Core Interference (Slowdown Eliminated, Higher is Better)

fectiveness of our CAER runtime environment and its applicability to current multicore architecture, we reserve further investigation of the heuristic tuning space for future work.

Figures 7 and 8 further illustrate CAER's effectiveness. As mentioned before, Figure 7 shows the utilization gained on the multicore processor when co-locating the latency-sensitive and batch applications using CAER. Figure 8 is another way to represent the decrease in cross-core interference penalty shown in Figure 6, showing the percentage of the cross-core interference penalty eliminated. For both of these Figures, higher is better. Running the latency-sensitive application alone will provide 100% cross-core interference elimination but 0% utilization gained. Running the applications together will provide 0% cross-core interference elimination but will have 100% utilization gained. Our goal is to maximize both while running both application on our CAER framework. It is important to note that utilization gained and cross-core interference eliminated are two separate units of measurement, so 50% cross-core interference eliminated for 50% more utilization can be a great result depending on the *cross-core interference sensitivity* of the latency-sensitive application. We explore *cross-core interference sensitivity* in the following section.

6.3 Understanding and Adapting to Cross-Core Interference Sensitivity

The amount of performance impact an application can experience due to contention for shared resources differs from application to

application. We call this application characteristic its *cross-core interference sensitivity*. This characteristic can also be determined by the amount of reliance an application puts on a shared resource. Applications whose working set fits in its core-specific private caches are *cross-core interference insensitive*. Applications whose working set uses shared cache, memory, etc, are *cross-core interference sensitive*.

When performing contention detection and response the handling of cross-core interference insensitive and cross-core interference sensitive applications should be different. More concretely, the amount of utilization that is sacrificed to reduce contention of a cross-core interference sensitive application should be higher than the cross-core interference insensitive application. For example, an application a is 50% slower when experiencing contention x, while another application b is 4% slower when contending with x. We say application a is more cross-core interference sensitive than b. To eliminate half of the cross-core interference penalty of a is more valuable than b, meaning the benefit gained, a 20% increase in speed, with a is better than the 1.9% speed up in b. Thus, we should be willing to sacrifice more utilization to eliminate 50% of the cross-core interference penalty for a than b since a is more cross-core interference sensitive.

Lets take mcf as application a and namd as b. As shown previously in Figure 6 mcf suffers a 36% slowdown when contending with lbm, namd only suffers a 2% performance degradation. Clearly mcf is more latency-sensitive than namd, therefor a good

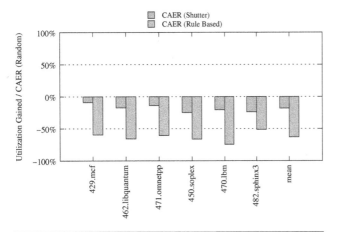

Figure 9. Utilization gained relative to random for 6 most cross-core interference sensitive applications.

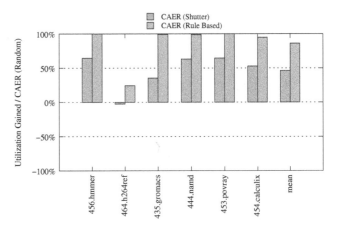

Figure 10. Utilization gained relative to random for 6 least cross-core interference sensitive applications.

contention detection and response approach will be able to detect these different cross-core interference sensitivities and sacrifice more utilization for the former case. CAER does exactly this. For `mcf` CAER *burst shutter* approach sacrifices 36% more utilization to accommodate `mcf`'s cross-core interference penalty, and CAER *rule based* sacrifices 80% more utilization.

6.4 Contention Detection Accuracy

When detecting contention it is possible to have both false positives and false negatives. A false positive occurs when contention is detected where there is none. A false negative occurs when no contention is detected where there is contention. To evaluate a heuristic's ability to accurately detect contention we have developed a baseline random heuristic. This heuristic reports contention with probability P and no contention with probability $1 - P$. In our experiments P equals 0.5. To respond to contention this heuristic uses the *red-light green-light* with a length of 1 period. To illustrate a CAER heuristic's ability to detect contention accurately we use the following

$$A = \frac{U_h}{U_r} - 1 \qquad (2)$$

where U_h is the utilization gained from a heuristic h, and U_r is the utilization gain with the random heuristic. Figures 9 and 10 demonstrates the contention detection accuracy of the *burst shutter* and *rule based* heuristics for the six most, and six least cross-core interference sensitive benchmarks respectively. The y-axis corresponds with the calculation of A from the equation. Figure 9 shows that, for cross-core interference sensitive benchmarks, our CAER heuristics sacrifices more utilization than the random technique, indicating that our detection is correctly responding to these applications as high contenders (i.e. cross-core interference sensitive). Figure 10 shows the opposite for cross-core interference insensitive benchmarks. The heuristics gain much more utilization than the random heuristics, indicating we are correctly responding to these workloads as low contenders.

Also note that any inversion in this response to cross-core interference penalty indicates inaccurate contention detection. Gaining more utilization for a cross-core interference sensitive application than the random heuristic represents a false negative (asserting no contention where there is contention). And contrarily, gaining less utilization for cross-core interference insensitive applications represents a false positive (asserting contention where there is none).

7. Related Work

QoS and Fairness techniques have received much research attention [11, 14, 15, 17, 21–23, 26]. These works propose QoS and fairness models, as well as hardware and platform improvement to enable QoS and fairness be enforced. Rafique et al. investigates micro-architectural extensions to support the OS for cache management [24]. There has been a number of works aimed at better understanding and modeling cache contention [2, 3, 8] and job co-scheduling [6, 10, 16]. Other hardware techniques to enable cache management have also received research attention [5, 12, 25, 27]. Suhendra [27] proposes partitioning and locking mechanisms to minimize unpredictable cache contention. Cache reconfiguration [25] has also been proposed as a mechanism to enable cache partitioning. Although these works show promising future directions for hardware and system designers to take when addressing these problems, unfortunately current commodity micro-architectures cannot support these solutions as they do not meet the micro-architectural assumptions made these works.

Another very promising direction based on what is likely to be future hardware capabilities, is to leverage core specific dynamic voltage scaling as is presented by Herdirch, Illikkal, Iyer, et al [11]. Instead of throttling down the execution of an application, this work proposes throttling down the frequency of the core hosting the batch application. This approach also has the added benefit of being energy efficient.

Hardware performance monitoring capabilities have been used heavily for online and adaptive solutions. Azimi et al. used these capabilities to enhance operating system support for multicore systems [1]. Mars et al. leverage performance monitoring hardware to enable online application adaptation via multiversioning [20].

8. Conclusion

Cross core cross-core interference on current multicore processors pose a significant challenge to providing application level quality of service (QoS) guarantees. This problem is especially prevalent with latency-sensitive applications (such as web-search) in the web services and data center domains. The commonly used solution to this problem is to disallow the co-location of latency-sensitive and batch applications on a single chip. This approach leaves much of the processing capabilities in multicore systems underutilized, and is a contributing factor to the low utilization in today's data centers (typically 15% or less [18]). In this work we have presented the **Contention Aware Execution Runtime (CAER)** environment, the first of its kind to our knowledge. The goals of CAER is to minimize the cross-core interference penalty of application co-location on multicore processors, while maximizing the utilization on the processor. In addition, CAER can be applied on today's commodity hardware.

By allowing co-location with CAER, as opposed to disallowing co-location, we are able to increase the utilization of the multicore CPU by 58% on average. Meanwhile CAER brings the overhead due to allowing co-location from 17% down to just 4% on average. CAER can be used in today's data centers and serve to increase utilization, resulting in savings in energy and cost.

References

[1] R. Azimi, D. K. Tam, L. Soares, and M. Stumm. Enhancing operating system support for multicore processors by using hardware performance monitoring. *SIGOPS Oper. Syst. Rev.*, 43(2):56–65, 2009.

[2] G. E. Blelloch and P. B. Gibbons. Effectively sharing a cache among threads. In *SPAA '04: Proceedings of the sixteenth annual ACM symposium on Parallelism in algorithms and architectures*, pages 235–244, New York, NY, USA, 2004. ACM.

[3] D. Chandra, F. Guo, S. Kim, and Y. Solihin. Predicting inter-thread cache contention on a chip multi-processor architecture. In *HPCA '05: Proceedings of the 11th International Symposium on High-Performance Computer Architecture*, pages 340–351, Washington, DC, USA, 2005. IEEE Computer Society.

[4] F. Chang, J. Dean, S. Ghemawat, W. C. Hsieh, D. A. Wallach, M. Burrows, T. Chandra, A. Fikes, and R. E. Gruber. Bigtable: A distributed storage system for structured data. *ACM Trans. Comput. Syst.*, 26(2):1–26, 2008.

[5] J. Chang and G. S. Sohi. Cooperative cache partitioning for chip multiprocessors. In *ICS '07: Proceedings of the 21st annual international conference on Supercomputing*, pages 242–252, New York, NY, USA, 2007. ACM.

[6] S. Chen, P. B. Gibbons, M. Kozuch, V. Liaskovitis, A. Ailamaki, G. E. Blelloch, B. Falsafi, L. Fix, N. Hardavellas, T. C. Mowry, and C. Wilkerson. Scheduling threads for constructive cache sharing on cmps. In *SPAA '07: Proceedings of the nineteenth annual ACM symposium on Parallel algorithms and architectures*, pages 105–115, New York, NY, USA, 2007. ACM.

[7] L. Cherkasova, Y. Fu, W. Tang, and A. Vahdat. Measuring and characterizing end-to-end internet service performance. *ACM Trans. Internet Technol.*, 3(4):347–391, 2003.

[8] C. Ding and Y. Zhong. Predicting whole-program locality through reuse distance analysis. In *PLDI '03: Proceedings of the ACM SIGPLAN 2003 conference on Programming language design and implementation*, pages 245–257, New York, NY, USA, 2003. ACM.

[9] S. Eranian. Perfmon2. http://perfmon2.sourceforge.net/.

[10] A. Fedorova, M. Seltzer, C. Small, and D. Nussbaum. Performance of multithreaded chip multiprocessors and implications for operating system design. In *ATEC '05: Proceedings of the annual conference on USENIX Annual Technical Conference*, pages 26–26, Berkeley, CA, USA, 2005. USENIX Association.

[11] A. Herdrich, R. Illikkal, R. Iyer, D. Newell, V. Chadha, and J. Moses. Rate-based qos techniques for cache/memory in cmp platforms. In *ICS '09: Proceedings of the 23rd international conference on Supercomputing*, pages 479–488, New York, NY, USA, 2009. ACM.

[12] J. Huh, C. Kim, H. Shafi, L. Zhang, D. Burger, and S. W. Keckler. A nuca substrate for flexible cmp cache sharing. In *ICS '05: Proceedings of the 19th annual international conference on Supercomputing*, pages 31–40, New York, NY, USA, 2005. ACM.

[13] Intel Corporation. *IA-32 Application Developer's Architecture Guide*. Intel Corporation, Santa Clara, CA, USA, 2009.

[14] R. Iyer. Cqos: a framework for enabling qos in shared caches of cmp platforms. In *ICS '04: Proceedings of the 18th annual international conference on Supercomputing*, pages 257–266, New York, NY, USA, 2004. ACM.

[15] R. Iyer, L. Zhao, F. Guo, R. Illikkal, S. Makineni, D. Newell, Y. Solihin, L. Hsu, and S. Reinhardt. Qos policies and architecture for cache/memory in cmp platforms. In *SIGMETRICS '07: Proceedings of the 2007 ACM SIGMETRICS international conference on Measurement and modeling of computer systems*, pages 25–36, New York, NY, USA, 2007. ACM.

[16] Y. Jiang, X. Shen, J. Chen, and R. Tripathi. Analysis and approximation of optimal co-scheduling on chip multiprocessors. In *PACT '08: Proceedings of the 17th international conference on Parallel architectures and compilation techniques*, pages 220–229, New York, NY, USA, 2008. ACM.

[17] S. Kim, D. Chandra, and Y. Solihin. Fair cache sharing and partitioning in a chip multiprocessor architecture. In *PACT '04: Proceedings of the 13th International Conference on Parallel Architectures and Compilation Techniques*, pages 111–122, Washington, DC, USA, 2004. IEEE Computer Society.

[18] S. Lohr. Demand for data puts engineers in spotlight. *The New York Times*, 2008. Published June 17th.

[19] K. London, J. Dongarra, S. Moore, P. Mucci, K. Seymour, and T. Spencer. End-user tools for application performance analysis using hardware counters. In *14th Conference on Parallel and Distributed Computing Systems*, August 2001.

[20] J. Mars and R. Hundt. Scenario based optimization: A framework for statically enabling online optimizations. In *CGO '09: Proceedings of the 2009 International Symposium on Code Generation and Optimization*, pages 169–179, Washington, DC, USA, 2009. IEEE Computer Society.

[21] M. Moreto, F. J. Cazorla, A. Ramirez, R. Sakellariou, and M. Valero. Flexdcp: a qos framework for cmp architectures. *SIGOPS Oper. Syst. Rev.*, 43(2):86–96, 2009.

[22] K. J. Nesbit, N. Aggarwal, J. Laudon, and J. E. Smith. Fair queuing memory systems. In *MICRO 39: Proceedings of the 39th Annual IEEE/ACM International Symposium on Microarchitecture*, pages 208–222, Washington, DC, USA, 2006. IEEE Computer Society.

[23] K. J. Nesbit, J. Laudon, and J. E. Smith. Virtual private caches. In *ISCA '07: Proceedings of the 34th annual international symposium on Computer architecture*, pages 57–68, New York, NY, USA, 2007. ACM.

[24] N. Rafique, W.-T. Lim, and M. Thottethodi. Architectural support for operating system-driven cmp cache management. In *PACT '06: Proceedings of the 15th international conference on Parallel architectures and compilation techniques*, pages 2–12, New York, NY, USA, 2006. ACM.

[25] R. Reddy and P. Petrov. Eliminating inter-process cache interference through cache reconfigurability for real-time and low-power embedded multi-tasking systems. In *CASES '07: Proceedings of the 2007 international conference on Compilers, architecture, and synthesis for embedded systems*, pages 198–207, New York, NY, USA, 2007. ACM.

[26] L. Soares, D. Tam, and M. Stumm. Reducing the harmful effects of last-level cache polluters with an os-level, software-only pollute buffer. In *MICRO '08: Proceedings of the 2008 41st IEEE/ACM International Symposium on Microarchitecture*, pages 258–269, Washington, DC, USA, 2008. IEEE Computer Society.

[27] V. Suhendra and T. Mitra. Exploring locking & partitioning for predictable shared caches on multi-cores. In *DAC '08: Proceedings of the 45th annual Design Automation Conference*, pages 300–303, New York, NY, USA, 2008. ACM.

An Adaptive Task Creation Strategy for Work-Stealing Scheduling

Lei Wang

[1]Institute of Computing Technology,
Chinese Academy of Sciences
[2]Graduate University of Chinese
Academy of Sciences
Beijing, China
wlei@ict.ac.cn

Huimin Cui

[1]Institute of Computing Technology,
Chinese Academy of Sciences
[2]Graduate University of Chinese
Academy of Sciences
Beijing, China
cuihm@ict.ac.cn

Yuelu Duan

Department of Computer Science,
University of Illinois at
Urbana-Champaign
duan11@illinois.edu

Fang Lu

[1]Institute of Computing Technology,
Chinese Academy of Sciences
[2]Graduate University of Chinese
Academy of Sciences
Beijing, China
flv@ict.ac.cn

Xiaobing Feng

Institute of Computing Technology,
Chinese Academy of Sciences
Beijing, China
fxb@ict.ac.cn

Pen-Chung Yew

[1]Department of Computer Science and
Engineering, University of Minnesota,
MN 55455 U.S.A
[2]Institute of Information Science,
Academia Sinica, Taiwan
yew@cs.umn.edu

Abstract

Work-stealing is a key technique in many multi-threading programming languages to get good load balancing. The current work-stealing techniques have a high implementation overhead in some applications and require a large amount of memory space for data copying to assure correctness. They also cannot handle many application programs that have an unbalanced call tree or have no definitive working sets.

In this paper, we propose a new adaptive task creation strategy, called AdaptiveTC, which supports effective work-stealing schemes and also handles the above mentioned problems effectively. As shown in some experimental results, AdaptiveTC runs 2.71x faster than Cilk and 1.72x faster than Tascell for the 16-queen problem with 8 threads.

Categories and Subject Descriptors D.3.3 [*Language Constructs and Features*]: Concurrent programming structures; D.3.4 [*Processors*]: Compilers, Run-time environments

General Terms Design, Languages, Management, Performance

Keywords adaptive, work-stealing, task granularity, backtracking search

1. Introduction

With the wide adoption of multi-threading techniques, many parallel programming languages such as Cilk [4] [10], X10 [5], and OpenMP3.0 [1], have provided their support for task-level parallelism. They define conceptually similar concurrent constructs, that include Cilk's *spawn-sync*, X10's *asyn-finish* and OpenMP3.0's *omp task-taskwait*. In their support, work-stealing is one of the key techniques used in the runtime system to help load balancing. Generally, in work-stealing, each thread maintains a double-ended queue (called *d-e-que*, in this paper) for ready tasks. An owner thread pushes and pops ready tasks to and from its own d-e-que's **tail** end. Each thread steals tasks from the **head** of the d-e-que in other threads when its own d-e-que is empty. Hence, when stealing tasks, the thief thread can run in parallel with the victim thread's execution. A thread could also suspend a waiting task to execute other ready tasks. With this scheme, work-stealing achieves good load balancing [4] [10] [3].

However, there are still problems in the current work-stealing techniques. Firstly, the overhead of task creation and d-e-que management could be very high in some applications. Secondly, in some popular applications such as backtracking search, branch-and-bound search and game trees, the overhead of allocating and copying workspaces for each child task to assure correctness, called *workspace copying* [13], could be quite high, and it could badly hurt the performance. Finally, the d-e-que is often implemented as a fixed-size array in Cilk, which is prone to overflow.

Tascell [13] uses an improved scheduling technique based on backtracking to solve some of these problems. In Tascell, the task is stored in a thread's execution stack instead of in a d-e-que. When a thread receives a task request from an idle thread, it backtracks through the chain of nested function calls, and creates a task for the requesting thread. It then returns to the top frame of its execution stack and resume its own execution. Hence, when responding to a request, the responding thread cannot run in parallel with the request thread. Tascell also delays workspace copying as much as possible. Its copying overhead could thus be significantly reduced, and it could often achieve a higher performance than Cilk in some important applications [13].

However, Tascell still could not achieve good load balancing in some applications. For example, Tascell cannot suspend a waiting task (and has to wait for its child tasks to complete) because it uses its execution stack to store the task information. If a waiting task is suspended and starts to run other ready tasks, the stack frame of the waiting task will be destroyed and cannot be resumed. Taking 16-queens as an example, the waiting time for child tasks could be as high as 16.73% of the total execution time with 8 threads (see section 5.2).

In this paper, we proposed a new adaptive task creation strategy, called AdaptiveTC, to support work-stealing. When executing a *spawn* statement, AdaptiveTC can generate a *task*, a function call (a *fake task*, refer to Section 3), or a *special task*. The *task* is responsible for keeping idle threads busy; the *fake task* is responsible for improving performance; and the *special task* is used to switch a thread from a *fake task* to a *task* for good load balancing. In addition, AdaptiveTC introduces a new data attribute, call *taskprivate*, for *workspace variables* common in applications such as backtracking search, branch-and-bound search and game trees. Allocating and copying a new *taskprivate* variable for a child task is only performed in the *task*, not in the *fake task*. AdaptiveTC can adaptively switch between *tasks* and *fake tasks* to get a better performance.

In AdaptiveTC, a specified number of *tasks* are created initially to keep all threads busy, and then a *fake task* is executed in each thread. During the execution, except when some thread becomes idle, at which point a busy thread generates a *special task* to transition back from the *fake task* to a *task*, each busy thread would avoid creating more *tasks* into its d-e-que. As a result, the number of tasks created is smaller than that of Cilk. Hence, it reduces the overhead of task creation, d-e-que management, and workspace copying, without sacrificing good load balancing, and is less prone to d-e-que overflow. The cost of managing d-e-que in AdaptiveTC is thus much less than that of managing nested functions on the execution stack in Tascell.

Our experiments show that AdaptiveTC outperforms Cilk and Tascell in many common applications. For example, it runs 2.71 times faster than Cilk and 1.72 times faster than Tascell for the 16-queen problem with 8 threads (see section 5.1).

The contributions of this paper are:

- An adaptive task creation strategy is proposed to support work-stealing techniques for better load balancing and lower system implementation overhead. It reduces the number of tasks created with a better control of the task granularities, hence, could significantly reduced the overhead of task creation. It is also less prone to d-e-que overflow. AdaptiveTC is very suitable for many applications that have no definitive working sets, and could achieve a much better load balancing for applications with unbalanced call trees.

- A new data attribute *taskprivate* is introduced for workspace variables to improve the programmability and to further reduce the cost of workspace copying, and thus achieving a higher performance.

The rest of the paper is organized as follows. We first present some related work in Section 2. In Section 3, we introduce our adaptive task creation strategy. In Section 4, we describe the implementation of our approach. Some experimental studies are presented in Section 5, and in Section 6, we conclude our paper.

2. Related work

Cut-off strategies: several prior studies [16] [14] [9] [8] [7] used cut-off strategies to control the recursion depth of function calls during the task generation, and thus could reduce the overhead of task creation. These strategies could also control the task granularities by reducing the number of small tasks. A basic cut-off strategy usually specifies a depth of recursion in a *computation tree* (or *call tree*) beyond which no tasks could be created (see Figure 1.a). It has been found that such strategies work very well for balanced computation trees. However, for unbalanced computation trees, such cut-off strategies are known to cause starvation, i.e. some threads might be forced to become idle for lack of tasks to work on [14].

Three approaches were generally used to implement a cut-off strategy. The first is to ask the programmer to provide a cut-off depth for the recursion [16] [14], or using the runtime system to set a common default depth, for all applications [9]. Both are very simple, but cannot adapt to a changing environment. The second approach is *batching*, i.e. to set the cut-off depth according to the current size of the d-e-que and adaptively control the granularity of parallel tasks [8]. However, this approach needs the programmers to set a sequential processing threshold, and to carry out performance tuning manually. The third approach is *profiling* [7]. It adopts a working set profiling algorithm, and then uses the profiling information to perform cut-offs. It works well for some divide-and-conquer applications in which all parallel tasks deal with different parts of a working set. However, it becomes less effective in some important applications such as backtracking search, branch-and-bound search and game trees, in which there are no definitive working sets during the execution.

The AdaptiveTC can adaptively create tasks to keep all threads busy, and also adaptively control the task granularities to reduce the overhead of task creation.

Workspace copying: This problem is introduced by work-stealing scheduling. In some popular applications such as backtracking search, branch-and-bound search and game trees, solution space variables and states of nodes, such as chessboards and pieces, are all stored in workspaces. In order to assure correctness, programmer needs to allocate memory space, and copy the value of the parent's workspace variables to each child task.

The work proposed in [2] pointed out that workspace variables increase programming difficulties. Workspace variables are usually C arrays or pointers of data structure, if a pointer is used in an OpenMP 3.0's *firstprivate* directive, only the pointer is captured. In order to capture the value of the data structure, the programmer must deal with them inside each task, including proper synchronization, and it could become quite complicated to write such parallel programs. We found that by supporting such workspace variables in a programming language such as providing a special attribute for those workspace variables, it significantly improves the programmability of those applications.

Cilk supports SYNCHED variables to conserve space resources [11]. A SYNCHED variable has a value of 1 if the scheduler can guarantee that there is no stolen child task in the current task and 0 otherwise. By testing the SYNCHED variable, it would allow some child tasks to reuse the same memory space and store their private data so that the *space overhead* could be drastically reduced. However, all child tasks still have to copy the data from their parent tasks, and hence, the *time overhead* is not reduced.

In AdaptiveTC, we propose a new data attribute ***taskprivate*** that works with the controlled task granularities to reduce both space and time overhead, and also improves the programmability as mentioned before.

D-e-que: In [6], it presents a work-stealing d-e-que using a buffer pool that does not have the overflow problem. In [15], it proposes techniques to expand the size of a d-e-que with automatic garbage collection. As AdaptiveTC pushes fewer tasks into d-e-ques, it is less prone to overflow.

Adaptive work-stealing scheduler: SLAW [12] adaptively switches between work-first and help-first scheduling policies, which has the possibility of running parallel programs to completion when the sequential version overflows stack. In contrast, AdaptiveTC adaptively switches between tasks and fake tasks to get a better performance.

3. An adaptive task creation strategy for work-stealing

As mentioned in Section 1, when executing a *spawn* statement, AdaptiveTC can generate a *task*, a function call (a *fake task*), or a *special task*. The *task* is pushed to the d-e-que's *tail* end and can be stolen by idle threads; the *fake task* is only a plain recursive function and is never pushed into the d-e-que; the *special task* is pushed into the *tail* of d-e-que and marks a transition point from the *fake task* back to the *task*. Allocating and copying a new *taskprivate* variable for a child task is only performed in a *task*, not in a *fake task*. AdaptiveTC can adaptively switch between *tasks* and *fake tasks* to get a better performance. In AdaptiveTC, a specified number of tasks are created initially to keep all threads busy. During the execution, except when some thread becomes idle, all busy threads would avoid creating additional tasks into their d-e-ques. A randomized work-stealing algorithm with our adaptive task creation strategy is described in more detail as follows.

If the number of active threads is capped at N, the *cut-off* of a recursive call tree beyond which no tasks should be created, is initially set to $\lceil \log N \rceil$ by the runtime system. The depth of the recursive call chain for the original task is considered to be 0.

At the beginning, all d-e-ques are empty. Then, the root task is placed in one thread's d-e-que, while other threads start work stealing. A thread obtains work by popping the task from the d-e-que's *tail* end, and continues executing this task's instructions until this task spawns, terminates, or reaches a synchronization point, in which case, it performs according to the following rules.

Each active *worker/victim thread* (a *victim thread* is a thread whose tasks in its d-e-que have been stolen by other worker threads) will use the following scheme:

Spawn: (a *spawn* statement, task α spawns a child task β)

1. As shown in Figure 1.a, when the depth of task α (the depth of the recursive call tree) is smaller than the *cut-off*, a thread will push task α into the *tail* of the d-e-que, generate a new task β, and begin to execute task β. If the *cut-off* has been reached, a thread will not push task α into the *tail* of the d-e-que, but continue the main execution of recursive functions down the call tree, called the *fake task* (because no real task was generated for its execution), without creating new tasks, thus will not incur any task creation overhead.

2. However, before the *fake task* continues to execute down the recursive call tree, it will first check whether there is an idle thread waiting to steal tasks. If *not*, no new tasks will be generated; if *yes*, it creates a *special task* for itself to resume, and pushes the *special task* into the *tail* of its d-e-que, and then continues its own execution. The depth of the special task's child will be set to 0. As the depth of the special task's child task is 0, it generates and pushes more child tasks into its own d-e-que later on. Other threads could steal the descendant tasks. The *special task* in the d-e-que marks a transition point from the main fake task to its child tasks. It stores all of the task information of the main fake task, and thus cannot be stolen. It also has to wait for its child tasks to complete before its resumption for execution; otherwise, we will not be able to resume the main fake task when we complete the child tasks.

Terminate: (a *return* statement, task α terminates and returns to its parent task γ)

- The task α is popped from the d-e-que's *tail* end first. If task α is the root task, the schedule ends. Otherwise, a thread checks its d-e-que. (1) If the d-e-que contains any task, the thread will pop a task γ from the d-e-que's *tail* end and begin to execute task γ. (2) If the d-e-que is empty, and task α is spawned by the thread, i.e. the parent task γ is stolen by another thread, the thread will return immediately. (3) If the d-e-que is empty, and task α is stolen by the thread, i.e. the thread returns to the runtime system code, the thread will inform the parent task γ that task α is completed, and check the status of the parent task γ. If the parent task γ is suspended, and all the child nodes of task γ are completed, the thread will begin to execute task γ; otherwise, the thread will begin its work stealing.

Reaching a synchronization point: (a *sync* statement, task α reaches a synchronization point)

- A thread checks whether all the child nodes of task α are completed. If *yes*, it will execute the instruction following the synchronization point in task α. If *no*, (1) if task α is a *task*, the thread will pop task α from the d-e-que's *tail* end, **suspend** task α, and then start stealing other task; (2) if task α is a *special task*, the thread will **wait** for its child tasks to complete before its resumption of execution.

Each *thief thread* will use the following scheme:
Steal: (when a thread begins work stealing)

1. A thread randomly selects a victim thread, and tries to steal task from the victim thread. If it succeeds, the thread will execute the new stolen task; if not, it will inform the victim thread that it needs a task, and try again, picking another victim thread at random. When a thief thread is attempting to steal a *special task*, it will steal the special task's child task instead, if there is any, to avoid the problem mentioned above (i.e. the resumption of the original fake task).

2. The thread executes the new stolen task, restores the task's state first, and then goes to the point after a spawn or synchronization instruction according to the new stolen task's state and executes the task's instructions.

In Figure 1, there are 4 threads (p0, p1, p2, p3) that execute nodes in the *computation tree* (i.e. *call tree*), and the default *cut-off* is 2. Note that not all of the nodes in the tree are generated as tasks by the threads. Figure 1.a illustrates the starting stage, in which each thread executes a sub-tree, respectively, from nodes 2, 41, 7 and 44. During the execution, p3 steals task 0 from p1, and suspends task 0 as neither child task 1 nor 40 is completed. p3 then steals task 40 from p1, and continues to execute node 44 (the second child of task 40), but not node 41 (the first child of task 40), because node 41 was already under execution by p1. Each thread will then execute nodes down its respective sub-tree sequentially.

Then, at the beginning stage of Figure 1.b, p0, p1 and p3 have finished these sub-trees, respectively, from nodes 2, 41 and 44; p2 is executing a certain node in the sub-tree rooted at node 7, and there is only task 1 in p2's d-e-que. When p1 steals task 1 from p2, it suspends task 1 as its child node 7 is not completed yet. There are no tasks to be stolen at this time. As the sub-tree rooted at the node 7 is larger than the other sub-trees, it is very likely that when p2 is executing a node in the sub-tree, say node 12, it could find that some other thread needs a task. As described in worker thread Spawn's step 2, p2 will create a *special task* 12 for node 12, and push it into the *tail* of its d-e-que. p2 will then create a task and push it into the *tail* of d-e-que for nodes 13 and 14 sequentially. In one scenario, p0 would steal task 13 from p2, and p1 would steal task 14 from p2. At this point, as $H >= T$ in the p2's d-e-que, there is no task in the p2's d-e-que to steal. p3 would steal task 13

268

from p0, suspend it as neither child tasks 14 nor 24 is completed, and then steal task 24 from p0 (illustrated in Figure 1.b). Now the threads p0, p1, p2 and p3 execute sub-trees 25, 18, 15 and 30.

Also, as illustrated in Figure 1.c, p2 finishes the sub-tree rooted at node 15 and returns to node 14. As task 14 is stolen by p1, p2 will return to node 13 immediately. Also, because task 13 is stolen as well, p2 will return to node 12 immediately and execute the sub-tree rooted at node 35. In this way, our adaptive task creation strategy only generates 20 tasks, while Cilk generates 49 tasks. Even though, Cilk could use its cut-off strategy to reduce the number of tasks generated, it could be at the risk of creating an unbalanced call tree.

With the same starting stage in Figure 1.a, Tascell would make p0 wait on task 1 for its child task 7's completion after it finishes its own sub-tree rooted at node 2. Thus, only p1, p2 and p3 could expect to execute the sub-tree rooted at node 7. However, as illustrated in Figure 1.b and 1.c, with the strategy of AdaptiveTC, all the four threads could expect to execute the sub-tree rooted at node 7 together, which would achieve better dynamic load balancing than Tascell.

4. AdaptiveTC - A comprehensive parallel programming environment

AdaptiveTC is a comprehensive parallel programming environment that includes a parallel programming language, a compiler and a runtime system. The parallel language is an extended Cilk. The key features of the Cilk language include the inclusion of parallelism and synchronization semantics through the *spawn* and *sync* keywords. AdaptiveTC extends the Cilk language further by providing the **taskprivate** keyword to specify data storage. Our compiler translates the extended Cilk program to a C program that could take advantage of an improved runtime library. The compiler generates five different versions of the code for each task, and these five versions will each generate a *task*, a function call (a *fake task*), or a *special task*. AdaptiveTC uses a finite state machine (FSM) in each thread, and executes a different version of the code depending on the state the thread is in. Transition from one state to another only requires a few concise steps followed by a transition to a different version of the code. This FSM implementation makes it easier to switch a thread from fake tasks to tasks, and then generate more tasks for other threads to steal, while at the same time minimizing the number of tasks stored in the d-e-que and the amount of workspace copying.

4.1 A new data attribute – *taskprivate*

A variable with a *taskprivate* attribute will have **no** storage association with the same named variable in other tasks. A *taskprivate* variable inherits the value of its parent task's *taskprivate* variable. Only parameters or local variables can be declared as *taskprivate*, and *taskprivate* could be declared on a pointer or an array. For example,

taskprivate: (*address) (an expression to calculate the size of the taskprivate variable);

In the n-queens problem, it computes the number of all possible placements for n queens in a chessboard with only one queen in any vertical, horizontal and diagonal line. It is a typical backtracking search problem. The implementation of the problem needs to maintain a chessboard that indicates all current positions of the queens. The chessboard variable can be declared as a *taskprivate* in AdaptiveTC as follows:

// *depth* is the numerical ID of a queen; n is the total number of queens; $x[]$ is the chessboard.

cilk int nqueens(int *depth*, int n, char* x)
taskprivate: (*x) (n * sizeof(char));

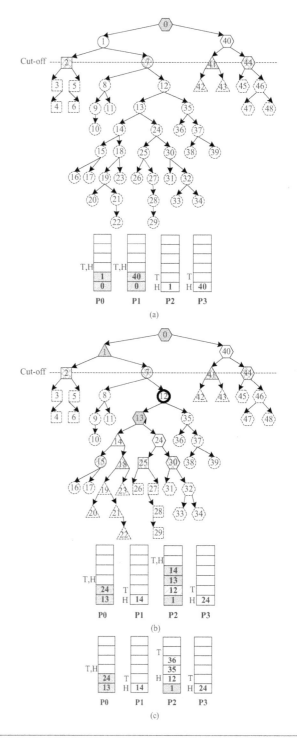

Figure 1. The status of a call tree and d-e-ques in active threads. In the call tree, nodes with a dotted boundary are executed sequentially in a thread and are not created as tasks. Solid boundary nodes are created as tasks, among which the grid-shaded ones are not pushed into d-e-ques and the non-shaded ones are pushed into d-e-ques. The grey ones are suspended. Node 12 is special task. The square nodes are executed in thread p0, the triangle ones are in p1, the circle ones in p2, and the hexagon ones in p3. In the d-e-ques, T indicates the *tail* of the d-e-que, H indicates the *head* of the d-e-que. Figure 1 (a) shows the starting stage. In Figure 1 (b), the special task 12 can be pushed into p2's d-e-que. Figure 1 (c) shows the next stage of Figure 1 (b).

As the chessboard variable could be accessed and modified by multiple tasks concurrently, in Cilk, the programmer needs to allocate memory space, and copy the value of the parent's chessboard variable to each child task in order to assure correctness. There are two ways to do it: one is to use Cilk_alloca() function to allocate a new chessboard variable for each child task; the other is to allocate a new chessboard variable using malloc function, and free it at the end of the child task. In either way, the programmer must take special care to the chessboard variable. Cilk also provides SYNCHED variables to conserve memory space [11]. Hence, the *taskprivate* data attribute we proposed significantly improves the programmability of those applications.

Sudoku is a logic-based, combinatorial number-placement puzzle. The objective is to fill a 9*9 grid so that each column, each row, and each of the nine 3*3 blocks contains the digits from 1 to 9 only one time each. Appendix A is an AdaptiveTC program for Sudoku. Here, the program Sudoku finds all solutions for a given grid. The parameter *st* is a *taskprivate* variable.

In AdaptiveTC, *fake tasks* and *tasks* handle *taskprivate* variable in different ways. In *fake tasks*, the *taskprivate* keyword is ignored. But in *tasks*, allocating and copying a new *taskprivate* variable for a child task is performed in order to assure correctness. The chessboard variable is handled as follows:

In a *fake task*,
$x[depth] = j$;
sn += nqueens($depth + 1, n, x$);
And in a *task*,
char *tmp_x;
$x[depth] = j$;
tmp_x = Cilk_alloca(n * sizeof(char));
memcpy(tmp_x, x, n * sizeof(char));
sn += nqueens($depth + 1, n, tmp\_x$);

In AdaptiveTC, as the number of tasks created is very small, it reduces the cost of workspace copying, and thus achieves a higher performance.

4.2 AdaptiveTC compilation strategy

To support the adaptive task creation strategy and to achieve a high performance, the AdaptiveTC compiler generates five different versions of the code for each task: a *fast* version, a *check* version, a *fast_2* version, a *sequence* version and a *slow* version. These five different versions provide the support of various work required at different stages of the execution. Figure 2 shows the relationship of these five versions at runtime during the adaptive task generation. The *fast*, *fast_2* and *slow* versions generate *tasks*. The *sequence* version generates *fake tasks*. The *check* version is similar to the *sequence* version when no other thread needs to steal a task. However, when any other thread needs a new task, it will generate a *special task* for its current sequential execution, and push it into the *tail* of d-e-que, so it could generate its child tasks into the d-e-que. The AdaptiveTC compiler ignores the *taskprivate* keyword in the *sequence* version and the *fake tasks* part of the *check* version, but allocates and copies a new *taskprivate* variable for a child task in the *fast*, *fast_2*, *slow* versions and the *special task* part of the *check* version (see section 4.1). The runtime system links together the actions of the five versions to produce a complete AdaptiveTC implementation with a high performance.

Appendix B shows a *fast* version of a Sudoku task in AdaptiveTC. When the *fast* version runs for the first time, the depth of the recursive call tree is 0. A task is created at the entry of the fast version and is freed at its exit. 1) When the depth is smaller than the *cut-off*, the state of the *fast* version is saved, and the task is pushed to the *tail* of the d-e-que. Then, the *fast* version of the child task is called with the depth incremented by 1. After the child task returns, it pops the saved task from the *tail* of the d-e-que, and

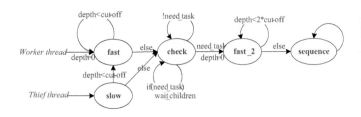

Figure 2. The relationship of the five versions in AdaptiveTC

check whether the task has been stolen. If *yes*, the *fast* version returns with a dummy value immediately. If *not*, it continues to run the next child task. 2) When the depth reaches *cut-off*, the *fast* version will call the *check* version without pushing the task into the d-e-que. In Figure 1, nodes 0, 1 and 40 use one of the fast versions before the *cut-off*, and nodes 2, 41, 7 and 44 use the fast versions beyond the *cut-off*.

In the *fast* version, all sync statements are translated to no-ops. Except for a *special task*, only parent tasks are allowed to be stolen, therefore all child nodes have completed when executing *sync* statements in the *fast* version. No operations are thus required for a *sync* statement.

Appendix C is a *check* version of a Sudoku task in AdaptiveTC. The *check* version checks whether other threads need tasks. If *not*, it calls its child task's *check* version recursively. If *yes*, it generates a *special task*, pushes the task into the tail of the d-e-que, and calls the child task's *fast_2* version with its depth set to 0. After the child task's *fast_2* version returns, it pops the *special task* and check whether its child task has been stolen. If *yes*, the *stolen_flag* variable is set to true. The *check* version continues to run the next child task's *fast_2* version until all child tasks are executed (using their *fast_2* version). At the synchronization point, if the *stolen_flag* variable is true, the *special task* will wait until all its child tasks are completed. In Figure 1, node 3, 5, 4, 6, 8, 9, 11, 10, 42, 43, 45, 46, 47 and 48 will use their *check* versions. The *special task* is node 12.

The *fast_2* version is a variant of the *fast* version with two differences. One is that the *cut-off* in *fast_2* is twice of that in the *fast* version. The other is that when the *cut-off* is reached, the *fast_2* version will call the *sequence* version, but not the *check* version as the *fast* version does. When the *fast_2* version is executed, the number of tasks generated by the *fast* version is not enough to keep all threads busy, so more tasks are generated in the *fast_2* version. The *sequence* version is a regular recursive function. In Figure 1, nodes 13, 14, 35, 36, 37 and 24 use their *fast_2* version before the *cut-off*, and nodes 15, 18, 25, 30, 38 and 39 use the *fast_2* version beyond the *cut-off*. Other nodes use their *sequence* version.

The *slow* version is used at the start of all stolen tasks. When a *thief thread* steals a task, the *slow* version of the task will be executed. It restores its program counter using a *goto* statement, and also restores its local variables and the depth for the task. Depending on whether the depth reaches the *cut-off* yet, the *slow* version will call either the *fast* version or the *check* version. At the synchronization point, a call to the runtime system, which checks whether all the child nodes of the task are completed, is inserted by compiler. If all the child nodes are completed, the thread will execute the next instructions of a synchronization point. If *not*, the thread will pop the task from the d-e-que's *tail* end, suspend the task, and then start stealing other task.

4.3 The runtime system

Cilk's work-stealing mechanism is based on a Dijkstra-like, shared-memory, mutual exclusive protocol called the THE protocol [10]. As both victim and thief operate directly on the victim's d-e-que,

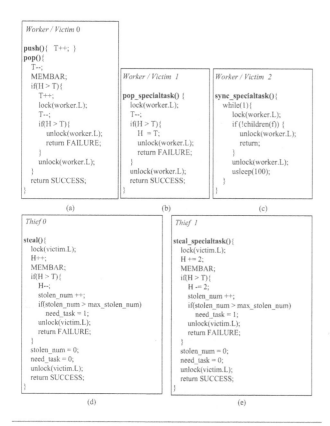

(a) (b) (c)

(d) (e)

Figure 3. Pseudo code of a simplified THE protocol. (a), (b) and (c) show the action performed by a victim thread; (d) and (e) show the action of a thief thread.

Nqueen-array(n)	The n-queens problem. It uses an array to record whether conflicts occur, and is more time efficient.
Nqueen-compute(n)	The n-queens problem. It traverses the chessboard to find out whether conflicts occur, and is more memory efficient.
Strimko	A logic puzzle. The objective is to fill in the given 7*7 grid so that each column, each row, and each stream contain the digits from 1 to 7 only once.
Knight's Tour	To find all solutions on a 6*6 chessboard. The knight is placed on an empty chessboard and moving according to the rules of the chess. It needs to visit each square on the chessboard exactly once.
Sudoku	To find all solutions for a given grid.
Pentomino(n)	To find all solutions to the Pentomino problem with n pieces (using additional pieces and an expanded board for $n > 12$).
Fib(n)	To compute recursively the n-th Fibonacci number.
Comp(n)	To compare array elements a_i and b_j for all $0 <= i, j < n$.

Table 1. Benchmark programs

As a result, the victim thread would notice that other threads need tasks. When the thief thread succeeds in stealing a task, it clears the victim thread's *stolen_num* and *need_task*. The default *max_stolen_num* is set to *20* in our runtime system.

pop_specialtask (in Figure 3.b): When $H < T$, no child task of the *special task* is stolen; otherwise, the child task is stolen, and H is reset to T. The intention of this reset is to ensure the *special task* to be the head of the d-e-que as the *special task* is never stolen.

sync_specialtask (in Figure 3.c): the *special task* awaits its child task to complete.

steal_specialtask (in Figure 3.e): the *special task* can never be stolen, and an attempt to steal it will lead to its child tasks being stolen.

5. Experimental results

In this section, we present some experimental results and try to compare the performance of our AdaptiveTC with those in Cilk-5.4.6 and Tascell. We first give detailed experimental results, and then analyze the overheads of three systems, finally give the performance in unbalanced trees to evaluate the dynamic load balancing.

We perform such measurements on Intel multi-core SMP, 2-processor quad core Intel Xeon E5520 (2.26GHz, 8G memory). We compile all parallel benchmark programs with the Cilk-5.4.6 compiler using gcc with option -O3. All serial benchmark programs are compiled with gcc -O3 as well. The speedup is computed using the serial execution time as the baseline, and using the median execution time of 3 successive executions of its corresponding parallel version. We evaluate the performance of our AdaptiveTC using the benchmark programs in Table 1.

5.1 Detailed experimental results

The results in Figure 4 and Figure 5 show a significant performance improvement of the AdaptiveTC over Cilk in the range of 1.15x to 2.78x using 8 threads. In addition, from Figure 4 we can see that AdaptiveTC has a good scalability when the threads number increases. In *Nqueen-array*, *Strimko*, *Knight's tour*, *Sudoku* and *Pentomino*, reducing the cost of the workspace copying is the major performance contributor. In *Nqueen-compute*, *fib* and *comp*, reducing the cost of creating tasks and managing d-e-ques is another major performance contributor. It shows that the proposed adaptive task creation strategy in AdaptiveTC could be very efficient and effective in the implementation of work-stealing strategy.

AdaptiveTC also achieves a higher performance than Tascell for most benchmarks. One reason is that the cost of creating tasks and managing d-e-ques in AdaptiveTC is much less than that of managing nested functions in Tascell; the other reason is that AdaptiveTC performs better dynamic load balancing than Tascell does(see sec-

race conditions will arise when a thief tries to steal the same task that its victim is attempting to pop. The THE protocol resolves such a race condition, and AdaptiveTC follows the THE protocol to implement the *special task* in the d-e-que.

Figure 3 shows the pseudo code of a simplified THE protocol used in AdaptiveTC. The code assumes that the d-e-que is implemented as a task array. T is the *tail* of the d-e-que, the first unused element in the array, and H is the *head* of the d-e-que, the first task in the array. Indices grow from the *head* to the *tail* so that under normal conditions, we have $T >= H$.

In *fast*, *fast_2* and *slow* versions, the *worker* thread uses a *push* operation to push a task into the *tail* of d-e-que before calling a *parallel* version. It also uses a *pop* operation to pop the task after calling the *parallel* version. In the *check* version, the worker thread uses a *push* operation to push a *special task* into the *tail* of the d-e-que before calling the *fast_2* version. It performs a *pop_specialtask* operation to pop the *special task* after calling the *fast_2* version, and a *sync_specialtask* operation to wait for the child tasks to complete at the synchronization point. In a *pop_specialtask* operation, when the *special task*'s child task is stolen, H is reset to T. The intention of this reset is to ensure the *special task* to be the *head* of the d-e-que because the *special task* could never be stolen.

A thief needs to get *victim.Lock* before attempting to steal the task at the *head* of d-e-que. Hence, only one thief may steal from the d-e-que at a time. When a thief attempts to steal a *special task*, it will steal the *special task*'s child task.

To notify a busy thread that some other idle thread needs tasks, the thief thread (an idle thread) increases the *stolen_num* of the victim thread (a busy thread). When the *stolen_num* exceeds the *max_stolen_num*, the *need_task* in the victim thread is set to *true*.

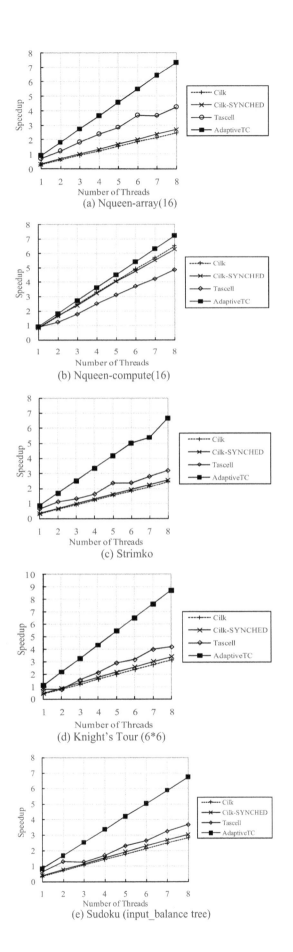

(a) Nqueen-array(16)

(b) Nqueen-compute(16)

(c) Strimko

(d) Knight's Tour (6*6)

(e) Sudoku (input_balance tree)

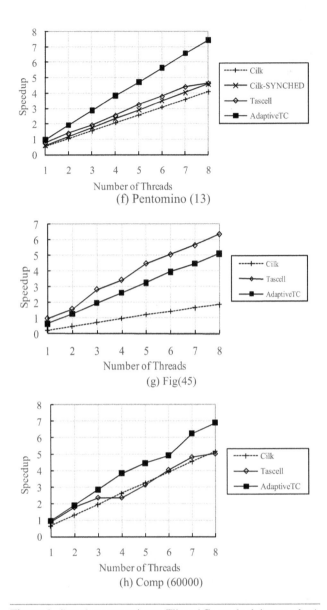

(f) Pentomino (13)

(g) Fig(45)

(h) Comp (60000)

Figure 4. Speedup comparisons. Fib and Comp don't have *taskprivate* variables, therefore the speedup in (g) and (h) are against Cilk and Tascell only.

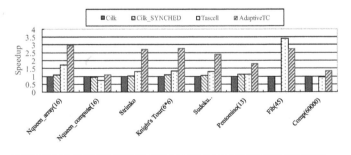

Figure 5. Speedup with 8 threads, baseline is Cilk's execution time.

	C	Tascell	Cilk	Cilk_SYN CHED	Adap tiveTC
Nqueen-array(16)	60.81	85.33 (1.4)	197.69 (3.25)	184.26 (3.03)	66.04 (1.09)
Nqueen-compute(16)	554.04	627.15 (1.13)	669.22 (1.21)	661.16 (1.19)	612.24 (1.11)
Strimko	262.97	423.24 (1.61)	839.03 (3.19)	813.01 (3.09)	315.55 (1.2)
Knight's Tour (6*6)	1322.51	1713.54 (1.3)	3307.32 (2.5)	3038.8 (2.3)	1217.56 (0.92)
Sudoku (balance_tree)	614.74	943.99 (1.54)	1717.09 (2.79)	1632.57 (2.66)	731.13 (1.19)
Pentomino (13)	8.74	11.64 (1.33)	16.73 (1.91)	14.83 (1.7)	9.176 (1.05)
Fib(45)	16.57	16.8 (1.01)	66.46 (4.01)	–	25.14 (1.52)
Comp(60000)	12.59	14.13 (1.12)	19.03 (1.51)	–	13.08 (1.04)

Table 2. Execution time in seconds (and relative time to sequential C programs) with one thread.

tion 5.2). The performance improvement over Tascell is in the range of 1.37x to 2.093x using 8 threads.

The only exception is *fib*. As shown in Figure 7.c, the cost of managing nested functions in Tascell is only 1.4% of the total execution time, while the cost of creating tasks and managing d-e-ques in AdaptiveTC is 51.7%; Tascell is thus 1.24x faster than AdaptiveTC. The main reason is that, in *fib*, there is almost no actual computation workload in each function. Hence, it increases the proportion of task creations and the d-e-que management cost substantially.

5.2 Overhead breakdown

We could basically break down the overheads of the three systems, AdaptiveTC, Cilk and Tascell as follows:

1. Overhead of AdaptiveTC = management of d-e-ques and task creations + *taskprivate* variables + THE protocol + waiting of child tasks to complete + task stealing overhead;

2. Overhead of Cilk = management of d-e-ques and task creations + workspace copying + THE protocol + task stealing overhead;

3. Overhead of Tascell = nested functions overhead + polling overhead+ waiting of child tasks to complete;

The cost of managing d-e-ques and creating tasks, workspace copying, *taskprivate* variables, and nested functions overhead could be measured by using only one thread, and the other costs need to be measured by running multiple threads.

From Table 2 and Figure 6, the overhead incurred in AdaptiveTC is lower than that in Cilk, and that is the main reason why AdaptiveTC could achieve a higher performance than Cilk for most benchmarks. However, in *fib*, the overhead in Tascell is much lower than that in the other two, thus Tascell gets the best performance on *fib*.

However, as shown in Figure 7, using Tascell, the waiting time for child tasks to complete takes 16.73%, 20.84%, and 11.31% of the total execution time in Nqueen-array, Nqueen-compute and fib, respectively, using 8 threads. The busy time in Cilk and AdaptiveTC is about 99% of the total execution time. Thus Nqueen-compute in AdaptiveTC is 1.485x faster than in Tascell, even though the cost of managing d-e-ques and creating tasks in AdaptiveTC is almost the same as the cost of managing nested functions in Tascell.

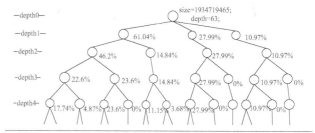

Figure 8. An unbalanced tree (input1)

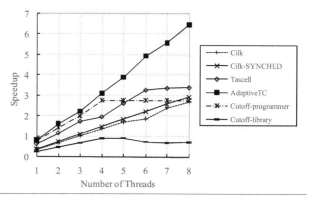

Figure 9. Speedup of Sudoku (input1)

5.3 The performance of unbalanced trees

5.3.1 The performance of AdaptiveTC and the cutoff strategy

Figure 8 shows a part of an unbalanced tree. The tree has a total of 1,934,719,465 nodes, and a depth of 63. The percentage on each node shows the size of the sub-tree rooted on the node compared to the entire tree. This unbalanced tree is dynamically generated by one of the inputs to Sudoku.

We implemented two cutoff strategies. In one strategy (Cutoff-programmer), the cutoff is assigned by the programmer, and in the other (Cutoff-library) the cutoff is assigned by the runtime system. The *cut-off* is $\lceil \log N \rceil$ in AdaptiveTC. In both Cutoff-programmer and Cutoff-library, some threads are in starvation when the numbers of threads are larger than 4, as shown in Figure 9. In Cutoff-library, the cost of workspace copying cannot be reduced as mentioned before. In comparison, AdaptiveTC gets a better speedup in an unbalanced tree than the other two strategies.

5.3.2 The dynamic load balancing in Cilk, Tascell and AdaptiveTC

The three systems use different tradeoff strategies between dynamic load balancing and system implementation overhead to get a high performance. Cilk can suspend a waiting task (to avoid its waiting time) and execute other ready tasks because it keeps each task's information in the d-e-que. Tascell cannot suspend a waiting task and has to wait for all its child tasks to complete because Tascell uses the execution stack to keep the task information. AdaptiveTC can suspend a waiting task to execute other ready tasks, except the *special task* which it has to wait for all its child tasks to complete.

Figure 10 shows the speedups of 4 unbalanced trees. In Figure 10(a), it uses the tree shown in Figure 8 and its reversed tree. In Figures 10(b), 10(c) and 10(d), it uses three randomly generated unbalance trees and their reversed trees.

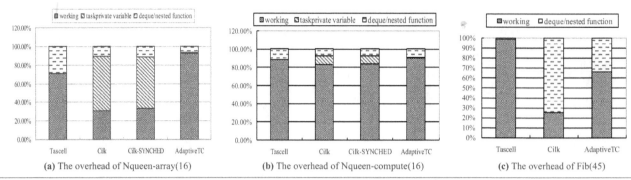

(a) The overhead of Nqueen-array(16) **(b)** The overhead of Nqueen-compute(16) **(c)** The overhead of Fib(45)

Figure 6. Breakdown of overheads with one thread. The overheads in AdaptiveTC are lower than Cilk for the three benchmarks and lower than Tascell for Nqueens, but higher than Tascell for fib.

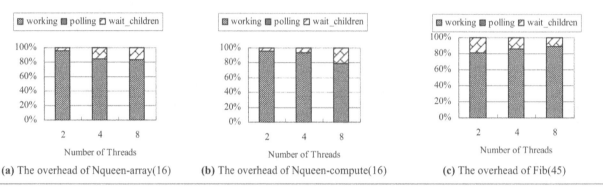

(a) The overhead of Nqueen-array(16) **(b)** The overhead of Nqueen-compute(16) **(c)** The overhead of Fib(45)

Figure 7. Breakdown of overheads with multiple threads in Tascell.

Input	Size(the number of nodes)	Leaf nodes	Depth	The percent numbers shows size of the depth 1 sub-tree comparing with the entire tree. (%)
Tree1L	1961025791	1245356982	48	42.512, 25.362, 13.019, 4.936, 0.416, 11.771, 1.984
Tree1R	1961025791	1245356982	48	1.984, 11.771, 0.416, 4.936, 13.019, 25.362, 42.512
Tree2L	1961025791	1192225858	52	74.492, 20.791, 1.106, 2.732, 0.637, 0.049, 0.193
Tree2R	1961025791	1192225858	52	0.193, 0.049, 0.637, 2.732, 1.106, 20.791, 74.492
Tree3L	1961025791	1182058030	51	89.675, 6.891, 1.836, 0.819, 0.645, 0.026, 0.108
Tree3R	1961025791	1182058030	51	0.108, 0.026, 0.645, 0.819, 1.836, 6.891, 89.675

Table 3. Randomly generated unbalanced trees. The six trees have the same size, but different shapes. Tree*L is a left-heavy tree. Tree*R is reversed of Tree*L and is a right-heavy tree.

We use a random function of $x_i = (x_{i-1} * A + C) mod M$ to generate a fixed random sequence of numbers for a given x_0 (the initial seed). x_i is localized in each node and is used to get the size of each sub-tree. When the tree size and the initial seed are defined, the same unbalanced tree can be generated in multiple executions.

We set the execution time of each node to the average time of the task in the benchmarks shown in Figure 4. Table 3 presents the details of the unbalanced search trees. Tree3 is the most unbalanced one among these trees.

In the experimental results (Figures 10(b), 10(c), 10(d)), Cilk shows the best dynamic load balancing among the three systems because it gets almost the same speedup in all six trees. Figure 10

also shows Cilk achieves a slightly higher performance in right-heavy trees than in left-heavy trees.

The performance of Tascell is impacted a lot by the shape of the tree. It gets worse performance on right-heavy trees than on left-heavy trees as the recursive call is a depth-first tree traversal. In Tascell, a *parallel-for* loop construct is implemented by spawning a half of the tasks for the requested threads. On a left-heavy tree, the first thread can run many tasks before waiting for its child tasks to complete. But on the right-heavy tree, the first thread could run fewer tasks before having to wait for its child tasks to complete. Therefore, it spends more time waiting on a right-heavy tree than on a left-heavy tree. For example, Tascell with 8 threads spends 8.08% of the total execution time in waiting on Tree3L, but almost 51.99% on Tree3R.

AdaptiveTC performs better dynamic load balancing than Tascell, but not always as good as Cilk. In Figures 10(a), 10(b) and 10(c), AdaptiveTC gets almost the same speedup on right-heavy and left-heavy trees. But in Figure 10(d), AdaptiveTC with 4, 7 and 8 threads, it gets worse load balancing on left-heavy tree than on right-heavy tree. AdaptiveTC with 4 threads in Tree3L spends 14.44% of total execution time waiting due to *steal fails* (i.e. it fails to steal a task) and 0.56% in waiting for child tasks to complete. About 2/3 of the *steal fails* are due to encountering an empty deque. Hence, in AdaptiveTC with 4, 7 and 8 threads in Tree3L, the number of tasks generated is not sufficient to keep all threads busy, and this leads to the runtime starvation. But in Tree3R with 4 threads, AdaptiveTC spends 0.95% of total execution time waiting due to *steal fail* and 1.46% due to waiting for child tasks to complete.

In the future, we will compare the number of steals in Cilk, the number of steals in AdaptiveTC and the number of respond-

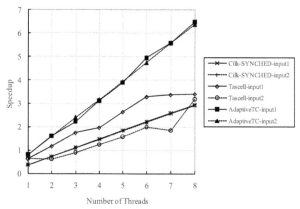

(a) Sodoku (input1/input2)

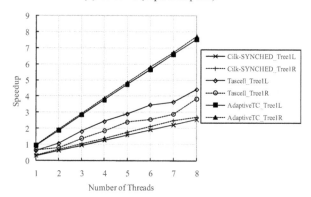

(b) Random unbalanced tree1L /tree1R

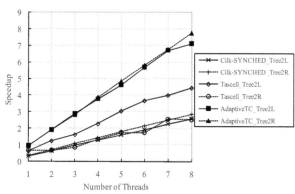

(c) Random unbalanced tree2L /tree2R

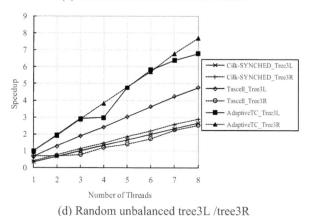

(d) Random unbalanced tree3L /tree3R

Figure 10. Speedup of unbalanced trees

ing requests in Tascell to analyze and evaluate the dynamic load balancing.

6. Conclusions

In this paper, we proposed an adaptive task creation strategy, called AdaptiveTC, to support work-stealing that could outperform Cilk and Tascell in several aspects. AdaptiveTC could adaptively create tasks to keep all threads busy most of the time, reduce the number of tasks created, and control the tasks granularity. It also introduced a new data attribute *taskprivate* for workspace variables that could reduce the workspace copying overhead in many important applications such as backtracking search, branch-and-bound search and game tree. As the result, it could reduce the overhead of managing the d-e-ques and creating tasks, the cost of workspace copying, and the chances of d-e-que overflow. Further, by using an adaptive task creation strategy, it improves load balancing on unbalanced call trees, and it is applicable to applications with or without definitive working set.

Acknowledgments

This research was supported in part by the National Basic Research Program of China (2005CB321602), the National Natural Science Foundation of China (60970024, 60633040), the National Science and Technology Major Project of China (2009ZX01036-001-002), the Innovation Research Group of NSFC (60921002), the U.S. National Science Foundation under the grant CNS-0834599 and a gift grant from Intel.

We would like to thank the reviewers for valuable comments and suggestions. We would like to thank Professor Zhiyuan Li at Purdue University for his many valuable suggestions and Tasuku Hiraishi for providing the Tascell system. Finally, we would like to thank Professor Vivek Sarkar for shepherding the paper.

References

[1] OpenMP Application Program Interface. Version 3.0, 2008.

[2] E. Ayguade, A. Duran, J. Hoeflinger, F. Massaioli, and X. Teruel. An Experimental Evaluation of the New OpenMP Tasking Model. In *the 20th International Workshop on Languages and Compilers for Parallel Computing*, pages 63–77, 2007.

[3] Robert D. Blumofe and Charles E. Leiserson. Scheduling multithreaded computations by work stealing. *Journal of the ACM*, 46(5): 720C–748, 1999.

[4] Robert D. Blumofe, Christopher F. Joerg, Bradley C. Kuszmaul, Charles E. Leiserson, Keith H. Randall, and Yuli Zhou. Cilk: an efficient multithreaded runtime system. In *the Fifth ACM SIGPLAN Symposium on Principles and Practice of Parallel Programming, PPoPP*, pages 207–216, 1995.

[5] Philippe Charles, Christian Grothoff, Vijay A. Saraswat, Christopher Donawa, Allan Kielstra, Kemal Ebcioglu, Christoph von Praun, and Vivek Sarkar. X10: an object-oriented approach to non-uniform cluster computing. In *the Twentieth Annual ACM SIGPLAN Conference on Object-Oriented Programming, Systems, Languages, and Applications, OOPSLA*, pages 519–538, 2005.

[6] David Chase and Yossi Lev. Dynamic circular work-stealing d-e-que. In *the seventeenth Annual ACM Symposium on Parallelism in Algorithms and Architectures, SPAA*, pages 21C–28, 2005.

[7] Shimin Chen, Phillip B. Gibbons, Michael Kozuch, Vasileios Liaskovitis, Anastassia Ailamaki, Guy E. Blelloch, Babak Falsofi, Limor Fix, Nikos Hardavellas, Tod C. Mowry, and Chris Wilkerson. Scheduling Threads for Constructive Cache Sharing on CMPs. In *the nineteenth annual ACM symposium on Parallel algorithms and architectures, SPAA*, pages 105–115, 2007.

[8] Guojing Cong, Sreedhar Kodali, Sriram Krishnamoorthy, Doug Lea, Vijay Saraswat, and Tong Wen. Solving large, irregular graph

problems using adaptive work-stealing. In *the 2008 37th International Conference on Parallel Processing*, pages 536–545, 2008.

[9] Alejandro Duran, Julita Corbaln, and Eduard Ayguad. Evaluation of Openmp Task Scheduling Strategies. In *the 4th International Workshop on OpenMP, IWOMP*, pages 100–110, 2008.

[10] Matteo Frigo, Charles E. Leiserson, and Keith H. Randall. The implementation of the cilk-5 multithreaded language. In *the ACM SIGPLAN Conference on Programming Language Design and Implementation, PLDI*, pages 212C–223, 1998.

[11] Supercomputing Technologies Group. Cilk 5.4.6 Reference Manual. Massachusetts Institute of Technology, Laboratory for Computer Science, Cambridge, Massachusetts, USA.

[12] Yi Guo, Jisheng Zhao, Vincent Cave, and Vivek Sarkar. Slaw: a scalable locality-aware adaptive work-stealing scheduler. In *the 24th IEEE International Parallel and Distributed Processing Symposium, IPDPS*, 2010. (To appear).

[13] Tasuku Hiraishi, Masahiro Yasugi, Seiji Umatani, and Taiichi Yuasa. Backtracking-based Load Balancing. In *the 14th ACM SIGPLAN Symposium on Principles and Practice of Parallel Programming, PPoPP*, pages 55–64, 2009.

[14] Hans Wolfgang Loidl, Kevin Hammond, Hans Wolfgang, and Loidl Kevin Hammond. On the Granularity of Divide-and-Conquer Parallelism. In *Glasgow Workshop on Functional Programming*, 1995.

[15] Maged M. Michael, Martin T. Vechev, and Vijay A. Saraswat. Idempotent Work Stealing. In *the 14th ACM SIGPLAN Symposium on Principles and Practice of Parallel Programming, PPoPP*, pages 45–54, 2009.

[16] Eric Mohr, David A. Kranz, and Jr Robert H. Halstead. Lazy task creation: A technique for increasing the granularity of parallel programs. *IEEE Transactions on Parallel and Distributed Systems*, 2 (3):264C–280, 1991.

A. An AdaptiveTC program for Sudoku

```
typedef struct {
unsigned char board[9][9];          // the chess board
unsigned char placed_block[9][9];   // whether a piece is placed
unsigned char placed_row[9][9];
unsigned char placed_col[9][9];
} Status_t;

cilk int search(int next_row, int next_col, Status_t *st)
  taskprivate: (*st) (sizeof(Status_t));
{
  int sn = 0;                       // the number of solutions
                                    // find the first free row and col.
  if(!find_free_cell(next_row, next_col, &free_row, &free_col)){
    sn++;    return sn;             // a solution found
  }

  for(x = 1; x <= 9; x++){          // iterate through all numbers
    if(conflict(st, free_row, free_col, x)) // check whether conflict
      continue;
    set(st, free_row, free_col, x);     // set the board and placed arrays
    sn += spawn search( free_row, free_col+1, st);
    undo(st, free_row, free_col, x); // undo the board and placed arrays
  }
  sync;
  return sn;
}
```

An AdaptiveTC program for Sudoku

B. A fast version of a Sudoku task in AdaptiveTC

```
typedef struct {
unsigned char board[9][9];          // the chess board
unsigned char placed_block[9][9];  //  whether a piece is placed
unsigned char placed_row[9][9];
unsigned char placed_col[9][9];
} Status_t;

int search(CilkWorkerState*const _cilk_ws, int _adpTC_dp,
           int next_row, int next_col, Status_t *st){
  search_info *f;                   // task_infor pointer
  f = alloc(sizeof(*f));            // allocate task_infor
  f->sig = search_sig;              // initialize task_infor
                                    // find the first free row and col.
  if(!find_free_cell(next_row, next_col, &free_row, &free_col)){
    sn++;                           // a solution found
    free(f);                        // free task_info
    return sn;
  }
  f->sn = sn;
  for(x = 1; x <= 9; x++){          // iterate through all numbers
    if(conflict(st, free_row, free_col, x)) // check whether conflict
      continue;
    set(st, free_row, free_col, x); // set the board and placed arrays
    if(_adpTC_dp < cut-off){
      tmp_st = Cilk_alloca(sizeof(Status_t)); // alloca a new space
      memcpy(tmp_st, st, sizeof(Status_t)); // copy parent status
      f->entry = 1;                 // save PC
      f->st = st;                   // save live vars
      f->mt = mt; f->depth = 0; f->x = x; f->sn = sn;
      f->free_row = free_row; f->free_col = free_col;
      *T = f;                       // store task_infor pointer
      push();                       // push task_infor into deque
      sn += search(_cilk_ws, _adpTC_dp+1, free_row,
                   free_col+1, tmp_st);
      if(pop(sn) == FAILURE)        // check task_info
        return 0;                   // child task stolen
    }else{
      sn += search_check(_cilk_ws, free_row, free_col+1, st);
    }
    undo(st, free_row, free_col, x); // undo board and placed arrays
  }

  free(f);
  return sn;
}
```

A fast version of a Sudoku task in AdaptiveTC

C. A check version of a Sudoku task in AdaptiveTC

```
typedef struct {
unsigned char board[9][9];          // the chess board
unsigned char placed_block[9][9];  // pieces whether placed
unsigned char placed_row[9][9];
unsigned char placed_col[9][9];
} Status_t;

int search_check(CilkWorkerState*const _cilk_ws, int next_row,
                  int next_col, Status_t *st){
                                    // find the first free row and col.
  if(!find_free_cell(next_row, next_col, &free_row, &free_col)){
    sn++;               // a solution found
    return sn;
  }

{   search_info *f = NULL;               // task_infor pointer
    int _adpTC_stolen = 0;
    int _adpTC_need_task = _cilk_ws->need_task;
    for(x = 1; x <= 9; x++){          // iterate through all numbers
      if(conflict(st, free_row, free_col, x))  // check whether conflict
        continue;
      set(st, free_row, free_col, x);  // set the board and placed arrays
      if(!_adpTC_need_task){
        sn += search_check(_cilk_ws, free_row, free_col+1, st);
      }else{
        if(!f){
          f = alloc(sizeof(*f));              // allocate task_infor
          f->sig = search_sig;                // initialize task_infor
          f->status = SPECIAL_TASK;
          f->sn = sn;
        }
        tmp_st = Cilk_alloca(sizeof(Status_t));     // alloca a new space
        memcpy(tmp_st, st, sizeof(Status_t));       // copy the parent status
        f->entry = 1;                // save PC
        f->st = st;                  // save live vars
        f->depth = 0; f->x = x;
        f->free_row = free_row; f->free_col = free_col;
        *T = f;                                 // store task_infor pointer
        push();                                 // push task_infor into d-e-que
        sn += search_2(_cilk_ws, 0, free_row, free_col+1, tmp_st);
        if(pop_specialtask() == FAILURE)     // pop and check special task_info
          _adpTC_stolen = 1;                  // child task stolen
      }
      undo(st, free_row, free_col, x);     // undo the board and placed arrays
    }

  if(_adpTC_stolen){
    f->sn += sn;
    sync_specialtask();               // wait children tasks
    sn = f->sn;                       // update the result
  }
  if(f) free(f);
  return sn;
  }
}
```

A check version of a Sudoku task in AdaptiveTC

Dynamic Interpretation for Dynamic Scripting Languages

Kevin Williams *   Jason McCandless*   David Gregg

Trinity College Dublin

{ kwilliam, mccandjm, dgregg } @ cs.tcd.ie

Abstract

Dynamic scripting languages offer programmers increased flexibility by allowing properties of programs to be defined at run-time. Typically, program execution begins with an interpreter where type checks are implemented using conditional statements. Recent JIT compilers have begun removing run-time checks by specializing native code to program properties discovered at JIT time.

This paper presents a novel intermediate representation for scripting languages that explicitly encodes types of variables. The dynamic representation is a flow graph, where each node is a specialized virtual instruction and each edge directs program flow based on control and type changes in the program. The interpreter thus performs specialized execution of whole programs. We present techniques for the efficient interpretation of our representation showing speed-ups of greater than 2x over *static interpretation*, with an average speed-up of approximately 1.3x.

Categories and Subject Descriptors D.3.4 [*Software*]: Programming Languages / Processors / Interpreters

General Terms Experimentation, Languages, Performance

Keywords Interpreter Optimization, Type Specialization, Dynamic Languages

1. Motivation

Scripting language virtual machines (VMs) typically compile high-level source code into an array of low-level opcodes (bytecodes). They then use a standard interpretation loop to execute the array of opcodes. Run-time type checks are implemented with either conditional statements or switch statements. Performing these type checks forms a significant

---

* Supported by Irish Research Council for Science, Engineering & Technology and IBM Dublin

portion of program execution. These costs seem unnecessary especially when we realize the same variable types are inevitably rechecked as loop iterations repeat the execution of the same block of code.

Recent research has shown the advantages of type specialization in JIT compilation [21, 11]. However, little research exists on the specialization of interpreters for scripting languages. We propose a scripting language representation and interpretation technique that performs specialized execution of dynamic code. We present a dynamic intermediate representation (DIR) which explicitly encodes the types of variables at each point of execution. The DIR is a flow graph, where each node is a specialized virtual instruction and each edge directs program flow based on control and type changes in the program. The proposed DIR therefore has a specialized path in the graph for every sequence of control and type changes found during execution.

In this paper we present the initial development of our prototype implementation in the Lua Virtual Machine [14, 15]. We present the design of our dynamic representation as well as the techniques used for its efficient interpretation. We illustrate our representation with a motivating example and present our plans for future interpreter optimizations. We compare the interpretation of our representation to the standard Lua implementation and show early speed-ups reaching a max of 2.13x and an average of 1.3x. We present reductions in the total number of instructions executed including reductions in conditional branches (used in interpreter type checking) as well as decreases in data and instruction cache accesses.

2. Background

All high level programming languages have type systems. A type system defines a set of valid values and a set of operations that can be applied to those values. The type system allows high level languages to detect and prevent invalid operations such as an arithmetic operation between two strings. The types of variables can be defined statically at compile time, or dynamically at run time. Languages such as C and Java have static type systems; whereas Perl, Python and Lua are dynamically typed. In a statically typed language, the type of a value that a variable can contain is determined at compile time. In dynamically typed languages however, variables can contain values of any type and each time an operation is applied to a variable during program execution the type of the variable must be checked. This typically adds a significant overhead to executing programs in dynamically typed languages. A goal of much research is to reduce or eliminate dynamic type checks in compilers or virtual machines for dynamically typed languages [3, 11, 21, 19].

The Lua VM supports nine variable types: NIL, BOOLEAN, LIGHTUSERDATA, NUMBER, STRING, TABLE, FUNCTION, THREAD, USERDATA. Variables are stored in a *(type,value)* pair called a *'tagged value'*. The type field of this structure is a byte and the value field is a union of values accessed by the VM depending on the value of the type tag.

The Lua VM is a register based machine. Instructions executed by the interpreter access *'virtual registers'* stored in the VM's call stack. There are thirty eight instructions in the Lua instruction set [18]. Instructions are 32 bits wide and contain an opcode and between one and three operands. Operands can either index a register or declare a constant value. Instructions are stored in arrays. The executing interpreter accesses this array through a program counter index. The index is updated by each instruction. Standard instructions simply increment the counter to the next index while conditional branch and loop instructions increment the counter by an offset value. The interpreter then *dispatches* the instruction indexed by the program counter. In interpretation, dispatching is the process of sending interpretation to the correct location for the implementation of the program's opcode. In this paper we will refer to this representation as the static intermediate representation (or SIR) and to the interpretation technique as static interpretation.

3. Dynamic Intermediate Representation

In this section we present the DIR we propose for the specialized interpretation of Lua programs. Our representation is a flow graph where nodes represent specialized instructions and edges represent either control-flow or type-flow. Type-flow provides a path for each variable type defined by the node's operation. These paths provide the opportunity for type specialization. As every type change results in a new path, all variable types are known at every point in execution. The interpreter therefore achieves complete specialization of whole programs.

Paths in the graph are built on demand, meaning only those control flow and type flow paths which occur during execution are ever created. Every constructed path is terminated with a *dummy* build instruction. This build instruction is dispatched inside the interpreter just like all other virtual machine instructions. When this build instruction is executed it builds a specialized node for the next instruction in the program path. When the build is complete the new node is dispatched. This use of dummy nodes and build instructions

allows seamless transitions between construction and execution of the DIR.

As complete knowledge of local types is available, creation of a new node and selection of its specialized instruction is directed by the types of the instruction's operands. The program's structure and behavior is defined by the SIR generated by the script compiler (the Lua compiler in our case). Hence construction of the dynamic flow graph is guided by the SIR. The rest of this section describes the structure of nodes forming our DIR followed by a discussion of some of the specializations performed on the Lua instruction set.

3.1 Standard Node

The most basic node in our representation contains three fields: (1) the opcode of the specialized instruction, (2) a pointer to the array of live types and (3) a pointer to the next node in the path. Instructions which use this basic node structure always result in the same control and type flow. Examples of such instructions include loading of constant values, arithmetic instructions and direct branches. Figure 1(a) sketches the structure of this node and Listing 1(e) shows a pseudo-implementation of its dispatch.

3.2 Conditional Node

Conditional nodes have all the fields of a standard node and an additional pointer to a target node. They are used to implement instructions that can result in two paths of control flow but never result in any type changes. Examples of such instructions include conditional instructions such as *equal to*, *greater than* and *less than*, as well as loop instructions which control the flow of loops. Figure 1(b) sketches the structure of this node and Listing 1(f) shows a pseudo-implementation of its dispatch. Here we can see a condition statement defining the direction of execution.

3.3 Type-Directed Node

Type-directed nodes dispatch the next node based on the type of the operation's result variable. This node has three fields, the first two fields are the same as the standard node fields. The third field is an array of target nodes. Each entry in the array is a pointer to the first node of a new path. During execution, the type of the result of the operation is used to index the target array. The node selected is dispatched and execution continues down that path.

These nodes are used at any point where there is a single change of variable type and no change in control flow (i.e. all paths exiting the node execute the same instructions, the difference between paths is the types they are specialized to). The Lua language has nine types and so the dispatch array for our implementation has nine entries. Figure 1(c) sketches the structure of this node and Listing 1(g) shows a pseudo-implementation of its dispatch. Here we can see that the instruction defines some variable in *dest_reg*. This

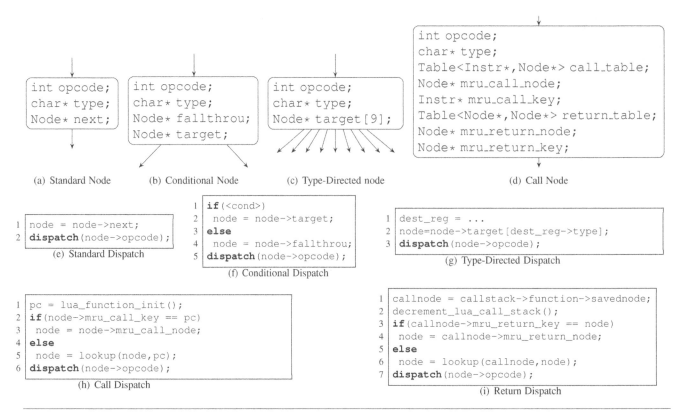

Figure 1. Node Structures and interpreter dispatch techniques.

register has two fields, a value and a type. The type is used to index the dispatch array.

3.4 Call Node

Recall that each node in the DIR is an instruction specialized to a set of local variable types. Therefore, call nodes represent a call site and a known set of parameter types. A key/value mapping structure maps the call node to a function and the set of parameter types. The key for this mapping is the address of the called function. The value returned is the entry node of the function in the dynamic representation. The effect of this mapping is a flow of types across function boundaries.

In dynamic languages, the function called at a given point may change from execution to execution as functions are treated as first-class values. In practice, our experiments show that the majority of call points have a single called function, with a few having more than one. As a result of this profile information, call node mappings are implemented efficiently using two arrays. One array to store keys of functions and the second to store the value of nodes. A linear search of the key array will find the index of the correct node in the value array. Once found, this node can be dispatched in the usual way. Our implementation further improves the efficiency of this search by storing the most recently used key and value in 'cached' fields of the node. This caching is analogous to Self's polymorphic inline cache technique [13].

In practice these cached fields are usually a correct match, so linear searches only occur in a small number of cases.

3.5 Return Node

Having completed execution of a function, control flow must return to the calling function. As is the case for call nodes, return nodes represent a return instruction and a set of return types. Hence, an equivalent table mechanism using *(key,value)* pairs to find the next node is also used in return nodes. The return table is located in the calling node, as functions may regularly be called from different call sites but individual call sites rarely call multiple functions. Storing the return table in the call site therefore reduces the number of *(key,value)* pairs in a table and improves the search time for the correct key. Call nodes are stored in stack frames on the Lua stack and accessed from the stack at the end of each function.

The combination of our call/return mappings results in the inter-procedural type profiling of all function calls for any number of parameter and return variables (a powerful asset for JIT compilation).

3.6 Instruction Specialization

This section provides a brief overview of the set of instructions in the Lua VM and the range of specialization our interpreter performs.

1. **Register Loads:** Several different instructions in the Lua instruction set implement different types of loads. A specialization applicable to all of these instructions is the assignment of type. A register in Lua stores a value and a type. Commonly a load instruction loads a variable of the same type from a source register to a destination register. In these cases we have removed the redundant assignment of type to the destination register.

2. **Arithmetic Operations:** The usual set of arithmetic instructions are available in the Lua instruction set. Static implementations of these operations first check that both operands are of type NUMBER before proceeding with the operation. Having full type knowledge of variables, our specialized implementations of arithmetic instructions do not require type checking and simply perform the desired operation. The same is true for string operations like concatenation.

3. **Table Access:** Tables are the sole data structuring mechanism in the Lua language. They are used to implement a wide range of data structures. They are associative structures and can be indexed by any value and can store values of any type. They contain two separate parts (1) a hash part, for storing values indexed by hashed values and (2) an array part for storing values indexed by integer keys. Our implementation provides specialized table access based on the type of the key. The wide use of tables in Lua makes this specialization an important optimization for overall performance.

4. **Conditional Branches:** The Lua instruction set has several different conditional instructions. These instructions compare two values and direct control flow based on the result of these comparisons. Valid comparisons can only be made between two values of the same type. Each conditional instruction in the instruction set is therefore specialized to the type of its operands. The value of this specialization is large because type checking in these instructions is performed by an expensive ANSI C switch statement.

4. Motivating Example

4.1 SIR

Figure 2 shows an example of a Lua implementation of the well known Sieve of Eratosthenes algorithm. The program calculates all prime numbers in the first N natural numbers. The implementation presented in Figure 2(a) marks all numbers which are not prime in the *flags* table with the boolean value *true*. At the end of this program all prime numbers will remain unmarked in the *flags* table.

Figure 2(b) is the SIR generated by the Lua compiler. Execution of this opcode results in the control flow pattern depicted in Figure 2(c). This graph is presented to illustrate the structure of a static flow graph to the reader and is never constructed at any point in static interpretation.

```
1  local N = 100
2  local flags = {}
3  for i = 2, N do
4     if not flags[i] then
5        for k = i+i, N, i do
6           flags[k] = true
7        end
8     end
9  end
```

(a) Lua source code, a high-level representation.

```
1   loadk     r0 k0    ; reg0 = constant0
2   newtable  r1 0 0   ; reg1 = new table(0,0)
3   loadk     r2 k1    ; reg2 = constant1
4   move      r3 r0    ; reg3 = reg0
5   loadk     r4 k2    ; reg4 = constant2
6   forprep   r2 L15   ; perform forloop prep, goto[15]
7   gettable  r6 r1 r5 ; reg6 = reg1[reg5]
8   test      r6 L15   ; if reg6, goto[9] else goto[15]
9   add       r6 r5 r5 ; reg6 = reg5 + reg5
10  move      r7 r0    ; reg7 = reg0
11  move      r8 r5    ; reg8 = reg5
12  forprep   r6 r1    ; perform forloop prep, goto[14]
13  settable  r1 r9 k3 ; reg9[reg1] = constant3
14  forloop   r6 L13   ; if loop, goto[13] else goto[15]
15  forloop   r2 L7    ; if loop, goto[7] else [end]
```

(b) Lua opcode, a low-level representation.

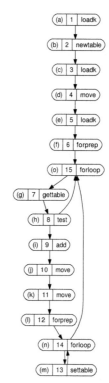

(c) An *'imaginary'* control flow graph for the static interpretation of the Sieve of Eratosthenes algorithm.

Figure 2. A Lua implementation of the Sieve of Eratosthenes algorithm.

4.2 DIR

Figure 3 is an illustration of the graph that is constructed and interpreted by our dynamic interpreter for the Sieve of Eratosthenes program. The graph has twenty-six nodes in total. Each node has three labels, the first is a letter (a–z) which the authors will use for referencing nodes during discussion. The second is a number (1–15) which identifies the equivalent static instruction that the node specializes (found in Figure 2(b)). The last label is the opcode name. Opcodes in our DIR are specialized to the types of variables they are operating on. For example, node *v* is an add operation operating on two numbers, therefore the opcode selected is *add_number_number*.

Edges in the graph represent program flow. Edges with no labels represent fall-through flow, i.e. instructions which always dispatch to the same next instruction in the program. Control flow edges are labeled *loop branch* and *cond branch*. These edges represent control flow dispatches for branch instructions. The remaining edges are type flow edges. In this graph, they are labeled either *nil* or *boolean*. An example of type flow can be found in nodes *g* and *r*. These nodes are table fetch instructions and return a value from a table. They therefore dispatch based on the type of the return value. In node *g* there is only a single path, for type *nil*, as only one type value is ever returned at this point. In contrast, node *r* has two paths where values of type *nil* and *boolean* are returned. The two paths exit to the same program instruction, however the next and all subsequent instructions are specialized to the returned type.

The Sieve of Eratosthenes program is implemented with fifteen static Lua instructions. When these instructions are specialized to the local variable set found during execution, twenty-six specialized instructions are generated. In Figure 3 we have clustered these nodes into three sets. The first cluster represents the instructions that initialize the variables of the program. The second cluster is the first iteration of the for-loop spanning the static instructions 5–15. The final cluster is all subsequent iterations of the same loop. Two separate paths are generated for iterations of the outer loop as there are uninitialized variables in the first iteration. Only after the first iteration completes does the graph become stable.

5. Experimental Evaluation

5.1 Experimental Setup

The following sections provide a comparison of hardware performance and running times between static and dynamic interpretation. The test machine used to run these experiments has two Intel Xeon Dual Core 2.13Ghz processors each with 4MB caches and 12GB of memory. The operating system is Ubuntu 9 with x86_64 GNU/Linux kernel 2.6.29.2. Lua source code is version 5.1.4. We have used the GNU gcc compiler version 4.3.3. Both the static and dynamic versions of code were compiled with the optimization options '-O3

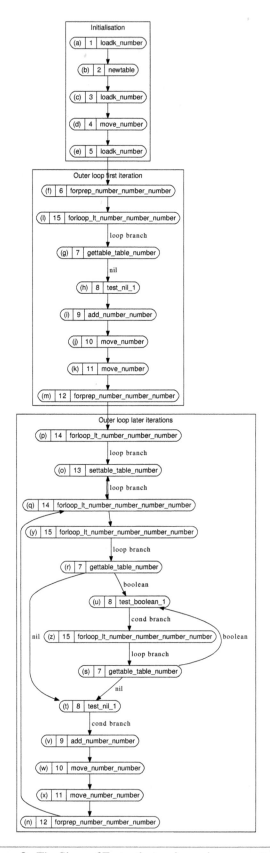

Figure 3. The Sieve of Eratosthenes dynamic representation built and executed by our interpreter.

-fomit-frame-pointer'. The hardware performance counters presented were collected using the PAPI profiling tool.

Our micro-benchmark set is taken from the Computer Language Benchmarks Game [8] and the Great Win32 Computer Language Shootout [12]. A lack of formal benchmark sets for scripting languages make these suites a common source of benchmarking for scripting language implementations [11, 3, 7, 19].

Figures 4(a) to 4(e) present hardware performance counters. Results are presented relative to the absolute result for the static interpreter. Hence, in all these figures, static bars are at 100% and the dynamic versions show percentage increases or decreases relative to the absolute static numbers.

5.2 Machine Instructions Issued

We first look at the total number of machine instructions issued to execute both static and dynamic interpreters (see Figure 4(a)). With the exception of one benchmark, all show a decrease in the number of machine instructions issued. This shows that the combination of dynamic interpreter dispatch and instruction specialization results in fewer instructions than the standard (and cheaper) static interpreter dispatch and (more expensive) run-time conditional type-check.

The benchmark that does not achieve a decrease in instructions issued is the *thread-ring* benchmark. This program benchmarks the Lua *coroutine* library, executing many coroutine yield and resumes. At the time of experimentation, our prototype interpreter had no efficient implementation for resuming from coroutines after yields and hence each resume requires a lookup of the correct resume node (removing this lookup is a future goal of the project).

5.3 Branch Instructions

The effect of interpreter specialization can be best seen in the dramatic decrease of conditional branch machine instructions (again across all benchmarks except *thread-ring*). By far the best performing benchmark in this experiment is the *mandelbrot* benchmark. This benchmark executes many arithmetic instructions. The greater than 75% reduction in conditional branches is achieved largely from specializing those arithmetic instructions. Other notable results are for *array-access* and *matrix-mul* both of which have many number-key table accesses. All of these accesses are specialized to the key type.

5.4 Cache Access

Figures 4(c) and 4(d) present Level 1 cache accesses for both the data cache and instruction cache. Interpreter dispatch of nodes requires more loads compared to an equivalent bytecode dispatch. Because of this, an overall increase in data cache accesses would be expected. Surprisingly, dynamic interpretation reduces the overall number of data cache accesses. The reduction in data cache accesses is a result of removing type accesses for run-time type checking. The in-

struction cache has an overall reduction in cache accesses as would be expected after a reduction in instructions issued.

5.5 Processor Stalls

Despite the reduction in cache accesses, Figure 4(e) shows that the DIR implementation leads to many more processor stalls across almost all benchmarks. There are several factors contributing to these stalls. An increase in data cache misses is recorded, caused by the inefficient allocation of nodes. Memory for individual nodes is currently allocated on a node-by-node basis. The result of this allocation is many nodes scattered inefficiently around memory. The allocation also contributes to an increase in TLB misses. Implementing specialized versions of interpreter instructions leads to an increase in instruction size which leads to a corresponding increase in instruction cache misses. A more compact allocation of nodes is expected to improve data cache performance in future iterations of our interpreter — where DIRs will be stored in contiguous blocks of memory, managed by the VM.

5.6 Memory

DIRs require a separate node for each specialization of an individual instruction. Programs which contain many changes in control and type flow will result in large graphs and an increase in memory use. Figure 4(f) shows this behavior in a couple of our benchmarks — *fasta* and *n-body*. They both contain large increases in memory use as the data sets they are operating on are small and hence the DIR is relatively large.

5.7 Performance

Figures 5(a) and 5(b) show running times and speed-ups for our benchmark set. Benchmarks whose bottleneck is the execution of instructions that perform lots of type checking achieve a very favorable speed-up. Other benchmarks whose bottleneck is system library calls and non-specializable Lua instructions see a smaller increase in performance. The interpreter dispatch overhead of our DIR approach is greater than that of bytecode dispatch. Despite this increased cost, the only benchmark which achieves a slow down is *thread-ring* (our current implementation lacks an efficient coroutine resume mechanism).

6. Scope for Optimization

This paper has presented a dynamic intermediate program representation that encodes both dynamic control flow and variable type flow through a whole program. It has shown interpreter dispatch techniques which enable the efficient execution of the representation. It finally presented analysis of the technique; comparing its performance to that of a static equivalent. In order to present a fair comparison of both techniques this paper has so far neglected the possibilities of optimization of the dynamic representation. In this

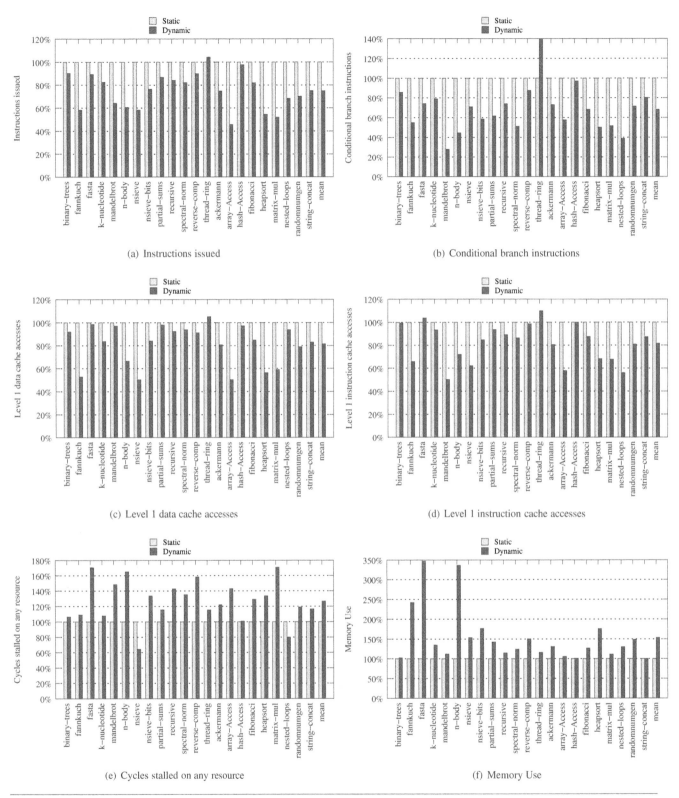

Figure 4. (a–e) present hardware performance counters collected using the PAPI profiling tool. All results are presented relative to the absolute result for static interpretation. (f) presents memory use in the heap and stack, collected by polling the process status information from the Linux proc file-system.

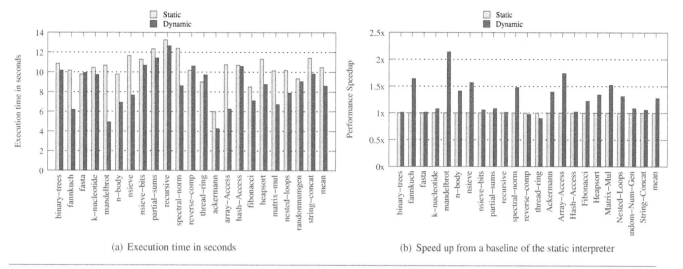

| (a) Execution time in seconds | (b) Speed up from a baseline of the static interpreter |

Figure 5. A comparison of run-time performance.

section we present some thoughts on our future work and the types of optimization we plan to improve performance in the future.

Interpreter Dispatch: The Lua 5.1 implementation is designed to be as portable as possible. For these reasons, the Lua authors have used a switch based interpreter dispatch. Our current representation copies this dispatch technique. More efficient dispatch techniques have been established in previous work. Threading techniques [2] such as token threading and direct threading are equally applicable to our representation. As specialization reduces the bottleneck of type checks, instruction dispatch becomes more and more important to overall performance.

Register Caching: A popular optimization among stack based virtual machines is to cache the top value(s) of the stack in machine registers [9]. An equivalent approach to caching virtual registers in machine registers is to date unestablished[1]. Using our dynamic representation we plan to specialize instructions with implicit register operands. Due to the number of virtual registers it is not advisable to cache all registers. The authors plan to create a mapping of machine registers to virtual registers. Region boundaries will be given header and footer nodes for loading and storing cached registers. Caching will be implemented by need, meaning only the most frequently used registers will be cached.

Super Nodes: Another optimization tecnhique is to concatenate common pairs of instructions together to form a single instruction [20]. This technique is equally applicable to dynamic representations. The authors plan to use established techniques to implement super node optimizations [10, 5].

Loop Optimizations: Loops often provide opportunities for optimization in compilers — as is the case in our interpreter. We plan to leverage the type knowledge of variables inside loops to eliminate array bounds checking and move memory allocation outside the loop body. Table access nodes can be further specialized to 'cache' the array pointer; we believe this will lead to a massive performance gain. The number type in Lua is implemented using 'doubles'. We plan to optimize loop counters by specializing them to integers when we know the loop bound is constant.

Dead Node Removal: Specialization of operations can lead to redundant nodes. For example in Figure 3, node t specializes the TEST instruction to an operand of type NIL. The result of this operation is always false and control flow will always follow the FALSE path. This is illustrated in Figure 3 as there is only a single path leaving the TEST node, which is a conditional node. The TRUE path is never built as it is never executed. Nodes specialized to this level can be removed and all entry nodes can be directed to the target exit node.

Library Nodes: Scripting languages often provide standard libraries to perform complex operations like STRING, MATH and IO functions. The authors plan to inline these operations into the interpreter. This will remove the stack incrementing and decrementing required for their execution and will improve performance of the functions themselves as they are heavily inlined into the interpreter.

7. General Applicability

The DIR presented in this paper is implemented in the Lua VM. However, the technique is applicable to other scripting languages — some require minor changes to their variable structures and some would specialize instructions in differ-

---

[1] It is in-fact a goal of the JavaScript Squirrel-fish VM, http://webkit.org/blog/189/announcing-squirrelfish/

ent ways to Lua. For example, in Python, arithmetic instructions can overflow from one type (*int*) into another (*long*). Arithmetic behavior like this would be modeled with a type-directed node (see Figure 1(c)). In general, dynamic scripting language implementations have some *'tagged value'* structure to define *(type,value)* pairs. In Lua, these tagged values have a byte which encodes one of the nine possible types. Our dynamic interpreter uses this byte to index the array of targets for node dispatch. In Python, tagged values use a pointer to a type object; however objects of 'built-in' types can be augmented with extra information. The data structure for objects of these types would need to be extended with a type indicator byte. In PHP, tagged values called *ZVals* have a type byte which encodes one of eight basic types. Javascript implementations differ in their bytecode format. In the SpiderMonkey implementation, the tagged value, termed *jsval*, is a machine word with three bits representing the type, thus some decoding would be required.

8. Related Work

The earliest work on efficient dynamic language implementations was completed in the Self project [6]. This project produced a large number of techniques for the efficient implementation of dynamic object-oriented programming languages. The technique in this paper, by contrast, is concerned with a whole program sepcialization based on all primitive local variable types. In the range of languages commonly referred to as scripting languages, only a few recent research efforts have focused on program specialization. All of these research efforts have been directed at either ahead-of-time compilation and analysis or just-in-time compilation and specialization of run-time variables.

Gal et al. wrote a tracing JIT compiler for the JavaScript VM running in the Firefox web browser [11]. They successfully showed that compiling at a trace granularity allowed for the specialization of JIT compiled code. They used *type guards* at trace entry and *side-exits* at selected points in the trace to guarantee type-safe execution. They used SSA-based *trace trees* to perform aggressive optimizations and presented trace formations to handle the problem of nested control flow. Their interpreter, which begins the execution of all programs and performs the profiling of control flow (but not type) uses *'static interpretation'* techniques. Zaleski *et al.* [25] presented a tracing JIT for the Java language. They used direct calling dispatch techniques in their interpreter to gradually develop a trace JIT of a hot region of code. Rigo's psyco [21] is a run time specialization technique for the Python programming language. It performs run time specialization *by need* using a mixed execution/specialization phase of execution to specialize JIT code fragments.

Biggar et al. presented *phc*, an ahead-of-time compiler for the PHP language. They performed static analysis of PHP programs and developed a compiler technique that links with the language's interpreter to enable correctness through future iterations of the language [3]. Jensen et al. present a static analysis infrastructure for the JavaScript language. Their technique uses type inference and pointer analysis to achieve precision rates greater than 90% in a large number of benchmarks. Their technique, while powerful, has some shortcomings. In their worst case they achieve 61% precision. These results show that the use of static analysis alone is not sufficient to infer large numbers of types in all programs. The dynamic representation presented in this paper guarantees 100% precision for all run-time local variables.

Bruening and Duesterwald [4] investigated strategies for finding optimal JIT compilation unit shapes for Java programs. They explored strategies for minimizing compiled code size and maximizing time spent in JIT code. They concluded that using multiple levels of granularity in JIT compilation could lead to greater performance. Work by Whaley [24], and later by Suganuma et al. [22, 23] used dynamic profiling inside the Java Virtual Machine's interpreter to reduce compilation time by selecting and compiling smaller sections of code they called *partial methods* (i.e. loops). Larus presented whole program paths which capture a program's complete control flow [17]. An outcome of this work was effective discovery of *hot subpaths* for programmers and compilers to optimize. In Ammons' and Larus' retrospective piece [1] they observe the success of program path optimizations in the JIT community. The DIR in this paper similarly builds program paths to improve interpreter efficiency.

Kistler and Franz [16] pioneered the concept of using tree structures in the Java VM. The advantage of their tree representation over the original bytecode was a more compact representation that contained more high-level information that improved JIT compilation.

9. Conclusions

This paper has presented a novel approach to scripting language specialization. The approach is the first stage of a project which plans to bring program specialization to all levels of execution from interpretation to post-JIT native execution. Our experiments have shown our interpretation technique to be more efficient than existing techniques for scripting languages. In future work we plan to bring further efficiency to both interpretation and JIT compilation.

While our approach has shown performance to encourage adoption of our technique in the wider community, we have not addressed some of the potential scaling issues with our representation. For the most part scripting languages are in general type-stable, but the possibility still exists for a dynamic representation to grow to an unsuitably large size. A study of potential profiles is required to analyze the risk of programs which are pathological in type and/or control flow. Possible solutions to any such programs could be to (1) limit the number of paths allowed by creating unspecialized paths in problem regions, (2) remove paths which may have become obsolete or (3) require the existence of a static interpreter as a fall back processing unit.

We have claimed that our dynamic representation will bring improvements to the area of JIT specialization. Our future work includes plans to build an experimental JIT compiler which will make run-time decisions about compilation units. Leaving these compilation decisions to run-time should improve the quality of JIT compilation as whole program profiles are available to guide appropriate compilation units.

Acknowledgements

The authors would like to express their gratitude to those who spared their time to review this work. They include: Roberto Ierusalimschy of PUC-Rio, Mike Pall of the LuaJIT project and the anonymous reviewers of the CGO committee.

References

[1] G. Ammons and J. R. Larus. Improving data-flow analysis with path profiles. *SIGPLAN Not.*, 39(4):568–582, 2004.

[2] J. R. Bell. Threaded Code. *Commun. ACM*, 16(6):370–372, 1973.

[3] P. Biggar, E. de Vries, and D. Gregg. A practical solution for scripting language compilers. In *SAC '09: Proceedings of the 2009 ACM symposium on Applied computing*, pages 1916–1923, New York, NY, USA, 2009. ACM.

[4] D. Bruening and E. Duesterwald. Exploring optimal compilation unit shapes for an embedded just-in-time compiler. In *In Proceedings of the 2000 ACM Workshop on Feedback-Directed and Dynamic Optimization FDDO-3*, pages 13–20, 2000.

[5] K. Casey, D. Gregg, and M. A. Ertl. Tiger – an interpreter generation tool. *Compiler Construction*, pages 246–249, 2005.

[6] C. Chambers. *The Design and Implementation of the Self Compiler, an Optimizing Compiler for Object-Oriented Programming Languages*. PhD thesis, Computer Science Department, Stanford University, 1992.

[7] M. Chang, E. Smith, R. Reitmaier, M. Bebenita, A. Gal, C. Wimmer, B. Eich, and M. Franz. Tracing for web 3.0: trace compilation for the next generation web applications. In *VEE '09: Proceedings of the 2009 ACM SIGPLAN/SIGOPS international conference on Virtual execution environments*, pages 71–80, New York, NY, USA, 2009. ACM.

[8] CLBG. The Computer Language Benchmarks Game. *Available at http://shootout.alioth.debian.org/*, 2008.

[9] M. A. Ertl. Stack Caching for Interpreters. In *PLDI '95: Proceedings of the ACM SIGPLAN 1995 conference on Programming language design and implementation*, pages 315–327, New York, NY, USA, 1995. ACM.

[10] M. A. Ertl, D. Gregg, A. Krall, and B. Paysan. Vmgen: a generator of efficient virtual machine interpreters. *Softw. Pract. Exper.*, 32(3):265–294, 2002.

[11] A. Gal. Trace-based just-in-time type specialization for dynamic languages. In *PLDI '09*, pages 465–478, New York, NY, USA, 2009. ACM.

[12] GWCLS. The Great Win32 Computer Language Shootout. *Available at http://dada.perl.it/shootout/*, 2008.

[13] U. Hölzle, C. Chambers, and D. Ungar. Optimizing dynamically-typed object-oriented languages with polymorphic inline caches. In *ECOOP '91: Proceedings of the European Conference on Object-Oriented Programming*, pages 21–38, London, UK, 1991. Springer-Verlag.

[14] R. Ierusalimschy, L. H. de Figueiredo, and W. Celes. The Implementation of Lua 5.0. *Journal of Universal Computer Science*, 11(7):1159–1176, July 2005.

[15] R. Ierusalimschy, L. H. de Figueiredo, and W. Celes. The evolution of lua. In *HOPL III*, pages 2–1–2–26, New York, NY, USA, 2007. ACM.

[16] T. Kistler and M. Franz. A tree-based alternative to java byte-codes. *International Journal of Parallel Programming*, 27(1):21–33, 1999.

[17] J. R. Larus. Whole program paths. *SIGPLAN Not.*, 34(5):259–269, 1999.

[18] K.-H. Man. A No-Frills Introduction to Lua 5.1 VM Instructions. In *http://chunkspy.luaforge.net/*. Lua Chunkspy Project, 2003.

[19] M. Pall. The LuaJIT Project. *Available at http://luajit.org*, 2008.

[20] T. A. Proebsting. Optimizing an ansi c interpreter with superoperators. In *POPL '95: Proceedings of the 22nd ACM SIGPLAN-SIGACT symposium on Principles of programming languages*, pages 322–332, New York, NY, USA, 1995. ACM.

[21] A. Rigo. Representation-based just-in-time specialization and the psyco prototype for python. In *Proceedings of the 2004 ACM SIGPLAN Workshop on Partial Evaluation and Semantics-based Program Manipulation*, pages 15–26. ACM Press, 2004.

[22] T. Suganuma, T. Yasue, and T. Nakatani. A region-based compilation technique for a java just-in-time compiler. In *PLDI '03: Proceedings of the ACM SIGPLAN 2003 conference on Programming language design and implementation*, pages 312–323, New York, NY, USA, 2003. ACM.

[23] T. Suganuma, T. Yasue, and T. Nakatani. A region-based compilation technique for dynamic compilers. *ACM Trans. Program. Lang. Syst.*, 28(1):134–174, 2006.

[24] J. Whaley. Partial method compilation using dynamic profile information. In *OOPSLA '01: Proceedings of the 16th ACM SIGPLAN conference on Object oriented programming, systems, languages, and applications*, pages 166–179, New York, NY, USA, 2001. ACM.

[25] M. Zaleski, A. D. Brown, and K. Stoodley. Yeti: a gradually extensible trace interpreter. In *VEE '07: Proceedings of the 3rd international conference on Virtual execution environments*, pages 83–93, New York, NY, USA, 2007. ACM.

Author Index

NOTES

NOTES